Creative Resources for the Early Childhood Classroom

Join us on the Web at
EarlyChildEd.delmar.com

Creative Resources for the Early Childhood Classroom

Fifth Edition

Judy Herr, Ed.D.
Yvonne Libby Larson

THOMSON
DELMAR LEARNING ™

Australia Canada Mexico Singapore Spain United Kingdom United States

THOMSON

DELMAR LEARNING

Creative Resources for the Early Childhood Classroom, Fifth Edition

Judy Herr and Yvonne Libby Larson

Vice President, Career Education Strategic Business Unit:
Dawn Gerrain

Director of Learning Solutions:
John Fedor

Managing Editor:
Robert L. Serenka, Jr.

Senior Acquisitions Editor:
Erin O'Connor

Product Manager:
Philip Mandl

Editorial Assistant:
Alison Archambault

Director of Production:
Wendy A. Troeger

Production Manager:
Mark Bernard

Technology Project Manager:
Sandy Charette

Director of Marketing:
Wendy E. Mapstone

Channel Manager:
Kristin McNary

Marketing Coordinator:
Scott A. Chrysler

Marketing Specialist:
Erica S. Conley

Art Director:
Joy Kocsis

Cover Design:
Joseph Villanova

For permission to use material from this text or product, submit a request online at http://www.thomsonrights.com
Any additional questions about permissions can be submitted by email to thomsonrights@thomson.com

Library of Congress Cataloging-in-Publication Data
Herr, Judy.
  Creative resources for the early childhood classroom / Judy Herr, Yvonne Libby-Larson—5th ed.
      p. cm.
  Includes bibliographical references and index.
  ISBN-13: 978-1-4283-1832-8 (pbk. : alk. paper)
  ISBN-10: 1-4283-1832-1 (pbk. : alk. paper) 1. Education, Preschool—Curricula. 2. Unit method of teaching. I. Libby-Larson, Yvonne. II. Title.
  LB1140.4.H47 2007
  372.19—dc22

                               2007010400

NOTICE TO THE READER

Contents

Contents by Subjects

CONTENTS BY SUBJECTS

CONTENTS BY SUBJECTS

Our Community

Plants

Seasons and Weather

Sports and Hobbies

Transportation

FEATURES

FIELD TRIPS/ RESOURCE PEOPLE

Field Trips

Resource People

CONTENTS BY SUBJECTS

FINGERPLAYS

All About Me

Animals

CONTENTS BY SUBJECTS

LARGE MUSCLE ACTIVITIES

MATH
Classification

Counting and Numerals

Matching

CONTENTS BY SUBJECTS

CONTENTS BY SUBJECTS

Preface

While reviewing early childhood curriculum resources, it becomes apparent that few books are available using a thematic or unit approach for teaching young children. As a result, our university students, colleagues, and alumni convinced us of the importance of such a book. Likewise, they convinced us of the contribution the book could make to early childhood teachers and, subsequently, the lives of young children.

Before preparing the manuscript, we surveyed hundreds of child care, preschool, and kindergarten teachers. Specifically, we wanted them to share their curriculum needs. Our response has been to design and write a reference book tailored to their teaching needs using a thematic approach for use with two-through six-year-old children. Each theme or unit contains a flowchart, theme goals, concepts for the children to learn, theme-related vocabulary words, music, fingerplays, science, dramatic play, creative art experiences, sensory, mathematics, cooking experiences, multimedia recordings, books, and song titles. In addition, creative ideas for designing child-involvement bulletin boards and family letters have been included. These resources were identified, by the teachers included in our survey, as being critical components that have been lacking in other curriculum guides. As the second, third, fourth, and fifth editions were developed, we continuously sought input from colleagues and other individuals using the book.

In addition to the themes included in this book, other themes can and should be developed for teaching young children. We, however, want to caution the readers that it is the teacher's responsibility to select, plan, and introduce developmentally appropriate themes and learning experiences for his or her group of children. Specifically, the teacher must tailor the curriculum to reflect the children's needs, interests, abilities, and background experiences. Consequently, we encourage all teachers to carefully select, adapt, or change any of the activities in this book to meet the needs, abilities, interests, and experiences of their group of children to ensure developmental appropriateness. The inside covers of this book should be used as handy references for checking developmental milestones.

As you use this guide, you will note that some themes readily lend themselves to particular curriculum areas. As a result, the number of activities listed under each curriculum area will vary from theme to theme.

The color insert in the center of this book, "Scrapbook of Teacher Made Materials," illustrates numerous additional activities. These pages include photos and lists of materials necessary to construct the teaching boards illustrated to accompany the activities. Themes where the use of these activities would be appropriate are also suggested.

The detailed Introduction that follows is designed to help teachers use the book most effectively. It includes:

1. a discussion on how to develop the curriculum using a thematic approach
2. a list of possible themes
3. suggestions for writing family letters
4. methods for constructing and evaluating creative interactive bulletin boards
5. criteria for selecting children's books
6. the importance of documentation boards

What's New in This Edition!

1. Activities. Over one hundred new activities enrich this fifth edition. These activities are spread throughout the book and complement the existing themes. Each thematic unit begins with a curriculum web. This webbing is designed as a tool to inform teachers of the major subconcepts that can be included under each theme. Ideally, the teacher will tailor the curriculum to make it developmentally appropriate and meet the needs, interests, and experiences of her or his children.

2. An entire **Multicultural Materials Appendix** has been added including books, music, and dramatic play ideas.

3. New and Expanded Reference Materials. The sections on books and multimedia that appear at the end of each theme have been carefully researched and updated to reflect the new publications related to each theme. Hundreds of new books have been added.

4. Introduction of Additional Recordings and Songs for the Thematic Units. A recording and song section containing music with related concepts has been revised for each theme where available. Again, special thanks to Elaine Murphy, Director of Sales and Marketing, Kimbo Educational, for assistance in developing this section for each edition. Free catalogs for these materials can be obtained by telephoning 800-631-2187, faxing 732-870-3340, or e-mailing kimboed@aol.com.

5. Documentation boards are available on the CD at the back of this book so that you may be able to print and copy them. A Documentation Board Evaluation Form is also included on the CD.

6. The CD that accompanies this Fifth Edition of *Creative Resources for the Early Childhood Classroom* contains forms for assessing young children's growth and development. Included are:

- Activity Preferences: Self Selected Play
- Anecdotal Record
- Block Plan Form
- Bulletin Board Letters: Lowercase
- Bulletin Board Letters: Uppercase
- Bulletin Board Numbers
- Curriculum Area Planning Web
- Evaluating Documentation Boards/Panels
- Emerging Competencies: Two-Year-Olds–Six-Year-Olds
- Emerging Competencies: Two-Year-Olds
- Emerging Competencies: Three-Year-Olds
- Emerging Competencies: Four-Year-Olds
- Emerging Competencies: Five-Year-Olds
- Emerging Competencies: Six-Year-Olds
- Evaluation of an Activity
- Individual Child Profile

- Lesson Plan
- Parent Letter
- Play Patterns Assessment Form
- A Shadow Study

Also included on the CD is the actual art taken from the suggested Bulletin Boards in each theme. Along with the Upper- and Lowercase Letters and Numbers, you should be able to recreate these Bulletin Boards without any art abilities necessary.

Acknowledgments

During the years between the first and fifth editions of this book, there were many individuals whose creative ideas, support, and encouragement helped us. Our sincere thanks to all of them.

First, we would like to thank our parents, who fostered our creativitiy, interest in teaching, and love of young children.

In addition, we extend our thanks to:

Our husbands, Jim Herr and Troy Larson.
Sara Anger, who provided insightful suggestions and encouragement.
Melissa Seehaver, for her technical support and curriculum ideas.
Moe Hendricks, the Director of the Child and Family Study Center, and her staff: Kathy Preusse, Jamie Lynch, Heidi Anderson, and Marcia Wolf.
Rachel Wegner, who assisted in the development of the documentation boards.
Sherri Post and Moe Hendricks for assisting with the development of the Documentation Board Evaluation Form.
Our colleagues in early childhood education who have worked with us at the University of Wisconsin–Stout and throughout the nation.
All students who have majored in early childhood education at the University of Wisconsin–Stout, the children who have participated in programs at the Child and Family Study Center, their families, and all children who have enjoyed the themes and activities presented in this book.
And, finally, to Jeffrey, Eva, Madelyn, Marena, Vivian, Evan, Josie, and all of the children throughout the world who have made our efforts worthwhile.

We are also grateful to our reviewers:

Patricia Capistron, B.A.
Lead Teacher at Rocking Unicorn Nursery School
Chatham, MA

Judith Lindman, M.Ed.
Professor at Rochester Community & Technical
  College
Rochester, MN

Leanna Manna, M.A.
Associate Professor at Villa Maria College
Buffalo, NY

Karen Ray, M.Ed.
Instructor at Wake Technical Community College
Raleigh, NC

Lois Wachtel, B.A. and Director's Credential
Education Director/Instructor at Temple Sinai
  Pre-School
Delray Beach, FL

Our special thanks to individuals whose assistance made this book possible: Erin O'Connor, our Delmar Learning editor, who provided continuous encouragement, support, and assistance; and Isabel Baker, President of Vines Books and a professional librarian, for selecting the multicultural books.

We also extend our special thanks to the fourteen individuals whose assistance made this book possible: Carol Hagness, the Director of the Educational Materials Center at the University of Wisconsin–Stout; Elaine Murphy of Kimbo Educational; Tracey Wellington and Dawn Tenneyson Grimm, who shared teacher made materials; Marty Springer, University of Wisconsin–Stout staff member, who photographed the teacher made materials; Erin O'Connor and Alexis Breen Ferraro, our Delmar Learning editors, who provided continuous encouragement, support, and assistance; our typists, Vicki Weber and Debra Hass; Rachel Wegner and Moe Hendricks, who provided assistance with the development of the documentation boards; Melissa Seehaver, who provided assistance with the activities; Joni Conlon, Project Manager for Thomson Delmar Learning; Christine Clark, who copy edited this edition; and Kelly Morrison, Project Manager at GEX Publishing Services.

Introduction

The purpose of this introduction is to explain the process involved in curriculum planning for preschool and kindergarten children using the thematic, or unit, approach. Why use themes? Children's learning does not occur in naturally defined subject areas, so learning and development are integrated. Activities that stimulate one area of development and learning affect other areas as well. By organizing the curriculum around a theme, teachers can plan a meaningful child-centered curriculum that focuses on children's emerging interests. The theme provides a central focus that lends itself to the integration of curriculum areas. Themes help children develop concepts more readily. Themes also provide concept development through a variety of "hands-on," "minds-on," and "feelings-on" activities. The curriculum is more interesting and also encourages parents to contribute to the curriculum. To support each theme, planning and construction ideas are included for bulletin boards, family letters, and a wide variety of classroom learning experiences.

Curriculum Planning

As you use this resource, remember that children learn best when they can control and interact with their environment. Therefore, many opportunities should be available for active learning—seeing, hearing, touching, tasting, self-expression, and problem solving. Children need an inviting environment with an abundance of hands-on, minds-on, and feelings-on learning experiences. They also need materials, equipment, and choices. To construct knowledge, they need to actively manipulate their environment. To provide these opportunities, the teacher's primary role is first to assess the children's needs, interests, abilities, experiences, and learning styles. Using this assessment data, the teacher's next step is to create a stimulating, engaging environment where children can explore materials and relationships. To be meaningful, these experiences should be consistent with the child's development and culture.

Children learn by doing, and play is their work. Development proceeds when children have appropriate tools to develop new skills. For this, they need large blocks of time and flexible schedules. As a result, it is the authors' intention that this book be used as a resource to help you design and carry out a child-centered curriculum. Specifically, the ideas in this book should help you to enrich, organize, and structure the children's environment, providing them an opportunity to make choices among a wide variety of activities that stimulate their natural curiosity.

Knowledge of child development and curriculum must be interwoven. To illustrate, play in the classroom should be child-centered and self-initiated. To provide an environment that promotes these types of play, it is the teacher's role to provide unstructured time, space, materials, and support. Using a theme-based approach to plan curriculum is one way to ensure that a wide variety of classroom experiences is provided. Successful early childhood programs have interesting, challenging, and engaging environments that are developmentally appropriate. Children need to learn to think, reason, and become active decision makers.

It is important that all curricula be adapted to match the developmental needs of children at a particular age or stage of development. An activity that is appropriate for one group of children may be inappropriate for another. To develop an appropriate curriculum, knowledge of the typical development of children is needed. For this reason, the inside covers of this book contain such information and may be helpful in making predictions about a child's developmental stage. Review these developmental milestones, or emerging competencies as they are often called, before selecting a theme or specific activities. The enclosed CD on the back cover of this book contains forms that should be helpful in assessing the children's needs, interest, abilities, and experiences.

Theme Planning

A developmentally appropriate curriculum for young children integrates the children's needs, interests, abilities, and experiences and focuses on the whole child. Cognitive, social, emotional, and physical development are all included. Before planning curriculum, use the forms on the CD to assess the children's development. Record your observations. At the same time, note the children's interests and listen carefully. Children's conversations provide clues; this information is vital in selecting a theme that follows the direction of the children's interests and is personally meaningful to the children. After this, review your observations by discussing them with other staff members. A developmentally appropriate curriculum for young children cannot be planned without understanding their development. The curriculum must be relevant to their lives and emerge from their interests.

There are many methods for planning a curriculum other than using themes. In fact, you may prefer not to use a theme during parts of the year. If this is your choice, you might want to use the book as a source of ideas, integrating activities and experiences from a variety of the themes outlined in the book.

Planning an emergent child-centered curriculum using a theme approach involves several steps. Based upon assessment, the first step involves selecting a theme that is appropriate for the developmental level and emerging interests of your group of children. Themes based on the children's conversations and interests provide intrinsic motivation for exploration and learning. Meaningful experiences are more easily comprehended, remembered, and lead to new understandings. Moreover, curiosity, enjoyment of participation, and self-direction are heightened.

After selecting a theme, the next step is developing a flowchart. From the flowchart, goals, conceptual understandings, and vocabulary words can easily be extracted. The final step in curriculum planning is selecting activities based on the children's stages of development and available resources. While doing this, the covers of this book should be used as a reference to review emerging milestones for children of different ages.

To help you understand the theme approach to curriculum development, each step of the process will be discussed. Included are assessing the children to identify themes related to the children's interests, needs, abilities, and experience. After selecting a theme, the next step is developing a flowchart, theme goals, concepts, vocabulary, and activities. In addition, suggestions are given for writing family letters, designing bulletin boards, and selecting children's books.

Assessment

Assessment is important for planning curriculum, identifying children with special needs, and communicating a child's progress to parents. Assessment provides a child's development status at a give time. It also provides information on a child or group of children's progress over time. Authentic assessment needs to be a continuous process of evaluating children's growth through their daily play activities. It involves a process of observing children during activities and engaging in thoughtful dialogue. Assessment is a process of observing children, recording their behaviors, and documenting their work. It involves showing what the children can do and have learned.

Assessment also involves records and descriptions of what you observe, see, and hear while the behavior is occurring. Logs and journals can be developed. The emerging milestones on the inside covers of this text can be used as a checklist of behavior. You can create a profile of each child's individualized progress in developing skills. Your observations should tell what the child likes, doesn't like, has discovered, knows, and wants to learn.

Samples of the children's work should be maintained in an individual portfolio collection. A portfolio is a purposeful collection that documents the children's progress, achievements, and efforts. Included should be samples of the children's paintings, drawings, storytelling experiences, and oral and written language. Thus, the portfolio will include products and evidence of the children's accomplishments. The portfolio can also be used to communicate with parents and to demonstrate teacher accountability. The CD contains documentation boards that can be used to showcase the children's or child's thinking and work.

Selecting a Theme

By reviewing the assessment materials, you can identify the children's emerging milestones and interests. This information will be important in selecting a theme that interests the children and in selecting developmentally appropriate learning experiences. A theme can be any topic of interest to young children.

When selecting a theme, remember that celebrating holidays can be controversial. You need to respect the diversity of the children and their families in your program. Therefore, it is important to seek input from parents regarding holiday themes. Ask parents how they feel. If some parents object, respect those objections. In some cases, you can talk about a holiday rather than celebrate it. Remember, if used, a holiday theme should not be the focus of the curriculum for an extended period.

Three-year-old children primarily view holiday celebrations in terms of their own families. They need to learn about holiday activities that are concrete with simple information that is connected to their own familial experiences. Like three-year-old children, four-year-olds view holidays from the experiences they have had in their own families. Often, children these ages can remember a celebration from the previous year. Five- and six-year-olds enjoy learning about holidays and understand the reasons they are celebrated. They particularly enjoy preparing decorations, foods, and even invitations.

Flowcharts/Webbings. Once you have identified a theme that emerges out of the children's interest, the next step is to develop a flowchart. The flowchart is a simple way to record all possible subconcepts that relate to the major concept or theme. It includes a graphic picture of what may be included in the theme. To illustrate, plan a theme on apples. Begin this process by printing a copy of the Curriculum Area Planning Web form provided on the accompanying CD. In the center on this form, print the word "apple." Then, using an encyclopedia as a resource, record the subconcepts that are related. Include origin, parts, colors, tastes, sizes, textures, food preparation, and nutrition. The following flowchart (see Figure I-1) includes these concepts. In addition, under each subconcept, list content that could be included. For example, apples may be colored green, yellow, or red. By using a thematic approach, we teach children the way environments and humans interconnect. This process helps children make sense out of the human experience.

Theme Goals. Once you have prepared a flowchart webbing, abstracting the theme goals is a simple process. Begin by reviewing the chart. Notice the subheadings listed. For the unit on apples, the subheadings include: preparation, tastes, parts, sizes, forms, origin, and colors. Writing each of these subheadings as a goal is the next step of the process.

Because there are seven subheadings, each of these can be included as a goal. In some cases,

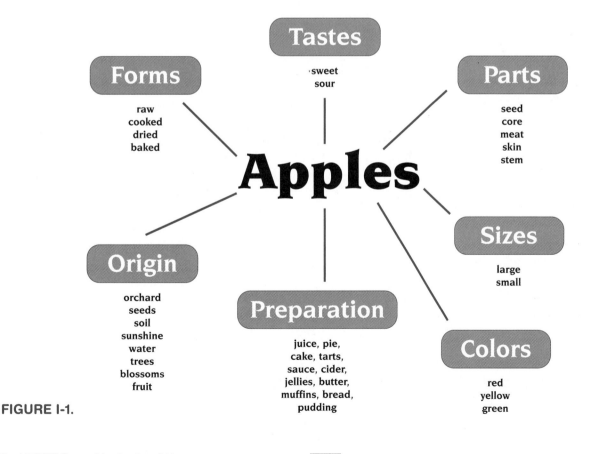

FIGURE I-1.

subheadings may be combined. For example, note the fourth goal listed. It combines several subheadings.

Through participation in the experiences provided by using apples as a curriculum theme, the children may learn

1. parts of an apple.
2. preparation of apples for eating.
3. forms of apples.
4. the colors of apples.
5. the origin of an apple.
6. the tastes of apples.
7. the sizes of apples.
8. the texture of apples.

Concepts. The concepts must be related to the goal; however, they are more specific. To write the concepts, study the goals. Then prepare sentences that are written in a simple form that children can understand. Examples of concepts for a unit on apples may include:

1. Apples grow on trees.
2. Seeds are planted in the soil to grow an apple tree.
3. A group of apple trees is called an orchard.
4. Water and sunshine are needed to make apple trees grow.
5. The flower on the apple tree is called a blossom.
6. An apple is a fruit.
7. An apple has five parts: seed, core, meat, skin, and stem.
8. Apples can be colored green, yellow, or red.
9. Apples can be large or small.
10. Bread, pies, puddings, and applesauce can be prepared from apples.
11. Cake, sauce, muffins, tarts, and juice may also be prepared from apples.

Vocabulary. The vocabulary should include new words that you want to informally introduce to the children. Vocabulary words need to be tailored to meet the specific needs of your group of children. The number of vocabulary words will vary, depending on the theme and the developmental level of the children. For example, it might be assumed that the children know the word sweet, but not tart. So, the definition of the word tart is included. Collectively, the following words

could be introduced in this unit: apple, apple blossom, apple butter, core, and texture. Definitions for these words could include:

1. **apple**—a fruit that is grown on a tree.
2. **apple blossom**—a flower on the apple tree.
3. **apple butter**—a spread for bread made from apples.
4. **core**—the part of the apple that contains the seeds.
5. **texture**—how something feels.

Activities. Now that you have learned how to develop goals related to a theme using a flowchart, you will need to learn how to select developmentally appropriate activities. You will discover that many theme goals can be accomplished by additions to the environment, bulletin boards, field trips, and stories or resource people at large group time. Your major role as an adult, or teacher, is that of a facilitator, planning and preparing the environment to stimulate the child's natural curiosity.

To begin this process, review each goal and determine how it can be introduced in the classroom. For example, review the goals if you were going to develop a theme on apples. A bulletin board or game could introduce the three colors of apples. The children could also learn these colors through cooking experiences. The third vehicle for teaching the colors of apples would be placing the three colors of apples on a science table.

The five parts of an apple could also be introduced through participation in a tasting or cooking experience, bulletin board, or even discussion on a field trip or at the snack table. Always remember that children need to observe and manipulate the concrete object while engaged in child-initiated or child-directed play that is teacher supported. For that reason, fresh apples could be cut horizontally and placed on the science table with a magnifying glass. Likewise, simultaneously, apple seeds and paper could be available on the art table to construct a collage. Always remember that the best activities for young children are hands-on and open-ended. That is: focus on the process, rather than the product. Children need to learn to think, reason, and become problem solvers. As a teacher, you should take the ideas in this book and use and adapt them for planning and preparing the environment. Always remember that successful early childhood programs provide interesting, challenging, and engaging environments.

xxxii

INTRODUCTION

Family Letters

Communication between the child's home and school is important. It builds mutual understanding and cooperation. With the efficiency of modern technology, family letters are a form of written communication that can be shared on a weekly basis. Samples of family letters that you can adapt for each theme have been included in this book. The most interesting family letters are written in the active voice. It states the subject did something. To illustrate: "Mark's favorite activities today were playing with blocks and listening to stories on a cassette player."

When writing the family letter, consider the family's educational level. Then write the letter in a clear, friendly, concise style. To do this, eliminate all words that are not needed. Limit the length of the letter to a page or two. To assist you with the process, an example of a family letter is included for each theme.

Family letters can be divided into three sections. Included should be a general introduction, school activities, and home activities. One way to begin the letter is by introducing new children or staff, or sharing something that happened the previous week. After this, introduce the theme for the coming week by explaining why it was chosen.

The second section of the family letter could include some of the goals and special activities for the theme. Share with the families all of the interesting things you will be doing at school throughout the week. By having this information, families can initiate verbal interaction with their child.

The third section of the family letter should be related to home activities. Suggest developmentally appropriate activities that the families can provide in the home. These activities may or may not relate to the theme. Include the words of new songs and fingerplays. This section can also be used to provide parenting information such as the developmental value of specific activities for young children. A format for writing family letters is introduced on the CD.

Bulletin Boards

Bulletin boards add color, decoration, and interest to the classroom. They also communicate what is happening in the classroom to parents and other visitors. The most effective bulletin boards involve the children and are placed at their eye level. That is, the child will manipulate some pieces of the board. As a result, they are called interactive or involvement bulletin boards. Through the concrete experience of interacting with the bulletin board materials, children learn a variety of concepts and skills. Included may be size, shape, color, visual discrimination, hand-eye coordination, problem solving, etc.

Carefully study the bulletin boards included for each theme in this book. They are simple, containing a replica of objects from the child's immediate environment. Each bulletin board has a purpose. It teaches a skill or concept.

As you prepare the bulletin boards provided in this book, you will become more creative. Gradually, you will combine ideas from several bulletin boards as you develop new themes for curriculum.

An opaque projector is a useful tool for individuals who feel uncomfortable with their drawing skills. Using the opaque projector, you can enlarge images from storybooks, coloring books, greeting cards, wrapping paper, etc. To do this, simply place the image to be copied in the projector. Then tape paper or tagboard on the wall. Turn on the projector. Using a pencil, color marker, or crayon, trace the outline of the image onto the paper or tagboard.

Another useful tool for preparing bulletin boards is the overhead projector. Place a sheet of acetate on the picture desired for enlargement. This may include figures from a coloring or storybook. Trace around the image using a washable marker designed for transparencies. Project the image onto a wall and follow the same procedures as with the opaque projector.

To make your bulletin board pieces more durable, laminate them. If your center does not have a laminating machine, use clear contact paper. This process works just as well, but it can be more expensive. Otherwise, some school specialty stores provide this service.

Titles for bulletin boards can be made from stencils, plastic lettering, or by using a word processor. Using a word processor, you can use Microsoft software to prepare titles or labels. To do this, click on boldface first. Then, select a lettering size that would be in proportion to the size of the bulletin board and figures. After this, select a font. Placard Condensed is recommended because it represents a manuscript style young children see in books. Uppercase and lowercase manuscript letters and numbers have been included on the accompanying CD that can be used for bulletin board titles. Prepare lettering for bulletin boards by using these letters and placing colored construction paper in the printer.

In addition to providing these letters and numbers on the CD, the simple art objects that are shown in the suggested Bulletin Boards in each theme are also included. You should be able to recreate these Bulletin Boards with very little effort or artistic skills.

Finally, the materials you choose to use on a bulletin board should be safe and durable. Careful attention should be given when selecting attachments. For two-, three-, and four-year-old children, adhesive Velcro and staples are preferred attachments. **Caution:** Pushpins may be used with older children under *careful supervision*.

Selecting Books

Books for young children need to be selected with care. Before selecting books, once again, refer to the covers and review the typical development for your group of young children. This information can provide a framework for selecting appropriate books.

There are some general guidelines for selecting books. First, children enjoy books that relate to their experiences. They also enjoy action. The words written in the book should be simple, descriptive, and within the child's understanding. The pictures should be large, colorful, and closely represent the actions.

A book that is good for one group of children may be inappropriate for another. You must know the child or group of children for whom the story is being selected. Consider their interests, attention span, and developmental level.

Developmental considerations are important. Two-year-olds enjoy stories about the things they do, know, and enjoy. Commonplace adventure is a preference for three-year-olds. They like to listen to things that could happen to them, including stories about community helpers. Four-year-old children are not as self-centered. These children do not have to be part of every situation that they hear about. Many are ready for short and simple fantasy stories. Five-year-olds like stories that add to their knowledge—that is, books that contain new information.

Documentation Boards/Panels

Documentation boards can illustrate the process and progress of learning. They can articulate the philosophy of the classroom and provide tangible evidence that the children are actively engaged in learning. Visual evidence such as photographs, work samples, and teacher's reflections can all be used. Documentation boards can communicate the theme, child development, celebration, skill acquisition, special events, and curricular milestones.

See the CD for examples of documentation boards.

Curriculum Planning Guide

We hope you find this book to be a valuable guide in planning curriculum for preschool and kindergarten children. The ideas should help you build a curriculum based on the children's natural interests. The book should also give you ideas so that your program will provide a wide variety of choices for children.

In planning a developmentally valid curriculum, consult the Contents by Subject. It has been prepared to allow you easy selection from all the themes. So pick and choose and make it your own! The subjects included are shown in Figure I-2. For easy reference, on the first page of each theme, the art icons are presented for those subject areas which are covered in that particular theme.

Caution: Check for children's allergies when any food products will be used.

Other Sources

Early childhood educators should refer to other Delmar Learning publications when developing appropriate curricula, including:

1. Ramirez, Gonzalo, Jr. and Ramirez, Jan Lee. *Multiethnic Children's Literature: A Comprehensive Resource Guide.*

2. Dolinar, Kathleen, Boser, Candace and Holm, Eleanor. *Learning through Play: Curriculum and Activities for the Inclusive Classroom.*

3. Allen, K. Eileen and Marotz, Lynn. *Developmental Profiles: Pre-birth through Twelve* (5th ed.).

4. Berns, Roberta M. *Topical Child Development.*

5. Mayesky, Mary. *Creative Activities for Young Children* (8th ed.).

FIGURE I-2.

6. Gestwicki, Carol. *Home, School, and Community Relations: A Guide to Working with Parents* (6th ed.).

7. Essa, Eva L. *A Practical Guide to Solving Preschool Behavior Problems* (5th ed.).

8. Sawyer, Walter E. and Jean, C. *Integrated Language Arts for Emerging Literacy*.

9. Charlesworth, Rosalind and Lind, Karen K. *Math and Science for Young Children* (5th ed.).

10. Bentzen, Warren R. *Seeing Young Children: A Guide to Observing and Recording Behavior* (4th ed.).

11. Davidson, Jane. *Children's Emerging Literacy Through Dramatic Play*.

12. Pica, Rae. *Experiences in Movement with Music, Activities, and Theory* (3rd ed.).

13. Gestwicki, Carol. *Developmentally Appropriate Practice: Curriculum and Development in Early Education* (2nd ed.).

14. Schirrmacher, Robert. *Art and Creative Development for Young Children* (4th ed.).

15. Click, Phyllis. *Caring for School Age Children* (3rd ed.).

16. Essa, Eva and Royce Rogers, Penelope. *Early Childhood Curriculum: From Developmental Model to Application*.

17. Herr, Judy. *Creative Learning Activities for Young Children*.

18. Herr, Judy and Swim, Terri. *Creative Resources for Infants and Toddlers* (2nd ed.).

1

Colors

black
brown
rust
gray
red

Foods

insects
fruit
plants

Growth Stages

egg
larvae
pupa
adult

Kinds

carpenter
weaver
leaf cutter
fire
cornfield
thief
army

Ants

Roles

queen
worker
soldier
male

Homes

underground,
earthen mounds,
inside trees or
hollow plants

Body Parts

head,
antennae, eyes,
mouth parts,
trunk, six legs,
wings
(males and
young queens)

Importance

eat large number of insects;
food source for birds, frogs, and
other animals

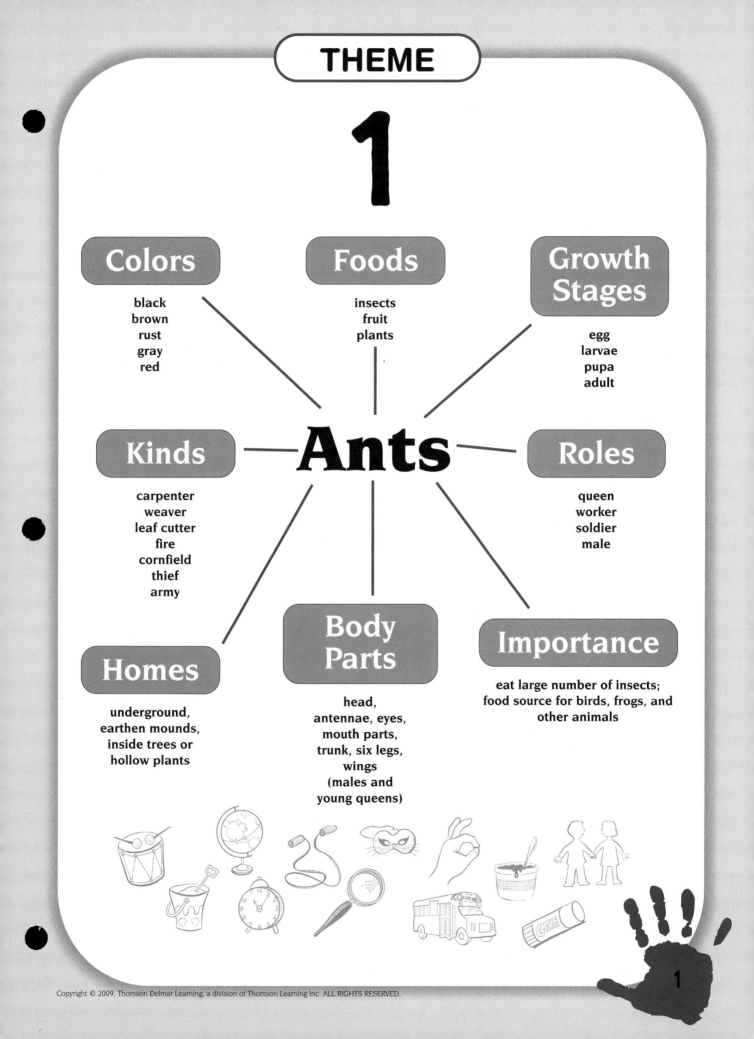

1

Theme Goals

Through participating in the experiences provided by this theme, the children may learn

1. Kinds of ants
2. Ant body parts
3. Colors of ants
4. Roles of ants
5. Ant growth stages
6. Foods ants eat
7. Ant homes
8. Importance of ants

Concepts for the Children to Learn

1. An ant is a small insect.
2. There are many kinds of ants.
3. An ant's body has three main parts.
4. An ant has six legs.
5. Ants can be black, brown, rust, gray, or red colored.
6. Ants use their mouth parts to grasp food, carry their young, and fight enemies.
7. Ants use their antennae to smell, touch, taste, and hear.
8. Ants build homes in many places.
9. Ants live in groups called colonies.
10. Ants eat other insects, plants, and fruits.
11. The queen ant lays the eggs.
12. Worker ants have many jobs.
13. A soldier ant is a large worker ant.
14. Ants can carry things larger than their bodies.
15. Ants are a food source for birds, frogs, and other animals.

Vocabulary

1. **ant**—a type of small insect.
2. **antennae**—feelers on the head of an insect.
3. **colony**—a community or group of ants.
4. **mandibles**—pair of jaws that move from side to side.
5. **queen**—female ant that lays eggs.
6. **soldiers**—largest worker ants.
7. **workers**—female ants that build the nest, search for food, care for the young, and fight enemies.

Bulletin Board

The purpose of this bulletin board is to promote mathematical skills. Sketch anthills on heavy construction paper or tagboard. As illustrated, on each anthill make a dot to represent each ant. Using a felt-tip magic marker, print a numeral on each hill that represents a number of dots. If desired for durability, laminate each anthill or cover with transparent contact paper. If desired, small rubber or plastic ants may be purchased commercially; otherwise, they can be constructed out of black construction paper.

Family Letter

Dear Families,

Another week has quickly come and gone. Before we know it, summer will be here again! Have you noticed the grass getting greener and the birds in the trees? Nature is full of small wonders. This week in school we will be learning about a group of "small wonders." We will find out many things about ants, those small picnic-joining insects! The children will learn about ant body parts, types of ants, foods ants eat, and places ants make homes, just to name a few!

AT SCHOOL

Learning experiences planned for this week include:

- finding ants to create an ant farm for the classroom
- going on a pretend picnic in the dramatic play area—ants included!
- using small plastic ants as game pieces for classroom games

AT HOME

Try some of these ant activities at home this week.

- Create egg-carton ants! Cut a cardboard egg carton into three-cup sections. Paint as desired. Use chenille stems or yarn pieces to represent six legs and antennae. Add small pompons, pebbles, or seeds for the eyes, or use purchased craft eyes. Fun!

- Check out books about ants from the library. Some titles to look for:
  Ant Cities by Arthur Dorros
  Two Bad Ants by Chris Van Allsburg

- Take a slow walk around your home or neighborhood with your child and look for ants. Are they all the same size? Color? Can you figure out where their homes are? What do you think they eat?

Have a f-*ant*-astic week!

Young children enjoy visually tracking ants crawling through the grass.

Arts and Crafts

1. Ant Prints

Set out several washable black and red ink pads and white paper. To create an ant, have each child press his or her index finger on the ink pad, and then make three prints in a row on the paper. Repeat process to make more ants. Provide black and red pens so children can add six legs and antennae.

2. Egg-Carton Ants

Cut cardboard egg cartons into three-section pieces. Children can paint their section as desired with "ant color" paints—black, brown, red, or gray. When dry, chenille stems or yarn pieces can be added to represent six legs and antennae. Eyes can be made from small pompons, pebbles, seeds, or purchased small craft eyes.

3. Clay Ants

Provide clay or play dough for children to create ants. Three small balls or circle shapes can be pushed together to create an ant body. Chenille stem pieces can be used for legs and antennae.

Cooking

Anthill Slaw

3 carrots, coarsely grated
3/4 cup raisins
1/2–3/4 cup mayonnaise
juice from 1/2 lemon
dash of salt and pepper

In a mixing bowl, combine carrots, raisins, and mayonnaise. Add more mayonnaise if needed. Add lemon juice, salt, and pepper. Mix again. Chill in the refrigerator for an hour.

Dramatic Play

Picnic (with ants, of course!)

Provide picnic props such as child-sized picnic table, backpack, tablecloth, picnic basket, cooler, thermos, plastic plates, and silverware. Plastic food items can be added. Have children assist in the preparation of paper ants that can be placed in the picnic area.

Field Trips/ Resource People

Insect Specialist

Contact your local Department of Natural Resources or county 4-H agent to find out if there are any insect specialists in your area who could talk about ants or show examples of types of ants.

Fingerplays

Little Ants

One little ant, two little ants,
   (point to a finger for each number)
Three little ants I see.
Four little ants, five little ants,
Lively as can be.
Six little ants, seven little ants,
Eight in a bowl of glass.
Nine little ants, ten little ants,
Entertain our class.

Anthill

Once I saw an anthill,
   (make fist with one hand)
With no ants about.
So I said, "Dear little ants,
Won't you please come out?"
Then as if the little ants
Had heard my call,
One, two, three, four, five came out.
   (extend fingers one at a time)
And that was all.

Caught an Ant

One, two, three, four, five,
   (extend a finger for each number)
I caught an ant alive.
Six, seven, eight, nine, ten,
   (extend fingers of other hand)
I let it go again.
Why did I let it go?
   (shrug shoulders)
It bit my finger so.
Which one did it bite?
   (shrug shoulders)
The little one on the right.
   (hold up right pinkie finger)

Group Time
(Games, Language)

Ant Partners

Draw and cut out small matching ants from
different colors of construction paper. Place the
ants in a paper bag and have each child take
one. Play music and let the children crawl
around the room to find their "ant partners" by
matching up their ants. Then have them hold
hands with their partners and sit to the side of
the group until all have found a partner. Collect
the ants and start the game again.

Large Muscle

Anthill Walk

Cut at least one large anthill shape out of brown
construction paper for each child. Also cut
several circles out of white construction paper.
Mix up the shapes and tape them to the floor in
a circle or trail. Play music and let the children
walk, skip, or hop around the shape circle or
trail. Stop the music and have each child find an
anthill to stand on. Continue the game as long
as there is interest.

Math

1. Ant Sort

Draw and cut out various-sized ants from
different colors of paper. Laminate pieces to
make them durable. Children can use the ant
pieces for counting activities, as well as for sorting by attributes such as color and size.

2. Anthill Math

Create several anthills from cardboard. Place a
numeral on each anthill. Have the children place
a corresponding number of ants on each hill.
The numerals you place on each anthill can vary
depending on the developmental abilities of the
children in your classroom.

Music

1. "The Ants Go Marching"
(*Sing to the tune of "When Johnny Comes Marching Home"*)

The ants go marching one by one.
Hurrah, hurrah.
The ants go marching one by one.
Hurrah, hurrah.
The ants go marching one by one.
The little one stopped to wiggle its thumb.
They all go marching,
Marching to escape the rain.

Continue with:

The ants go marching two by two.
The little one stopped to tie its shoe.

The ants go marching three by three.
The little one stopped to disagree.

The ants go marching four by four.
The little one stopped to shut the door.

The ants go marching five by five.
The little one stopped to learn to dive.

The ants go marching six by six.
The little one stopped to do some tricks.

The ants go marching seven by seven.
The little one stopped to wait for Devon.

The ants go marching eight by eight.
The little one stopped to shut the gate.

The ants go marching nine by nine.
The little one stopped to walk a line.

The ants go marching ten by ten.
The little one stopped to shout, "The End!"

2. "Six Little Ants"
(*Sing to the tune of "Six Little Ducks"*)

Six little ants that I once knew,
Black ants, brown ants, gray ants, too.
But the busiest ants are the workers of
    the bunch.
They feed the babies with a munch,
    munch, munch.
Munch, munch, munch. Munch, munch, munch.
They feed the babies with a munch,
    munch, munch.

3. "Ants"
(*Sing to the tune of "Mary Had a Little Lamb"*)

There's an ant trail underground,
Underground, underground.
There's an ant trail underground.
An ant colony lives down there.

The job of the queen is to lay the eggs,
Lay the eggs, lay the eggs.
The job of the queen is to lay the eggs,
That's all she has to do.

The worker ants have many jobs,
Many jobs, many jobs.
The worker ants have many jobs,
They do all the work.

4. "Little Black Ant"
(*Sing to the tune of "I'm a Little Teapot"*)

I'm a little black ant on the ground.
I'm so tiny I can hardly be found.
Look very closely, then you'll see.
I'm scurrying around—just look at me!

Science

1. Ant Farm

If you and the children would like to watch ants close up, try making an ant farm. Begin by sifting soil and/or sand into a clean, clear container that has a lid or cover with holes punched in it. Next, search for some ants. Select ants from the same area so they will likely be from the same colony. Scoop the ants into a separate collecting jar and transfer them to the viewing container. Place a small piece of damp sponge into the container so the ants will have something to drink. Every three days or so, use an eyedropper to add a teaspoon of water to the sponge. Put a little food into the jar. Try to see what the ants are eating. Some ants like sweets, some like other insects, and some like seeds. Keep the ant farm in a dark place or cover it with a cloth when the ants are not being viewed. Ants will tend to dig deep tunnels, away from the light. You could also purchase an ant farm for classroom use.

2. Ant Watch

Place a cut piece of fruit or candy outside as ant bait. Check on the food piece periodically with the children to observe if ants have found it. Similarly, cracker or bread crumbs could be placed outside. Children may then be able to watch ants attempt to carry pieces to their nest.

Sensory

Additions to the Sensory Table

- sand and small plastic ants with plastic jars and spoons

- play dough, rolling pins, circle cookie cutters (to create ants and anthills)

Social Studies

Ant Jobs

Ants work together to keep the ant colony alive. Each ant has work to do. Talk about the various roles or jobs that ants have in the colony.

Queen: The queen ant lays thousands and thousands of eggs. There is usually only one queen in a colony.

Workers: Workers are all females. They do the work in the ant city. They find food, store food, and take care of the ant eggs. They will also fight to protect the nest.

New Queens: New queens have wings. They use them to fly away to start new ant colonies. Their wings drop off, and then the queens lay eggs.

Books

The following books can be used to complement this theme:

Chinery, Michael. (1991). *Ant*. Mahwah, NJ: Troll. (Pbk.)

Climo, Shirley. (1995). *The Little Red Ant and the Great Big Crumb*: A Mexican Fable. New York: Clarion Books.

Cole, Joanna. (1996). *The Magic School Bus Gets Ants in Its Pants*: A Book about Ants. New York: Scholastic.

Demuth, Patricia Brennan. (1994). *Those Amazing Ants*. Illus. by S. D. Schindler. New York: Simon & Schuster.

Dorros, Arthur. (1987). *Ant Cities*. Bellevue, WA: Ty Crowell.

Fowler, Allan. (1998). *Inside an Ant Colony*. Chicago: Children's Press.

Hartley, Karen and Chris Marco. (2001). *Ant*. Des Plaines, IL: Heinemann Library.

Hepworth, Catherine. (1992). *Antics! An Alphabetical Anthology*. New York: G. P. Putnam.

Nickle, John. (1999). *The Ant Bully*. New York: Scholastic.

Pinczes, Elinor. (1993). *One Hundred Hungry Ants*. Illus. by Bonnie MacKain. Boston: Houghton Mifflin.

Poole, Amy Lowry. (2000). *The Ant and the Grasshopper*. Aesop fable retold and illustrated by Amy Lowry Poole. New York: Holiday House.

Multimedia

The following multimedia products can be used to complement this theme:

Ants: Hunters and Gardeners [video]. (1986). National Geographic Society.

The Ants Go Marching [cassette and book]. (1992). Bothell, WA: Wright Group.

"Ants on Parade" on *Songs about Insects, Bugs and Squiggly Things* [compact disc]. (1993). Kimbo Educational.

"Little Ant's Hill." (2004). Laugh N Learn Silly Songs. Long Branch, NJ: Kimbo.

Magic School Bus Gets Ants in Its Pants [video]. (1997). New York: Distributed by Kidvision.

Scruggs, J. *Ants* [compact disc or cassette]. (1994). Shadow Play Records and Video/Educational Graphics Press.

2

Tastes

sweet
sour

Forms

raw
cooked
dried
baked

Parts

seed
core
meat
skin
stem

Apples

Origin

orchard
seeds
soil
sunshine
water
trees
blossoms
fruit

Preparation

juice, pie,
cake, tarts,
sauce, cider,
jellies, butter,
muffins, bread,
pudding

Sizes

large
small

Colors

red
yellow
green

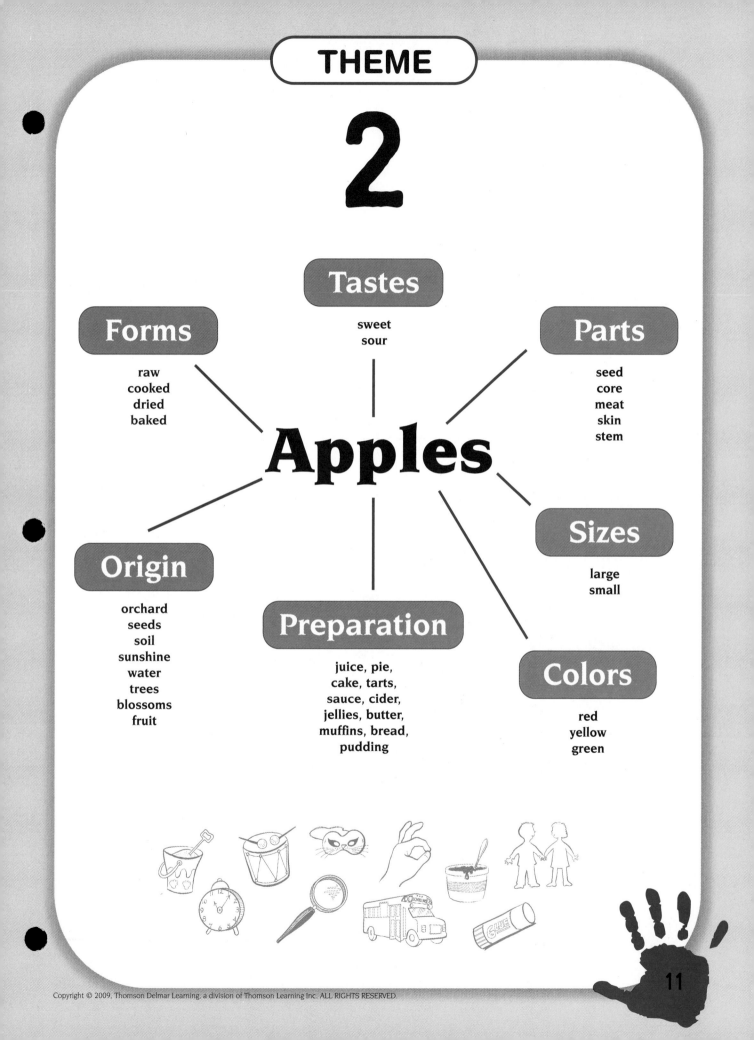

Theme Goals

Through participating in the experiences provided by this theme, the children may learn

1. Parts of an apple
2. Preparation of apples for eating
3. Apple tastes
4. Textures, sizes, and colors of apples
5. The origin of an apple

Concepts for the Children to Learn

1. An apple is a fruit.
2. An apple has five parts: seed, core, meat, skin, and stem.
3. Apples grow on trees.
4. A group of apple trees is an orchard.
5. Bread, butter, cakes, pies, pudding, applesauce, dumplings, butter, and jelly can be prepared from apples.
6. Some apples are sweet; others are sour.
7. Apples can be green, yellow, or red.
8. Apples can be large or small.
9. Apples can be hard or soft.
10. Seeds from an apple can grow into a tree.

Vocabulary

1. **apple**—a fruit that is grown on a tree.
2. **apple blossom**—a flower on the apple tree.
3. **apple butter**—a spread for bread made from apples.
4. **core**—the part of the apple that contains seeds.
5. **texture**—how something feels.

Bulletin Board

The purpose of this bulletin board is to develop the mathematical skill of sets, as well as to identify written numerals. Construct apples from red, green, and/or yellow tagboard. The number will depend on the developmental level of the children. Laminate the apples. Collect containers for baskets, such as large cottage cheese or pint berry containers. Cover the containers with paper if necessary. Affix numerals on baskets, beginning with the numeral 1. Staple the baskets to the bulletin board. The object is for the children to place the appropriate number of apples in each basket.

Family Letter

Dear Families,

Is it true that "an apple a day keeps the doctor away"? I'm not sure, but the children will make many discoveries as we begin a new unit on apples at school. Through active exploration and interaction, they will become more aware of the origin of apples, different flavors of apples, parts of apples, colors of apples, and ways apples can be prepared and eaten.

AT SCHOOL

Some classroom activities for this unit include:

- preparing applesauce for Thursday's snack

- drying apples in the sun

- creating apple-shaped sponge prints in the art area

- visiting the apple orchard! Arrangements have been made for a tour of the apple orchard on Wednesday morning. We will be leaving the center at 10:00 a.m. Feel free to join us.

AT HOME

Apples are a tasty and nutritious food—and most children enjoy eating them. Try a variety of apples for meals or snacks. You might also enjoy preparing caramel apples with your child. A recipe is as follows:

1 pound of vanilla caramels
2 tablespoons of water
dash of salt
6 crisp apples
6 wooden skewers or popsicle sticks

Melt the caramels with water in a microwave oven or double boiler, stirring frequently until smooth. Stir in the salt and stick a wooden skewer or popsicle stick in each apple. Dip the apple into the syrup, turning until the surface of the apple is completely covered.

Cooking is a great way to learn by experience because it involves the whole child—physically, emotionally, socially, and intellectually. It also builds vocabulary and involves counting and measuring, which are mathematical concepts. When a recipe is used, your child will also learn to follow a sequence. Enjoy cooking with your child.

Enjoy an apple with your child today!

THEME 2

Arts and Crafts

1. Apple Printing

Cut apple shapes from sponges. Have available individual shallow pans of red, yellow, and green tempera paint. Provide paper. The apple can be used as a painting tool. To illustrate, the children can place an apple half in the paint. After removing the excess paint, the apple can be placed on paper to create a print.

2. Seed Pictures

Collect: apple seeds along with other seeds
colored paper
glue

Each child who chooses to participate should be provided with a small number of seeds. As they are distributed, discuss the seeds' similarities and differences. Provide uninterrupted time for the children to glue seeds onto paper and create pictures.

3. Shakers

Collect: apple seeds
paper plates (two per child)
glue or stapler
color crayons or felt-tip markers

The children can decorate the paper plates with color crayons or felt-tip markers. After this, the seeds can be placed between the two plates. To create the shakers, staple or glue the two plates together by securing the outer edges of the plates. The children can use the shakers as a means of self-expression during music or self-directed play.

Cooking

1. Caramel Apple Slices

Prepare the following recipe, which should serve 12 to 14 children.

1 pound caramels
2 tablespoons water

A teacher-made chart can help children learn the sequence of preparing applesauce.

dash of salt
6 crisp apples

Melt caramels with water in the microwave oven or double boiler, stirring frequently until melted. Stir in the salt. Pour the melted caramel over the sliced apples and cool before serving.

2. Applesauce

30 large apples
2 1/2 cups water
1 1/2 cups sugar
1 tablespoon Red Hots

1. Clean apples by peeling, coring, and cutting into small pieces.
2. Place the apples in a large kettle containing water.
3. Simmer the apples on low heat, stirring occasionally until soft.
4. Add the remaining ingredients.
5. Stir and simmer a few minutes.
6. Cool before eating.

3. Persian Apple Dessert

3 medium apples, cut up
2 to 3 tablespoons sugar
2 tablespoons lemon juice
dash of salt

Place half the apples and the remaining ingredients in a blender. Cover and blend until coarsely chopped, about 20 to 30 seconds. Add remaining apples and repeat. Makes 3 servings.

4. Charoses

6 medium apples
1/2 cup raisins
1/2 teaspoon cinnamon
1/2 cup chopped nuts
1/4 cup white grape juice

Chop the peeled or unpeeled apples. Add the remaining ingredients. Mix well and serve.

5. Fruit Leather

2 cups applesauce
vegetable shortening or oil

Preheat oven to 400 degrees. Pour applesauce onto greased, shallow pan. Spread to 1/8 inch in thickness. Place pan in oven and lower temperature to 180 degrees. Cook for approximately 3 hours until the leather can be peeled from the pan. Cut with scissors to serve.

6. Dried Apples

5 or 6 apples
2 tablespoons salt
water

Peel, core, and cut apples into slices or rings 1/8 inch thick. Place apple slices in saltwater solution (2 tablespoons per 1 gallon water) for several minutes. Remove from the water. Place in 180-degree oven for 3 to 4 hours until dry. Turn apples occasionally.

Dramatic Play

Set Up an Apple Stand

Prepare an apple stand by providing the children with bags, plastic apples, cash register, money, stand, and bushels. Encourage buying, selling, and packaging.

Field Trips

1. Visit an Apple Orchard

Observe the workers picking, sorting, and/or selling the apples. Call attention to the colors and types of apples.

2. Visit a Grocery Store

Observe all the forms of apples sold in a grocery store. Also, in the produce department, observe the different colors and sizes of apples. To show children differences in weight, take a large apple and place it on a scale. Note the weight. Then take a small apple and repeat the process.

Fingerplays

Apple Tree

Way up high in the apple tree
   (stretch arm up high)
Two little apples smiled at me.
   (hold up two fingers)
I shook that tree as hard as I could
   (make shaking motion)
Down came the apples.
   (make downward motions)
Mmmm—they were good.
   (smile and rub stomach)

Picking Apples

Here's a little apple tree.
   (left arm up, fingers spread)
I look up and I can see
   (look at fingers)
Big red apples, ripe and sweet,
   (cup hands to hold apple)
Big red apples, good to eat!
   (raise hands to mouth)
Shake the little apple tree.
   (shake tree with hands)
See the apples fall on me.
   (raise cupped hands and let fall)
Here's a basket, big and round.
   (make circle with arms)
Pick the apples from the ground.
   (pick and put in basket)
Here's an apple I can see.
   (look up to the tree)
I'll reach up. It's ripe and sweet.
   (reach up to upper hand)
That's the apple I will eat!
   (hands to mouth)

An Apple

An apple is what I'd like to be.
My shape would be round.
   (fingers in circular shape)
My color would be green.
   (point to something green)
Children could eat me each and every day.
I'm good in tarts and pies and cakes.
   (make these food shapes)
An apple is good to eat or to bake.
   (make stirring motion)

Apple Chant

Apples, apples, good to eat.
Apples, apples, juicy and sweet.
Pick them off the tree.
Buy them at the store.
Apples, apples,
We want more.

The Apple

Within its polished universe
The apple holds a star.
   (draw design of star with index finger)
A secret constellation
To scatter near and far.
   (point near and far)

Let a knife discover
Where the five points hide.
Split the shiny ruby
And find the star inside.
After introducing the fingerplay, the teacher can
   cut an apple crosswise to find a star.

Apple Tree

This is the tree
With leaves so green.
   (make leaves with fingers outstretched)
Here are the apples
That hang in-between.
   (make fist)
When the wind blows
   (blow)
The apples will fall.
   (falling motion with hand)
Here is the basket to gather them all.
   (use arms to form basket)

Group Time

(Games, Language)

1. **What Is It?**

Collect a variety of fruits such as apples, bananas, and oranges. Begin by placing one fruit in a bag. Choose a child to touch the fruit, describe it, and name it. Repeat with each fruit, discussing the characteristics. During the activity, each child should have an opportunity to participate.

2. **Transition Activity**

The children should stand in a circle. As a record is played, the children pass an apple. When the record stops, the child holding the apple can get up to get a snack, put on outdoor clothes, clean up, etc. Continue until all children have a turn. For older children, more than one apple may be successfully passed at a time.

3. **Picking Apples**

Draw or paste a tree on a piece of tagboard or large piece of cardboard. Cut out apples from tagboard and place an alphabet letter on each apple. Laminate and attach Velcro to the back-side of the apple. Place apples (letter-side down) on the tree with Velcro. Invite children to pick an apple and then try to identify the letter name.

Sing the following song while the child picks the apple:

Pick an apple from the apple tree,
Say the letter (number, shape, color) name for me.

Note: Shapes, colors, or numbers can be substituted for the alphabet letters on the apples.

Math

1. Cut apple shapes of various sizes from construction paper. Let the children sequence the shapes from smallest to largest.

2. Place a scale and various-sized apples on the math table. The children can experiment by weighing the apples.

Music

1. **"Little Apples"**
(*Sing to the tune of "Ten Little Indians"*)

One little, two little, three little apples,
Four little, five little, six little apples,
Seven little, eight little, nine little apples,
All fell to the ground.

A variation for older children would be to give each child a number card (with a numeral from 1 through 9). When that number is sung, that child stands up. At the end of the fingerplay all the children fall down.

2. **"Apples Off My Tree"**
(*Sing to the tune of "Skip to My Lou"*)

Pick some apples off my tree,
Pick some apples off my tree,
Pick some apples off my tree,
Pick them all for you and me.

3. **"My Apple Tree"**
(*Sing to the tune of "The Muffin Man"*)

Did you see my apple tree,
Did you see my apple tree,
Did you see my apple tree,
Full of red apples?

Science

1. **Dried Apples**

Using plastic knives, peel, core, and cut apples into slices or rings about 1/8 inch thick. Prepare a saltwater solution by mixing a tablespoon of salt in a gallon of water. Place the apples in this solution for several minutes. Remove from the solution. Place the apples in an 180-degree oven for 3 to 4 hours or until dry. Turn the apples occasionally.

2. **Oxidation of an Apple**

Cut and core an apple into sections. Dip half the apple into lemon juice and place it on a plate. Place the remaining sections of apple on another plate. What happens to each plate of apples? Discuss the effects of the lemon juice coating, which keeps oxygen from the apples. As a result, they do not discolor as rapidly.

3. **Explore an Apple**

Discuss the color, size, and shape of an apple. Then discuss the parts of an apple. Include the skin, stem, core, meat, etc. Feel the apple. Then cut the apple in half. Observe the core and seeds. An apple is a fruit because it contains seeds.

Sensory

1. Cut different varieties of apples for a tasting party. This activity can easily be extended. On

another day provide the children applesauce, apple pie, apple juice, or apple cider to taste during snack or lunch.

2. Place several different kinds of seeds on the sensory table. In addition, to create interest provide scoops, bowls, and bottles to fill.

Books

The following books can be used to complement this theme:

Aliki. (1991). *The Story of Johnny Appleseed.* New York: Simon & Schuster.

Early, Margaret. (1991). *William Tell.* New York: Harry N. Abrams.

Fisher, Leonard Everett. (1996). *William Tell.* New York: Farrar, Straus & Giroux.

Hall, Zoe. (1996). *The Apple Pie Tree.* Illus. by Shari Halpern. New York: Scholastic.

Hodges, Margaret. (1997). *The True Tale of Johnny Appleseed.* New York: Holiday House.

Hutchins, Pat. (2000). *Ten Red Apples.* New York: Greenwillow.

Lindbergh, Reeve. (1990). *Johnny Appleseed.* Illus. by Kathy Jakobsen. Boston: Little, Brown.

Maestro, Betsy. (1992). *How Do Apples Grow?* New York: HarperCollins.

Marzollo, Jean. (1997). *I Am an Apple.* Illus. by Judith Moffatt. St. Paul, MN: Cartwheel Books. (Pbk.)

Micucci, Charles. (1992). *The Life and Times of the Apple.* New York: Orchard Books.

Naslund, Gorel Kristina. (2005). *Our Apple Tree.* Illus. by Kristina Digman. New Milford, CT: Roaring Brook Press.

Patent, Dorothy Hinshaw. (1998). *Apple Trees.* Photos by William Munoz. Minneapolis, MN: Lerner Publications.

Priceman, Marjorie. (1994). *How to Make an Apple Pie and See the World.* New York: Knopf.

Rickert, Janet Elizabeth and Pete McGahan (Photographer). (1999). *Russ and the Apple Tree Surprise.* Bethesda, MD: Woodbine House.

Rockwell, Anne. (1991). *Apples and Pumpkins.* New York: Simon & Schuster.

Slawson, Michele Benoit. (1994). *Apple Picking Time.* Illus. by Deborah Kogan Ray. New York: Crown Publishers.

Tryon, Leslie. (1993). *Albert's Field Trip.* New York: Simon & Schuster.

Wallace, Nancy Elizabeth. (2000). *Apples, Apples, Apples.* Delray Beach, FL: Winslow Press.

Wellington, Monica. (2001). *Apple Farmer Annie.* New York: Dutton Books.

Multimedia

The following multimedia products can be used to complement this theme:

Apples [video]. (1996). DeBeck Educational Video.

Kunstler, James Howard. (1992). *Johnny Appleseed* [video]. Told by Garrison Keillor. Rabbit Ears.

Occupations

artist, weaver,
designer, potter,
painter, glassblower,
cartoonist

Tools

paintbrushes, paper,
crayons, pencils,
paint, chalk,
watercolors,
felt-tip markers,
needles, scissors,
sewing machine,
pottery wheel, food

Places

art studios,
museums, parks,
stores, homes,
schools, craft shops,
historical sites

Art

Uses

expressions of feelings
thoughts
beauty
decoration
communication
enjoyment

Kinds

folk art
impressionist
modern
child created
crafts
romantic

Surfaces

paper, canvas,
wood, metal,
fabric, yarn,
glass, ceramic,
plastic, cement

Theme Goals

Through participating in the experiences provided by this theme, the children may learn

1. The uses of art
2. Places where works of art can be found
3. Art tools
4. Surfaces used for art
5. Occupations associated with art
6. Kinds of art

Concepts for the Children to Learn

1. Art is an expression of feelings and thoughts.
2. Brushes, scissors, paints, pencils, felt-tip markers, crayons, watercolors, chalk, and paper are all tools for teaching art.
3. Art can be used for decoration and beauty.
4. An artist uses art tools to make designs, pictures, or sculptures.
5. Art is a form of communication.
6. A museum has art objects.
7. An art gallery sells art objects for people to look at.
8. Paper, canvas, and wood can all be painted.
9. We are all artists.
10. Artists create for many reasons—personal enjoyment, gift giving, and career.
11. Artwork can be displayed in our homes.

Vocabulary

1. **art**—a form of beauty.
2. **artist**—a person who creates art.
3. **chalk**—a soft stone used for writing or drawing.
4. **crayon**—an art tool made of wax.
5. **gallery**—a place to display works of art.
6. **paint**—a colored liquid used for decoration.
7. **paintbrush**—a tool for applying paint.

Bulletin Board

The purpose of this bulletin board is to reinforce color-matching skills. Construct a crayon match bulletin board by drawing 16 crayons on white tagboard. Divide the crayons into pairs. Color each pair of crayons a different color. Include the colors pink, red, blue, yellow, purple, orange, brown, and green. Hang one from each pair on the top of the bulletin board and attach a corresponding colored string from the crayons. Hang the second set of crayons on the lower end of the bulletin board. A pushpin can be added to the bottom set of crayons and the children can match the top crayons to their corresponding match on the bottom of the bulletin board.

Adjust the bulletin board to match the developmental needs and level of the children. For younger children, use fewer color choices. Let the children use the bulletin board during self-directed and self-initiated play periods. Repetition of this activity, providing it is initiated by the child, is important for assimilation.

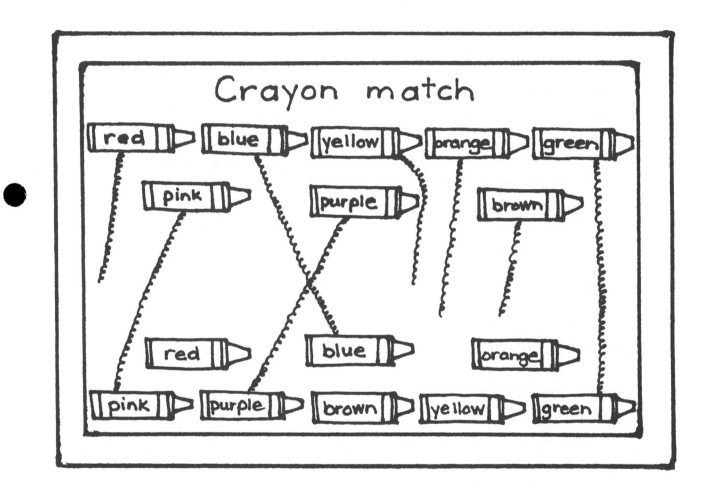

Family Letter

Dear Families,

Art is an expressive and aesthetic activity that can be enjoyed throughout life. It is also a curriculum theme that children always enjoy. During our focus on art, the children will be exploring many different types of art tools and supplies. They will also be learning where works of art can be found. Moreover, the artwork that they create will be displayed in an outdoor art gallery. You are invited to browse the gallery when you pick up your child from the center.

AT SCHOOL

Some of the artistic experiences planned include:

- creating chalk murals on the sidewalk
- staging an art gallery in the dramatic play area
- visiting on Tuesday with Bob Jones, a tour guide at the city museum. Mr. Jones will be sharing several art objects with us in our classroom.
- sorting art tools
- participating in a wide variety of art activities and exploring painting surfaces

AT HOME

You can introduce the concepts of this unit into your home by collecting art tools and exploring them together. A fun art idea is applying tempera paint on paper using kitchen tools as applicators. Forks, potato mashers, and slotted spoons all work well for this activity. Through this and other art activities, your child will be discovering interesting and creative ways for using materials. Art also provides opportunities for experimenting with color.

Have fun exploring art with your child!

Through art, children can experience new outlets for self-expression.

Arts and Crafts

1. Frames

During the course of this unit, the children can, with your assistance, frame their works of art by mounting them on sheets of colored tagboard and trimming them with a frame-like border. Older children may be able to do this unassisted. Display the works of art in the lobby or classroom—or outdoors, if weather permits.

2. Experimenting

In a unit on art, many kinds of art media need to be explored. Include the following art experiences:

- markers (both jumbo and skinny)
- chalk (both wet and dry)
- charcoal
- pencils (both colored and lead)
- crayons (jumbo, regular-sized, and shavings)
- paint (watercolors, tempera, fingerpaint)
- paper (colored construction, white, typing, tissue, newsprint, fingerpaint, tagboard)
- other (tin foil, cotton, glitter, glue and paste, lace, scraps, crepe paper, bags, waxed paper, yarn, and string)
- tools for painting (marbles, string, fingers, brushes of all sizes, straws, sponges)
- play dough and clay
- printing tools (stamps and ink pads, kitchen tools, sponges, potatoes, apples, and carrot ends)
- seeds

Cooking

1. Graham Cracker Treat

Give each child a graham cracker, honey, and a brush to spread the honey. Top with grated cheese, raisins, or coconut.

ART

2. Cookie Decorating

Sugar cookies can be purchased commercially or baked and decorated. Recipes for the cookies and frosting follow.

3. Drop Sugar Cookies

2 eggs
2/3 cup vegetable oil
2 teaspoons vanilla
3/4 cup sugar
2 cups flour
2 teaspoons baking powder
1/2 teaspoon salt

Beat eggs with fork. Stir in oil and vanilla. Blend in sugar until mixture thickens. Add flour, baking powder, and salt. Mix well. Drop dough by teaspoons about 2 inches apart on an ungreased baking sheet. Flatten with the bottom of a plastic glass dipped in sugar. Bake at 400 degrees for 8 to 10 minutes or until delicate brown. Remove from baking sheet immediately. Makes about 4 dozen cookies that are 2 1/2 inches in diameter.

4. Favorite Icing

1 cup sifted confectioner's sugar
1/4 teaspoon salt
1/2 teaspoon vanilla
1 tablespoon water
food coloring

Blend salt, sugar, and vanilla. Add enough water to make frosting easy to spread. Tint with food coloring. Allow children to spread on cookie with spatula or paintbrush.

Dramatic Play

1. Artist

Smocks, easels, and paint tables can be placed in the dramatic play area. The children can use the materials to pretend they are artists.

2. Art Gallery

Mount pictures from magazines on sheets of tagboard. Let the children hang the pictures

around the classroom. A cash register and play money for buying and selling the paintings can extend the play.

Field Trips/ Resource People

1. Museum

Take a field trip to a museum, if one is available. Observe art objects. Point out and discuss color and form.

2. Art Store

Take a walk to a nearby art store. Observe the many kinds of pencils, markers, crayons, paints, and other art supplies that are available.

3. Resource People

Invite the following people to show the children their artwork.

- painter
- potter
- weaver
- glassblower
- sculptor

Fingerplays

Clay

I stretch it.
    (pulling motion)
I pound it.
    (pounding motion)
I make it firm.
    (pushing motion)
I roll it.
    (rolling motion)
I pinch it.
    (pinching motion)
I make a worm.
    (wiggling motion)

Painting

Hands are blue.
  (look at outstretched hands)
Hands are green.
Fingers are red,
In between.
  (wiggle fingers)
Paint on my face.
  (touch face)
Paint on my smock.
  (touch smock)
Paint on my shoes.
  (touch shoes)
Paint on my socks.
  (touch socks)

Group Time
(Games, Language)

Toward the end of the unit, collect all art projects and display them in an art gallery at your center. The children can help hang their own projects and decide where to have the gallery. If weather permits, the art gallery can be set up on the playground using low clotheslines and easels to display the art. If weather does not permit, a gallery can be set up in the classroom or center lobby, using walls and tables to display the art.

Large Muscle

1. Sidewalk Chalk

Washable colored chalk can be provided for the children to use outside on the sidewalk. After the activity, the designs can be removed with a hose. The children may even enjoy using scrub brushes to remove the designs.

2. Painting

Provide large paintbrushes and buckets of water for the children to paint the sidewalks, walls, and fences surrounding your center or school.

3. Foot Art

Prepare a thick tempera paint and pour a small amount in a shallow pan. Roll out long sheets of paper. The children can take off their shoes and socks, step into the tempera paint, and walk or dance across the sheets of paper. Provide buckets with soapy water and towels at the end of the paper for the children to wash their feet. Dry the foot paintings and send them home with the children.

 # Math

1. Counting Cans

Counting cans for this unit can be made from empty soup cans with filed edges. On each can write a numeral. The number prepared will depend on the developmental needs of the children. Then provide an equal number of the following objects: pencils, pens, felt-tip markers, paintbrushes, crayons, chalk sticks, sponges, etc. The object is for the children to relate the number of objects to numerals on the can.

2. Measuring Art Tools

Art tools come in all different lengths. Provide a variety of art tools and rulers, or a tape measure that has been taped to the table. The children can measure the objects to find which one is the longest. Make a chart showing the longest tool and continuing to the shortest.

3. Sorting Art Supplies

A large ice cream pail can be used to hold pencils, pens, markers, crayons, glue bottles, and other supplies that can be sorted into shoeboxes.

 # Music

"Let's Pretend"
(Sing to the tune of "Here We Are Together")

Let's pretend that we are artists,
are artists, are artists.

Let's pretend that we are artists
How happy we'll be.
We'll paint with our brushes,
and draw with our crayons.
Let's pretend that we are artists
How happy we'll be.

Science

1. Art Tools

A variety of art tools can be placed on the science table. Included may be brushes, pencils, felt-tip markers, crayons, and chalk. The children can observe, smell, and feel the difference in the tools.

2. Charcoal

Place charcoal pieces and magnifying glasses on the science table.

3. Rock Writing

Provide the children with a variety of soft rocks. The children can experiment drawing on the sidewalks with them.

Sensory

Additions to the Sensory Table

1. Goop

Mix together food coloring, 1 cup cornstarch, and 1 cup water in the sensory table. If a larger quantity is desired, double or triple the recipe.

2. Silly Putty

Mix food coloring, 1 cup liquid starch, and 2 cups of glue together. Stir constantly until the ingredients are well mixed. Add more starch as needed.

3. Wet sand and sand mold containers

Social Studies

The Feel of Color

This activity can be introduced at large group time. Begin by collecting colored construction paper. Individually hold each color up and ask

Painting Surfaces

There are many types of interesting surfaces that children can successfully use for painting. The list of possibilities is limited only by one's imagination. Included are:

- construction paper
- newsprint (plain/printed)
- tissue paper
- tracing paper
- tin foil
- clear/colored acetate
- wood
- cardboard—sheets, boxes
- shelf paper
- paper tablecloths
- paper place mats
- waxed paper
- boxes
- leather scraps
- sandpaper
- paper toweling
- mirror
- plexiglass
- paper bags
- cookie sheets
- meat trays—plastic, styrofoam
- table surfaces
- shopping bags
- wrapping paper

the children how that particular color makes them feel. Adjectives that may be used include: hot, cold, cheerful, warm, sad, tired, happy, clean.

Books

The following books can be used to complement this theme:

Anholt, Laurence. (1994). *Camille and the Sunflowers: A Story about Vincent Van Gogh*. Hauppauge, NY: Barron's Educational Series.

Auch, Mary Jane. (1996). *Eggs Mark the Spot*. New York: Holiday House.

Beaumont, Karen. (2005). *I Ain't Gonna Paint No More!* Illus. by David Catrow. Orlando, FL: Harcourt.

Blizzard, Gladys. (1991). *Enjoying Art with Children*. West Palm Beach, FL: Lickle. (*Come Look with Me* series.)

Blizzard, Gladys. (1992). *Animals in Art*. West Palm Beach, FL: Lickle. (*Come Look with Me* series.)

Blizzard, Gladys. (1992). *Exploring Landscape with Children*. West Palm Beach, FL: Lickle. (*Come Look with Me* series.)

Blizzard, Gladys. (1993). *Words of Play*. West Palm Beach, FL: Lickle. (*Come Look with Me* series.)

Catalanotto, Peter. (1995). *The Painter*. New York: Orchard Books.

Cooney, Barbara. (1990). *Hattie and the Wild Waves*. New York: Viking.

Crespi, Francesca. (1995). *A Walk in Monet's Garden: Full Color Pop-Up with Guided Tour*. Boston: Little, Brown.

De Paola, Tomie. (1989). *Art Lesson*. New York: G. P. Putnam.

Dixon, Annabelle. (1990). *Clay*. Photographs by Ed Barber. Ada, OK: Garrett.

Dunrea, Olivier. (1995). *The Painter Who Loved Chickens*. New York: Farrar, Straus & Giroux.

Ehlert, Lois. (1997). *Hands*. San Diego, CA: Harcourt Brace.

Florian, Douglas. (1993). *Painter*. New York: Greenwillow Books.

Gutman, Anne and Georg Hallensleben. (2001). *Gaspard & Lisa at the Museum*. New York: Knopf.

Hest, Amy. (1996). *Jamaica Louise James*. Illus. by Sheila White Samton. Cambridge, MA: Candlewick Press.

Hurd, Thacher. (1996). *Art Dog*. New York: HarperCollins.

Jeunesse, Gallimard. (1991). *Colors*. Illus. by P. M. Valet. New York: Scholastic.

Le Tord, Bijou. (1995). *Blue Butterfly: A Story about Claude Monet*. New York: Bantam.

Lynn, Sara. (1993). *Play with Paint*. Minneapolis, MN: Carolrhoda Books.

Micklethwait, Lucy. (1992). *I Spy: An Alphabet in Art*. New York: Greenwillow Books.

Micklethwait, Lucy. (1993). *I Spy a Lion: Animals in Art*. Nashville, TN: Ideals.

Micklethwait, Lucy. (1995). *Spot a Cat*. New York: Dorling Kindersley.

Micklethwait, Lucy. (1995). *Spot a Dog*. New York: Dorling Kindersley.

Micklethwait, Lucy. (1996). *I Spy a Freight Train: Transportation in Art*. New York: Greenwillow Books.

Moon, Nicola. (1997). *Lucy's Picture*. Illus. by Lynn Munsinger. New York: Dial Books.

Nikola, Lisa W. (2004). *Setting the Turkeys Free*. Illus. by Ken Wilson-Max. New York: Hyperion Books for Children.

Porte, Barbara Ann. (1995). *Chickens Chickens*. Illus. by Greg Henry. New York: Orchard Books.

Reynolds, Peter. (2005). *The Dot*. Denton, TX: BrailleInk.

Richardson, Joy. (1993). *Inside the Museum: A Children's Guide to the Metropolitan Museum of Art*. New York: Abrams.

Rockwell, Anne F. (1993). *Mr. Panda's Painting*. New York: Simon & Schuster.

Stanley, Diane. (1994). *The Gentleman and the Kitchen Maid*. Illus. by Dennis Nolan. New York: Dial Books.

Venezia, Mike. (1988–1997). *Getting to Know the World's Greatest Artists* [Series]. Chicago: Children's Press. 23+ titles.

Watson, A. and the Staff of the Abby Aldrich Rockefeller Folk Art Center. (1992). *Folk Art Counting Book*. New York: Abrams.

Winter, Jeanette. (1996). *Josefina*. Orlando: Harcourt Brace.

Wolestein, Diane. (1992). *Little Mouse's Painting*. Illus. by Maryjane Begin. New York: William Morrow.

Yenawine, Philip. (1991). *Colors*. The Museum of Modern Art. New York: Delacorte Press.

Ziefert, Harriet. (2003). *Lunchtime for a Purple Snake*. Paintings by Todd McKie. Boston, MA: Houghton Mifflin.

Kid Pix Studio [CD-ROM]. (1994). Novato, CA: Broderbund.

New Kid Pix [CD-ROM]. (1996). Novato, CA: Broderbund.

Paint, Write and Play [CD-ROM]. (1996). Fremont, CA: Learning Company.

Polisar, Barry Louis. *Barry's Scrapbook: A Window into Art* [video]. (1994). ALA Video/Library Video Network.

Rylant, Cynthia. *All I See* [video]. (1990). Hightstown, NJ: McGraw-Hill Media.

Multimedia

The following multimedia products can be used to complement this theme:

I Want to Be an Artist [video]. (1993). Glenview, IL: Crystal Productions.

4

Origin

eggs

Colors

blue, brown,
black, red, gray,
orange, green, pink

Body

feathers, wings,
tails, beaks,
legs, eyes

Birds

Foods

seeds, insects,
crumbs, berries,
worms, fish,
small animals

Types

turkeys
ducks
chickens
wild
pets

Help

eat insects
create beauty

Homes

nests
trees
houses
cages

Sizes

small
medium
large

Theme Goals

Through participating in the experiences provided by this theme, the children may learn

1. The bird's body parts
2. Types of birds
3. Bird homes
4. Foods that birds eat
5. Ways birds help
6. Sizes of birds
7. Colors of birds
8. Origins of birds

Concepts for the Children to Learn

1. There are many types of birds.
2. Birds hatch from eggs.
3. Birds have feathers, wings, tails, legs, eyes, and beaks.
4. Birds live in nests, trees, houses, and cages.
5. Birds eat seeds, insects, crumbs, berries, and worms.
6. Some birds eat fish and small animals.
7. Some birds help us by eating insects.

Vocabulary

1. **beak**—the part around a bird's mouth.
2. **bird feeder**—a container for bird food.
3. **birdwatching**—watching birds.
4. **feathers**—cover skin of a bird.
5. **hatch**—to come from an egg.
6. **nest**—bed or home prepared by a bird.
7. **perch**—a pole for a bird to stand on.
8. **wing**—movable body part that helps most birds fly.

Bulletin Board

The purpose of this bulletin board is to develop skills in eye-hand coordination, problem solving, and matching. To construct the board, cut 10 bird nests out of brown-colored tagboard. Draw a set of dots, beginning with 1, on each bird nest. Tack the nest on the bulletin board. Next, construct the same number of birds out of tagboard. Write a numeral on each bird beginning with 1. By matching the numeral on each bird to the number of dots on the nests, the children can help each bird find a home. The number of birds and nests on this bulletin board should match the children's developmental abilities.

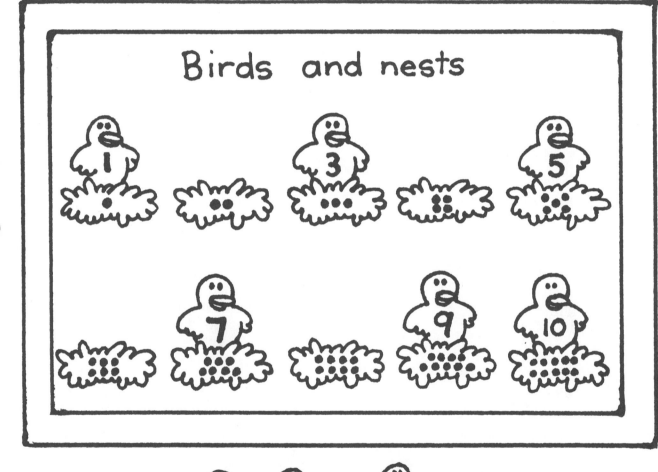

Family Letter

Dear Families,

The children will be discussing our "feathered friends"—birds—during our next unit. They will be introduced to birds kept as pets and birds in the wild. In addition, they will discover the unique body parts of birds and the homes in which they live. By participating in class activities, the children will learn that birds are more similar than they are dissimilar.

AT SCHOOL

Some of the activities planned for the unit on birds include:

- observing different types of bird nests with a magnifying glass at the science table
- visiting with Jodi's pet canary on Wednesday
- creating collages using birdseed and glue in the art area
- making bird feeders to hang outdoors in our play yard
- building birdhouses

AT HOME

Whether you live in the city or country, chances are there are birds nearby. If you have birds in your yard, the following game may be fun to play with your child. Set an egg or kitchen timer for 3 to 5 minutes. Then look out the window and see how many birds you can see. For each bird, drop a button in a jar. When the timer goes off, count how many buttons are in the jar. This game will strengthen your child's observation skills and increase his or her understanding of number concepts. Variations of this game would be to observe for cars, squirrels, or any other object that can be counted.

Happy birdwatching!

Children enjoy exploring bird habitats.

Arts and Crafts

1. Feather Painting

On the art table, place feathers, thin paper, and paint. Let the children experiment with different paint consistencies and types of feathers. *Suggestion:* Inexpensive feather dusters from discount stores are a good source of feathers. Individual feathers can be cut off as needed.

2. Birdseed Collages

Birdseed, paper, and white glue are needed for this activity. Apply glue to paper and sprinkle birdseed over the glue. For a variation, use additional types of seeds such as corn and sunflower seeds.

3. Eggshell Collage

Save eggshells and dye them. Crush the dyed shells into small pieces. Using glue, apply the eggshells to paper.

4. Robin Eggs

Cut easel paper into the shape of an egg. Provide light blue paint with sand for speckles.

5. Dyeing Eggs

Boil an egg for each child. Then let the children paint the eggs with non-toxic paint and easel brushes. The eggs can be eaten at snack time or taken home.

Cooking

1. Egg Salad Sandwiches

eggs
bread
mayonnaise
dry mustard (just a pinch)
salt
pepper

Boil, shell, and mash the eggs, adding enough mayonnaise to provide a consistent texture. Add salt, pepper, and dry mustard to flavor. Spread on the bread.

2. French Bread Recipe

1/2 cup water
2 packages rapid rise yeast
1 tablespoon salt
2 cups lukewarm water
7 to 7 1/2 cups all-purpose flour

Soften the yeast in 1/2 cup lukewarm water. Be careful that the water isn't too warm or the activity of the yeast will be destroyed. Add salt to 2 cups of lukewarm warm water in a large bowl. Gradually, add 2 cups of flour and beat well. Add the softened yeast and gradually add the remaining flour, beating well after each addition. Turn the soft dough out on a lightly floured surface and knead until elastic. Lightly grease a bowl and place the dough into it, turning once to grease surface. Let rise until double. Divide into 2 portions. Bake in a 375-degree oven until light brown, about 35 minutes.

3. Bird's Nest Salad

1 grated carrot
1/2 cup canned Chinese noodles
mayonnaise to moisten
peas or grapes

Have the children grate a carrot. Next have them mix the carrot with 1/2 cup canned Chinese noodles and mayonnaise to moisten. Put a mound of this salad on a plate and push in the middle with a spoon to form a nest. Peas or grapes can be added to the nest to represent bird eggs. The nest could also be set on top of a lettuce leaf. Makes 2 salads.

Note: From *Super Snacks*, by J. Warren, 1982, Alderwood Manor, WA: Warren. Reprinted with permission.

4. Egg Foo Young

12 eggs
1/2 cup finely chopped onion
1/3 cup chopped green pepper
3/4 teaspoon salt
dash of pepper
2 16-ounce cans bean sprouts, drained
Sauce:
2 tablespoons cornstarch
2 teaspoons sugar
2 cubes or 2 teaspoons chicken bouillon
dash of ginger
2 cups water
3 tablespoons soy sauce

Heat oven to 300 degrees. Beat eggs in a large bowl. Add remaining ingredients, except sauce ingredients; mix well. Heat 2 tablespoons of oil in a large skillet. Drop egg mixture by tablespoons into skillet and fry until golden. Turn and brown other side. Drain on a paper towel. Continue to cook the remaining egg mixture, adding oil to skillet if necessary. Keep warm in 300-degree oven while preparing sauce. Combine the first four sauce ingredients in a saucepan. Add water and soy sauce. Cook until mixture boils and thickens, stirring constantly.

5. Bird Nest Treat

Prepare Rice Krispies bar.

- 1/4 cup butter or margarine (1/2 stick)
- 6–10 oz. regular marshmallows (about 40) or 4 cups miniature marshmallows
- 6 cups Rice Krispies

Melt butter in 3-quart saucepan. Add marshmallows and cook over low heat, stirring constantly, until marshmallows are melted and mixture is syrupy. Remove from heat.

Add Rice Krispies and stir until well coated.

Before cooling, shape into a bird's nest.

Dramatic Play

1. Birdhouse

Construct a large birdhouse out of cardboard. Place in the dramatic play area, allowing the children to imitate birds. Unless adequate room is available, this may be more appropriate for an outdoor activity. Bird accessories such as teacher-made beaks and wings may be supplied to stimulate interest.

2. Bird Nest

Place several bales of hay in the corner of a play yard, confining the materials to one area. Let the child rearrange the straw to simulate a bird nest.

3. Hatching

Here is a general idea of what you can say to create the hatching experience with young children. Say, "Close your eyes. Curl up very small, as small as you can. Lie on your side. Think of how dark it is inside your egg. Yes, you're in an egg! You're tiny and curled up and quiet. It's very dark. Very warm. But now, try to wiggle a little—just a little! Remember, your eggshell is all around you. You can wiggle your wingtips a little, and maybe your toes. You can shake your head just a little. Hey! Your beak is touching something. I think your beak is touching the eggshell. Tap the shell gently with your beak. Hear that? Yes, that's you making that noise. Keep tapping. A little harder. Something is happening. The shell has cracked—oh, close your eyes. It's bright out there. Now you can wiggle a little more. The shell is falling away. You can stretch out, stretch to be as long as you can make yourself.

Stretch your feet. Stretch your wings. Doesn't that feel good, after being in that little egg? Stretch! You're brand new—can you stand up slowly? Can you see other new baby birds?"

Field Trips/ Resource People

1. Pet Store

Take a field trip to a pet store. Arrange to have the manager show the children birds and birdcages. Ask the manager how to care for birds.

2. Bird Sanctuary

Take a field trip to a bird sanctuary, nature area, pond, or park. Observe where birds live.

3. Museum

Arrange to visit a nature museum or taxidermy studio to look at stuffed birds. Extend the activity by providing magnifying glasses.

4. Zoo

Visit the bird house. Observe the colors and sizes of birds.

5. Resource People

Invite resource people to visit the classroom. Suggestions include:

- wildlife management people
- ornithologists
- veterinarians
- bird owners
- birdwatchers
- pet store owners

# Fingerplays

Houses

Here is a nest for a robin.
    (cup both hands)

Here is a hive for a bee.
    (fists together)
Here is a hole for the bunny;
    (finger and thumb make circle)
And here is a house for me!
    (fingertips together to make roof)

Two Little Blackbirds

Two little blackbirds sitting on a hill,
    (close fists, extend index fingers)
One named Jack. One named Jill.
    (talk to one finger; talk to other finger)
Fly away, Jack. Fly away, Jill.
    (toss index fingers over shoulder separately)
Come back, Jack. Come back, Jill.
    (bring back hands separately with index fingers extended)

Bird Feeder

Here is the bird feeder. Here are seeds and crumbs.
    (left hand out flat, right hand cupped)
Sprinkle them on and see what comes.
    (sprinkling motion with right hand over left hand)
One cardinal, one chickadee, one junco, one jay,
    (join fingers of right hand and peck at the bird feeder once for each bird)
Four of my bird friends are eating today.
    (hold up four fingers of left hand)

If I Were a Bird

If I were a bird, I'd sing a song
And fly about the whole day long.
    (twine thumbs together and move hands like wings)
And when the night comes, go to rest,
    (tilt head and close eyes)
Up in my cozy little nest.
    (cup hands together to form nest)

Tap Tap Tap

Tap, tap, tap goes the woodpecker
    (tap with right pointer finger on inside of left wrist)
As he pecks a hole in a tree.
    (make hole with pointer finger and thumb)
He is making a house with a window
To peep at you and me.
    (hold circle made with finger and thumb in front of eye)

Stretch, Stretch

Stretch, stretch away up high:
On your tiptoes, reach the sky.
See the bluebirds flying high.
   (wave hands)
Now bend down and touch your toes.
Now sway as the North Wind blows.
Waddle as the gander goes!

Group Time

(Games, Language)

1. Little Birds

This is a movement game that allows for activity. To add interest, the teacher may use a tambourine for rhythm. One child can be the mother bird and the remainder of the children can act out the story.

All the little birds are asleep in their nest.
All the little birds are taking a rest.
They do not even twitter, they do not even tweet.
Everything is quiet up and down the street.
Then came the mother bird and tapped them on
   the head.
They opened up one little eye and this is what
   was said,
"Come little birdies, it's time to learn to fly,
Come little birdies, fly way up in the sky."
Fly fly, oh fly away, fly, fly, fly
Fly fly, oh fly away, fly away so high.
Fly fly, oh, fly away, birds can fly the best.
Fly fly, oh, fly away, now fly back to your nest.

2. Who Is Inside?

The purpose of this game is to encourage the child to develop listening skills. To prepare for the activity, find a piece of large muscle equipment such as a jungle gym to serve as the birdhouse. Cover it with a large blanket. To play the game, one child looks away from the group or covers his or her eyes. A second child should go into the birdhouse. The first child says, "Who is inside?" The second child replies, "I am inside the birdhouse." Then the first child tries to guess who is in the birdhouse by recognizing the voice. Other clues may be asked for, if voice alone does not work.

3. Little Red Hen

Tell the story of the Little Red Hen. After they have heard the story, let the children help make bread.

Large Muscle

1. Bird Nest Search

Hide strips of brown fabric around the room. Invite children to search for "twigs" for a bird nest. When strips are found, glue onto small plastic pool and place "nest" in dramatic play area.

2. Penguin Waddle

Explain to children how a penguin waddles. Place a small rubber ball between the knees of the children, so they can imitate the waddle of a penguin.

3. Egg Drop

Have the children walk while balancing a plastic egg on a large wooden spoon.

4. Egg Hunt

Hide plastic eggs on the outdoor playground or in the classroom. Ask children to search for eggs.

Math

1. Feather Sorting

During the self-directed activity period, place a variety of feathers on a table. Encourage the children to sort them according to attributes such as color, size, and/or texture. This activity can be followed with other sorting activities including egg shapes and pictures of birds.

2. Cracked Eggs

Cut tagboard egg shapes. Using scissors, cut the eggs in half making a jagged line. Record a numeral on one side of the egg and corresponding dots on the other side. The number of eggs prepared should reflect the children's developmental level.

3. **Clothesline Birds**

Create a clothesline stand by placing two wooden dowels into opposite ends of a board. Drill holes through each dowel near the top. Tie a rope from one dowel to another. Make birds in a variety of sizes. Have the children clip the birds onto the clothesline with clothespins, in order from smallest to largest or largest to smallest.

Music

1. **"Birds"**
(Sing to the tune of "Here We Go Round the Mulberry Bush")

The first verse remains the same, with the children walking around in a circle holding hands.

This is the way we scratch for worms, scratch for worms, scratch for worms.
This is the way we scratch for worms
    so early in the morning.
    (children move foot in a scratching motion like a chicken)
This is the way we peck our food . . .
    (children peck)
This is the way we sit on our eggs . . .
    (children squat down)
This is the way we flap our wings . . .
    (bend arms at elbows and put thumbs under armpits, flap)
This is the way we fly away . . .
    (children can "fly" anywhere they want, but return to the circle at the end of the verse)

2. **"Pretty Birds"**
(Sing to the tune of "Ten Little Indians")

One pretty, two pretty
Three pretty birdies.
Four pretty, five pretty,
Six pretty birdies.
Seven pretty, eight pretty,
Nine pretty birdies,
All sitting in a tree.

Science

1. **Bird Feeders**

Make bird feeders. Suet can be purchased from a butcher shop or meat department of a supermarket. For each feeder, purchase 1/2 pound of suet, a 12-inch × 12-inch piece of netting, and birdseed. Begin by rolling the suet in birdseed. Place the seeded suet in the netting. Tie the four corners of the netting together and hang in a tree or set outside on a window ledge for children to observe.

2. **Grapefruit Cup Feeders**

Place seeds in an empty grapefruit half. If possible, place the feeder in an observable location for the children. Some children may wish to take their feeders home.

3. **Science Table**

On the science table, provide magnifying glasses and the following items:

- feathers
- eggs
- nests

4. **Observing a Bird**

Arrange for a caged parakeet to visit the classroom. A parent may volunteer or a pet store may lend a bird for a week. Encourage the children to note the structure of the cage, the beauty of the bird, food eaten, and the behavior of the bird.

5. **Feed the Hummingbirds**

Hang a hummingbird feeder near a classroom window. Encourage the children to help you mix the liquid to fill the hummingbird feeder. The recipe is as follows:

Hummingbird Food
2 cups water
1 cup sugar
Stir until dissolved.

Pour liquid into feeder and encourage the children to watch for hummingbirds. Be sure to clean the feeder between refills.

6. Birds I Have Seen

Prepare a chart with all of the children's names and birds that can be identified in the local area. Title the chart "Bird Watch." Place a pair of binoculars and the chart on the science shelf. Encourage children to look outside for birds. If they see a bird, they can mark "yes" or place their picture on the corresponding bird chart behind their name.

Sensory

Additions to the Sensory Table

- feathers and sand
- eggshells
- sticks and twigs for nests
- worms and soil
- water, rubber ducks, and other water toys
- birdseed and measuring tools

Social Studies

1. Caring for Birds

Arrange for a pet canary to visit the classroom. The children can take turns feeding and caring for the bird. Responsibilities include cleaning the cage and providing water and birdseed. Also, a cuttlebone should be inserted in the bars of the cage within reach of the bird's bill. This bone will help keep the bird's bill sharp and clean, providing the bird uses it.

2. Bird Feeders

Purchase birdseed and small paper cups. The children can fill a cup with a small amount of seed. After this, the teacher can attach a small string to the cup for use as a handle. The bird feeders can then be hung in bushes outdoors. If bushes are not available, they can be placed on window sills.

Books

The following books can be used to complement this theme:

Appelt, Kathi and Jane Dyer. (2000). *Oh My Baby, Little One*. San Diego, CA: Harcourt Brace.

Arnosky, Jim. (1992). *Crinkleroot's Guide to Knowing the Birds*. New York: Simon & Schuster.

Arnosky, Jim. (1993). *Crinkleroot's 25 Birds Every Child Should Know*. Minneapolis, MN: Bradbury.

Arnosky, Jim. (1997). *Watching Water Birds*. Washington, DC: National Geographic Society.

Bates, Ivan. (2006). *Five Little Ducks*. Illus. by Ivan Bates. New York: Scholastic.

Bennett, Penelope. (1995). *Town Parrot*. Illus. by Sue Heap. Cambridge, MA: Candlewick Press.

Berger, Bruce. (1995). *A Dazzle of Hummingbirds*. Illus. by John Chellman. Morristown, NJ: Silver Burdett.

Bernhard, Emery. (1994). *Eagles: Lions of the Sky*. Illus. by Durga Bernhard. New York: Holiday House.

Brenner, Barbara and Julia Takaya. (1996). *Chibi: A True Story from Japan*. Illus. by June Otani. New York: Clarion Books.

Cannon, Janell. (1993). *Stellaluna*. Orlando, FL: Harcourt Brace.

Carle, Eric. (2005). *10 Little Rubber Ducks*. New York: HarperCollins.

Cherry, Lynne. (1997). *Flute's Journey: The Life of a Wood Thrush*. San Diego, CA: Gulliver Books.

Demuth, Patricia. (1994). *Cradles in the Trees: The Story of Bird Nests*. Illus. by Suzanne Barnes. New York: Simon & Schuster.

Ehlert, Louis. (1997). *Cuckoo: A Mexican Folktale*. Orlando, FL: Harcourt Brace.

Esbensen, Barbara Juster. (1991). *Tiger with Wings: The Great Horned Owl*. Illus. by Mary Barrett Brown. New York: Orchard Books.

Ezra, Mark. (1997). *The Frightened Little Owl*. Illus. by Gavin Rowe. New York: Crocodile Books.

Flanagan, Alice K. (1996). *Desert birds*. Chicago: Children's Press. (*New True Book* series.)

Flanagan, Alice K. (1996). *Night birds*. Chicago: Children's Press. (*New True Book* series.)

Flanagan, Alice K. (1996). *Seabirds*. Chicago: Children's Press. (*New True Book* series.)

Flanagan, Alice K. (1996). *Songbirds*. Chicago: Children's Press. (*New True Book* series.)

Flanagan, Alice K. (1996). *Talking birds*. Chicago: Children's Press. (*New True Book* series.)

Fontanel, Beatrice. (1992). *The Penguin*. Illus. by Valerie Tracqui. Watertown, MA: Charlesbridge. (Pbk.)

Foster, Joanna. (1995). *The Magpies' Nest*. Illus. by Julie Downing. New York: Clarion Books.

Gans, Roma and Paul Mirocha. (1996). *How Do Birds Find Their Way?* New York: HarperCollins.

Gibbons, Gail. (1997). *Gulls—Gulls—Gulls*. New York: Holiday House.

Gibbons, Gail. (1998). *Soaring with the Wind: The Bald Eagle*. New York: William Morrow.

Horacek, Petr. (2005). *Bird, Fly High*. Cambridge, MA: Candlewick Press. (First U.S. edition.)

Inches, Alison and Cheryl Mendenhal. (2001). *Dizzy's Bird Watch*. New York: Simon Spotlight.

Jenkins, Priscilla Belz. (1995). *Nest Full of Eggs*. Illus. by Lizzy Rockwell. New York: HarperCollins.

Kalbacken, Joan. (1997). *Peacocks and Peahens*. Chicago: Children's Press.

Lewin, Betsy. (1995). *Booby Hatch*. New York: Clarion Books.

Maslowski, Steve. (2002). *Birds in the Fall*. North Mankato, MN: Smart Apple Media.

Maslowski, Steve. (2002). *Birds in the Spring*. North Mankato, MN: Smart Apple Media.

Maslowski, Steve. (2002). *Birds in the Summer*. North Mankato, MN: Smart Apple Media.

Maslowski, Steve. (2002). *Birds in the Winter*. North Mankato, MN: Smart Apple Media.

Massie, Diane Redfield and Steven Kellogg. (2000). *The Baby BeeBee Bird*. Illus. by Steven Kellogg. New York: HarperCollins.

Maynard, Thane. (1997). *Ostriches*. Mankato, MN: Child's World.

Mazzola, Frank. (1997). *Counting Is for the Birds*. Watertown, MA: Charlesbridge Publishers.

McMillan, Bruce. (1995). *Nights of the Pufflings*. Boston: Houghton Mifflin.

Morrison, Gordon. (1998). *Bald Eagle*. Boston: Houghton Mifflin.

Murphy, Mary. (2002). *I Like It When*. San Diego, CA: Red Wagon Books.

Neitzel, Shirley. (1997). *The House I'll Build for the Wrens*. New York: Greenwillow Books.

Owens, Mary Beth. (1993). *Counting Cranes*. Boston: Little, Brown.

Parry-Jones, Jemima. (1992). *Amazing Birds of Prey*. Illus. by Mike Dunning. New York: Knopf.

Pfeffer, Wendy. (1996). *Mute Swans*. Morristown, NJ: Silver Burdett Press.

Polacco, Patricia. (2001). *Mr. Lincoln's Way*. New York: Philomel Books.

Rau, Dana Meachen. (1995). *Robin at Hickory Street*. Illus. by Joel Snyder. Norwalk, CT: Soundprints/Smithsonian Institution.

Rockwell, Anne. (1992). *Our Yard Is Full of Birds*. New York: Macmillan.

Royston, Angela. (1992). *Birds*. New York: Aladdin Books.

Savage, Stephen. (1995). *Duck*. Illus. by Steve Lings. Cincinnati, OH: Delmar Learning.

Savage, Stephen. (1995). *Seagull*. Illus. by Andre Boos. Cincinnati, OH: Thomson Learning.

Sill, Cathryn P. (1991). *About Birds: A Guide for Children*. Illus. by John Sill. Atlanta, GA: Peachtree Publishers.

Swinburne, Stephen R. (1996). *Swallows in the Birdhouse*. Illus. by Robin Brickman. Brookfield, CT: Millbrook Press.

Torres, Leyla. (1993). *Subway Sparrow*. New York: Farrar, Straus & Giroux.

Waddell, Martin. (1992). *Owl Babies*. Illus. by Patrick Benson. Cambridge, MA: Candlewick Press.

Warren, J. (1982). *Super Snacks*. Alderwood Manor, WA: Warren.

Willis, Nancy Carol. (1996). *The Robins in Your Backyard*. Montchanin, DE: Cucumber Island Storytellers.

Multimedia

The following multimedia products can be used to complement this theme:

"Birds and How They Grow" on *Animals and How They Grow* [CD-ROM]. (1993). Washington, DC: National Geographic Society.

Eastman, P. D. (1991). *Are You My Mother? Plus Two More P. D. Eastman Classics* [video]. New York: Random House Video.

Flying, Trying, and Honking Around [video]. (1994). Washington, DC: National Geographic Kids Video.

Recordings and Song Titles

The following recordings can be used to complement the theme:

"Mary's Canary," "The Little Bird," "The Robin," "Sing a Song of Sixpence," "Swan." (1986). *Singable Nursery Rhymes*. Long Branch, NJ: Kimbo Educational.

"Six Little Ducks," "Little White Duck," "Old MacDonald Had a Farm." (1997). *Six Little Ducks*. Long Branch, NJ: Kimbo Educational.

"The Little Bird." (1999). *Moving with Mozart*. Long Branch, NJ: Kimbo Educational.

"The Rooster's Song." (1999). *On the Farm with RONNO*. Long Branch, NJ: Kimbo Educational.

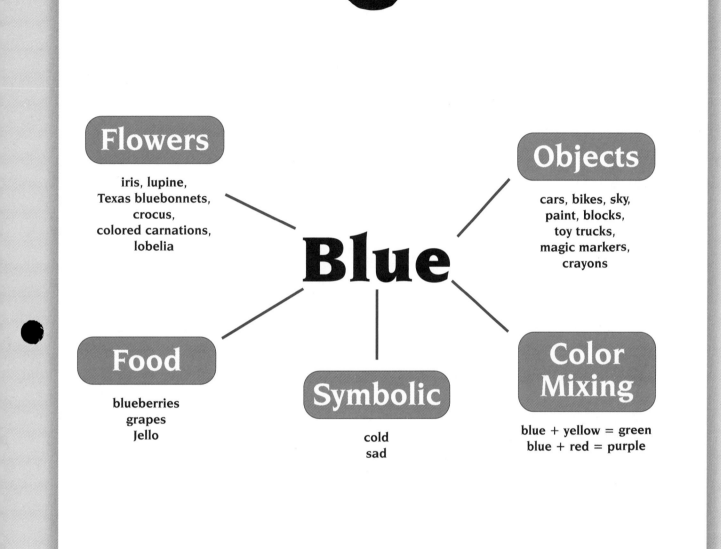

Flowers

iris, lupine,
Texas bluebonnets,
crocus,
colored carnations,
lobelia

Objects

cars, bikes, sky,
paint, blocks,
toy trucks,
magic markers,
crayons

Blue

Food

blueberries
grapes
Jello

Symbolic

cold
sad

**Color
Mixing**

blue + yellow = green
blue + red = purple

Theme Goals

Through participating in the experiences provided by this theme, the children may learn

1. Blue is the color of many objects.
2. Some foods are a blue color.
3. Some flowers are colored blue.
4. Blue can be mixed with other colors.
5. The color blue can be symbolic.

Concepts for the Children to Learn

1. Blue is the name of a color.
2. Mixing blue with yellow makes green.
3. Many objects are colored blue.
4. Cars, bikes, blocks, and toy trucks can be colored blue.
5. Magic markers and crayons can be colored blue.
6. On sunny, clear days the sky is a blue color.
7. Blueberries and grapes are examples of blue-colored foods.
8. Flowers can be colored blue.
9. Iris, Texas bluebonnet, crocus, colored carnation, and lobelia are flowers that can be colored blue.
10. Blue is symbolic for being cold or sad.

Vocabulary

1. **blue**—a primary color.
2. **primary colors**—red, yellow, and blue.

Bulletin Board

The purpose of this bulletin board is to develop hand-eye coordination, visual discrimination, and problem-solving skills. A blue bulletin board can be constructed by focusing on familiar objects. Draw pictures of many familiar objects on tagboard. Color them various shades of blue. Cut out the objects and laminate. Next, trace the pictures, allowing 1/4-inch borders, on black construction paper. Cut out shadow pieces and hang on the bulletin board. Add a magnet piece to each shadow and picture. The children can match each picture to its corresponding shadow.

Blue objects

BLUE

Family Letter

Dear Families,

Colors! Colors! Colors! Colors are all around us. In our curriculum, we will be focusing our activities on the color blue. The children will learn that blue can be mixed with red to make purple. When the color yellow is mixed with blue, green is created. The children will also become aware that many familiar objects are blue in color. Moreover, they will learn that the color blue has many associations, including sadness, cold, and music.

AT SCHOOL

Some of the learning experiences planned for this unit include:

- singing a song called "Two Little Bluejays"
- looking out our blue windows in the classroom
- playing a paint store in the dramatic play area
- fingerpainting with blue paint
- eating blueberries for snack

AT HOME

You can make almost any meal entertaining by occasionally adding a small amount of food coloring to one of your food items. Children often find this amusing. The food coloring adds interest to your food and mealtimes become fun! Try adding a drop or two to milk, vanilla pudding, mashed potatoes, scrambled eggs, or cottage cheese. Does the color of a food affect its taste? (Try drinking green milk!) You be the judge! To further develop an awareness of color, identify foods that are red, blue, yellow, etc. This improves memory, classification, and receptive and expressive language skills.

Have a great time helping your child discover the color blue!

THEME 5

Mixing blue paint with yellow paint will give us green.

Arts and Crafts

1. Arm Dancing

Provide each child with two blue crayons and a large sheet of paper. Play music, encouraging the children to color, using both arms. Because of the structure of this activity, it should be limited to older children.

2. Sponge Painting

Collect sponge pieces, thick blue tempera paint, and sheets of light blue paper. If desired, clothespins can be clipped on the sponges and used as handles. To use as a tool, dip the sponge into blue paint and print on light blue paper.

3. Easel Ideas

- Feature different shades of blue paint at the easel.
- Use blue paint on aluminum foil.
- Add whipped soap flakes to blue paint.
- Add a container of yellow paint to the easel. Allow the children to mix the yellow and blue paints at the easel. This activity can be extended by providing red and blue tempera paint.

4. Fingerpainting

Blue fingerpaint and large sheets of paper should be placed in the art area.

5. Melted Crayon Design

Grate broken blue crayons. Place the shreddings on one square of waxed paper 6 inches × 6 inches. On top of the shreddings, place another 6-inch × 6-inch piece of waxed paper. Cover with a dishtowel or old cloth. Apply heat with a warm iron for about 30 seconds. Let the sheets cool, and the child can trim them with scissors. These melted crayon designs can be used as nice sun catchers on the windows. **Caution:** This activity needs to be supervised closely. Only the teacher should handle the hot iron.

Cooking

1. Blueberries

Wash and prepare fresh or frozen blueberries for snack. Blueberry muffins are also appropriate for this theme.

2. Blueberry Muffins

2 tablespoons sugar
1 3/4 cups flour
2 1/2 teaspoons baking powder
3/4 teaspoon salt
1 egg
1/2 cup milk
1/3 cup salad oil

Spray a muffin tin with a non-stick spray or line it with paper liners. Mix all of the ingredients together. Add 2 tablespoons of sugar to 1 cup frozen or fresh blueberries. Mix slightly and gently add to the batter. Bake at 400 degrees for approximately 25 minutes.

3. Cream Cheese and Crackers

Tint cream cheese blue with food coloring and spread on crackers.

4. Cupcakes

Add blue food coloring to a white cake mix. Fill paper cupcake holders with the batter and bake as directed.

Dramatic Play

Paint Store

Provide paintbrushes, buckets, and paint sample books. The addition of a cash register, play money, and pads of paper will extend the children's play.

Field Trips

1. "Blue" Watching

Walk around your center's neighborhood and observe blue items. Things to look for include cars, bikes, birds, houses, flowers, etc. When you return, have the children dictate a list. Record their responses.

2. Paint Store

Visit a local paint store. Observe all the different shades of blue paint. Look carefully to see if they look similar. Ask the store manager for discarded sample cards. These cards can be added to the materials to use in the art area.

Group Time

(Games, Language)

1. Bluebird, Bluebird

The children should join hands and stand in a circle. Construct one bluebird necklace out of yarn and construction paper. Choose one child to be the first bluebird. This bluebird weaves in and out of the children's arms while the remainder of the children chant:

"Bluebird, bluebird through my window
Bluebird, bluebird through my window
Bluebird, bluebird through my window
Who will be the next bluebird?"

At this time the child takes off the necklace and hands it to a child he or she would like to be the next bluebird.

2. I Spy

The teacher says, "I spy something blue that is sitting on the piano bench," or other such statements. The children will look around and try to figure out what the teacher has spied. Older children may enjoy taking turns repeating, "I spy something on the _____."

Large Muscle

1. Painting

Provide a bucket of blue-colored water and large paintbrushes. Encourage the children to paint the sidewalks, building, fence, sandbox, etc.

2. Blue Ribbon Dance

Make blue streamer ribbons by attaching blue crepe paper to unsharpened pencils. Play lively music and encourage the children to move to the music.

Math

1. Muffin Math

Make muffin cutouts on white or brown construction paper. Print a numeral on the top of each muffin. Use blue fingerpaint to place the corresponding number of "blueberries" on each muffin.

2. Cube Tower

Place blue Unifix cubes on a table. Roll a die and stack the corresponding number of cubes. Continue rolling and stacking until the tower falls over.

3. Colored Craft Sticks

Purchase a pack of colored craft sticks (or color your own). Have children sort the sticks into a matching colored cup.

Music

1. "Two Little Bluejays"
(*Sing to the tune of* "*Two Little Blackbirds*")

Two little bluejays
sitting on a hill
One named Sue
One named Bill.

Fly away, Sue
Fly away, Bill.
Come back, Sue
Come back, Bill.

Two little bluejays
sitting on a hill

One named Sue
One named Bill.

To add interest, you can substitute names after the song has been sung several times. The children will enjoy hearing their names.

2. "Finding Colors"
(*Sing to the tune of* "*The Muffin Man*")

Oh, can you find the color blue,
The color blue, the color blue?
Oh, can you find the color blue,
Somewhere in this room?

Science

1. Just One Drop

Each child will need a smock for this activity. Provide a glass of water and blue food coloring. Encourage the children to add a drop of blue food coloring to the water. Watch as the water becomes a light blue. Add a few more drops of food coloring, observing as the blue water turns a darker shade.

2. Blue Color Paddles

Construct blue color paddles out of stiff tagboard and blue overhead transparency sheets. Make a form for the paddle out of tagboard, leaving the inside empty. Put the sheet of blue transparency paper on the back, glue, and trim. The children can hold the paddle up to their eyes and see how the colors have changed.

3. Blue Windows

Place blue-colored cellophane or acetate sheets over some of the windows in the classroom. It is fun to look out the windows and see the blue world.

4. Dyeing Carnations

On the science table, place the stem of a white carnation in a bottle of water with blue food coloring added. Observe the change of the petal colors.

Sensory

Additions to the Sensory Table

1. Water with blue food coloring

2. **Blue Goop**

   Mix together blue food coloring, 1 cup cornstarch, and 1 cup of water.

Social Studies

Eye Color

Prepare an eye color chart with the children. Colors on the chart should include blue, brown, and green. Under each category, record the names of children who have that particular eye color. Extend the activity by adding the number of children with each color.

Transitions: Dismissal of Children

- colors of clothing/types of clothing/patterns of fabrics (stripes, polka dots, plaid)
- shoes (boots, shoes with buckles, shoes with ties, shoes with Velcro, slip-on shoes, jelly shoes); also, number of eyelets on shoes, number of buckles
- ages in years
- number of brothers/sisters
- hair/eye color
- birthdays in certain months
- name cards
- first letter of names
- last names
- rhyming names
- animal or word that starts with same sound as your name (Tiger-Tom)
- give each child a turn at something while putting rugs away (blowing a bubble, strumming a guitar, hugging puppet).
- play "I Spy" by saying, "I spy someone wearing blue pants and a Mickey Mouse sweatshirt."

- play a quick game of "Simon Says" and then have Simon tell where the children are to go next.
- "Two Little Blackbirds"

Two little blackbirds sitting on a hill
One named Jack, one named Jill.
Fly away Jack, fly away Jill.
Come back Jack, come back Jill.
Two little blackbirds sitting on a hill,
One named Jack, one named Jill.

- "I Have a Very Special Friend" (*Sing to the Tune of* "B*ingo*")

I have a very special friend,
Can you guess his name-o?
J-A-R-E-D, J-A-R-E-D, J-A-R-E-D,
And Jared is his name-o.

- "I'm Looking for Someone"

I'm looking for someone named Kristen,
I'm looking for someone named Kristen,
If there is someone named Kristen here now,

Stand up and take a bow. (Or, Stand up and go to lunch.)

- "Where, Oh, Where Is My Friend"

Where, oh, where is my friend Travis?
Where, oh, where is my friend Travis?
Where, oh, where is my friend Travis?
Please come to the door.

- "How Did You Come to School Today?"

How did you come to school today,
How did you come on Monday? (Child responds)
He came in a blue car,
Came in a blue car on Monday.

- "One Elephant Went Out to Play"

One elephant went out to play
Upon a spider's web one day.
He had such enormous fun
That he called for another elephant to come.

- Good-Bye Song
  (*Sing to the tune of "Yankee Doodle"*)

  Now it's time to say goodbye,
  We've had a lot of fun.
  Goodbye (child) goodbye (child)
    and goodbye (child).
  We had a lot of fun!
  Goodbye (child) goodbye (child)
    and goodbye (child).
  Our time at school is done.

Group Dismissal

- hop like a bunny
- walk as quiet as a mouse
- tiptoe
- walk backward
- count steps as you walk
- have footsteps for group to
  walk on or a winding trail
  to follow
- "This Train" (Tune: "This Train
  Is Bound for Glory")

This train is bound for the
  lunchroom,
This train is bound for the
  lunchroom,
This train is bound for the
  lunchroom,
Katie, get on board.
Matthew, get on board.

Zachary, get on board.
Afton, get on board.
(Change lunchroom to fit
  situation.)

Fillers

- "One Potato"

One potato, two potato, three
  potato, four
Five potato, six potato, seven
  potato, more.

- "And One and Two"

And one and two and three
  and four,
And five and six and seven
  and eight.
(Repeat faster)

- "Colors Here and There"

Colors here and there,
Colors everywhere.
What's the name of this
  color here?

- "This Is What I Can Do"

This is what I can do,
Everybody do it, too.
This is what I can do,
Now I pass it on to you.

- "A Peanut Sat on a
  Railroad Track"

A peanut sat on a railroad track,
Its heart was all a-flutter.
Engine Nine came down
  the track,
Toot! Toot! Peanut butter!
  - apple—applesauce
  - banana—banana split
  - orange—orange juice

- "Lickety Lick"

Lickety lick, lickety lick,
The batter is getting all
  thickety thick.
What shall we bake?
What shall we bake?
A great, big beautiful carrot cake.
(Change "carrot" to any kind
  of cake.)

- "I Clap My Hands"

I clap my hands. (Echo)
I stamp my feet. (Echo)
I turn around. (Echo)
And it's really neat. (Echo)
I touch my shoulders. (Echo)
I touch my nose. (Echo)
I touch my knees. (Echo)
And that's how it goes. (Echo)

Books

The following books can be used to
complement this theme:

Bogacki, Tomek and Tomasz Bogacki. (1998).
  Story of a Blue Bird. New York: Farrar,
  Straus & Giroux.

Burnett, Frances H. (1993). *Land of the Blue
  Flower*. Illus. by Judith Ann Griffith.
  Tiburon, CA: H. J. Kramer.

Campilonga, Margaret S. (1996). *Blue Frogs*.
  Illus. by Carl Lindahl. Circleville, NY:
  Chicken Soup Press.

Childress, Mark. (1996). *Joshua and the Big Bad
  Blue Crabs*. Illus. by Mary B. Brown.
  Boston: Little, Brown.

Davies, Nicola. (1997). *Big Blue Whale*. Illus. by
  Nick Maland. Cambridge, MA:
  Candlewick Press.

Demarest, Chris L. (1995). *My Blue Boat*.
  Orlando, FL: Harcourt Brace.

Foster, Kelli C., Kerri Gifford, and Gina Clegg
  Erickson. (1994). *Pink & Blue*. Illus. by
  Gina Clegg Erickson. Hauppauge, NY:
  Barron Juveniles.

BLUE

Hausman, Gerald. (1998). *The Story of Blue Elk.* Illus. by Kristina Rodanas. Boston: Houghton Mifflin.

Inkpen, Mick. (1996). *The Blue Balloon,* (Vol. 1). Boston: Little, Brown.

Jensen, Patsy. (1993). *Paul Bunyan and His Blue Ox.* Illus. by Jean Pidgeon. Mahwah, NJ: Troll.

Lewin, Betsy. (1995). *Booby Hatch.* New York: Clarion Books.

Lionni, Leo. (1995). *Little Blue and Little Yellow.* New York: Mulberry Books. (Pbk.)

Martin, Bill Jr. (1992). *Brown Bear, Brown Bear, What Do You See?* Illus. by Eric Carle. New York: H. Holt.

Onyefulu, Ifeoma. (1997). *Chidi Only Likes Blue: An African Book of Colors.* New York: Cobblehill.

Oram, Hiawyn. (1993). *Out of the Blue: Poems about Color.* Illus. by David McKee. New York: Hyperion.

Ostheeren, Ingrid et al. (1996). *The Blue Monster.* New York: North South Books.

Pulver, Robin. (1994). *Mrs. Toggle's Beautiful Blue Shoe.* Illus. by R. W. Alley. New York: Simon & Schuster.

Salzmann, Mary Elizabeth. (2000). *Blue* (*Sandcastle* I: *What Color Is It?*). Minneapolis, MN: Abdo Publishing.

Whitman, Candaceaut. (1998). *Bring on the Blue.* New York: Abbeville Press.

Winne, Joanne. (2000). *Blue in My World.* New York: Children's Press.

Woolfitt, Gabrielle. (1992). *Blue (Colors).* Minneapolis, MN: Carolrhoda Books.

Multimedia

The following multimedia products can be used to complement this theme:

"The Big Piece of Blue Corn" on *Tall Tales, Yarns and Whoppers* [video]. (1991). Atlas Video, Inc.

Colors, Shapes, and Counting [video]. Kimbo Educational.

"Look Blue" on *There's Music in the Colors* [cassette]. Kimbo Educational.

Peter's Colors Adventure [CD-ROM]. (1994). Arborescence.

Breads

Purpose
food
good health

Sizes
many

Places Prepared
homes
restaurants
bakeries
supermarkets

Flat Breads
taco shells
pita bread
tortilla
lefse

Shapes
round
twisted
oblong

Basic Ingredients
flour
water
milk
yeast
shortening

Yeast Breads
Danish pastries
croissants
rolls
breads
bagels
sweet rolls

Quick Breads
cornbread, biscuits,
coffee cakes, muffins,
popovers, scones,
pancakes, waffles

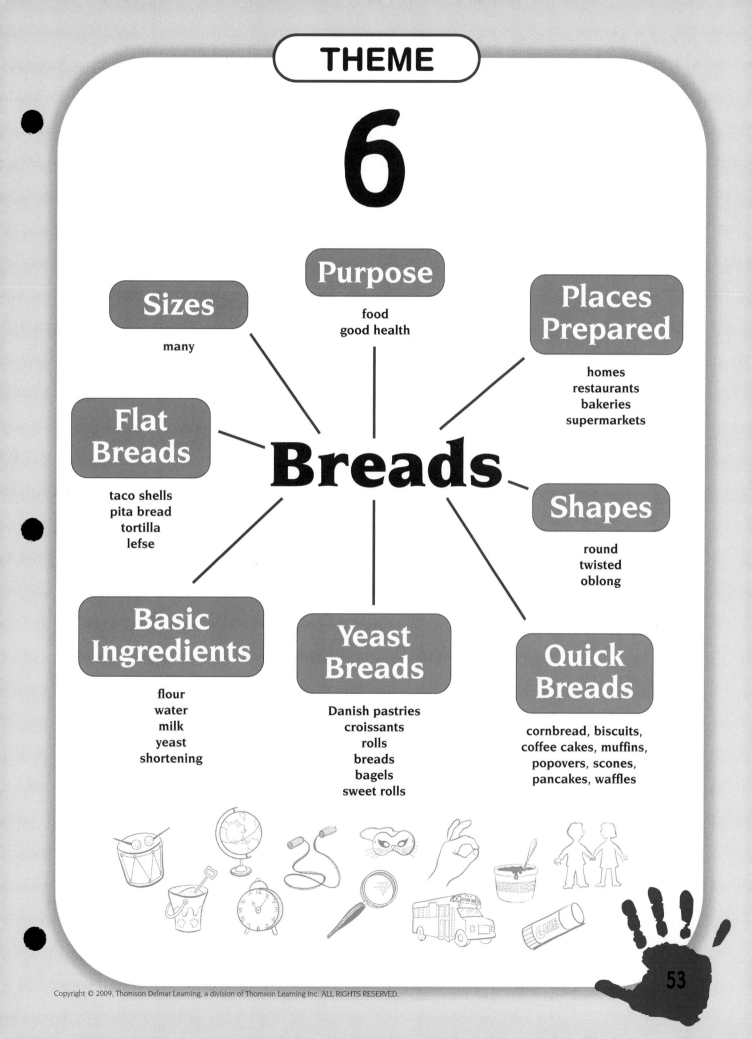

Theme Goals

Through participating in the experiences provided by this theme, the children may learn

1. The purpose of bread
2. The basic ingredients of bread
3. Places bread is prepared
4. Types of yeast bread
5. Types of flat bread
6. Types of quick bread
7. Shapes of bread
8. Sizes of bread

Concepts for the Children to Learn

1. Bread is a healthy food.
2. There are many kinds of breads.
3. Eating bread helps us keep our bodies healthy.
4. The basic ingredients used in preparing bread are flour, water and/or milk, and shortening.
5. Bread can be prepared in homes, bakeries, supermarkets, and restaurants.
6. Breads can be large or small in size.
7. Some breads contain a fruit filling and are called sweet rolls.
8. Breads can be shaped into different forms: round, twisted, and oblong.
9. Breads can be hard or soft.
10. Breads can be part of a meal or snack.

Vocabulary

1. **bread**—a food prepared by mixing flour or grain meal with water or milk and shortening.
2. **crust**—the outside part of the bread.
3. **flour**—wheat that has been ground to a soft powder.
4. **yeast**—a food that makes the bread dough rise.

Bulletin Board

The purpose of this bulletin board is to promote hand-eye coordination, visual discrimination, and problem-solving skills and call attention to various types of baked goods. Create this bulletin board by drawing baked goods on a piece of tagboard as illustrated. Pictures from magazines or computer-generated clip art could also be used. If drawn, color and add detail to the bakery items with felt-tip markers, cut out, and laminate. Trace these pieces onto black construction paper. Count out the pieces and attach to the bulletin board. Use map tacks or adhesive magnet pieces for children to match the corresponding baked good to its shadow.

Family Letter

Dear Families,

Did you know that bread is one of the most widely eaten foods? It is often called the "staff of life" and it provides a large share of people's energy and a small amount of plant protein. Special breads are also used in different cultural ceremonies. Our curriculum next week will focus on a theme related to breads. Activities will help your child learn the different types of bread and the ingredients of bread, including the purpose of yeast. Your child will also participate in making bread.

AT SCHOOL

Some of the curriculum activities related to the theme will include:

- tasting many different kinds of breads
- taking a field trip to the bakery
- baking bread on Thursday and observing the action of yeast
- making and selling baked goods in the Bakery Shop located in the dramatic play area

FAMILY INVOLVEMENT

If you prepare any special ethnic breads, we invite you to share them with our class. Please contact me so a time can be arranged. The children will enjoy having you in our class and learning about other types of breads.

AT HOME

We encourage you to participate in our celebration of bread. The next time you and your child are in the grocery store, find the bakery or bread department. Point out the different types and sizes of breads. Ask questions to help your child recognize similarities and differences.

Bake breads with your child and create warm family memories. Here is a simple recipe that you may want to try:

Zucchini Bread

1 1/2 cups all-purpose flour
3/4 cup sugar
1 teaspoon ground cinnamon
1/2 teaspoon baking soda
1/4 teaspoon salt
1/4 teaspoon baking powder

1/4 cup cooking oil
1/4 teaspoon nutmeg
1 beaten egg
1/4 teaspoon finely shredded lemon peel
1 cup shredded zucchini
1/2 cup chopped walnuts

Grease an 8×4×2-inch loaf pan. In a medium bowl mix together flour, sugar, cinnamon, baking powder, and nutmeg. Make a well in the center of the dry mixture and add the zucchini. Stir only until mixture is folded in. Add the chopped walnuts.

Pour batter into the prepared loaf pan. Bake in a preheated oven set at 350 degrees for 55 to 60 minutes. Remove from the oven and cool on a wire rack for 10–12 minutes. Remove the bread from the pan and continue cooling on the wire rack. Wrap when cooled and let sit overnight before slicing.

A variation of this recipe would be to substitute shredded apples for the zucchini.

Enjoy a slice of bread with your child today!

It's tasty trying different kinds of bread and pastries.

Arts and Crafts

1. Bread Collage

Provide magazines for the children to find and cut out pictures of different types of breads. These pictures can be glued or pasted to a piece of construction paper or a paper plate, creating a bread collage.

2. Play Dough

The children can assist in preparing play dough. If the mixture is left uncolored, it will resemble bread dough and have a similar consistency. Place three cups of flour and one cup of salt in a mixing bowl. Add 3/4 cup of water and stir. Keep adding small amounts of water and mix until the dough is workable but not sticky.

3. Muffin Tin Paint Trays

Fill muffin tins with various colors of paint in the art area for the children to use. Pastry brushes could be used as paint applicators.

4. Biscuit Cutter Prints

Place biscuit cutters and a shallow pan of paint out at the art table. The children can dip the biscuit cutter into the paint. After this, the biscuit cutter can be placed on a piece of construction paper. The children can repeat the process as desired.

5. Bread Sponge Painting

Cut sponges into different shapes and types of bread. Place the sponges and shallow trays of tempera paint on the art table. The children can dip a sponge into the paint and then press it onto a piece of paper to create a bread-shaped print.

Cooking

1. Bag Bread

Collect the following ingredients:

3 cups of bread flour
2 packages of fast-rising yeast
1/4 cup sugar
1 1/2 teaspoon salt
1 1/2 cup warm water (125 to 130 degrees)
4 teaspoons vegetable oil

In a gallon-size, heavy plastic, zipper seal freezer bag, place 1 1/2 cups flour, dry yeast, and salt. Close. Let the children mix

BREADS

the ingredients by shaking and working the bag with their fingers.

Add the oil and warm water to the ingredients in the bag. Reseal the bag and demonstrate to the children how to mix the ingredients. Gradually add the remaining flour until the mixture forms a stiff ball.

Grease your hands with a solid vegetable oil. Remove the dough from the bag and place on a lightly floured surface. Knead about 5 minutes. Small air pockets that appear as bubbles will form under the surface of the dough when it has been sufficiently kneaded. When they appear, let the children observe them.

Let the dough rest for 5–10 minutes. Grease two bread pans. Divide the dough in half. Shape into two loaves. Place each loaf in a greased bread pan. Cover with a kitchen towel. Let rise for an hour. Bake at 375 degrees for 25–30 minutes.

2. Pretzels

Collect the following ingredients:

1 teaspoon salt
2 1/2 teaspoons sugar
1 package of fast-rising yeast
1 cup warm water (125 to 130 degrees)
1 tablespoon vegetable oil
1 egg yolk, beaten with 1 tablespoon water
3–3 1/2 cups flour

Combine 1 1/2 cups of flour, the dry yeast, sugar, and salt in a large bowl. Add the warm water and vegetable oil and mix at low speed with an electric mixer for 3 minutes. Add an additional 1/2 cup flour and beat at high speed for 2–3 minutes. Stir in the remaining flour to form a soft dough. **Caution:** Use of the electric mixer needs to be carefully supervised.

Lightly flour a surface. Place the soft dough on the floured surface and knead for approximately 10 minutes. Grease a bowl with vegetable oil and place the dough in it to rise. Cover with a dish towel for 30–45 minutes.

Punch the air out of the dough and divide into 20 equal pieces. Demonstrate to the children how to roll a piece into a rope 12–14 inches long. Form the rope into a pretzel. Place on a greased baking sheet. Cover again and let rise in a warm place for about 25 minutes.

Brush each of the pretzels with the egg yolk mixture. Preheat the oven to 375 degrees. Bake for 15 minutes and remove from pan. Place on a wire rack to cool.

3. Chappatis

This recipe, which comes from India, serves six; consequently, it will need to be adjusted to accommodate the number of children who need to be served.

1 1/2 cups of whole wheat flour
1/2 teaspoon salt
2/3 cup warm water
a small amount of cooking oil

Mix the flour and salt together in a bowl. Stir in water a small amount at a time until the mixture forms a ball.

On a floured surface, knead dough for 5–10 minutes until it is a smooth, sticky ball. Let rise in a covered bowl for 30 minutes.

Cut the dough into six pieces. Roll each piece out into a circle that is about 8 inches in diameter.

Lightly oil a frying pan with oil and heat until it smokes. **Caution:** This portion of the activity needs to be carefully supervised to promote a safe environment.

Cook each circle of dough until it is brown and puffy on both sides. The chappatis are more flavorful when eaten warm.

4. Cheesey Puff Bread

3 3/4 cups of bread flour
1 package rapid-rise dry yeast
1 teaspoon salt
1/2 cup milk
2 tablespoons margarine
2 eggs
1 cup grated cheddar cheese
1/2 cup warm water
3 tablespoons sugar

Combine the dry yeast, sugar, salt, and 1 1/2 cups of flour in a large mixing bowl. Heat the milk, water, and margarine on the stove or in the microwave oven until warm to the touch. Add the dry ingredients. Then beat at low speed with an electric mixer. Add 1/2 cup of flour and the eggs. Beat at high speed for 2–3 minutes. Stir in the cheese and enough flour to make a soft dough.

On a lightly floured surface, knead the dough until it is elastic and smooth. Typically this will take 6–10 minutes. Place the dough in a greased bowl and let rise for 15–30 minutes.

Grease the entire inner surface of two 1 lb. coffee cans. Divide the dough into two equal pieces. Place each piece in a can. Cover the top of the can with a piece of aluminum foil. Let the dough rise for 35 minutes.

Bake for 30 minutes in a 375-degree oven. Remove from cans and cool on a wire rack.

5. **Alphabet Toast**

Pour milk into small container and color with food coloring. (Make as many colors as desired). Give each child a piece of bread and alphabet cookie cutters.

Encourage them to find the letter that their name begins with. Press the cutter lightly into the bread. Use a cotton swab to spread the colored milk on the letter. Place in toaster. The toast will come out brightly colored.

Dramatic Play

1. **Bakery**

Prepare the housekeeping area to resemble a bakery where the children can pretend to make breads and bake goods to sell to their classmates as customers. Provide the following items: aprons, baker's hats, bowls, mixing spoons, pans, rolling pins, muffin tins, measuring cups, egg cartons, empty bread/roll mix boxes, oven mitts or hot pads, a cash register, and poster/pictures depicting baked goods.

2. **Restaurant**

Prepare the housekeeping area as a restaurant. Provide props such as a tablecloth, dishes, cooking utensils, and a cash register with play money. Create menus by cutting pictures from magazines and gluing onto construction paper. Include pictures of different baked goods.

Field Trips

1. **Bakery**

Arrange a visit to a local bakery. Observe the process of bread and baked goods production. Discuss a baker's job and uniform.

2. **Farm**

Take a trip to a farm where grains are grown. Notice the equipment and machinery used to plant and harvest the crops.

3. **Grocery Store**

Tour a grocery store and find the bakery department. The children can look at the many types of breads and ways they are packaged.

Fingerplays

Five Little Donuts

Down around the corner, at the bakery shop
There were five little donuts with sugar on top.
(hold up five fingers)
Along came _____ (child's name), all alone.
And she/he took the biggest one home.

Continue the verses until all the donuts are gone.

Group Time
(Games, Language)

1. **Bread-Tasting Party**

Bake or purchase various types and flavors of breads. Cut the bread into small pieces and place these samples on paper plates for the children to taste. Discuss the types of breads, textures, flavors, and scents.

2. **Yeast Experiment**

To demonstrate the effects of yeast, try this experiment. Pour one package of dry yeast, 1/2 cup of sugar, and one cup of warm water into an empty soda bottle. Cover the bottle opening with a balloon and watch it expand.

3. ***The Little Red Hen***

Read the story of *The Little Red Hen* by Paul Galdone. After reading the story several times so that the children are familiar with the content, it can be acted out. Simple props can be

BREADS

provided to assist the children in creative dramatics and re-creating the story.

4. Bread Basket Upset

This game is played in a circle formation on chairs or carpet squares. One child is asked to sit in the middle of the circle as the baker. Hand a picture of a different type of bread—bagel, roll, muffin, and others—to each of the other children. To play the game, the baker calls out the name of a bread. The children holding that particular bread exchange places. The game continues. When the baker calls out, "Bread Basket Upset," all of the children must exchange places, including the baker. The child who is unable to find a place is the new baker.

Large Muscle

1. Tricycles

During outdoor play, encourage children to use the tricycles for making bakery deliveries.

2. Bread Trail

Set up a bread trail in the classroom. Tape pictures of the bread creating a trail on the floor. Have the children follow the trail by walking or hopping.

Math

1. Favorite Bread Graph

After tasting various types of breads, the children can assist in making a class graph of their favorite types of breads. Across the top of a piece of tagboard, print the caption "Our Favorite Breads." Draw or paste pictures of different types or flavors of breads along the left-hand side of the tagboard.

On the chart, place each child's name or picture next to the picture of his or her favorite bread. The results of the graph can be shared with the children using math vocabulary words such as most, more, fewer, least, etc. Display the graph for future reference.

2. Muffin Tin Math

Muffin tins can be used for counting and sorting activities based on the children's developmental level. For example, numerals can be printed in each cup, and the children can place the corresponding set of corn or toy pieces in each cup. Likewise, colored circles can be cut out of construction paper and glued to the bottom of the muffin cups. The children then can place objects of matching colors in the corresponding muffin cups.

3. Pretzel Sort and Count

Provide each child with a cup containing various sizes and shapes of pretzels. Encourage the children to empty the cup onto a clean napkin or plate and sort the pretzels by size or shape. If appropriate, the children can count how many pretzels they have of each shape. Upon completion of the activity, the pretzels can be eaten by the children.

4. Breadstick Seriation

Provide breadsticks or pictures of breadsticks of varying lengths. The children can place the breadsticks in order from shortest to longest.

Music

1. "If I Had a Bagel"
(*Sing to the tune* "If I Had a Hammer")

If I had a bagel.
I'd eat it in the morning,
I'd eat it in the evening,
All over this land.
I'd eat it for breakfast,
I'd eat it for supper,
I'd eat it with all my friends and sisters and brothers,
All, all over this land.

2. "Little Donuts"
(*Sing to the tune of* "Ten Little Indians")

One little, two little, three little donuts
Four little, five little, six little donuts
Seven little, eight little, nine little donuts
Ten donuts in the bakery shop.

60

THEME 6

3. "Let's Pretend"

(Sing to the tune of "Here We Are Together")

Let's pretend that we are bakers,
Are bakers, are bakers
Let's pretend that we are bakers,
As busy as can be.
We'll knead all the dough out
And bake loaves of bread.
Let's pretend that we are bakers
As busy as can be.

4. "Down at the Bakery"

Down at the bakery what did I see?
Five little cookies smiling at me.
Along came (child's name) with a nickel one day.
He bought the (color) one and took it away.
(Continue singing until all cookies are gone.)

Note: Make five different-colored cookies from construction paper. Laminate and attach Velcro or magnets to the back. Place on either a magnet board or a flannel board. Give five children a nickel. As you call their name, invite them to take the corresponding color of cookie off the flannel or magnet board.

Science

1. Bread Grains

On the science table, set out containers of grains used to make bread for the children to examine. Examples include wheat, corn, oats, and rye. Provide magnifying glasses for children to explore the grains.

2. Weighing Bread Grains

The property of mass can be explored by providing a balance scale and bread grains at the science table. Scoops and spoons could be available to assist the children. The children can compare the grains. Encourage the use of vocabulary words such as heavier, lighter, more than, and less than.

3. Baking Bread

The process of bread baking is definitely a science activity. The children can observe

changes in substances and make predictions about the final outcome. Choose a bread recipe listed under the cooking section of this theme. Prepare a recipe chart for classroom use. Stress cooking safety with the children.

Sensory

1. Different types of grains can be placed in the sensory table. Examples include corn, rice, wheat, barley, and oats. Provide pails, scoops, measuring cups, flour sifters, and spoons to encourage active exploration.

2. Place play dough in the sensory table with rolling pins, measuring cups, muffin tins, and plastic knives.

3. Cooking utensils used for preparing baked goods can be placed in the sensory table with soapy water and dish cloths. The children can "wash" the items.

Social Studies

1. Baker

The occupation of baker can be examined through books and discussion.

2. Sharing Breads

Bake breads or muffins to give to a home for the elderly, the homeless, or some other organization. If possible, take a walk and have the children deliver them.

3. Visitor

Invite people from various cultural backgrounds to bake or share breads originating from their native countries. As a follow-up activity, assist the children in writing thank-you notes.

Books

The following books can be used to complement this theme:

Barton, Byron. (1993). *The Little Red Hen*. New York: HarperCollins.

Brett, Jan. (1999). *Gingerbread Baby*. New York: G. P. Putnam.

Carle, Eric. (1995). *Walter the Baker*. New York: Simon & Schuster.

Curtis, Neil and Peter Greenland. (1992). *How Bread Is Made (I Wonder)*. Minneapolis, MN: Lerner Publications.

Czernecky, Stefan et al. (1992). *The Sleeping Bread*. New York: Hyperion.

De Paola, Tomie. (1997). *Antonio the Bread Boy*. New York: G. P. Putnam.

Dooley, Norah. (1995). *Everybody Bakes Bread*. Illus. by Peter J. Thornton. Minneapolis, MN: Carolrhoda Books.

Dragonwagon, Crescent. (1991). *This Is the Bread I Baked for Ned*. Illus. by Isadore Seltzer. New York: Simon & Schuster.

Edelman, Julie and Omar H. Davis. (2000). *Once Upon A Recipe: Favorite Tales, Food and FUNtivities*. Illus. by Omar H. Davis. Maplewood, NJ: Once Upon A Recipe Press.

Flanagan, Romie and Alice K. (1998). *Mr. Santizo's Tasty Treats*. Chicago: Children's Press.

Gershator, David et al. (1995). *Bread Is for Eating*. New York: Holt.

Granowsky, Alvin. (1996). *Help Yourself, Little Red Hen! (Another side to the story.)* Illus. by Wendy Edelson and Jane K. Manning. Austin, TX: Raintree/Steck Vaughn.

Heath, Amy. (1992). *Sophie's Role*. Illus. by Sheila Hamanaka. New York: Simon & Schuster.

Hoban, Russell. (1993). *Bread and Jam for Frances*. Illus. by Lillian Hoban. New York: HarperCollins.

Hoopes, Lyn Littlefield. (1996). *The Unbeatable Bread*. Illus. by Brad Sneed. New York: Dial Books.

Levenson, George. (2004). *Bread Comes to Life: a Garden of Wheat and a Loaf to Eat*. Photography by Shmuel Thaler. Berkeley, CA: Tricycle Press.

Pellam, David. (1991). *Sam's Sandwich*. New York: Dutton. (flap book.)

Wolff, Ferida. (1993). *Seven Loaves of Bread*. Illus. by Katie Keller. New York: William Morrow.

Multimedia

The following multimedia products can be used to complement this theme:

"The Donut Song." (2004). *Laugh N Learn Silly Songs*. Long Branch, NJ: Kimbo.

Greg and Steve. "Muffin Man" on *We All Live Together*, Volume 2 [compact disc]. Youngheart Records.

"The Muffin Man" on *Toddler Tunes: 26 Classic Songs for Toddlers* [compact disc]. (1995). Franklin, TN: Cedarmont Music; distributed by Benson Music Group.

7

Parts

handle
bristles

Hair Styles

long
short
thick
thin

Users

all people
hairstylists
janitors/maids
dentists
artists
painters
animal groomers
manicurists

Brushes

Kinds

paint brush
scrub brush
toothbrush
hairbrush
clothes brush
vegetable brush
pastry brush
pet brush
eyebrow brush
nail brush
picks
makeup brush

Uses

cleaning
grooming/hygiene
painting
cooking

Materials

plastic
wood
nylon
hair

Theme Goals

Through participating in the experiences provided by this theme, the children may learn

1. Parts of a brush
2. Kinds of brushes
3. Uses of brushes
4. Materials used to make brushes
5. Community helpers who need brushes for their work

Concepts for the Children to Learn

1. A brush is a tool.
2. Brushes come in many sizes.
3. Brushes have handles and bristles.
4. Brushes can be used for cleaning, grooming, painting, and cooking.
5. Scrub brushes are used for cleaning in our homes.
6. Toothbrushes help clean our teeth.
7. Hairbrushes and eyebrow brushes are used for grooming.
8. A pastry brush is used for cooking.
9. Brushes can be made of plastic, wood, nylon, or hair.
10. Some people use brushes while working.
11. Animal groomers use pet brushes to groom dogs and horses.
12. Janitors and maids use scrub brushes.
13. Dentists use toothbrushes.
14. Hairstylists use hairbrushes.
15. Manicurists use nailbrushes.
16. Makeup brushes are used to apply powder and coloring to the face.
17. Painting brushes are tools to apply paint to surfaces.
18. Eyebrow brushes are tools for brushing the eyebrows.

Vocabulary

1. **bristle**—a short, stiff hair or threadlike object.
2. **brush**—a tool made of bristles or wires attached to a handle.
3. **dog brush**—a brush used to clean a dog's hair.
4. **groom**—to clean.
5. **handle**—the part of a brush that is held.
6. **powder brush**—a brush that is used to apply facial powder.
7. **toothbrush**—a small brush used to clean teeth.
8. **vegetable brush**—a stiff brush used to clean vegetables.

Bulletin Board

The purpose of this bulletin board is to promote the development of color identification and matching skills. Construct paint palettes and brushes out of tagboard. Use a different colored marker to draw paint spots on each palette and to "paint" the bristles of each brush. Laminate all the pieces. Attach the palettes to the bulletin board. Map tacks, putty, or Velcro may be used to place the brushes next to the corresponding color of paint palette.

Family Letter

Dear Families,

Did you ever stop to think about the number and types of brushes we use in a day? Brushes will be the next subject that we will explore. Each one has a different function and helps us do a different job. Through the activities related to the theme, the children will become aware of the many types and uses of brushes. In addition, they will be exposed to materials used in constructing brushes.

AT SCHOOL

Some of the learning experiences this week will include:

- setting up a hairstylist shop in the dramatic play area (and discussing different hairstyles and colors)
- "painting" outside with buckets of water and brushes
- observing teeth being cleaned with electric and handheld brushes as we visit Dr. Smith's dental office on Thursday morning
- painting with a variety of brushes at the easel each day

AT HOME

With your child, go through your home and locate brushes. Examples include: toothbrushes, hairbrushes, paintbrushes, fingernail polish brushes, pastry brushes, and makeup brushes. Compare and sort the various brushes. This will help your child discriminate among weights, colors, sizes, textures, and shapes. The brushes can also be counted to determine which room contains the most and which contains the least number of brushes, which will promote the understanding of number concepts.

Paint a picture with your child today!

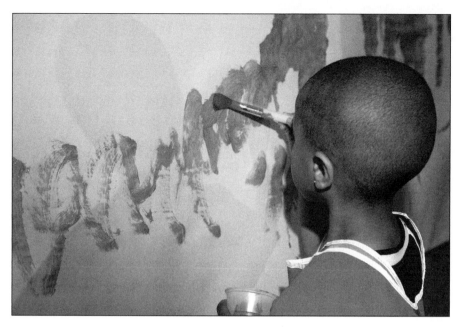

Children enjoy using a brush as a tool to apply paint.

 # Arts and Crafts

1. Brush Painting

Place various brushes such as hairbrushes, makeup brushes, toothbrushes, and clothes brushes on a table in the art area. In addition, thin tempera paint and paper should be provided. Let the children explore the painting process with a variety of brushes.

2. Easel Ideas

Each day change the type of brushes the children can use while painting at the easel. Variations may include sponge brushes, discarded toothbrushes, nail polish brushes, vegetable brushes, and makeup brushes.

3. Box House Painting

Place a large cardboard box outside. To decorate it, provide smocks, house painting brushes, and tempera paint for the children.

 # Cooking

1. Cleaning Vegetables

Place several washtubs filled with water in the cooking area. Then provide children with fresh carrots and brushes. Encourage the children to clean the carrots using a vegetable brush. The carrots can be used to make carrot cake or muffins, or they can be added to soup.

2. Pretzels

1 1/2 cups warm water
1 envelope yeast
4–5 cups flour
1 teaspoon salt
1 tablespoon sugar
1 egg white
coarse salt (optional)

Dissolve the dry yeast in 1 1/2 cups of warm water and 1 tablespoon of sugar. Mix 4 cups of the flour and the salt in a large bowl. Add the dry yeast mixture. Stir and add additional flour if needed to make the dough stiff and easy to handle. Then place the dough on a floured surface. Provide each child with dough to roll and shape into pretzels. Beat the egg white and apply the egg white glaze with a pastry brush. Sprinkle with salt if desired. Bake at 400 degrees for approximately six minutes.

Dramatic Play

1. Hairstylist

Collect hairspray bottles, brushes, empty shampoo bottles, chairs, mirrors, hair dryers, and curling irons, and place in the dramatic play area. **Caution:** Cut the cords off the electrical appliances.

2. Water Painting

In an outdoor area, provide children with buckets of water and house paintbrushes. They can pretend to "paint" the building, sidewalks, equipment, and fence.

3. Shining Shoes

In the dramatic play area, place clear shoe polish, shoes, brushes, and shining cloths for the children to use to polish shoes. **Caution:** This activity needs to be carefully supervised.

Field Trips/ Resource People

1. The Street Sweeper

Contact the city maintenance department. Invite them to clean the street in front of the center or school for the children to observe.

2. Artist's Studio

Visit a local artist's studio. Observe the various brushes used.

3. Dentist's Office

Visit a dentist's office. Ask the dentist to demonstrate and explain the use of various brushes.

4. Animal Groomer

Invite an animal groomer to school. Ask the groomer to show the equipment, emphasizing the importance of brushes.

Fingerplays

Brushes in My Home

These brushes in my home
Are simply everywhere.
I use them for my teeth each day,
   (brushing teeth motion)
And also for my hair.
   (hair brushing motion)

We use them in the kitchen sink
   (scrubbing motion)
And in the toilet bowls,
   (scrubbing motion)
For putting polish on my shoes
   (touch shoes and rub)
And to waterproof the soles.

Brushes are used to polish the floors
   (polishing motions)
And also paint the wall,
   (painting motion)
To clean the charcoal barbecue,
   (brushing motion)
It's hard to name them all.

My Toothbrushes

I have a little toothbrush.
   (use pointer for toothbrush)
I hold it very tightly.
   (make tight fist)
I brush my teeth each morning
   (pretend to brush teeth)
And then again at night.

Shiny Shoes

First I loosen mud and dirt,
My shoes I then rub clean.
For shoes in such a dreadful sight,
Never should be seen.

I spread the polish on the shoes.
And then I let it dry.
I brush the shoes until they shine.
And sparkle in my eye.

THEME 7

Group Time

(Games, Language)

1. **Brush Hunt**

   Hide several brushes in the classroom. Have one child search for the brushes. When she or he gets close to them, clap loudly. When she or he is farther away, clap quietly.

2. **Brush of the Day**

   At group time each day introduce a new brush. Discuss the shape, color, materials, and uses. Then allow the children to use the brush in the classroom during self-selected play period.

Large Muscle

Sidewalk Brushing

Place buckets of water and paintbrushes for use outdoors on sidewalks, fences, and buildings.

Math

1. **Sequencing**

   Collect various-sized paintbrushes. Encourage the children to sequence them by height and width.

2. **Weighing Brushes**

   Place a balance scale and several brushes in the math area. Encourage the children to weigh and balance the brushes.

3. **Toothbrush Counting**

   Collect toothbrushes and cans. Label each can with a numeral. The children can place the corresponding number of brushes into each labeled can. If desired, the toothbrushes can be constructed out of tagboard.

Music

"Using Brushes"
(*Sing to the tune of "Mulberry Bush"*)

This is the way we brush our teeth,
brush our teeth, brush our teeth.
This is the way we brush our teeth
So early in the morning.

Variations:

- This is the way we brush our hair. . . .
- This is the way we polish our nails. . . .
- This is the way we paint the house. . . .

Act out each verse, and allow the children to make up more verses.

Science

1. **Identifying Brushes**

   Inside the feely box, place various small brushes. The children can reach into the box, feel each object, and try to identify it by name.

2. **Exploring Bristles**

   Add to the science table a variety of brushes and magnifying glasses. Allow the children to observe the bristles up close, noting similarities and differences.

Sensory

Place play plastic fruits and vegetables in the sensory table. Provide scrub brushes for the children to clean and scrub the fruits and vegetables.

Social Studies

1. **Brushes Chart**

   Design a "Brushes in Our Classroom" chart. Encourage the children to find all that are used in the classroom.

2. **Helper Chart**

   Design a helper chart. Include tasks such as sweeping floors, cleaning paintbrushes, and putting away brushes and brooms. This chart can encourage the children to use brushes every day in the classroom.

Books

The following books can be used to complement this theme:

Lillegard, Dee. (1987). *I Can Be a Beautician*. Chicago: Children's Press.

Tripp, Valerie. (1987). *The Penguins Paint*. Chicago: Children's Press.

De Paola, Tomie. (1988). *The Legend of the Indian Paintbrush*. New York: G. P. Putnam.

Hoban, Tara. (1987). *Dots, Spots, Speckles, & Stripes*. New York: Greenwillow.

Langreuter, Jutta and Vera Sobat. (1997). *Little Bear Brushes His Teeth*. Illus. by Vera Sobat. Brookfield, CT: Millbrook Press Trade.

Small, David. (1985). *Imogene's Antlers*. New York: Crown.

Testa, Fulvio. (1986). *If You Take a Paintbrush*: A *Book of Colors*. New York: Dial Books.

Quinlan, Patricia. (1992). *Brush Them Bright*. New York: Walt Disney Publishing.

Recordings and Song Titles

The following recordings can be used to complement the theme:

"Brush Your Teeth." (1994). *Get Up & Grow*. Long Branch, NJ: Kimbo Educational.

"Combing My Hair." (1979). *Self Help Skills*. Long Branch, NJ: Kimbo Educational.

Paint Applicators

There are many ways to apply paint. The size and shape of the following applicators produce unique results. Although some are recyclable, others are disposable.

Recyclable Examples		**Disposable Applicators to Use with Paint**
paintbrushes, varying sizes and widths	string/yarn	twigs and sticks
whisk brooms	roll-on deodorant bottles	string/yarn
fingers and hands	squeeze bottles (plastic ketchup containers)	feathers
tongue depressors or craft sticks	marbles and beads	pinecones
potato mashers	styrofoam shapes	rocks
forks and spoons	sponges	cloth
toothbrushes	feet	cardboard tubes
aerosol can lids	spools	straws
cookie cutters	rollers	leaves
spray bottles	rags	cotton balls
	gauze	cotton swabs

8

Coloring

food coloring

Purpose

bathing
cleaning
playing

Bubbles

Places Found

foods
bath
water/drinks

Sizes

large
medium
small

Tools for Making

straws,
bubble rings,
strings, funnels,
coat hangers,
pipes,
berry baskets,
six-pack rings

Ingredients

soap
water

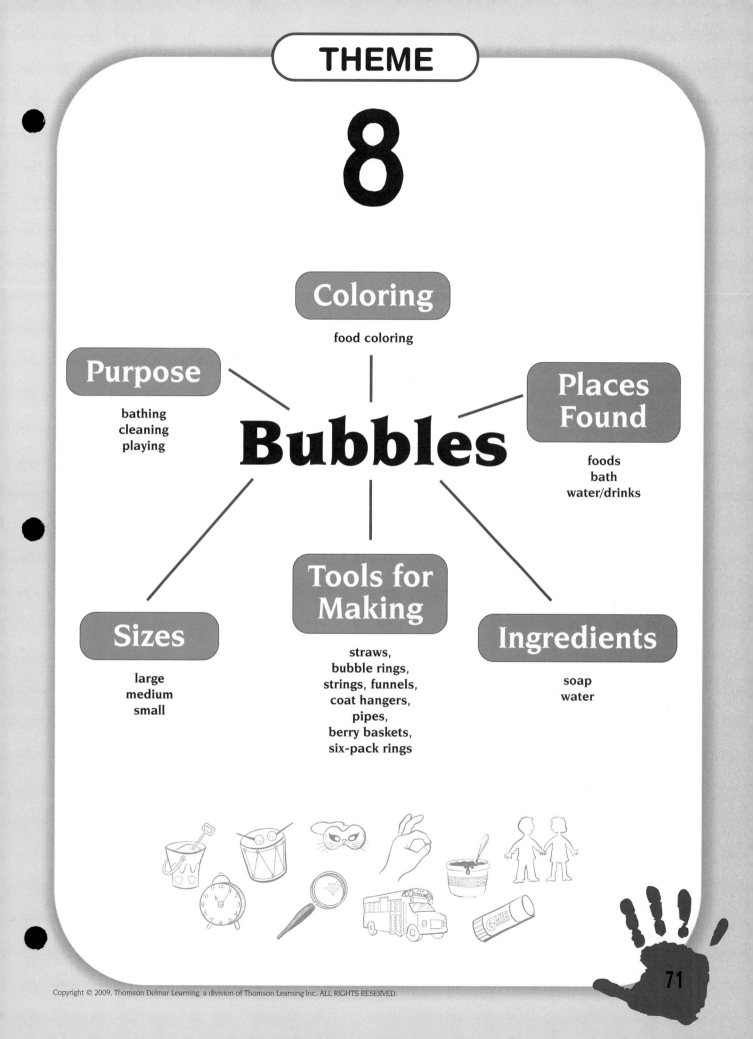

71

Theme Goals

Through participating in the experiences provided by this theme, the children may learn:

1. Purposes of bubbles
2. Bubble ingredients
3. Tools for making bubbles
4. Colors of bubbles
5. Sizes of bubbles
6. Places bubbles are found

Concepts for the Children to Learn

1. Bubbles are made with soap and water.
2. Bubbles are all around us in foods, baths, water, and drinks.
3. Food coloring can be used to add color to bubbles.
4. Bubbles can be made with straws, bubble rings, strings, and funnels.
5. Coat hangers, pipes, berry baskets, and six-pack rings can also be used to make bubbles.
6. Bubbles can be used for bathing, cleaning, and playing.
7. Bubbles have a skin that holds air inside of them.

Vocabulary

1. **bubble**—a circle that has a skin and contains air.
2. **bubble skin**—the outside of the bubble that holds the air.
3. **bubble solution**—a mixture of water and liquid soap.
4. **bubble wand**—a tool used to make bubbles.

Bulletin Board

The purpose of this bulletin board is to promote the active exploration of household items that can be used to make bubbles. Collect items such as chenille stems, funnels, spools, six-pack rings, berry baskets, and scissors. Construct and label boxes and/or pockets to hold items on the bulletin board. Containers of bubble solution should be placed near the bulletin board for the children to experiment with to make bubbles with household items. Provide towels in the area to encourage the children to assist in wiping up spills.

Family Letter

Dear Families,

What do you get when you mix water and soap? Bubbles! The children will make many fascinating discoveries as we focus on a bubbles theme. Through the experiences provided, the children will learn the ingredients used in making bubbles, sizes of bubbles, and tools for making bubbles.

AT SCHOOL

Some of the learning experiences planned to highlight bubble concepts include:

- washing dolls and dishes in the sensory table
- testing many bubble solution recipes
- making bubbles with common household items such as plastic berry baskets, funnels, straws, chenille stems, spools, and scissors
- creating prints of bubbles in the art area

AT HOME

Try the following activities with your child to reinforce bubble concepts at home.

- Allow your child to assist in washing dishes after a meal. This experience will give your child a sense of responsibility and promote self-esteem, as well as heighten his or her awareness of the purpose of bubbles for cleaning.
- Prepare the following bubble solution with your child, then blow some bubbles with straws, bubble wands, and funnels! You need one cup of water, two tablespoons of liquid dish soap, and one tablespoon of glycerine (optional). Enjoy!

Have a good time with your child!

THEME 8

Catching bubbles outdoors is a good science experience.

 # Arts and Crafts

Bubble Prints

For each bubble-print color desired, mix one part liquid tempera paint with two parts liquid dish soap in a small container. Place a straw in the solution and blow until the bubbles rise above the rim of the container. Remove the straw and place a piece of paper over the bubbles. As the bubbles break, they will leave a print on the paper. (Each child will need a straw for this activity. A pin may be used to poke holes near the top of the straws to prevent the children from accidentally sucking in the paint mixture.)

Variation: Small bubble wands can be dipped into the paint bubble solution and blown so the bubbles will land on a piece of paper, either at the easel or on the ground outdoors.

 # Cooking

1. **Bubbly Beverage**

    6 oz. can frozen orange juice
    6 oz. can frozen lemonade
    6 oz. can frozen limeade
    6 oz. can frozen pineapple juice (optional)
    1 liter lemon-lime soda, chilled
    1 liter club soda, chilled

    Combine ingredients in a punch bowl or other large bowl. Stir to blend the ingredients. Serve over ice, if desired.

2. **Root Beer**

    5 gallons cold water
    5 lb. white sugar
    3 oz. bottle root beer extract
    5 lb. dry ice

In a large stone crock or plastic container (do not use metal) mix sugar with 1 gallon of water. Add the remainder of the water and root beer extract. Stir. Carefully add the dry ice. After the ice melts, the root beer can be transferred into other containers to store for 2–3 days.

Dramatic Play

1. **Housekeeping**

   Fill the sink in the dramatic play area with soapy water. Provide dishes, dishcloth, towels, and a dish rack for the children to wash the dishes.

2. **Hairstylist**

   Set up a hairstylist studio in the dramatic play area. Include props such as a cash register, empty shampoo and hair spray containers, mirrors, brushes, combs, barrettes, curlers, discarded hair dryers and curling irons, towels, and smocks. Display pictures of hairstyles and hair products. **Caution:** Cut the electric cords off the hair dryers and curling irons to prevent possible injuries.

Field Trips/ Resource People

1. **Hairstylist**

   Visit a hairstylist to watch a customer receive a shampoo.

2. **Pet Groomer**

   Invite a pet groomer to demonstrate giving a dog a bath.

Fingerplays

Here Is a Bubble

Here is a bubble
   (make a circle with thumb and index finger)
And here is a bubble
   (make a bigger circle with two thumbs and index finger)
And here is a great big bubble I see.
   (make a large circle with arms)
Let's count the bubbles we've made.
One, two, three.
   (repeat prior actions)

Draw a Bubble

Draw a bubble, draw a bubble.
Make it very round.
   (make a shape in the air with index finger)
Draw a bubble, draw a bubble.
No corners can be found.
   (repeat actions)

Group Time

(Games, Language)

1. **What's Missing?—Game**

   Place several items used to prepare bubbles on a tray. At group time, show and discuss the items. To play the game, cover the tray with a towel and carefully remove one item. Have children then identify the missing item. The game can be made more challenging by adding more items to the tray, or by removing more than one item at a time.

2. **Bubbles—Creative Dramatics**

   Guide the children through a creative dramatics activity as they pretend to be bubbles. They can act out being

   - a tiny bubble

   - a giant bubble

- a bubble floating on a windy day
- a bubble landing on the grass
- a bubble floating high in the air
- a bubble in a sink
- a bubble in a piece of bread

3. **Favorite Bubble Gum Chart**

At the top of a piece of tagboard, print the caption "Our Favorite Bubble Gum." Along the left-hand side, glue bubble gum wrappers representing different brands or flavors. Present the chart at group time and ask each child to choose one as his or her favorite. Record the children's names or place their pictures next to the response. If appropriate, count the number of "votes" each brand received and print them on the chart. Display the chart in the classroom and refer to it throughout the unit.

Math

1. **Bubble Count**

If appropriate, encourage the children to blow a set of bubbles that you specify. For example, if you say the number "three," the children would try to blow three bubbles.

2. **Bubble Wand Sort**

Collect small commercially manufactured bubble wands and place them in a small basket. These wands can be sorted by size or color. They could also be counted or placed in order by size.

3. **Geometric Bubble Shapes**

Attach the ends of two straws together with duct tape or paper clips, creating the desired shapes. Six straws will be needed to make a pyramid and 12 to make a cube. The frames can be dipped into bubble solutions and observed.

Music

1. **"Pop! Goes the Bubble"**
(Sing to the tune of "Pop! Goes the Weasel")

Soap and water can be mixed.
To make a bubble solution.
Carefully blow,
Now, watch it go!
Pop! Goes the bubble!

2. **"Can You Blow a Big Bubble?"**
(Sing to the tune of "The Muffin Man")

Can you blow a big bubble?
A big bubble, a big bubble?
Can you blow a big bubble,
With your bubble gum?

3. **"I'm a Little Bubble"**
(Sing to the tune of "I'm a Little Teapot")

I'm a little bubble, shiny and round.
I gently float down to the ground.
The wind lifts me up and then I drop.
Down to the dry ground where I pop.

4. **"Ten Little Bubbles"**
(Sing to the tune of "Ten Little Indians")

One little, two little, three little bubbles.
Four little, five little, six little bubbles.
Seven little, eight little, nine little bubbles.
Ten bubbles floating to the ground.

5. **"Here's a Bubble"**
(Sing to the tune of "Frere Jacques")

Here's a bubble, here's a bubble.
Big and round; big and round.
See it floating gently,
See it floating gently,
To the ground; to the ground.

Science

1. Bubble Solutions

Encourage the children to assist in preparing the following bubble solutions. (**Note:** The use of glycerine in preparing the bubble solution is optional. It helps to provide a stronger skin on the bubble, but the solutions can be prepared without this ingredient.)

Recipe #1

1/4 cup liquid dish soap
1/2 cup water
1 teaspoon sugar

Recipe #2: Outdoor Use

3 cups water
2 cups liquid dish soap (Joy detergent)
1/2 cup light corn syrup

Recipe #3

2/3 liquid dish soap
1 gallon of water
1 tablespoon glycerine

2. Bubble Gadgets

Prepare a bubble solution and make some bubbles! Use the following to make great bubbles.

- plastic berry baskets
- chenille stems or thin electrical wire shaped into wands
- six-pack holders
- egg poacher trays
- funnels
- children's scissors—hold the blades and dip the finger holders into the bubble solution.
- tin cans—open at both ends.
- paper cups—poke a hole in the bottom of a paper cup. Dip the rim into a bubble solution and blow through the hole.
- plastic straws—use a single straw or tape several together in a bundle.
- straws and string—thread 3 feet of thin thread through two plastic straws. Tie the string together. Hold the straws and pull them to form a rectangle with the string. Dip into a bubble solution and pull upward. As you move the frame, a bubble will form. Bring the two straws together to close off the bubble. This technique requires practice.
- Hula Hoop—fill a small wading pool with 2 inches of bubble solution. The Hula Hoop can be used as a giant wand by dipping the hoop in a solution and lifting it up carefully.

3. Wet/Dry

While blowing bubbles with the children, try touching a bubble with a dry finger. Repeat using a wet finger. What happens? You will observe that bubbles break when they touch an object that is dry.

4. Bubble Jar

Fill a small plastic bottle half-full of water. Add a few drops of food coloring, if desired. Add baby oil or mineral oil to completely fill the jar. Secure the bottle tightly. Then slowly tilt the bottle from side to side. When this occurs, the liquid in the jar resembles waves. Bubbles can be created by shaking the bottle. Encourage the children to observe these reactions.

5. Air Bubbles in Food

Examine the air bubbles in pieces of bread, Swiss cheese, and carbonated drinks.

6. Bubbling Raisins

Place two or three raisins in a small bottle of sparkling mineral water. Secure the cap and watch the bubbles form as the raisins sink and float.

Sensory

1. Wash Dolls

Fill the sensory table with warm water and add a few tablespoons of dish soap. Provide plastic dolls, washcloths, and towels.

2. Dishwashing

Place plastic dishes and dishcloths in a sensory table filled with warm soapy water. A dish-drying rack could be set up nearby or towels could be provided to dry the dishes.

3. Bubble Bath

Purchase or make bubble bath soap to put at the sensory table along with scoops, measuring cups, and pails.

4. Bubble Solution

The sensory table can be used to hold a bubble solution and bubble-making tools.

5. Pumps and Water

Fill the sensory table with water. Add water pumps, turkey basters, and siphons to create air bubbles in the water.

Books

The following books can be used to complement this theme:

Arnold, Tedd. (1995). *No More Water in the Tub*. New York: Dial Books.

Bennett, Andrea T., James H. Kessler, and Melody Sarecky. (1996). *Apples, Bubbles, and Crystals: Your Science ABCs*. Illus. by Melody Sarecky. New York: Learning Triangle Press.

Bergen, Stuart. (1996). *Fozzie's Bubble Bath*. Illus. by Rick Brown. New York: Grosset & Dunlap.

Bradbury, Judy. (1997). *Double Bubble Trouble!* Illus. by Cathy Trachok. Hightstown, NJ: McGraw-Hill.

Bradley, Kimberly Brubaker and Margaret Miller. (2001). *Pop: A Book about Bubbles*. Illus. by Margaret Miller. New York: HarperCollins.

Buxbaum, Susan Kovacs et al. (1992). *Splash! All about Baths*. Boston: Little, Brown.

Cowley, Joy. (1990). *Mrs. Wish-Washy*. Bothell, WA: Wright Group.

De Paola, Tomie and Margaret Frith (Editor). (2000). *Strega Nona Takes a Vacation*. Illus. by Tomie De Paola. New York: Putnam.

Edwards, Frank B. (1998). *Troubles with Bubbles*. Illus. by John Bianchi. Kingston, Ont: Bungalo Books. (New Reader Series.)

Everett, Louise. (1989). *Bubble Gum in the Sky*. Illus. by Paul Harvey. Mahwah, NJ: Troll. (Pbk.)

Goodman, Joan Elizabeth. (1996). *Bernard's Bath*. Illus. by Dominic Catalano. Honesdale, PA: Boyds Mills Press.

Mayer, Mercer. (1997). *Just a Bubble Bath*. Utica, NY: Good Times Publishing.

Mooney, E. S. and Brothers Thompson. Illus. by Brothers Thompson. (2001). *Bubbles' Best Adventure Ever*. New York: Scholastic.

Noble, Kate. (1994). *Bubble Gum*. Illus. by Rachel Bass. Chicago: Silver Seahorse Press.

O'Connor, Jane. (1997). *Benny's Big Bubble*. Illus. by Tomi De Paola. New York: Price Stern Sloan.

Wood, Audrey. (1991). *King Bidgood's in the Bathtub*. Orlando, FL: Harcourt Brace.

Multimedia

The following multimedia products can be used to complement this theme:

De Paola, Tomie. *The Bubble Factory* [cassette and book]. (1997). New York: Scholastic.

Johnson, Laura. "Be a Bubble" on *Fun Activities for Toddlers* [cassette]. Available from Kimbo Educational.

The Tots and the Lovely Bubbly Surprise [video]. (1997). Troy, MI: Ragdoll Productions; distributed by Anchor Bay Entertainment.

Walcoff, Larry et al. *Bubbles: How Do Insects Walk on Water?* [video]. (1992). Bloomington, IN: Agency for Instructional Technology. (*Science for You* series.)

Recordings and Song Titles

The following recording can be used to complement this theme:

"Bubblehouse." (1976). *Pop Rock Parachute*. Long Branch, NJ: Kimbo Educational.

THEME

9

Materials

brick, wood,
cement, steel,
glass

Purpose

shelter
storage

Buildings

Parts

basement
rooms
windows
doors
roof
walls
chimney
ceilings
floors
frame

Construction Workers

carpenters
electricians
architects
masons
plumbers

Types

homes, schools, offices,
stores, malls,
hospital/clinic,
police station, fire station,
library, church, bank,
restaurant,
handicapped-accessible

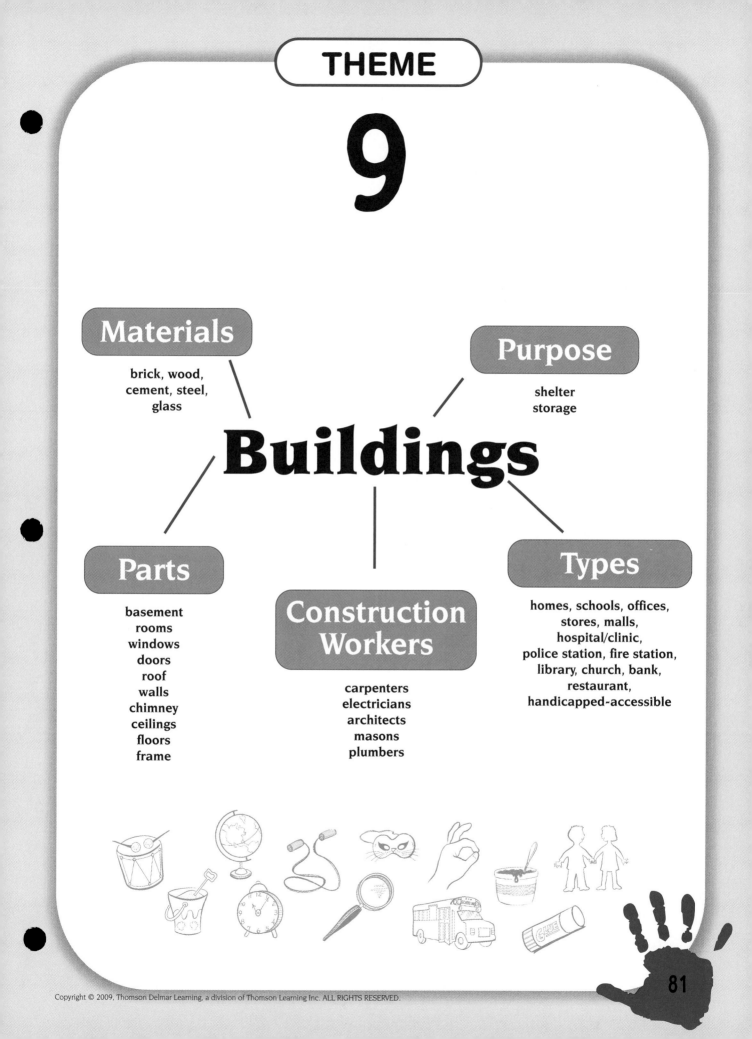

Theme Goals

Through participating in the experiences provided by this theme, the children may learn

1. Types of buildings
2. Purposes of buildings
3. Materials used to make buildings
4. Parts of a building
5. Workers who construct buildings

Concepts for the Children to Learn

1. There are many types of buildings: homes, offices, stores, hospitals, malls, etc.
2. Buildings can be made of brick, wood, cement, steel, and glass.
3. Many workers help construct buildings: architects, carpenters, electricians, plumbers, and masons.
4. Buildings can be used for shelter and storage.
5. Most buildings have a roof and rooms with ceilings, walls, windows, doors, and a floor.
6. Some buildings have a basement and chimney.

Vocabulary

1. **architect**—a person who designs a building.
2. **building**—a structure.
3. **carpenter**—a person who builds.
4. **ceiling**—the top "wall" of a room.
5. **electrician**—a person who wires a building for light, heat, and cooking.
6. **mall**—a building containing many stores.
7. **mason**—a person who lays cement, blocks, and bricks.
8. **plumber**—a person who installs water pipes, toilets, and sinks.
9. **roof**—the top covering of a building.
10. **room**—a part of a building set off by walls.
11. **skyscraper**—a very tall building.

Bulletin Board

The purpose of this bulletin board is to develop awareness of size as well as visual discrimination skills and hand-eye coordination. Construct house shapes out of tagboard ranging in size from small to large. Color the shapes and laminate. Punch a hole in the top of each house. Trace each house shape on black construction paper and cut out. Hang the shadow pieces on the bulletin board with a pushpin inserted in the top of each. During self-directed and self-initiated play, the children can match each colored house to the corresponding shadow piece by hanging it on the pushpin.

Family Letter

Dear Families,

Your home, the library, our school . . . these are all buildings with which your child is familiar. Buildings will be our next theme. Discoveries will be made regarding different kinds and parts of buildings, materials used to construct buildings, and construction workers who erect buildings.

AT SCHOOL

A sampling of the learning experiences includes:

- building with various materials—such as cardboard boxes and milk cartons
- working at the woodworking bench to practice supervised hammering, drilling, and sawing
- weighing and balancing bricks
- taking a walk to a construction site and observing the building process
- identifying different types of buildings

AT HOME

You can reinforce building concepts on your way to and from the center by pointing out any buildings of interest, such as the fire station, police station, hospital, library, shopping mall, and restaurants. Children are naturally curious about why and how things happen. If you pass any construction sites, point out the materials and equipment used, as well as the jobs of the workers. This will help your child develop receptive and expressive language skills as well as stimulate his or her interest. Concepts of time can also be fostered if you are able to visit the construction site over an extended period of time. You and your child will be able to keep track of progress in the development of the building.

Enjoy your child as you reinforce concepts related to buildings.

Together we will build a big house.

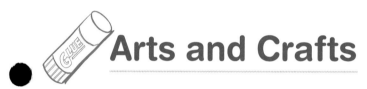 # Arts and Crafts

1. Our Home

Provide paper, crayons, and markers for each child to draw his or her home. Collect all of the drawings and place them in mural fashion on a large piece of paper to create a town. To extend this activity, have the children also draw buildings in the town to extend the mural. (This activity may be limited to kindergarten children or children who have reached the representational stage of art development.)

2. Blueprints

Blueprint paper, pencils, and markers should be placed in the art area. The children will enjoy marking on it. Older children may also enjoy using rulers and straight edges.

3. Building Shapes

Cut out building shapes from easel paper. Place at the easel, allowing children to paint their buildings.

4. Creating Structures

Save half-pint milk cartons. Rinse well and allow the children to paint, color, and decorate the cartons to look like buildings.

 # Cooking

Sugar Cookies

1 1/2 cups powdered sugar
1 cup margarine or butter
1 egg
1 teaspoon vanilla
2 1/2 cups all-purpose flour
1 teaspoon baking soda
1 teaspoon cream of tartar
granulated sugar

Mix the powdered sugar, margarine, egg, and vanilla together. Stir in the flour, baking soda, and cream of tartar. Chill, to prevent sticking while rolling the dough out. Heat the oven to

BUILDINGS

375 degrees. Roll out the dough. Cut into squares, triangles, diamonds, rectangles, and circles. Sprinkle with sugar. Place on a lightly greased cookie sheet. Bake until lightly browned, about 7 to 8 minutes. Give each child 3 to 5 cookies. Allow them to make buildings with their shapes before eating.

Dramatic Play

1. **Library**

   Rearrange the dramatic play area to resemble a library. Include books, library cards, book markers, tables, and chairs for the children's use.

2. **Buildings**

   Collect large cardboard boxes from an appliance dealer. The children can construct their own buildings and paint them with tempera paint.

3. **Construction Site**

   Place cardboard boxes, blocks, plastic pipes, wheelbarrows, hard hats, paper, and pencils in the dramatic play area to represent a construction site.

Field Trips/ Resource People

1. **Building Site**

   Visit a local building site if available. Observe and discuss the people who are working, how buildings look, and talk about safety. Take pictures. When the pictures are developed, post them in the classroom.

2. **Neighborhood Walk**

   Take a walk around the neighborhood. Observe the various kinds of buildings. Talk about the different sizes and colors of the buildings.

3. **Library**

   Visit a library. Observe how books are stored. Read the children a story while there. If possible, allow the children to check out books.

4. **Browsing at the Mall**

   Visit the shopping mall. Talk about the mall being a large building that houses a variety of stores. Visit a few of the stores that may be of special interest to the children. Included may be a toy store, a pet store, and a sporting goods store.

5. **Resource People**

   Invite people to visit the classroom, such as

   - construction worker
   - carpenter
   - electrician
   - architect
   - decorator/designer
   - plumber

Fingerplays

The Carpenter's Tools

The carpenter's hammer goes rap, rap, rap
   (make hammering motion with fist)
And his saw goes see, saw, see.
   (make sawing motion with arm and hand)
He planes and hammers and saws
   (make motions for each)
While he builds a building for me.
   (point to yourself)

Carpenter

This is the way he saws the wood
   (make sawing motion)
Sawing, sawing, sawing.

This is the way she nails a nail
   (make hammering motion)
Nailing, nailing, nailing.

This is the way he paints a building
    (make brushing motion)
Painting, painting, painting.

My House

I'm going to build a little house.
    (draw house with fingers by outlining in the
    air)
With windows big and bright,
    (spread out arms)
With chimney tall and curling smoke
    (show tall chimney with hands)
Drifting out of sight.
    (shade eyes with hands to look)
In winter when the snowflakes fall
    (use fingers to make the motion of
    snow falling downward)
Or when I hear a storm,
    (place hand to ear)
I'll go sit in my little house
    (draw house again)
Where I'll be snug and warm.
    (hug self)

Group Time

(Games, Language)

1. **Identifying Buildings**

Collect several pictures of buildings that are easily identified such as school, fire station, hospital, and home. Talk about each picture. Ask, "How do you know this is a school?" Discuss the function of each building. To help the children, pictures of buildings in their community can be used.

2. **Exploring Our Center**

Explore your center. Walk around the outside and observe walls, windows, roof, etc. Explore the inside also. Check out the rooms, floor, walls, ceiling, and stairs. Colors, materials, and size are some things you can discuss. Allow the children to help make an "Our Center Has . . ." chart.

Large Muscle

Workbench

Call attention during group time to the wood-working bench and explain the activities that can occur there. Try to encourage the children to practice pounding nails, sawing, drilling, and so forth, during self-initiated play. **Caution:** This activity needs constant supervision.

Math

1. **Weighing Bricks**

Set out a heavy-duty balance scale and small bricks. The children can weigh and balance the bricks.

2. **Wipe-off Windows**

Cut out and laminate a variety of buildings with varying numbers of windows. Provide children with grease markers or watercolor markers. Encourage the children to count the number of windows of each building and print the corresponding numeral on the building. The numerals can be wiped off with a damp cloth. (This activity would be most appropriate for kindergarten children.)

3. **Blocks**

Set out blocks of various shapes, including triangles, rectangles, and squares, for the children to build with.

Music

"Go In and Out the Window"

Form a circle with the children and hold hands. While holding hands, have the children raise

their arms up to form windows. Let each child have a turn weaving in and out the windows. Use the following chant as you play.

_____ goes in and out the windows,
In and out the windows,
In and out the windows.
_____ goes in and out the windows,
As we did before.

Fill in child's name in the _____.

Science

1. **Building Materials**

   Collect materials such as wood, brick, cement, metal, and magnifying glasses and place on the science table. Encourage the children to observe the various materials up close.

2. **Mixing Cement**

   Make cement using a small amount of cement and water. Mix materials together in a large plastic ice cream bucket. Allow the children to help. The children can also observe and feel the wet cement.

3. **Building Tools**

   Collect and place various tools such as a hammer, level, wedge, and screwdriver on the science table for the children to examine. Discuss each tool and demonstrate how it is used. Then place the tools in the woodworking area. Provide wood and styrofoam so that the children are encouraged to use the tools as a self-selected activity with close adult supervision.

Sensory

1. **Wet Sand**

   Fill the sensory table with sand and add water. Provide cups, square plastic containers, bowls, and so forth, for children to create molds with the sand.

2. **Wood Shavings**

   Place wood shavings in the sensory table.

3. **Scented Play Dough**

   Prepare scented play dough and place in the sensory table.

Social Studies

1. **Buildings in Our Town**

   Make a chart with the children's names listed vertically on the right-hand side. Across the top of the chart draw buildings or glue pictures of buildings that the children have visited. Suggestions include a theater, supermarket, clinic, museum, post office, fire station, etc. At group time, ask the children what buildings they have visited. Mark the sites for each child.

2. **Unusual Buildings**

   Show pictures of unusual buildings cut from various magazines, travel guides, etc. Allow the children to use their creative thinking by asking them the use of each building. All answers and possibilities should be acknowledged.

3. **Occupation Match**

   Cut out pictures of buildings and the people who work in them. Examples would include: hospital—nurse, fire station—firefighter. Glue these pictures to a tagboard and laminate. The children should be encouraged to match each worker to the appropriate building.

Books

The following books can be used to complement this theme:

Ackerman, Karen. (1995). *The Sleeping Porch*. Illus. by Elizabeth Sayles. New York: William Morrow.

Barton, Byron. (1997). *Machines at Work*. New York: HarperCollins.

Dorros, Arthur. (1992). *This Is My House*. New York: Scholastic.

Gibbons, Gail. (1986). *Up Goes the Skyscraper!* New York: Macmillan.

Gibbons, Gail. (1990). *How a House Is Built*. New York: Holiday House.

Hautzig, David. (1994). *At the Supermarket*. New York: Orchard Books.

Hoban, Tana. (1997). *A Construction Zone*. New York: Greenwillow Books.

James, Alan. (1989). *Homes on Water*. Minneapolis, MN: Lerner.

Jaspersohn, William. (1994). *My Hometown Library*. Boston: Houghton Mifflin.

Kalman, Bobbie. (1994). *Homes Around the World*. New York: Crabtree Publishing.

Keats, Ezra Jack. (1999). *Apt. 3*. New York: Viking.

Korman, Justine, Jan Gerardi, Justine Dorman-Fontes, and Jeffrey Scott. (2000). *Emmy's Dream House*. Illus. by Jan Gerardi. New York: CTW Books/Random House. (*Jellybean Books Just for Preschoolers*.)

McDonald, Megan. (1996). *My House Has Stars*. Illus. by Peter Catalanotto. New York: Orchard Books.

Miller, Marilyn. (1996). *Behind the Scenes at the Shopping Mall*. Illus. by Ingo Fast. Austin, TX: Raintree/Steck Vaughn.

Morris, Ann. (1992). *Houses and Homes*. Photos by Ken Heyman. New York: Lothrop, Lee & Shepard.

Novak, Matt. (1996). *Elmer Blunt's Open House*. New York: Orchard Books. (Pbk.)

Richardson, Joy. (1994). *Skyscrapers*. New York: Franklin Watts.

Rounds, Glen. (1995). *Sod Houses on the Great Plains*. New York: Holiday House.

Seltzer, Isadore. (1992). *The House I Live In: At Home in America*. Colchester, CT: Atheneum.

Shelby, Anne. (1996). *The Someday House*. Illus. by Rosanne Litzinger. New York: Orchard Books.

Shemie, Bonnie. (1990). *Houses of Bark*. San Francisco: Children's Book Press.

Santoro, Christopher. (1998). *It's Haunted!* New York: Random House.

Yeoman, John. (1995). *The Do-It-Yourself House That Jack Built*. Illus. by Quentin Blake. Colchester, CT: Atheneum.

Multimedia

The following multimedia products can be used to complement this theme:

Building Skyscrapers [video]. (1994). New York: David Alpert Associates, Inc.

Community Construction Kit [CD-ROM]. (1998). Watertown, MA: Tom Snyder Productions.

Dig Hole, Build House [video]. (1994). Gig Harbor, WA: Real World Video.

The Fire Station [video]. (1990). Washington, DC: National Geographic Society.

Gryphon Bricks [CD-ROM]. (1996). San Diego, CA: Gryphon Software Corp.

Let's Build a House [video]. (1996). San Diego, CA: Video Connections.

Equipment

tent, camper,
lantern/flashlight,
sleeping bag

Activities

boating,
waterskiing, hiking,
cooking outdoors,
horseback riding,
telling stories,
fishing,
birdwatching,
observing wild animals

Camping

Places

woods,
campgrounds,
parks, lakes,
backyards

Transportation

camper, car, pickup truck,
motorcycle, van, canoe,
bicycle, horse

Foods

hot dogs
marshmallows
beans
fish

91

Theme Goals

Through participating in the experiences provided by this theme, the children may learn

1. Places where people camp
2. Equipment used for camping
3. Camping transportation
4. Camping activities
5. Foods we eat while camping

Concepts for the Children to Learn

1. A tent is a shelter used for camping.
2. We can camp in the woods or at a campground.
3. We can also camp in a park, at a lake, or in our backyard.
4. Hot dogs, fish, marshmallows, and beans are all camping foods.
5. Foods can be cooked outdoors while camping.
6. A camper can be driven or attached to the back of a car or pickup truck.
7. Lanterns and flashlights are sources of light used for camping.
8. A sleeping bag is a blanket used for camping.
9. Some people camp by a lake to waterski and go boating and fishing.
10. Some people take their bicycles and canoes on camping trips.
11. Bird watching, hiking, and observing wild animals can be camping activities.
12. Some people enjoy storytelling while camping.

Vocabulary

1. **backpack**—a zippered bag worn on one's back to carry objects.
2. **campfire**—a controlled fire that is made at a campground.
3. **camping**—living outdoors in sleeping bags, tents, cabins, or campers.
4. **campsite**—a place for tents and campers to park.
5. **hiking**—taking a long walk.
6. **lantern**—a covered light used for camping.
7. **recreational vehicle**—a living and sleeping area on wheels.
8. **sleeping bag**—a zippered blanket used for camping.
9. **tent**—a movable shelter made out of material.
10. **woods**—an area with many trees.

Bulletin Board

The purpose of this bulletin board is to develop skills in recognizing colors and color words. In addition, visual discrimination, hand-eye coordination, and problem-solving skills are promoted. Construct several tents out of tagboard as illustrated. Make an identical set out of white tagboard. Color the first set of tents using the primary colors. Print the color names using corresponding colored markers onto the second set of tents. Laminate the materials. Staple the tents with color names to the bulletin board. Punch holes in the colored tents. Children can attach the tent to a pushpin on the corresponding color word tent.

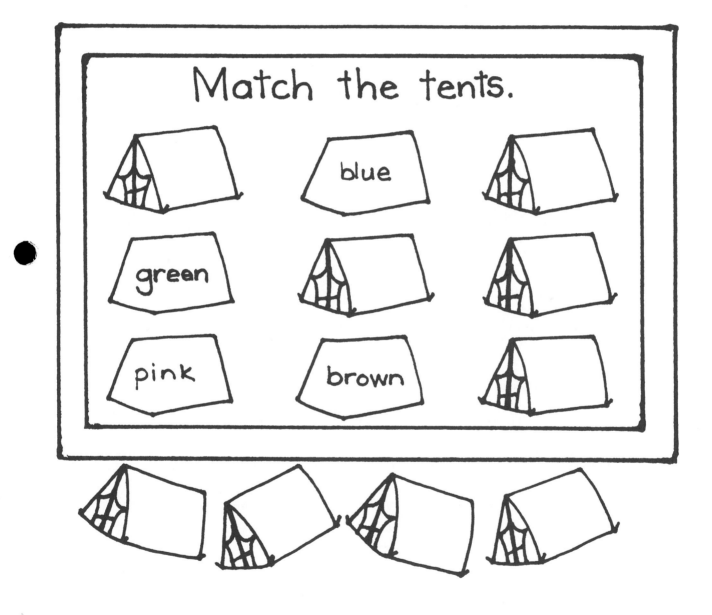

Family Letter

Dear Families,

With summer approaching, we will begin focusing on a fun family activity—camping! The children will become aware of camping activities. They will also learn about items and equipment that are commonly used while camping. From listening to the children's conversations, it sounds as if many have already been camping with their families. It should be fun to hear the camping stories they share!

AT SCHOOL

Some of the learning experiences planned include:

- setting up the dramatic play area with a tent, sleeping bags, and other camping items
- singing songs around a pretend campfire
- going on a "bear hunt" (a rhythmic chant)
- preparing foods that are eaten while camping
- cleaning up after camping

AT HOME

Help your child create a tent by draping a sheet over a table. Provide a flashlight and a blanket or sleeping bag, and your child will be prepared for hours of indoor camping fun! Through dramatic play experiences children relive and clarify situations and roles. They act out how they see the world and how they view relationships among people.

If you have any photographs or slides of family camping trips, we would be delighted if you would share them with us. Contact me and we can work out a time that would be convenient for you. Thanks!

Plan a camping trip with your child today!

Having a picnic is one of the best things about camping.

Arts and Crafts

1. **Easel Ideas**

   - Paint with leaves, sticks, flowers, and rocks.

   - Paint with colors seen in the forest such as brown, green, yellow, and orange.

   - Cut easel paper into the following shapes: tent, rabbits, chipmunks, and fish.

2. **Camping Collage**

   Collect leaves, pebbles, twigs, pine cones, etc. Provide glue and sturdy tagboard. Encourage the children to create a collage on the tagboard using the materials found while camping.

3. **Tackle Box**

   Make two holes approximately 3 inches apart in the center of the lid of an egg carton. To form the handle, thread a cord through the holes and tie. Paint the box. In the box, place paper clips for hooks and S-shaped styrofoam pieces for worms.

Cooking

1. **S'Mores**

   Place a large marshmallow on a square graham cracker. Next place a square of sweet chocolate on top of the marshmallow. After this, place the graham cracker on a baking sheet into a 250-degree oven for about 5 minutes or until the chocolate starts to melt. Remove the s'more and press a second graham cracker square on top of the chocolate. Let cool for a few minutes, and serve while still slightly warm.

2. **Venezuela Breakfast Cocoa**

   1/4 cup water
   3 tablespoons cocoa
   2 tablespoons sugar
   2 cups milk
   1 teaspoon vanilla

   1. Bring the water to a boil in a saucepan.

   2. Stir in the cocoa and sugar until they are blended. Turn the heat very low.

3. Slowly pour the milk into the saucepan with the cocoa mixture. Stir steadily to keep the mixture from burning. Continue cooking the mixture over low heat for about 2 minutes. Do not let it boil or skin will form on the top.

4. When the cocoa is hot, remove it from the stove and stir in the vanilla.

5. Carefully pour the cocoa into the cups. Serve warm.

Note: From *Many Hands Cooking*, by Terry Touff and Marilyn Ratner, 1974, New York: Thomas Y. Crowell. Reprinted with permission.

Dramatic Play

1. **Camping**

   Collect various types of clothing and camping equipment and place in the dramatic play area or outdoors. Include items such as hiking boots, sweatshirts, raincoats, sleeping bags, back-packs, cooking tools, and a tent.

2. **Puppets**

   Develop a puppet corner in the dramatic play area, including various animal puppets, that would be seen while camping.

3. **Going Fishing**

   Set up a rocking boat or a large box in the class-room or outdoors. Prepare paper fish with paper clips attached to them. Include a fishing pole made from a wooden dowel and a long string with a magnet attached to the end.

4. **Going to the Beach**

   In the dramatic play area, set up lawn chairs, beach towels, buckets, shovels, sunglasses, etc. Weather permitting, these items could also be placed outdoors.

Field Trips

1. **Department Store**

   Visit a department store or a sporting goods store where camping tents and other equipment are displayed.

2. **Picnic**

   Pack a picnic lunch or snack and take it to an area campground.

3. **Camper Salesperson**

   Visit a recreational vehicle dealer and tour a large mobile home.

Fingerplays

Five Little Bear Cubs

Five little bear cubs
Eating an apple core.
One had a sore tummy
And then there were four.

Four little bear cubs
Climbing in a tree.
One fell out
And then there were three.

Three little bear cubs
Playing peek-a-boo.
One was afraid
And then there were two.

Two little bear cubs
Sitting in the sun.
One ran away
And then there was one.

One little bear cub
Sitting all alone.
He saw his mommy
And then he ran home.

Group Time

(Games, Language)

1. What's Missing

Have different pieces of camping equipment available to show the children. Include a canteen, portable stove, sleeping bag, cooking tools, lantern, etc. Discuss each item, and then have the children close their eyes. Take one of the objects away and then have the children guess which object is missing.

2. Camping Safety

Discuss camping safety. Include these points:

- Always put out fires before going to sleep.
- Swim in safe areas and with a partner.
- When walking, or hiking away from your campsite, always have an adult with you.
- Always wear a life jacket in the boat.

3. Pack the Backpack

Bring a large backpack into the classroom. Also have many camping items available such as sweatshirts, flashlights, lanterns, food, raincoats, etc. The teacher gives the children instructions that they are going to pretend to go on a hike to the beach. What is one thing they will need to bring along? Why? Continue until all of the children have had a chance to contribute.

4. Campfire Story

Build a "campfire" by gluing empty toilet paper tubes or paper towel tubes together. (These will represent the logs.) Glue red, orange, and yellow tissue paper to the tops of the "logs" to represent the fire. Spread out a large blanket and place the "fire" in the middle. Turn off the lights and use a flashlight to read a camping story.

Large Muscle

Caves

Using large packing boxes or barrels placed horizontally on the playground, allow the children to pretend to be wild animals in caves.

Math

1. Camping Scavenger Hunt

Before the children go outdoors, instruct them to find things on your playground that you would see while camping. Sort them and count them when they bring them into the classroom (five twigs, three rocks, etc.).

2. Campers

Draw or paste tents onto the outside of a milk carton. Place a numeral on each tent.

The children will place the corresponding number of campers into the tent. Use small people figurines for the campers. (If none are available, make people from construction paper.)

Music

1. "A Camping We Will Go"
(*Sing to the tune of "The Farmer and the Dell"*)

A camping we will go.
A camping we will go.
Hi ho, we're off to the woods.
A camping we will go.

Saba will bring the tent.
Oh, Saba will bring the tent.
Hi ho, we're off to the woods.
A camping we will go.

(continued)

Juan will bring the food.
Oh, Juan will bring the food.
Hi ho, we're off to the woods.
A camping we will go.

The names in the song can be changed to different children's names.

2. **"Two Little Black Bears"**
(*Sing to the tune of* "Two Little Blackbirds")

Two little black bears sitting on a hill,
One named Jack, one named Jill.
Run away, Jack,
Run away, Jill.
Come back, Jack,
Come back, Jill.
Two little black bears sitting on a hill,
One named Jack, one named Jill.

3. **Campfire Songs**

Pretend that you are sitting around a campfire. Explain to the children that often people sing their favorite songs around a campfire. Encourage the children to name their favorite songs, and then sing some of them.

Science

1. **Scavenger Hunt**

While outside, have the children find plants growing, insects crawling, insects flying, a plant growing on a tree, a vine, a flower, bird feathers, a root, a seed, etc.

2. **Sink/Float**

Collect various pieces of camping equipment. Fill the water table with water and let the children test which objects sink or float. If desired, make a chart.

3. **Magnifying Glasses**

Provide magnifying glasses for looking at objects seen on a camping trip.

4. **Binoculars**

Make binoculars by gluing or stapling toilet paper tubes together. If desired, children can decorate their binoculars with paint. Encourage children to find specific camping items by looking outside with their binoculars.

5. **Flashlight Fun**

Give children flashlights to experiment with during naptime or when the lights have been dimmed. Encourage them to try to create shadows by holding their hands or other objects in front of the light.

Sensory

Sensory Table Additions

- leaves
- rocks
- pebbles
- mud and sand
- twigs
- evergreen needles and branches
- water

Social Studies

1. **Pictures**

Collect pictures of different campsites. Share them by displaying them in the classroom at the children's eye level.

2. **Camping Experiences**

At group time ask if any of the children have been camping. Let them tell the rest of the children what they did while they were camping. Ask where they slept, what they ate, where the bathroom was, etc.

Books

The following books can be used to complement this theme:

Bauer, Marion Dane. (1995). *When I Go Camping with Grandma*. Illus. by Allen Garns. Morago, CA: Bridgewater Books.

Brillhart, Julie. (1997). *When Daddy Took Us Camping*. Niles, IL: Albert Whitman.

Brown, Mark Tolon. (1984). *Arthur Goes to Camp*. Madison, WI: Demco Media.

Brown, M. K. (1995). *Let's Go Camping with Mr. Sillypants*. New York: Crown.

Christelow, Eileen. (1998). *Jerome Camps Out*. New York: Clarion Books.

Duffey, Betsy. (1996). *Camp Knock Knock*. Illus. by Fiona Dunbar. New York: Delacorte Press.

Henkes, Kevin. (1997). *Bailey Goes Camping*. New York: Mulberry Books.

Hoff, Syd. (1996). *Danny and the Dinosaur Go to Camp*. New York: HarperCollins.

Howe, James. (1995). *Pinky and Rex and the Double-Dad Weekend*. Illus. by Melissa Sweet. New York: Atheneum.

Huneck, Stephen. (2001). *Sally Goes to the Mountains*. New York: Harry N. Abrams.

Kalman, Bobbie D. (1995). *Summer Camp*. New York: Crabtree Publishing.

Rand, Gloria. (1996). *Willie Takes a Hike*. Illus. by Ted Rand. Orlando, FL: Harcourt Brace.

Rosen, Michael. (1989). *We're Going on a Bear Hunt*. Illus. by Helen Oxenbury. New York: Margaret K. McElderry Books.

Say, Allen. (1989). *The Lost Lake*. Boston: Houghton Mifflin.

Shaw, Nancy E. (1994). *Sheep Take a Hike*. Illus. by Margot Apple. Boston: Houghton Mifflin.

Tafuri, Nancy. (1987). *Do Not Disturb*. New York: William Morrow.

Touff, Terry and Marilyn Ratner. (1974). *Many Hands Cooking*. New York: Thomas Y. Crowell.

Wallace, Ian. (1997). *A Winter's Tale*. Washington, DC: Groundwood Books.

Williams, Vera B. (1983). *Three Days on a River in a Red Canoe*. New York: Greenwillow.

Multimedia

The following multimedia products can be used to complement this theme:

Barney's Campfire Sing-Along [video]. (1990). Allen, TX: Lyons Group.

Let's Go Camping [video]. (1995). Burlington, VT: Vermont Story Works.

Mercer Mayer's Just Me and My Dad [CD-ROM]. (1996). New York: GT Interactive Software.

Uses

move objects
move people

Care

wash
wax
vacuum
repair

Sizes

small
medium
large

Cars, Trucks, and Buses

Inside Parts

horn, steering wheel,
seats, blinkers,
seat belts, radio,
mirrors, clock, motor

Outside Parts

wheels, hood,
headlights,
trunk, mirrors,
windshield wipers,
antenna

Safety

speed, seatbelts,
noise, activities,
air bags, gasoline,
handicapped-accessible,
number of people,
sit until stopped

Kinds

TRUCKS	CARS	BUSES
dump	compact, van,	school
fire	station wagon,	city
pickup	convertible,	tour
tank	police, taxi,	
semi	ambulance	

Colors

white, black,
blue, green,
yellow, gray,
red

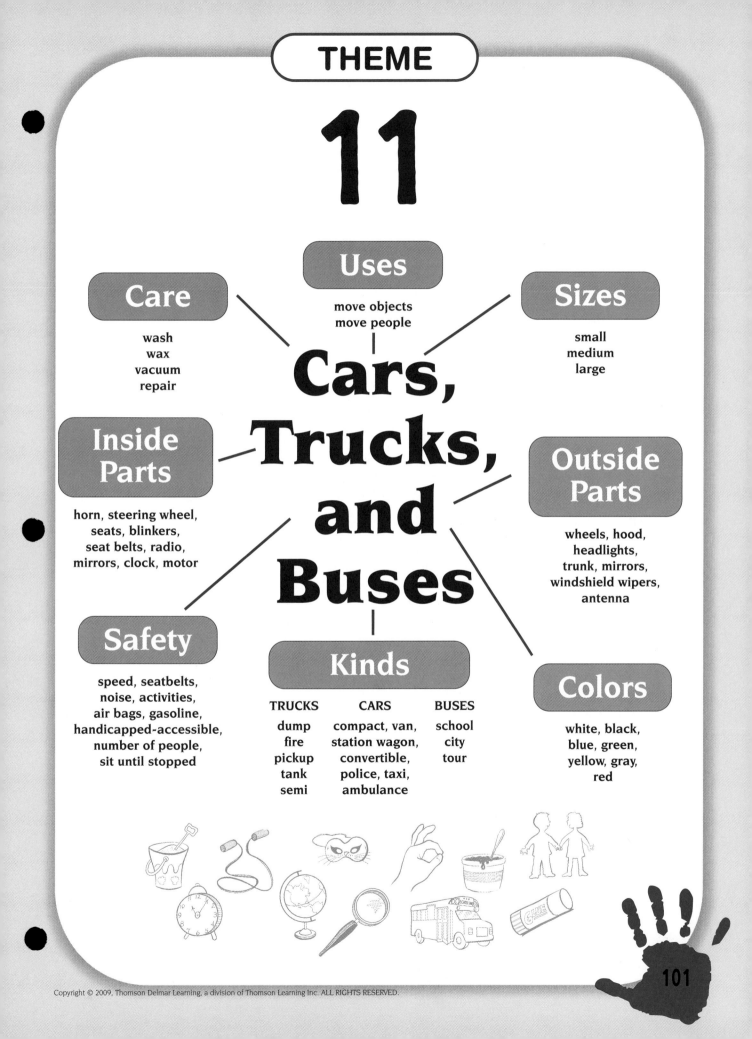

101

Theme Goals

Through participating in the experiences provided by this theme, the children may learn

1. Kinds of cars, trucks, and buses
2. Care of vehicles
3. Uses of vehicles
4. Inside and outside parts of vehicles
5. Colors and sizes of vehicles
6. Safety factors

Concepts for the Children to Learn

1. Cars, trucks, and buses are used to move people.
2. There are many kinds of cars, trucks, and buses.
3. Trucks and buses are usually bigger than cars.
4. Trucks can be used to haul objects.
5. There are dump, pickup, tank, and semi trucks.
6. Compact van, station wagon, and convertible are kinds of cars.
7. Special cars include police cars, taxis, and ambulances.
8. There are several kinds of buses, such as a city bus.
9. Cars, trucks, and buses come in many colors and sizes.
10. Cars, trucks, and buses have inside and outside parts.
11. The horn, steering wheel, seats, blinkers, seat belt, mirror, clock, and motor are inside parts.
12. The wheels, hood, headlights, trunk door, mirrors, and windshield wipers are outside parts.
13. Seat belts help keep people safe; so does remaining seated until the vehicle stops.
14. Vehicles need care.
15. Vehicles need to be vacuumed, washed, waxed, and repaired.

Vocabulary

1. **bus**—a vehicle that carries many people.
2. **car**—a vehicle used for moving people.
3. **driver**—operates the vehicle.
4. **fuel**—gas, diesel, and so forth, used to produce power.
5. **gas**—produces power to move a vehicle.
6. **motor**—makes the vehicle move by creating energy.
7. **passenger**—the rider.
8. **truck**—a wheeled vehicle used to move people and big objects.

102

THEME 11

Bulletin Board

The purpose of the bulletin board is to reinforce color recognition and matching skills, as well as to develop one-to-one correspondence concepts. In addition, visual discrimination, problem solving, and hand-eye coordination are promoted. Construct garage shapes out of tagboard. Color each garage a different color and hang on the bulletin board. Hang a pushpin or attach a Velcro piece in the center of each garage. Next, construct the same number of cars as garages from tagboard. Color each car a different color to correspond with the colors of the garages. Use a paper punch to make a hole in each car. The children can park each car in its corresponding colored garage. (**Note:** Carefully supervise the use of pushpins.)

CARS, TRUCKS, AND BUSES

Family Letter

Dear Families,

Cars, trucks, and buses—these are all transportation vehicles that your child sees daily. Because of the children's interest, we are beginning a unit on "Cars, Trucks, and Buses." Through participating in the planned activities, the children will learn that there are many colors, sizes, and kinds of cars, trucks, and buses. They will also learn the care of the inside and outside parts of a car.

AT SCHOOL

Some of the activities planned for this unit include:

- painting with small cars at the art table
- looking at and listening to many books and stories about trucks, buses, and cars
- setting up a gas station in the dramatic play area
- visiting with Officer Lewis from the police department, who will show the children his squad car at 10:30 a.m. on Thursday

AT HOME

You can foster the concepts of this unit at home by taking your child with you the next time you need to buy gas for your vehicle. There are many different types of trucks and cars to observe at the filling station. Also, provide soapy water and a sponge and let your child help you wash the family vehicle. Children enjoy taking part in grown-up activities, and this helps build a sense of responsibility and self-esteem.

Enjoy your child as you explore concepts related to cars, trucks, and buses.

Cars, trucks, and buses are used to move people.

 Arts and Crafts

1. License Plate Rubbings

Place paper on top of a license plate. Using the side of a large crayon, rub across the top of the license plate.

2. Car Track Painting

Provide several small plastic cars and trucks and large sheets of white paper. Also, have available low, flat pans of thin tempera paint. Encourage the children to take the cars and trucks and roll the wheels in the paint. They can then transfer the car to their own paper and make car or truck tracks on the paper.

3. Designing Cars

Provide the children with large, appliance-sized cardboard boxes. To protect the floor surface, place a large sheet of plastic underneath. Provide the children with paint, markers, and collage materials to decorate the boxes as cars. When the cars dry, they can be moved into the block building, dramatic play area, or outdoor area.

 Cooking

1. Cracker Wheels

For this recipe each child will need:

4 round crackers
1/2 hot dog
1/2 a slice of 4-inch × 4-inch cheese

Slice hot dogs and place on a cracker. Place cheese over the top. Place in oven at 350 degrees for 3 to 5 minutes or microwave for 30 seconds. Let cool and eat.

2. Greek Honey Twists

3 eggs, beaten
2 tablespoons vegetable oil
1/2 teaspoon baking powder
1/4 teaspoon salt
1 3/4 to 2 cups all-purpose flour
vegetable oil
1/4 cup honey
1 tablespoon water
ground cinnamon to taste

Mix eggs, 2 tablespoons oil, baking powder, and salt in a large bowl. Gradually stir in enough flour to make a very stiff dough. Knead 5 minutes. Roll half the dough at a time as thin as possible on well-floured surface with a stockinet-covered rolling pin. Cut into wheel shapes. Twist into the shape of the numeral eight. Cover with damp towel to prevent drying.

Heat 2 to 3 inches of oil to 375 degrees. Fry three to five twists at a time until golden brown, turning once, about 45 seconds on each side. Drain on paper towels. Heat honey and water to boiling; boil 1 minute. Cool slightly. Drizzle over twists; sprinkle with cinnamon. Makes 32 twists.

Note: From *Betty Crocker's International Cookbook*, 1980, New York: Random House. Reprinted with permission.

Dramatic Play

1. Filling Station

Provide cardboard boxes for cars and hoses for the gas pumps. Also, make available play money and steering wheels.

2. Bus

Set up a bus situation by lining up chairs in one or two long rows. Provide a steering wheel for the driver. A money bucket and play money can also be provided. If a steering wheel is unavailable, heavy round pizza cardboards can be used to improvise.

3. Taxi

Set up two rows of chairs side by side to represent a taxi. Use a pizza cardboard, or other round object, as the steering wheel. Provide a telephone, dress-up clothes for the passengers, and a hat for the driver. A "TAXI" sign can also be placed by the chairs to invite play.

4. Fire Truck

Contact the local fire chief and ask to use old hoses, fire hats, and firefighter clothing.

Field Trips/ Resource People

1. City Bus

Take the children for a ride around town on a city bus. When boarding, allow each child to place his or her own money in the meter. Observe the length of the bus. While inside, watch how the bus driver operates the bus. Also, have a school bus driver visit and tell about the job and the importance of safety on a bus.

2. Taxi Driver

Invite a taxi driver to visit and show the features of the taxi.

3. Patrol Car

Invite a police officer to bring a squad car to the center. The radio, siren, and flashing lights can be demonstrated. Let the children sit in the car.

4. Fire Truck

Invite a local firefighter to bring a fire truck to the center. Let the children climb in the truck and observe the parts.

5. Semi-truck Driver

Invite a semi driver to bring the truck to school. Observe the size, number of wheels, and parts of the cab. Let the children sit in the cab.

6. Ambulance

Invite an ambulance driver to bring the vehicle to school. Let the children inspect the contents.

Fingerplays

Windshield Wiper

I'm a windshield wiper
   (bend arm at elbow with fingers pointing up)
This is how I go
   (move arm to left and right, pivoting at elbow)
Back and forth, back and forth
   (continue back and forth motion)
In the rain and snow.
   (continue back and forth motion)

Here Is a Car

Here is a car, shiny and bright.
   (cup one hand and place on other palm)
This is the windshield that lets in the light.
   (hands open, fingertips touching)
Here are wheels that go round and round.
   (two fists)
I sit in the back seat and make not a sound.
   (sit quietly with hands in lap)

The Car Ride

(Left arm, held out with bent elbow and open palm, is road; right fist is car.)

106

THEME 11

"Vroom!" says the engine
(place car on left shoulder)
As the driver starts the car.
(shake car)

"Mmmm," say the windows
As the driver takes it far.
(travel over upper arm)

"Errr," say the tires
As it rounds the final bend,
(turn at elbow, proceed over forearm)

"Ahhh," says the driver
As his trip comes to an end.
(stop car on left flattened palm)

School Bus

I go to the bus stop each day
(walk one hand across table)
Where the bus comes to take us away.
(stop, have other hand wait also)
We stand single file
(one behind the other)
And walk down the aisle
(step up imaginary steps onto bus)
When the bus driver talks, we obey.

Group Time

(Games, Language)

1. **Thank-You Note**

   Write a thank-you note to a resource person. Allow the children to dictate and sign it.

2. **Red Light, Green Light**

   Select one child to pretend to be a traffic light. The traffic light places his or her back to children lined up at the other end of the room. When the traffic light says, "Green Light," or holds up green paper, the other children attempt to creep up on the traffic light. At any time the traffic light can say, "Red Light," or hold up a red paper, and quickly turn around. Creeping children must freeze. Any child caught moving is sent back to the starting line. Play continues until one child reaches the traffic light. This child becomes the new traffic light.

Large Muscle

1. **"Fill 'er Up"**

   The trikes, wagons, and scooters can be used outside on the playground. A gas pump can be constructed out of an old cardboard box with an attached hose.

2. **Car, Car, Truck**

   Play this simple variation of Duck, Duck, Goose by substituting the words, "Car, Car, Truck."

3. **Wash a Car**

   If possible, wash a compact-size car. Provide a hose, sponges, brushes, a bucket, and soapy water. If an actual car is not available, children can wash tricycles, bicycles, scooters, and wagons.

4. **Road Map Shower Curtain**

   Use permanent markers to color roads, trees, train tracks, buildings, etc. on a shower curtain. Place curtain on floor and encourage children to drive cars, trucks, or buses on the roads.

Math

1. **Cars and Garages**

   Car garages can be constructed out of empty half-pint milk cartons. Collect and carefully wash the milk cartons. Cut out one side and write a numeral, starting with one, on each carton. Next, collect a corresponding number of small miniature cars. Attach a strip of paper with a numeral from one to the appropriate number on each car's top. The children can drive each car into the garage with the corresponding numeral.

2. **License Plate Match**

   Construct two sets of identical license plates. Print a pattern of letters or numerals on each set. Mix them up. Children can try to match the pairs.

3. **Car, Truck, or Bus Sequencing**

Cut out various-sized cars, trucks, or buses and laminate. Children can sequence them from largest to smallest and vice versa.

4. **Sorting**

Construct cars, trucks, and buses of different colors and laminate. Children can sort according to color.

5. **Car Ramp**

Roll a bus, car, and truck toy down a wooden ramp. Encourage children to determine which vehicle went the farthest or shortest distance.

Science

1. **License Plates**

Collect license plates from different states and different vehicles and place them on a table for the children to explore.

2. **Feely Box**

Put transportation toys in a feely box. Include cars, trucks, and buses. Individually, let the children feel inside the box and identify the type of toy.

3. **Road Materials**

Place pieces of dirt, blacktop, and concrete in containers and place them on a table for the children to explore.

Sensory

Sensory Table Additions

- cars and trucks with wet sand
- baby oil and water

Social Studies

Discussion on Safety

Have a group discussion on safety when riding in a car. Allow children to come up with suggestions. Write them down on a chart and display in classroom during the unit. The addition of pictures or drawings would be helpful for younger children.

Books

The following books can be used to complement this theme:

Barton, Byron. (2001). *My Car*. New York: Greenwillow.

Betty Crocker's International Cookbook. (1980). New York: Random House.

Bingham, Caroline. (1995). *Fire Truck: And Other Emergency Machines*. New York: Dorling Kindersley. (Mighty Machine series.)

Bingham, Caroline. (1996). *Big Rig*. Illust. by M. Ling. New York: Dorling Kindersley. (Mighty Machine series.)

Bingham, Caroline. (1996). *Race Car*. New York: Dorling Kindersley. (Mighty Machine series.)

Bingham, Caroline. (1998). *Monster Machines*. New York: Dorling Kindersley. (Mighty Machine series.)

Blanchard, Arlene. (1995). *The Dump Truck*. Illus. by Tony Wells. Cambridge, MA: Candlewick Press.

Bloom, Suzanne. (2001). *The Bus for Us*. Honesdale, PA: Boyds Mills Press.

Crews, Donald. (1984). *School Bus*. New York: William Morrow.

Eick, Jean. (1997). *Giant Dump Trucks*. Illus. by Michael Sellner. Minneapolis, MN: Abdo & Daughters.

Gray, Libba Moore. (1994). *The Little Black Truck*. Illus. by Elizabeth Sayles. New York: Simon & Schuster.

Haldane, Elizabeth. (2005). *Truck*. New York: DK Publishing.

Hort, Lenny. (2000). *The Seals on the Bus*. Illus. by Karas, G. Brian. New York: Henry Holt.

Howland, Naomi. (1994). *ABCDrive!: A Car Trip Alphabet*. New York: Clarion Books.

Katz, Bobbi. (1997). *Truck Talk: Rhymes on Wheels*. St. Paul, MN: Cartwheel Books.

Kirk, Daniel. (1997). *Trash Trucks*. New York: G. P. Putnam.

Kirk, David. (1999). *Miss Spider's New Car*. New York: Scholastic.

Oxlade, Chris. (1997). *Car (Take It Apart)*. Morristown, NJ: Silver Burdett.

Mahy, Margaret. (1994). *The Rattlebang Picnic*. Illus. by Steven Kellogg. New York: Dial Books.

Marston, Hope Irvin. (1993). *Big Rigs*. New York: Cobblehill Books.

Patrick, Denise Lewis. (1993). *The Car Washing Street*. Illus. by John Ward. New York: William Morrow.

Radford, Derek. (1997). *Harry at the Garage*. Cambridge, MA: Candlewick Press.

Ready, Dee. (1998). *School Bus Driver*. New York: Capstone.

Rex, Michael. (2004). *Truck Duck*. New York: G.P. Putnam.

Richardson, Joy. (1994). *Cars*. New York: Franklin Watts.

Rockwell, Anne F. (1992). *Cars*. New York: Dutton.

Royston, Angela. (1991). *Cars*. Photos by Tim Ridley. New York: Macmillan.

Scarry, Richard. (1997). *Richard Scarry's Cars and Trucks and Things That Go*. New York: Golden Book.

Skultety, Nancy. (2005). *From Here to There*. Illus. by Tammie Lyon. Honesdale, PA.: Boyds Mills Press.

Strickland, Paul. (2000). *Truck Jam: A Pop-Up Book*. Brooklyn, NY: Ragged Bear.

Wheelie Board Books: Bus. (1999). London: DK Publishing.

Wilkins, Verna Allette et al. (1993). *Mum Can Fix It*. Lawrenceville, NJ: Red Sea Press.

Multimedia

The following multimedia products can be used to complement this theme:

Big Red [video]. (1993). Mill Valley, CA: Fire Dog Pictures.

Firefighter [CD-ROM]. (1994). New York: Simon & Schuster Interactive.

How a Car Is Built [video]. (1995). Think Media.

K. C.'s First Bus Ride [video]. (1994). KidSafety of America.

Murphy, Jane Lawliss. *Cars, Trucks and Trains* [compact disc]. (1997). Long Branch, NJ: Kimbo Educational.

Snowplows at Work [video]. (1994). Truckee, CA: Bill Aaron Productions.

Recordings and Song Titles

The following recordings can be used to complement the theme:

"Car Goes Beep." (1974). *Put Your Finger in the Air*. Long Branch, NJ: Kimbo Educational.

"Car, Car Song." (1990). *Car Songs*. Long Branch, NJ: Kimbo Educational.

"Car, Car Song." (1999). *Five Little Monkeys*. Long Branch, NJ: Kimbo Educational.

Cars, Trucks, and Trains. (1997). Long Branch, NJ: Kimbo Educational.

"Hooray for Farm Machines." (1999). *On the Farm with RONNO*. Long Branch, NJ: Kimbo Educational.

"Motoring." (1996). *People in Our Neighborhood*. Long Branch, NJ: Kimbo Educational.

"Stop at the Red Light." (1993). *Pre-K Hooray*. Long Branch, NJ: Kimbo Educational.

"The Wheels on the Bus." (1997). *Six Little Ducks*. Long Branch, NJ: Kimbo Educational.

12

Cats

Body Parts

fur
paws and claws
tail
whiskers
eyes
ears
nose
mouth

Food

water
cat food

Care

food
water
grooming
exercise
shelter
medical
gentle handling

Colors

black
brown
white
gray
yellow
calico

Places Cats Live

homes
barns
outdoors

Types

long-haired
short-haired
different colors
calico

Communication

purring
meowing

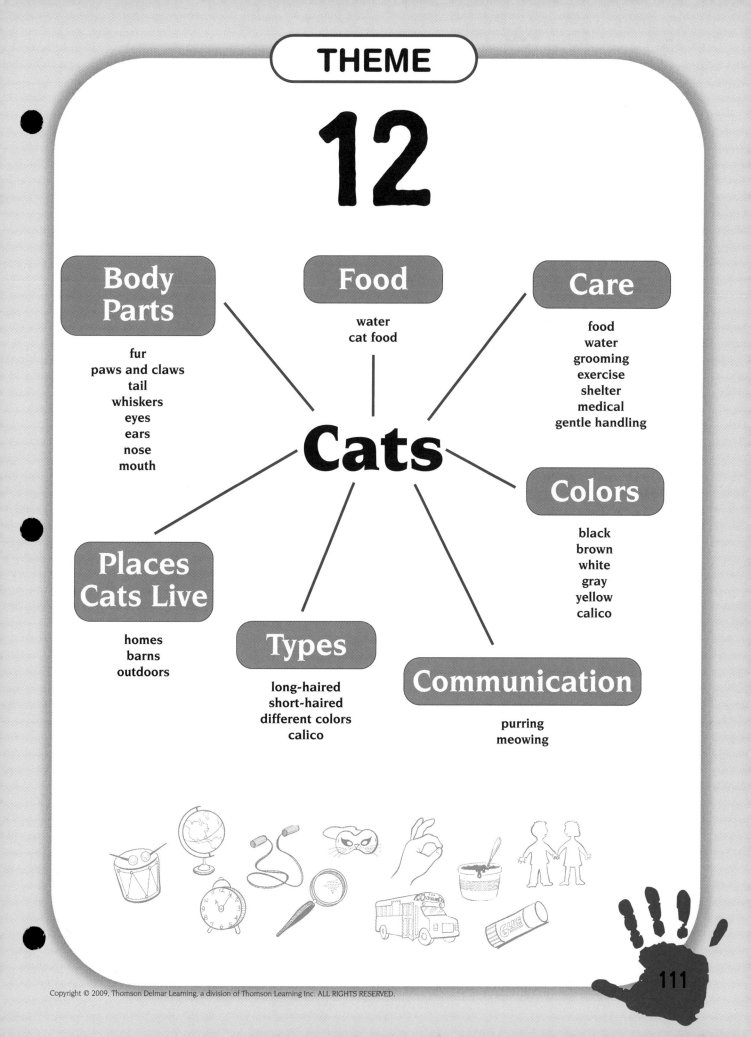

Theme Goals

Through participating in the experiences provided by this theme, the children may learn

1. Types of cats
2. Body parts of a cat
3. Cats need special care
4. Foods cats need
5. Places cats live
6. Colors of cats
7. How cats communicate

Concepts for the Children to Learn

1. Cats can be black, brown, white, gray, yellow, or calico.
2. Cats meow and purr to communicate.
4. Cats have legs, eyes, ears, a mouth, nose, whiskers, paws, and a tail.
5. Cats have fur on their skin.
6. Cats should be handled gently.
7. There are many different colors of cats.
8. Cats need food, water, and exercise everyday.

Vocabulary

1. **calico**—a cat that has fur of many colors.
2. **coat**—hair covering the skin.
3. **collar**—a band worn around the cat's neck.
4. **kitten**—a baby cat.
5. **leash**—a rope, chain, or cord that attaches to a collar.
6. **paw**—the cat's foot.
7. **pet**—an animal kept for pleasure.
8. **veterinarian**—an animal doctor.
9. **whiskers**—stiff hair growing around the cat's nose, mouth, and eyes.

Bulletin Board

The purpose of this bulletin board is to promote visual discrimination, pattern-matching, problem-solving, and hand-eye coordination skills. Construct cats' bodies and heads out of tagboard, coloring each a different color and fur pattern. Laminate all pieces. Attach cats' bodies to the bulletin board. Children then match the heads to the corresponding body.

Family Letter

Dear Families,

We have many exciting activities planned at school as we begin our study on cats. We will be learning about a cat's body structure, how to care and feed our cats, and different types of cats.

AT SCHOOL

Some of the learning experiences planned include:

- taking field trips to the veterinarian's office and pet store
- making a chart of different types of cats
- setting up a cat grooming area in dramatic play
- listening to stories about cats
- looking at pictures of cats

AT HOME

We will be learning the fingerplay "Two Little Kittens." You may want to try it with your child at home.

Two little kittens found a ball of yarn

(hold up two fingers . . . cup hands together to form a ball)

As they were playing near a barn.

(bring hands together pointed upward for barn)

One little kitten jumped in the hay,

(hold up one finger . . . make jumping then wiggling motion)

The other little kitten ran away.

(make running motion with other hand)

Fingerplays and rhymes help children develop language vocabulary and sequencing skills. The actions that often accompany fingerplays develop fine motor development.

Have fun with your child!

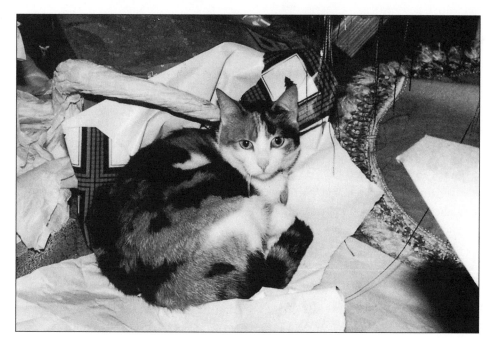

What is your favorite color of cat?

Arts and Crafts

1. **Pom Pom Painting**

    Set out several different colors of tempera paint. Using pom-pom balls, let children create their own designs on construction paper.

2. **Cat Mask**

    Using paper plates or paper bags along with paper scraps, yarn, crayons, scissors, and paint, let the children design cat masks.

3. **Paw Prints**

    Let children pretend they are cats, using their hands and paint to make prints.

Cooking

1. **Cheese Cat**

    English muffins
    cheese slices

Allow the children to cut out a cat face on their own slice of cheese. Put the cheese on top of the English muffin and bake long enough to melt the cheese.

2. **Cat Face**

    1/2 peach (head)
    dried prunes (ears)
    red hots (eyes)
    raisin (nose)
    stick pretzels (whiskers)

    Create a cat face using the ideas above or a variety of other items.

Dramatic Play

1. **Cat Grooming**

    Provide the children with empty shampoo and conditioner bottles, brushes, combs, ribbons, collars, plastic bathtub, towels, and stuffed animal cats.

2. Veterinarian's Office

Provide various medical supplies such as a stethoscope, bandages, and thermometers along with stuffed cats.

3. Cats!

Let children pretend they are cats by using cat masks or costumes. Also, you may want to try using yarn balls, boxes to curl up in, and empty cat food boxes. Allow the children to act out the story "The Three Little Kittens" or other cat stories.

4. Circus or Zoo

Lions, cheetas, panthers, leopards, and tigers are also cats. Use large boxes for cages.

Field Trips/ Resource People

1. Pet Store

Take a field trip to a pet store. Ask the manager how to care for cats. Observe the different types of cats, cages, collars, leashes, and food.

2. Veterinarian's Office

Take a field trip to a veterinarian's office or animal hospital. Compare the similarities and differences to a doctor's office.

3. Pet Supply Store

Visit a pet supply store and observe pet accessories.

4. Resource People

Invite resource people. Suggestions include:

- cat groomer
- humane society representative
- pet store owner
- veterinarian
- parents to bring in pet cats

Fingerplays

Mrs. Kitty's Dinner

Mrs. Kitty, sleek and fat,
    (put thumb up with fingers folded on
    right hand)
With her kittens four.
    (hold up four fingers on right hand)
Went to sleep upon the mat
    (make a fist)
By the kitchen door.

Mrs. Kitty heard a noise.
Up she jumped in glee.
    (thumb up on right hand)
"Kittens, maybe that's a mouse?
    (all five fingers on right hand up)
Let's go and see!"

Creeping, creeping, creeping on.
    (slowly sneaking with five fingers on floor)
Silently they stole.
But the little mouse had gone
    (mouse is thumb on left hand)
Back into his hole.

Three Cats

One little cat and two little cats
went out for a romp one day.
    (hold up one finger and then two fingers with
    other hand)

One little cat and two little cats
make how many cats at play?
    (ask how many that makes)
Three little cats had lots of fun
till growing tired away ran _____?
    (take one finger away and ask how many
    ran away)
I really think that he was most unkind to the
    _____ little cats that were left behind.
    (ask how many are left)

Kitten Is Hiding

A kitten is hiding under a chair,
    (hide one thumb in other hand)
I looked and looked for her everywhere.
    (peer about with hand on forehead)
Under the table and under the bed,
    (pretend to look)

I looked in the corner and then I said,
"Come Kitty, come Kitty, I have milk for you."
   (cup hands to make dish and extend)
Kitty came running and calling, "Mew, mew."
   (run fingers up arm)

Two Little Kittens

Two little kittens found a ball of yarn
   (hold up two fingers . . . cup hands together
   to form a ball)
As they were playing near a barn.
   (bring hands together pointed upward
   for barn)
One little kitten jumped in the hay,
   (hold up one finger . . . make jumping, then
   wiggling motion)
The other little kitten ran away.
   (make running motion with other hand)

I Love Little Pussy

I love little pussy,
Her coat is so warm.
And if I don't hurt her,
She'll do me no harm.
So I'll not pull her tail,
Nor drive her away.
But pussy and I,
Very gently will play.

Group Time

(Games, Language)

1. Copycats

Have one child be the cat and clap a rhythm for the group. The other children listen and then act as copycats. They clap the same rhythm as the cat did. Another child now becomes the cat and creates a rhythm for the copycats to imitate.

2. Nice Kitty

One child is chosen to be the kitty. The rest of the children sit in a circle. As the kitty goes to each child in the circle, he or she pets the kitty and says, "nice kitty," but the kitty makes no

reply. Finally, the kitty meows in response to one child. That child must run around the outside of the circle as the kitty chases him. If the child returns to his or her original place before the kitty can catch him or her, the child becomes the new kitty. This activity is appropriate for four-, five-, and six-year-old children.

3. Listen Carefully

The children should sit in a circle. One child is selected to be the mother cat. After mother cat has left the room, choose several other children to be kittens. All of the children cover their mouths with both hands and the kittens start saying, "meow, meow, meow." When the mother cat returns she should listen carefully to find all of her kittens. When she has found them all, another child should be chosen mother cat and the game can continue.

4. Farmer in the Dell

The children can play "Farmer in the Dell."

Large Muscle

1. Bean Bag Toss

Make a cat shape on plywood with holes of different sizes cut out. The children can try from varying distances to throw bean bags through the holes.

2. Yarn Balls

Set up baskets at varying distances from a masking tape line on the floor. Toss yarn balls into the baskets.

3. Cat Pounce

Children pretend to be cats and pounce from one tape line to another.

4. Climbing Cats

Bring a wooden climber into the classroom or set it up outside. The children can pretend to be cats and climb on the climber.

5. Cat Movements

Write down all the words that describe how cats move. Allow the children to demonstrate the movements. Also, use music in the background.

6. Kitty, Kitty, Cat

Play a variation of Duck, Duck, Goose by saying "Kitty, Kitty, Cat."

Math

1. Matching Game

Have the children match the number of cats on a card to the correct numeral. (Cat stickers work well.)

2. How Many Paper Clips

Make several different sizes of cats out of tagboard. Children measure each cat with the paper clips.

3. Whisker Count

Make several cat faces with one numeral on each face. Children attach the correct number of whiskers (chenille stems, felt, paper strips, etc.) according to the numeral on the cat.

Music

1. "Two Little Kittens"
(Sing to the tune of "Two Little Blackbirds")

Two little kittens sitting on a hill
One named Jack, one named Jill
Run away, Jack, run away, Jill
Come back, Jack, come back, Jill
Two little kittens sitting on a hill
One named Jack, one named Jill.

2. "Kitty"
(Sing to the tune of "Bingo")

I have a cat. She's very shy.
But she comes when I call Kitty.

K-I-T-T-Y
K-I-T-T-Y
K-I-T-T-Y
And Kitty is her name-o.

Variation: Let children think of other names.

3. "Three Little Kittens"

Three little kittens lost their mittens;
And they began to cry,
"Oh, mother dear, we very much fear
Our mittens we have lost."
"What! Lost your mittens! You naughty kittens!
Then you shall have no pie."
"Mee-ow, mee-ow, mee-ow, mee-ow."
"No, you shall have no pie."
The three little kittens they found their mittens;
And they began to cry,
"Oh, Mother dear, see here, see here!
Our mittens we have found."
"What! Found your mittens! You good little kittens!
Now you shall have some pie."
"Purr, purr, purr, purr,
Purr, purr, purr."

Science

1. Provide a scale and different cat items (such as cat toys, collar, food dish, etc.) to weigh.

2. During the social studies activity, "Share Your Cat," arrange for a cat and a kitten to be in the classroom at the same time. With the help of parents, weigh the cats or kittens and discuss the differences with the children.

3. Set out a magnifying glass to observe different kinds of dry cat food.

4. Talk about a cat that has claws and one that is declawed. Ask various questions such as: Why do cats have claws? Why are cats declawed? Where do cats go to be declawed?

5. Discuss the various parts of a cat's body and how they can protect the cat (examples: fur, whiskers, etc.).

6. Discuss what a cat's body does when the cat senses danger.

Social Studies

1. **Chart**

   With the children, make a chart of different types of cats.

2. **Displays**

   Display different pictures of cats around the room.

3. **Share Your Cat**

   Invite the children and the parents to bring in a pet cat on specified days. (Have your camera ready! Take pictures and display them on a bulletin board.) Encourage the children to talk about their cat's colors, likes, body, etc.

4. **Cat Safety**

   Discuss cat safety with the class. Items that may be discussed include why cats use their claws, what to do if you find a stray cat, and the uses of collars and leashes.

Books

The following books can be used to complement this theme:

Brown, Margaret Wise, Alice Provensen, and Martin Provensen. (2000). *The Color Kittens*. Illus. by Alice Provensen & Martin Provensen. New York: Golden Books.

Carle, Eric. (1991). *Have You Seen My Cat?* Saxonville, MA: Picture Book Studio.

Dupont, Marie. (1991). *Your First Kitten*. Neptune City, NJ: TFH.

Ehlert, Lois. (1990). *Feathers for Lunch*. San Diego, CA: Harcourt Brace.

Farjeon, Eleanor. (1990). *Cats Sleep Anywhere*. New York: HarperCollins Children's Books.

Gag, Wanda. (1996). *Millions of Cats*. New York: Putnam.

Hutchins, Hazel. (1992). *And You Can Be the Cat*. Buffalo, NY: Firefly Books.

Kherdian, David and Nonny Hogrogian. (1990). *The Cat's Midsummer Jamboree*. New York: Philomel Books.

Mantegazza, Giovanna. (1992). *The Cat*. Honesdale, PA: Boyds Mills Press.

Martin, Bengt. (1992). *Olaf the Ship's Cat*. Yardley, PA: Checkerboard.

Marzello, Jean. (1990). *Pretend You're a Cat*. New York: Dial Books for Young Readers.

McCue, Lisa. (1990). *Kittens Love*. New York: Random House.

Moncure, Jane. (1990). *Caring for My Kitty*. Mankato, MN: Children's World.

Nottridge, Rhoda. (1990). *Let's Look at Big Cats*. New York: Franklin Watts.

Petty, Kate. (1992). *Baby Animals: Kittens*. Hauppauge, NY: Barron's Educational Series.

Piers, Helen. (1992). *Taking Care of Your Cat*. Hauppauge, NY: Barron's Educational Series.

Pittman, Helena C. (1990). *Miss Hindy's Cats*. Minneapolis, MN: Carolrhoda Books.

Polushkin, Maria. (1990). *Here's That Kitten!* New York: Macmillan.

Rylant, Cynthia. (2006). *Mr. Putter & Tabby Spin the Yarn*. Illus. by Arthur Howard. Orlando, FL: Harcourt.

Simon, Seymour. (1991). *Big Cats*. New York: HarperCollins.

Spinelli, Eileen and Anne Mortimer. (2001). *Kittycat Lullaby*. Illus. by Anne Mortimer. New York: Hyperion Press.

Tan, Amy and Gretchen Shields. (2001). *SAGWA, the Chinese Siamese Cat*. Illus. by Gretchen Shields. New York: Alladin Paperbacks.

Multimedia

The following multimedia products can be used to complement this theme:

Crume, Marion. *I Like Cats* [record].

Carr, Rachel. "Stretch Like a Cat" on *Be a Frog, a Bird, or a Tree* [record].

Sharon, Lois, & Bram. "The Cat Came Back" on *Singing, Swinging* [record].

Seeger, Pete. "My Little Kitty" on *Birds, Beasts, Bugs and Little Fishes* [record].

Kittens, Kids and a Frog [Apple/IBM software (Ages: 6–7)]. Hartley.

Sugar and Snails and Kitty-Cat Tails [Mac/Apple software, PK-2]. Entrex.

"Cat Who Clowns Around." (1994). *A to Z, the Animals and Me*. Long Branch, NJ: Kimbo Educational.

"The Cat and the Mouse." (1975). *I Like Myself*. Long Branch, NJ: Kimbo Educational.

Recordings and Song Titles

The following recordings can be used to complement this theme:

"Cat Stretch." (1987). *Animal Walks*. Long Branch, NJ: Kimbo Educational.

13

Sounds

songs (carols)
bells

Colors

red
green
white

Foods

cookies
eggnog
candy canes
candy

Christmas

Symbols

ornaments,
lights, gifts,
stockings,
Christmas cards,
Santa Claus,
star, garland,
elves, wreaths,
reindeer

Activities

decorating tree
hanging wreath
shopping
wrapping
visiting families and friends

Plants

trees
poinsettias
mistletoe
holly

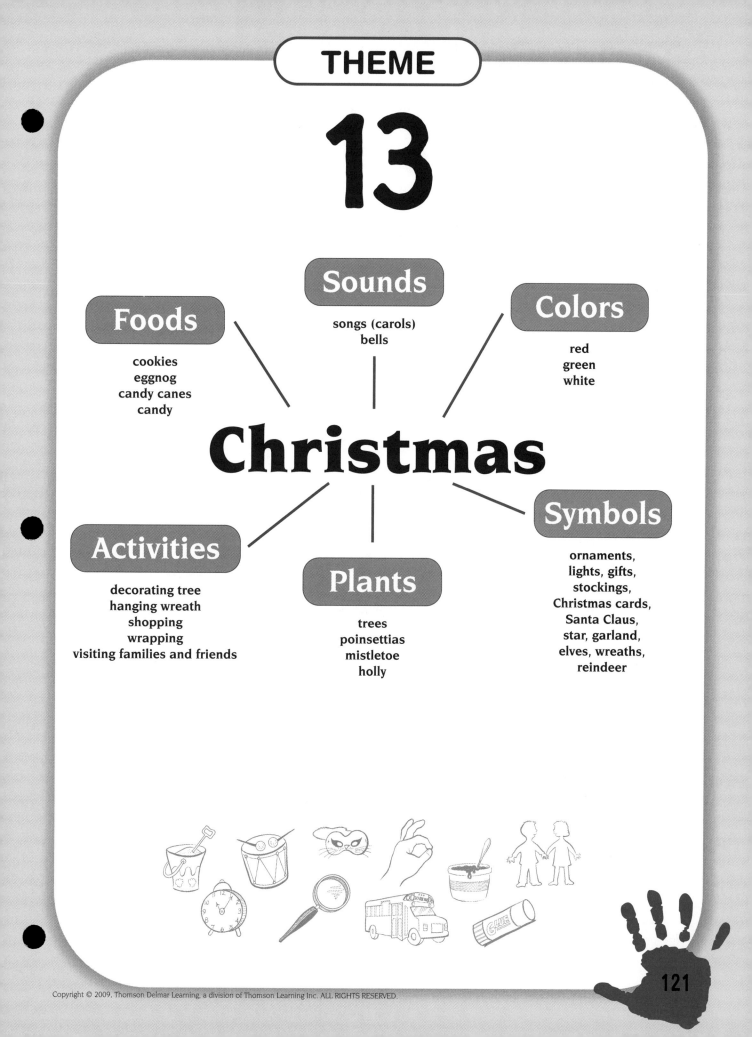

Theme Goals

Through participating in the experiences provided by this theme, the children may learn

1. Christmas colors
2. Christmas foods
3. Christmas plants
4. Christmas symbols
5. Christmas sounds

Concepts for the Children to Learn

1. Red, green, and white are Christmas colors.
2. Christmas cookies and candies are special treats for Christmas.
3. Santa Claus, reindeer, stockings, and Christmas trees are symbols of Christmas.
4. Decorating Christmas trees and hanging a wreath are Christmas activities.
5. Christmas ornaments, lights, and garlands are hung on Christmas trees.
6. There are special Christmas songs.
7. A star is an ornament that can be placed on the top of the tree.
8. Bells and Christmas carols are sounds heard at Christmas.
9. Poinsettias, evergreen trees, and mistletoe are Christmas plants.
10. Many people spend Christmas with their families and friends.
11. Some people hang special stockings that are filled with candy and small gifts.
12. Christmas is a time for giving and receiving gifts for some people.
13. Christians believe that Jesus was born on Christmas day.
14. People shop for gifts and wrap them in bright, pretty papers.
15. People send Christmas cards to their family and friends.

Vocabulary

1. **carol**—a Christmas song.
2. **elf**—Santa's helper.
3. **evergreen tree**—a tree decorated for the Christmas holidays.
4. **ornament**—decoration for the home or tree.
5. **piñata**—brightly colored papier-mâché figure that is filled with candy and gifts.
6. **present**—a gift.
7. **reindeer**—animals used to pull Santa's sleigh.
8. **Santa Claus**—a jolly man who wears a red suit and symbolizes Christmas.
9. **star**—a treetop decoration.
10. **stocking**—a large Christmas sock.
11. **wreath**—a decoration made from evergreen branches.

122

THEME 13

Bulletin Board

The purpose of this bulletin board is to foster a positive self-concept, as well as name-recognition skills. Construct a stocking out of tagboard for each child in your class. Print the name across the top and punch a hole in the top with a paper punch. Hang a Christmas poster or teacher-made poster in the center of the bulletin board. Next, attach pushpins to the bulletin board, allowing enough room for each stocking to hang on a pin. The children can hang their own stockings on the bulletin board as they arrive each day.

Family Letter

Dear Families,

The holiday season is approaching. All we need to do is drive through our neighborhoods to see decorations and busy shoppers everywhere. Holiday songs are heard, and Santa is in the thoughts and sentences of many children. At school we will be participating in many Christmas activities. The children will learn the colors, plants, and symbols that are associated with the Christmas season. Perhaps not all children and families in our program celebrate this holiday, but we feel it is very important for children to learn about and respect others' beliefs. A general understanding of other cultures is also interesting and fun. However, if you wish that your child not participate in this, please let us know.

AT SCHOOL

A few of the Christmas learning experiences planned include:

- creating ornaments to decorate the classroom Christmas tree
- painting with pine boughs at the easel
- making Christmas cookies
- designing Christmas cards in the art area
- practicing songs for our holiday program. Keep your eyes open for a special invitation! The program will be held on December 19th at 3:30 p.m. Mark your calendar.

AT HOME

Music and singing are wonderful ways to communicate our feelings, and we often have many feelings this time of year! When singing Christmas carols, encourage traditional songs as well as this new song:

"I'm a Little Pine Tree"
(Sing to the tune of "I'm a Little Teapot")

I'm a little pine tree tall and straight
Here are my branches for you to decorate.   *(extend arms)*
First we'll put the shiny star on top.   *(touch head)*
Just be careful the balls don't drop.   *(clap hands)*
Now be sure to plug in all the lights
So I will look very cheerful and bright.
Then put all the presents under me.
I'm all set for Christmas, as you can see!

REMINDER

Our last day of school will be December 23. School will open again on January 3 of the new year.

Happy holidays to you and yours!

Santa Claus and Christmas make winter fun.

Arts and Crafts

1. Christmas Chains

Cut sheets of red, green, and white construction paper into strips. Demonstrate how to form the links. The links can be pasted, taped, or stapled, depending on the developmental level of the children.

2. Cookie Cutter Painting

Provide Christmas cookie cutters, paper, and shallow pans containing red and green paint. The children can apply the paint to the paper using the cookie cutters as printing tools.

3. Rudolph

Begin the activity by encouraging the children to trace their shoe. This will be used for Rudolph's face. Then the children should trace both of their hands, which will be used as the reindeer's antlers. Finally, cut out a red circle to be used as the reindeer's nose. Have the children paste all the pieces together on a sheet of paper and add facial features.

4. Designing Wrapping Paper

The children can design their own wrapping paper using newsprint, ink stampers, felt-tip colored markers, tempera paint, etc. Glitter can also be glued onto the paper.

5. Pine Bough Painting

Collect short pine boughs to use as painting tools. The tools can be placed at the easel or used with a shallow pan of tempera paint at tables.

6. Candy Cane Marble Painting

Cut red construction paper into candy cane shapes. Marble paint with white tempera paint.

7. Glittery Pinecones

Paint pinecones with tempera paint, sprinkle with glitter, and allow the paint to dry. The glittery pinecones can be used for classroom decorations, presents, or taken home.

8. Paper Wreaths

Purchase green muffin tin liners. To make the paper wreaths, cut out a large ring from light tagboard or construction paper for each child in the class. The children can glue the green muffin tin liners to the ring, adding small pieces of red yarn, crayons, or felt-tip marker symbols to represent berries if desired.

9. Play Dough Cookies

Using red, green, and white play dough and Christmas cookie cutters, the children can make play dough cookies.

10. Favorite Play Dough

Combine and boil until dissolved:

2 cups water
1/2 cup salt
food coloring or tempera

Mix while very hot:

2 tablespoons salad oil
2 tablespoons alum
2 cups flour

Knead approximately 5 minutes until smooth. Store in an airtight covered container.

11. Gingerbread Play Dough

1 1/4 cup flour
1/2 cup salt
3 teaspoons cream of tartar
1 cup water
1 1/2 teaspoon vegetable oil
2 tablespoons ground cinnamon
1 teaspoon ground ginger

Mix all ingredients and cook in a saucepan over medium heat while stirring frequently. When mixture begins to pull away from the sides of the pan, remove from heat and knead until smooth. Store in an air-tight container.

Cooking

1. Candy Canes

Prepare the basic sugar dough recipe for cookie cutters. Divide the recipe in half. Add red food coloring to one half of the dough. Show the children how to roll a piece of red dough in a strip about 3 inches long by 1/2-inch wide. Repeat this process using the white dough. Then twist the two strips together, shaping into a candy cane. Bake the cookies in a 350-degree oven for 7 to 10 minutes.

2. Basic Sugar Dough for Cookie Cutters

1/2 cup butter
1 cup sugar
1 egg
1/2 teaspoon salt
2 teaspoons baking powder
2 cups flour
1/2 teaspoon vanilla

Cut into desired shapes. Place on lightly greased baking sheets. Bake 8 minutes at 400 degrees. This recipe makes approximately three to four dozen cookies.

3. Eggnog

4 eggs (pasteurized)
2 teaspoons vanilla
4 tablespoons honey
4 cups milk

Beat all of the ingredients together until light and foamy. Pour into glasses or cups and shake a little nutmeg on the top of the eggnog. This adds color and flavor. The recipe makes one quart. Eggnog should always be served immediately or refrigerated until snack or lunch. It should not be served to children who are allergic to eggs.

Dramatic Play

1. Gift Wrapping

Collect and place in the dramatic play area empty boxes, scraps of wrapping paper, comic paper, wallpaper books, and scraps. Scissors, tape, bows, and ribbon should also be provided.

2. North Pole

Create a sleigh out of cardboard or wood. Make reindeer headbands for the children to wear and pretend to pull the sleigh. Cover the floor with white felt or a white sheet.

Field Trips

1. Christmas Tree Farm

Plan a trip to a Christmas tree farm so the children can cut down a Christmas tree. Check your state's licensing requirements regarding the use of fresh Christmas trees and decorations in the center or classroom.

2. Caroling

Plan to go Christmas caroling at a local nursing home or even for another group of children. After caroling, Christmas cookies could be shared.

126

Fingerplays

Santa's Workshop

Here is Santa's workshop.
   (form peak with both hands)
Here is Santa Claus.
   (hold up thumb)
Here are Santa's little elves
   (wiggle fingers)
Putting toys upon the shelves.

Here Is the Chimney

Here is the chimney.
   (make fist and tuck in thumb)
Here is the top.
   (cover with hand)
Open it up quick
   (lift hand up)
And out Santa will pop.
   (pop out thumb)

Five Little Christmas Cookies

(hold up five fingers, take one away as directed
by poem)

Five little Christmas cookies on a plate by
the door,
One was eaten and then there were four.

Four little Christmas cookies, gazing up at me,
One was eaten and then there were three.

Three little Christmas cookies, enough for me
and you,
One was eaten and then there were two.

Two little Christmas cookies sitting in the sun,
One was eaten and then there was one.

One little Christmas cookie, better grab it fast,
As you can see, the others surely didn't last.

Presents

See all the presents by the Christmas tree?
   (hand shades eyes)
Some for you,
   (point)
And some for me—
   (point)
Long ones,
   (extend arms)

Tall ones,
   (measure hand up from floor)
Short ones, too.
   (hand to floor—low)
And here is a round one
   (circle with arms)
Wrapped in blue.
Isn't it fun to look and see
   (hand shades eyes)
All of the presents by the Christmas tree?
   (arms open wide)

Group Time

(Games, Language)

1. **Find the Christmas Bell**

For this activity the children should be standing
in a circle. One child is given a bell. Then the
child should hide, while the remainder of the
children cover their eyes. After the child has
hidden, he or she begins to ring the bell, signal-
ing the remainder of the children to listen for
the sound and identify where the bell is hidden.
Turns should be taken, allowing each child an
opportunity to hide and ring the bell.

2. **"Guess What's Inside"**

Place a familiar object inside a box. Let the children shake, feel, and try to identify the object.
After this, open the box and show the children
the object. This activity works well in small
groups as well as large groups.

Math

1. **Christmas Card Sort**

Place a variety of Christmas cards on a table
in the math area. During self-selected or self-
initiated periods, the children can sort by
color, pictures, size, etc.

2. Christmas Card Puzzles

Collect two sets of identical Christmas cards. Cut the covers off the cards. Cut one of each of the identical sets of cards into puzzle pieces. The matching card can be used as a form for the children to match the pieces.

Music

1. "Rudolph the Red-Nosed Reindeer"
(*traditional*)

2. "Jingle Bells"
(*traditional*)

3. "The Twelve Days of Christmas"
(*traditional*)

4. "We Wish You a Merry Christmas"
(*traditional*)

5. "Peppermint Stick Song"

Oh I took a lick of my
   peppermint stick
And I thought it tasted yummy.
Oh it used to hang on my
   Christmas tree,
But I like it better in my tummy.

6. "S-A-N-T-A"
(*Sing to the tune of* "B-I-N-G-O")

There was a man on Christmas Day
And Santa was his name-o.
S-A-N-T-A
S-A-N-T-A
S-A-N-T-A
And Santa was his name-o.

7. "Up on the House Top"
(*traditional*)

8. "Santa Claus Is Coming to Town"
(*traditional*)

9. "Circle Christmas Verse"

Two, four, six, eight.
Santa Claus don't be late;

Here's my stocking, I can't wait!
Two, four, six, eight.

10. "Christmas Chant"

With a "hey" and a "hi" and a "ho-ho-ho,"
Somebody tickled old Santa Claus's toe.
Get up ol' Santa, there's work to be done,
The children must have their holiday fun.
With a "hey" and a "hi" and a "ho-ho-ho,"
Santa Claus, Santa Claus,
GO-GO-GO!

11. "Santa's in His Shop"
(*Sing to the tune of* "The Farmer in the Dell")

Santa's in his shop
Santa's in his shop
What a scene for Christmas
Santa's in his shop.
Other verses:
Santa takes a drum
The drum takes a doll
The doll takes a train
The train takes a ball
The ball takes a top
They're all in the shop
The top stays in the shop
Pictures could be constructed for use singing
   about each toy.

Science

1. Making Candles

Candles can be made for Christmas gifts. This experience provides an opportunity for the children to see how a substance can change from solid to liquid and back to a solid form. The children can place pieces of paraffin in a tin can that is bent at the top, forming a spout. A red or green crayon piece can be used to add color.

The bottom of the tin cans should be placed in a pan of water and heated on the stove until the paraffin is melted. Meanwhile, the children can prepare small paper cups.

In the bottom of each paper cup mold place a wick. Wicks can be made by tying a piece of string to a paper clip and a pencil. Then lay the pencil horizontally across the cup allowing the string to hang vertically into the cup. When the wax is melted, the teacher should carefully pour the wax into the cup. After the wax hardens, the candles can be used as decorations or presents.

Caution: This activity should be restricted to four- and five-year-old children. Constant supervision of this activity is required for safety.

2. **Add to the Science Area**

   - pine needles and branches with magnifying glasses
   - pinecones with a balance scale
   - red, green, and white materials representing different textures

3. **Bells**

   Collect bells of various shapes and sizes. Listen for differences in sounds in relation to the sizes of the bells.

4. **Feely Box**

   A feely box containing Christmas items such as bows, cookie cutters, wrapping paper, nonbreakable ornaments, stockings, bells, candles, and so forth, can be placed on the science table.

Sensory

1. **Add to the Sensory Table**

   - pine branches, needles, and cones
   - scented red and green play dough
   - icicles or snow (if possible) with thermometers
   - water for a sink and float activity; add different Christmas objects such as bells, plastic stars, and cookie cutters
   - scents such as peppermint and ginger added to water

2. **Holiday Cubes**

   Prepare ice cube trays using water that is colored with red and green food coloring. Freeze. Place in the sensory table.

Books

The following books can be used to complement this theme:

Ammon, Richard. (1996). *An Amish Christmas.* Illus. by Pamela Patrick. New York: Atheneum.

Barracca, Debra et al. (1994). A *Taxi Dog Christmas.* Illus. by Alan Ayers. New York: Dial Books.

Brett, Jan. (1990). *Christmas Reindeer.* New York: G. P. Putnam.

Brett, Jan. (2001). *Jan Brett's Christmas Treasury.* New York: G. P. Putnam.

Brimmer, Larry Dane. *Merry Christmas Old Armadillo.* (1995). Illus. by Dominic Catalano. Honesdale, PA: Boyds Mills Press.

Brown, Margaret Wise. (1996). *On Christmas Eve.* Newly illus. by Nancy Edwards Calder. New York: HarperCollins.

Brown, Margaret Wise. (1994). A *Pussycat's Christmas.* Newly illus. by Anne Mortimer. New York: HarperCollins.

Burningham, John. (1993). *Harvey Shumfenburger's Christmas Present.* Cambridge, MA: Candlewick Press.

Carle, Eric. (2000). *Dream Snow.* New York: Philomel Books.

Carlstrom, Nancy White. (1995). *I Am Christmas.* Illus. by Lori McElrath-Eslick. Grand Rapids, MI: Wm. B. Eerdmans Publishing Co.

Ciavonne, Jean. (1995). *Carlos, Light the Farolito.* Illus. by Donna Clair. New York: Clarion Books.

Cummings, E. E. and Chris Raschka. (2001). *Little Tree.* Illus. by Chris Raschka. New York: Hyperion Press.

Davis, Rebecca. (1995). *The 12 Days of Christmas.* Illus. by Linnea Asplind Riley. New York: Simon & Schuster.

Day, Alexandra. (1994). *Carl's Christmas.* Orlando, FL: Harcourt Brace.

De Paola, Tomie. (1994). *Legend of the Poinsettia.* New York: G. P. Putnam.

(continued on page 132)

Gifts for Families and Friends

Wax Paper Placemats

wax paper that is heavily waxed
crayon shavings
paper designs
dish towel
scissors

Use at least one of the following:

yarn	lace
fabric	dried leaves

Cut the wax paper into 12-inch × 20-inch sheets (two per mat). Place crayon shavings between the wax paper. Then decorate with other items. Place towel on wax paper and press with warm iron until crayon melts. Fringe the edges.

Craft Stick Picture Frames

craft sticks (10 per frame)
glue
picture

Make a background of sticks and glue picture in place. Add additional sticks around the edges, front, and back for the frame and for support. For a freestanding frame, add more craft sticks to both the front and the back at the bottom.

Refrigerator Magnets

small magnets
glue
any type of decoration (paper cutouts, plaster of Paris molds, yarn, styrofoam pieces, buttons, etc.)

Glue the decorations to the magnet.

Service Certificate

paper	lace
crayons	ribbon
pencils	

Have the children write and decorate a certificate that states some service they will do for their parents (example: This certificate is good for washing the dishes; sweeping the floor; picking up my toys; etc.).

Ornaments

plaster of Paris	yarn
any mold	straw
glitter	

Pour the plaster of Paris into the mold. Decorate with glitter and let dry. If so desired, place a straw into the mold and string with yarn or thread.

Refrigerator Clothespin

clothespins
glue
sequins/glitter/beads
small magnet

Let the children put glue on one side of the clothespin. Sprinkle this area with glitter, sequins, or beads. Then assist the child in gluing the magnet to the other side.

Patchwork Flowerpot

precut fabric squares
glue
tins (for glue)
flower pots

Let the children soak the fabric squares one at a time in the glue. Press onto the pot in a patchwork design. Let dry overnight.

Snapshot Magnet

snapshot
plastic lid
scissors (preferably pinking shears)
glue
magnet

Trace the outline of the lid onto the back of the picture. Cut the picture out and glue it onto the lid. Glue the magnet to the underside of the lid.

Holiday Pin

outline of a heart, wreath, and so forth, cut out of tagboard
glue
sequins, beads, buttons, yarn
purchased backing for a pin

Let the children decorate the cardboard figure with glue and other decorating items. Glue onto purchased backing for a pin.

Flowers with Vase

styrofoam egg carton
chenille stem
scissors
glass jar or bottle
liquid starch
colored tissue paper (cut into squares)
glue
yarn
paintbrush

Cut individual sections from egg carton and punch a hole in the bottom of each. Insert a chenille stem through the hole as a stem. Use the scissors to cut the petals.

For the vase: Using the paintbrush, cover a portion of the jar with liquid starch. Apply the tissue paper squares until the jar is covered. Add another coat of liquid starch. Dip the yarn into the glue and wrap it around the jar. Insert the flower for a decoration.

Pinecone Ornament

pinecones	glue
paint	glitter
paintbrush	yarn

Paint the pinecones. Then roll the pinecones in the glue and then into a dish filled with glitter. Tie a loop of yarn for hanging.

Paperweights

glass furniture glides
crepe paper
crayons
glue
plaster of Paris
felt piece
scissors

Children decorate a picture and then cut it to fit the glide. Place the picture face down into the recessed part of the glide. Pour plaster of Paris over the top of the picture and let it dry. Glue a felt piece over the plaster.

Rock Paperweight

large rocks
paint

Let the children paint a design on a rock they have chosen and give to their parents as a present.

Soap Balls

1 cup Ivory Snow
  detergent
1/8 cup water
food coloring
colored nylon netting
ribbon

Add the food coloring to the water and then add the Ivory Snow detergent. Shape the mixture into balls or any shape. Wrap in colored netting and tie with ribbon.

Closet Clove Scenter

orange
cloves
netting
ribbon

Have the children push the pointed ends of the cloves into an orange. Cover the orange completely. Wrap netting around the orange and tie it with the ribbon. These make good closet or dresser drawer scenters.

Handprint Wreath

colored construction paper
scissors
glue
pencil
cardboard/tagboard circle

Let the children trace their hand and cut it out. Glue the palm of the hand to the cardboard circle. Using a pencil, roll the fingertips of the hand until curly.

Bird's Nest

1 can sweetened condensed milk
2 teaspoons vanilla
3 to 4 cups powdered milk
1 cup confectioners' sugar
yellow food coloring

Mix all the ingredients together and add food coloring to tint the mixture to a yellow-brown color. Give each child a portion and let him or her mold a bird's nest. Chill for 2 hours. If so desired, green tinted coconut may be added for grass and put in the nest. Add small jelly beans for bird's eggs.

Flower Pots

plaster of Paris
1/2-pint milk containers
straws (three to four for each
  container)
scissors

construction paper
paint
paintbrush
stapler

Cut the cartons in half and use the bottom half. Pour 1 to 3 inches of plaster into the containers. Stick three or four straws into the plaster and let harden. After plaster has hardened, remove the plaster very carefully from the milk carton. Let the children paint the plaster pot, make flowers from construction paper, and staple the flowers to the straws.

Cookie Jar

coffee can with lid or
  oatmeal box
construction paper
crayons or felt-tip markers
glue
scissors

Cover the can with construction paper and glue to seal. Let the children decorate their cans with crayons or felt-tip markers. For an added gift, make cookies in the classroom to send home in the jars.

Felt Printing

felt
glue
wood block
tempera paint
scissors

Let the children cut the felt pieces into any shape. Glue the shape onto the wood block. Dip into a shallow pan of tempera paint. Print on newspaper to test.

Napkin Holder

paper plates
scissors

(continued)

Gifts for Families and Friends
(continued)

yarn
paper punch
crayons
clear shellac

Cut one paper plate in half. Place the inside together and punch holes through the lower half only. Use yarn to lace the plates together. Punch a small hole at the top for hanging. Decorate with crayons or felt-tip markers. Coat with shellac. May be used as a potholder, napkin, or card holder. **Caution:** This needs to be carefully supervised.

Clay Figures
4 cups flour
1 1/2 cup water
1 cup salt paint
paintbrush

Combine flour, water, and salt. Knead for 5 to 10 minutes. Roll and cut dough into figures. (Cookie cutters work well.) Make a hole at the top of the figure. Bake in a 250-degree oven for 2 hours or until hard. When cool, paint to decorate.

Key Holder
8 craft sticks

construction paper or a cutout from a greeting card
self-adhesive picture hanger
yarn

Glue five sticks together edge to edge. Cut one 3/4-inch piece of stick and glue it across the five sticks. Glue two sticks across the top parallel to the five sticks. Turn the sticks over. Cut paper or a greeting card to fit between the crossed sticks. Place on the self-adhesive hanger and tie yarn to the top for hanging.

Planter Trivets
7 craft sticks
glue

Glue four craft sticks into a square, the top two overlapping the bottom ones. Fill in the open space with the remaining three and glue into place.

Pencil Holder
empty soup cans
construction paper or contact paper
crayons or felt-tip markers
glue
scissors

Cover the can with construction or contact paper. Decorate with crayons or markers and use as a pencil holder.

Plaster Hand Prints
plaster of Paris
1-inch-deep square container
paint
paintbrush

Pour plaster of Paris into the container. Have the child place his or her hand in the plaster to make a mold. Let the mold dry and remove it from the container. Let the child paint the mold and give as a gift with the following poem:

My Hands
Sometimes you get discouraged
Because I am so small
And always have my fingerprints
On furniture and walls.
But every day I'm growing up
And soon I'll be so tall
That all those little handprints
Will be hard for you to recall.
So here's a little handprint
Just for you to see
Exactly how my fingers looked
When I was little me.

Fearrington, Ann. (1996). *Christmas Lights*. Boston: Houghton Mifflin.

Francisco, X. Mora. (1993). *La Gran Fiesta*. Port Atkinson, WI: Highsmith Co.

Frazee, Marla. (2005). *Santa Claus: the World's Number One Toy Expert*. Orlando, FL: Harcourt.

George, William T. (1992). *Christmas at Long Pond*. Illus. by Lindsay Barrett George. New York: Greenwillow.

Hobbie, Holly. (2001). *Toot & Puddle: I'll Be Home for Christmas*. Boston: Little Brown.

Hoffman, Mary. (1997). *An Angel Just Like Me*. Illus. by Cornelius Van Wright. New York: Dial Books.

Jordan, Sandra. (1993). *Christmas Tree Farm*. New York: Orchard Books.

Numeroff, Laura Joffe. (2000). *If You Take a Mouse to the Movies*. Illus. by Felicia Bond. New York: Laura Geringer Books.

Packard, Mary. *Christmas Kitten*. Illus. by Jenny Williams. San Francisco: Children's Book Press, 1997.

Rahaman, Vashanti. (1996). *O Christmas Tree*. Illus. by Frane Lessac. Honesdale, PA: Boyds Mills Press.

Rylant, Cynthia. (1997). *Silver Packages: An Appalachian Christmas Story*. Illus. by Chris K. Soentpiet. New York: Orchard Books.

Say, Allen. (1991). *Tree of Cranes*. Boston: Houghton Mifflin.

Stevenson, James. (1996). *The Oldest Elf*. New York: William Morrow.

Tompert, Ann. (1994). *A Carol for Christmas*. Illus. by Laura Kelly. New York: Simon & Schuster.

Waldron, Jan L. (1997). *Angel Pig and the Hidden Christmas*. Illus. by David M. McPhail. New York: Dutton.

Multimedia

The following multimedia products can be used to complement this theme:

De Paola, Tomie. *Merry Christmas, Strega Nona* [talking book]. (1991). Read by Celeste Holm. Old Greenwich, CT: Listening Library.

A Multicultural Christmas [video]. (1993). Niles, IL: United Learning.

The Night before Christmas [CD-ROM]. (1991). Toronto, Ont.: Discis Knowledge Research.

Palmer, Hap. *Holiday Songs and Rhythms* [compact disc]. (1997). Educational Activities.

Raffi. *Raffi's Christmas Album* [cassette]. (1983). Kimbo Educational.

Recordings and Song Titles

The following recordings can be used to complement this theme:

A Children's Christmas (*The Learning Station*). (2000). Long Branch, NJ: Kimbo Educational.

"Christmas in Killarney." (1993). *Pre-K Hooray*. Long Branch, NJ: Kimbo Educational.

"December." (1984). *Singing Calendar*. Long Branch, NJ: Kimbo Educational.

"I've Been Waiting for Christmas," "Where Is Santa?" "Did You Ever See a Reindeer?" "Little Green Tree." (1998). *Holiday Piggyback Songs*. Long Branch, NJ: Kimbo Educational.

"Jingle Bells," "Rudolph the Red-Nosed Reindeer," "Mrs. Claus," "Up on the Housetop," "The Twelve Days of Christmas," "The Little Drummer Boy," "Silver Star," "We Wish You Happy Holidays." (2001). *Sing 'n Sign Holdiay Time with Gaia*. Long Branch, NJ: Kimbo Educational.

"My Christmas Wish." (1978). *Holiday Songs for All Occasions*. Long Branch, NJ: Kimbo Educational.

Raffi's Christmas Album. (1983). Long Branch, NJ: Kimbo Educational.

14

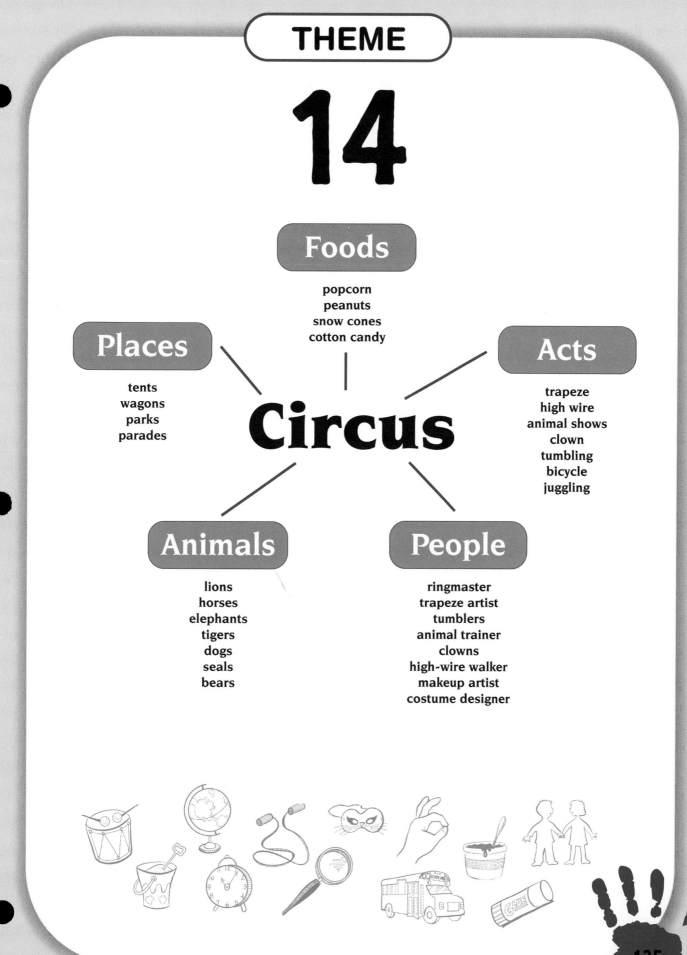

Foods

popcorn
peanuts
snow cones
cotton candy

Places

tents
wagons
parks
parades

Acts

trapeze
high wire
animal shows
clown
tumbling
bicycle
juggling

Circus

Animals

lions
horses
elephants
tigers
dogs
seals
bears

People

ringmaster
trapeze artist
tumblers
animal trainer
clowns
high-wire walker
makeup artist
costume designer

Theme Goals

Through participating in the experiences provided by this theme, the children may learn

1. Different circus acts
2. People who work for a circus
3. Animals that perform in a circus
4. Places to watch a circus
5. Foods eaten at a circus

Concepts for the Children to Learn

1. The circus is a traveling show with people and animals.
2. The circus is fun.
3. Many adults and children enjoy the circus.
4. The circus can be performed under a big tent.
5. Often there are circus parades.
6. An animal trainer teaches animals tricks.
7. Circus wagons, people, and animals are in the parade.
8. Circus shows have colorful clowns.
9. Clowns wear makeup.
10. Clowns often do tumbling, juggling, and bicycle acts.
11. Music is played at the circus.
12. People and animals do special tricks in the circus.
13. Many people work at the circus.
14. The circus has a ringmaster, trapeze artist, animal trainers, high-wire walkers, makeup artists, and costume designers.
15. Popcorn, peanuts, snow cones, and cotton candy are foods that can be eaten at a circus.

Vocabulary

1. **circus**—traveling show with people and animals.
2. **circus parade**—a march of people and animals at the beginning of the performance.
3. **clowns**—people who wear makeup and dress in silly clothes.
4. **makeup**—colored face paint.
5. **ringmaster**—person in charge of the circus performance.
6. **stilts**—long sticks a performer stands on to be taller.
7. **trapeze**—short bar used for swinging.

Bulletin Board

The purpose of this bulletin board is to develop color recognition and matching skills. Construct eight clown faces with collars out of tagboard. Color each collar a different color using felt-tip markers. Hang these pieces on the bulletin board. Next, construct eight hat pieces out of tagboard. Color each one a different color, to correspond with the colors of the clowns' collars. Punch holes in the hats, and use pushpins to hold the hats above the appropriate clown. The children can match the colored hats to the clown wearing the same-colored collar.

Family Letter

Dear Families,

We are starting a unit that will be fun and exciting for everyone—the circus! Developing an awareness of special people and animals enhances an appreciation of others. It also stimulates children's curiousity to learn more about other people and people's jobs. The children will be learning about the many acts and performances of circus people and animals.

AT SCHOOL

Some of the many fun and exciting things we will be doing include:

- listening to the story *Harriet Goes to the Circus* by Betsy and Guilio Maestro
- dressing up in clown suits and applying makeup in the dramatic play area
- acting out a small circus of our own
- making clown face puppets
- imitating circus clowns
- looking at books containing circus animals
- viewing the video *Circus*

We will have a very special visitor come to our room on Friday—a clown! He will show us how he applies his makeup and will perform for us. You are invited to join us for the fun at 3:00 p.m. to share in this activity.

AT HOME

It has been said that the circus is perhaps the world's oldest form of entertainment. Pictures of circus acts drawn over 3,000 years ago have been discovered on walls of caves. Most children enjoy clowns and dressing up as clowns. Prepare clown makeup with your child by adding a few drops of food coloring to cold cream. Have your child use his or her fingers or a clean paintbrush to paint his or her face. This activity will help develop an awareness of colors, as well as help him or her realize that appearances can change but the person remains the same!

Enjoy your child!

138

THEME 14

Clowns like to make people laugh.

4. Play Dough Animals

Prepare play dough by combining:

2 cups flour
1 cup salt
1 cup hot water
2 tablespoons oil
4 teaspoons cream of tartar
food coloring

Mix the ingredients. Then knead the mixture until smooth. This dough may be kept in a plastic bag or covered container. If the dough becomes sticky, add additional flour.

Cooking

Clown Snack

Place a pear in the middle of a plate. Sprinkle grated cheese on the pear for hair. Add raisin eyes, a cherry nose, and a raisin mouth. Finally, make a ruffle collar from a lettuce leaf.

Dramatic Play

1. Clown Makeup

Prepare clown makeup by mixing 1 part cold cream with 1 drop food coloring. Place clown makeup by a large mirror in the dramatic play area. The children apply makeup to their faces. Clown suits can also be provided if available. (Some programs may require parental permission slips for activities such as this.)

2. Circus

Set up a circus in your classroom. Make a circle out of masking tape on the floor. The children can take turns performing in the ring. The addition of hula hoops, animal and clown costumes, tickets, and chairs would extend the children's play in this area.

3. Animal Trainers

Each child can bring in his or her favorite stuffed animals on an assigned day. The children

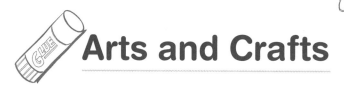

Arts and Crafts

1. Easel Ideas

- clown face–shaped paper
- circus tent–shaped paper

2. Circus Wagons

Collect old cardboard boxes and square food containers. The children can make circus wagons by decorating the boxes. When each child is through making his or her wagon, all of the boxes can be placed together for a circus train.

3. Clown Face Masks

Provide paper plates and felt-tip markers to make paper plate clown masks. Glue the plate to a tongue depressor. The children can use the masks as puppets.

CIRCUS

can pretend to be animal trainers for the circus. They may choose to act out different animal performances.

Field Trips/ Resource People

1. Clown Makeup

Invite a clown to demonstrate putting on makeup. Then have the clown put on a small skit and talk about the circus.

2. The Circus

If possible, go to a circus or circus parade in your area.

Fingerplays

Going to the Circus

Going to the circus to have a lot of fun.
  (hold closed fist, and raise fingers to
  indicate number)
The animals parading one by one.
Now they are walking 2 by 2,
A great big lion and a caribou.
Now they are walking 3 by 3,
The elephants and the chimpanzee.
Now they are walking 4 by 4,
A striped tiger and a big old bear.
Now they are walking 5 by 5,
It makes us laugh when they arrive.

Elephants

Elephants walk like this and like that.
  (sway body back and forth)
They're terribly big; they're terribly fat.
  (spread arms wide in a circular motion)
They have no hands, they have no toes,
And goodness gracious, what a NOSE!
  (put arms together and sway for
  elephant nose)

Five Little Clowns

Five little clowns running through the door.
  (hold up one hand, put down one finger at
  each verse)
One fell down and then there were four.
Four little clowns in an apple tree.
One fell out and then there were three.
Three little clowns stirring up some stew.
One fell in and then there were two.
Two little clowns having lots of fun.
One ran away and then there was one.
One little clown left sitting in the sun.
He went home and then there were none!

Circus Clown

I'd like to be a circus clown
And make a funny face,
  (make a funny face)
And have all the people laugh at me
As I jump around the place.
  (act silly and jump around)

Group Time

(Games, Language)

1. Circus Pictures

Place pictures of clowns and circus things around the room at the children's eye level. Introduce the pictures at group time and discuss each picture.

2. Who Took My Nose?

Prepare red circles from construction paper. Seat the children in a circle. Give each child a red circle to tape on his or her nose. Then have everyone close their eyes. Tap one child. This child should get up and go to another child and take his or her nose. When the child returns to his or her place, the teacher claps her or his hands and all the children open their eyes. The children then try to identify the child who took the nose.

3. Clown Lotto

Adhere clown face stickers, or draw simple clown faces, on several 2-inch × 2-inch pieces of tagboard. Also, prepare lotto boards using the same stickers or drawings. To play, turn all cards face down. Children take turns choosing a card from the table and seeing if it matches a picture on their game boards.

Large Muscle

1. Tightrope Walker

Provide a balance beam and a stick for the children to hold perpendicular to their bodies.

2. Dancing Elephants

Provide each child with a scarf and play music. The children can pretend to be dancing elephants.

3. Bean Bag Toss

Make a large clown or other circus person or animal bean bag toss out of thick cardboard. Cut the eyes, nose, and mouth holes all large enough for the bean bags to go through. For older children, assign each hole a certain number of points and maintain a score chart or card.

4. Can Stilts

Provide large tin cans with prebored holes on sides and thick string or twine for the children to make can stilts. Once completed, the children stand on the cans and walk around the room.

5. Tightrope Transition

As a transition, place a 10-foot line of masking tape on the floor. The children can pretend to tightrope walk over to the next activity.

6. Monkey, Monkey, Clown

Play Duck, Duck, Goose but change the words to "Monkey, Monkey, Clown."

These games are most appropriate for older children—four-, five-, six-, and seven-year-olds.

Math

1. Clown Hat Match

Make sets of matching colored hats. On one set print a numeral. On the matching hats print an identical number of dots. The children match the dots to the numbers.

2. Circus Sorting

Find several pictures of symbols that represent a circus. Also include other pictures. Place all pictures in a pile. The children can sort pictures into two piles. One pile will represent circus objects.

3. Growing Chart

Make a growing chart in the shape of a giraffe. If desired, another animal can be substituted. Record each child's height on the chart at various times during the year.

4. Unicycle Riders

Make unicycle cutouts and write numerals on them. Have children stack the corresponding number of cutout clowns on each unicycle with Velcro.

Music

1. "Circus"
(Sing to the tune of "Did You Ever See a Lassie")

Let's pretend that we are clowns, are clowns, are clowns.
Let's pretend that we are clowns.
We'll have so much fun.
We'll put on our makeup and make people laugh hard.
Let's pretend that we are clowns.
We'll have so much fun.

Let's pretend that we are elephants, are elephants, are elephants.

Let's pretend that we are elephants.
We'll have so much fun.
We'll sway back and forth and stand on just
    two legs.
Let's pretend that we are elephants.
We'll have so much fun.
Let's pretend that we are on a trapeze, a
    trapeze, a trapeze.
Let's pretend that we are on a trapeze.
We'll have so much fun.
We'll swing high and swoop low and make
    people shout "oh!"
Let's pretend that we are on a trapeze.
We'll have so much fun!

2. **"The Ringmaster"**
(*Sing to tune of* "*The Farmer and the Dell*")

The ringmaster has a circus.
The ringmaster has a circus.
Hi-ho the clowns are here.
The ringmaster has a circus.

The ringmaster takes a clown.
The ringmaster takes a clown.
Hi-ho the clowns are here.
The ringmaster takes a clown.

The clown takes an elephant . . .

Use clowns, elephants, lions, tigers, tight-rope
    walker, trapeze artist, acrobat, etc.

Science

1. **Circus Balloons**

Cut several pieces of tagboard into circles. If
desired, cover the balloons with transparent
contact or lamination paper. On each table have
three cups of colored water—red, yellow, and
blue—with a brush in each cup. The children
can mix all or any two colors and see which colors they can create for their circus balloons.

2. **Seal and Ball Color/Word Match**

Cut several seals out of different-colored tagboard. Out of the same colors cut several balls.

Write the correct color on each ball. The children match each ball with the word on it to the
correct seal.

3. **Sizzle Fun**

Pour 1 inch of vinegar in a soda or catsup bottle. Put 2 teaspoons of baking soda inside a balloon. Quickly slip the open end of the balloon
over the soda bottle. Watch the balloon fill with
gas created by the interaction of the vinegar
with the baking soda.

4. **Texture Clown**

Construct a large clown from tagboard. Use different textured materials to create the clown's
features. Make two sets. Place the extra set in a
box or a bag. The children may pick a piece of
textured material from the bag and match it to
the identical textured piece used as a clown
feature.

5. **High-Wire Balancers**

Cut out the outline of a person, resembling an
"x" shape with legs and arms apart, on tagboard
or light cardboard. Tape a penny to the back of
each foot. This will help the "high-wire walker"
balance almost anywhere.

Sensory

1. Provide rubber or plastic animal figurines for the
   children to play with in the water table.

2. Make face paint to have the children practice
   painting on their cheeks or a friend's cheek. (Be
   sure to get parental permission first!) Encourage
   them to paint shapes or letters.

   Face Paint Recipe
   2 tsp. shortening
   1 tsp. flour
   food coloring
   5 tsp. cornstarch
   3–4 drops glycerin
   fragrance-free cream or lotion

Social Studies

1. Circus Life

Read *You Think It's Fun to Be a Clown!* by David A. Adler. When finished, discuss the lives of circus people.

2. Body Parts

Make a large clown out of tagboard. Make corresponding matching body parts such as arms, legs, ears, shoes, hands, and fingers. The children can match the parts.

Books

The following books can be used to complement this theme:

Bond, Michael. (1992). *Paddington at the Circus.* Illus. by John Lobban. New York: HarperCollins.

Burmingham, John. (1994). *Cannonball Simp.* Cambridge, MA: Candlewick Press.

Chwast, Seymour. (1993). *The Twelve Circus Rings.* Orlando, FL: Harcourt Brace.

De Paola, Tomie. (1992). *Jingle, the Christmas Clown.* New York: G. P. Putnam.

Duncan, Lois. (1993). *The Circus Comes Home: When the Greatest Show on Earth Rode the Rails.* Illus. by Joseph Janney Steinmetz. New York: Doubleday.

Ehlert, Lois. (1992). *Circus.* New York: HarperCollins.

Ernst, Lisa Campbell. (1996). *Ginger Jumps.* Madison, WI: Demco Media.

Flaconer, Ian. (2001). *Olivia Saves the Circus.* New York: Atheneum.

Johnson, Neil. (1995). *Big-Top Circus.* New York: Dial Books.

Langen, Annette, Constanza Droop, and Laura Lindgren. (2000). *Felix Joins the Circus.* Illus. by Constanza Droop. New York: Abbeville Press.

McCully, Emily Arnold. (1992). *Mirette on the Highwire.* New York: G. P. Putnam.

Paxton, Tom. (1997). *Engelbert Joins the Circus.* Illus. by Roberta Wilson. New York: William Morrow.

Schumaker, Ward. (1997). *Sing a Song of Circus.* Orlando, FL: Harcourt Brace.

Spier, Peter. (1992). *Peter Spier's Circus.* New York: Delacorte Press.

Vincent, Gabrielle. (1989). *Ernest and Celestine at the Circus.* New York: Greenwillow.

Ziefert, Harriet M. (1992). *Clown Games.* Illus. by Larry Stevens. New York: Viking.

Multimedia

The following multimedia products can be used to complement this theme:

"Circus Baby" by Maud and Miska Petersham on *Max's Chocolate Chicken and Other Stories for Young Children* [video]. (1993). Weston, CT: Children's Circle Home Video; Los Angeles, CA: distributed by Wood Knapp Video.

Circus [video]. (1984). Edited by Steven Rosofsky. Chicago: Encyclopaedia Britannica Educational Corporation.

Do It Yourself Kid's Circus [cassette]. Available from Kimbo Educational.

Hanna, Jack. (1994). *A Day with the Greatest Show on Earth.* Glastonbury, CT: VideoTours.

Rogers, Fred. *Circus Fun* [video]. (1995, ©1987). Beverly Hills, CA: CBS/Fox Video.

Seuss, Dr. *Horton Hatches the Egg/If I Ran the Circus* [video]. (1992). Narrated by Billy Crystal. Random House.

Recordings and Song Titles

The following recordings can be used to complement this theme:

"Animal Parade." (1987). *Animal Walks*. Long Branch, NJ: Kimbo Educational.

Do It Yourself Kids Circus. (1980). Long Branch, NJ: Kimbo Educational.

15

Colors and Sizes

many

Uses

ceremonial
protection
decoration
identification
costumes

Workers

tailor
seamstress
salesperson
laundromat assistant
shoe repair person

Clothing

Care

wash
dry
mend
press
steam
polish
brush

Kinds

pants
uniforms
dresses
sweaters
skirts
shirts
shoes
socks
hats
gloves
coats
pajamas
scarves

Equipment

sewing machine,
washing machine,
dryer, washboard,
iron, ironing board,
brushes, steamer,
needle, clothespins,
hangers

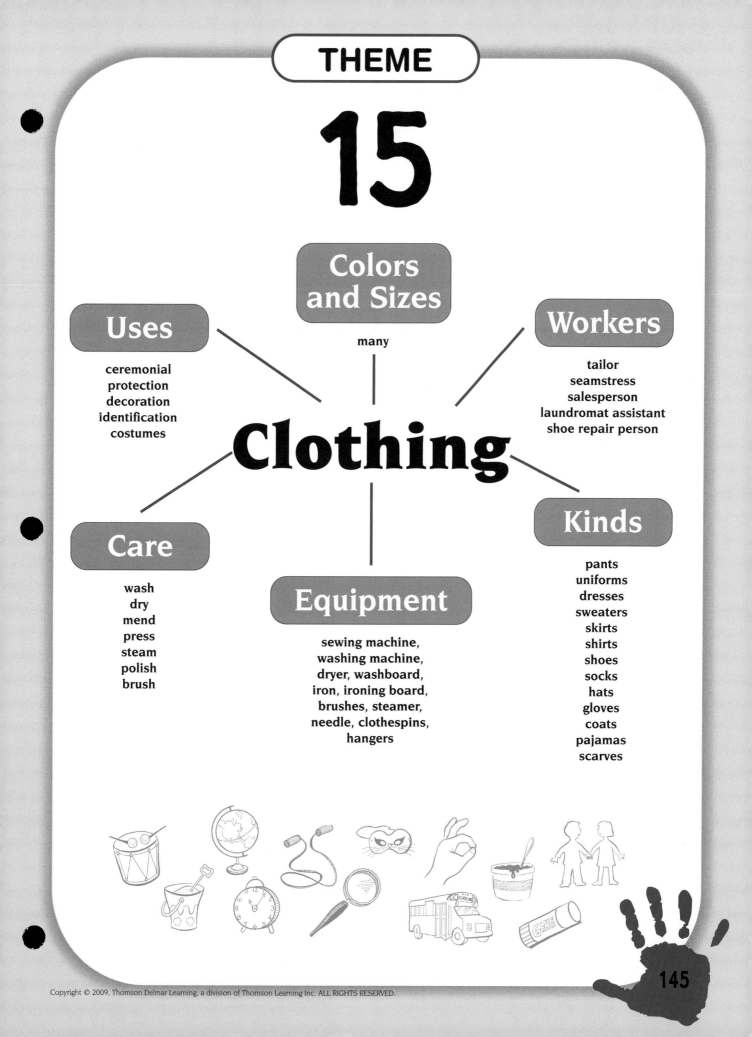

145

Theme Goals

Through participating in the experiences provided by this theme, the children may learn

1. Kinds of clothing
2. Clothing workers
3. Uses of clothing
4. Care of clothing
5. Clothing equipment
6. Colors and sizes of clothing

Concepts for the Children to Learn

1. Clothing is a covering for our body.
2. Pants, dresses, shirts, skirts, coats, pajamas, uniforms, and sweaters are some of the clothing we wear on our bodies.
3. Shoes, socks, and boots are clothing for our feet.
4. Gloves and mittens are coverings for our hands.
5. Hats and scarves are coverings for our head.
6. Protection, decoration, and identification are uses for clothing.
7. Clothes identify workers.
8. Policemen and firefighters wear uniforms.
9. There are many colors and sizes of clothing.
10. Clothing can be washed, dried, steamed, pressed, and mended.
11. Clothing needs to be cleaned.
12. Tailors and seamstresses help make and mend clothing.
13. People wear clothing for ceremonies.
14. Brides may wear a bridal gown.
15. Costumes, such as at Halloween, are also clothing.
16. A shoe repair person mends shoes.
17. Clothespins and hangers are used to hang clothes.
18. Needles and thread, brushes, and irons are needed to care for clothing.

Vocabulary

1. **clothespin**—a clip used to hang clothes on a clothesline or a hanger.
2. **clothing**—a covering for the body.
3. **coat/jacket**—a piece of clothing that is often used for warmth and is worn over other clothing.
4. **dryer**—an appliance that dries clothes.
5. **hat**—clothing that covers our head.
6. **laundromat**—a place to clean clothes.
7. **shirt**—clothing that covers the chest and sometimes the arms.
8. **shoes**—clothing for our feet.
9. **skirt**—clothing that hangs from the waist.
10. **washing machine**—an appliance used to clean clothes.

Bulletin Board

The purpose of this bulletin board is to develop visual perception and discrimination skills. A "Sort the Clothes" bulletin board can be an addition to the clothing unit. Construct shorts and shirt pieces out of tagboard. The number used will be dependent on the size of the bulletin board and the development appropriateness for the children. Draw a pattern on a pair of shorts and the same pattern on one of the shirts. Continue, drawing a different pattern for each shorts and shirt set. Hang the shorts on the bulletin board, and hang a pushpin on top of the shorts, so the children can hang the corresponding patterned shirt on top of the shorts.

Family Letter

Dear Families,

We will be beginning a unit on clothing. Through participation in this unit, the children will learn about many different kinds of clothing. They will also become aware of the purposes and care of clothing.

AT SCHOOL

Some of the learning experiences planned for this unit include:

- sorting clothes hangers by color
- going to a laundromat in the dramatic play area
- making newspaper skirts at the art table
- washing doll clothes in the sensory table

We will also be taking a walk to the Corner Laundromat on Tuesday afternoon. We will be looking at the big laundry carts, washers and dryers, and folding tables. If you would like to join us, please contact me. We will be leaving the center at 3:00 p.m.

PARENT INVOLVEMENT

If you have any special clothes worn for celebrations or ceremonies, we invite you to share them with our class. Please contact me so a time can be arranged for your visit. The children will enjoy having you in the class and learning about the significance of the apparel.

AT HOME

You can foster the concepts introduced in this unit by encouraging your child to select what he or she will wear to school each day. To promote independence, begin by placing your child's clothes in a low drawer, allowing easy access to the clothing. To make mornings more enjoyable, encourage your child to select clothes at night that can be worn the next day. Find a location to place the clothes. Also, if your child has doll clothes, fill the kitchen sink or a tub with soapy water, and let your child wash the doll clothes. This will help your child learn how to care for clothing.

Have fun exploring clothing concepts.

We take turns washing the clothes.

 # Arts and Crafts

1. Dress the Paper Doll

Prepare clothing out of construction paper scraps to fit paper dolls. For younger children, the dolls can be precut. Older children may be able to cut their own dolls if the lines are traced on paper and a simple pattern is provided.

2. Newspaper Skirts

Depending on the developmental level of the children, newspaper skirts can be constructed in the classroom. Begin by stapling about 10 sheets of newspaper across at the top. Draw a bold line about 2 inches from the staples. Then instruct the children to vertically cut from the bottom edge of the paper, all the way up to the bold line, creating strips. String pieces can be attached by stapling to the top of both sides to enable the skirt to be tied in the back.

3. Easel Ideas

- feature clothes-shaped easel paper

- paint using tools created by attaching small sponges to a clothespin

 # Cooking

1. Graham Crackers

Wear chef uniforms, and make your own graham crackers for snack.

1/2 cup margarine
2/3 cup brown sugar
1/2 cup water
2 3/4 cups graham flour
1/2 teaspoon salt
1/2 teaspoon baking powder
1/8 teaspoon cinnamon

Beat margarine and sugar till smooth and creamy. Add the remainder of the ingredients and mix well. Let the mixture sit for 30 to 45 minutes. Sprinkle flour on a board or table-top. Roll out dough to 1/8 inch thick. Cut the dough into squares, logs, or other shapes. Place on an oiled cookie sheet. Bake at 350 degrees for 20 minutes until lightly browned. This recipe should produce a sufficient quantity for eight children.

2. Irish Gingerbread

1 or 2 teaspoons butter
2 cups flour
1 1/2 teaspoon baking soda
1 teaspoon cinnamon
1 teaspoon ground ginger
3/4 teaspoon salt
1 egg
2 egg yolks
1 cup molasses
1/2 cup soft butter
1/2 cup sugar
1/2 cup quick-cooking oatmeal
1 cup hot water

Preheat the oven to 350 degrees. Grease the bottom of the baking pan with 1 or 2 teaspoons of butter. Measure the flour, baking soda, cinnamon, ginger, and salt; sift them together onto a piece of waxed paper. In a mixing bowl, combine the butter with the sugar by stirring them with the mixing spoon until they are blended. Add the egg and egg yolks. With the mixing spoon, beat the mixture until it is fluffy. Stir in the molasses.

Add the sifted dry ingedients, the oatmeal, and the hot water one fourth at a time to the egg and molasses mixture, stirring after each addition. Pour the mixture into the greased pan. Bake 50 to 55 minutes. Test with a toothpick. Make gingerbread people with cookie cutters. Decorate: make clothes for the gingerbread people using coconut, nuts, raisins, etc.

Note: From *Many Hands Cooking*, by Terry Touff and Marilyn Ratner, 1974, New York: Thomas Y. Crowell. Reprinted with permission.

3. Pita or Pocket Bread

1 package of yeast
1/4 cup lukewarm water
3 cups flour
  (white, whole wheat, or any combination)
2 teaspoons salt

Dissolve the yeast in the water and add the flour and salt. Stir into a rough sticky ball. Knead on a floured board or table until smooth, adding more flour, if necessary. Divide the dough into six balls and knead each ball until smooth and round.

Flatten each ball with a rolling pin until 1/4 inch thick and about 4 to 5 inches in diameter.

Cover the dough with a clean towel and let it rise for 45 minutes. Arrange the rounds upside down on baking sheets. Bake in a 500-degree oven for 10 to 15 minutes or until brown and puffed in the center. The breads will be hard when they are removed from the oven but will soften and flatten as they cool. When cooled, split or cut the bread carefully and fill with any combination of sandwich filling.

Dramatic Play

1. Clothing Store

Place dress-up clothing on hangers and a rack. A cash register, play money, bags, and small shopping carts can also be provided to extend the play.

2. Party Clothes

Provide dressy clothes, jewelry, shoes, hats, and purses.

3. Uniforms

Collect occupational clothing and hats, such as police officer shirts and hats, a firefighter's hat, nurse and doctor lab coats, and artist smocks. High school athletic uniforms can also be provided. After use, store this box so the uniforms are available upon request for other units.

4. Hanging Clothes

String a low clothesline in the classroom or outdoors. Provide clothespins and doll clothes for the children to hang up.

5. Laundromat

Collect two large, appliance-sized boxes. Cut a hole in the top of one to represent a washing machine, and cut a front door in the other to represent a dryer. A laundry basket, empty soap box, and play clothing may be welcome additions to extend the play.

Field Trips/ Resource People

Group Time
(Games, Language)

1. Clothing Store

Visit a children's clothing store. Look at the different colors, sizes, and types of clothing.

2. Tailor/Seamstress

Invite a seamstress to visit your classroom to show the children how she makes, mends, and repairs clothing. The seamstress can demonstrate tools and share some of the clothing articles she has made.

3. Laundromat

Take a walk to a local laundromat. Observe the facility. Point out the sizes of the different kinds of washing machines and dryers. Explain the use of the laundry carts and folding tables.

Look Closely

While the children are sitting on the floor in a circle, call out the clothes items that one child is wearing. For example, say, "I see someone who is wearing a red shirt and pants." The children can look around the circle and say the name of the child who is wearing those items.

Large Muscle

1. Clothespin Drop

Collect clothespins and a series of jars with mouth openings of varying widths. The children can stand near the jar and drop the clothespins into it. To ensure success, the younger children should be guided to try the jar with the largest opening.

2. Bean Bag Toss

Bean bags can be tossed into empty laundry baskets.

3. Clothes Race

Fill bags with large-sized clothing items. Give a bag to each child. Signal the children to begin dressing up with the clothing. The object is to see how quickly they can put all of the clothes items in the bag over their own clothing. This activity is more appropriate for five-, six-, and seven-year-olds, who have better large motor coordination and development.

Fingerplays

Three Buttons

Here's a button
(make circle shape with thumb and
index finger)
And here's a button
(make circle shape with other thumb and
index finger)
A great big button, I see.
(make circle shape with arms above head)
Shall we count them?
Are you ready?
One, two, three!
(make all three circles in succession)

Math

1. **Clothes Seriation**

   Provide a basketful of clothes for the children to line up from largest to smallest. Include hats, sweatshirts, shoes, and pants. Use clothing items whose sizes are easily distinguishable.

2. **Line 'em Up**

   Print numerals on clothespins. The children can attach the clothespins on a low clothesline and sequence them in numerical order.

3. **Hanger Sort**

   Colored hangers can be sorted into laundry baskets or on a clothesline by color.

4. **Sock Match**

   Collect many different pairs of socks. Combine in a laundry basket. The children can find the matching pairs and fold them.

Music

1. **"Love Somebody"**

   Love somebody, yes I do!
   Love somebody, yes I do!
   Love somebody, yes I do!
   Love somebody but I won't tell who!

   Give the children a clue to which child you are thinking about by telling them what color shirt, pants, shorts, shoes, etc. the child is wearing. Whoever guesses correctly gets to think of the next person.

2. **"Head, Shoulders, Knees, and Toes"**

   Head, shoulders, knees, and toes,
   Knees and toes.
   Head, shoulders, knees, and toes,
   Knees and toes.
   Eyes and ears and mouth and nose.
   Head, shoulders, knees, and toes,
   Knees and toes!

Science

1. **Fabric Sink and Float**

   Provide various kinds of clothing and fabric on the science table along with a large tub of water. The children can test the different types of clothing to see which will sink and which will float. Some clothing articles will sink, whereas other clothing articles float until they become saturated with water. After a test has been made, the clothes can be hung to dry.

2. **Cleaning Fabric**

   Give each child a piece of fabric. Set a bowl of mud, paint, ketchup, and markers on the table. Ask them to get their fabric dirty. After the children have gotten their fabric dirty, give them a brush and water and ask them to try to clean it. After a few minutes of trying with water ask them to report their progress and ask what they think might help clean it. Provide laundry soap for the children to rub into the fabric. Discuss the difference in cleaning the fabric. What changes do they see? Why?

   Note: This activity will require the table to be covered and should be completed near the sink and on non-carpeted floors.

Sensory

1. **Washing Clothes**

   Fill the sensory table with soapy water and let the children wash doll clothing. After being washed, the clothes can be hung on a low clothesline.

2. **Add to the Sensory Table**

   Place a variety of clothespins in the sensory table. Encourage the children to clip the pins together to create various forms.

   - clothespins

Social Studies

1. Weather Clothing

Bring in examples of clothing worn in each of the four seasons. Provide four laundry baskets. Label each basket with a picture representing a sunny, hot day, a rainy day, a cold day, and a fall or spring day. Then encourage the children to sort the clothing according to the weather label on the basket.

2. Who Wears It?

At group time, hold up clothing items and ask the children who would wear it. Include baby clothes, sports uniforms and occupational clothing, ladies clothes, men's clothes, etc.

Books

The following books can be used to complement this theme:

Blankenship, Lee Ann. (2005). *Mr. Tuggle's Troubles*. Illus. by Karen Dugan. Honesdale, PA: Boyds Mills Press.

Burton, Marilee Robin. (1994). *My Best Shoes*. Illus. by James E. Ransome. New York: William Morrow.

Havill, Juanita. (1993). *Jamaica and Brianna*. Illus. by Anne Sibley O'Brien. Boston: Houghton Mifflin.

Hilton, Nette. (1991). *The Long Red Scarf*. Illus. by Margaret Power. Minneapolis, MN: Carolrhoda Books.

Howard, Elizabeth Fitzgerald. (1991). *Aunt Flossie's Hats and Crab Cakes Later*. Illus. by James Ransome. New York: Clarion Books.

Hurwitz, Johanna. (1993). *New Shoes for Silvia*. Illus. by Jerry Pinkney. New York: William Morrow.

Karon, Jan and Toni Goffe. (2001). *Miss Fannie's Hat*. Illus. by Toni Goffe. New York: Puffin.

Keller, Holly. (1995). *Rosata*. New York: Greenwillow.

Lewis, J. Patrick and Chris Sheban. (2000). *The Shoe Tree of Chagrin*: A Christmas Story. Illus. by Chris Sheban. Mankato, MN: Creative Editions.

London, Jonathan. (1992). *Froggy Gets Dressed*. Illus. by Frank Remkiewicz. New York: Viking.

Dramatic Play Clothes

The following list contains names of male and female clothing articles to save for use in the dramatic play area:

aprons	leotards	shoes	shorts
boots	swimsuits	slippers	sweatsuits
pajamas	socks	robes	suspenders
shirts	purses	slacks	billfolds
dresses	jewelry	sweaters	ties
skirts	rings	coats	belts
hats	bracelets	earmuffs	tutus
gloves/mittens	necklaces	raincoats	bridal veils
scarves	clip-on earrings	snow pants	capes

Lucas, David. (2004). *Halibut Jackson*. New York: Knopf. (Distributed by Random House.)

Mendel, Lydia J. (1993). *All Dressed Up and Nowhere to Go*. Illus. by Normand Chartier. Boston: Houghton Mifflin.

Morris, Ann. (1995). *Shoes, Shoes, Shoes*. New York: Lothrop, Lee & Shepard.

Murphy, Stuart. (1996). *A Pair of Socks*. Illus. by Lois Ehlert. New York: HarperCollins.

Neitzel, Shirley. (1992). *The Dress I'll Wear to the Party*. Illus. by Nancy Winslow Parker. New York: Greenwillow.

Neitzel, Shirley. (1989). *The Jacket I Wear in the Snow*. Illus. by Nancy Winslow Parker. New York: Greenwillow.

O'Brien, Claire. (1997). *Sam's Sneaker Search*. Illus. by Charles Fuge. New York: Simon & Schuster.

Patrick, Denise Lewis. (1993). *Red Dancing Shoes*. Illus. by James Ransome. New York: William Morrow.

Pearson, Tracey Campbell. (1997). *The Purple Hat*. New York: Farrar, Straus & Giroux.

Serfozo, Mary. (1993). *Benjamin Bigfoot*. Illus. by Joseph A. Smith. New York: Margaret McElderry.

Small, David. (1996). *Fenwick's Suit*. New York: Farrar, Straus & Giroux.

Stoeke, Janet Morgan. (1994). *A Hat for Minerva Louise*. New York: Dutton.

Touff, Terry and Marilyn Ratner. (1974). *Many Hands Cooking*. New York: Thomas Y. Crowell.

Multimedia

The following multimedia products can be used to complement this theme:

Jenkins, Ella. "One Two Buckle My Shoe" on *Ella Jenkins Live at the Smithsonian* [video]. (1991). Washington, D.C.: Smithsonian/Folkways.

London, Jonathan. *Froggy Gets Dressed* [cassette and book]. (1997). New York: Penguin Books.

Parker, Dan. *Teach Me About Getting Dressed* [cassette and book]. (1988). Fallbrook, CA: Living Skills Music.

Scullard, Sue. *The Flyaway Pantaloons* [video]. (1992). Pine Plains, NY: Live Oak Media.

Recordings and Song Titles

The following recordings can be used to complement this theme:

"Blue Suede Shoes." (2000). *Bean Bag Rock & Roll*. Long Branch, NJ: Kimbo Educational.

"If You Have This On . . . Stand Up, Sit Down." (1974). *More Songs about Me*. Long Branch, NJ: Kimbo Educational.

"I Wear Clean Clothes." (1979). *Self Help Skills*. Long Branch, NJ: Kimbo Educational.

"My Space Suit." (1988). *Journey into Space*. Long Branch, NJ: Kimbo Educational.

"Shoes." (2004). *Circle Time Activities*. Long Branch, NJ: Kimbo Educational.

Alarm

flashing lights,
car horns,
fire alarms, sirens

Written

books, newspapers,
magazines, letters,
greeting cards,
printed words

Verbal

talking
singing
sounds
foreign accents
disabilities

Communication

Equipment

telephone,
television,
telegraph,
FAX, radio, records,
video recorder,
cassette player,
computer, e-mail,
compact disc player,
cell phone

Visual

letters
numbers
greeting cards
signs
pictures
art
artifacts

Nonverbal

listening
body movements
sign language
dancing
pantomime
drawings

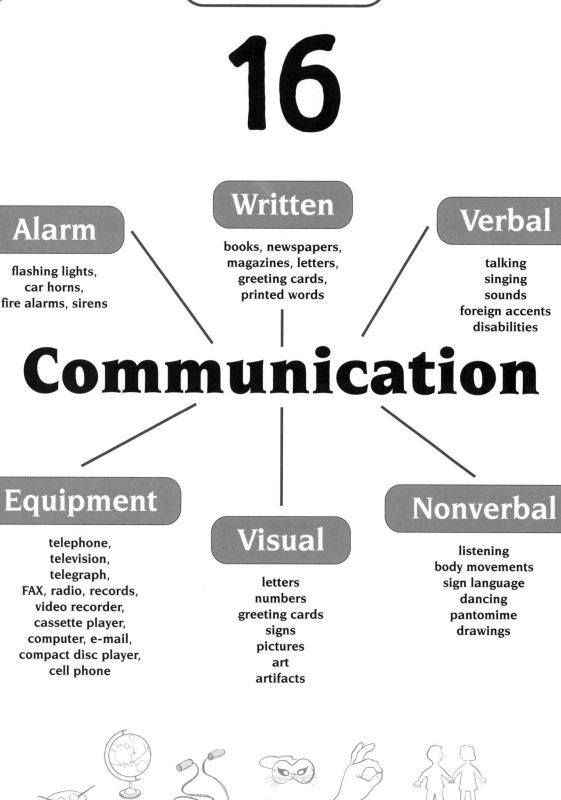

Theme Goals

Through participating in the experiences provided by this theme, the children may learn

1. Visual communication skills
2. Nonverbal communication skills
3. Verbal communication skills
4. Communication equipment
5. Types of written communication
6. Ways of communicating alarm

Concepts for the Children to Learn

1. Talking is a form of communication.
2. Listening is a way to communicate.
3. Our hands and face can communicate.
4. Sign language is a way of communication.
5. Body movements, dancing, and pantomiming are nonverbal communication.
6. Singing and making sounds are forms of communication.
7. The telephone is a communication tool.
8. Letters and greeting cards are a way of communicating.
9. Machines can transmit messages.
10. Numbers and signs are a way of communicating.
11. Books, magazines, letters, greeting cards, and printed words are forms of written communication.
12. Telephones, televisions, radios, video records, computer disks, computers, and cell phones are equipment for communicating.
13. Pictures, artifacts, and art are forms of visual communication.
14. Flashing lights, car horns, fire alarms, and sirens communicate alarm.
15. Books are a form of communication.

Vocabulary

1. **alphabet**—letter symbols that are used to write a language.
2. **Braille**—a system of printing for people who are blind.
3. **card**—a piece of folded paper with a design. Cards are sent to people on special occasions: birthdays, holidays, celebrations, or when ill.
4. **communication**—sharing information.
5. **computer**—a machine that keeps and gives back information.
6. **fax machine**—a machine that copies a message and sends it to another person or place.
7. **letter**—paper with a written or typed message.
8. **newspaper**—words printed on paper.
9. **sign language**—making symbols with our hands to communicate.
10. **signs**—symbols.
11. **cell phone**—a cell phone is used to talk to someone in another place.

Bulletin Board

The purpose of this bulletin board is to help older children learn their home telephone number. Construct a telephone handset and phone base for each child. See the illustration. Affix each child's telephone number to the handset. Laminate this card. For younger children, handsets can be attached to the telephone base, but left off the hook. The children can place their handsets on the bases when they arrive at school. Older children can match their handset to their number and correct themselves by the color match. Later, white handsets could be used to see if the children know their telephone number. Telephones can be prepared for dialing by constructing a number pad for each handset and gluing the pads on the handsets. The children can practice dialing their home phone numbers by "pressing" the appropriate pad on the handset.

THEME 16

Family Letter

Dear Families,

We will begin talking about communication or how we share our ideas with others. Through this unit the children will become aware of the different ways we communicate: through our voices, letters, using hand signals, and body language. They will also become familiar with machines that are used to communicate, such as the television, radio, computer, cell phone, and telephone.

AT SCHOOL

Some of the learning experiences planned for this unit include:

- a sign language demonstration
- a phone booth in the dramatic play area
- a computer in the writing center
- songs and books about communication
- a wireless telephone on the science table

AT HOME

It is important for children to learn their telephone number for safety purposes. Help your children learn your home telephone number. (This is also something we will be practicing at school.) To make practicing more fun, construct a toy telephone with your child. Two paper cups or empty tin cans and a long piece of rope, string, or yarn are needed to make a telephone. Thread the string through the two cups and tie knots on the ends. Have two people hold the cups and pull the string taut. Take turns talking and listening. The sound vibrations travel through the string—and you won't hear a busy signal!

Enjoy your children as you share concepts and experiences related to communication.

It is important for children to know their home telephone numbers.

 Arts and Crafts

1. Easel Idea

Cut easel paper in the shape of a book, record, radio, or other piece of communication equipment.

2. Stationery

Provide the children with various stencils or stamps to make their own stationery. It can be used for a gift for a parent or a special person. Children could then dictate a letter to a relative or friend.

 Dramatic Play

1. Post Office

In the dramatic play area, place a mailbox, envelopes, old cards, paper, pens, old stampers, ink pads, hats, and mailbags. During self-selected or self-initiated play periods, the children can play post office.

2. Television

Obtain a discarded television console to use for puppetry or storytelling experiences. Remove the back and set, leaving just the wooden frame. If desired, make curtains.

3. Radio Station

Place an old microphone, or one made from a styrofoam ball and cardboard, with records in the dramatic play area.

4. Puppet Show

Place a puppet stand and a variety of puppets in the dramatic play area for the children to use during the self-selected or self-directed play period.

Field Trips/ Resource People

1. Post Office

Visit a local post office. Encourage the children to observe how the mail is sorted.

2. Radio Station

Visit a local disc jockey at the radio station.

3. Television Station

If available, visit a local television station. Observe the cameras, microphones, and other communication devices.

4. Sign Language Demonstration

Invite someone to demonstrate sign language.

Fingerplays

Body Talk

When I smile, I tell you I'm happy.
   (point at the corner of mouth)
When I frown I tell you that I'm sad.
   (pull down corners of mouth)
When I raise my shoulders and tilt my head I tell you "I don't know."
   (raise shoulders, tilt head, raise hands, shake head)

Helpful Friends

Mail carriers carry a full pack
Of cards and letters on their backs.
   (hold both hands over one shoulder)
Step, step, step! Now ring, ring, ring!
   (step in place and pretend to ring bell)
What glad surprises do they bring?

My Hands

My hands can talk
In a special way.
These are some things

They help me to say:
"Hello"
   (wave)
"Come Here"
   (beckon toward self)
"It's A-OK"
   (form circle with thumb and pointer)
"Now Stop"
   (hand out, palm up)
"Look"
   (hands shading eyes)
"Listen"
   (cup hand behind ear)
Or "It's far, far away"
   (point out into the distance)
And "Glad to meet you, how are you today?"
   (shake neighbor's hand)

Group Time

(Games, Language)

1. Telephone

Play the game "telephone" by having the children sit in a circle. Begin by whispering a short phrase into a child's ear. That child whispers your message to the next child. Continue until the message gets to the last child. The last child repeats the message out loud. It is fun to see how much it has changed. (This game is most successful with older children.)

2. What's Missing?

Place items that are related to communication on a tray. Include a stamp, a telephone, a record, a portable radio, etc. The children can examine the objects for a few minutes. After this, they should close their eyes while you remove an object. Then let the children look at the tray and identify which object is missing.

3. Household Objects Sound Like . . .

Make a tape of different sounds around the house. Include a radio, television, alarm clock, telephone, vacuum cleaner, flushing toilet, door bells, egg timer, etc. Play the tape for the children, letting them identify the individual sounds.

Fingerpaint Recipes

Liquid Starch Method

liquid starch
   (put in squeeze bottles)
dry tempera paint in shakers

Put about 1 tablespoon of liquid starch on the surface to be painted. Let the child shake the paint onto the starch. Mix and blend the paint. **Note:** If this paint becomes too thick, simply sprinkle a few drops of water onto the painting.

Soap Flake Method

Mix in a small bowl:

soap flakes
a small amount of water

Beat until stiff with an eggbeater. Use white soap on dark paper, or add colored tempera paint to the soap and use it on light-colored paper. This gives a slight three-dimensional effect.

Wheat Flour Paste

3 parts water
1 part wheat flour
coloring

Stir flour into water. Add coloring.

Uncooked Laundry Starch

A mixture of 1 cup laundry/liquid starch, 1 cup cold water, and 3 cups soap flakes will provide a quick fingerpaint.

Flour and Salt I

1 cup flour
1 1/2 cups salt
3/4 cup water
coloring

Combine flour and salt. Add water. This has a grainy quality, unlike the other fingerpaints, providing a different sensory experience. Some children enjoy the different touch sensation when 1 1/2 cups salt are added to the other recipes.

Flour and Salt II

2 cups flour
2 teaspoons salt
3 cups cold water
2 cups hot water
coloring

Add salt to flour, then pour in cold water gradually and beat mixture with egg beater until it is smooth. Add hot water and boil until it becomes clear. Beat until smooth, then mix in coloring. Use 1/4 cup food coloring to 8 to 9 ounces of paint for strong colors.

Instantized Flour Uncooked Method

1 pint water (2 cups)
1 1/2 cups instantized flour (the kind used to thicken gravy)

Put the water in the bowl and stir the flour into the water. Add color. Regular flour may be lumpy.

Cooked Starch Method

1 cup laundry starch dissolved in a small amount of cold water
5 cups boiling water added slowly to dissolve starch
1 tablespoon glycerine (optional)

Cook the mixture until it is thick and glossy. Add 1 cup mild soap flakes. Add color in separate containers. Cool before using.

Cornstarch Method

Gradually add 2 quarts water to 1 cup cornstarch. Cook until clear and add 1/2 cup soap flakes (like Ivory Snow). A few drops of glycerine or oil of wintergreen may be added.

Flour Method

Mix 1 cup flour and 1 cup cold water. Add 3 cups boiling water and bring all to a boil, stirring constantly. Add 1 tablespoon alum and coloring. Paintings from this recipe dry flat and do not need to be ironed.

Large Muscle

Charades

Invite children one at a time to come to the front of the group. Then whisper something in the child's ear, such as "You're very happy." The child then uses his or her hands, face, feet, arms, and so forth, to communicate this feeling to the other children. The group of children then identifies the demonstrated feeling.

Math

1. **Phone Numbers**

   Make a list of the children's names and telephone numbers. Place the list by a toy telephone.

2. **Stamp Sort**

   Paste a variety of samples of different shapes and colors onto construction paper. Laminate and cut out. Encourage the children to sort the stamps by size and color.

Music

1. **"Call a Friend"**
   (*Sing to the tune of "Row, Row, Row Your Boat"*)

   Call, call, call a friend.
   Friend, I'm calling you.
   Hi, hello, how are you?
   Very good, thank you!

2. **"Twinkle, Twinkle Traffic Light"**
   (*Sing to the tune of "Twinkle, Twinkle Little Star"*)

   Twinkle, twinkle traffic light
   Standing on the corner bright.
   Green means go, we all know
   Yellow means wait, even if you're late.
   Red means STOP!
      (pause)
   Twinkle, twinkle traffic light
   Standing on the corner bright.

3. **"I'm a Little Mail Carrier"**
   (*Sing to the tune of "I'm a Little Teapot"*)

   I'm a little mail carrier, short and stout.
   Here is my hat, and here is my pouch.
      (point to head, point to side)
   I walk around from house to house,
   Delivering mail from my pouch.
      (pretend to take things out of a bag)

Science

1. Telephones

Place telephones, real or toy, in the classroom to encourage the children to talk to each other. Also, make your own telephones by using two large empty orange juice concentrate cans. After washing the cans, connect with a long string. The children can pull the string taut. Then they can take turns talking and listening to each other.

2. Sound Shakers

Using identical small orange juice cans, pudding cups, or empty film containers, fill pairs of the containers with different objects. Included may be sand, coins, rocks, rice, salt, etc. Replace the lids. Make sure to secure the lids with glue or heavy tape to avoid spilling. To make the containers self-correcting, place numbers or like colors on the bottoms of the matching containers.

3. Feely Box

Prepare a feely box that includes such things as tape cassette, pen, pencil, block letters, an envelope, and anything else that is related to communication. The children can place their hand in the box and identify objects using their sense of touch.

4. Training Telephones

Contact your local telephone company to borrow training telephones. Place the telephone on the science table along with a chart listing the children's telephone numbers. The children can sort, match, and classify the wires.

5. Vibrations

Encourage the children to gently place their hand on the side of the piano, guitar, record player, radio, television, and so forth, in order to feel the vibrations. Then have the children feel their own throats vibrate as they speak. A tuning fork can also be a teaching aid when talking about vibrations.

6. Telephone Parts

Dismantle an old telephone and put it on the science table for the children to discover and explore the parts.

Social Studies

1. Thank You

Let the children dictate a group thank-you letter to one of your resource visitors or field trip representatives. Before mailing the letter, provide writing tools for children to sign their names.

2. Sign Language

Learn some simple sign language to teach the children in your classroom. Some ideas include: thank you (touch hand to chin and pull down), please (rub chest), and friend (cross pointer fingers).

Books

The following books can be used to complement this theme:

Aliki. (1993). *Communication*. New York: Greenwillow.

Aliki. (1996). *Hello! Good-Bye*. New York: Greenwillow.

Austin, Margot and David McPhail. (1999). *A Friend for Growl Bear*. Illus. by David McPhail. New York: HarperCollins.

Bornstein, Harry. (1992). *Nursery Rhymes from Mother Goose: Told in Signed English*. Washington, DC: Kendall Green.

Brown, Marc Tolon. (1997). *Arthur's TV Trouble*. Boston: Little, Brown. (Pbk.)

Brown, Ruth. (1991). *Alphabet Times Four: An International ABC*. New York: Dutton.

Buck, Nola. (1996). *Sid and Sam*. Illus. by G. Brian Karas. New York: HarperCollins.

Coffelt, Nancy. (1995). *The Dog Who Cried Woof*. Orlando, FL: Harcourt Brace.

Gibbons, Gail. (1993). *Puff—Flash—Bang: A Book about Signals*. New York: William Morrow.

Hubbard, L. Ron. (2000). *Grammar & Communication for Children*. Los Angeles: Effective Education.

King, Mary Ellen. (1997). *A Good Day for Listening*. Harrisburg, PA: Morehouse Publishing.

Klove, Lars. (1996). *I See a Sign*. New York: Aladdin Paperbacks.

Leedy, Loreen. (1990). *The Furry News: How to Make a Newspaper*. New York: Holiday House.

Lester, Helen. (1995). *Listen, Buddy*. Illus. by Lynn Munsinger. Boston: Houghton Mifflin.

Nelson, Nigel. (1994). *Codes*. Illus. by Tony De Saulles. Cincinnati, OH: Thomson Learning.

Nelson, Nigel. (1994). *Writing and Numbers*. Illus. by Tony De Saulles. Cincinnati, OH: Thomson Learning.

Oxlade, Chris. (1997). *Electronic Communication*. Illus. by Colin Mier. New York: Franklin Watts.

Peterson, Jeanne Whitehouse. (1994). *My Mama Sings*. Illus. by Sandra Speidel. New York: HarperCollins.

Rankin, Laura. (1991). *The Handmade Alphabet*. New York: Dial Books.

Shapiro, Arnold. (1997). *Mice Squeak, We Speak*. Illus. by Tomie de Paola. New York: G. P. Putnam.

Showers, Paul. (1991). *Listening Walk*. Revised ed. New York: HarperCollins.

Weller, Janet. (1997). *The Written Word*. Illus. by Colin Mier. New York: Franklin Watts.

Wheeler, Cindy. (1998). *More Simple Signs*. New York: Viking.

Multimedia

The following multimedia products can be used to complement this theme:

Bailey's Book House [CD-ROM]. (1995). Redmond, WA: Edmark.

Be a Better Listener [video]. (1995). Pleasantville, NY: Sunburst Communications.

Exciting People, Places and Things [video]. (1989). Washington, DC: Gallaudet University Press.

Lonnquist, Ken and others. *Sign Songs: Fun Songs to Sign and Sing* [video]. (1994). Madison, WI: Aylmer Press.

Reader Rabbit's Ready for Letters [computer program]. (1994). Learning Company.

Tossing, Gaia. *Sing 'n Sign for Fun!* [compact disc]. (1995). Glenview, IL: Heartsong.

Recordings and Song Titles

The following recordings can be used to complement this theme:

Gaia—Sign 'n Sing for Fun (Sign Language). (1996). Long Branch, NJ: Kimbo Educational.

Gaia—Sign, Dance 'n Sing (Sign Language). (1998). Long Branch, NJ: Kimbo Educational.

"Imagination, Communication." (1997). *Tony Chestnut (The Learning Station)*. Long Branch, NJ: Kimbo Educational.

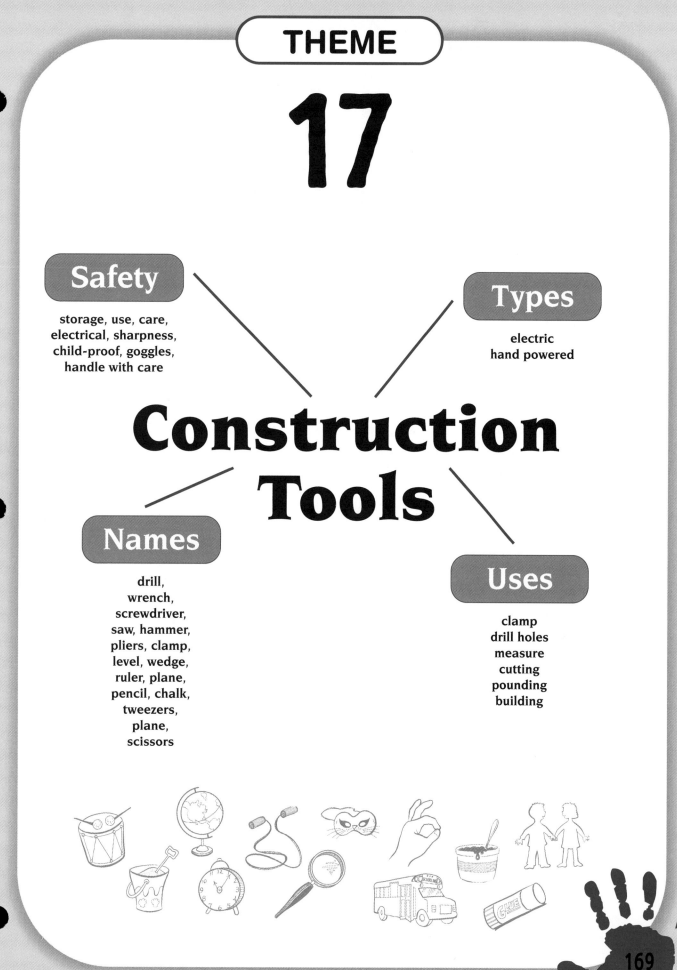

THEME

17

Safety

storage, use, care,
electrical, sharpness,
child-proof, goggles,
handle with care

Types

electric
hand powered

Construction Tools

Names

drill,
wrench,
screwdriver,
saw, hammer,
pliers, clamp,
level, wedge,
ruler, plane,
pencil, chalk,
tweezers,
plane,
scissors

Uses

clamp
drill holes
measure
cutting
pounding
building

Theme Goals

Through participating in the experiences provided by this theme, the children may learn

1. Types of tools
2. Names of common tools
3. Uses of tools
4. Tool safety

Concepts for the Children to Learn

1. Something that helps you do work is called a tool.
2. Tools can be electric or hand-powered.
3. Tools are helpful when building.
4. Pliers, tweezers, and clamps hold things.
5. Tools can be used for measuring, cutting, pounding, and building.
6. Tools can also be used for drilling holes and clamping.
7. Drills, nails, and screws make holes.
8. Planes, saws, and scissors cut materials.
9. Hammers and screwdrivers are used to put in and remove nails and screws.
10. A level and plane are tools to help make wood straight.
11. A wrench is used to open or tighten things.
12. A wedge is used to split materials.
13. Rulers are used for measuring.
14. To be safe, tools need to be handled with care.
15. Goggles should be worn to protect our eyes when using tools.
16. Pencils and chalk are marking tools.
17. After use, tools need to be put away and stored.
18. Some tools are made for left-handed people.
19. Other tools are for right-handed people.

Vocabulary

1. **clamp**—a tool used to join or hold things.
2. **drill**—a tool that cuts holes.
3. **hammer**—a tool used to insert or remove objects such as nails.
4. **plane**—a tool used for shaving wood.
5. **pliers**—a tool used for holding.
6. **ruler**—a measuring tool.
7. **saw**—a cutting tool with sharp edges.
8. **screwdriver**—a tool that turns screws.
9. **tool**—an object to help us.
10. **wedge**—a tool used for splitting.
11. **wrench**—a tool that opens and tightens things.

Bulletin Board

The purpose of this bulletin board is to develop awareness of tool types, as well as to foster visual discrimination skills. A shadow tool match bulletin board can be constructed by drawing six or seven tool pieces on tagboard. See the illustration. These pieces can be colored and then cut out. Next, trace the tools on black construction paper to make shadows of each piece. These shadow pieces can be attached to the bulletin board. Magnet pieces can be applied to both the shadows and the colored tool pieces. Otherwise, a pushpin can be placed above the shadow and a hole can be punched in the colored tool piece. The children can match the colored tool piece to its corresponding-shaped shadow.

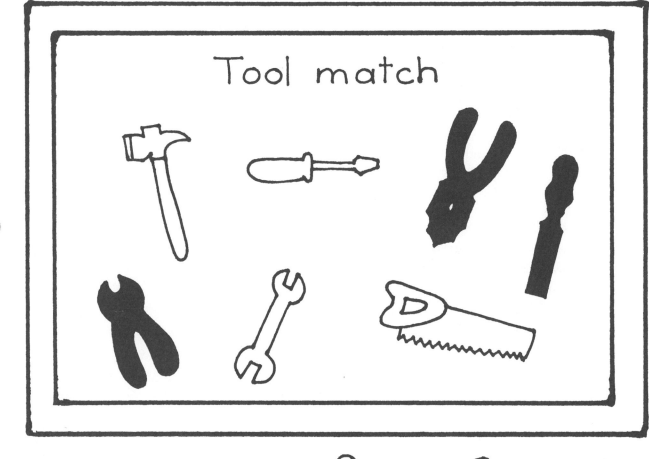

Tool match

CONSTRUCTION TOOLS

Family Letter

Dear Families,

Construction tools will be the focus of our next curriculum unit. This unit will help your child become more aware of many kinds of tools, their purposes, and tool safety. While exploring the classroom activities, the children will have opportunities to use many hand tools at the woodworking bench.

AT SCHOOL

Some of the activities the children will participate in include:

- painting with screwdrivers and wrenches
- exploring wood shavings in the sensory table
- setting up a mechanic's shop where the children can pretend to fix cars
- a visit on Wednesday from Mr. Smith, a local shoe repairman. Mr. Smith will show us the tools and techniques he uses to repair shoes.
- On Friday, Bob the builder will show us how to use woodworking tools.

AT HOME

To develop language skills, recall with your child the tools you use in your home—from cooking and cleaning tools to gardening tools. Count the number of tools that are in each room of your house. Which room contains the most tools? This will promote the mathematical concepts of rational counting and vocabulary concepts of most and least.

Have fun with your child!

Cooking

"Hands On" Cookies

3 cups brown sugar
3 cups margarine or butter
6 cups oatmeal
1 tablespoon baking soda
3 cups flour

Place all of the ingredients in a bowl. Let the children use clean, child-size wooden hammers to mash and knead. Form into small balls and place on ungreased cookie sheet. Butter the bottom of a glass. Dip the bottom of the glass into a saucer with sugar. Use the glass to flatten the balls. Bake in an oven preheated to 350 degrees for 10 to 12 minutes. Makes 15 dozen.

Dramatic Play

1. The Carpenter

Place a carpentry box with scissors, rulers, and masking tape in the woodworking area. Also, provide large cardboard boxes and paint, if desired.

2. Shoemaker Store

Set up a shoemaker's store. Provide the children with shoes, toy hammers, smocks, cash registers, and play money. The children can act out mending, buying, and selling shoes.

Learning to use the correct tool for the job is important.

Arts and Crafts

1. Rulers

Set rulers and paper on the table. The children can then experiment creating lines and geometric shapes.

2. Tool Print

Pour a small amount of thick, colored tempera paint in a flat pan. Also, provide the children with miniature tools such as wrenches, screwdrivers, and paper. The children then can place the tools in the paint pan, remove them, and print on paper.

Field Trips/ Resource People

1. Shoe Repair Store

Visit a shoe repair store. Observe a shoe being repaired.

2. Woodworker

Invite into the classroom a parent or other person who enjoys woodworking as a hobby.

Fingerplays

Carpenter's Hammer

The carpenter's hammer goes rap, rap, tap
(make hammer motion)
And his saw goes see, saw, see.
(make saw motions)
He planes and measures and hammers and saws
(act out each one)
While he builds a house for me.
(draw house with index fingers)

Johnny's Hammer

Johnny works with one hammer, one hammer,
one hammer.
Johnny works with one hammer, then he works
with two.

Say the same words adding one hammer each
time. Children are to pretend to hammer using
various body parts.

Verse 1:   one hand hitting leg.
Verse 2:   two hands hitting legs.
Verse 3:   use motions for verses 1 and 2,
            plus tap one foot.
Verse 4:   verses 1, 2, and 3 plus tap other
            foot.
Verse 5:   verses 1 to 4, plus nod head. At the
            end of verse 5 say, "Then he goes to
            sleep," and place both hands by
            side of head.

You can also change the name used in the fingerplay to include names of children in your
classroom.

The Cobbler

Cobbler, cobbler, mend my shoe.
(point to shoe)
Get it done by half past two.
(hold up two fingers)
Half past two is much too late.
Get it done by half past eight.
(hold up eight fingers)

Group Time

(Games, Language)

1. **Tool of the Day**

   Each day of this unit, introduce a "tool of the
   day." Explain how each tool is used and who
   uses it. If possible, leave the tool out for
   children to use on the woodworking bench.

   Caution: The use of tools needs to be closely
   supervised.

2. **Thank-You Letter**

   Using a pencil as a tool, let the children dictate
   a thank-you note to any resource person or
   field trip site coordinator who has contributed
   to the program.

Large Muscle

The Workbench

In the woodworking area place various tools,
wood, and goggles for the children to use. It
is very important to discuss the safety and
limits used when at the workbench before this
activity. An extra adult is helpful to supervise
this area.

Math

1. **Use of Rulers**

   Discuss how rulers are used. Provide children
   with rulers so that they may measure various
   objects in the classroom. Allow them to
   compare the lengths. Also, measure each
   child and construct a chart including each
   child's height.

2. Weighing Tools

Place scales and a variety of tools on the math table. Let the children explore weighing the tools.

Music

1. "This Is the Way"

(*Sing to the tune of* "Mulberry Bush")

This is the way we saw our wood,
  saw our wood, saw our wood.
This is the way we saw our wood,
  so early in the morning.

Other verses: pound our nails
                  drill a hole
                  use a screwdriver

2. "Johnny Works with One Hammer"

Johnny works with one hammer,
One hammer, one hammer.
  (make hammering motion with right hand)
Johnny works with one hammer
Then he works with two.
Johnny works with two hammers . . .
  (motion with left and right hands)
Johnny works with three hammers . . .
  (motion with both hands and right foot)
Johnny work with four hammers . . .
  (motion with both hands and both feet)
Johnny works with five hammers . . .
  (motion with both hands and feet and with head)
Then he goes to bed.

Science

1. Exploring Levels

Place levels and wood scraps on a table for the children to explore while being closely supervised.

2. Hammers

Collect a variety of hammers, various-sized nails, and wood scraps or styrofoam. Allow the children to practice pounding using the different tools and materials.

3. The Wide World of Rulers

Set up a display with different types and sizes of rulers. Paper and pencils can also be added to create interest.

Sensory

1. Scented Play Dough

Prepare play dough and add a few drops of extract such as peppermint, anise, or vanilla. Also, collect a variety of scissors, and place in the art area with the play dough.

2. Wood Shavings

Place wood shavings in the sensory table along with scoops and pails.

Social Studies

1. Tool Safety

Discuss the safe use of tools. Allow the children to help decide what classroom rules are necessary for using tools. Make a chart containing these rules to display in the wood-working area.

2. Helper Chart

Design a helper chart for the children to assist with cleanup and care of the classroom tools. Each day select new children to assist, assuring that everyone gets a turn. To participate, the children can be responsible for cleaning the dirty tools and putting them away.

Science Materials and Equipment

Teachers need to continuously provide science materials for the classroom. Materials that can be collected include:

acorns and other nuts
aluminum foil
ball bearings
balloons
binoculars
bird nests
bones
bowls and cups
cocoons
corks
de-corded clock
dishpans
drinking straws
drums
egg cartons
eggbeaters
eyedroppers and basters
fabric scraps
filter paper
flashlights
flowers
gears
insect nests
insects
jacks
kaleidoscopes

locks and keys
magnets of varying strengths, sizes
magnifying glasses with good lenses
marbles
measuring cups and spoons
microscopes
milk cartons
mirrors—all sizes
moths
musical instruments
newspapers
nails, screws, bolts
paper bags
paper of various types
paper rolls and spools
plants
plastic bags
plastic containers with lids—many sizes
plastic tubing
pots, pans, trays, muffin tins
prisms
pulleys
rocks

rubber tubing
rulers
safety goggles—child size
sandpaper
scales
scissors—assorted sizes
screen wire
sieves, sifters, and funnels
seeds
spatulas
sponges
stones
string
styrofoam
tape
thermometers
tongs and tweezers
tools—hammer, pliers
tuning forks
waxed paper
weeds
wheels
wood and other building materials

Books

The following books can be used to complement this theme:

Barton, Byron. (1995). *Tools*. New York: HarperCollins. (Board book.)

Brady, Peter. (1996). *Bulldozers*. Mankato, MN: Bridgestone Books.

Gibbons, Gail. (1990). *How a House Is Built*. New York: Holiday House.

Hoban, Tana. (1997). *Construction Zone*. New York: Greenwillow.

Klinting, Lars. (1996). *Bruno the Carpenter*. New York: Holt.

Miller, Margaret. (1990). *Who Uses This?* New York: Greenwillow.

Morris, Ann. (1992). *Tools*. Photos by Ken Heyman. New York: Lothrop, Lee & Shepard.

Neitzel, Shirley. (1997). *The House I'll Build for the Wren*. Illus. by Nancy Winslow Parker. New York: Greenwillow.

Radford, Derek. (1994). *Building Machines and What They Do*. Reprint ed. Cambridge, MA: Candlewick Press.

Robbins, Ken. (1993). *Power Machines*. New York: Holt.

Rockwell, Anne F. (1990). *Toolbox*. New York: Aladdin.

Wallace, John. (1997). *Building a House with Mr. Bumble*. Cambridge, MA: Candlewick Press.

Winne, Joanne. (2001). *A Day with a Carpenter*. New York: Children's Press.

Multimedia

The following multimedia products can be used to complement this theme:

Big Job [CD-ROM]. (1995). Bethesda, MD: Discovery Communications, Inc.

Let's Build a House [video]. (1996). San Diego, CA: Video Connections.

Macaulay, David. *The Way Things Work* [CD-ROM]. (1994). New York: Dorling Kindersley Multimedia.

There Goes a Bulldozer [video]. (1993). Van Nuys, CA: Live Action Video for Kids.

Recordings and Song Titles

The following recordings can be used to complement this theme:

"Cement Mixer," "Ding Dong Digger (The Power Shovel)." (1997). *Cars, Trucks and Trains*. Long Branch, NJ: Kimbo Educational.

"The Community Helper Hop" (Construction Workers)—Builders, Carpenters, Bricklayers, Plasterers, Painters, Plumbers, Electricians. (1996). *People in Our Neighborhood*. Long Branch, NJ: Kimbo Educational.

THEME

18

Uses

packaging liquids/solids
carrying items

Containers

Types

boxes
jars
cans
bags
bottles
pockets
baskets
bowls

Materials

glass
aluminum
steel
cardboard
paper
plastic
fabric
wood

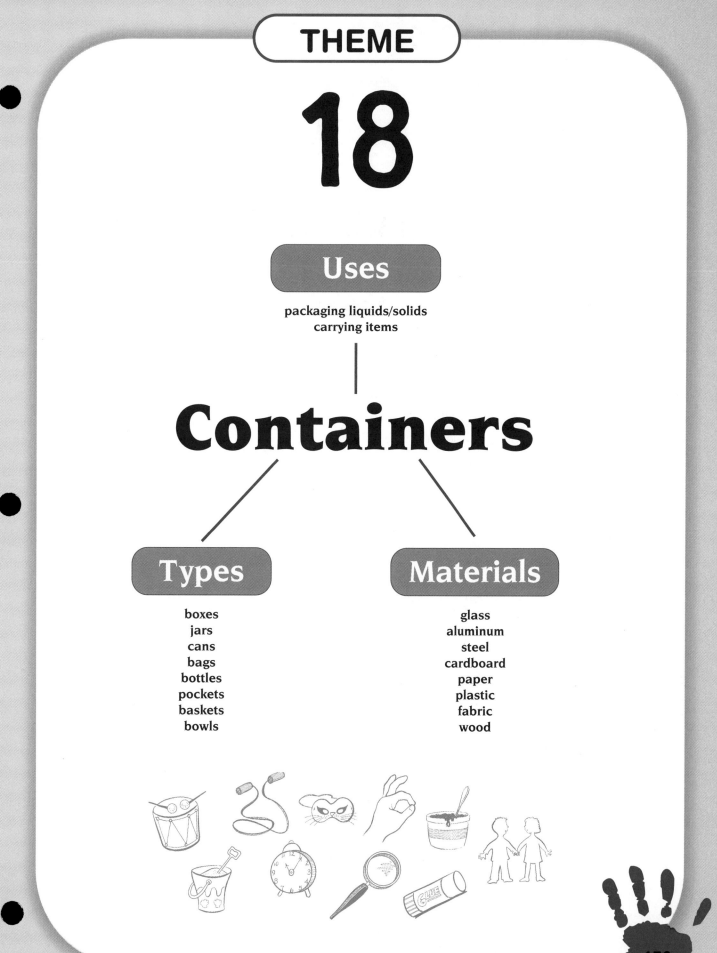

Theme Goals

Through participating in the experiences provided by this theme, the children may learn

1. Types of containers
2. Materials used to make containers
3. Container uses

Concepts for the Children to Learn

1. There are many kinds of containers.
2. Boxes, jars, cans, bags, and bottles are containers.
3. Bowls, baskets, and pockets are containers.
4. Containers are used to hold some things.
5. Containers can be made from many materials.
6. Boxes are usually made from cardboard and paper.
7. Cans are made from aluminum or steel.
8. Fruit juice, soup, and paint are stored in cans.
9. Jars are usually made from glass.
10. Bags can be paper, plastic, or fabric.
11. Bottles are made from glass or plastic.
12. Bottles usually have caps on them.
13. Pockets are usually made from fabric.
14. Baskets can be made from wood or plastic.
15. Many items are sold in containers.

Vocabulary

1. **bag**—container made of paper, cloth, or plastic that can be closed at the top.
2. **basket**—a container used to hold objects and foods.
3. **bottle**—container for holding liquids that has a narrow neck that can be closed with a stopper.
4. **bowl**—a deep dish.
5. **can**—a container that can hold food or paint.
6. **container**—a box, jar, can, and so forth, used to hold something.
7. **pocket**—a small bag sewn into clothing.

Bulletin Board

The purpose of this bulletin board is to promote the development of visual discrimination, hand-eye coordination, problem-solving, and memory skills. Create the containers by sketching them onto heavy tagboard. Use felt-tip markers to add color and/or details. Laminate and cut out the containers. Trace the cutout container pieces onto black construction paper. Cut out these pieces and attach to the bulletin board. A magnet strip should be attached to the containers and the shadow pieces. The children can match each container shape to its shadow on the bulletin board.

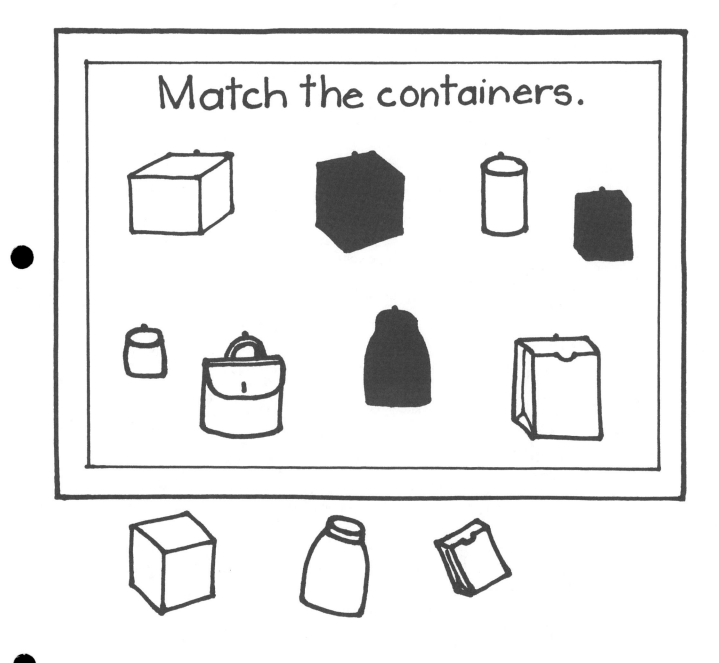

Family Letter

Dear Families,

Try to imagine a world without boxes, jars, bags, baskets, bowls, or pockets. It's hard to do! There are so many kinds of containers—we use them every day and probably never realize it. This week at school we will focus on the subject of containers. The children will learn about types of containers, typical materials used to make containers, and items that come in containers.

AT SCHOOL

As we learn about containers this week at school, the children will

- make prints with plastic berry baskets and paint in the art area

- work in our classroom grocery store set up in the dramatic play area. We could use your help. Please save and send empty, clean food containers to school. We will use the boxes, bottles, and jars as grocery items in the dramatic play area. Thank you.

- sort various containers by type and materials

PARENT INVOLVEMENT

If you have special containers reflecting your culture or heritage, we invite you to share them with our class. Please contact me so a time can be arranged for your visit. The children will enjoy having you share with us!

AT HOME

You can help your child make discoveries about containers. A few things to try include:

- Look in your refrigerator or kitchen and find containers. How many are boxes, cans, bottles, etc.?

- Make a milk carton bird feeder. Cut a large rectangle in the side of a half-gallon milk carton. Fill the bottom of the carton with birdseed. Hang the bird feeder outside where it can be observed.

- Find some books at the library about containers. A few to look for include:

  The Paper Bag Princess by Robert Munsch

  Katy-No-Pocket by Emmy Payne

  Pocket for Corduroy by Don Freeman

Have a good week!

Children develop hand-eye coordination skills by pouring liquids from one container to another.

Arts and Crafts

1. Basket Prints

Collect plastic berry baskets, construction paper, and paints. Pour paint(s) into shallow trays. Have the children dip the bottom of the plastic berry baskets in paint, and then press them on construction paper.

2. Jar Prints

Save and clean baby food jars. Provide the jars, construction paper, and paint(s). Pour the paint(s) into individual trays, just covering the bottoms. Children can turn the jars over and dip the tops of the baby food jars in the paint, and then press them on their paper to create prints.

3. Zipper Seal Plastic Bag Painting

Materials needed include tempera paints and small zipper seal plastic bags—one per child. Ask each child which two colors of paint he or she would like. Put a small amount of the two colors of paint into a zipper seal plastic bag. Carefully seal the bags. Apply cellophane or masking tape for added safety. The children can then squeeze their bags to mix the colors. The bag can be placed on a table and fingers can be used to fingerpaint without getting messy.

4. Colored Salt Jars

Create several colors of salt (or sand) by adding teaspoons of tempera paint powder to bowls of salt. Stir well. Collect baby food jars and lids. To create a colored salt jar, the children spoon colored salt into the jar, creating layers of beautiful colors. Fill jars to the top and secure lid tightly. If desired, squeeze glue around the jar rim before placing lid on.

Cooking

1. Container Cookies

1/2 cup butter or margarine
1/2 cup shortening
1 cup sugar
1 egg

2 tablespoons milk
1/2 teaspoon vanilla
2 1/4 cups flour
1/2 teaspoon baking soda
1/2 teaspoon salt
Filling choices:
pie filling—any flavor
jam or jelly
chocolate chips
raisins
toasted coconut
sugar

Beat butter (or shortening) in a large mixing bowl with an electric mixer on medium speed, about 30 seconds. Add sugar and beat until fluffy. Add egg, milk, and vanilla. Beat well. In a medium mixing bowl, combine flour, baking soda, and salt. With electric mixer on low, gradually add the flour mixture to the butter mixture, beating well. Cover and chill dough in the freezer about 20 minutes or until firm to handle. Divide dough in half. Shape each half into a roll 3 inches thick and 3 inches long. Wrap in plastic wrap. Freeze at least 6 hours or up to 6 months.

When ready to bake the cookies, preheat oven to 375 degrees. Unwrap one roll of dough. Slice the roll crosswise to make 16 slices about 1/8-inch thick. Repeat with the other roll. Place half of the slices 2 inches apart on ungreased cookie sheets. In the center of the circles, place 2 teaspoons of desired filling(s). Top each with a plain slice of dough. Press a floured fork around the edges to seal well. Sprinkle with a little sugar.

Bake for 12 to 15 minutes or until edges are golden brown. Place cookies on rack to cool.

2. Butter in a Jar

Pour 1/3 cup of whipping cream in a clean small jar. Secure lid tightly. Allow children to take turns shaking the jar until a lump of butter forms. This will take several minutes. Pour off liquid, add a dash of salt, and stir. Spread butter on crackers to enjoy.

3. Pita Pocket Sandwiches

Use pita bread to create yummy pocket sandwiches. Cut rounds of pita bread in half, creating pocket-shaped pieces. Fill with favorite sandwich ingredients.

Try

sloppy joes
tuna salad
ham and cheese

Dramatic Play

Grocery Store

To create a grocery store in the dramatic play area, provide props such as a cash register, posters of various foods, smocks or shirts, paper and plastic grocery bags, and empty, clean food containers. A note can be sent home requesting help with this project. Set food containers on shelves or in baskets to resemble a grocery store.

Fingerplays

There Was a Little Turtle
by *Vachel Lindsay*

There was a little turtle,
    (make small circle with hands)
He lived in a box.
    (make box with both hands)

He swam in a puddle,
    (wiggle hands)
He climbed on the rocks.
    (climb fingers of one hand up over the other)

He snapped at a mosquito,
    (clap hands)
He snapped at a flea,
    (repeat)
He snapped at a minnow,
    (repeat)
He snapped at me!
    (point to self)
He caught the mosquito,
    (catching motion with hands and arms)
He caught the flea,
    (repeat)
He caught the minnow,
    (repeat)

But he didn't catch me!
(shake head from side to side)

Group Time

(Games, Language)

1. Mystery Box

Collect a box with a lid. Color or decorate as desired. Secretly place an object inside the box. At group time, begin by saying, "There is something in my box. What do you think it might be?" Give identifying clues until the children guess what the object is.

2. Cookie Jar

Have the children sit on the floor, with their legs crossed, in a circle formation. The children should repeat a rhythmic chant with the teacher while clapping their hands together and then clapping their hands on their thighs. The chant is as follows:

Someone took a cookie from the cookie jar.
Who took a cookie from the cookie jar?
Mara took a cookie from the cookie jar.
(Mara): Who me?
(All): Yes, you!
(Mara): Couldn't be!
(All): Then who?
(Mara, naming another child): ———— took a cookie from the cookie jar.

Use each child's name.

3. Hiding Game

Collect three small boxes. Set out the boxes in a row and place a bean or button under one of the boxes. While the children watch, move the order of the cups several times. Ask the children to guess which cup the bean is under. The bean or button can be hidden again and the game repeated.

Large Muscle

Box Obstacle Course

Collect large cardboard boxes. Open the tops and bottoms and lay boxes on their sides to create tunnels. Place the boxes in a maze-type course and let children discover ways to complete the course. They could run, walk, crawl, or hop from beginning to end.

Math

1. Container Sort

Collect various containers and place in a laundry basket. Encourage children to find ways to sort the containers. Containers could be sorted by type, size, or construction material.

2. Pocket Count

During a group time, have the children individually stand up and take note of the pockets on their clothes. Assist in counting the number of pockets each child has. If appropriate, the information could be recorded and put on a graph to be displayed. Repeat the activity on a different day and compare the results.

3. How Many?

Place a number of small objects (such as paper clips, dice, marbles, buttons) in a clear plastic bag or a jar. Let children guess how many of the objects are in the bag. Count the objects together. Repeat with a different number of objects.

4. Container Stack

Roll a die. The number that is rolled is the number of containers to be stacked. Continue rolling and stacking. See how many containers can be stacked before the containers fall.

Music

1. "I Have Something in My Pocket"
(*traditional*)

I have something in my pocket that belongs
    across my face.
I keep it very close at hand in a most convenient
    place.
I'm sure you couldn't guess it if you'd take a
    long, long while.
So, I'll take it out and put it on,
It's a great, big, happy smile.

2. "Tony Has Three Pockets"
(*Sing to the tune of* "Mary Wore a Red Dress")

Tony has three pockets,
Three pockets, three pockets.
Tony has three pockets,
On his shirt today.
Insert individual children's names and substitute
    articles of clothing that could have pockets,
    such as a dress, slacks, jacket, etc.

3. "A Tisket, a Tasket"
(*traditional*)

A tisket, a tasket, a green and yellow basket.
I wrote a letter to my love
And on the way I dropped it.
I dropped it, I dropped it
And on the way I dropped it.
I wrote a letter to my love
And on the way I dropped it.

Science

1. Insect Keeper

Collect milk cartons or similar-sized cardboard boxes. For each insect keeper, cut a rectangle out of each side of a clean carton or box. Glue or tape the top closed. Decorate if desired. After an insect or two are found, put the insects, along with a twig and grass, in the carton. Quickly insert box in the leg portion of an old nylon stocking (or cover with netting) and use a twist tie or rubber band to fasten the top.

2. Rubber Band Guitar

Each child will need a small box or carton, such as an individual cereal box, check box, or half-pint milk carton. For each "guitar" cut a rectangle in one side of a box or carton. Decorate as desired. Wrap each container with four or five rubber bands. The children can pluck or strum the rubber bands to create sounds.

3. Wave Jar

Fill a clear jar half full with water. Add a few drops of food coloring, if desired. Pour mineral oil to fill the jar. Secure the lid tightly. Watch what happens as the jar is gently tilted back and forth. Individual wave jars can be made using baby food jars.

4. Sound Jars or Boxes

Collect 10 film canisters or 10 identical small boxes. Fill the containers, as pairs, with five different materials such as popcorn kernels, pennies, sand, nails, cotton balls, rubber bands, paper clips, etc. Secure caps or lids and place containers on a table. Encourage children to shake the containers to find the matching sound containers.

5. Musical Jars

Fill five or six identical-sized jars with varying amounts of water. Add drops of food coloring to water if desired. Encourage children to gently tap the sides of the jars with a metal spoon to create sounds. The jars will produce low to high sounds. Some children may be able to arrange the jars from lowest to highest sounds.

6. Fish in a Bottle

Save and clean a 2-liter plastic soda bottle. Fill the bottle one-quarter full with water. Add a few drops of blue food coloring to the water and swirl to mix. Barely blow up some small balloons and tie ends closed. Use a permanent marker to draw eyes, gills, and mouths on balloons to make them look like fish. Push the balloons into the bottle and securely fasten the cap of the bottle. Hold the bottle on its side and it will look like fish in the water. Gently rock bottle back and forth to create waves.

Sensory

The following materials can be added to the sensory table:

- plastic bottles, funnels, and colored water
- plastic jars, animals, and sand
- berry baskets, plastic zoo animals, and grains
- zipper-seal plastic bags, scoops, and sand

Books

The following books can be used to complement this theme:

Boivin, Kelly. (1991). *What's in a Box?* Illus. by Janice Skivington. Chicago: Children's Press.

Carter, David A. (1990). *More Bugs in Boxes Pop-Up Book: A Pop-Up Book about Color.* New York: Simon & Schuster.

Cressy, Judith and Edward Heina. (2001). *What Can You Do with a Paper Bag?* Illus. by Edward Heina. San Francisco: Chronicle Books.

King, Stephen Michael. (1996). *A Special Kind of Love.* New York: Scholastic.

Lillegard, Dee. (1992). *Sitting in My Box.* Illus. by Jon Agee. New York: Puffin. (Pbk.)

Rau, Dana Meachen. (1997). *A Box Can Be Many Things.* Illus. by Paige Bellin-Frye. Chicago: Children's Press.

Stevenson, James. (1997). *The Mud Flat Mystery.* New York: Greenwillow.

Stock, Catherine. (1994). *Sophie's Bucket.* Orlando, FL: Harcourt Brace. (Pbk.)

Tibo, Gilles. (1995). *Simon and His Boxes.* Plattsburgh, NY: Tundra Books.

Westcott, Nadine. (1990). *There's a Hole in the Bucket.* New York: Harper & Row.

Multimedia

The following multimedia product can be used to complement this theme:

Carter, David A. *How Many Bugs in a Box?* [CD-ROM]. (1996). Simon & Schuster Interactive.

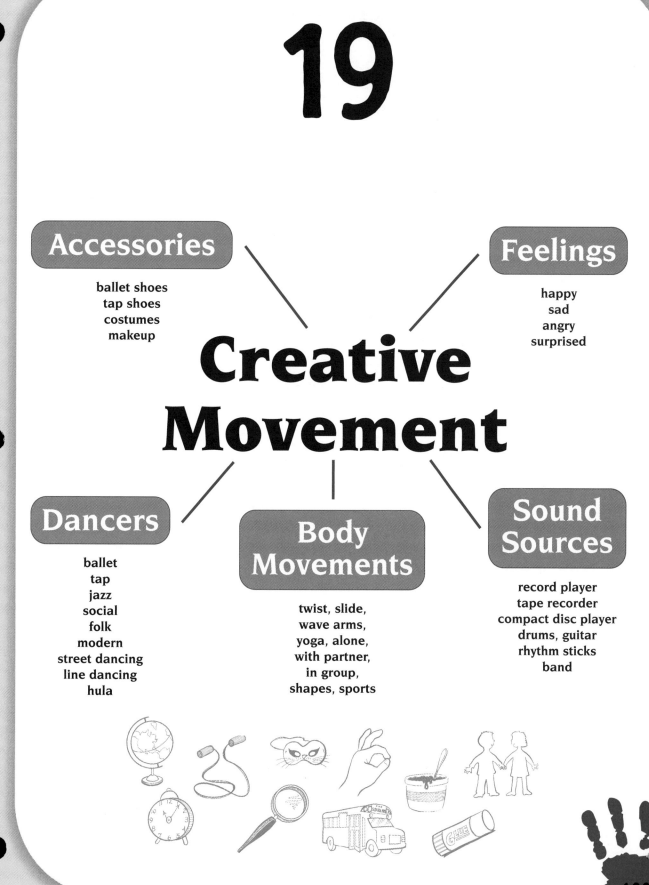

Creative Movement

Accessories

ballet shoes
tap shoes
costumes
makeup

Feelings

happy
sad
angry
surprised

Dancers

ballet
tap
jazz
social
folk
modern
street dancing
line dancing
hula

Body Movements

twist, slide,
wave arms,
yoga, alone,
with partner,
in group,
shapes, sports

Sound Sources

record player
tape recorder
compact disc player
drums, guitar
rhythm sticks
band

Theme Goals

Through participating in the experiences provided by this theme, the children may learn

1. Creative movement accessories
2. Creative movement sound sources
3. Body movements used in creative movement
4. Expression of feelings through creative movement
5. Types of dancers

Concepts for the Children to Learn

1. People can dance to music.
2. The record player, tape recorder, compact disc player, and drums are all sound sources used for dance.
3. The guitar, rhythm sticks, and a band are also sound sources for creative movement.
4. Dancing and moving can be done alone, with a partner, or in a group.
5. Our bodies can move in many different ways.
6. Ballet, tap, jazz, and social are some types of dances.
7. Happy, sad, angry, and surprised are feelings that can be expressed through dance.
8. There are many types of dances.
9. Some dancers wear special costumes and makeup.
10. Ballet and tap dancers wear special shoes.
11. Ballet, tap, and jazz are types of dances.
12. Folk, modern, street, and line are other types of dances.
13. Our bodies can move to the sound of drums, guitars, and rhythm sticks.
14. We can twist, slide, and wave our arms during dance.

Vocabulary

1. **ballet**—movement that usually tells a story.
2. **dance**—a pattern of body movements.
3. **movement**—change in body position.
4. **music**—sounds made by instruments or voices.

190

THEME 19

Bulletin Board

The purpose of this bulletin board is to promote the development of one-to-one correspondence skills and to match a set to a written numeral. Construct tank tops, each of a different color, from a sheet of tagboard. See the illustration. Print a numeral that would be developmentally appropriate for the group of children on each tank top. Draw a corresponding number of black dots below each numeral. Construct a tutu ruffle from white tagboard for each top. Place colored dots on each ruffle. Trace ruffles onto black construction paper. Laminate all pieces. Staple tank tops and shadow ruffles to bulletin board. The children can match the ruffles with dots to the corresponding tank top, using holes in white ruffles and pushpins in shadow ruffles.

Family Letter

Dear Families,

Children love to dance, and they are constantly on the move. We will begin a curriculum unit on creative movement. Throughout the classroom activities the children will discover the different ways our bodies move, and also learn about various forms of dance. Some of the activities include:

- singing songs and moving to music
- dancing in the dance studio that will be set up in the dramatic play area
- watching other people move
- participating in an aerobics class

PARENTAL INVOLVEMENT

If you have any special ethnic dances you enjoy, we invite you to share them with our class. Please contact me so a time for your visit can be arranged. The children will enjoy having you visit our class and learning new types of dances.

FIELD TRIP

On Thursday, at 2:30 p.m., we will be taking a bus to a dance studio. At the studio, we will observe dancers and learn a few steps from a dance instructor. To assist with the trip, we need several parents to accompany us. Please call the school if you are available.

AT HOME

As your child develops, you will observe increased control and interest in perfecting and improving motor skills. To foster the development of large muscle skills, balance, and body coordination, provide opportunities each day for vigorous play. Give suggestions such as "How fast can you hop?" "How far can you hop on one foot?" etc. Also, ask your child to walk on a curved line, a straight line, or a balance beam.

Enjoy your child!

Exercise can be a form of creative movement.

Cooking

1. Orange Buttermilk Smoothie

1 quart buttermilk
3 cups orange juice
1/2 teaspoon cinnamon
1/4 cup honey

Blend in a blender until the mixture is smooth. Enjoy!

2. Indian Flat Bread

2 cups all-purpose flour
1/4 cup unflavored yogurt
1 egg, slightly beaten
1 1/2 teaspoons baking powder
1 teaspoon sugar
1/4 teaspoon salt
1/4 teaspoon baking soda
1/2 cup milk
vegetable oil
poppy seeds

Mix all ingredients except milk, vegetable oil, and poppy seeds. Stir in enough milk to make a soft dough. Turn dough onto lightly floured surface. Knead until smooth, about 5 minutes. Place in greased bowl; turn greased side up. Cover and let rest in warm place 3 hours.

Divide dough into 6 or 8 equal parts. Flatten each part on lightly floured surface, rolling it into a 6-inch × 4-inch leaf shape about 1/4 inch thick. Brush with vegetable oil; sprinkle with poppy seeds.

Place 2 cookie sheets in oven; heat oven to 450 degrees. Remove hot cookie sheets from oven; place breads on cookie sheets. Bake until firm, 6 to 8 minutes. Makes 6 to 8 breads.

Note: From *Betty Crocker's International Cookbook*, 1980, New York: Random House. Reprinted with permission.

Arts and Crafts

1. Stencils

The teacher can construct stencils from tagboard. Shapes such as shoes, ballerinas, circles, and so forth, can be made and added to the art table for use during self-selected activity periods.

2. Musical Painting

Provide a tape recorder with headphones and a tape of children's music or classical music at the easel. The children can listen and move their brushes to the music if desired.

Dramatic Play

1. Dance Studio

Add to the dramatic play area tap shoes, tutus, ballet shoes, tights, and leotards. Provide a record player with records or tape player with tapes.

2. Fitness Gym

Add to the dramatic play area a small mat, headbands, wristbands, sweatshirts, sweatpants, leotards, and music.

Field Trips/ Resource People

1. Field Trips

- dance studio
- health club
- gymnasium

2. Resource People

Invite the following people to class to talk with the children:

- a dancer or dance instructor
- gymnast
- aerobics instructor

Fingerplays

Hands on Shoulders

Hands on shoulders (follow actions described
   for each line)
Hands on knees.
Hands in front of you, if you please.
Touch your shoulders,
Now your nose,
Now your head and now your toes.
Hands go up high in the air,
Now touch your ears,
Then touch your hair.
Hands way up high just like before.
Now clap your hands,
One, two, three, four!

Clap, Two, Three, Four!

Clap, two, three, four, five, six, seven.
   (clap hands)
Shake, two, three, four, five, six, seven.
   (shake fingers)
Slap, two, three, four, five, six, seven.
   (slap knees)
Roll, two, three, four, five, six, seven.
   (rotate hands over each)
Snap, two, three, four, five, six, seven.
   (snap fingers)
Tap, two, three, four, five, six, seven.
   (pound fists)
Push, two, three, four, five, six, seven.
   (push hands forward)
Clap, two, three, four, five, six, seven.
   (clap hands)

My Wiggles

I can reach high. (stretch up high)
I can reach low. (touch the ground)
I'll touch my head. (touch head)
And then my toes. (touch toes)
I'll wiggle my fingers. (move fingers)
And touch them, too. (touch fingers)
I'm having fun. (point to self)
And so are you! (point to another person)
We'll stretch up to the ceiling. (stretch up high)
And reach out to the wall. (reach arms to
   the side)
We'll bend to touch our knees and toes.
   (touch knees, then toes)
Then stand up straight and tall.
   (stand up straight)

Taller, Smaller

When I stretch up, I feel so tall. (stand up and
   reach hands up into the air)
When I bend down, I feel so small. (crouch down)
Taller, taller, taller, taller. (slowly stand and
   raise arms)
Smaller, smaller, smaller, smaller. (slowly
   crouch down)
Into a tiny ball. (tuck in arms and head)

Group Time

(Games, Language)

1. Balloon Bounce

Blow up balloons for the children to use at group time. Play music and have children bounce the balloons up in the air. Let the balloons float to the ground when the music ends. Supervision is required for this activity. Broken balloons should be immediately removed from the environment.

2. Toy Movements

Form a circle and move like different toys. Try to include as many actual toys as you can, so that the children can observe each toy moving, and then can more easily pretend to be that toy.

- jack-in-the-box
- wind-up dolls
- roll like a ball
- skates

3. Rag Doll

Repeat the following poem as the child creates a dance with a rag doll:

If I were a rag doll
And I belonged to you,
Whenever I would try to dance,
This is what I'd do.

Large Muscle

1. Streamer/Music Activity

In the music area provide streamers. Play a variety of music, allowing the children, if desired, to move to the different rhythms.

2. Do As I Say

Provide the children verbal cues for moving. For example, say, "Move like you are sad," "Show me that you are tired," "You just received a special present," or "Show me how you feel."

3. Animal Movement

Ask a child to act out the way a certain animal moves. Examples include frog, spider, caterpillar, butterfly, etc.

4. Balance

Add a balance beam or balance strip to the indoor or outdoor environment.

5. Roly-Poly

The children can stretch their bodies out on the floor. When touched by a teacher, the child rolls into a tight ball.

6. Dancing Cloud

Using an inflated white balloon or ball, let the children stand in a circle and bounce or hit it to each other.

7. Obstacle Course

Set up an obstacle course indoors or outdoors depending on the weather. Let the children move their bodies in many different ways. They can run or crawl through the course. Older children may enjoy hopping or skipping.

Math

1. Matching Leotards to Hangers

Using plastic hangers, prepare a numeral on each of the hangers. Provide the children with a box of leotards. Have a printed numeral on each. Encourage the children to match the numbered leotard with the identically numbered hanger.

2. Following Steps

Using tagboard, cut out some left feet and right feet. Write the numerals from one to ten on the feet and arrange them in numerical order. Place the footprints on the floor, securing them with masking tape. Encourage the children to begin the walk on the numeral one and continue in the correct sequence.

3. Ballet Puzzle

Purchase a large poster of a ballet dancer. Laminate the poster or cover it with clear contact paper. Cut the poster into several large shapes. Place the puzzle in the manipulative area. During self-selected play periods, the children can reconstruct the puzzle.

Movement Activities

Listen to the Drum

Accessory: drum
fast
slow
heavy
soft
big
small

Choose a Partner

Make a big shape
go over
go under
go through
go around

To Become Aware of Time

Run very fast
Walk very slowly
Jump all over the floor quickly
Sit down on the floor slowly
Slowly grow up as tall as you can
Slowly curl up on the floor as
  small as possible

To Become Aware of Space

Lift your leg up in front of you
Lift it up backward, sideways
Lift your leg and step forward,
  backward, sideways, and
  around and around
Reach up to the ceiling
Stretch to touch the walls
Punch down to the floor

To Become Aware of Weight

To feel the difference between heavy and light, the child should experiment with his own body force.

Punch down to the floor hard
Lift your arms up slowly
  and gently
Stomp on the floor
Walk on tiptoe
Kick out one leg as hard as
  you can
Very smoothly and lightly slide
  one foot along the floor

Moving Shapes

1. Try to move about like something huge and heavy: elephant, tugboat, bulldozer.
2. Try to move like something small and heavy: a fat frog, a heavy top.
3. Try moving like something big and light: a beach ball, a parachute, a cloud.
4. Try moving like something small and light: a feather, a snowflake, a flea, a butterfly.

Put Yourself Inside Something

(bottle, box, barrel)
You're *outside* of something—
  now get into it
You're *inside* of something—
  now get out of it
You're *underneath* something
You're *on top of* something
You're *beside* or *next to* something
You're *surrounded* by it

Pantomime

1. You're going to get a present. What is the shape of the box? How big is the box? Feel it. Hold it. Unwrap it. Take it out. Put it back in.
2. Think about an occupation. How does the worker act?
3. Show me that it is cold, hot.
4. You are two years old (sixteen, eighty, etc.)
5. Show me: It's very early in the morning, late in the afternoon.
6. Show me: What is the weather like?
7. Pretend you are driving, typing, raking leaves.
8. Take a partner. Pretend you're playing ball.

Science

1. Magnet Dancers

On a piece of tagboard, draw pictures of 3-inch dancers. Stickers or pictures from magazines can also be used. Cut the dancers out and attach paper clips to the back side. Use a small box and a magnet to make these dancers move. Hold the dancers up on one side of the box and move the dancer up by holding and moving a magnet on the other side of the box.

2. Kaleidoscopes

On the science table, put a number of kaleidoscopes. The tiny figures inside appear to be dancing.

3. Dancing Shoes

Place various types of dancing shoes at the science table. Let the children compare the shape, size, color, and texture of the shoes. The children may also enjoy trying the shoes on for size and dancing in them.

Social Studies

Social Dancing

Let each child choose a partner. Encourage the children to hold hands. Play music as a background, so the partners can move together.

Books

The following books can be used to complement this theme:

Asher, Sandy and Kathryn Brown. (2001). *Stella's Dancing Days*. Illus. by Kathryn Brown. San Diego, CA: Harcourt Brace.

Auch, Mary Jane. (1995). *Hen Lake*. New York: Holiday House.

Duvall, Jill D. (1997). *Meet Rory Hohenstein, a Professional Dancer*. Photos by Lili S. Duvall. Chicago: Children's Press.

Esbensen, Barbara Juster. (1995). *Dance with Me*. Illus. by Megan Lloyd. New York: HarperCollins.

Gauch, Patricia Lee. (1992). *Bravo, Tanya*. Illus. by Satomi Ichikawa. New York: Philomel Books.

Gauch, Patricia Lee. (1994). *Tanya and Emily in a Dance for Two*. Illus. by Satomi Ichikawa. New York: Philomel Books.

Gray, Libba Moore. (1995). *My Mama Had a Dancing Heart*. Illus. by Raul Colon. New York: Orchard Books.

Grimm, Jakob. (1996). *The Twelve Dancing Princesses*. Retold by Jane Ray. New York: Dutton.

Holabird, Katharine and Helen Craig. (2000). *Angelina and the Princess*. Illus. by Helen Craig. Middleton, WI: Pleasant Company.

Isadora, Rachel. (1993). *Lili at Ballet*. New York: G. P. Putnam.

Isadora, Rachel. (1997). *Lili Backstage*. New York: G. P. Putnam.

King, Sandra. (1993). *Shannon: An Ojibway Dancer*. Minneapolis, MN: Lerner Publications.

Kroll, Virginia L. (1996). *Can You Dance, Dalila?* Illus. by Nancy Carpenter. New York: Simon & Schuster.

Lee, Jeanne M. (1991). *Silent Lotus*. New York: Farrar, Straus & Giroux.

Loredo, Elizabeth. (1997). *Boogie Bones*. Illus. by Kevin Hawkes. New York: G. P. Putnam.

Lowery, Linda. (1995). *Twist with a Burger, Jitter with a Bug*. Boston: Houghton Mifflin.

O'Connor, Jane. (1993). *Nina, Nina Ballerina*. Illus. by DyAnne DiSalvo-Ryan. New York: Grosset & Dunlap.

Patrick, Denise Lewis. (1993). *Red Dancing Shoes*. Illus. by James E. Ransome. New York: Tambourine.

Schomp, Virginia. (1997). *If You Were a . . . Ballet Dancer.* Tarrytown, NY: Marshall Cavendish.

Sis, Peter. (2001). *Ballerina!* New York: Greenwillow.

Thomassie, Tynia. (1996). *Mimi's Tutu.* Illus. by Jan Spivey Gilchrist. New York: Scholastic.

Walsh, Ellen Stoll. (1993). *Hop Jump.* New York: Harcourt Brace.

Waters, Kate. (1990). *Lion Dancer: Ernie Wan's Chinese New Year.* New York: Scholastic.

Wilder, Laura Ingalls. (1994). *Dance at Grandpa's.* New York: HarperCollins. (Adapted from the *Little House* Books.)

Multimedia

The following multimedia products can be used to complement this theme:

All-Time Favorite Dances [compact disc or cassette]. (1991). Longbranch, NJ: Kimbo Educational.

Dance with Us: A Creative Movement Video [video]. (1994). Pleasantville, NY: Sunburst.

Jack, David. *David Jack . . . Live!: Makin' Music, Makin' Friends* [video]. (1991). Leucadia, CA: Ta-Dum Productions.

Jack, David. *Gotta Hop* [cassette]. (1990). Leucadia, CA: Ta-Dum Productions.

Jenkins, Ella. *Growing Up with Ella Jenkins: Rhythms, Songs and Rhymes* [cassette]. (1990). Rockville, MD: Smithsonian Folkways.

Stewart, Georgiana Liccione. *Children of the World: Multi-Cultural Rhythmic Activities* [cassette]. (1991). Long Branch, NJ: Kimbo Educational.

Recordings and Song Titles

The following recordings can be used to complement this theme:

A to Z, the Animals and Me. (1994). Long Branch, NJ: Kimbo Educational.

A World of Parachute Play. (1997). Long Branch, NJ: Kimbo Educational.

"Alligator Stomp." (2001). *Jack in the Box.* Lang Branch, NJ: Kimbo Educational.

Children of the World. (1991). Long Branch, NJ: Kimbo Educational.

"Cho, Cho, Cho." (2001). *Jack in the Box.* Long Branch, NJ: Kimbo Educational.

Dance Party Fun. (2001). Long Branch, NJ: Kimbo Educational.

Everybody Dance. (1993). Long Branch, NJ: Kimbo Educational.

Gotta Dance. (1996). Long Branch, NJ: Kimbo Educational.

Joining Hands in Other Lands. (1993). Long Branch, NJ: Kimbo Educational.

"Mexican Hat Dance." (2001). *Jack in the Box.* Long Branch, NJ: Kimbo Educational.

Motown Dances. (1998). Long Branch, NJ: Kimbo Educational.

Moving with Mozart. (1997). Long Branch, NJ: Kimbo Educational.

People in Our Neighborhood. (1996). Long Branch, NJ: Kimbo Educational.

Physical Ed. (2000). Mebourne, FL: The Learning Station.

Preschool Action Time. (1988). Long Branch, NJ: Kimbo Educational.

"Shake, Rattle and Roll." (2001). *Dance Party Fun.* Long Branch, NJ: Kimbo Educational.

"Shake, Rattle and Roll," "Peppermint Twist," "Whole Lotta Shakin'." (2000). *Bean Bag Rock & Roll.* Long Branch, NJ: Kimbo Educational.

"Stretch," "Stomp and Clap," "Side Slide," "Musical Hula Hoops," "Can You Keep Your Balance?" (2000). *Physical Ed.* Long Branch, NJ: Kimbo Educational.

Where Is Thumbkin? (1996). Long Branch, NJ: Kimbo Educational.

Yes, I Can Sing Songs with RONNO. (1994). Long Branch, NJ: Kimbo Educational.

20

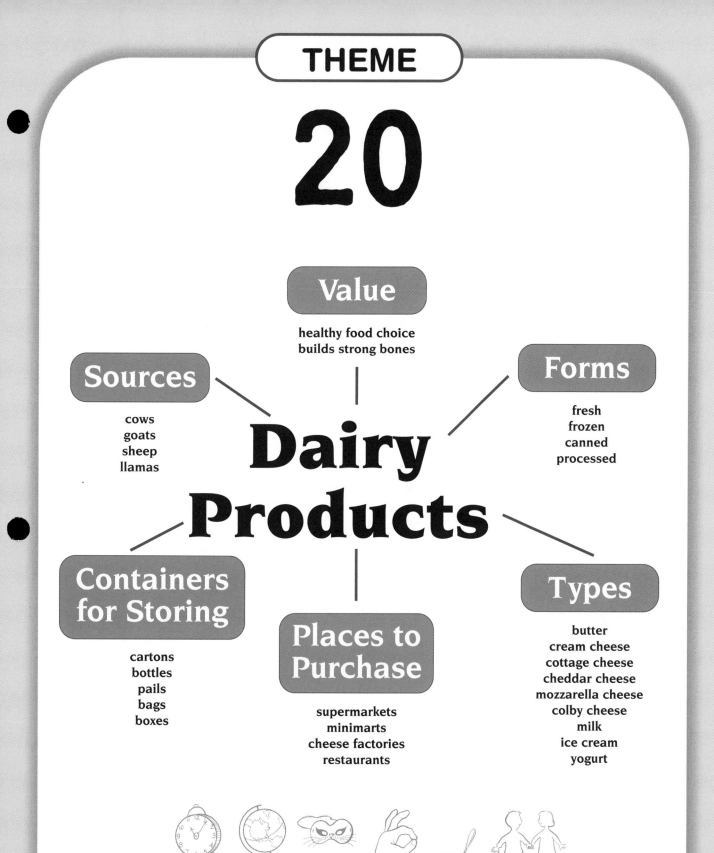

Value

healthy food choice
builds strong bones

Sources

cows
goats
sheep
llamas

Forms

fresh
frozen
canned
processed

Dairy Products

Containers for Storing

cartons
bottles
pails
bags
boxes

Places to Purchase

supermarkets
minimarts
cheese factories
restaurants

Types

butter
cream cheese
cottage cheese
cheddar cheese
mozzarella cheese
colby cheese
milk
ice cream
yogurt

Theme Goals

Through participating in the experiences provided by this theme, the children may learn

1. Sources of dairy products
2. Types of dairy products
3. Forms of dairy products
4. Places to purchase dairy products
5. Containers used to store dairy products
6. Value of dairy products

Concepts for the Children to Learn

1. Cows, goats, sheep, and llamas provide milk.
2. Milk can be used to make butter, cheese, ice cream, and yogurt.
3. There are many kinds of cheese, such as cottage cheese, cream cheese, cheddar cheese, mozzarella, and colby.
4. Dairy products can be purchased fresh, frozen, canned, or processed.
5. We can buy dairy products at supermarkets, minimarts, cheese factories, and restaurants.
6. Cartons, bottles, pails, bags, and boxes are used to store dairy products.
7. Dairy products are good, healthy choices.
8. Dairy products help build strong bones and bodies.

Vocabulary

1. **can**—to prepare food for future use.
2. **carton**—a box or container to hold food or other objects.
3. **cheese factory**—a place where cheese is made or sold.
4. **cream**—the yellowish part of milk.
5. **dairy product**—a product made from milk.
6. **frozen**—food that is kept cold.
7. **minimart**—a very small store.
8. **yogurt**—a milk product that can be flavored with fruit.

Bulletin Board

The purpose of this bulletin board is to help children become aware of ice cream as a dairy product, as well as recognize the printed word. This is designed as a check-in or attendance bulletin board. Each child is provided a bulletin board piece with his or her name on it. When the children arrive each day at school, they should be encouraged to place their names on the bulletin board.

To create the bulletin board, cut an ice cream cone out of tagboard or construction paper for each child in the class. Color or decorate each cone as desired. Print the child's name on the ice cream cone. Laminate the pieces or cover with clear contact paper. Use pushpins or adhesive magnet pieces to attach the ice cream cones to the bulletin board.

DAIRY PRODUCTS

Family Letter

Dear Families,

Did you know that the average person in the United States consumes about 550 pounds of dairy products each year? Dairy products provide us with one of our main sources of protein. We will be learning about dairy products in our classroom. The children will learn sources of dairy products, values of dairy products, types of dairy products, forms of dairy products, places dairy products can be purchased, and containers used to hold dairy products.

AT SCHOOL

Some of the learning activities the children will participate in include

- preparing milkshakes, homemade vanilla pudding, and strawberry yogurt in the cooking area
- creating a dairy collage, yogurt print cups, and ice cream cone sponge paints in the art area
- hearing stories related to the dairy theme
- visiting the dairy department of a grocery store
- looking at books featuring dairy products
- identifying foods prepared with dairy products

AT HOME

At home, to reinforce the dairy product concepts, you can

- encourage your child to prepare instant pudding with you for snack or a dessert.
- have your child identify the foods being served at mealtimes that are dairy products.
- browse through newspaper ads or magazines and have your child identify dairy products.
- take your child grocery shopping and have him or her show you where the dairy section of the store is located.

Enjoy your child!

Milk is a dairy product.

Arts and Crafts

1. Buttermilk Chalk Pictures

Dip colored chalk into a small container of buttermilk or brush construction paper with buttermilk. Use the chalk to create designs on construction paper.

2. Dairy Product Paint Containers

Use empty dairy product containers to hold paint for use at the art table or easel. Examples include milk cartons, yogurt cups, and cottage cheese containers.

3. Whipped Soap Painting

The following mixture can be made to represent ice cream or cottage cheese. Mix one cup of Ivory Snow flakes with 1/2 cup of warm water in a bowl. The children can beat the mixture with a hand eggbeater until it is fluffy. Add more water, if necessary. Apply mixture with paint brushes or fingers to construction paper. For a variation, food coloring can be added to the paint mixture.

4. Ice Cream Cone Sponge Painting

Cut sponges into shapes of ice cream cones and scoops of ice cream. Provide shallow trays of various colors of paints. Designs are created by dipping the sponge in the paint and then pressing it onto a piece of construction paper.

5. Yogurt Cup Prints

Collect empty yogurt cups of various shapes and sizes. Wash them thoroughly. Prepare shallow trays of paint. Create designs by inverting a yogurt cup, dipping it into the paint, and then applying it to construction paper. Repeat the process as desired.

Cooking

1. Milk Shake

For each shake, combine 1/2 cup of vanilla ice cream and one cup of milk in a blender. If desired, flavor the shake with one of the following: 1/2 cup fresh berries, 1/2 banana, or two tablespoons chocolate syrup.

2. Grilled Cheese Sandwich

Assist the children in making cheese sandwiches. Provide plastic knives for the children to spread soft butter or margarine on the outside of sandwiches. Turn over and place a cheese slice between the two pieces of bread.

Under adult supervision, place the sandwiches on a heated skillet or electric grill until golden brown, turning once.

3. Homemade Vanilla Pudding

1/8 teaspoon salt
2 cups milk
2 slightly beaten egg yolks
1 tablespoon softened butter or margarine
2 teaspoons vanilla

Combine cornstarch, sugar, and salt in a medium saucepan. Stir in the milk. Over medium heat, cook and stir constantly until the mixture thickens and comes to a boil. Stir and boil 1 minute. In a small bowl, blend half of the hot mixture into the egg yolks. Pour the egg mixture back into the saucepan and cook until the mixture boils, stirring constantly. Remove the pan from the heat and add the butter and vanilla. Allow the pudding to cool slightly and spoon into a serving bowl or individual dishes. Refrigerate. (This recipe makes four servings.)

4. Strawberry Yogurt Surprise

3 oz. package strawberry-flavored gelatin
1 cup boiling water
1/2 cup cold water
1 cup strawberry yogurt

Dissolve gelatin in the boiling water. Stir in cold water. Chill until thickened but not set. Beat gelatin and fold in yogurt. Pour into serving dish. Refrigerate until firm. (This recipe makes four servings.)

Dramatic Play

1. Ice Cream Shop

Clothes and props for an ice cream shop can be placed in the dramatic play area. Include items such as empty, clean ice cream pails and cartons, ice cream scoops, plastic parfait glasses and bowls, plastic spoons, empty ice cream cone boxes, napkins, aprons, and a cash register with play money. Prepare and display posters in the area that portray various ice cream products and flavors.

2. Dairy Farm

Turn the dramatic play center into a dairy farm where the children can pretend to do chores. Display pictures of farms and cows and provide overalls, boots, hats, pails, hoses, and other appropriate props.

3. Grocery Store—Dairy Department

Set up the dramatic play area to resemble the dairy department of a grocery store. Include

props such as milk cartons, cottage cheese containers, yogurt cups, sour cream containers, ice cream pails and cartons, butter boxes, cheese packages, and a cash register. Display pictures of dairy foods.

Field Trips

1. The Grocery Store

Visit a grocery store and locate the dairy section. Look at the types of dairy products available.

2. Ice Cream Shop

Take a trip to an ice cream shop. Count the flavors of ice cream available. Purchase a cone for each of the children.

3. Dairy Farm

Visit a dairy farm. Ask the farmer to show the housing, equipment, and food supplies needed to care for dairy cows.

Fingerplays

Ice Cream

I'm licking my ice cream.
I'm licking it fast.
It's dripping down my arm.
It's disappearing fast.

Little Miss Muffet

Little Miss Muffet
Sat on a tuffet
Eating her curds and whey.
Along came a spider
And sat down beside her
And frightened Miss Muffet away!

This Little Cow

This little cow eats grass.
    (hold up fingers of one hand, bend down
    one finger)

204

This little cow eats hay.
   (bend down another finger)
This little cow drinks water.
   (bend down another finger)
And this little cow does nothing.
   (bend down another finger)
But lie and sleep all day.

Group Time

(Games, Language)

1. Dairy Charts

Print the caption, "Foods Made from Milk," across the top of a piece of tagboard. During group time, present the chart and record the children's responses. Display the chart and refer to it throughout the theme.

Additional language charts could be made about types of cheeses, ice cream, and yogurt.

2. Cheese Tasting Party

Cut various types of cheese into small slices or pieces. Place the cheese pieces on paper plates for the children to taste. Discuss types of cheeses, textures, flavors, and colors.

Math

1. Dairy Sort

Collect different types of food-product containers, including dairy products. Place all of the containers in a basket. Encourage the children to sort out the containers representing dairy products from the other food-product containers.

2. Dairy Lids

Collect lids and caps from milk jugs. They can be recycled and used for game pieces, creating patterns, and counting activities.

3. Favorite Ice Cream Graph

The children can assist in making a graph of their favorite ice cream flavors. Begin by printing

the caption, "Our Favorite Ice Cream Flavors," across the top of a piece of tagboard. Draw or paste pictures of different flavors of ice cream along the left-hand side of the tagboard. Each child's name or picture is placed next to the picture of his or her favorite ice cream flavor. The results of the graph should be shared with the children using math vocabulary words: most, more, fewer, least, etc. Display the graph for further reference.

Additional graphs could be made depicting the children's favorite flavors of yogurt, cheese, or milk.

Music

1. "The Farmer in the Dell"

The farmer in the dell,
The farmer in the dell,
Hi-ho, the dairy-o
The farmer in the dell.

Continue with additional verses:

The farmer takes the wife/husband.
The wife/husband takes the nurse.
The nurse takes the dog.
The dog takes the cat.
The cat takes the rat.
The rat takes the cheese.

The final verse:

The cheese stands alone.
The cheese stands alone.
Hi-ho, the dairy-o,
The cheese stands alone.

2. "Old MacDonald Had a Farm"
(traditional)

Old MacDonald had a farm,
Ee i ee i oh!
And on his farm he had some chicks,
Ee i ee i oh!
With a cluck-cluck here,
And a cluck-cluck there
Here a cluck, there a cluck,
Everywhere a cluck-cluck
Old MacDonald had a farm
Ee i ee i oh!

Old MacDonald had a farm,
Ee i ee i oh!
And on his farm he had some cows,
Ee i ee i oh!
With a moo-moo here,
And a moo-moo there
Here a moo, there a moo,
Everywhere a moo-moo
Old MacDonald had a farm
Ee i ee i oh!

Old MacDonald had a farm,
Ee i ee i oh!
And on his farm he had some pigs,
Ee i ee i oh!
With an oink-oink here,
And an oink-oink there
Here an oink, there an oink,
Everywhere an oink-oink,
Old MacDonald had a farm
Ee i ee i oh!

3. **"We Like Ice Cream"**
(S*ing to the tune of "Are You Sleeping?"*)

We like ice cream, we like ice cream.
Yes, we do! Yes, we do!
Vanilla and strawberry,
Chocolate and mint.
Yum, yum, yum.
Yum, yum, yum!

4. **"Drink Your Milk"**
(S*ing to the tune of "My Darling Clementine"*)

Drink your milk.
Drink your milk.
Drink your milk every day.
It is good for your teeth and bones.
Drink your milk every day.

5. **"Cows"**
(S*ing to the tune of "Mulberry Bush"*)

This is the way we feed the cows,
Feed the cows, feed the cows.
This is the way we feed the cows,
On the dairy farm each day.

This is the way we milk the cows,
Milk the cows, milk the cows.
This is the way we milk the cows,
On the dairy farm each day.

Science

1. **Making Butter**

Fill baby food jars half-full with whipping cream and replace lids. The children can take turns shaking the jars until the cream separates. (The mixture will first look like whipping cream, then like overwhipped cream, and finally it will be obvious that separation has occurred.) Pour off the remaining liquid. Rinse the butter in cold water several times and drain. Add salt to taste. Let the children spread the butter on crackers or bread. **Caution:** Supervise this activity carefully because of the use of glass jars.

2. **Making Ice Cream**

Collect the following ingredients:

1 cup milk
1/2 cup sugar
1/4 teaspoon salt
3 beaten egg yolks
1 tablespoon vanilla
2 cups whipping cream

In a saucepan, combine milk, sugar, salt, and egg yolks. Stir constantly over medium heat until bubbles appear around the edge of the pan. Cool mixture at room temperature. Stir in vanilla and whipping cream. Pour into an ice cream maker and follow the manufacturer's directions. (Recipe makes 1 quart of ice cream.)

3. **Science Table Additions**

Additions to the science table may include:

- pictures of dairy cows
- books about milking cows and dairy animals
- containers of grain, corn, and hay along with magnifying glasses
- pictures of goats, sheep, and llamas

Sensory

Additions to the Sensory Table

- sand, scoops, and empty milk cartons.
- water and empty, clean yogurt and cottage cheese containers.
- cotton balls, spoons, ice cream scoops, bowls, and empty, clean ice cream pails.

Social Studies

1. **Sharing a Treat**

   Prepare a dairy food with the children and share it with another class, senior citizens' group, or other community group.

2. **Role of the Dairy Farmer**

   Invite a dairy farmer to the classroom to discuss his or her occupation. The equipment and tools used to farm could also be shown and discussed.

3. **Dairy Allergies**

   Discuss dairy allergies. Provide dairy-free alternatives for the children to sample. Differences in taste and smell can be discussed. Some ideas include soymilk and rice milk.

Books

The following books can be used to complement this theme:

Aliki. (1992). *Milk: From Cow to Carton*. Rev. ed. New York: HarperCollins.

Asch, Frank. (1992). *Milk and Cookies*. Milwaukee: Gareth Stevens.

Barton, Byron. (1995). *Wee Little Woman*. New York: HarperCollins.

Brady, Peter. (1996). *Cows*. Illus. by William Munoz. Mankato, MN: Bridgestone Books.

Cazet, Denys. (2000). *Minnie and Moo and the Thanksgiving Tree*. New York: DK.

Daly, Kathleen N. and Tibor Gergeby. (2001). *The Good Humor Man*. Illus. by Tibor Gergeby. New York: Golden Books.

Ericsson, Jennifer A. (1993). *No Milk*. Illus. by Ora Eitan. New York: Tambourine Books.

Fowler, Allan. (1992). *Thanks to Cows*. Chicago: Children's Press.

Godfrey, Neale S. (1995). *Here's the Scoop: Follow an Ice-Cream Cone Around the World*. Illus. by Randy Verougstraete. Morristown, NJ: Silver Burdett Press.

Grossman, Bill and Victoria Chess. (1991). *Tommy at the Grocery Store*. New York: HarperCollins. (Pbk.)

Jackson, Ellen. (1995). *Brown Cow, Green Grass, Yellow Mellow Sun*. Illus. by Victoria Raymond. New York: Hyperion.

Keillor, Garrison. (1996). *The Old Man Who Loved Cheese*. Illus. by Anne Wilsdorf. Boston: Little, Brown.

Keller, Stella and John Holm. (1990). *Ice Cream*. Austin, TX: Raintree/Steck Vaughn.

Mazan, Barbara S. (1994). *Pass the Cheese Please*. Illus. by Paul Harvey. Littleton, MA: Newbridge. (Pbk.)

Older, Jules. (1997). *Cow*. Illus. by Lyn Severance. Watertown, MA: Charlesbridge Publishers.

Peterson, Cris. (1994). *Extra Cheese, Please! Mozzarella's Journey from Cow to Pizza*. Illus. by Alvis Upitis. Honesdale, PA: Boyds Mills Press.

Reid, Mary Ebeltoft. (1997). *Let's Find Out About Ice Cream*. New York: Scholastic. (Pbk.)

Root, Phyllis and Will Hillenbrand. (2000). *Kiss the Cow!* Illus. by Will Hillenbrand. Cambridge, MA: Candlewick Press.

Schertle, Alice. (1994). *How Now Brown Cow?* Illus. by Amanda Schaffer. San Diego, CA: Browndeer Press.

Seymour, Tres. (1993). *Hunting the White Cow*. Illus. by Wendy Anderson Halperin. New York: Orchard Books.

Smith, Linda and Kathryn Brown. (2001). *When Moon Fell Down*. Illus. by Kathryn Brown. New York: HarperCollins.

Van Laan, Nancy. (1993). *Tiny Tiny Boy and the Big Big Cow: A Scottish Folk Tale.* Illus. by Marjorie Priceman. New York: Knopf.

Multimedia

The following multimedia products can be used to complement this theme:

From Moo to You [CD-ROM]. (1996). Westmont, IL: Dairy Council of Wisconsin.

Let's Go to the Ice Cream and Yogurt Factory [video]. (1996). Burlington, VT: Vermont Story Works.

Make Mine Milk [video]. Sky Dog Productions.

Milk Cow, Eat Cheese [video]. (1995). Gig Harbor, WA: Real World Video.

Paterson, Katherine. *Smallest Cow in the World* [cassette and book]. (1996). Harper Audio.

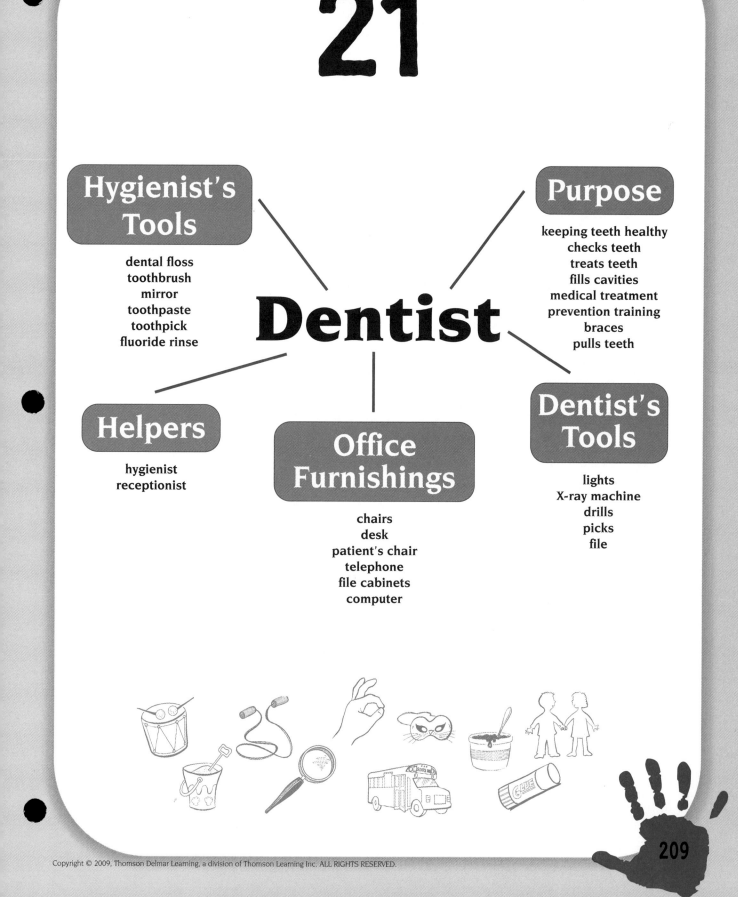

Dentist

Hygienist's Tools

dental floss
toothbrush
mirror
toothpaste
toothpick
fluoride rinse

Purpose

keeping teeth healthy
checks teeth
treats teeth
fills cavities
medical treatment
prevention training
braces
pulls teeth

Helpers

hygienist
receptionist

Office Furnishings

chairs
desk
patient's chair
telephone
file cabinets
computer

Dentist's Tools

lights
X-ray machine
drills
picks
file

Theme Goals

Through participating in the experiences provided by this theme, the children may learn

1. The dentist's purpose
2. How the dentist helps us
3. The dentist's tools
4. Hygienist's tools
5. Dental office furnishings

Concepts for the Children to Learn

1. The dentist helps keep our teeth healthy.
2. Teeth are used to chew food.
3. Teeth should be brushed after each meal.
4. A hygienist helps the dentist.
5. The dentist checks teeth, treats teeth, fills cavities, and pulls teeth.
6. The dentist places braces on some people to straighten their teeth.
7. A dentist has helpers.
8. A receptionist makes a time for people to see the dentist.
9. A hygienist cleans and X-rays people's teeth.
10. A dentist removes decay from our teeth with a drill.
11. Pictures of our teeth are called X-rays.
12. Dental floss and toothpicks help clean between teeth.
13. The dentist's office has special machines.
14. The dentist has office furniture.
15. Chairs, desks, a telephone, computer, and file cabinets are office furniture.

Vocabulary

1. **cavity**—decay on the tooth.
2. **dental floss**—a string used to clean between the teeth.
3. **dentist**—a person who helps to keep our teeth healthy.
4. **hygienist**—the dentist's assistant.
5. **teeth**—used to chew food.
6. **toothbrush**—a brush to clean our teeth.
7. **toothpaste**—a paste to clean our teeth.
8. **toothpick**—a stick-like tool used for removing food particles between our teeth.
9. **X-ray**—to take a picture.

Bulletin Board

The purpose of this bulletin board is to promote the development of a positive self-concept and assist in developing name recognition skills. Prepare an attendance bulletin board by constructing a toothbrush out of tagboard for each student and teacher. See the illustration. Color the toothbrushes with colored felt-tip markers and print the children's and teachers' names on them. Laminate. Punch holes in each toothbrush. Check who has brushed their teeth by observing the toothbrush hung on the bulletin board.

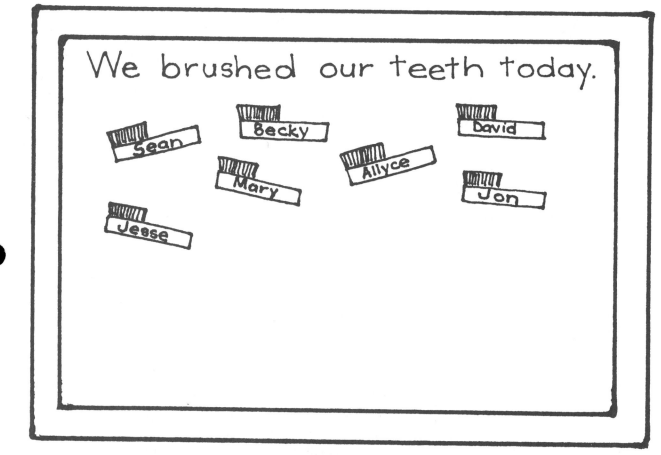

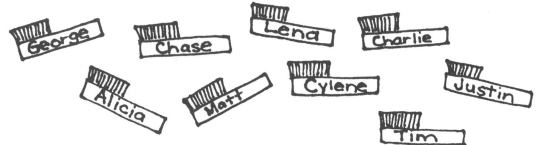

Family Letter

Dear Families,

We are continuing our study of community helpers with a unit on the dentist. The dentist is an important helper for us because our teeth are very important. Children are very aware of their teeth at this age. Many of the older five-year-olds will soon begin losing their baby teeth. Through the experiences provided in this curriculum unit, the children may learn that the dentist is a person who helps us keep our teeth healthy. They will also spend some time learning about the importance and techniques of proper tooth care.

AT SCHOOL

Some of the experiences planned for the unit include:

- making toothpaste
- string painting with dental floss at the art table
- painting with discarded toothbrushes at the easel
- exploring tools that a dentist uses

SPECIAL VISITOR

On Tuesday, we will meet Mrs. Jones, the dental hygienist at Dr. Milivitz's dental clinic. Mrs. Jones will discuss proper toothbrushing and will pass out toothbrush kits. You are invited to join our class at 10:00 a.m. for her visit.

AT HOME

Good habits start young! Dental cavities are one of the most prevalent diseases among children. It has been estimated that 98 percent of school-aged children have at least one cavity. You and your child can spend some time each day brushing your teeth together. Sometimes a child will more effectively brush if someone else is with him or her. It is important for children to realize that they are the primary caretakers of their teeth!

Have fun with your child!

Children usually enjoy brushing their teeth.

Arts and Crafts

1. **Easel Ideas**

   • Paint with discarded toothbrushes.

   • Paint on tooth-shaped easel paper.

2. **Toothbrushes and Splatter Screen**

   Provide construction paper, splatter screens, and discarded toothbrushes. The children can splatter paint onto the paper using the toothbrush as a painting tool.

3. **Dental Floss Painting**

   Provide thin tempera paint, paper, and dental floss. The child can spoon a small amount of paint onto the paper and can hold on to one end of the dental floss while moving the free end through the paint to make a design.

Cooking

Happy Teeth Snacks

• apple wedges

• orange slices

• asparagus

• cheese chunks

• milk

• cucumber slices

• cauliflower pieces

Dramatic Play

Dental Office

Provide white shirts, cotton balls, paper and pencils, phone, clipboards, and chairs in the dramatic play area. Set up as a dental office with a front desk, waiting area, and examination office. **Note:** Remind children to not put cotton balls or fingers in each other's mouths.

Field Trips/ Resource People

1. **The Dentist**

   Visit the dentist's office. Observe the furnishings and equipment.

2. **The Hygienist**

   Invite a dental hygienist to visit the classroom. Ask the hygienist to discuss tooth care and demonstrate proper brushing techniques. After the discussion, provide each child with a disclosing tablet to check his or her brushing habits.

Fingerplays

My Toothbrush

I have a little toothbrush.
   (use pointer finger)
I hold it very tight.
   (make hand into fist)
I brush my teeth each morning,
   and then again at night.
   (use pointer finger and pretend to brush)

Brushing Teeth

I move the toothbrush back and forth.
   (pretend to brush teeth)
I brush all of my teeth.
I swish the water to rinse them and then,
   (puff out cheeks to swish)

I look at myself and smile.
   (smile at one another)

My Friend the Toothbrush

My toothbrush is a tool.
I use it every day.
I brush and brush and brush and brush
   to keep the cavities away.
   (pretend to brush teeth)

Group Time

(Games, Language)

Pass the Toothpaste

Play music and pass a tube of toothpaste around the circle. When the music stops, the person who is holding the toothpaste stands up and claps his or her hands three times (or some similar action). Repeat the game.

Large Muscle

1. **Drop the Toothbrush**

   Set a large, plastic, open-mouth bottle on the floor. Encourage the children to try to drop the toothbrushes into the mouth of the bottle.

2. **Sugar, Sugar, Toothbrush**

   Play like "Duck, Duck, Goose." The "toothbrush" tries to catch the "sugar" before it gets around the circle to where the "toothbrush" was sitting. Game can continue until interest diminishes.

Music

1. **"Brushing Teeth"**
   (Sing to the tune of "Mulberry Bush")

   This is the way we brush our teeth,
      brush our teeth, brush our teeth.

This is the way we brush our teeth,
so early in the morning.

2. **"Clean Teeth"**
(*Sing to the tune of "Row, Row, Row Your Boat"*)

Brush, brush, brush your teeth
Brush them every day.
We put some toothpaste on our brush
To help stop tooth decay.

Science

1. **Tools**

Place some safe dental products on the sensory table. Include a mirror, dental floss, toothbrush, toothpaste, etc. A dentist may even lend you a model of a set of teeth.

2. **Acid on Our Teeth**

Show the children how acid weakens the enamel of your teeth. Place a hard-boiled egg into a bowl of vinegar for 24 hours. Observe how the eggshell becomes soft as it decalcifies. The same principle applies to our teeth if the acid is not removed by brushing. (This activity is most appropriate with older children.)

3. **Making Toothpaste**

In individual plastic bags, place 4 teaspoons of baking soda, 1 teaspoon salt, and 1 teaspoon water. Add a drop of food flavoring extract such as peppermint, mint, or orange. The children can mix their own toothpaste.

4. **Sugar on Our Teeth**

Sugar found in sweet food can cause cavities on tooth enamel if it is not removed by rinsing or brushing. To demonstrate the effect of brushing, submerge white eggshells into a clear glass of cola for 24 hours. Observe the discoloration of the eggshell. Apply toothpaste to toothbrush. Brush the eggshell, removing the stain. Ask the children, "What caused the stain?"

5. **Flossing Teeth**

Use empty egg cartons to represent teeth. Cut pieces of yarn for the children to practice "flossing" teeth. Discuss the importance of flossing teeth daily.

Sensory

Additions to the Sensory Table

- toothbrushes and water

- peppermint extract added to water

Books

The following books can be used to complement this theme:

Adler, David A. (1997). *A Young Cam Jansen and the Lost Tooth*. Illus. by Susanna Natti. New York: Viking.

Falwell, Cathryn. (1996). *Dragon Tooth*. New York: Clarion Books.

Finnegan, Evelyn M. (1995). *My Little Friend Goes to the Dentist*. Illus. by Diane R. Houghton. Scituate, MA: Little Friend Press.

Frost, Helen. (1999). *Brushing Well*. Mankato, MN: Pebble Books.

Frost, Helen. (1999). *Going to the Dentist*. Mankato, MN: Pebble Books.

Gomi, Taro. (1994). *The Crocodile and the Dentist*. Brookfield, CT: Millbrook Press.

Hall, Kirsten. (1994). *The Tooth Fairy*. Illus. by Nan Brooks. Chicago: Children's Press.

Hoban, Lillian. (1987). *Arthur's Loose Tooth: Story and Pictures*. New York: HarperCollins.

Keller, Laurie. (2000). *Open Wide: Tooth School Inside*. New York: Holt.

Luttrell, Ida. (1997). *Milo's Toothache*. Illus. by Enzo Giannini. New York: Puffin. (Pbk.)

MacDonald, Amy. (1996). *Cousin Ruth's Tooth*.
Illus. by Marjorie Priceman. Boston:
Houghton Mifflin.

Paxton, Tom. (1996). *The Story of the Tooth Fairy*.
Illus. by Rob Sauber. New York:
William Morrow.

Ready, Dee. (1997). *Dentists*. Chicago:
Children's Press.

Showers, Paul. (1991). *How Many Teeth?*
New York: HarperCollins. (Pbk.)

Sis, Peter. (2000). *Madlenka*. New York: Frances
Foster Books.

Multimedia

The following multimedia products can be
used to complement this theme:

Goofy over Dental Health [video]. (1991). Newton,
PA: Disney Educational Productions.

McPhail, David M. *The Bear's Toothache* [book
and cassette]. (1986). Pine Plains, NY: Live
Oak Media.

Parker, Dan. *Teach Me about the Dentist* [cassette
and book]. (1988). Fallbrook, CA: Living
Skills Music.

Recordings and Song Titles

The following recording can be used to
complement this theme:

"Doctor, Doctor." (1996). *People in Our
Neighborhood*. Long Branch, NJ:
Kimbo Educational.

22

Doctors and Nurses

Tools

rubber hammer,
stethoscope,
thermometer,
scale, medicine

Kinds

eye, ear,
feet, teeth,
animal, baby

Clothing

white lab coat
gloves
masks

Places of Work

hospitals
clinics
home care
schools

Purposes

community helpers
help people
help animals

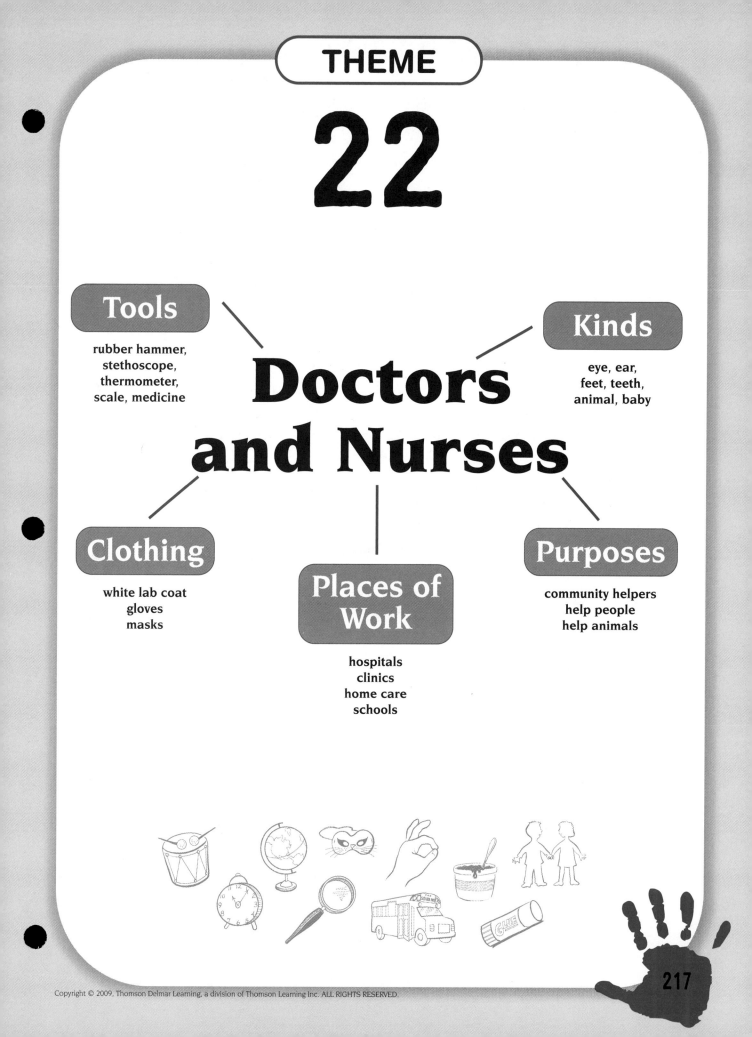

Theme Goals

Through participating in the experiences provided by this theme, the children may learn

1. The purpose of doctors and nurses
2. Kinds of doctors and nurses
3. Places doctors and nurses work
4. Tools used by doctors and nurses
5. Clothing worn by doctors and nurses

Concepts for the Children to Learn

1. Doctors and nurses are community helpers.
2. Doctors and nurses help to keep people and animals healthy.
3. Doctors and nurses work in clinics, hospitals, schools, and homes.
4. Lab coats, gloves, and masks are clothing doctors and nurses may wear.
5. Special doctors and nurses care for our eyes, ears, feet, and teeth.
6. An animal doctor is called a veterinarian.
7. A pediatrician is a children's doctor.
8. Doctors and nurses use many tools.
9. A stethoscope is a tool used to check heartbeats and breathing.
10. Thermometers are used to check body temperature.
11. A scale is used to check people's weight.
12. A rubber hammer is used to check reflexes.
13. Sometimes doctors give people medicine to make them feel better.

Vocabulary

1. **doctor**—a man or woman who helps keep our bodies healthy.
2. **nurse**—a man or woman who usually assists the doctor.
3. **ophthalmologist**—an eye doctor.
4. **patient**—a person who goes to see a doctor.
5. **pediatrician**—a children's doctor.
6. **stethoscope**—a tool for checking heartbeat and breathing.
7. **thermometer**—a tool for checking body temperature.
8. **veterinarian**—an animal doctor.

Bulletin Board

The purpose of this bulletin board is to develop skills in identifying written numerals and matching sets to numerals. Construct bandages out of manila tagboard as illustrated, or use purchased adhesive bandages. Laminate. Collect small boxes and cover with white paper if necessary. The number of boxes will be dependent on the developmental age of children. Plastic bandage boxes or 16-count crayon boxes may be used. On each box place a numeral. Affix the box to a bulletin board by stapling. The children can place the proper number of bandages in each box.

Family Letter

Dear Families,

I hope everyone in your family is happy and healthy! Speaking of healthy, we are starting a unit on doctors and nurses. The children will be learning about the different types of doctors and nurses and how they help people. They also will be introduced to some of the tools used by doctors and nurses.

AT SCHOOL

A few of the learning experiences planned include:

- listening to the story, *Tommy Goes to the Doctor*
- taking our temperatures with forehead strips and recording them on a chart in the science area
- dressing up as doctors and nurses in the dramatic play area
- experimenting with syringes (no needles!) and water at the sensory table
- listening to and looking at books related to doctors and nurses
- viewing the video titled *Hospital*

AT HOME

There are many ways to integrate this curriculum unit into your home. To begin, discuss the role of your family doctor. Talk about your child's visit to a physician. This will help to alleviate anxiety and fears your child may have about the procedures and setting.

Let your child help you prepare this nutritious snack at home. We will be making it for Wednesday's snack as well.

Fruit Smoothie

1 cup low fat yogurt
2 cups fresh or frozen berries
2 tablespoons frozen orange concentrate

Combine all of the ingredients and blend. Process the mixture until smooth. If desired, thin adding additional orange juice.

Model positive attitudes toward health for your child.

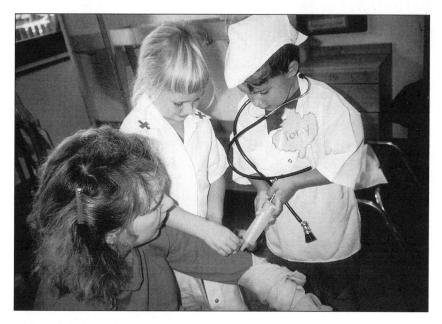

Girls and boys can be doctors or nurses.

Arts and Crafts

1. Cotton Swab Painting

Place cotton swabs, cotton balls, and tempera paint on a table in the art area. The cotton swabs and balls can be used as painting tools.

2. Body Tracing

Trace the children's bodies by having them lie down on a large piece of paper. The body shape can be decorated at school by the child with crayons and felt-tip markers. The shapes could also be taken home and decorated with parental assistance.

3. Eyedropper Painting

Provide eyedroppers, thin tempera paint, and absorbent paper. Designs can be made by using the eyedropper as a painting tool. Another method is to prepare water colored with food coloring in muffin tins. Using heavy paper towels with construction paper underneath for protection, the children will enjoy creating designs with the colored water.

Cooking

1. Mighty Mixture

Mix any of the following:

A variety of dried fruit (apples, apricots, pineapple, raisins)
A variety of seeds (pumpkin, sunflower)

2. Vegetable Juice

Prepare individual servings of vegetable juice in a blender by adding 1/2 cup of cut-up vegetables and 1/4 cup water. Salt to taste. Vegetables that can be used include celery, carrots, beets, tomatoes, cucumbers, and zucchini.

Dramatic Play

Fingerplays

1. Doctors and Nurses

Make a prop box for a doctor and nurse. Include a white coat, rubber gloves, a forehead strip thermometer, gauze, tape, masks, eyedroppers, eye chart, cots, blankets, pencil and paper, empty and washed medicine bottles, a stethoscope, a scale, and syringes without needles. A first-aid kit including gauze and tape, bandages, a sling, and ace bandages can be placed in this box. Place the prop boxes in the dramatic play area.

2. Animal Clinic

Place stuffed animals with the doctor tools in the dramatic play area.

3. Eye Doctor Clinic

Ask a local eye doctor for discontinued eyeglass frames. Place the frames with a wall chart in the dramatic play area.

Field Trips/ Resource People

1. Doctor's Office

Visit a doctor's office.

2. Resource Person

Invite a nurse or doctor to visit the classroom. Encourage him or her to talk briefly about his or her job. He or she can also share some of the tools with the children.

3. The Hospital

Visit a local hospital.

Miss Polly's Dolly

Miss Polly had a dolly that was sick, sick, sick.
(cradle arms and look sad)
She called for the doctor to come quick, quick, quick.
(clap hands three times)
The doctor came with his coat and his hat.
(point to your shirt and head)
And rapped on the door with a rap, rap, rap.
(pretend to knock three times)
He looked at the dolly and he shook his head
(shake head)
And he said, "Miss Polly, put her straight to bed."
(shake finger)
Then he wrote on a paper for some pills,
pills, pills.
(hold left hand out flat, pretend to write with right hand)
I'll be back in the morning with my bill, bill, bill.
(hold left hand out flat, wave it up and down as if waiting to be handed cash)

Note: The doctor may be male or female. Substitute pronouns.

Five Little Children

Five little children, playing in a tree. (hold up five fingers)
One fell out and broke his knee. (touch knee)
Mommy (Daddy) called the doctor,
(hold fist to ear)
And the doctor said,
"No more children playing in a tree!" (shake pointed index finger)
Four little children . . . (repeat actions as above)
Three little children . . .
Two little children . . .
One little child . . .

Group Time
(Games, Language)

1. Doctor, Doctor, Nurse

Play "Duck, Duck, Goose" inserting the words, "Doctor, Doctor, Nurse."

2. What's Missing?

Place a variety of doctors' and nurses' tools on a large tray. Tell the children to close their eyes. Remove one item from the tray. Then have the children open their eyes and guess which item has been removed. Continue playing the game using all of the items as well as providing an opportunity for each child.

Math

1. Weight and Height Chart

Prepare a height and weight chart out of tagboard. Record each child's height and weight on this chart. Repeat periodically throughout the year to note physical changes.

2. Tongue Depressor Dominoes

Make a set of dominoes by writing on tongue depressors. Divide each tongue depressor in half with a felt-tip marker. On each half place a different number of dots. Consider the children's developmental level in determining the number of dots to be included. Demonstrate to interested children how to play dominoes.

3. Bandage Lotto

Construct a bandage lotto game using various sizes and shapes of bandages. Place it on a table for use during self-selected activity time.

Music

1. "The Doctor in the Clinic"
(*Sing to the tune of* "Farmer in the Dell")

The doctor in the clinic.
The doctor in the clinic.
Hi-ho the derry-o,
The doctor in the clinic.

The doctor takes a nurse . . .
The nurse takes a patient . . .
The patient gets help . . .
The patient gets better . . .

2. "To the Hospital"
(*Sing to the tune of* "Frere Jacques")

To the hospital, to the hospital,
We will go, we will go.
We will see the doctors,
And we'll see the nurses,
Dressed in white, dressed in white.

Science

1. Thermometer

Place a variety of unbreakable thermometers on the science table. Include a candy, a meat, and an outdoor thermometer. Also include a strip thermometer that can be safely used on children's foreheads.

2. Casts

Ask personnel at a local hospital to save clean, discarded casts. Place the casts on the science table, allowing the children to observe the materials, try them on for size, as well as feel their weight. The children may also enjoy decorating the casts.

3. Stethoscope

Place a stethoscope on the science table for the children to experiment with. After each child uses it, wipe the ear plugs with alcohol to prevent the transmission of disease.

4. Doctors' Tools

In a feely box place several tools that a doctor uses. Include a thermometer, gauze, stethoscope, rubber hammer, and tongue depressor.

5. Making Toothpaste

Mix 4 teaspoons baking soda, 1 teaspoon salt, and 1 teaspoon peppermint flavoring. Then add just enough water to form a thick paste.

Social Studies

Pictures

Display various health-related pictures in the room at the children's eye level. Include doctors and nurses. Pictures should depict males and females in these health-related fields.

Books

The following books can be used to complement this theme:

Bond, Michael, Karen Jankel, and R. W. Alley. (2001). *Paddington Bear Goes to the Hospital*. Illus. by R. W. Alley. New York: HarperCollins.

Brazelton, T. Berry. (1996). *Going to the Doctor*. Photos by Alfred Womack. Reading, MA: Addison Wesley.

Cousins, Lucy. (2001). *Doctor Maisy*. Cambridge, MA: Candlewick Press.

Dooley, Virginia. (1996). *Tubes in My Ears: My Trip to the Hospital*. Illus. by Miriam Katin. Greenvale, NY: Mondo Publications. (Pbk.)

Fine, Anne. (1992). *Poor Monty*. Illus. by Clara Vulliamy. New York: Clarion Books.

Flanagan, Alice K. (1997). *Ask Nurse Pfaff, She'll Help You*. Photos by Christine Osinski. Chicago: Children's Press.

Gutman, Anne and Georg Hallensleben. (2001). *Gaspard in the Hospital*. New York: Knopf.

Howe, James. (1994). *The Hospital Book*. Photos by Mal Warshaw. New York: William Morrow.

Miller, Marilyn. (1996). *Behind the Scenes at the Hospital*. Illus. by Ingo Fast. Austin, TX: Raintree/Steck Vaughn.

Moses, Amy. (1997). *Doctors Help People*. Mankato, MN: Child's World.

Murkoff, Heidi E. (2001). *What to Expect When You Go to the Doctor*. New York: HarperFestival.

Ready, Dee. (1997). *Doctors*. Chicago: Children's Press.

Ready, Dee. (1997). *Nurses*. Chicago: Children's Press.

Redberg, Rita F. et al. (1996). *You Can Be a Woman Cardiologist*. Culver City, CA: Cascade Pass. (Pbk.)

Rogers, Fred. (1997). *Going to the Hospital*. Illus. by Jim Judkis. New York: G. P. Putnam.

Rosenberg, Maxine B. (1997). *Mommy's in the Hospital Having a Baby*. Photos by Robert Maass. New York: Clarion Books.

Schomp, Virginia. *If You Were a Veterinarian*. (1998). Tarrytown, NY: Marshall Cavendish.

Multimedia

The following multimedia products can be used to complement this theme:

Come See What the Doctor Sees [video]. (1994). Half Moon Bay, CA: Visual Mentor.

Emergency 911 [video]. (1994). Washington, DC: National Geographic.

Hospital [video]. (1990). Washington, DC: National Geographic.

Rogers, Fred. *Mister Rogers' Neighborhood: Doctor* [video]. (1996). CBS/Fox Home Video.

Ronno. "Doctor Doctor" on *People in Our Neighborhood* [cassette]. (1996). Long Branch, NJ: Kimbo Educational.

When I Grow Up I Wanta Be [video]. (1994). Birmingham, AL: Five Points South.

Recordings and Song Titles

The following recording can be used to complement this theme:

"Doctor, Doctor." (1996). *People in Our Neighborhood*. Long Branch, NJ: Kimbo Educational.

23

Body Parts

fur, four legs,
paws, tail,
ears, eyes,
nose, mouth

Communicate

growling, barking,
wagging tail,
pawing, licking

Food

water
dog food
table scraps

Safety

diseases
rabies
wild dogs
strange dogs

Supplies

collars, bones
leashes, brushes

Dogs

Care

exercise,
food, water,
sleep, grooming

Occupational Uses

police/security dog,
Seeing Eye dog,
hunting, farming,
ranching

Colors

yellow, brown,
black, white,
mixed

Sizes

large
medium
small

Homes

dog houses
kennels
house

Theme Goals

Through participating in the experiences provided by this theme, the children may learn

1. Dog's body parts
2. Sizes of dogs
3. Foods dogs eat
4. Supplies dogs need
5. Occupational uses of dogs
6. Dog homes
7. Dog safety
8. Colors of dogs
9. Dogs need special care

Concepts for the Children to Learn

1. There are many different sizes of dogs.
2. Dogs have keen senses of smell and hearing.
3. Dogs growl, paw, lick, wag their tail, and bark to communicate.
4. Dogs may bark at strangers to protect their owners and their space.
5. Dogs have four legs, eyes, ears, a mouth, a nose, paws, and a tail.
6. Dogs have fur on their skin.
7. Dogs need water and dog food.
8. Some dogs eat table scraps.
9. Police dogs help police officers.
10. Seeing Eye dogs help people who are blind.
11. Hunting dogs help hunters.
12. Some dogs help farmers or ranchers.
13. There are many different colors, sizes, and kinds of dogs.
14. Dogs need exercise every day.
15. Dogs can live in dog houses, kennels, or in a house.
16. Dogs can be many different colors.

Vocabulary

1. **bone**—an object a dog chews on.
2. **coat**—hair or fur covering the skin.
3. **collar**—a band worn around the dog's neck.
4. **doghouse**—a place for dogs to sleep and keep warm.
5. **guide dog**—a dog trained to help people who are blind or need help.
6. **leash**—a rope, chain, or cord that attaches to a collar.
7. **obedience school**—a school where dogs are taught to obey.
8. **paw**—the dog's foot.
9. **pet**—an animal kept for pleasure.
10. **puppy**—a baby dog.
11. **veterinarian**—an animal doctor.
12. **whiskers**—stiff hair growing around the dog's nose, mouth, and eyes.

Bulletin Board

The purpose of this bulletin board is to develop visual discrimination, problem-solving, color recognition, and matching skills. Prepare the bulletin board by cutting dog shapes out of tagboard or construction paper. Add details using felt-tip markers. Use rubber cement to attach a different colored paper collar to each dog's neck. Also, cut out dog dishes from colored construction paper. Attach the pieces to the bulletin board as illustrated. Attach lengths of yarn or string for children to match the color of each dog's collar to the corresponding dog dish.

Family Letter

Dear Families,

We will begin a curriculum unit on a favorite subject of children of all ages—dogs! Through the classroom activities, we will be learning about a dog's basic physical features such as coat and body parts. We will also learn about caring for a dog, the roles of dogs in people's lives, dog training, as well as factors families need to consider when choosing a dog. This curriculum unit is designed to encourage the children to develop an awareness of and respect for dogs as pets.

AT SCHOOL

Some of the learning experiences planned include:

- creating paw prints at the art table (dipping paw-shaped sponges into paint and applying them to paper)
- sorting various-sized dog biscuits
- listening to the children's stories about their own dogs
- setting up a "pet store" in the dramatic play area, complete with stuffed animals and many dog accessories
- baking dog biscuits

AT HOME

To foster parent-child interaction and reinforce some of the concepts we are working on at school, try some of the following ideas:

- Look through magazines to find pictures of dogs and puppies. Help your child tear out some of the pictures. This activity is good for the development of fine motor and visual discrimination skills. An interesting collage can be made by gluing these pictures onto a piece of paper.
- If you don't have access to a dog, visit a pet shop to observe the puppies. At the same time, note all of the dog supplies available.

Enjoy your child!

What is your favorite size of dog?

Arts and Crafts

1. Dog Puppets

Provide socks, paper bags, and/or paper plates to make dog puppets.

2. Dog Masks

Use fake fur ears and chenille stems for whiskers.

3. Bone Printing

Provide different meat bones, a tray of tempera paint, and paper to make prints.

4. Bone Painting

Cut easel paper in bone shapes.

Cooking

1. Hot "Dog" Kebabs on a Stick

paper plates and napkins
skewers
1 package hot dogs, cut up
2 green peppers, cut up
cherry tomatoes

Place two pieces of green pepper, two cherry tomatoes, and two hot dog pieces on each child's plate. Show the children how to thread the ingredients on skewers. Bake the kabobs in a preheated oven for 15 minutes at 350 degrees.

2. Dog Biscuits—For Dogs!

2 1/2 cups whole wheat flour
1/2 cup powdered dry milk
1/2 teaspoon salt
1/2 teaspoon garlic powder
6 tablespoons margarine, shortening,
   or meat drippings
1 egg
1 teaspoon brown sugar
1/2 cup ice water

Combine flour, milk, salt, and flour. Cut in the shortening. Mix in egg. Add enough water that mixture forms a ball. Pat the dough to a half-inch thickness on a lightly oiled cookie sheet. Cut with cutters and remove scraps. Bake 25 to 30 minutes at 350 degrees. This recipe may be varied by adding pureed soup greens, protein powder, etc.

3. Healthy Dog Biscuits

Makes 30 (6-inch) biscuits:

1 3/4 cups beef or chicken broth
1 package dry yeast

2 cups whole-wheat flour
1/2 cup cornmeal
1 teaspoon salt
1/3 cup safflower oil
1/3 cup finely chopped fresh mint
1 egg, lightly beaten with 1 teaspoon
of water

To proof yeast:

Heat broth in small saucepan to 105 degrees. Sprinkle in yeast. Stir to dissolve. Let mixture stand at room temperature for 5 minutes. **Caution:** If the broth is too hot it will kill the yeast.

To make biscuits:

Pour yeast mixture into bowl of standing mixer fitted with paddle attachment. Add whole-wheat, cornmeal, salt, oil, and mint. Mix on medium speed until soft dough is formed.

Remove to well-floured surface. Knead 10–12 times, or just until texture is smooth. Cover dough with kitchen towel. Let stand for 20 minutes.

To shape biscuits:

Roll out into 1/4-inch-thick rectangle. Using bone-shaped cookie cutter, cut shapes starting from edge of dough and working toward the center so that fewer scraps remain. Gather up scraps. Knead together until smooth. Reroll to cut additional biscuits. Place 1/2-inch apart on parchment-linked baking sheets.

To bake biscuits:

Brush tops with egg mixture. Place on center oven rack. Bake in 400-degree oven for 45–50 minutes or until lightly browned, reversing baking sheets halfway through baking time. Turn oven off. Keep biscuits inside oven for 30 minutes to crisp. Remove. Cool. Store in plastic bags.

When finished:

Dog biscuits can be sent home with children or donated to a local animal shelter.

4. **Hush Puppies**

vegetable oil
2 1/4 cups yellow cornmeal
1 teaspoon salt
2 tablespoons finely chopped onion
3/4 teaspoon baking soda
1 1/2 cups buttermilk

Heat oil (about 1-inch deep) to 375 degrees. Mix cornmeal, salt, onion, and baking soda in a bowl. Add buttermilk. Drop by spoonfuls into hot oil. Fry until brown, about 2 minutes. **Caution:** This activity should be carefully supervised.

Dramatic Play

1. **Pet Store**

Simulate a pet store using stuffed animals. Include a counter complete with cash register and money. Post a large sign that says, "Pet Store." Set out many stuffed dogs with collars and leashes. Children will enjoy pretending they have a new pet.

2. **Veterinarian's Office**

Use some medical equipment and stuffed dogs to create a veterinarian's office.

3. **Pet Show**

Encourage the children to bring a stuffed animal to school. Children can pretend that their stuffed animals can do tricks. Have ribbons available for them to look at and award to each other.

4. **Doghouse**

Construct a doghouse from a large cardboard box. Provide dog ears and tails for the children to wear as they imitate the pet.

Field Trips/ Resource People

1. **Pet Store**

Take a field trip to a pet store. While there ask the manager how to care for dogs. Observe the different types of cages, collars, leashes, food, and toys.

2. Veterinarian's Office

Take a field trip to a veterinarian's office or animal hospital. Compare its similarities and differences with a doctor's office.

3. Kennel

Visit a kennel and observe the different sizes of cages and dogs.

4. Variety Store

Visit a variety store and observe pet accessories.

5. Grocery Store

Take a field trip to the grocery store and purchase the ingredients needed to make dog biscuits.

6. Dog Trainer

Invite an obedience trainer to talk about teaching dogs.

7. Additional Resource People

- veterinarian
- pet store owner
- parents (bring in family dogs)
- humane society representative
- representative from a kennel
- dog groomer
- person with a Seeing Eye dog (guide dog)

Fingerplays

Frisky's Doghouse

This is Frisky's doghouse;
   (pointer fingers touch to make a roof)
This is Frisky's bed;
   (motion of smoothing)
Here is Frisky's pan of milk;
   (cup hands)
So that he can be fed.

Frisky has a collar
   (point to neck with fingers)

With his name upon it, too;
Take a stick and throw it,
   (motion of throwing)
He'll bring it back to you.
   (clap once)

Five Little Puppies

Five little puppies were playing in the sun.
   (hold up hands, fingers extended)
This one saw a rabbit, and he began to run.
   (bend down first finger)
This one saw a butterfly, and he began to race.
   (bend down second finger)
This one saw a cat, and he began to chase.
   (bend down third finger)
This one tried to catch his tail, and he went round and round.
   (bend down fourth finger)
This one was so quiet, he never made a sound.
   (bend down thumb)

Five Little Puppies

Five little puppies jumping on the bed,
   (hold up five fingers)
One fell off and bumped his head,
   (hold up one finger—tap head)
Mama called the doctor and the doctor said,
"No more puppies jumping on the bed."
   (shake index finger)

Group Time

(Games, Language)

1. The Dog Catcher

Hide stuffed dogs or those cut from construction paper around the classroom and have children find them.

2. Child-Created Stories

Bring in a picture of a dog or stuffed dog. Encourage the children to tell you a story about the picture or the stuffed dog. While the child speaks, record the words. Place the story in the book corner.

3. Dog Chart

Make a chart listing the color of each child's dog. A variation would be to have the children state their favorite color of dog. This activity can be repeated using size.

4. Doggie, Doggie, Where's Your Bone?

Bring in a clean bone or a bone cut from construction paper. Sit the children in a circle. Choose one child to be the dog. Have the child pretending to be the dog sit in the middle. The doggie closes his or her eyes. A child from the circle sneaks up and takes the bone. Children call, "Doggie, doggie, where's your bone? Someone stole it from your home!" The "dog" gets three guesses to find out who has the bone.

5. The Lost Dog

(This is a variation of the "Dog Catcher" game.) Using the children's stuffed animals from home, have the children trade dogs so that each is holding another's pet. One child begins by hiding the dog he or she is holding while the other children cover their eyes. He or she tells the owner, "Your dog is lost, but we can help you find it." As the dog owner looks, he or she can put the pet he or she is holding on his or her carpet square to free both hands. The group gives "hot" and "cold" clues to indicate whether the child is close to or far away from the pet. When the child finds his or her pet, he or she is the next one to hide a pet.

Large Muscle

1. Encourage the children to dramatize the following movements:

- a big dog
- a tiny dog
- a dog with heavy steps
- a dog with light steps
- a happy dog
- a sad dog
- a mad dog

- a loud dog
- a quiet dog
- a hungry dog
- a tired dog
- a curious dog
- a sick dog

2. Dog Hoops

Provide hoops for the children to jump through as they imitate dogs.

3. Scent Walk

Place prints of dog paws on the play yard leading to different activities. Encourage the child to crawl to each activity.

4. Tracks

If snow is available, make tracks with boots that have different treads. Encourage children to follow one track.

5. Bean Bag Bones

Provide round bean bags or make special bone-shaped bean bags. Encourage the children to throw them into a large dog food bowl.

Math

1. Dog Bones

Cut dog bone shapes of four different sizes from tagboard. Encourage the children to sequence them.

2. Classifying Dog Biscuits

Purchase three sizes of dog biscuits. Using dog dishes, have the children sort them according to size and type.

3. Weighing Biscuits

Using the scale, encourage the children to weigh different sizes and amounts of dog biscuits.

Music

1. "Bingo"

There was a farmer who had a dog
And Bingo was his name-o.
B-I-N-G-O

B-I-N-G-O
B-I-N-G-O
And Bingo was his name-o.

2. **"Six Little Dogs"**
(*Sing to the tune of "Six Little Ducks"*)

Six little dogs that I once knew,
fat ones, skinny ones, fair ones too.
But the one little dog with the brown curly fur,
He led the others with a grr, grr, grr.
Grr, grr, grr
Grr, grr, grr
He led the others with a grr, grr, GRR!

Science

1. Additions to the science table or area may include:

   - a magnifying glass with bones, dog hair, and dog food

   - dog toys of different sizes, including some with squeakers

   - a balance scale and dry dog food

2. During a cooking activity, prepare dog biscuits. The recipe is listed under Cooking.

Social Studies

1. **Share Your Dog**

   Individually invite the parents to bring their child's pet to school.

2. **Pictures of Dogs**

   Display pictures of different types of dogs.

3. **Bulletin Board**

   Prepare a bulletin board with pictures of the children's dogs.

4. **Slides**

   Take slides of field trips and of resource people. Share them at group time. (This slide series may be shared with parents at meetings or coffees.)

5. **Dog Biscuits**

   Prepare dog biscuits and donate to the local animal shelter. (See Cooking.)

6. **Chart**

   Make a chart including the children's name, type of pet, size of pet, and the name of the pet. Count the number of dogs, cats, birds, etc. Discuss the most popular names.

7. **Dogs**

   Using pictures or a real dog, talk about a dog's body. Some dogs have long noses so they can smell things very well; others have short hair to live in hot climates. Discuss why some dogs are good guard dogs. Discuss how dogs' tongues help them to cool off on hot days. Also talk about what else a dog's rough tongue is used for.

Books

The following books can be used to complement this theme:

Boland, Janice and Brian G. Karas. (1998). *A Dog Named Sam*. New York: Puffin.

Coffelt, Nancy. (1995). *Dog Who Cried Woof*. New York: Harcourt Brace.

Cole, Joanna. (1991). *My Puppy Is Born*. Revised and newly illustrated. Photos by Margaret Miller. New York: William Morrow.

Copeland, Eric. (1994). *Milton, My Father's Dog*. Plattsburgh, NY: Tundra.

Demas, Corinne. (2004). *Saying Goodbye to Lulu*. Illus. by Ard Hoyt. Boston, MA: Little Brown.

Ernst, Lisa Campbell. (1992). *Walter's Tail*. New York: Simon & Schuster.

Gibbons, Gail. (1996). *Dogs*. New York: Holiday House.

Gliori, Debi. (1996). *The Snow Lambs*. New York: Scholastic.

Gregory, Nan. (1995). *How Smudge Came*. Illus. by Ron Lightburn. New York: Red Deer College Press.

Gutman, Anne and Georg Hallensleben. (2001). *Gaspard & Lisa at the Museum*. New York: Knopf.

Hall, Donald. (1994). *I Am the Dog, I Am the Cat*. Illus. by Barry Moser. New York: Dial Books.

Harper, Isabelle. (1994). *My Dog Rosie*. Illus. by Barry Moser. New York: Scholastic.

Harper, Isabelle. (1996). *Our New Puppy*. Illus. by Barry Moser. New York: Scholastic.

Herman, R.A. (2005). *Gomer & Little Gomer*. Illus. by Steve Haskamp. New York: Dutton Children's Books.

Hesse, Karen. (1993). *Lester's Dog*. Illus. by Nancy Carpenter. New York: Crown.

Hill, Eric. (2001). *Spot Goes to School*. New York: G.P. Putnam's Sons. (First American Board Book Edition.)

Kasza, Keiko. (2005). *The Dog Who Cried Wolf*. New York: G.P. Putnam's Sons.

King, Stephen Michael. (2005). *Mutt Dog!* Orlando, FL: Harcourt.

Masurel, Claire. (1997). *No, No, Titus!* Illus. by Shari Halpern. New York: North South Books.

McGeorge, Constance W. (1994). *Boomer's Big Day*. Illus. by Mary Whyte. San Francisco: Chronicle.

Moore, Eva. (1996). *Buddy: The First Seeing Eye Dog*. Illus. by Don Bolognese. New York: Scholastic.

Osofsky, Audrey. (1992). *My Buddy*. Illus. by Ted Rand. New York: Holt.

Robertus, Polly M. (1991). *The Dog Who Had Kittens*. Illus. by Janet Stevens. New York: Holiday House.

Rylant, Cynthia. (1991). *Bookshop Dog*. New York: Scholastic.

Rylant, Cynthia. (1994). *Mr. Putter and Tabby Walk the Dog*. Illus. by Arthur Howard. Orlando, FL: Harcourt Brace.

Rylant, Cynthia. (2006). *Mr. Putter & Tabby Spin the Yarn*. Illus. by Arthur Howard. Orlando, FL: Harcourt.

Siracusa, Catherine. (1991). *Bingo, the Best Dog in the World*. Illus. by Sidney Levitt. New York: HarperCollins.

Wells, Rosemary. (1997). *McDuff Moves In*. Illus. by Susan Jeffers. New York: Hyperion.

Wells, Rosemary and Susan Jeffers. (2001). *McDuff Goes to School*. Illus. by Susan Jeffers. New York: Hyperion Press.

Wild, Margaret. (1994). *Toby*. Illus. by Noela Young. New York: Ticknor & Fields.

Zolotow, Charlotte. (1995). *Old Dog*. Revised and newly illustrated. Illus. by James Ransome. New York: HarperCollins.

Multimedia

The following multimedia products can be used to complement this theme:

"Bingo" on *Six Little Ducks: Classic Children's Songs* [cassette or CD]. (1997). Long Branch, NJ: Kimbo Educational.

Dog [video]. Eyewitness Videos. Available from Kimbo Educational, Long Branch, NJ.

World of Pets: Dogs [video]. (1985). National Geographic Society.

Pets: See How They Grow [video]. Sony. Available from Kimbo Educational, Long Branch, NJ.

"Puppy Dog" on *Walk Like the Animals* by Georgiana Liccione Stewart [cassette]. Kimbo Educational.

Robertus, Polly M. *The Dog Who Had Kittens* [video]. (1992). Pine Plains, NY: Live Oak Media.

Wagging Tails: The Dog and Puppy Music Video [video]. (1994). Forney Miller Film & Video; distributed by New Market Sales.

Recordings and Song Titles

The following recordings can be used to complement this theme:

"My Dog Rags" (2004). *Laugh N Learn Silly Songs*. Long Branch, NJ: Kimbo.

"Who Let the Dogs Out?" (2001). *Dance Party Fun*. Long Branch, NJ: Kimbo Educational.

24

Special Foods

colored eggs
hot cross buns
candies

Easter

Symbols

baskets
rabbits
eggs
chicks/ducks
bonnets

Spring Holiday

new life,
religious for
some people*

Celebrations

egg hunts
parades

* Some center personnel may elect to include an Easter theme with an emphasis on the spring holiday as opposed to the traditional religious emphasis.

Theme Goals

Through participating in the experiences provided by this theme, the children may learn

1. Easter celebrations
2. Easter symbols
3. Special foods served at Easter
4. Easter as a spring holiday

Concepts for the Children to Learn

1. Easter is a holiday.
2. Many families celebrate Easter.
3. At Eastertime eggs are colored and decorated.
4. There are many symbols of Easter, including baby animals, baskets, rabbits, and eggs.
5. Baskets filled with colored eggs and candy may be hidden.
6. Baby animals born in the spring are a sign of new life.
7. Bonnets (hats) may be worn at Easter time.
8. There are many shapes of eggs.
9. Eggs may be round, oval, or spherical.

Vocabulary

1. **basket**—a woven container.
2. **bonnet**—a kind of hat.
3. **bunny**—a baby rabbit.
4. **chick**—a baby chicken.
5. **duckling**—a baby duck.
6. **dye**—to change the color.
7. **Easter**—a holiday in spring.
8. **hatch**—to break out of a shell.
9. **holiday**—a day of celebration.
10. **spring**—the season of the year when plants begin to grow.

Bulletin Board

The purpose of this bulletin board is to promote correspondence of sets to the written numerals. Construct baskets out of stiff tagboard. Write a numeral beginning with the number one on each basket as illustrated. Carefully attach these to the bulletin board by stapling all the way around the bottom of the baskets. Construct many small Easter eggs. Encourage the children to deposit the corresponding number of Easter eggs in the numbered baskets. Care needs to be taken when removing the eggs. The number of baskets provided should reflect the developmental level of the children. If available, you might want to try using lightweight Easter baskets. They are harder to hang up but may prove to be more sturdy.

Family Letter

Dear Families,

"Here comes Peter Cottontail, hopping down the bunny trail...." Easter is on its way and is the curriculum theme we will explore. This is an exciting holiday for children. Through the planned learning experiences, the children will learn ways that families celebrate Easter and the symbols representing Easter. Included will be customs such as the Easter bunny, Easter baskets, and foods that are usually associated with Easter. Perhaps not all children and families celebrate this holiday, but we feel it is very important for children to learn about and respect others' beliefs. A general understanding of other cultures is also interesting and fun. However, if you wish that your child not participate in this theme, please let us know.

AT SCHOOL

Learning experiences planned to reinforce concepts of Easter include:

- a special visitor for the week—a rabbit! The children will assist in taking care of the rabbit.
- a hat shop in the dramatic play area with materials to create Easter bonnets
- Easter grass and plastic eggs in the sensory table
- an egg hunt! On Friday, we will search our play yard for hidden eggs and place them in our baskets.
- listening to Easter stories

AT HOME

To establish a sense of family history, recall family Easter celebrations that you have had in the past with your child. What special things does your family do together on this holiday? And, of course, dye some Easter eggs!

Be adventurous and try some dyes from natural materials. Natural dying is not new; natural dyes were the original Easter egg colors the world over. To make purple eggs, purchase a box of frozen blackberries. Thaw and place in a saucepan. Add eggs and cover with water plus 1 tablespoon of vinegar. Bring the water to a boil and simmer for 20 minutes. Afterward, take the pan off the heat source and let stand for approximately 20 minutes.

To make gold eggs, use powdered turmeric. Place eggs in a saucepan and add enough water to cover. Then, add 3 tablespoons of turmeric and bring to a boil. Simmer for 20 minutes. Remove from heat source and cool.

To create pale green eggs, cut spinach and place in the bottom of a pan. Add enough water to cover and add eggs. Bring to a boil and simmer for 20 minutes. Remove from heat and allow to set for more intense color.

Enjoy the holiday with your children!

242

Baby chicks are a symbol of Easter and need to be treated gently.

Arts and Crafts

1. Easter Collages

Collect eggshells, straw, Easter grass, or plant seeds for making collages. Place on art table with sheets of paper and glue.

2. Colorful Collages

Use pastel-colored sand and glue to make collages.

3. Wet Chalk Eggs

Use wet chalk to decorate paper cut in the shape of eggs in pastel colors. Show the children the difference between wetting the chalk in vinegar and in water. The vinegar color will be brighter.

4. Easel Ideas

Cut egg-shaped easel paper or basket-shaped paper. Clip to the easel. Provide pastel paints at the easel. To make the paint more interesting, add glitter.

5. Milk Carton Easter Baskets

Cut off the bottom 4 inches of milk cartons. Provide precut construction or wallpaper to cover the baskets and yarn. Include small bits of paper or bright cloth to glue on the cartons. Make a handle using a thin strip of paper that is stapled to the carton. Use the baskets for the children's snack.

6. Plastic Easter Baskets

Easter baskets can be made by using the green plastic baskets that strawberries and blueberries come in from the grocery store. Cut thin strips of paper that children can practice weaving through the holes. This activity is most successful with older children.

7. Color Mixing

Provide red, yellow, and blue dyed water in shallow pans. Provide the children with medicine droppers and absorbent paper cut in the shape of eggs. Also, the children can use medicine droppers to apply color to the paper. Observe what happens when the colors blend together.

8. Rabbit Ears

Construct rabbit ears out of heavy paper. Attach them to a band that can be worn around the head, fitting it for size. These ears may stimulate creative movement as well as dramatic play.

Cooking

1. Decorating Cupcakes

Let the children use green frosting, dyed coconut, and jelly beans to decorate cupcakes and put them into an Easter basket. As a last touch, add a chenille stem handle. Cake mixes can be used to make the cupcakes. Follow the directions on the box. Place paper liners in a muffin pan to ensure easy removability.

2. Bunny Food

Carrot sticks, celery, and lettuce can be available for snack.

3. Egg Sandwiches

Use the boiled eggs the children have decorated to make egg salad or deviled eggs for snack time.

4. Carrot and Raisin Salad

4 cups grated carrots
1 cup raisins
1/2 cup mayonnaise or whipped salad dressing

Place ingredients in a bowl and mix thoroughly.

5. Bunny Salad

For each serving place one lettuce leaf on a plate. Put one canned pear half with the cut side down on top of the lettuce leaf. Add sections of an orange to represent the ears. Decorate the bunny face by adding grated carrots, raisins, or maraschino cherries to make eyes, a nose, and a mouth.

Dramatic Play

1. Flower Shop

Plan a flower shop for the dramatic play area. Include spring plants, baskets, and Easter lilies.

2. Egg Center

Create a colored egg center to be used during self-directed play. Some children put stickers on plastic eggs, some sell the eggs, and others buy them.

3. Costume Shop

Place costumes for bunny use, Easter baskets, and Easter eggs in the dramatic play area. The children can take turns hiding the eggs and going on hunts.

4. A Bird Nest

Place a nest with eggs in the dramatic play area. Also provide bird masks, a perch, and other bird items in the area for use during self-initiated play.

5. Easter Clothes

Bring in Easter clothes for the children to dress up in. Suits, dresses, hats, purses, gloves, and dress-up shoes should be included.

6. Hat Shop

Make a hat shop. Place hats, ribbons, flowers, netting, and other decorations in the dramatic play area. The children can decorate the hats. If appropriate, plan an Easter Parade.

Field Trips

1. The Farm

Take a trip to a farm to see baby animals.

2. The Hatchery

Visit a hatchery on a day that they are selling chicks.

3. Neighborhood Walk

Take a walk around the neighborhood and look for signs of new life.

4. Rabbit Visit

Bring some rabbits to school for the children to observe.

Fingerplays

The Duck

I waddle when I walk.
   (hold arms elbow high and twist trunk side to
   side, or squat down)
I quack when I talk.
   (place palms together and open and close)
And I have webbed toes on my feet.
   (spread fingers wide)
Rain coming down
Makes me smile, not frown
   (smile)
And I dive for something to eat.
   (put hands together and make diving motion)

My Rabbit

My rabbit has two big ears
   (hold up index and middle fingers for ears)
And a funny little nose.
   (join other three fingers for nose)
He likes to nibble carrots
   (move thumb away from other two fingers)
And he hops wherever he goes.
   (move whole hand jerkily)

Group Time

(Games, Language)

1. The Last Bunny

This is a game for 10 or more players. It is more fun with a large number. An Easter rabbit is chosen by counting out or drawing straws. All the other players stand in a circle. The Easter rabbit walks around the circle and taps one player on the back saying, "Have you seen my bunny helper?" "What does it look like?" asks the player and the Easter rabbit describes the bunny helper. He or she may say, "She is wearing a watch and blue shoes." The player tries to guess who it is. When he or she names the right person, the Easter rabbit says, "That's my helper!" and the other player chases the bunny helper outside and around the circle. If the chaser catches the bunny helper before he or

she can return to his or her place, the chaser becomes the Easter rabbit. If the bunny helper gets there first, then the first Easter rabbit must try again. The Easter rabbit takes the place in the circle of whoever is the new Easter rabbit.

Note: From *Games and How to Play Them*, by Anne Rockwell, 1973, New York: Thomas Y. Crowell.

2. Outdoor Egg Hunt

Plan an egg hunt outdoors, if possible. Hide the boiled eggs that the children have decorated, candy eggs in wrappers, or small Easter candies in clear plastic bags. The children can use the baskets they have made to collect their eggs, then, weather permitting, eat the boiled eggs for a snack outdoors.

Large Muscle

1. Bunny Trail

Set up a bunny trail in the classroom. Place tape on the floor and have children hop over the trail. To make it more challenging, add a balance beam to resemble a bridge.

2. Eggs in the Basket

The children can practice throwing egg-shaped or regular beanbags into a large basket or bucket.

3. Rabbit Tag

Make egg-shaped beanbags to play rabbit tag. To play the game, the children stand in a circle, with one child being the rabbit. The rabbit walks around the circle with a beanbag balanced on his or her head and drops a second beanbag behind the back of another child. The second child must put the beanbag on his or her head and follow the rabbit around the circle once. Each child must keep the beanbag balanced—if it drops, it must be picked up and replaced on the head. If the rabbit is tagged, he or she chooses the next rabbit. If the rabbit returns to the empty spot in the circle, the second child becomes the rabbit. This is an unusual game in that the action is fairly slow but it's still very exciting.

4. Egg Rolling

Place mats on the floor and have children roll across with their arms at their sides. For older children, you can place the mat on a slightly inclined plane and have children roll down, and to then try to have them roll back up, which is more challenging.

Math

1. Egg Numerals

Collect five large plastic eggs, such as the kind that nylon stockings can be purchased in. Put numerals from 1 to 5 (or 10, for older children) on the eggs. Let the children place the correct number of cotton balls or markers into each egg.

2. Easter Seriation

Cut different-sized tagboard eggs, chicks, ducks, and rabbits. The children can place the items in a row from the smallest to the largest.

Music

1. "Did You Ever See a Rabbit?"
(Sing to the tune of "Did You Ever See a Lassie?")

Did you ever see a rabbit, a rabbit, a rabbit?
Did you ever see a rabbit, a rabbit, on
    Easter morn?
He hops around so quietly
And hides all the eggs.
Did you ever see a rabbit, on Easter morn?

2. "Easter Bunny"
(Sing to the tune of "Ten Little Indians")

Where, oh, where is the Easter Bunny,
Where, oh, where is the Easter Bunny,
Where, oh, where is the Easter Bunny,
Early Easter morning?

Find all the eggs and put them in a basket,
Find all the eggs and put them in a basket,
Find all the eggs and put them in a basket,
Early Easter morning.

3. "Easter Eggs"
(Sing to the chorus of "Jingle Bells")

Easter eggs, Easter eggs,
Hidden all around.
Come my children look about
And see where they are found.

Easter eggs, Easter eggs,
They're a sight to see.
One for Tom and one for Ann
And a special one for me!

Insert names of children in your classroom.

4. "Easter Eggs"
(Sing to the tune of "Mama's Little Baby Loves Shortnin'")

Easter eggs here and there,
Easter eggs everywhere.
What's the color of the
Easter egg here?

Science

1. Incubate and Hatch Eggs

Check the yellow pages of your telephone book to see if any hatcheries are located in your area.

2. Dyeing Eggs

Use natural products to make egg dye. Beets—deep red; cranberries—light red; spinach leaves—green; and blackberries—blue. To make dyed eggs, pick two or three colors from the list. Make the dye by boiling the fruit or vegetable in small amounts of water. Let the children put a cool hard-boiled egg in a nylon stocking and dip it into the dye. Keep the egg in the dye for several minutes. Pull out the nylon and check the color. If it is dark enough, place the egg on a paper towel to dry. If children want to color the eggs with crayons before dying, you can show how the wax keeps liquid from getting on the egg.

3. **Science Table Additions**

- bird nests
- empty bird eggs
- different kinds of baskets
- an incubator
- newly planted seeds
- flowers still in bud (children can watch them open)
- pussy willows

4. **Basket Guessing**

Do reach-and-feel using a covered basket. Place an egg, a chick, a rabbit, a doll's hat, some Easter grass, and so on, in a large Easter basket. Let the children place their hands into the basket individually and describe the objects they are feeling.

Sensory

1. **Sensory Table Activities**

Add to the sensory table

- cotton balls with scoops and measuring cups
- birdseed or beans
- straw or hay and plastic eggs
- plastic chicks and ducks with water
- Easter grass, eggs, small straw mats
- dirt with plastic flowers and/or leaves
- dyed, scented water and water toys
- sand, shovels, and scoops

2. **Clay Cutters**

Make scented clay. Place on the art table with rabbit, duck, egg, and flower cookie cutters for the children to use during self-directed or self-initiated play.

Social Studies

1. **Family Easter Traditions**

During large group, ask the children what special activities their families do to celebrate Easter. Their families may go to church, eat together, have egg hunts, or do other things that are special on this day.

2. **Sharing Baskets**

Decorate eggs or baskets to give to a home for the elderly. If possible, take a walk and let the children deliver them.

Books

The following books can be used to complement this theme:

Adams, Adrienne. (1991). *Easter Egg Artists*. Madison, WI: Demco Media.

Auch, Mary Jane. (1992). *The Easter Egg Farm*. New York: Holiday House.

Auch, Mary Jane. (1996). *Eggs Mark the Spot*. New York: Holiday House.

Fisher, Aileen Lucia. (1997). *The Story of Easter*. Illus. by Stefano Vitale. New York: HarperCollins.

Garfield, Valarie and Julie Durrell. (2001). *Sergeant Sniff's Easter Egg Mystery*. Illus. by Julie Durrell. New York: HarperFestival.

Hallinan, P. K. (1993). *Today Is Easter!* Nashville, TN: Ideals Children's Books. (Pbk.)

Hopkins, Lee Bennett. (1993). *Easter Buds Are Springing: Poems for Easter*. Illus. by Tomie De Paola. Honesdale, PA: Boyds Mills Press.

Kennedy, Pamela. (1991). *An Easter Celebration: Traditions and Customs from around the World*. Nashville, TN: Ideals Children's Books.

McDonnell, Janet. (1993). *The Easter Surprise*. Illus. by Linda Hohag. Chicago: Children's Press.

Milich, Melissa. (1997). *Miz Fannie Mae's Fine New Easter Hat*. Illus. by Yong Chen. Boston: Little, Brown.

Easter Eggs

Where did the custom of coloring Easter eggs come from? No one knows for sure. In any case, the Easter holiday centers around eggs for young children. Here are some projects you might like to try.

- To hard-cook eggs: Place eggs in a saucepan and add enough cold water to cover at least 1 inch above the eggs. Heat rapidly to boiling and remove from heat. Cover the pan and allow to stand for 22 to 24 minutes. Immediately cool the eggs in cold water.
- Make a vegetable dye solution by adding a teaspoon of vinegar to 1/2 cup of boiling water. Drop in food coloring and stir. The longer the egg is kept in the dye, the deeper the color will be.
- Add a teaspoonful of salad oil to a dye mixture and mix in the oil well. This results in a dye that produces swirls of color. Immerse the egg in the dye for a few minutes.
- Draw a design on an egg with a crayon before dying it. The dye will not stay on the areas with the crayon marks and the design will show through.
- Wrap rubber bands, string, yarn, or narrow strips of masking tape around an egg to create stripes and other designs. Dip the egg in dye and allow to dry before removing the wrapping.
- Draw a design on the egg using a piece of wax. Place the egg in dye. Repeat the process again, if desired, dipping the egg in another color of dye. (**Caution:** The lighted candle is to be used by an adult only.)
- Felt-tip markers can be used to decorate dyed or undyed eggs.
- Small stickers can be used on eggs.
- Craft items such as sequins, glitter, ribbons, and small pom-poms can be used with glue to decorate eggs.
- Apply lengths of yarns, string, or thread to the eggs with glue, creating designs, and allow to dry.
- Egg creatures can be created by using markers, construction paper, feathers, ribbon, lace, cotton balls, fabric, and buttons. To make an egg holder, make small cardboard or construction paper cylinders. A toilet paper or paper towel tube can be cut to make stands as well.
- Save the shells from the eggs to use for eggshell collages. Crumble the shells and sprinkle over a glue design that has been made on paper or cardboard.

Nielsen, Shelly. (1992). *Celebrating Easter*. Minneapolis, MN: Abdo & Daughters.

Polacco, Patricia. (1992). *Chicken Sunday*. New York: Philomel Books.

Tudor, Tasha. (2001). *A Tale for Easter*. New York: Simon & Schuster.

Walburg, Lori and James Bernadin. (1999). *The Legend of the Easter Egg*. Illus. by James Bernadin. Grand Rapids, MI: Zondervan.

Zolotow, Charlotte. (1998). *The Bunny Who Found Easter*. Boston: Houghton Mifflin.

Multimedia

The following multimedia products can be used to complement this theme:

Auch, Mary Jane. *Easter Egg Farm* [book and cassette]. (1995). Pine Plains, NY: Live Oaks Media.

"Easter Egg Hunt" on *Holiday Songs for All Occasions* [cassette]. Long Branch, NJ: Kimbo Educational.

"Easter Time Is Here Again" on *Holiday Songs and Rhythms* [compact disc]. (1997). Freeport, NY: Activity Records, Inc.; Educational Activities, Inc.

Max's Chocolate Chicken and Other Stories for Young Children [video]. (© 1993). Weston, CT: Children's Circle Home Video; Los Angeles, distributed by Wood Knapp Video.

"Peter Cottontail" on *Holidays and Special Times* [cassette] (1989). Sung by Greg Scelsa and Steve Millang. Los Angeles, CA: Youngheart Records.

"Easter Egg Hunt." (1978). *Holiday Songs for All Occasions*. Long Branch, NJ: Kimbo Educational.

"So Early Easter Morning," "Bunny-Pokey," "Like a Bunny Would." (1993). *Holiday Piggyback Songs*. Long Branch, NJ: Kimbo Educational.

Recordings and Song Titles

The following recordings can be used to complement this theme:

"April." (1984). *Singing Calendar*. Long Branch, NJ: Kimbo Educational.

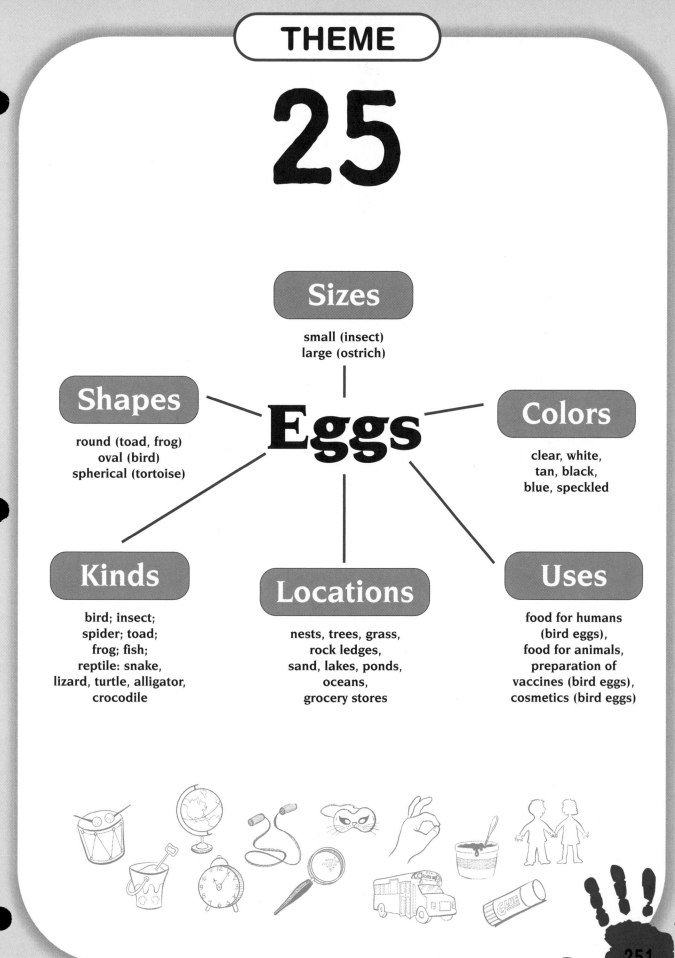

Sizes

small (insect)
large (ostrich)

Shapes

round (toad, frog)
oval (bird)
spherical (tortoise)

Eggs

Colors

clear, white,
tan, black,
blue, speckled

Kinds

bird; insect;
spider; toad;
frog; fish;
reptile: snake,
lizard, turtle, alligator,
crocodile

Locations

nests, trees, grass,
rock ledges,
sand, lakes, ponds,
oceans,
grocery stores

Uses

food for humans
(bird eggs),
food for animals,
preparation of
vaccines (bird eggs),
cosmetics (bird eggs)

Theme Goals

Through participating in the experiences provided by this theme, the children may learn:

1. Animals that produce eggs
2. Colors of eggs
3. Sizes of eggs
4. Shapes of eggs
5. Places to find eggs
6. Uses of eggs

Concepts for the Children to Learn

1. There are many kinds of eggs.
2. Birds, insects, spiders, toads, frogs, fish, and reptiles, including snakes, lizards, turtles, and alligators, lay eggs.
3. Eggs can be found in many locations.
4. Eggs can be found in nests, trees, grass, and rock ledges.
5. Eggs can also be found in the sand, lakes, ponds, oceans, and grocery stores.
6. An egg is the first stage in the development of an animal.
7. Eggs are made by the female.
8. Birds are the only animals that sit on their eggs to keep them warm.
9. Eggs can be different colors.
10. Eggs range in size from tiny eggs, such as insects' eggs, to very large eggs, like those of an ostrich.
11. Birds lay only a few eggs at a time. Other animals may lay thousands of small eggs.
12. Bird eggs are generally oval in shape. Other animals have eggs that are different shapes.
13. Eggs can be found in a variety of places.
14. Some people eat chicken eggs.
15. Chicken eggs can be prepared to be eaten in many ways (boiled, scrambled, fried, poached).
16. Chicken eggs are sold in grocery stores by the dozen.
17. Chicken eggs are also used to prepare vaccines, animal feeds, fertilizers, and some cosmetics.
18. Eggs have many uses.
19. Bird eggs can be food for humans or other animals.

Vocabulary

1. **egg**—a roundish object covered with a shell or membrane that is laid by the female of birds, reptiles, fish, and amphibians.
2. **hatch**—to come out of an egg.
3. **incubate**—to sit on eggs in order to hatch them.
4. **incubator**—a machine-type box for keeping bird eggs at a certain temperature so that they will hatch.
5. **shell**—the outer covering of most eggs.

Bulletin Board

The purpose of this bulletin board is to promote correspondence skills. To prepare the bulletin board pieces, trace and cut the nests from yellow tagboard. Then trace and cut the eggs from white tagboard. Attach dots and print numerals on each nest as illustrated. The number of nests prepared and numerals utilized should be developmentally appropriate for the group of children.

Family Letter

Dear Families,

We will be having an "egg-stra" special week as we make discoveries about eggs. We usually think of chicken eggs when we hear the word "egg"—but there are so many different kinds of animals that lay eggs. Your child will learn about many animals that lay eggs, places eggs can be found, and uses of eggs during our week focusing on the theme of eggs.

AT SCHOOL

A few of the week's highlights include:

- going on an egg walk! Weather permitting, we plan on walking through the park to look for various types of eggs, looking underneath logs and leaves. Care to join us?

- creating mosaic designs with eggshells. You can help us by saving and cleaning eggshells. Please bring them to school by Friday morning.

- observing chicken eggs in an incubator. Mr. Johnson (Matt's Dad) will be bringing an incubator and five fertilized eggs for us to watch. Chicken eggs hatch in about 21 days. We'll keep you posted!

AT HOME

There are many ways to bring our egg unit into your home. Some ideas to try include:

- preparing a meal or snack with your child that uses eggs as an ingredient

- comparing the sizes of small, medium, large, and extra-large eggs while at a grocery store with your child

- going to the library and checking out children's books about eggs. Some titles to look for include:

    Hatch, Egg, Hatch! by Shen Roddie

    Chickens Aren't the Only Ones by Ruth Heller

    Egg: A Photographic Story of Hatching by Robert Burton

Have an "egg-cellent" week!

Arts and Crafts

1. Eggshell Mosaic

Save and clean eggshells. Children can color eggshells with markers or paint. Then, have children spread glue on a piece of cardboard, tagboard, or construction paper. Eggshells can be broken into smaller pieces and placed in the glue to create a design.

2. Egg Carton Caterpillar

Collect cardboard egg cartons, chenille stems, crayons, markers, and paint. Cut egg cartons in half lengthwise. Help children fold a chenille stem in half and poke it into the top of the first section of the egg carton to represent the antennas. Children can then use the other materials as desired to decorate their caterpillar.

3. Painting with Feathers

Provide construction paper, feathers (available at craft stores), and paint. Children can use the feathers to apply the paint to the paper.

4. Clay Eggs

Children can use clay or play dough to create various sizes and colors of eggs. Allow to dry if desired.

Observing eggs hatching is a good science experiment.

Cooking

1. Noodle Nests

12 ounces butterscotch chips
3 cups chow-mein noodles
optional: jelly beans

Melt butterscotch chips in microwave or saucepan over low heat. Stir in noodles. Drop by teaspoonfuls onto waxed paper. Immediately top with jelly beans if desired. Let stand until firm. Makes about 36 pieces.

2. Egg Foo Young

6 eggs
1/4 cup instant minced onion
2 tablespoons chopped green pepper
1/2 teaspoon salt
dash of pepper
16-ounce can bean sprouts, drained

Sauce:
1 tablespoon cornstarch
2 teaspoons sugar
1 cube chicken bouillon
dash of ginger
1 cup water
2 tablespoons soy sauce

Heat oven to 300 degrees. In large bowl, beat eggs well. Add remaining ingredients, except sauce ingredients. Mix well. Heat 2 tablespoons oil in large skillet. Drop egg mixture by table-spoonfuls into skillet. Fry until golden. Turn and brown other side. Drain on paper towel. If necessary, add additional oil to skillet and cook remaining egg mixture. Keep warm in 300-degree oven while preparing sauce. Combine first four ingredients in small saucepan. Add water and soy sauce. Cook until mixture boils and thickens, stirring constantly.

3. Southwestern Eggs

1 pound bulk chorizo or pork sausage
1/2 cup chopped onion
1 1/4 cups mild salsa
4 eggs
3/4 cup shredded mozzarella cheese

Cook sausage and onion in 10-inch skillet until sausage is brown; drain. Stir in salsa and heat. Spread mixture evenly in skillet. Make four indentations in mixture with back of spoon. Break one egg into each indentation. Cover and cook over low heat about 12 minutes or until whites are set and yolks have thickened. Sprinkle with cheese. Serve with sour cream if desired.

4. Painted Egg Cookies

1/3 cup butter or margarine
1/4 cup sugar
1 egg
2/3 cup honey
3/4 teaspoon vanilla
2 3/4 cups flour
1 teaspoon baking soda
1/2 teaspoon salt

"Paint":
1 egg yolk
1/4 teaspoon water
food coloring

In a large mixing bowl, beat butter and sugar until fluffy. Add egg, honey, and vanilla. Beat well. Combine flour, baking soda, and salt. Gradually add flour mixture to butter mixture. Beat well. Cover and chill for 1 hour.

Set oven to 350 degrees. Grease cookie sheets if necessary. Divide dough in half, keeping one-half chilled. Roll dough on a lightly floured surface to a 1/4-inch thickness. Cut with egg-shaped (oval) cookie cutter. Place 1 inch apart on cookie sheets. Repeat with remaining dough.

Beat egg yolk and water in a small mixing bowl. Divide yolk mixture between three or four small bowls. Add two to three drops of different food colors to each bowl and mix well. With a clean small paint or pastry brush or cotton swab, paint cookies as desired. Bake 6 to 8 minutes or until golden.

Dramatic Play

1. Grocery Store

Ask parents to save empty, clean food containers (boxes, jars, plastic bottles, etc.) to be used as props and supplies for a grocery store. Include empty, clean egg cartons of various-sized eggs.

2. House

Provide empty, clean egg cartons, egg beaters, wire whips, bowls, small frying pans, and turners as additional props to the housekeeping area.

3. Bird Store

Create a bird store in the dramatic play area. Display posters and pictures of birds. Provide clean bird cages, stuffed toy and craft birds, and plastic bird eggs. Check out bird books from the library and include in the area.

Field Trips/ Resource People

1. Farm

Plan a field trip to a farm where children can observe young chickens, turkeys, or ducks.

2. Zoo

Eggs of many reptiles, amphibians, and birds may be observed at some zoos.

3. **4-H Agent**

   Contact your local 4-H agent for information regarding area people involved in hatcheries. Invite one to talk to the children about eggs and incubators.

4. **Grocery Store**

   While at the grocery store, observe the egg section.

Fingerplays

Eggs in a Nest

Here's an egg in a nest up in a tree.
   (make fist with right hand and place in palm of cupped left hand)
What's inside? What can it be?
   (shrug shoulders)
Peck, peck, peck,
Peep, peep, peep.
Out hatches a little bird,
   (wiggle fingers or fisted hand)
Cute as can be!

My Turtle

This is my turtle,
   (make fist and extend thumb)
He lives in a shell.
   (hide thumb in fist)
He likes his home very well.
He pokes his head out when he wants to eat
   (extend thumb)
And pulls it back in when he wants to sleep.
   (hide thumb in fist)

Hatching Chickens

Five eggs and five eggs
   (hold up one hand and then the other)
Are underneath a hen.
Five eggs and five eggs
   (hold up all fingers)
And that makes 10.
The hen keeps the eggs warm for three
   long weeks
   (hold up three fingers)

Snap go the shells with tiny little beaks.
   (snap fingers)
Crack, crack, the shells go.
   (clap four times)
The chickens, every one,
Fluff out their feathers
In the warm spring sun.
   (make circle of arms)

Group Time

(Games, Language)

1. **Egg Habitats**

   Ask the children, "If you could go looking for an egg right now, where would you look?" Have children name places eggs can be found—nests, grass, water, sand, ponds, sea, or trees. Record the children's responses on a large sheet of paper or tagboard. Display the sheet in the classroom.

2. **Game: "Egg, Egg, Who's Got the Egg?"**

   For this game, a plastic, paper, or hard-boiled egg can be used. The children sit in a circle formation. One child is chosen to be the chicken or bird and sits in the center of the circle with the egg in front of him or her. The "chicken" closes his or her eyes. A child from the circle is silently chosen to sneak up and take the egg. All children then put their hands behind their backs and call, "Egg, egg, who's got the egg?" The "chicken" then has three chances to guess who is holding the egg.

Large Muscle

1. **Egg Maze**

   Create a maze on the floor using classroom blocks. Older children may be able to help! Then, encourage children to roll and push a hard-boiled or plastic egg through the maze as quickly as possible. Tools such as brushes, small brooms, or spoons could be used to roll the egg.

EGGS

2. Egg Relay

In this activity, a spoon is used to transport a hard-boiled egg from one location to another. The game can be played individually or children can be in teams, if appropriate.

Math

1. Balancing Eggs

Provide a balance scale and a hard-boiled egg. If appropriate, children can estimate how many of a specific object (crayons, cubes, blocks) they think will balance the egg. Then the children can count (and possibly record) the actual number it takes to balance the egg. The activity can be repeated with various objects. Results can be compared.

2. Egg Sort

Create and cut various egg shapes out of construction paper or tagboard. Decorate pieces as desired. Laminate pieces for durability. Encourage children to sort the eggs by various attributes such as size, color, and patterns.

3. Egg Carton Math

Using a permanent marker, randomly number the egg cups in an egg carton from 1 to 12 (or use fewer numerals or sets of dots, if appropriate). Put a button or bread tag in the carton and close the lid. Children shake the carton, open the lid, and identify the number the piece landed on.

Music

1. "Here's a Little Birdie"
(*Sing to the tune of* "I *Know a Little Pussy*")

Here's a little birdie
Hatching from its shell.
First comes its beak,
Then comes its head.

He's working very, very hard,
His wings he gives a flap.
Then he lies down to rest and dry off,
Now what do you think of that?!
Peck, peck, peck, peck, peck, peck, peck, peck,
Peep!

2. "Egg Choices"
(*Sing to the tune of* "If *You're Happy and You Know It*")

If you like your eggs scrambled,
Clap your hands. (clap, clap)
If you like your eggs scrambled,
Clap your hands. (clap, clap)
If you like your eggs scrambled,
And it's your favorite way to make 'em,
If you like your eggs scrambled,
Clap your hands. (clap, clap)

Additional verses:

If you like your eggs fried,
Touch your toes . . .

If you like your eggs hard-boiled,
Snap your fingers . . .

3. "Red Hen, Red Hen"
(*Sing to the tune of* "Baa, Baa, Black Sheep")

Red hen, red hen, have you eggs for me?
Yes, sir. Yes, sir. A lot as you can see.
One to hard-boil.
Another one to fry.
One to scramble.
And Easter eggs to dye.
Red hen, red hen, have you eggs for me?
Yes, sir. Yes, sir. A lot as you can see.

Science

1. Eggshell Garden

Save and clean eggshell halves. Provide potting soil and seeds (such as radish or marigold). Have children fill each shell with soil and a few seeds. Add a spoonful of water to each shell. Place eggshell halves in the cups of an empty egg carton. Once the plants have grown, they can be transplanted into the ground or a larger container after crushing the eggshells.

2. Will an Egg Float?

All fresh, raw chicken eggs sink in water. However, salt mixed or dissolved in water can make an egg float. Place a raw egg in a clear glass filled with water. If appropriate, older students can count and record how many individual teaspoons of salt are mixed in the water to make the egg float.

3. Vinegar and Eggs

Gently place a raw egg in a clear glass or jar filled with vinegar. Observe what happens to the egg over a period of three to four days. (After two days, the shell will soften and begin to disappear. After three days, most of the calcium will have dissolved, leaving only a bladder.)

4. Egg to Frog (or Toad)

Hatching frog or toad eggs is a great way to observe eggs. In the spring, search local ponds for jelly-like masses of eggs. They are usually found underwater among weeds or grasses near shore. Prepare a tank or glass jar for the eggs/tadpoles. Changes occur fast and children will be able to observe them. (If ponds are not locally accessible, check a biological supply house or ask a high school biology teacher.)

5. Hatching Chicken Eggs

Contact a chicken farmer or your high-school biology department to find out about borrowing an incubator and obtaining fertilized eggs. Follow the directions closely for setting up the incubator and maintaining its temperature and humidity. Stress to the children the importance of not disturbing the incubator. Keep a camera handy to record the hatching process.

Sensory

Additions to the Sensory Table

- grains, egg cartons, and plastic eggs
- water, plastic fish, and strainers
- water, plastic frogs/toads, and berry baskets
- sand and plastic reptile and amphibian toys

Social Studies

Ukrainian Eggs

Ukrainian Easter eggs, known as pysanky, feature colorful, intricate designs. Some people are skilled in this Ukrainian art. If possible, a collection of Ukrainian eggs could be shown to the children. Ideally, the art could be demonstrated to the children. Contact your high school art department, library, or university for names of individuals who could share this art with the children.

Books

The following books can be used to complement this theme:

Brett, Jan. (2000). *Hedgie's Surprise*. New York: G. P. Putnam.

Burton, Robert. (1994). *Egg: A Photographic Story of Hatching*. Photos by Kim Taylor. New York: Dorling Kindersley.

Butrum, Ray. (1998). *I'm Sorry You Can't Hatch an Egg*. Sisters, OR: Multnomah Press.

De Bourgoing, Pascale. (1992). *The Egg*. Illus. by René Mettle. New York: Scholastic.

Ernst, Lisa Campbell. (1992). *Zinnia and Dot*. New York: Viking.

Fowler, Allan. (1993). *The Chicken or the Egg!* Chicago: Children's Press.

Gill, Shelley and Jo-Ellen Bosson. (2001). *The Egg*. Watertown, MA: Charlesbridge.

Heller, Ruth. (1981). *Chickens Aren't the Only Ones*. New York: G. P. Putnam.

Humphrey, Paul. (1996). *Frog's Eggs*. Austin, TX: Raintree/Steck Vaughn. (Pbk.)

Jenkins, Priscilla Belz. (1995). *A Nest Full of Eggs*. Illus. by Lizzy Rockwell. New York: HarperCollins.

Johnson, Sylvia A. (1992). *Inside an Egg*. Photos by Kiyoshi Shimizu. Minneapolis: Lerner Publishing. (Pbk.)

Joyce, William. (1992). *Bently and Egg*. New York: HarperCollins.

Kellogg, Steven. (2001). *A Penguin's Pup for Pinkerton*. New York: Dial Books.

Krauss, Ruth. (2005). *The Happy Egg*. Illus. by Crockett Johnson. New York: Harper-Collins Publishers. (1st HarperCollins edition.)

Lionni, Leo. (1994). *An Extraordinary Egg*. New York: Knopf.

Polacco, Patricia. (1988). *Rechenka's Eggs*. New York: G. P. Putnam.

Reasoner, Charles. (1994). *Who's Hatching*? New York: Price Stern Sloan. (A *Sliding Surprise* Book.)

Ruurs, Margriet. (1997). *Emma's Eggs*. Illus. by Barbara Spurll. New York: Stoddart Kids.

Seuss, Dr. (1992). *Scrambled Eggs Super*! New York: Random House.

Multimedia

The following multimedia products can be used to complement this theme:

Kids Get Cooking: The Egg [video]. (1987). Newton, MA: Kidviz.

Palmer, Hap. "Humpty Dumpty" on *Hap Palmer Sings Classic Nursery Rhymes* [cassette]. (1991). Freeport, NY: Educational Activities.

Polacco, Patricia. *Rechenka's Eggs* [video]. (1992). Lincoln, NE: GNP.

Changes

leaves turn color and fall
temperature cooler
darker earlier
days are shorter

Clothing

sweaters
coats
scarves
long-sleeved shirts
long pants

Fall

Holidays

Labor Day
Halloween
Thanksgiving

Activities

football
raking leaves
walks
bike rides
harvesting foods
camping
soccer

Theme Goals

Through participating in the experiences provided by this theme, the children may learn

1. Changes in fall
2. Fall holidays
3. Fall clothing
4. Fall activities

Concepts for the Children to Learn

1. There are many changes in the fall.
2. Leaves turn color in the fall.
3. It gets dark outside earlier in the day.
4. In some places the weather becomes cooler in the fall.
5. The day becomes shorter in the fall.
6. Leaves fall from some trees in the fall.
7. Labor Day, Halloween, and Thanksgiving are some fall holidays.
8. Scarves and sweaters may need to be worn in the fall in some areas.
9. Long-sleeved shirts, long pants, and coats may also need to be worn in the fall.
10. Pumpkins and apples can be harvested in the fall.
11. Football and soccer are fall sports.
12. People take walks, ride bikes, and camp in the fall.
13. Leaves may also be raked in the fall.

Vocabulary

1. **fall**—the season between summer and winter.
2. **Halloween**—the holiday when people wear costumes and go trick-or-treating.
3. **Labor Day**—a holiday to honor working people.
4. **season**—a time of the year.
5. **Thanksgiving**—a holiday to express thanks.

Bulletin Board

The purpose of this bulletin board is to foster a positive self-concept as well as develop name-recognition skills. Construct an acorn for each child. Print the children's names on the acorns. See illustration. Laminate and punch holes in the acorns. Children can hang their acorns on pushpins on the bulletin board when they arrive.

Family Letter

Dear Families,

Where we live, the days are getting shorter, the temperature is getting colder, and the leaves are changing color. It's the perfect time to introduce our next unit—fall. By participating in the experiences provided throughout this unit, children will become more aware of changes that take place in the fall. They will also learn the fall holidays, clothing, and activities.

AT SCHOOL

A few of this week's learning experiences include:

- recording the temperature and the changing colors of the leaves
- making leaf rubbings in the art area
- raking leaves on our playground during outdoor time

We will also be taking a fall walk around the neighborhood to observe the trees in their peak changes. We will be leaving Thursday at 10:00 a.m. Please feel free to join us. It will be a scenic tour.

AT HOME

To develop classification skills, help your child sort leaves by their color, type, or size.

Fingerplays promote language and vocabulary skills. This fingerplay is one we will be learning this week. Enjoy it with your child at home!

Autumn

Autumn winds begin to blow.
   (blow)
Colored leaves fall fast and slow.
   (make fast and slow motions with hands)
Twirling, whirling all around,
   (turn around)
'Til at last, they touch the ground.
   (fall to the ground)

Enjoy your child as you explore experiences related to the unit on fall.

264

THEME 26

Fall leaves can be collected and used for many different craft projects.

Arts and Crafts

1. Fall Collage

After taking a walk to collect objects such as grass, twigs, leaves, nuts, and weeds, collages can be made in the art area.

2. Leaf Rubbings

Collect leaves, paper, and crayons and show the children how to place several leaves under a sheet of paper. Using the flat edge of the crayon, rub over paper. The image of the leaves will appear.

3. Pumpkin Seed Collage

Wash and dry pumpkin seeds and place them in the art area with glue and paper. The children can make pumpkin seed collages.

4. Leaf Spatter Painting

Use a lid from a box that is approximately 9 inches × 12 inches × 12 inches. Cut a rectangle from the lid top, leaving a 1 1/2-inch border. Invert the lid and place a wire screen over the opening. Tape the screen to the border. Arrange the leaves on a sheet of paper. Place the lid over the arrangement. Dip a toothbrush into thin tempera paint and brush across the screen. When the tempera paint dries, remove the leaves.

Cooking

1. Apple Banana Frosty

1 golden delicious apple, diced
1 peeled, sliced banana
1/4 cup milk
3 ice cubes

Blend all the ingredients in a blender. Serves four children.

2. Apple Salad

6 medium apples
1/2 cup raisins
1/2 teaspoon cinnamon
1/4 cup white grape juice

Peel and chop the apples. Mix well and add the remaining ingredients. Serves 10 children.

Dramatic Play

1. Fall Wear

Set out warm clothes such as sweaters, coats, hats, and blankets to indicate cold weather coming. The children can use the clothes for dressing up.

2. Football

Collect football gear, including balls, helmets, and jerseys, and play on the outdoor playground.

Nature Recipes

Cattails

Use them in their natural color or tint by shaking metallic powder over them. Handle carefully. The cattail is dry and feels crumbly. It will fall apart easily.

Crystal Garden*

Place broken pieces of brick or terra-cotta clay in a glass bowl or jar. Pour the following solution over this:

4 teaspoons water
1 teaspoon ammonia
4 teaspoons bluing
1 teaspoon Mercurochrome
4 teaspoons salt

Add more of this solution each day until the crystal garden has grown to the desired size. (Adult supervision required.)

*This activity should be carefully observed if in a classroom with preschool children.

Drying Plants for Winter Bouquets

Strip the leaves from the flowers immediately. Tie the flowers by their stems with string and hang them with the heads down in a cool, dry place away from the light. Darkness is essential for preserving their color. Thorough drying takes about two weeks.

Preserving Fall Leaves

Place alternate layers of powdered borax and leaves in a box. The leaves must be completely covered. Allow them to stand for four days. Shake off the borax and wipe each leaf with liquid floor wax. Rub a warm iron over a cake of paraffin, then press the iron over the front and back of leaves.

Preserving Magnolia Leaves

Mix two parts of water with one part of glycerine. Place stems of the magnolia leaves in the mixture and let them stand for several days. The leaves will turn brown and last several years. Their surface may be painted or sprayed with silver or gold paint.

Pressing Wildflowers

When gathering specimens, include the roots, leaves, flowers, and seed pods. Place between newspapers, laying two layers of blotters underneath the newspaper and two on top to absorb the moisture. Change the newspapers three times during the week. Place between two sheets of corrugated cardboard and press. It usually takes 7 to 10 days to press specimens. Cardboard covered with cotton batting is the mounting base. Lay the flower on the cotton and cover with cellophane or plastic wrap to preserve the color.

Treating Gourds

Soak gourds in water for two hours. Scrape them clean with a knife. Rub with fine sandpaper. While still damp, cut an opening to remove seeds.

 **Field Trips**

1. **Neighborhood Walk**

   Take a walk around the neighborhood when the leaves are at their peak of changing colors. Discuss differences in color and size.

2. **Apple Orchard**

   Visit an apple orchard. Observe the apples being picked and processed. If possible, let children pick their own apples from a tree.

3. **Pumpkin Patch**

   Visit a pumpkin patch. Discuss and observe how pumpkins grow, their size, shape, and color. Let the children pick a pumpkin to bring back to the classroom.

THEME 26

Fingerplays

Autumn

Autumn winds begin to blow.
(blow)
Colored leaves fall fast and slow.
(make fast and slow falling motions with hands)
Twirling, whirling all around
(turn around)
'Til at last, they touch the ground.
(fall to the ground)

Leaves

Little leaves fall gently down
Red and yellow, orange and brown.
(flutter hands like leaves falling)
Whirling, whirling around and around.
(turn around)
Quietly without a sound.
(put finger to lips)
Falling softly to the ground
(begin to fall slowly)
Down and down and down and down.
(lie on floor)

Little Leaves

The little leaves are falling down
(use hands to make falling motion)
Round and round, round and round.
(turn around)
The little leaves are falling down,
(use hands to make falling motion)
Falling to the ground.
(fall to ground)

Twirling Leaves

The autumn wind blows—Oooo Oooo Oooo.
(make wind sounds)
The leaves shake and shake then fly into the sky
so blue.
(children shake)
They whirl and whirl around them, twirl and
twirl around.
(turn around in circles)
But when the wind stops, the leaves sink slowly
to the ground.
Lower, lower, lower, and land quietly without
a sound.
(sink very slowly and very quietly)

Large Muscle

Raking Leaves

Child-sized rakes can be provided. The children
can be encouraged to rake leaves into piles.

Math

1. **Weighing Acorns and Pinecones**

   A scale, acorns, and pinecones for the children
   to weigh can be added to the science table.

2. **Leaf Math**

   Out of construction paper or tagboard, prepare
   pairs of various-shaped leaves. The children can
   match the identical leaves.

Music

1. **"Little Leaves"**
   (*Sing to the tune of* "*Ten Little Indians*")

   One little, two little, three little leaves.
   Four little, five little, six little leaves.
   Seven little, eight little, nine little leaves.
   Ten little leaves fall down.

2. **"Happy Children Tune"**
   (*Sing to the tune of* "*Did You Ever See a Lassie?*")

   Happy children in the autumn,
   In the autumn, in the autumn.
   Happy children in the autumn
   Do this way and that.

   While singing the song, children can keep time
   by pretending to rake leaves, jump in the
   leaves, etc.

3. **"Pretty Leaves Are Falling Down"**
   (*Sing to the tune of* "*London Bridge*")

   Pretty leaves are falling down, falling down,
   falling down.

FALL

Pretty leaves are falling down, all around the town.
   (wiggle fingers)

Let's rake them up in a pile, in a pile, in a pile.
Let's rake them up in a pile, all around the town.
   (make raking motions)

Let's all jump in and have some fun,
   have some fun, have some fun.
Let's all jump in and have some fun, all around
   the town.
   (jump into circle)

Science

1. Leaf Observation

Collect leaves from a variety of trees. Place them and a magnifying glass on the science table for the children to explore.

2. Temperature Watch

Place a thermometer outside. A large cardboard thermometer can also be constructed out of tagboard with movable elastic or ribbon for the mercury. The children can match the temperature on the cardboard thermometer with the outdoor one.

3. Weather Calendar

Construct a calendar for the month. Record the changes of weather each day by attaching a symbol to the calendar. Symbols should include clouds, sun, snow, rain, etc.

4. Color Change Sequence

Laminate or cover with contact paper several leaves of different colors. The children can sort, count, and classify the leaves.

Sensory

1. Leaves

Place a variety of leaves in the sensory table. Try to include moist and dry examples for the children to compare.

2. Pumpkins

Place pumpkins, hammers, and golf tees in the sensory table. The children can practice pounding the golf tees into the pumpkins.

Note: This activity must be carefully supervised.

Social Studies

Bulletin Board

Construct a bulletin board using bare branches to represent a tree. Cut out leaves from colored construction paper and print one child's name on each. At the beginning of the day, children can hang their name on the tree when they arrive.

Books

The following books can be used to complement this theme:

Arnosky, Jim. (1993). *Every Autumn Comes the Bear*. New York: G. P. Putnam.

Bunting, Eve. (1997). *The Pumpkin Fair*. Illus. by Eileen Christelow. New York: Clarion Books.

Bunting, Eve and James Ransome. (2001). *Peepers*. Illus. by James Ransome. San Diego, CA: Harcourt Brace.

Ehlert, Lois. (1991). *Red Leaf, Yellow Leaf*. Orlando, FL: Harcourt Brace.

Ehlert, Lois. (2005). *Leaf Man*. Orlando, FL: Harcourt.

Fleming, Denise. (1993). *In the Small, Small, Pond*. New York: H. Holt.

Fowler, Allan. (1992). *How Do You Know It's Fall?* Chicago: Children's Press.

Fowler, Allan. (1993). *It Could Still Be a Leaf*. Chicago: Children's Press.

George, Lindsay Barrett. (1995). *In the Woods: Who's Been Here?* New York: Greenwillow.

Hall, Zoe. (1994). *It's Pumpkin Time!* Illus. by Shari Halpern. New York: Scholastic.

Hall, Zoe and Shari Halpern. (2000). *Fall Leaves Fall!* Illus. by Shari Halpern. New York: Scholastic.

Harshman, Marc, Cheryl Ryan, and Wade Zahares. (2001). *Red Are the Apples*. Illus. by Wade Zahares. San Diego, CA: Gulliver Books.

Hoban, Lillian. (1996). *Arthur's Back to School Day*. New York: HarperCollins.

Hunter, Anne. (1996). *Possum's Harvest Moon*. Boston: Houghton Mifflin.

Hutchings, Amy. (1994). *Picking Apples and Pumpkins*. Illus. by Richard Hutchings. St. Paul, MN: Cartwheel Books. (Pbk.)

Lotz, Karen E. (1993). *Snowsong Whistling*. Illus. by Elisa Kleven. New York: Dutton.

Maass, Robert. (1990). *When Autumn Comes*. Holt: New York. (Pbk.)

Maestro, Betsy C. (1994). *Why Do Leaves Change Color?* Illus. by Loretta Krupinski. New York: HarperCollins.

Moore, Elaine. (1995). *Grandma's Smile*. Illus. by Dan Andreasen. New York: Lothrop, Lee & Shepard.

Robbins, Ken. (1998). *Fall Leaves*. New York: Scholastic.

Rockwell, Anne F. (1989). *Apples and Pumpkins*. Illus. by Lizzy Rockwell. New York: Simon & Schuster.

Russo, Marisabina. (1994). *I Don't Want to Go Back to School*. New York: Greenwillow.

Rylant, Cynthia and Jill Kastner. (2000). *In November*. Illus. by Jill Kastner. San Diego, CA: Harcourt Brace.

Saunders-Smith, Gail. (1997). *Autumn Leaves*. Mankato, MN: Pebble Books.

Schweninger, Ann. (1993). *Autumn Days*. New York: Puffin. (Pbk.)

Simon, Seymour. (1993). *Autumn Across America*. New York: Hyperion.

White, Linda. (1996). *Too Many Pumpkins*. Illus. by Megan Lloyd. New York: Holiday House.

Zagwyn, Deborah Turney. (1997). *The Pumpkin Blanket*. Berkeley, CA: Tricycle Press.

Multimedia

The following multimedia products can be used to complement this theme:

Bingham, Bing. "The First Day of School" on *A Rainbow of Songs* [cassette]. Available from Kimbo Educational, Long Branch, NJ.

James, Dixie and Linda Becht. *The Singing Calendar* [cassette]. Kimbo Educational, Long Branch, NJ.

Maestro, Betsy C. *Why Do Leaves Change Color?* Illus. by Loretta Krupinski. [Book and cassette]. (1996). Harper Audio.

Seasonal Songs in Motion. (2001). Melbourne, FL: The Learning Station.

What Is a Leaf? [video]. (1991). Washington, DC: National Geographic.

White, Linda. *Too Many Pumpkins* [video]. (1997). Live Oak Productions.

Recordings and Song Titles

The following recordings can be used to complement this theme:

"Autumn," "Season Song," "Leaves." (1995). *Piggyback Songs*. Long Branch, NJ: Kimbo Educational.

"It's Fall Again." (2001). *Seasonal Songs in Motion*. Long Branch, NJ: Kimbo Educational.

Activities

celebrations
eating
reading
playing
working
reunions
vacationing
camping

Families

Purpose

care
protect
teach

Members

mothers, fathers,
stepparents,
sisters, brothers,
grandmothers,
grandfathers,
aunts, uncles,
nephews, nieces,
cousins,
adopted members,
deceased members

Theme Goals

Through participating in the experiences provided by this theme, the children may learn

1. The members in a family
2. Purpose of families
3. Family activities

Concepts for the Children to Learn

1. A family is a group of people who live together.
2. Mothers, fathers, sisters, and brothers are family members.
3. Grandmothers, grandfathers, aunts, uncles, cousins, nephews, nieces, and stepparents are family members.
4. Camping, eating, working, reading, and playing are all family activities.
5. Families often vacation together.
6. Families may often have reunions.
7. Families teach us about our world.
8. Family members care for and protect us.
9. There are many types of families: one-parent, two-parent, blended, and extended.

Vocabulary

1. **aunt**—sister of a parent.
2. **blended**—people from two or more families living together.
3. **brother**—a boy having the same parents as another person.
4. **children**—young people.
5. **cousin**—son or daughter of an uncle or aunt.
6. **extended**—includes aunts, uncles, grandparents, and cousins.
7. **family**—people living together.
8. **father**—male parent.
9. **grandfather**—father of a parent.
10. **grandmother**—mother of a parent.
11. **love**—feeling of warmth toward another.
12. **mother**—female parent.
13. **nephew**—son of a brother or sister.
14. **niece**—daughter of a brother or sister.
15. **one-parent family**—a child or children who lives with only one parent, a father or mother.
16. **sister**—a girl having the same parents as another person.
17. **uncle**—brother of a parent.

Bulletin Board

The purpose of this bulletin board is to foster an awareness of various family sizes, as well as to identify family members. Construct a name card for each child from tagboard. Print each child's name on one of the tagboard pieces. Then cut people figures as illustrated. Laminate the name cards and people. Staple the name cards to a bulletin board as illustrated. Individually, the children can affix the people in their family after their name using tape, sticky putty, or a stapler.

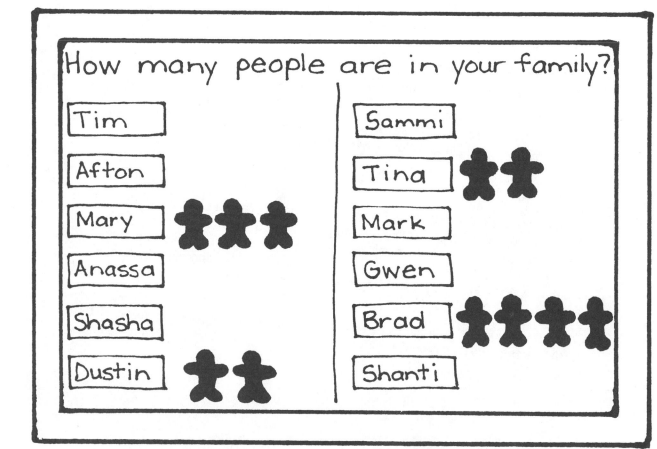

Family Letter

Dear Families,

Our next unit will focus on families. Through this unit, the children will develop an understanding of various family patterns. They will also discover what family members do for each other, as well as activities that families can participate in together.

AT SCHOOL

A few of this unit's highlights include:

- creating pictures of our families on a bulletin board

- looking at photographs of classmates' families. To assist us with this unit, please send a picture of your family to school with your child. We will place the photograph in a special photo album to look at in the reading area.

AT HOME

There are several activities you can do at home to foster the concepts of this unit. Begin by looking through family photographs with your child. While doing this, discuss family traditions or customs. You can also encourage your child to dictate a letter to you to write to a grandparent or other relative. Plan and participate in a family activity. This could be as simple as taking a walk together or going on a picnic.

We invite you and your family to visit us. This includes moms, dads, brothers, sisters, grandparents, and other relatives! If you are interested in coming, please let me know!

Enjoy your family this week!

Families are an important part of life.

Arts and Crafts

1. Family Collage

The children can cut out pictures of people from magazines. The pictures can be pasted on a sheet of paper to make a collage.

2. My Body

Trace each child's body on a large piece of paper. The children can use crayons and felt-tip markers to color their own body picture. When finished, display the pictures around the room or in the center's entrance.

Cooking

1. Jelly

Cut whole wheat bread into house shapes for snack one day. Put raisins and jelly on the table with knives. Let children choose their own topping.

2. Gingerbread Families

Use the following recipe to create gingerbread families.

1 1/2 cups whole-wheat pastry flour
1 teaspoon baking soda
1/2 teaspoon salt
1/2 teaspoon ginger
1 teaspoon cinnamon
1/4 cup oil
1/4 cup maple syrup
1/4 cup honey
1 large egg

Preheat oven to 350 degrees. Measure all of the dry ingredients into a bowl and mix well. Measure all wet ingredients into a second bowl and mix well. Add the two mixtures together. Pour the combined mixture into an 8-inch-square pan and bake for 30 to 35 minutes. When cool, roll the gingerbread dough into thin slices and provide cookie cutters for children to cut out their family. Decorate the figures with standard icing and candies/cookie decorations or sprinkles/jimmies. Enjoy for snack time.

3. Raisin Bran Muffins

4 cups raisin bran cereal
2 1/2 cups all-purpose flour
1 cup sugar
2 1/2 teaspoons baking soda
1 teaspoon salt
2 eggs, beaten
2 cups buttermilk
1/2 cup cooking oil

Stir the cereal, flour, sugar, baking soda, and salt together in a large mixing bowl. In a separate bowl beat the eggs, buttermilk, and oil together. Add this mixture to the dry ingredients and stir until moistened. The batter will be thick. Spoon the batter into greased or lined muffin cups, filling 3/4 full. Bake in a 375-degree oven for 20 to 25 minutes and remove from pans.

4. Kabbat Hamudth

(*Meatball soup served during Ramadan, a Muslim celebration*)

For the meatballs:

1 pound choice ground beef
14 oz. box cream of rice cereal
1/2 teaspoon salt

Combine ingredients and mix well. Add a little water if necessary. Puree in small batches. Divide mixture into 30 balls. Cover and chill.

For the stuffing:

1 medium onion, chopped
1/2 pound choice ground beef
1/2 cup drained chickpeas
1/4 cup chopped fresh parsley
1 scant teaspoon ground allspice

Brown onions and beef in a 10-inch skillet. Drain fat and add remaining stuffing ingredients. Set aside.

To form meatballs, flatten each ball with your fingertips. Place 2–3 teaspoons of the stuffing in the center and re-form beef into a ball around the stuffing. Cover and chill.

For the soup:

2–3 medium onions, quartered
1 pound turnips, chopped
2 tablespoons olive oil
16 cups beef broth
1 pound Swiss chard, coarsely chopped
1/2 cup drained canned chickpeas

1 teaspoon ground allspice (optional)
Salt and pepper to taste
3–4 tablespoons finely chopped fresh mint
leaves or 2 teaspoons dried
1/2 cup lemon juice

Sauté onions and turnips in olive oil until onions are translucent. Bring broth to boil, lower heat, add onions, turnips, Swiss chard, and chickpeas. Season with allspice, salt, and pepper. Simmer until turnips are soft. Add mint and lemon juice. About 20 minutes before serving add meatballs.

Serve in bowls with two to three meatballs per serving. Caution must be taken regarding the temperature of the soup.

Dramatic Play

1. Baby Clothing

Arrange the dramatic play area for washing baby dolls. Include a tub with soapy water, washcloths, drying towels, play clothes, brush, and comb.

2. Family Picnic

Collect items to make a picnic basket. Include paper napkins, cups, plates, plastic eating utensils, etc.

3. Dollhouse

Set up a large dollhouse for children to play with. These can be constructed from cardboard. Include dolls to represent several members of a family.

Fingerplays

Grandma's and Grandpa's Glasses

Here are Grandma's glasses.
(make small circles with fingers over eyes)
Here is Grandma's hat.
(fold hands over head)
This is the way she folds her hands
(fold hands)

(*continued*)

276

Snack Ideas

Milk
1. Dips (yogurt, cottage cheese, cream cheese)
2. Cheese (balls, wedges, cutouts, squares, faces, etc.)
3. Yogurt and fruit
4. Milk punches made with fruits and juices
5. Conventional cocoa
6. Cottage cheese (add pineapple, peaches, etc.)
7. Cheese fondues (preheated, no open flames in classroom)
8. Shakes (mix fruit and milk in a blender)

Meat
1. Meat strips, chunks, cubes (beef, pork, chicken, turkey, ham, fish)
2. Meatballs, small kabobs
3. Meat roll-ups (cheese spread, mashed potatoes, spinach, lettuce leaves, or tortillas)
4. Meat salads (tuna, other fish, chicken, turkey, etc.) as spreads for crackers, stuffing for celery, rolled in spinach or lettuce
5. Sardines
6. Stuffing for potatoes, tomatoes, squash

Eggs
1. Hard-boiled
2. Deviled (use different flavors)
3. Egg salad spread
4. Eggs any style that can be managed
5. Egg as a part of other recipes
6. Eggnog

Fruits
1. Use standard fruits, but be adventurous: pomegranates, cranberries, pears, peaches, apricots, plums, berries, pineapples, melons, grapes, grapefruit, tangerines
2. Kabobs and salads
3. Juices and juice blends
4. In muffins, yogurt, milk beverages
5. Fruit "sandwiches"
6. Stuffed dates, prunes, etc.
7. Dried fruits (raisins, currants, prunes, apples, peaches, apricots, dates, figs)

Vegetables
1. Variety—sweet and white potatoes, cherry tomatoes, broccoli, cauliflower, radishes, peppers, mushrooms, zucchini, all squashes, rutabaga, avocados, eggplant, okra, pea pods, turnips, pumpkin, sprouts, spinach
2. Almost any vegetable can be served raw with or without dip
3. Salads, kabobs, cutouts
4. Juices and juice blends
5. Soup in a cup (hot or cold)
6. Stuffed—celery, cucumbers, zucchini, spinach, lettuce, cabbage, squash, potatoes, tomatoes
7. Vegetable spreads
8. Sandwiches

Dried Peas and Beans
1. Kidney beans, garbanzos, limas, lentils, yellow and green peas, pintos, black beans
2. Beans and peas mashed as dips or spreads
3. Bean, pea, or lentil soup in a cup
4. Roasted soybeans
5. Three-bean salad

Pastas
1. Different shapes and thicknesses
2. Pasta with butter and poppy seeds
3. Cold pasta salad
4. Lasagne noodles (cut for small sandwiches)
5. Chow mein noodles (wheat or rice)

Breads
1. Use a variety of grains— whole wheat, cracked wheat, rye, cornmeal, oatmeal, bran, grits, etc.
2. Use a variety of breads— tortillas, pocket breads, crepes, pancakes, muffins, biscuits, bagels, popovers, English muffins
3. Toast—plain, buttered, with spreads, cinnamon
4. Homemade yeast and quick breads
5. Fill and roll up crepes, pancakes
6. Waffle sandwiches

Cereals, Grains, Seeds
1. Granola
2. Slices of rice loaf or rice cakes
3. Dry cereal mixes (not pre-sweetened)
4. Seed mixes (pumpkin, sunflower, sesame, poppy, caraway, etc.)
5. Roasted wheat berries, wheat germ, bran as roll-ins, toppings, or as finger mix
6. Popcorn with toppings of grated cheese or flavored butters
7. Stir into muffins or use as a topping

(*continued from page 276*)

And lays them in her lap.
(place hands in lap)

Here are Grandpa's glasses.
(make bigger circles with fingers over eyes)
Here is Grandpa's cap.
(pretend to put baseball cap on head)
This is the way he folds his arms
(fold arms across chest)
Just like that!

Children

"It's time for my children to go to bed,"
The nice and happy mother (father) said.
"Now I must count them up to see,
If all my children are home with me."
One child, two children, three children, dear,
(hold up three fingers in succession)
Four children, five children, YES, they are all here.
(hold up remaining fingers in succession)
They're the dearest little children alive,
One, two, three, four, five.
(hold up each finger in succession)

Five Little Robins

Five little robins lived in a tree.
A father, mother, and babies three.
(hold up fingers of one hand)
Father caught a worm,
(point to thumb)
Mother caught a bug,
(point to index finger)
This one got the bug,
(point to middle finger)
This one got the worm,
(point to ring finger)
And this one sat and waited his turn.
(point to pinky finger)

Home Sweet Home

A nest is a home for a blue jay.
(cup hands to form a nest)
A hive is a home for a bee.
(turn cupped hands over)
A hole is a home for a rabbit.
(make a hole shape with hands)

And a house is a home for me.
(make roof shape with peaked hands)

Group Time

(Games, Language)

A Hundred Ways to Get There

During outdoor or group play, form a large circle. Begin the game by choosing a child to cross the circle by skipping, hopping, jumping, crawling, running, etc. Once the circle has been crossed, the child takes the place of another person, who then goes across the circle in another manner. Each child can try to think of something new.

Large Muscle

Neighborhood Walk

Take a walk through a neighborhood and have children identify different homes. Observe the colors and sizes of the homes.

Math

1. **Families—Biggest to Smallest**

   Cut out from magazines several members of a family. The children can place the members from largest to smallest, and then smallest to largest. They can also identify which family member is the biggest and the smallest.

2. **Family Member Chart**

   Graph the number of family members for each child's family on a chart.

Music

"Family Helper"

(*Sing to the tune of "Here We Are Together"*)

It's fun to be a helper, a helper, a helper.
It's fun to be a helper, just any time.
Oh, I can set the table, the table, the table.
Oh, I can set the table at dinner time.
Oh, I can dry the dishes, the dishes, the dishes.
Oh, I can dry the dishes, and make them shine.

Resource People

Family Day

Invite moms, dads, sisters, brothers, grandfathers, grandmothers, and other family members to a tea at your center.

Science

1. **Sounds**

   Tape different sounds from around the house that families hear daily, such as a crying baby, teeth being brushed, telephone ringing, toilet flushing, doorbell ringing, water running, electric shaver, alarm clock, etc. Play the tape for the children to identify the correct sound.

2. **Feely Box**

   Place objects pertaining to a family into a box. Include items such as a baby rattle, a toothbrush, a comb, a baby bottle, etc. The children feel the objects and try to identify them.

3. **Animal Families**

   Gerbils or hamsters with young babies in a cage can be placed on the science table. Observe daily to see how they raise their babies. Compare the animal behavior with the children's own families.

Sensory

1. Washing baby dolls in lukewarm, soapy water

2. Washing dishes in warm water

3. Washing doll clothes and hanging them up to dry

4. Cars and houses placed on top of several inches of sand

Social Studies

Family Pictures

1. Display posters of all types of families. At group time discuss ways that families help and care for each other.

2. Ask each child to bring in a family picture. Label each child's picture and place on a special bulletin board with the caption, "Our Families."

3. Discuss the Muslim celebration of Ramadan. Each year Muslims around the world observe the religious period of Ramadan by refraining from food, water, television, and other activities from sunrise to sunset. The fasting lasts for 28 days. Fasting teaches patience, discipline, and humility. Families and friends gather before sunrise (*Suhour*) and after sunset for meals. When it is time to break the fast (*Iftar*), the first thing one should eat is dates. Children learn that the Prophet Mohammed broke his fast on dates. Families then mostly have soup, because it is easy on the stomach and also helps rehydrate the thirsty.

Books

The following books can be used to complement this theme:

Bailey, Debbie. (1999). *Families*. Illus. by Susan Huszar. Toronto, Canada: Annick Press.

Bee, William. (2005). *Whatever*. Cambridge, MA: Candlewick Press.

Brown, Margaret Wise. (2005). *The Runaway Bunny*. Illus. by Clement Hurd. New York: HarperCollins Publishers.

Buckley, Helen E. (1994). *Grandfather and I*. Illus. by Jan Ormerod. New York: Lothrop, Lee & Shepard.

Buckley, Helen E. (1994). *Grandmother and I*. Illus. by Jan Ormerod. New York: Lothrop, Lee & Shepard.

Buller, Jon and Susan Schade. (2006). *I Love You, Good Night*. Illus. by Bernadette Pons. New York: Little Simon. (Board Book.)

Carle, Eric. (2000). *Does a Kangaroo Have a Mother, Too?* New York: HarperCollins Publishers.

Clements, Andrew. (2005). *Because Your Daddy Loves You*. Illus. by Andrew Clements. New York: Clarion Books.

Combs, Bobbie, Desiree Keane and Brian Rappa. (2001). ABC: *A Family Alphabet Book*. Illus. by Desiree Keane and Brian Rappa. Ridley Park, PA: Two Lives.

De Paola, Tomie. (1996). *The Baby Sister*. New York: G. P. Putnam.

Downey, Roma and Justine Gasquet. (2001). *Love Is a Family*. Illus. by Justine Gasquet. New York: HarperCollins.

Edmonds, Barbara Lynn. (2000). *When Grown-Ups Fall in Love*. Eugene, OR: Barby's House Books.

Flournoy, Valerie. (1995). *Tanya's Reunion*. Illus. by Jerry Pinkney. New York: Dial Books.

Genechten, Guido Van. (2005). *The Cuddle Book*. New York: HarperCollins Publishers. (First U.S. Ed.)

Gutman, Anne and Georg Hallensleben. (2005). *Daddy Cuddles*. San Francisco, CA: Chronicle Books.

Gutman, Anne and Georg Hallensleben. (2005). *Mommy Loves*. San Francisco, CA: Chronicle Books.

Hausherr, Rosemarie. (1997). *Celebrating Families*. New York: Scholastic.

Hest, Amy. (2001). *Kiss Good Night*. Illus. by Anita Jeram. Cambridge, MA: Candlewick Press.

Johnson, Angela. (1990). *When I Am Old with You*. Illus. by David Soman. New York: Orchard Books.

Johnson, Angela. (1991). *One of Three*. Illus. by David Soman. New York: Orchard Books.

Jones, Rebecca C. (1995). *Great Aunt Martha*. Illus. by Shelley Jackson. New York: Dutton.

Joosse, Barbara. (2005). *Nikolai, the Only Bear*. Illus. by Renata Liwska. New York: Philomel Books.

Knight, Margy Burns. (1994). *Welcoming Babies*. Illus. by Anne Sibley O'Brien. Gardner, ME: Tilbury House.

Kroll, Virginia L. (1994). *Beginnings: How Families Came to Be*. Illus. by Stacey Schuett. Niles, IL: Albert Whitman.

Kuklin, Susan. (1992). *How My Family Lives in America*. Minneapolis, MN: Bradbury Press.

Lakin, Patricia. (1994). *Dad and Me in the Morning*. Illus. by Robert G. Steele. Niles, IL: Albert Whitman.

Leedy, Loreen. (1995). *Who's Who in My Family*. New York: Holiday House.

Long, Sylvia. (2002). *Hush Little Baby*. San Francisco, CA: Chronicle Books.

Maynard, Christopher. (1997). *Why Are All Families Different? Questions Children Ask about Families*. New York: Dorling Kindersley.

Medearis, Angela. (2004). *Snug in Mama's Arms*. Illus. by John Sandford. Columbus, OH: Gingham Dog Press.

Meyers, Susan. (2004). *Everywhere Babies*. Illus. by Marla Frazee. San Diego, CA: Harcourt.

Morris, Ann. (1995). *The Daddy Book*. Photos by Ken Heyman. Parsippany, NJ: Silver Press.

Morris, Ann. (1995). *The Mommy Book*. Photos by Ken Heyman. Parsippany, NJ: Silver Press.

Murphy, Mary. (2003). *I Kissed the Baby!* Cambridge, MA: Candlewick Press.

Norac, Carl. (2005). *My Daddy Is a Giant*. Illus. by Ingrid Godon. New York: Clarion Books.

Pellegrini, Nina. (1991). *Families Are Different*. New York: Holiday House.

Penn, Audrey. (2006). *The Kissing Hand*. Illus. by Ruth Harper & Nancy Leak. Terre Haute, IN: Tanglewood Press.

Polacco, Patricia. (2005). *Mommies Say Shhh!* New York: Philomel Books.

Porter-Gaylord, Laurel. (2004). *I Love My Daddy Because*. Illus. by Ashley Wolf. New York: Dutton Children's Books.

Porter-Gaylord, Laurel. (2004). *I Love My Mommy Because*. Illus. by Ashley Wolf. New York: Dutton Children's Books.

Rathmann, Peggy. (2003). *The Day the Babies Crawled Away*. New York: G.P. Putnam's Sons.

Rosenberg, Maxine B. (1991). *Brothers and Sisters*. Photos by George Ancona. New York: Clarion Books.

Rotner, Shelley and Sheila M. Kelly. (1996). *Lots of Moms*. New York: Dial Books.

Rotner, Shelley and Sheila M. Kelly. (1997). *Lots of Dads*. New York: Dial Books.

Russo, Marisabina. (1998). *When Mama Gets Home*. New York: Greenwillow Press.

Schindel, John. (1995). *Dear Daddy*. Illus. by Dorothy Dononue. Niles, IL: Albert Whitman.

Schwartz, Amy. (1994). *A Teeny Tiny Baby*. New York: Orchard Books.

Spelman, Cornelia. (2004). *When I Miss You*. Illus. by Kathy Parkinson. Morton Grove, IL: Albert Whitman & Co.

Stevenson, Harvey. (1994). *Grandpa's House*. New York: Hyperion.

Vigna, Judith. (1997). *I Live with Daddy*. Niles, IL: Albert Whitman.

Wild, Margaret. (1994). *Our Granny*. Illus. by Julie Vivas. New York: Ticknor & Fields.

Williams, Vera B. (1990). *More More More Said the Baby*. New York: Greenwillow.

Winthrop, Elizabeth. (2005). *Squashed in the Middle*. Illus. by Pat Cummings. New York: Henry Holt.

Wolff, Ashley. (2004). *Me Baby, You Baby*. New York: Dutton Children's Books.

Zamorano, Ana. (1997). *Let's Eat!* Illus. by Julie Vivas. New York: Scholastic.

Zemach, Margot. (2005). *Eating Up Gladys*. Illus. by Kaethe Zemach. New York: Arthur A. Levine Books.

Multimedia

The following multimedia products can be used to complement this theme:

A Kid's Guide to Families [video]. Available from Kimbo Educational, Long Branch, NJ.

Byars, Betsy. *My Brother Ant* [cassette and book]. (1998). Prince Frederick, MD: Recorded Books.

Daddy Doesn't Live with Us [video]. (1994). Sunburst.

My Family, Your Family [video]. (1994). Sunburst.

New Baby in My House [video]. (1993). Children's Television Workshop/ distributed by Sony Wonder.

We're a Family [video]. (1992). Sunburst.

Recordings and Song Titles

The following recordings can be used to complement this theme:

"A Family Song." (1985). *Songs for You and Me*. Long Branch, NJ: Kimbo Educational.

"Farm Families." (1999). *On the Farm with RONNO*. Long Branch, NJ: Kimbo Educational.

"Mi Casa, My House." (1993). *Joining Hands in Other Lands*. Long Branch, NJ: Kimbo Educational.

28

Farm Animals

Shelters

barns
stables
sheds

Kinds

horses
cows
chickens
pigs
goats
sheep

Sounds

hee-haw
moo
cluck
oink
baa

Food

corn
hay
oats
silage
water

Uses

transportation
milk
food

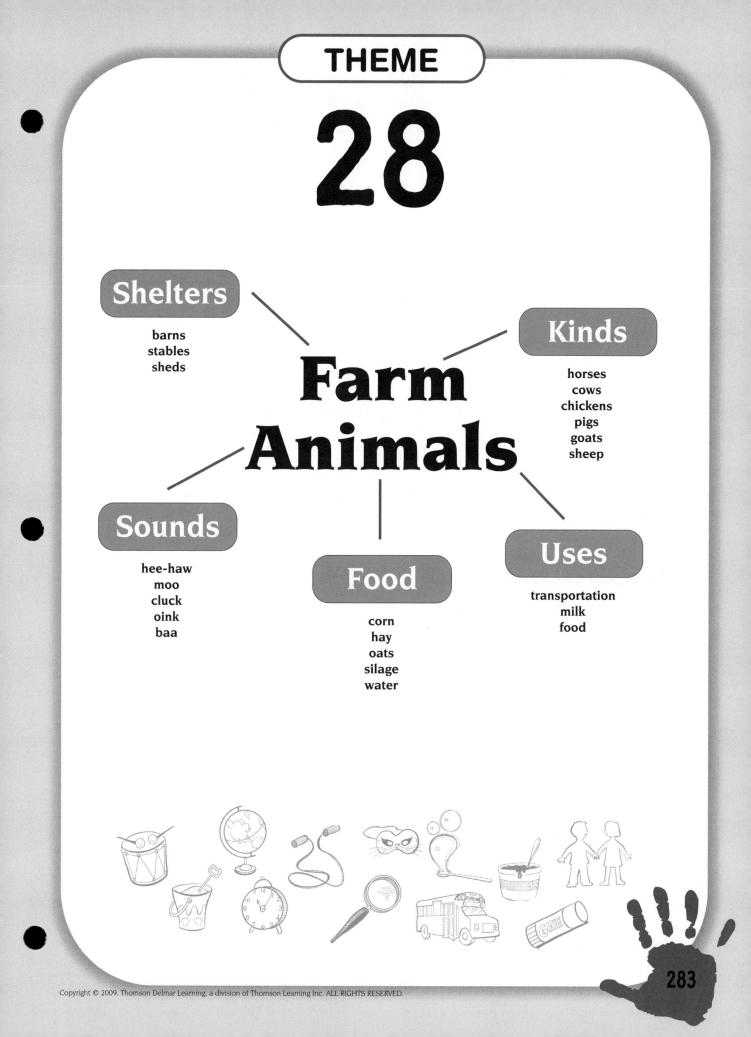

Theme Goals

Through participating in the experiences provided by this theme, the children may learn

1. Kinds of farm animals
2. Uses for farm animals
3. Farm animal shelters
4. Food for farm animals
5. Sounds of farm animals

Concepts for the Children to Learn

1. A farm animal lives on a farm.
2. Barns, stables, and sheds are homes for farm animals.
3. Horses are farm animals that can be used for transportation.
4. Cows, chickens, pigs, sheep, and goats are farm animals that can be used for food.
5. Some cows and goats give milk.
6. Farm animals eat corn, hay, oats, and silage.
7. We can recognize some farm animals by their sounds.
8. Some farm animals supply us with food such as milk, meat, and eggs.

Vocabulary

1. **barn**—building to house animals and store grain.
2. **farmer**—person who cares for farm animals.
3. **herd**—a group of animals.
4. **stable**—building for horses and cattle.

Bulletin Board

The purpose of this bulletin board is to foster visual discrimination, problem-solving, perceptual, and numeral-recognition skills. Out of tagboard, construct red barns as illustrated. The number of barns constructed will depend on the developmental level of your group of children. Place a numeral on each red barn. Construct the same number of black barns by tracing around the red barns onto black construction paper. After cutting out, place small white circles (dots from a paper punch) onto the black barns. Laminate all barns. Staple black barns to the board. Punch a hole in each red barn window. During self-selected activity periods the children can hang red barns on pushpins of corresponding black barns.

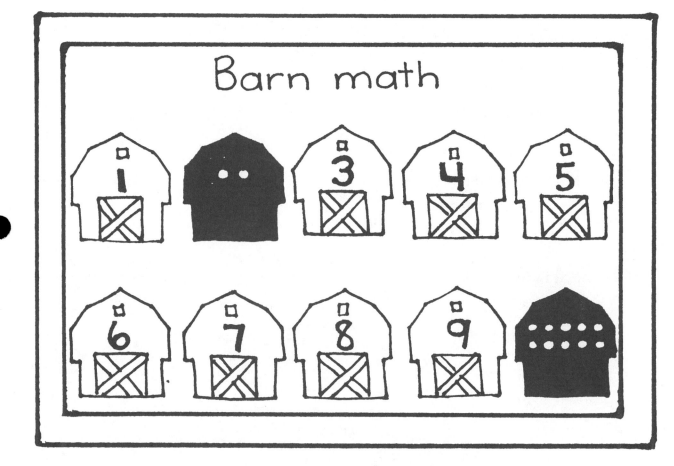

FARM ANIMALS

Family Letter

Dear Families,

Farm animals will be the focus of our next curriculum unit. The children will be learning the many different ways that farm animals help us. They will become aware of the difference between pets and farm animals. The children will also discover that farm animals need homes and food.

AT SCHOOL

Some of the learning activities scheduled for this week include:

- making a barn out of a large cardboard box for the dramatic play area
- tasting different kinds of eggs, milk, and cheese for breakfast one day
- at the science table, observing and comparing the many grains and seeds farm animals eat
- dressing up like farmers and farm animals
- making buttermilk chalk pictures
- listening to stories about farm animals
- reciting fingerplays representing farm animals

AT HOME

There are many ways you can integrate this unit into your family life. To stimulate imagination and movement skills, ask your child to imitate different farm animals by walking and making that animal's noise. Also, your child will be learning this rhyme at school. You can also recite it at home to foster language skills.

If I Were a Horse

If I were a horse, I'd gallop all around.
(slap thighs and gallop in a circle)
I'd shake my head and say "Neigh, neigh."
(shake head)
I'd prance and gallop all over town.

Enjoy your child as you explore experiences related to farm animals.

Farm animals come in many shapes and sizes.

Arts and Crafts

1. Yarn Collage

Provide the children with several types and lengths of yarn. Include clipped yarn, yarn fluffs, and frayed yarn in several different colors, along with paper.

2. Texture Collage

On the art table provide several colors, shapes, and types of fabric for creating a texture collage during the self-selected activity period for the children.

3. Buttermilk Chalk Picture

Brush a piece of cardboard with 2 to 3 tablespoons of buttermilk or dip chalk in buttermilk. Create designs using colored chalk as a tool.

4. Eggshell Collages

Collect eggshells and crush into pieces. Place the eggshells in the art area for the children to glue on paper. Let dry. If desired, the shells can be painted. If preparation time is available, eggshells can be dyed with food coloring by the teacher before the activity.

5. Sponge Prints

Cut farm animal shapes out of sponges. If a pattern is needed, cut out of a coloring book. Once cut, the sponge forms can be dipped into a pan of thick tempera paint and used as a tool to apply a design.

Cooking

1. Make Butter

Fill baby food jars half-full with whipping cream. Allow the children to take turns shaking the jars until the cream separates. First it will appear like whipping cream, then like overwhipped cream, and, finally, an obvious separation will occur. Pour off the liquid and taste. Wash the butter in cold water in a bowl several times. Drain off milky liquid each time. Taste, and then wash again until nearly clear. Work the butter in the water with a wooden spoon as you wash. Add salt to taste. Let the children spread the butter on crackers or bread. (**Note:** Carefully supervise the use of glass jars in this activity.)

2. Purple Cow Drink Mix

1/2 gallon milk
1/2 gallon grape juice
6 ice cubes

Mix the ingredients in a blender for one minute. Drink. Enjoy! This recipe will serve approximately 20 children.

3. Animal Crackers

Serve animal crackers for snack.

4. Corn Bread

2 cups cornmeal
1 teaspoon salt
1/2 teaspoon baking soda
1 1/2 teaspoons baking powder
1 tablespoon sugar
2 eggs
1 1/2 cups buttermilk
1/4 cup cooking oil

Heat oven to 400 degrees. Sift cornmeal, salt, soda, baking powder, and sugar into a bowl. Stir in unbeaten eggs, buttermilk, and cooking oil until all ingredients are mixed. Pour the batter into a greased 9-inch × 9-inch pan or cob-shaped pans. Bake for 30 minutes until lightly browned.

5. Hungry Cheese Spread

8 ounces of goat cheese or soft cream cheese
1/4 cup soft butter
1 teaspoon salt
1 tablespoon paprika
1 teaspoon dry mustard
1 1/2 tablespoons caraway seeds

Blend the cheese and butter in the mixing bowl. Add the remaining ingredients. Mix them well. Put the blended cheese into a small serving bowl. Chill in the refrigerator for at least 30 minutes before serving.

Note: From *Many Hands Cooking*, by Terry Touff Cooper and Marilyn Ratner, 1974, New York: Thomas Y. Crowell.

Dramatic Play

1. Farmer

Clothes and props for a farmer can be placed in the dramatic play area. Include items such as hats, scarves, overalls, boots, etc.

2. Saddle

A horse saddle can be placed on a bench in the classroom. The children can take turns sitting on it, pretending they are riding a horse.

3. Barn

A barn and plastic animals can be added to the classroom. The children can use blocks as accessories to make pens, cages, etc.

4. Veterinarian

Collect materials to make a veterinarian prop box. Stuffed animals can be used as patients.

Field Trips/ Resource People

1. Farmer

Invite a farmer to talk to the children. If possible, have him bring a small farm animal for the children to touch and observe.

2. The Farm

Visit a farm. Observe the animals and machinery.

3. Milk Station

Visit a milk station if there is one in your area.

4. Grocery Store

Visit the dairy section of a grocery store. Look for dairy products.

Group Time

(Games, Language)

1. **Duck, Duck, Goose**

   Sit the children in a circle. Then choose one child to be "it." This child goes around the circle and touches each of the other children on the shoulder and says "Duck, Duck, Goose." The child who is tapped as "goose" gets up and chases the other child around the circle. The first child who returns to the empty spot sits down, and the other child proceeds with the game of tapping children on the shoulder until someone else is tapped as the goose.

2. **Thank You**

   Write a thank-you note as a follow-up activity after a field trip or a visit from a resource person.

Large Muscle

1. **Trikes**

   During outdoor play, encourage children to use trikes and wagons for hauling.

2. **Barn**

   Construct a large barn out of a large cardboard box. Let all the children help paint it outdoors. When dry, the children can play in it.

Math

1. **Puzzles**

   Laminate several pictures of farm animals; coloring books are a good source. Cut the pictures into puzzles for the children.

2. **Grouping and Sorting**

   Collect plastic farm animals. Place in a basket and let the children sort them according to size, color, where they live, how they move, etc.

3. **Hen and Chick Match**

   Make 10 hen cutouts and place a numeral from 1–10 and corresponding dots on each hen. Give each child one hen cutout. Make 10 chick cutouts that will fit inside a plastic Easter egg and again place a numeral from 1–10 and corresponding dots on each chick. Place chicks inside eggs and place eggs in a basket. The children will take turns picking an egg and determining if the chick matches the number on their hen. The children should continue taking turns picking eggs until they find a match.

Miscellaneous

Transition

During transition time, encourage the children to imitate different farm animals. They may gallop like a horse, hop like a bunny, waddle like a duck, move like a snake, etc.

Music

1. **"Old MacDonald Had a Farm"**
   (*traditional*)

2. **"The Animals on the Farm"**
   (*Sing to the tune of "The Wheels on the Bus"*)

   The cows on the farm go moo, moo, moo.
   Moo, moo, moo, moo, moo, moo.
   The cows on the farm go moo, moo, moo
      all day long.

   The horses on the farm go neigh, neigh, neigh.
   Neigh, neigh, neigh, neigh, neigh, neigh.
   The horses on the farm go neigh, neigh, neigh
      all day long.

   (pigs—oink)   (chicken—cluck)
   (sheep—baa)   (turkeys—gobble)

3. **"The Farmer in the Dell"**
(*traditional*)

The farmer in the dell,
The farmer in the dell,
Hi-ho the dairy-o
The farmer in the dell.

The farmer takes a wife/husband.
The farmer takes a wife/husband.
Hi-ho the dairy-o
The farmer in the dell.

(The other verses are:)
The wife/husband takes the child
The child takes the nurse
The nurse takes the dog
The dog takes the cat
The cat takes the rat
The rat takes the cheese.

(The final verse:)
The cheese stands alone.
The cheese stands alone.
Hi-ho the dairy-o
The cheese stands alone.

4. **"This Little Piggy"**

This little piggy went to market, (wiggle big toe)
This little piggy stayed home, (wiggle second toe)
This little piggy had roast beef, (wiggle third toe)
This little piggy had none, (wiggle fourth toe)
And this little piggy cried, "Wee-wee-wee!" all
    the way home. (wiggle little toe)

Science

1. **Sheep Wool**

Place various types of wool on a table for the children to observe. Included may be wool clippings, lanolin, dyed yarn, yarn spun into thread, wool cloth, and wool articles such as mittens and socks.

2. **Feathers**

Examine various types of feathers. Use a magnifying glass. Discuss their purposes, such as keeping birds warm and helping ducks to float on water. Add the feathers to the water table to see if they float. Discuss why they float.

3. **Tasting Dairy Products**

Plan a milk-tasting party. To do this, taste and compare the following types of milk products: cow milk, goat milk, cream, skimmed milk, whole milk, cottage cheese, sour cream, butter, margarine, and buttermilk. **Caution:** Check for children's allergies before all food-related activities.

4. **Eggs**

Taste different kinds of eggs. Let children choose from scrambled, poached, deviled, hard-boiled, and fried. This could also be integrated as part of the breakfast menu.

5. **Cheese Types**

Observe, taste, and compare different kinds of cheese. Examples include Swiss, cheddar, colby, cottage cheese, and cheese curds.

6. **Egg Hatching**

If possible, contact a hatchery to borrow an incubator. Watch the eggs hatch in the classroom.

7. **Feels like the Farm**

Construct a feely box containing farm items. Examples may include an ear of corn, hay, sheep wool, a turkey feather, a hard-boiled egg, etc.

Sensory

1. **Farm Animal Sound Bingo**

Record a child making a farm animal sound or download the sound from the Internet. Find photographs or clipart of the animal and glue them onto a cardboard bingo card. Play each sound and ask the child to put a button over the corresponding animal.

2. **Additions to the Sensory Table**

- different types of grain, such as oats, wheat, barley, and corn, and measuring devices

- wool and feathers

- sand and plastic farm animals
- provide materials to make a barnyard. Include soil, hay, farm animals, barns, farm equipment toys, etc.

Social Studies

Farm Animal of the Day

Throughout the week let children take care of and watch baby farm animals. Suggestions include a piglet, chicks, small ducks, rabbit, or lamb.

Books

The following books can be used to complement this theme:

Aliki. (1992). *Milk from Cow to Carton*. Revised ed. New York: HarperCollins.

Baker, Keith. (1994). *Big Fat Hen*. San Diego, CA: Harcourt Brace.

Bates, Ivan. (2006). *Five Little Ducks*. Illus. by Ivan Bates. New York: Scholastic.

Battaglia, Aurelius. (2005). *Animal Sounds*. Illus. by Aurelius Battaglia. New York: Random House.

Beaumont, Karen. (2004). *Duck, Duck, Goose! A Coyote's on the Loose!* New York: Harper Collins Publishers.

Blackstone, Stella. (2006). *There's a Cow in the Cabbage Patch*. Cambridge, MA: Barefoot Books.

Brown, Craig. (1994). *In the Spring*. New York: Greenwillow.

Brown, Margaret Wise. (2002). *Big Red Barn*. New York: Rayo.

Bruss, Deborah and Tiphanie Beeke. (2001). *Book! Book! Book!* Illus. by Tiphanie Beeke. New York: Arthur A. Levine.

Carter, David A. (2001). *Old MacDonald Had a Farm*. New York: Scholastic Trade.

Cowley, Joy. (2003). *Mrs. Wishy-Washy's Farm*. Illus. by Elizabeth Fuller. New York: Philomel Books.

Cowley, Joy. (2003). *Mrs. Wishy-Washy Makes a Splash*. Illus. by Elizabeth Fuller. New York: Philomel Books.

Cronin, Doreen and Betsy Lewin. (2000). *Click, Clack, Moo: Cows That Type*. Illus. by Betsy Lewin. New York: Simon & Schuster.

Edwards, Pamela Duncan. (1998). *The Grumpy Morning*. Illus. by Loretta Krupinski. New York: Hyperion.

Ehrlich, Amy. (1993). *Parents in the Pigpen, Pigs in the Tub*. Illus. by Steven Kellogg. New York: Dial Books.

Fleming, Denise. (1994). *Barnyard Banter*. New York: Holt.

Fowler, Allan. (1992). *Thanks to Cows*. San Francisco: Children's Book Press.

Gibbons, Gail. (1998). *Farming*. New York: Holiday House.

Gorbachev, Valeri. (2005). *That's What Friends Are For*. New York: Philomel Books.

Gray, Libba Moore. (1997). *Is There Room on the Feather Bed?* Illus. by Nadine Bernard Westcott. New York: Orchard Books.

Henderson, Kathy. (1996). *Counting Farm*. Cambridge, MA: Shaw's Candlewick Press.

Hutchins, Pat. (1994). *Little Pink Pig*. New York: Greenwillow.

Jackson, Ellen. (1995). *Brown Cow, Green Grass, Yellow Mellow Sun*. Illus. by Victoria Raymond. New York: Hyperion.

Kasza, Keiko. (2003). *My Lucky Day*. New York: G.P. Putnam's Sons.

Landstrom, Lena. (2005). *Four Hens and a Rooster*. New York: Douglas & McIntyre Publishing Group.

Lesser, Carolyn. (1995). *What a Wonderful Day to Be a Cow*. Illus. by Melissa Bay Mathis. New York: Knopf.

MacLachlan, Patricia. (1994). *All the Places to Love*. Illus. by Mike Wimmer. New York: HarperCollins.

Masurel, Claire. (1997). *No, No, Titus!* Illus. by Shari Halpern. New York: North South Books.

McDonnell, Flora. (1994). *I Love Animals*. Cambridge, MA: Candlewick Press.

Milord, Susan. (2005). *Three About Thurston*. Boston, MA: Houghton Mifflin.

Older, Jules. (1997). *Cow*. Illus. by Lyn Severance. Watertown, MA: Charlesbridge.

Palatini, Margie and Richard Egielski. (2001). *The Web Files*. Illus. by Richard Egielski. New York: Hyperion Press.

Perl, Erica S. (2004). *Chicken Bedtime Is Really Early*. Illus. by George Bates. New York: Abrams.

Plourde, Lynn. (1997). *Pigs in the Mud in the Middle of the Road*. Illus. by John Schoenherr. New York: Scholastic.

Scarry, Richard. (2004). *The Rooster Struts*. New York: Golden Books.

Skultety, Nancy. (2005). *From Here to There*. Illus. by Tammie Lyon. Honesdale, PA: Boyds Mills Press.

Stohner, Anu. (2005). *Brave Charlotte*. Illus. by Henrike Wilson. New York: Bloomsbury Children's Books.

Sturghes, Philemon. (1999). *The Little Red Hen Makes a Pizza*. New York: Dutton Children's Books.

Sykes, Julie. (1996). *This and That*. Illus. by Tanya Linch. New York: Farrar, Straus & Giroux.

Tafuri, Nancy. (1994). *This Is the Farmer*. New York: Greenwillow.

Tresselt, Alvin. (1991). *Wake Up, Farm*. Newly illus. by Carolyn Ewing. New York: Lothrop, Lee & Shepard.

Waddell, Martin. (1992). *Farmer Duck*. Illus. by Helen Oxenbury. Cambridge, MA: Candlewick Press.

Waring, Richard. (2001). *Hungry Hen*. Illus. by Caroline Jayne Church. New York: Harper Collins Publishers.

Wormell, Christopher. (1995). *A Number of Animals*. Mankato, MN: Creative Editions.

Ziefert, Harriet. (1996). *Who Said Moo?* Illus. by Simms Taback. New York: HarperCollins.

Multimedia

The following multimedia products can be used to complement this theme:

Cows [video]. (1995). Churchill Media.

Let's Go to the Farm [video]. (1994). With Mac Parker. Burlington, VT: Vermont Story Works.

Rosenthal, Phil. "Little White Duck" on *Animal Songs* [sound disc]. (1996). Guilford, CT: American Melody.

See How They Grow: Farm Animals [video]. (1993). New York: Sony Music Entertainment.

We're Goin' to the Farm [video]. (1994). Minneapolis, MN: Shortstuff Entertainment.

Recordings and Song Titles

The following recordings can be used to complement this theme:

"Animal Farm." (2001). *Four Baby Bumblebees*. Long Branch, NJ: Kimbo Educational.

"Animal Parade." (1990). *Musical Playtime Fun*. Long Branch, NJ: Kimbo Educational.

"Animal Pig-nic Day," "Farm Families," "Someplace on the Farm." (1999). *On the Farm with RONNO*. Long Branch, NJ: Kimbo Educational.

"Farmer in the Dell." (1983). *Preschool Aerobic Fun, Diaper Gym*. Long Branch, NJ: Kimbo Educational.

"Farmer's Friends." (1988). *Preschool Action Time*. Long Branch, NJ: Kimbo Educational.

"Five Fat Turkeys Are We." (1996). *Where Is Thumbkin?* Long Branch, NJ: Kimbo Educational.

"Here Comes the Cow," "Hop Like a Bunny." (1974). *It's Fun to Clap*. Long Branch, NJ: Kimbo Educational.

"Neat Nanny Goat," "Piggly, Wiggly, Pizza Pig," "Skiing Sheep." (1994). *A to Z, the Animals and Me*. Long Branch, NJ: Kimbo Educational.

"Old MacDonald Had a Farm," "Six Little Ducks," "Little White Duck," "B-I-N-G-O." (1997). *Six Little Ducks*. Long Branch, NJ: Kimbo Educational.

"This Little Piggy," "Mary Had a Little Lamb," "Baa, Baa Black Sheep." (1986). *Singable Nursery Rhymes*. Long Branch, NJ: Kimbo Educational.

29

Causes

people
situations
sickness

Verbal

yelling
crying
talking
singing
laughing

Feelings

Types

happy
sad
lonely
tired
surprised
angry
excited
friendly
afraid
hungry
loving
depressed

Nonverbal

smiling
frowning
jumping
hitting
petting
hugging
kissing

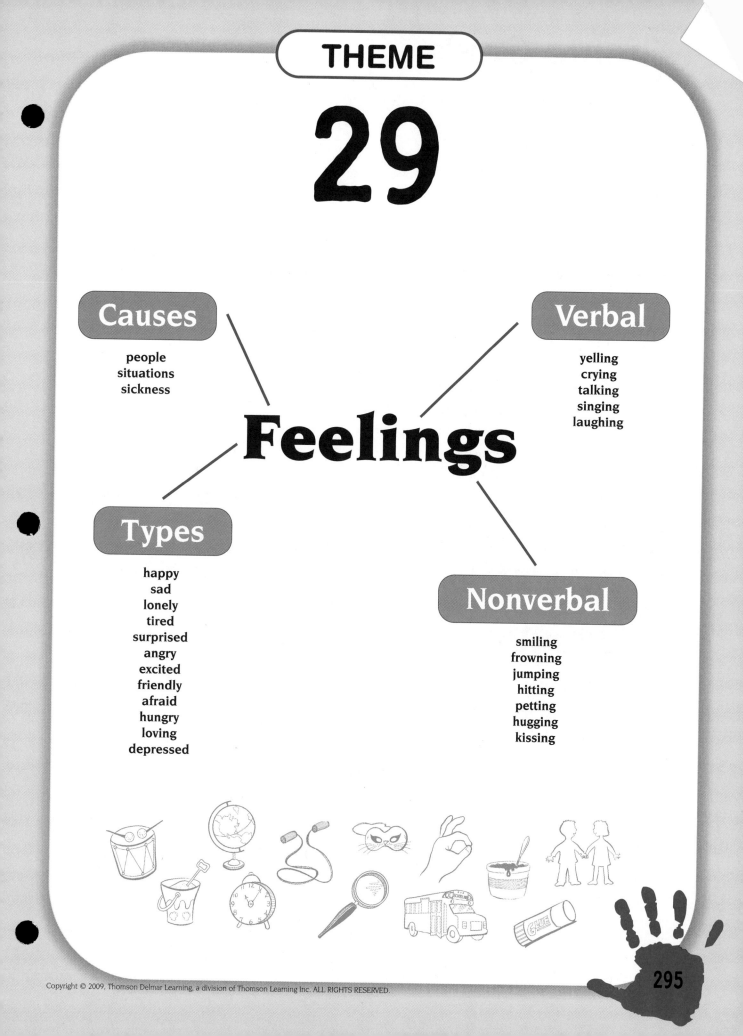

Theme Goals

Through participating in the experiences provided by this theme, the children may learn

1. Types of feelings
2. Verbal expressions of feelings
3. Nonverbal expressions of feelings
4. Causes for our feelings

Concepts for the Children to Learn

1. Everyone has feelings.
2. Feelings show how we feel.
3. Feelings change.
4. Feelings are caused by people, situations, and sickness.
5. Happy, sad, excited, and surprised are types of feelings.
6. Lonely, tired, angry, afraid, hungry, and depressed are feelings.
7. Friendliness and loving are also feelings.
8. People can show their feelings verbally.
9. Yelling, crying, talking, singing, and laughing are ways to verbally express feelings.
10. People show their feelings nonverbally.
11. Kissing, hugging, and petting are examples of showing feelings nonverbally.
12. Frowning, jumping, and hitting are other ways people can show feelings nonverbally.

Vocabulary

1. **afraid**—the feeling of being unsure of or frightened about something.
2. **feelings**—expressed emotions.
3. **happy**—a feeling of being glad.
4. **sad**—the feeling of being hurt or unhappy.
5. **smile**—a facial expression of pleasure or happiness.
6. **surprise**—a feeling from something unexpected.

Bulletin Board

The purpose of this bulletin board is to help the children become aware of happy, sad, and mad feelings, as well as recognize their printed names. Prepare individual name cards for each child. Then prepare different expressive faces such as happy, sad, and angry. Staple faces to top of bulletin board. See the illustration for an example. If available, magnetic strips may be added to the bulletin board under faces and pieces affixed to name cards, or pushpins may be placed on the board and holes punched in name cards. The children may place their names under the face they decide they feel like when arriving at school. Later, during large group time, the board can be reviewed to see if any of the children's feelings have changed.

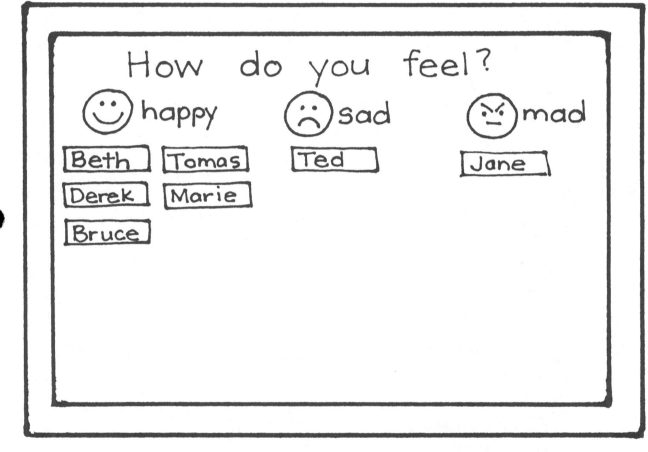
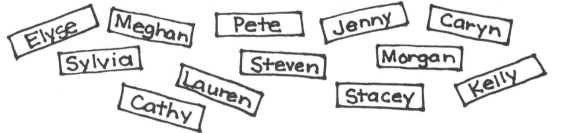

Family Letter

Dear Families,

Emotions and feelings will be the focus of our next curriculum unit. Throughout each day, the children experience many feelings, ranging from happiness to sadness. The purpose of this unit is to have the children develop an understanding of feelings. Feelings are something we all share, and feelings are acceptable. We will also be exploring ways of expressing different feelings.

AT SCHOOL

Some of the learning experiences planned for this unit include:

- listening and discussing the book *Alexander and the Terrible, Horrible, No Good, Very Bad Day* by Judith Viorst
- singing songs about our feelings
- drawing and painting to various types of music
- expressing feelings through music

OUR SPECIAL VISITOR

"Clancy the Clown" will be visiting the children on Thursday at 3:00 p.m. The children are all looking forward to this special visitor. You are encouraged to join us and share their excitement.

AT HOME

To help your child identify situations that elicit feelings, have your child cut or tear pictures from discarded magazines that depict events or situations that make your child feel happy or sad. These pictures can then be glued or pasted on paper to create a feelings collage.

Talking with your child about your feelings will encourage parent-child communication. Tell your child what things make you feel various ways. Then ask your child to share some feelings.

Make your child happy today!

How do you feel today?

 # Arts and Crafts

 # Cooking

1. Drawing to Music

Play various types of music, including jazz, classical, and rock, and let the children draw during the self-selected activity period. Different tunes and melodies might make us feel a certain way.

2. Play Dough

Using play dough is a wonderful way to vent feelings. Prepare several types and let the children feel the different textures. Color each type a different color. Add a scent to one and to another add a textured material such as sawdust, rice, or sand. A list of play doughs can be found later in this theme.

3. Footprints

Mix tempera paint. Pour the paint into a shallow jelly roll pan approximately 1/4-inch deep. The children can dip their feet into the pan. After this, they can step directly onto paper. Using their feet as an application tool, footsteps can be made. This activity could be used to create a mural to hang in the hall or lobby.

1. Happy Rolls

1 package of fast-rising dry yeast
1 cup warm water
1/3 cup sugar
1/3 cup cooking oil
3 cups flour
a dash of salt

Measure the warm water and pour it into a bowl. Sprinkle the yeast on top of the water. Let the yeast settle into the water. Mix all of the ingredients in a large bowl. Place the dough on a floured board to knead it. Demonstrate how to knead, letting each of the children take turns kneading the bread. This is a wonderful activity to work through emotions. After kneading it for about 10 minutes, put the ball of dough into a greased bowl. If kneaded sufficiently, the top of the dough should have blisters on it. Cover the bowl and put in the sun or near heat. Let it rise for about an hour or until doubled. Take the dough out of the bowl. Punch it down, knead for several more minutes, and then divide the dough into 12 to 15 pieces. Roll each piece of dough into a ball. Place each ball on a greased cookie sheet. Let the dough rise again until doubled. Bake at 450 degrees for 10 to 12 minutes. A happy face can be drawn on the roll with frosting.

2. **Berry "Happy" Shake—Finland**

   10 fresh strawberries or 6 tablespoons frozen
      sliced strawberries in syrup, thawed
   2 cups cold milk
   1 1/2 tablespoons sugar or honey

   Wash the strawberries (if fresh) and cut out the stems. Cut the strawberries into small pieces. (If you are using frozen strawberries, drain the syrup into a small bowl or cup and save it.) Pour the milk into the mixing bowl. Add the strawberries. If you are using fresh strawberries, add the sugar or honey. If you are using frozen strawberries, add 3 tablespoons of the strawberry syrup instead of sugar. Beat with the egg beater for 1 minute. Pour the drink into glasses.

   Note: From *Many Hands Cooking*, by Terry Touff Cooper and Marilyn Ratner, 1974, New York: Thomas Y. Crowell.

3. **Danish Smile Berry Pudding**

   1 10-ounce package frozen raspberries, thawed
   1 10-ounce package frozen strawberries, thawed
   1/4 cup cornstarch
   2 tablespoons sugar
   1/2 cup cold water
   1 tablespoon lemon juice

   Puree berries in blender or press through sieve. Mix cornstarch and sugar in 1 1/2-quart saucepan. Gradually stir in water; add puree. Heat to boiling, stirring constantly. Boil and stir 1 minute. Remove from heat. Stir in lemon juice. Pour into dessert dishes or serving bowl. Cover and refrigerate at least 2 hours. Serve with half-and-half if desired. Makes 6 servings.

   Note: From *Betty Crocker's International Cookbook*, 1980, New York: Random House.

Dramatic Play

1. **Flower Shop**

   Plastic flowers, vases, and wrapping paper can be placed in the dramatic play area. Make a sign that says "Flower Shop." The children may want to arrange, sell, deliver, and receive flowers.

2. **Post Office**

   Collect discarded greeting cards and envelopes. The children can stamp and deliver the cards to one another.

3. **Puppet Center**

   A puppet center can be added to the dramatic play area. Include a variety of puppets and a stage.

Fingerplays

I Looked inside My Looking Glass

I looked inside my looking glass
   (Pinch index finger and thumb together to
   form a circle.)
To see what I could see.
   (Hold a circle over each eye.)
It looks like I'm happy today,
   (Smile.)
Because that smiling face is me.
   (Continue smiling and point to oneself.)

Stand Up Tall

Stand up tall
   (Stand up straight.)
Hands in the air.
   (Hold hands over head in the air.)
Now sit down
In your chair.
   (Sit on chair.)
Clap your hands
   (Clap hands.)
And make a frown.
   (Frown.)
Smile and smile.
   (Smile.)
Hop like a clown.
   (Stand up and hop.)

Recipes for Doughs and Clays

Clay Dough

3 cups flour
3 cups salt
3 tablespoons alum

Combine ingredients and slowly add water, a little at a time. Mix well with spoon. As mixture thickens, continue mixing with your hands until it has the feel of clay. If it feels too dry, add more water. If it is too sticky, add equal parts of flour and salt.

Play Dough

2 cups flour
1 cup salt
1 cup hot water
2 tablespoons cooking oil
4 teaspoons cream of tartar
food coloring

Mix well. Knead until smooth. This dough may be kept in a plastic bag or covered container and used again. If it gets sticky, more flour may be added.

Favorite Play Dough

Combine and boil until dissolved:
2 cups water
1/2 cup salt
food coloring or tempera paint

Mix in while very hot:

2 tablespoons cooking oil
2 tablespoons alum
2 cups flour

Knead (approximately 5 minutes) until smooth. Store in covered, airtight containers.

Oatmeal Dough

2 cups oatmeal
1 cup flour
1/2 cup water

Combine ingredients. Knead well. This dough has a very different texture, is easily manipulated, and looks different. Finished projects can be painted when dry.

Baker's Clay #1

1 cup cornstarch
2 cups baking soda
1 1/2 cups cold water

Combine ingredients. Stir until smooth. Cook over medium heat, stirring constantly until mixture reaches the consistency of slightly dry mashed potatoes.

Turn out onto plate or bowl, covering with damp cloth. When cool enough to handle, knead thoroughly until smooth and pliable on cornstarch-covered surface.

Store in tightly closed plastic bag or covered container.

Baker's Clay #2

4 cups flour
1 1/2 cups water
1 cup salt

Combine ingredients. Mix well. Knead 5 to 10 minutes. Roll out to 1/4-inch thickness. Cut with decorative cookie cutters or with a knife. Make a hole at the top.

Bake at 250 degrees for 2 hours or until hard. When cool, paint with tempera paint

and spray with clear varnish or paint with acrylic paint.

Cloud Dough

3 cups flour
1 cup oil
scent (oil of peppermint, wintergreen, lemon, etc.)
food coloring

Combine ingredients. Add water until easily manipulated (about 1/2 cup).

Sawdust Dough

2 cups sawdust
3 cups flour
1 cup salt

Combine ingredients. Add water as needed. This dough becomes very hard and is not easily broken. It is good to use for making objects and figures that one desires to keep.

Salt Dough

4 cups salt
1 cup cornstarch

Combine with sufficient water to form a paste. Cook over medium heat, stirring constantly.

Cooked Clay Dough

1 cup flour
1/2 cup cornstarch
4 cups water
1 cup salt
3 or 4 pounds flour
food coloring if desired

Stir slowly and be patient with this recipe. Blend the flour and

(continued)

Recipes for Doughs and Clays
(continued)

cornstarch with cold water. Add salt to the water and boil. Pour the boiling salt and water solution into the flour and cornstarch paste and cook over high heat until clear. Add the flour and coloring to the cooked solution and knead. After the clay has been in use, if too moist, add flour; if dry, add water. Keep in covered container. Wrap dough with damp cloth or towel. This dough has a very nice texture and is very popular with all age groups. May be kept 2 or 3 weeks.

Play Dough

5 cups flour
2 cups salt
4 tablespoons cooking oil
add water to right consistency

Powdered tempera may be added in with flour, or food coloring may be added to finished dough. This dough may be kept in plastic bag or covered container for approximately 2 to 4 weeks. It is better used as play dough rather than leaving objects to harden.

Used Coffee Grounds

2 cups used coffee grounds
1/2 cup salt
1 1/2 cups oatmeal

Combine ingredients and add enough water to moisten. Children like to roll, pack, and pat this mixture. It has a very different feel and look, but it's not good for finished products. It has a very nice texture.

Mud Dough

2 cups sterile potting soil
2 cups sand
1/2 cup salt

Combine ingredients and add enough water to make pliable. Children like to work with this mixture. It has a nice texture and is easy to use. This cannot be picked up easily to save for finished products. It can be used for rolling and cutouts.

Soap Modeling

2 cups soap flakes

Add enough water to moisten and whip until consistency is right for molding. Use soap such as Ivory Snow, Dreft, Lux, etc. Mixture will have very slight flaky appearance when it can be molded. It is very enjoyable for all age groups and is easy to work. Also, the texture is very different from other materials ordinarily used for molding. It may be put up to dry, but articles are very slow to dry.

Soap and Sawdust

1 cup whipped soap
1 cup sawdust

Mix well together. This gives a very different feel and appearance. It is quite easily molded into different shapes by all age groups. May be used for 2 to 3 days if stored in tight plastic bag.

Bath Time Soap Flake Play Dough

4 cups soap flakes
1 cup water

Put the soap flakes into a large bowl. Gradually add the water, mixing constantly until the mixture is dough-like. Make a variety of figures. Save the figures on a plate for next bath time.

Best Play Dough Ever

1 cup flour
1 cup water
2 teaspoons cream of tartar
1/2 cup salt
1 tablespoon oil
food coloring (optional)

Stir all ingredients together and cook over medium-high heat for 5 minutes or until the right consistency. Store in a plastic bag or airtight container.

Changes in Your Hands Play Dough

2 cups baking soda
1/2 cups water
1 cup cornstarch

Add soda and starch to water. Mix with fork until smooth. Boil mixture over medium heat for 1 minute or until it thickens. Spoon onto wax paper or plate until it cools. This dough will respond to the warmth of the hands and will change as the child works with it. If the play dough is still soft and a little sticky, it is too fresh. Provide time for it to cool slightly.

Easy Play Dough

3/4 cup water
1 1/2 teaspoons oil
1 cup flour
1/4 cup salt
1 tablespoon alum
food coloring

Mix salt and water and bring to full rolling boil. Set on a cooling rack. Stir in oil, alum, and food coloring. Quickly mix in flour and knead.

Cookie Cutter Play Dough

2 cups flour
1/2 cup water
1/2 cup salt
1/4 cup water

Mix flour and salt in a bowl. Add 1/2 cup water and stir for a few minutes. Slowly add 1/4 cup water while turning dough in a bowl. Form dough into a ball. Knead for 5 minutes. Shape dough into desired shapes, adding enough water to join pieces together, or use cookie cutters. Bake at 250 degrees for 15–30 minutes until hard. Let cool completely. Paint with acrylic paints.

Cornstarch Play Dough

1/2 cup salt
1/4 cup water
1 cup cornstarch
food coloring

Mix ingredients thoroughly and cook over low heat, stirring constantly until it forms a lump. Add food coloring of desired color.

Creamy Play Dough

2 cups flour
water
2 cups salt

Mix flour and salt. Add enough water to make a creamy consistency. Add powdered paint or other coloring.

Crepe Paper Clay

1 cup crepe paper clippings (one color)
1 cup warm water
1/2 to 2/3 cup non-self-rising wheat flour

Cut crepe paper very finely. Place clippings in bowl and cover with water. Set aside for several hours until soft. Pour off excess water. Add 1/2 cup flour and stir thoroughly. Pour onto floured board and knead. Add flour until piecrust-like.

Fun Play Dough

2 cups water
2 tablespoons oil
2 cups flour
1/2 cup salt
2 tablespoons alum
food coloring or tempera paints

Combine water, salt, and coloring, and boil until salt is dissolved. While very hot, mix in oil, alum, and flour. Knead until smooth. Store in airtight container.

Indefinitely Pliable Play Dough

1 cup salt
3/4 cup water
1/2 cup cornstarch

Mix cold ingredients on top of a double boiler, preferably with a wooden spoon. For colored play dough, add a few drops of food coloring. Heat over boiling water; keep stirring until balls form around the spoon. Cover with a damp cloth until cool enough to handle, then work into a smooth ball. This hardens in the air but keeps pliable indefinitely in a plastic bag in the refrigerator. It can be formed into shapes and painted when hard.

Kool-Aid Play Dough #1

1 cup sifted flour
3 tablespoons oil
1 cup boiling water
1/2 cup salt
1 package Kool-Aid (unsweetened)

Mix flour, salt, oil, and Kool-Aid. Add boiling water. Stir together. Knead mixture until it forms into a soft dough.

Kool-Aid Play Dough #2

2 1/2 cups flour
1/2 cup salt
1/2 teaspoon alum
2 packages unsweetened Kool-Aid
3 tablespoons vegetable oil
2 cups boiling water

Mix flour, Kool-Aid, salt, oil, and alum. Stir in water. Knead.

Microwave Play Dough

2 cups flour
1/2 cup cornstarch
2 cups water
food coloring
1 cup salt
1 tablespoon alum
1 tablespoon cooking oil

Combine flour, salt, cornstarch, and alum into a 2-quart bowl. Microwave 4 1/2 to 5 minutes until thick, stirring every minute. Cool mixture. Knead on table, knead in color.

(continued)

Recipes for Doughs and Clays
(continued)

Salt Modeling Clay

1 cup non-self-rising wheat flour
1/2 cup salt
1/3 to 1/2 cup water
1 teaspoon powdered alum
food coloring

Combine flour, salt, and alum in a bowl. Add water a little at a time and stir into the flour mixture until it is like pie dough. Knead until dough is thoroughly mixed and has a smooth consistency. This clay is white.

Sand and Cornstarch Play Dough

1 cup sand
1 teaspoon powdered alum
1/2 cup cornstarch
3/4 cup hot water
food coloring

Mix sand, cornstarch, alum. Add hot water, stirring vigorously. Add food coloring if desired. Cook over medium heat until thick, stirring constantly.

Stretch Play Dough

1 cup liquid starch
2 cups white glue
food coloring

Mix ingredients in a bowl. Knead with hands until smooth. Food coloring may be added with starch. Store in covered container.

Goop

2 cups salt
1 cup cornstarch
1 cup water

Cook salt and 1/2 cup water for 4–5 minutes. Remove from heat. Add cornstarch and 1/2 cup water. Return to heat. Stir until mixture thickens. Store goop in plastic bag.

Group Time
(Games, Language)

Happy Feeling

Discuss happiness. Ask each child for one thing that makes him or her happy. Record each answer on a "Happiness Chart." Post the chart for the parents to observe as they pick up their children.

is. A variation of this activity would be to have partners face each other. When one child smiles, the partner is to imitate his or her feelings.

2. Simon Says

Play "Simon Says" using emotions:
"Simon Says walk in a circle feeling happy . . ."
"Simon Says walk in a circle feeling sad . . ."

Large Muscle

1. Mirrors

The children should sit as pairs facing each other. Select one child to make a "feeling face" at the partner. Let the other child guess what feeling it

Math

Face Match

Collect two small shoe boxes. On one shoe box draw a happy face. On the other box, draw a sad face. Cut faces of people from magazines. The children can sort the pictures accordingly.

Music

1. **"Feelings"**
   (*Sing to the tune of* "Twinkle, Twinkle Little Star")

   I have feelings.
   You do, too.
   Let's all sing about a few.

   I am happy.
     (smile)
   I am sad.
     (frown)
   I get scared.
     (wrap arms around self)
   I get mad.
     (make a fist and shake it)

   I am proud of being me.
     (hands on hips)
   That's a feeling, too, you see.
   I have feelings.
     (point to self)
   You do, too.
     (point to someone else)
   We just sang about a few.

2. **"If You're Happy and You Know It"**
   (*traditional*)

   If you're happy and you know it
   Clap your hands.
     (clap twice)
   If you're happy and you know it
   Clap your hands.
     (clap twice)
   If you're happy and you know it
   Then your face will surely show it.
   If you're happy and you know it
   Clap your hands.
     (clap twice)

   For additional verses, change the emotions
   and actions.

3. **"I Have Something in My Pocket"**

   I have something in my pocket.
   It belongs across my face.
   I keep it very close at hand.
   In a most convenient place.
   I bet you could guess it,
   If you guessed a long, long while

So I'll take it out and put it on,
It's a great big happy SMILE!

4. **"For He's a Jolly Good Fellow"**

   For he's a jolly good fellow,
   For he's a jolly good fellow,
   For he's a jolly good fellow,
   Which nobody can deny.
   Which nobody can deny,
   Which nobody can deny,
   For he's a jolly good fellow,
   For he's a jolly good fellow,
   For he's a jolly good fellow,
   Which nobody can deny.

   We won't go home until morning,
   We won't go home until morning,
   We won't go home until morning,
   'Till daylight doth appear.
   'Till daylight doth appear,
   'Till daylight doth appear,
   We won't go home until morning,
   We won't go home until morning,
   We won't go home until morning,
   'Till daylight doth appear.

Resource People

1. **A Clown**

   Invite a clown to the classroom. You may ask
   the clown to dress and apply makeup for the
   children. After the clown leaves provide makeup
   for the children.

2. **Musician**

   Invite a musician to play a variety of music for
   the children to express feelings.

3. **Florist**

   Invite a florist to visit your classroom and
   show how flowers are arranged. Talk about
   why people send flowers. If convenient, the
   children could visit the florist, touring the
   greenhouses.

Science

1. **Sound Tape**

   Tape various noises that express emotions; suggestions include sounds such as laughter, cheering, growling, shrieking, crying, etc. Play these sounds for the children, letting them identify the emotion. They may also want to act out the emotion.

2. **Communication without Words**

   Hang a large screen or sheet with a bright light behind it. The children can go behind the screen and act out various emotions. Other children guess how they are feeling.

3. **How Does It Feel?**

   Add various pieces of textured materials to the science table. Include materials such as soft fur, sandpaper, rocks, and cotton. Encourage the children to touch each object and explain how it feels.

Sensory

Texture Feelings

Various textures can create feelings. Let the children express their feelings by adding the following to the sensory table:

- cotton
- water (warm or with ice)
- black water
- blue water
- sand
- pebbles
- dirt with scoops
- plastic worms with water

Social Studies

Pictures

Share pictures of individuals engaged in different occupations such as doctors, firefighters, beauticians, florists, nurses, bakers, etc. Discuss how these individuals help us and how they make us feel.

Books

The following books can be used to complement this theme:

Berry, Joy. (1996). *Feeling Afraid*. Illus. by Maggie Smith. New York: Scholastic. (*Let's Talk About* series.) (Pbk.)

Berry, Joy. (1996). *Feeling Angry*. Illus. by Maggie Smith. New York: Scholastic. (*Let's Talk About* series.) (Pbk.)

Berry, Joy. (1996). *Feeling Sad*. Illus. by Maggie Smith. New York: Scholastic. (*Let's Talk About* series.) (Pbk.)

Brown, Laurie Krasny. (1996). *When Dinosaurs Die: A Guide to Understanding Death*. Illus. by Marc Tolon Brown. Boston: Little, Brown.

Cabrera, Jane. (2005). *If You're Happy and You Know It!* New York: Holiday House.

Carle, Eric. (1995). *The Very Lonely Firefly*. New York: Philomel Books.

Carlson, Nancy L. (1997). *ABC I Like Me*. New York: Viking.

Conlin, Susan et al. (1991). *All My Feelings at Preschool: Nathan's Day*. Seattle, WA: Parenting Press.

Cooper, Terry Touff and Marilyn Ratner. (1974). *Many Hands Cooking*. New York: Thomas Y. Crowell.

Crary, Elizabeth. (1992). *I'm Frustrated*. Illus. by Jean Whitney. Seattle, WA: Parenting Press. (*Dealing with Feelings* series.)

306

Crary, Elizabeth. (1992). *I'm Mad*. Illus. by Jean Whitney. Seattle, WA: Parenting Press. (*Dealing with Feelings* series.)

Crary, Elizabeth. (1992). *I'm Proud*. Illus. by Jean Whitney. Seattle, WA: Parenting Press. (*Dealing with Feelings* series.)

Crary, Elizabeth. (1996). *I'm Excited*. Illus. by Jean Whitney. Seattle, WA: Parenting Press. (*Dealing with Feelings* series.)

Crary, Elizabeth. (1996). *I'm Furious*. Illus. by Jean Whitney. Seattle, WA: Parenting Press. (*Dealing with Feelings* series.)

Crary, Elizabeth. (1996). *I'm Scared*. Illus. by Jean Whitney. Seattle, WA: Parenting Press. (*Dealing with Feelings* series.)

Curtis, Munzee. (1997). *When the Big Dog Barks*. Illus. by Susan Ayishai. New York: Greenwillow.

Cusimano, Maryann K. and Satomi Ichikawa. (2001). *You Are My I Love You*. New York: Philomel Books.

Danneberg, Julie and Judith Dufour Love. (2000). *First Day Jitters*. Illus. by Judith Dufour Love. Watertown, MA: Charlesbridge.

Egan, Tim. (1996). *Metropolitan Cow*. Boston: Houghton Mifflin.

Emberley, Ed. (1993). *Go Away, Big Green Monster!* Boston: Little, Brown.

Emberley, Ed. (1997). *Glad Monster, Sad Monster: A Book about Feelings*. Illus. by Anne Miranda. Boston: Little, Brown.

Freymann, Saxton and Joost Elffers. (1999). *How Are You Feeling?* New York: Arthur A. Levine.

Genechten, Guido Van. (2005). *The Cuddle Book*. New York: HarperCollins Publishers. (First U.S. Ed.)

Hamilton, Dewitt. (1995). *Sad Days, Glad Days: A Story about Depression*. Illus. by Gail Owens. Morton Grove, IL: Albert Whitman.

Havill, Juanita. (1993). *Jamaica and Brianna*. Illus. by Anne Sibley O'Brien. Boston: Houghton Mifflin.

Henkes, Kevin. (2000). *Wemberly Worried*. New York: Greenwillow.

Joosse, Barbara M. (1991). *Mama, Do You Love Me?* Illus. by Barbara Lavalle. San Francisco: Chronicle Books.

Julian, Alison. (2001). *Brave as a Bunny Can Be*. Minneapolis, MN: Waldman House.

Krueger, David. (1996). *What Is a Feeling?* Seattle, WA: Parenting Press.

Lachner, Dorothea. (1995). *Andrew's Angry Words*. Illus. by Tjong-Khing The. New York: North South Books.

Markes, Julie. (2001). *Good Thing You're Not an Octopus!* Illus. by Maggie Smith. New York: HarperCollins.

Mayer, Mercer. (1990). *There's a Nightmare In My Closet*. New York: Dial Books for Young Readers.

Miller, J. Phillip and Greene, Sheppard. (2001). *We All Sing With the Same Voice*. Illus. by Paul Meisel. New York: HarperCollins.

Penn, Audrey. (2006). *The Kissing Hand*. Illus. by Ruth Harper & Nancy Leak. Terre Haute, IN: Tanglewood Press.

Raffi. (2005). *If You're Happy and You Know It*. Illus. by Cyd Moore. New York: Alfred A. Knopf: distributed by Random House.

Roth, Susan L. (1997). *My Love for You*. New York: Dial Books.

Seeger, Pete and Jacobs, Paul DuBois. (2005). *Some Friends to Feed: the Story of Stone Soup*. Illus. by Michael Hays. New York: G.P. Putnam's Sons.

Seuss, Dr. (1996). *My Many Colored Days*. Edited by Lou Fancher; illus. by Steve Johnson. New York: Knopf.

Spelman, Cornelia. (2004). *When I Miss You*. Illus. by Kathy Parkinson. Morton Grove, IL: Albert Whitman & Co.

Tyler, Anne. (2005). *Timothy Tugbottom Says No!* Illus. by Mitra Modarressi. New York: G.P. Putnam's Sons.

Vail, Rachel. (2002). *Sometimes I'm Bombaloo*. Illus. by Yumi Heo. New York: Scholastic Press.

Waddell, Martin. (1993). *Let's Go Home, Little Bear*. Illus. by Barbara Firth. Cambridge, MA: Candlewick Press.

Ward, Heather P. (1994). *I Promise I'll Find You*. Illus. by Sheila McGraw. Buffalo, NY: Firefly Books.

Weeks, Sarah. (2002). *My Somebody Special*. Illus. by Ashley Wolff. Sand Diego, CA: Harcourt.

FEELINGS

Multimedia

The following multimedia products can be used to complement this theme:

Berenstain Bears in the Dark [CD-ROM]. (1996). New York: Random House/Broderbund.

Groark Learns about Prejudice [video]. (1996). Featuring Randel McGee. Elkind & Sweet Communications/distributed by Live Wire Media.

I Get So Mad! [video]. (1993). Sunburst Communications.

Murphy, Jane. *Songs for You and Me: Kids Learn about Feelings and Emotions* [cassette]. Kimbo Educational, Long Branch, NJ.

Recordings and Song Titles

The following recordings can be used to complement this theme:

"A Friend in Need," "It's a Great Day," "It's All Right," "Squabbles Hugs." (1994). *Get Up and Grow.* Long Branch, NJ: Kimbo Educational.

"Angry," "Sad," "Scared." (1986). *Singing, Moving and Fun.* Long Branch, NJ: Kimbo Educational.

"Friends." (1992). Nelson Gill/*Friends.* Long Branch, NJ: Kimbo Educational.

"Happy." (2004). *Circle Time Activities.* Long Branch, NJ: Kimbo Educational.

"Happy Days." (2000). *Bean Bag Rock & Roll.* Long Branch, NJ: Kimbo Educational.

"Happy Rappy." (1994). *Yes, I Can Songs (with RONNO).* Long Branch, NJ: Kimbo Educational.

"How Are You Today—Please?" (1995). *Piggyback Songs.* Long Branch, NJ: Kimbo Educational.

"If You Feel It." (2000). *Seasonal Songs in Motion.* Long Branch, NJ: Kimbo Educational.

"If You're Happy and You Know It." (1996). *Where Is Thumbkin?* Long Branch, NJ: Kimbo Educational.

"I Sign Like This," "Feeling Signs." (1996). Gaia—*Sing 'n Sign for Fun.* Long Branch, NJ: Kimbo Educational.

"Moods." (1985). *Toddlers on Parade.* Long Branch, NJ: Kimbo Educational.

"The Angry Song." (1985). *Songs for You and Me.* Long Branch, NJ: Kimbo Educational.

30

Purpose

Parts

Purpose

walking
hopping
running
jumping
balance

Care

Parts

toes
toenails
sole
heel
bones
ligaments
muscles

Care

keep feet clean and dry
cut toenails when needed
wear correctly fitting footwear

Feet

Coverings

SOCKS	SLIPPERS	SHOES	BOOTS	SPORTS
		sandles	rain	roller skates
		slip-on	snow	roller blades
		Velcro® closure	hiking	ice skates
		tie	cowboy	golf shoes
		buckle	ski	water shoes
				football shoes
				baseball shoes
				tennis shoes
				ballet shoes

309

Theme Goals

Through participating in the experiences provided by this theme, the children may learn

1. Parts of the foot
2. Ways to take care of feet
3. Coverings worn on the feet
4. Purpose of feet

Concepts for the Children to Learn

1. Our feet help us balance while standing.
2. Our feet also help us to walk, hop, run, jump, and dance.
3. There are six parts to our feet.
4. Toe, toenails, sole, heel, bones, ligaments, and muscles are all parts of our feet.
5. Feet need special care.
6. Our feet need to be kept clean and dry.
7. Toenails need to be cut.
8. Only correctly fitting footwear should be worn on our feet.
9. There are many types of coverings for our feet.
10. Socks, slippers, shoes, boots, and sports shoes are all coverings for our feet.
11. There are many types of shoes.
12. Sandals, slip-on, Velcro closure, tie, and buckled are different types of shoes.
13. Cowboy, hiking, snow, and rain are types of boots.
14. Special footwear is worn for some sports and activities.
15. Roller skates and ice skates can also cover our feet.
16. Golf, water, football, tennis, and ballet shoes are also coverings for our feet.

Vocabulary

1. **cobbler**—a person who mends shoes.
2. **foot**—end part of the leg, on which a person stands.
3. **podiatrist**—foot doctor.
4. **shoe**—a covering for the foot.
5. **sole**—bottom of the foot.
6. **toe**—a digit at the end of the foot.
7. **toenail**—a nail that grows on the end of each toe.

Bulletin Board

The purpose of this bulletin board is to develop beginning graphing skills. Create this bulletin board by drawing a buckle shoe, slip-on shoe, Velcro closure shoe, and tie shoe. Decorate each shoe as desired. Cut out tagboard squares and print a child's name on each one. Laminate all pieces. Staple each shoe to the left side of the bulletin board. Attach a row of pushpins to the right of each shoe. As each child arrives, he or she can hang a name card in the row that corresponds with the shoe type he or she is wearing that day. After all name cards have been placed on the bulletin board, count the number of shoes in each row. Which has more? Which has less?

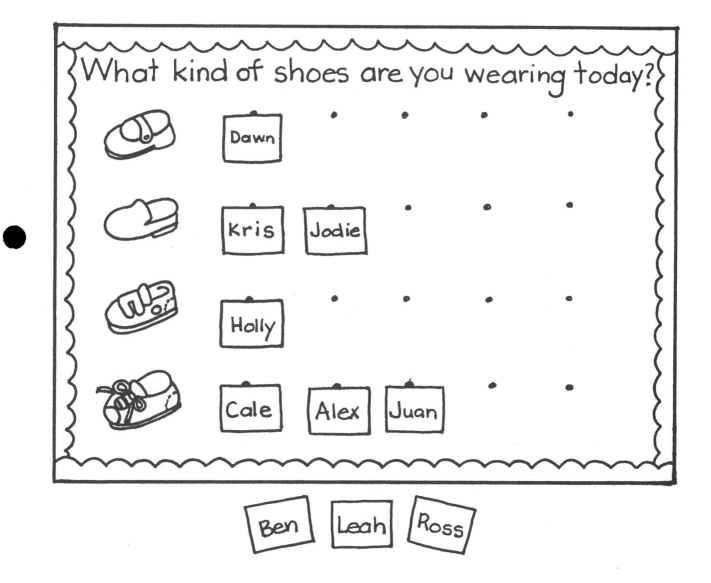

Family Letter

Dear Families,

Did you know that the human foot has 26 bones—14 of which are in the toes? No wonder your feet can ache at the end of a long day! This week we will learn the purpose and parts of our feet. We will also learn about foot care and coverings.

AT SCHOOL

During this busy week we will

- make prints of our feet with paint!
- find matching pairs of socks (sounds like doing laundry, doesn't it?)
- experiment with various shoe fasteners—such as laces, buckles, and Velcro
- look at footwear worn for different activities, including relaxing, sports, and weather

AT HOME

To reinforce the concepts of this unit at home, go on a "shoe hunt" with your child. Count the number of shoes each family member has. Count the total number of shoes and boots in your house. How many have laces? How many are slip-on shoes? Do any have Velcro® or buckles? How many are worn indoors? Which ones are worn outdoors? Also, have your child help with the laundry. He or she can help by finding matching pairs of socks and distributing them to the person who wears them!

Have a nice week!

Shoes can be sorted by color, size, and weight.

 # Arts and Crafts

1. Foot Painting

Set out different colors of tempera paint in trays on the floor. The children can take turns dipping a bare foot (or feet) in the paint and then stepping on butcher or construction paper, creating footprints. Have buckets of warm soapy water and towels nearby to assist in the cleanup process.

2. Sock Puppets

Collect clean, discarded socks, yarn, buttons, fabric scraps, pompons, and glue. Place materials on the art table. Children can use the supplies to design sock puppets.

3. Shoebox Art

Save shoeboxes of various sizes. Place the boxes on the art table with construction paper, markers, crayons, glue, and craft odds and ends. Children can use the materials to design creations of their choice.

4. Shoelace Painting

Provide containers of paint, paper, and shoelaces. The children can apply the paint to the paper using the shoelaces as painting tools.

5. Shoe Prints

On the art table, place a few discarded shoes, trays of paint, and construction paper. Children can dip the soles of the shoes in the paint and then press on paper, creating a print of the shoe.

 # Cooking

Foot French Toast

Cut slices of bread into sock or foot shapes and make French toast.

2 eggs, slightly beaten
1 tablespoon sugar
1/2 teaspoon salt
1/4 teaspoon cinnamon
1/2 cup milk
2 tablespoons margarine or butter
6 slices of bread

Heat griddle or frying pan to medium heat (340 degrees). Combine the first five ingredients in a shallow bowl. Melt margarine on griddle. Dip bread in egg mixture, coating both sides. Cook about 4 minutes on each side or until golden brown. Serve with maple syrup or powdered sugar.

FEET

Dramatic Play

Shoe Store

Collect a variety of shoes, shoeboxes, pictures of shoes, rulers, cash register, and play money. Arrange materials and chairs in the dramatic play area to resemble a shoe store.

Field Trips/ Resource People

1. Shoe Store

Plan a trip to a shoe store. Note the selection and variety of sizes. Which shoes are worn for special activities or sports?

2. Podiatrist

Make arrangements for the children to visit a podiatrist's office. What special equipment does the doctor have to take care of feet?

Fingerplays

I Clap My Hands

I clap my hands,
    (clap)
I touch my feet,
    (touch feet)
I jump up from the ground.
    (jump)

I clap my hands,
    (clap)
I touch my feet,
    (touch feet)
And turn myself around
    (turn around)

I clap my hands,
    (clap)

I touch my feet,
    (touch feet)
I sit myself right down,
    (sit on floor)

I clap my hands,
    (clap)
I touch my feet,
    (touch feet)
I do not make a sound.

I Am a Cobber

I am a cobbler,
    (point to self)
And this is what I do:
Rap-tap-a-tap
To mend my shoe.
    (pound fist into palm of other hand)

Night Time

Before I jump into my bed,
    (jump)
Before I dim the light,
    (pretend to turn light off)
I put my shoes together,
    (put hands together)
So they can talk at night.
I'm sure they would be lonesome,
If I tossed one here and there,
    (move one hand to right—one hand to left)
So I put them close together,
    (put hands together)
For they're a friendly pair.

Shiny Shoes

First I loosen mud and dirt,
    (pretend to brush off dirt)
My shoes I then rub clean.
    (rubbing motion)
For shoes in such a dreaful sight,
Never should be seen.
    (move hands behind back)
Next I spread the polish on,
    (slow, rubbing motion)
And then I let it dry.
I brush, and brush, and brush, and brush.
    (brushing motion)
How those shoes shine! Oh, my!
    (extend hand and smile)

Walking in the Snow

Let's go walking in the snow,
    (walking motion with legs)
Walking, walking, on tiptoe.
    (tiptoe)
Lift your one foot way up high,
    (lift one foot)
Then the other to keep it dry.
    (lift other foot)
All around the yard we skip,
    (skip)
Watch your step or you might slip.
    (pretend to slip)

Two Little

Two little feet go tap, tap, tap.
    (tap feet on floor)
Two little hands go clap, clap, clap.
    (clap)
A quiet leap up from a chair,
    (jump)
Two little arms reach high in the air.
    (raise hands above head)
Two little feet go jump, jump, jump.
    (hop)
Two little fists go thump, thump, thump.
    (pound fists)
One little body goes round, round, round.
    (turn around)
And one little child sits quietly down.
    (sit down)

This Little Piggy

This little piggy went to market.
    (touch big toe)
This little piggy stayed home.
    (touch second toe)
This little piggy had roast beef.
    (touch third toe)
This little piggy had none.
    (touch fourth toe)
And this little piggy cried, "Wee, wee, wee,"
All the way home.
    (touch little toe)

Group Time
(Games, Language)

1. **"One, Two, Buckle My Shoe"**

One, two, buckle my shoe.
Three, four, shut the door.
Five, six, pick up sticks.
Seven, eight, lay them straight.
Nine, ten, a big fat hen.

Using teacher-made materials or commercially available pictures, teach or review this nursery rhyme with the children. Upon mastery of the rhyme, encourage children to act it out.

2. **"Cobbler, Cobbler, Mend My Shoe"**

To play the game, have the children sit in a circle formation. Select one child to be the cobbler and sit in the center with his or her eyes closed. The children in the circle pass a shoe around as they chant the following nursery rhyme:

Cobbler, cobbler, mend my shoe.
Have it done by half past two.
Stitch it up and stitch it down.
Now see with whom the shoe is found.

When the chant is finished, the shoe is no longer passed. At this point, all children in the circle put their hands behind their backs. Then the "cobbler" opens his or her eyes and tries to guess who has the shoe.

Large Muscle

1. **Feet Movement**

Have the children think of movements and activities that require their feet, such as walking, running, skipping, hopping (on one foot, two feet), and jumping. Practice these movements outdoors or in a large indoor area.

2. Follow the Footprints

Cut foot shapes out of construction paper. Place them on the floor and have children follow the paper footprint trail.

Math

1. Sock Sort

Collect pairs of clean socks of a variety of sizes, materials, and colors. Place the socks in a laundry basket. Children can find matching pairs of socks.

2. Shoe Seriation

Collect shoes of various sizes. Encourage the children to put the shoes in order by size from smallest to largest.

3. How Many Footsteps?

Have the children count how many footsteps it takes to get from a designated beginning spot (such as a chair) to the window. How many footsteps does it take to reach the door? The sink? The calendar? If appropriate, record the information on a chart and compare results.

Music

1. "Tie Your Shoes"
(Sing to the tune of "Row Your Boat")

Tie, tie, tie your shoes.
Pull the laces tight.
Make two loops and twist them 'round.
Until you've got it right!

2. "What Are You Wearing on Your Feet?"
(Sing to the tune of "Mary Had a Little Lamb")

What are you wearing on your feet,
On your feet, on your feet?
What are you wearing on your feet,
On your feet today?

Tony is wearing tie shoes,
Tie shoes, tie shoes.
Tony is wearing tie shoes
On his feet today.

Suzanne is wearing buckle shoes . . .
Chandler is wearing hiking boots . . .
(insert child's name and footwear as appropriate)

3. "I Have Something Very Special"
(Sing to the tune of "She'll Be Coming 'Round the Mountain")

I have something very special on my legs,
They are right at the very end of my legs.
They help me walk and run,
They help me jump and hop.
Have you guessed what's very special?
They're my feet!

Science

1. Foot X-Rays

Contact the local hospital radiation department and ask to borrow x-rays of feet. In the classroom, hold the x-rays up to a light source and let the children observe the many bones of a foot.

2. Animal Tracks

With the children, look for animal tracks in the soil, sand, or snow. Use reference books to try to identify the animal that created the prints.

Sensory

Sensory Walk

Collect several plastic washtubs. Fill each with a few inches of various materials such as water, dry oats, cornmeal, rocks, sand, birdseed, cotton balls, etc. Have the children remove shoes and socks and get in a line formation. Place the buckets on the floor, and have the children follow the "leader" as he or she walks carefully through the tubs of materials. How did each feel on your feet?

316

THEME 30

Social Studies

Footwear of Long Ago

Borrow old shoes and boots from a local museum, historical society, or theater group. Have the children make comparisons of footwear worn long ago and today's footwear. What materials were used to make the boots and shoes? What kinds of fasteners were used?

Books

The following books can be used to complement this theme:

Aliki. (1990). *My Feet*. New York: Harper Trophy.

Badt, Karin Luisa. (1994). *On Your Feet!* Chicago: Children's Press.

Binch, Caroline. (2001). *Silver Shoes*. New York: DK Publishing.

Burton, Marilee Robin. (1994). *My Best Shoes*. Illus. by James E. Ransome. New York: William Morrow.

Carle, Eric. (1997). *From Head to Toe*. New York: HarperCollins.

Cleary, Beverly. (1997). *The Growing-Up Feet*. New York: Mulberry Books.

Daniels, Teri and Travic Foster. (1999). *The Feet in the Gym*. New York: Winslow Press.

Defelice, Cynthia C. and Robert Andrew Parker. (2000). *Cold Feet*. New York: DK Publishing.

Emerson, Scott and Howard Post. (1999). *The Magic Boots*. Layton, UT: Gibbs Smith.

Hamm, Diane Johnston and Kate Salley Palmer. (1994). *How Many Feet in the Bed?* New York: Aladdin Paperbacks.

Hughes, Shirley. (1982). *Alfie's Feet*. New York: Mulberry Books.

Hurwitz, Johanna. (1993). *New Shoes for Silvia*. Illus. by Jerry Pinkney. New York: William Morrow.

Knowlton, Laurie Lazzaro. (1995). *Why Cowboys Sleep with Their Boots On*. Gretna, LA: Pelican.

May, Kara and Jonathon Allen. (2000). *Joe Lion's Big Boots*. New York: Larousse Kingfisher Chambers.

Morris, Ann. (1998). *Shoes, Shoes, Shoes*. New York: Mulberry Books.

Murphy, Stuart. (1996). *A Pair of Socks*. Illus. by Lois Ehlert. New York: HarperCollins.

O'Brien, Claire. (1997). *Sam's Sneaker Search*. Illus. by Charles Fuge. New York: Simon & Schuster.

Patrick, Denise Lewis. (1993). *Red Dancing Shoes*. Illus. by James Ransome. New York: William Morrow.

Quinlan, Patricia and Linda Hendry. (1996). *Baby's Feet*. Willowdale, Ontario, Canada: Annick Press.

Seuss, Dr. (1996). *Foot Book*. New York: Random House.

Simmons, Jane. (2001). *Daisy: The Little Duck with Big Feet*. Boston: Little, Brown.

Waller, Barrett. (1992). *New Feet for Old*. Illus. by Harvey Stevenson. New York: Four Winds Press.

Recordings and Song Titles

The following recording can be used to complement this theme:

"Meet De Feet." (2001). *Fittersitters*. Long Branch, NJ: Kimbo Educational.

Clothing

hats, coats,
masks, boots,
gloves, uniforms

Job

fight fires,
inspect buildings,
teach fire safety,
provide medical
treatment

Vehicles

fire trucks
water trucks
fire chief car
rescue vehicles

Firefighters

Safety

when to use
house
person
how to contact
false alarms
matches
cooking
smoking

Equipment

fire hydrant,
fire extinguisher,
hose, nozzle, ax,
ladder, telephone,
communication radio,
water

Fire Station

garage
workroom
kitchen
sleeping room
bathrooms
dalmatians

Theme Goals

Through participating in the experiences provided by this theme, the children may learn

1. The firefighter's job
2. Clothing worn by firefighters
3. Vehicles used by firefighters
4. Firefighting equipment
5. Areas inside a fire station

Concepts for the Children to Learn

1. Men and women who fight fires are called firefighters.
2. Firefighters help keep our community safe.
3. Firefighters fight fires, inspect buildings, teach fire safety, and provide medical treatment.
4. Firefighters wear special hats and clothing.
5. Firefighters wear hats, coats, boots, masks, and uniforms.
6. The fire station has a garage, kitchen, workroom, and sleeping rooms.
7. The fire station has a special telephone number.
8. Firefighters have special equipment.
9. Ladders, hoses, and water are needed to fight fires.
10. Nozzles control the water.
11. The hoses are connected to the fire hydrant.
12. Firefighters have special vehicles.
13. The chief has a fire chief car.
14. Rescue vehicles assist in accidents.
15. Fire and water trucks are driven to fires.
16. Firefighters check buildings to make sure they are safe.
17. Firefighters teach us fire safety.
18. Fire extinguishers can be used to put out small fires.
19. Fire drills teach us what to do in case of a fire.

Vocabulary

1. **fire alarm**—a sound that warns people about fire.
2. **fire drill**—practice for teaching people what to do in case of a fire.
3. **fire engines**—trucks carrying tools and equipment needed to fight fires.
4. **fire extinguisher**—equipment that puts out fires.
5. **fire station**—a building that provides housing for firefighters and fire trucks.
6. **helmet**—a protective hat.
7. **hose**—a tube that water flows through.

Bulletin Board

The purpose of this bulletin board is to develop an awareness of clothing worn by firefighters and to reinforce color-matching skills. Likewise, this board promotes the development of hand-eye coordination, visual discrimination, and problem-solving skills. From tagboard, construct five firefighter hats. Color each hat a different color. Then construct five firefighter boots from tagboard. Color-coordinate boots to match the hats. Laminate all of the pieces. Staple hats in two rows across the top of the bulletin board as illustrated. Staple boots in a row across the bottom of the bulletin board. Affix matching yarn to each hat. Children can match each hat to its correspondingly colored boot by winding the string around a push-pin in the top of the boot.

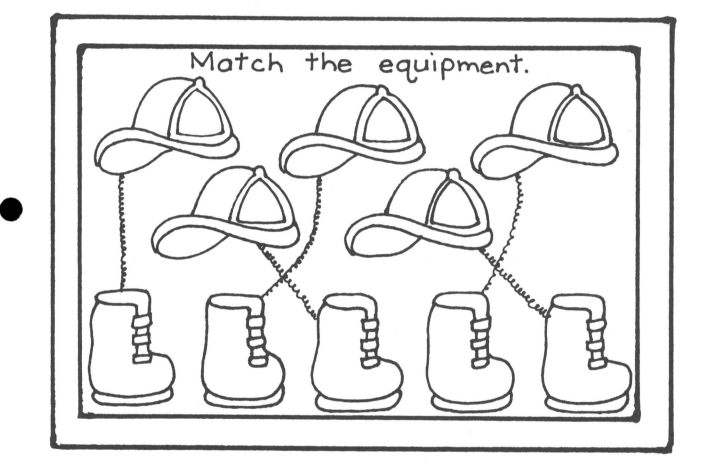

Family Letter

Dear Families,

Because next week is Fire Prevention Week, we have decided that it would be fun and educational to focus on some very important community helpers—firefighters. The children will become more aware of the role of the firefighter, clothing worn by firefighters, and the fire station. We will also learn how to use the telephone to call the emergency fire number.

AT SCHOOL

We have many activities planned for this unit! On Monday, we will paint a large box to create our own fire engine to use during the week in the dramatic play area. On Tuesday, a real fire engine will visit the parking lot so the children can see how many tools firefighters need to take along on the job. We'll also be making fire helmets and practicing our fire drill procedures.

AT HOME

To ensure your family's safety, talk with your child about what would happen in the event of a fire in your house. You can do this calmly, without frightening your child. Practice taking a fire escape route from the child's bedroom, the playroom, kitchen, and other rooms of your house. Establish a meeting place so that family members can go to the same location in the event of a fire.

Enjoy your child as you share the importance of safety in the event of a fire.

iron. Show the children the effect of heat. This activity needs to be carefully supervised. The caption "crayon melting" may be printed on a bulletin board. On the board, place the children's pictures, identifying each by name in the upper-left corner.

Having a fire truck visit school is very exciting!

Cooking

Firehouse Baked Beans

Purchase canned baked beans. To the beans, add cut-up hot dogs, cut lengthwise, and extra catsup. Heat and serve for snack.

Dramatic Play

1. **Firefighters**

   Place firefighting clothes such as hats, boots, and coats for children to wear. Sometimes fire station personnel will allow schools to borrow some of their clothing and equipment. Also, provide a bell to use as an alarm. To extend play, a vacuum cleaner hose or a length of garden hose can be included to represent a water hose.

2. **Fire Truck**

   A fire truck can be cut from a cardboard refrigerator box. The children may want to paint the box yellow or red. A steering wheel and chairs may be added.

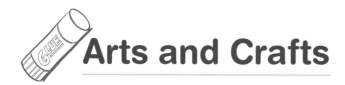

Arts and Crafts

1. **Firefighters' Hats**

   Provide materials for the children to make fire hats. The hats can be decorated with foil, crayons, or paint. The emergency number 911 may be printed on the crown.

2. **Charcoal Drawings**

   Provide real charcoal at the easels to be used as an application tool.

3. **Crayon Melting**

   Place wax crayons and paper on the art table for the children to create a design during self-initiated or self-directed play. Place a clean sheet of paper over the picture. Apply a warm

Field Trips/ Resource People

1. **Fire Station**

   Take a trip to a fire station. Observe the clothing worn by firefighters, the building, the vehicles, and the tools.

FIREFIGHTERS

2. Firefighter

Invite a firefighter to bring a fire truck to your school. Ask the firefighter to point out the special features such as the hose, siren, ladders, light, and special clothing kept on the truck. If permissible and safe, let the children climb onto the truck.

Fingerplays

The Firefighter

This brave firefigher is going to bed.
    (hold up right thumb)
Down on the pillow he lays his head.
    (place right thumb on left palm)
He wraps himself in a blanket tight
    (curl fingers around thumb)
And wants to sleep this way all night.
    (close eyes)
But the fire alarm rings! He opens his eyes!
    (open eyes wide)
Quickly he's dressed and down the pole he slides.
    (right hand slides down left arm in a
        grip motion)
Then he climbs on the truck, to the fire he goes.
    (hands grip imaginary steering wheel)
Out goes the fire with water from a hose.
    (pretend to hold hose and spray)

Group Time

(Games, Language)

Language Experience

Review safety rules. Write the rules on a large piece of paper. These rules can also be included in a family letter as well as posted in the classroom.

Large Muscle

1. Firefighter's Workout

Lead children in a firefighter's workout. Do exercises such as jumping jacks, knee bends, leg lifts, and running in place. Ask children why they think firefighters need to be in good physical condition for their job.

2. Obstacle Course

Make an obstacle course. Let children follow a string or piece of tape under chairs or tables, over steps, and across ladders. This activity can be planned for indoors or outdoors.

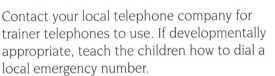

Math

1. Sequencing

Cut a piece of rubber tubing into various lengths. The children can sequence the pieces from shortest to longest.

2. Emergency Number

Contact your local telephone company for trainer telephones to use. If developmentally appropriate, teach the children how to dial a local emergency number.

Music

"Down by the Station"

Down by the station early in the morning
See the great big fire trucks all in a row.
Hear the jangly fire bell sound a loud alarm now—
Chug chug, clang clang, off we go!

Science

"Fire" Paintings

Provide red and yellow paint. Invite children to experiment mixing the colors with their hands. What did they observe? The finished paintings can be "fires."

Sensory

1. Fill the sensory table with water. Provide cups and rubber tubing to resemble hoses and funnels.
2. Place sand in the sensory table. Add fire engines, firefighter dolls, craft sticks to make fences, and blocks to make buildings or houses.

Social Studies

1. **Safety Rules**

   Discuss safety rules dealing with fire. Let children generate ideas about safety. Write their ideas on chart paper and display. Discuss why fire drills are a good idea. Practice "stop, drop, and roll" procedures.

2. **Fire Inspection Tour**

   Tour the classroom or building looking for fire extinguishers, emergency fire alarm boxes, and exits.

3. **Fire Drill**

   Schedule a fire drill. Before the drill, talk to the children about fire drill procedures.

Books

The following books can be used to complement this theme:

Bingham, Caroline. (2003). *Fire Truck*. New York: DK Publisher.

Cuyler, Margery and Arthur Howard. (2001). *Stop, Drop, and Roll* (A *Book about Fire Safety*). Illus. by Arthur Howard. New York: Simon & Schuster.

Demarest, Chris. (2000). *Firefighters* (A *to* Z). New York: Margaret McElderry.

Flanagan, Alice K. (1997). Ms. *Murphy Fights Fires*. Photos by Christine Osinski. Chicago: Children's Press.

Hines, Gary. (1993). *Flying Firefighters*. Illus. by Anna Grossnickle Hines. New York: Clarion Books.

Kallen, Stuart A. (1997). *The Fire Station*. Minneapolis, MN: Abdo & Daughters.

Kottke, Jan. (2000). A *Day with Firefighters* (*Hard Work*). New York: Children's Press.

Kuklin, Susan. (1993). *Fighting Fires*. New York: Simon & Schuster.

Kunhardt, Edith. (1995). I'm *Going to Be a Fire Fighter*. St. Paul, MN: Cartwheel Books. (Pbk.)

Lakin, Pat. (1995). *The Fire Fighter*: *Where There's Smoke*. Austin, TX: Raintree/Steck Vaughn.

McMullan, Kate and Mavis Smith. (1999). *Fluffy and the Firefighters*. Illus. by Mavis Smith. New York: Scholastic.

Packard, Mary. (1995). I'm *a Fire Fighter*. Illus. by Julie Durrell. Madison, WI: Demco Media.

Ready, Dee. (1997). *Fire Fighters*. Danbury, CT: Grolier.

Simon, Norma. (1995). *Fire Fighters*. Illus. by Pam Paparone. New York: Simon & Schuster.

Winkleman, Katherine. (1994). *Firehouse*. Illus. by John S. Winkleman. New York: Walker.

Multimedia

The following multimedia products can be used to complement this theme:

Big Job [CD-ROM]. (1995). Bethesda, MD: Discovery Communications, Inc.

Big Red [video]. (1993). Mill Valley, CA: Fire Dog Pictures.

Fire and Rescue [video]. (1993). Montpelier, VT: Focus Video Productions.

Fire Safety for Kids [video]. (1995). South Burlington, VT: Children's Video Development.

Fire Station [video]. (1990). Washington, DC: National Geographic.

Firefighter [CD-ROM]. (1994). New York: Simon & Schuster Interactive.

Sound the Alarm: Firefighters at Work [video]. (1994). Bohemia, NY: Rainbow Educational Media.

Recordings and Song Titles

The following recording can be used to complement this theme:

"Safety Pros Know" (firefighter, fire chief, fire inspector, police). (1996). *People in Our Neighborhood*. Long Branch, NJ: Kimbo Educational.

32

Fish

Habitat

lakes
oceans
ponds
rivers
fish farms
aquariums

Size

small
medium
large
very large

Foods

insects
snails
worms
other fish
fish food
cornmeal

Colors

blue
brown
gray
black
orange
white
red
yellow
green

Parts

eyes
fins
gills
scales
mouth
tail

Kinds

northern pike
seahorse
guppy
catfish
shark
eel

Importance

food
entertainment
sports
pets

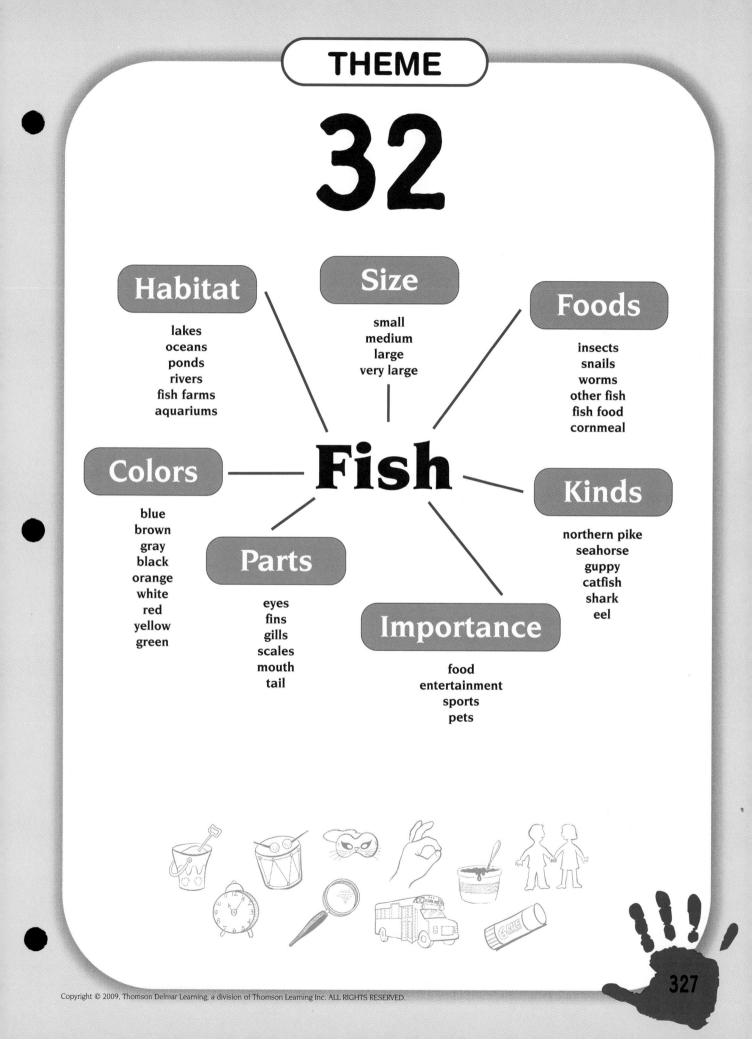

Theme Goals

Through participating in the experiences provided by this theme, the children may learn

1. Homes for fish
2. The importance of fish
3. Colors of fish
4. Foods for fish
5. Kinds of fish
6. Sizes of fish
7. Parts of fish

Concepts for the Children to Learn

1. Most fish have two eyes, fins, gills, scales, a mouth, and a tail.
2. Fish vary in size.
3. They may be small, medium, large, or very large.
4. Blue, brown, gray, white, black, red, yellow, green, and orange are colors of fish.
5. Fish may live in lakes, oceans, ponds, rivers, fish farms, and aquariums.
6. Fish need food and water to live.
7. Insects, snails, other fish, plants, worms, fish food, and cornmeal are foods fish eat.
8. There are many kinds of fish.
9. Some kinds include northern pike, seahorse, guppy, catfish, shark, and eel.
10. Fish are important to people.
11. Fish provide food and entertainment.
12. Fishing can be a sport.

Vocabulary

1. **fin**—the part that moves to help fish swim.
2. **fish farm**—a place to raise fish for food.
3. **gills**—the part of the fish's body that helps it get air.
4. **scales**—skin covering of fish and other reptiles.
5. **school**—a group of fish.
6. **tail**—the end body part that helps fish move.

Bulletin Board

The purpose of this bulletin board is to promote identification of written numerals, as well as matching a set to a written numeral. To prepare the bulletin board, begin by drawing and cutting fish shapes from construction paper. Decorate the fish as desired and print a numeral on each fish. Make another set of identical fish shapes from black construction paper to create fish "shadows." Cut small circles out of white construction paper to represent the fishes' air bubbles. Staple the fish shadows to the bulletin board. Above each fish shadow, staple a set of air bubbles. Children can then match the numerals on the fish to the corresponding set of air bubbles. The fish can be attached to the bulletin board with pushpins or small adhesive magnet pieces.

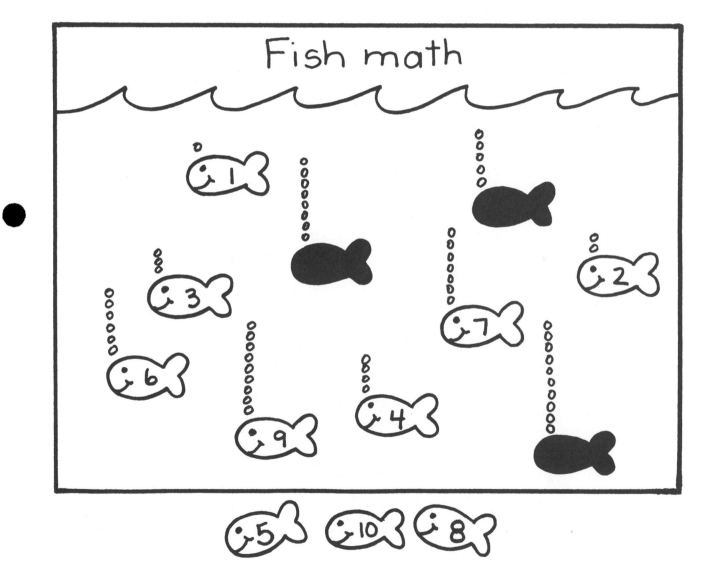

Family Letter

Dear Families,

Our next theme will focus on fish. Through participating in the experiences provided by this theme, the children will learn the color, size, kinds, and parts of a fish. They will also learn where fish live and the role fish play in our lives.

AT SCHOOL

Learning experiences that have been planned to complement this theme include:

- visiting a pet store to observe different types and colors of fish. We will also purchase fish to bring back to our classroom.
- listening to the story *Fish Eyes* by Lois Ehlert
- sorting, counting, and eating various fish-shaped crackers
- fishing in the dramatic play area
- observing minnows at the sensory table

AT HOME

- Prepare a tuna salad using a favorite recipe with your child.
- Point out fishing gear in the sports section of a department store or in a catalog.
- Check out children's books about fish from the library. Look for

  Fishes by Brian Wildsmith

  Fish Is Fish and *Swimmy* by Leo Lionni

  Gone Fishing by Earlene R. Long

  A Million Fish . . . More or Less by Patricia C. McKissack

Enjoy your child as you explore experiences related to fish!

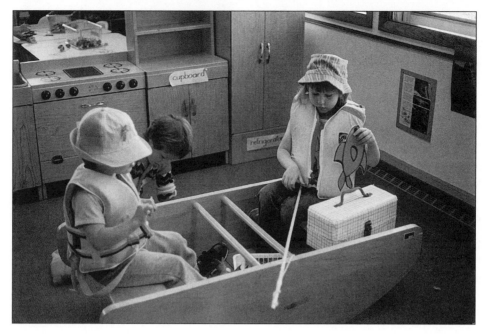

How many fish can you catch?

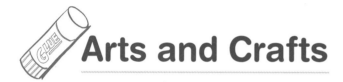

Arts and Crafts

1. Aquarium Crayon Resist

After observing fish or listening to stories about them, encourage the children to use crayons to draw fish on a piece of white construction paper. Then, the children can paint over their crayon drawing with a thin wash of blue tempera or water color. The wax will repel the water paints, leaving an interesting effect.

2. Fish Sponge Painting

Cut sponges into fish shapes. Place the sponges on the art table with paper and several shallow trays of paint. Use thick tempera paint the color of fish. Also provide paper. The children can make prints by dipping the sponges into the paint and then pressing them onto paper.

3. Fish Rubbings

Cut fish shapes out of tagboard, adding details as desired. Place the fish shapes on the art table along with paper and crayons. The children can create designs by placing a tagboard fish beneath a piece of paper and rubbing over the top of the paper with a crayon. Repeat as discussed.

4. Tackle Box Paint Container

Use a discarded, clean tackle box as a container to hold paints at the art table. Paints can be placed in individual compartments, providing several choices for the children.

Cooking

1. Swimming Fish Snack

8 ounces soft cream cheese
blue food coloring
1 box rectangular-shaped crackers
2 cups small fish-shaped crackers (any flavor)

Add a few drops of blue food coloring to the cream cheese and stir. For each serving, spread cream cheese on a large, rectangular cracker. Place a few fish-shaped crackers on top of the cream cheese.

2. Fish Mix Snack

2 cups toasted oat cereal
2 cups pretzel sticks
2 cups small fish-shaped crackers (any flavor)

1/4 cup melted margarine
2 teaspoons Worcestershire sauce

Combine oat cereal, pretzels, and fish-shaped crackers in a bowl. In a small bowl, stir together melted margarine and Worcestershire sauce. Drizzle over cereal mixture and toss to coat evenly. Transfer into 13 × 9 baking pan and bake in a 300-degree oven for 30 minutes, stirring occasionally. Remove from oven and cool. Makes approximately six cups.

3. Tuna Salad

1 can of tuna (3 1/4 ounces), drained
1/4 cup mayonnaise, salad dressing, or
 plain yogurt
1/4 cup finely chopped apple
3 tablespoons sunflower seeds
4 slices of bread or 2 English muffins

Combine the tuna, mayonnaise, apple, and sunflower seeds in a bowl. Chill if desired. Toast the bread or English muffins. Spread tuna mixture on toasted muffins. (Makes four servings.)

4. Tartar Sauce for Fish Sticks

1/2 cup mayonnaise or salad dressing
1 tablespoon finely chopped pickle or pickle relish
1 teaspoon dried parsley
1/2 teaspoon grated onion or onion flakes

Combine all ingredients and chill. Bake frozen fish sticks as directed on the package and serve with tartar sauce.

Dramatic Play

1. Gone Fishing

Set up a fishing area in the dramatic play center. Provide props such as a wooden rocking boat, small wading pool, life vests, hats, tackle boxes, nets, and fishing poles. Fishing poles can be made by attaching string to a short dowel or paper towel tube. Tie a small magnet to the end of the string. Attach paper clips to the construction paper fish. Then, go fishing!

2. Bait and Tackle Shop

Provide props to simulate a bait and tackle shop in the dramatic play area. Items can include a cash register, play money, plastic or paper fish of varying sizes, nets, fishing lures (remove hooks), tackle boxes, coolers, fishing poles, and life vests. Display pictures of fish and people fishing.

Field Trips/ Resource People

1. Lake, Pond, or Stream

If possible, visit a small body of water to observe a fish habitat. Watch for people fishing. (For safety purposes, the body of water will have to be carefully chosen. Likewise, additional supervision may be required.)

2. Pet Store

Visit a pet store to see many types of fish as well as aquariums and fish supplies. Purchase one or more goldfish to take back to your classroom. (**Note:** Water needs to be de-chlorinated before placing goldfish in it.)

3. Bait and Tackle Shop

Make arrangements to visit a bait and tackle shop. Observe the many types of fishing poles and lures as well as boat safety items.

4. State or National Fish Hatchery

These make a wonderful field trip. They also have coloring books, and so on, for the children.

5. Fish Sportsman or Sportswoman

Invite a parent or another person who enjoys fishing to come talk with the children. Ask the person to bring fishing gear and pictures of fishing trips as well as fish caught.

Fingerplays

Fish Story

One, two, three, four, five
   (hold up fingers while counting)
Once I caught a fish alive.
Six, seven, eight, nine, ten
   (hold up additional fingers)
Then I let it go again.
Why did I let it go?
Because it bit my finger so.
Which finger did it bite?
The little finger on the right.
   (hold up pinky on the right hand)

Group Time

(Games, Language)

1. Fish Memory Game

Collect items associated with fish and place on a tray. At group time, show the tray containing the items and name them. To play the game, cover the tray with a towel. Then ask the children to recall the names of items on the tray. To vary the game, play again, this time removing an item from the tray while covered. The children then try to name the item missing from the tray. To ensure success, begin the activity with few objects. Additional objects can be added depending on the developmental maturity of the children.

2. Go Fish!

Cut fish shapes out of various colors of construction paper. Attach a paper clip to each fish. Make a fishing pole by tying a string to a short dowel. Attach a small magnet to the end of the string. At group time, present the fishing pole and fish. Place the fish on the floor and allow the children to take turns fishing. As a fish is caught, the child removes it from the magnet and names the color. Repeat until all of the children have had a turn. The game can be varied by drawing a basic shape and printing a numeral or a letter on each fish for the children to identify.

Math

1. Sort the Fish

Purchase a variety of small plastic fish or construct some out of tagboard. Put them in a large pail. The children can sort the fish by size, color, and type.

2. Fish Seriation/Measurement

Trace and cut fish shapes out of construction paper. Encourage the children to place them in order from smallest to largest. If developmentally appropriate, provide rulers and yardsticks for the children to measure the fish.

3. Fishbowl Math

Print numerals or sets of dots on small plastic fish. Place the fish in a clean bowl or container. The children can use small nets to take turns scooping out a fish and stating the numeral or counting the dots.

4. Fish Cracker Sort

Purchase a variety of flavors of small, fish-shaped crackers. For each child, place a few of each kind of cracker in a paper cup. Before eating the crackers, encourage the children to sort the crackers. If appropriate, the children can count the number of each cracker flavor.

Music

1. "I'm a Little Fish"
(Sing to the tune of "I'm a Little Teapot")

I'm a little fish in the lake so blue,
There are so many things that I can do.
I can swim around with my tail and fin.
The water's fine—just jump right in.

2. "Goldfish"
(Sing to the tune of "Have You Ever Seen a Lassie?")

Have you ever seen a goldfish, a goldfish, a goldfish?

(continued)

Have you ever seen a goldfish, just swimming
all around?
He swims this way and that way,
And this way and that way.
Have you ever seen a goldfish, just swimming
all around?

3. **"Six Little Fish"**
(*Sing to the tune of* "Six Little Ducks")

Six little fish that I once knew,
Fat ones, skinny ones, fair ones, too.
But the one little fish who was the leader of
the crowd.
He led the other fish around and around.

Science

1. **Aquarium**

Set up an aquarium to place on the science
table. Let the children take turns feeding the
fish. Provide pictures and books about fish.

2. **Balance Scale**

On the science table, place a balance scale and
clean aquarium rocks. The children can use
spoons and measuring cups to transfer the
rocks into the scale containers. After this, they
can experiment with the balance.

3. **Fish-Tasting Party**

Plan a tasting party. Prepare fish using different
methods, such as baked, broiled, fried, and prepared in a casserole. The results of the children's
favorite fish-preparation method can be discussed and charted.

Sensory

1. **Aquarium Rocks**

Place a bag of clean aquarium rocks at the
sensory table. Provide cups, bowls, and pails for
the children's use. Add water, if desired.

2. **Plastic Fish**

Purchase small plastic fish and place at the
sensory table with water, strainers, and pails.

3. **Minnows**

Purchase minnows from a bait store. Place the
minnows in a sensory table filled with cold
water. Stress the importance of being gentle
with the fish and follow through with limits set
for the activity. After participating in this activity,
the children need to wash their hands.

4. **Plastic Boats**

Place small plastic boats in a sensory table filled
with water. Also provide small plastic people to
ride in and fish from the boats.

Books

The following books can be used to
complement this theme:

Adams, Georgie. (1993). *Fish, Fish, Fish.*
New York: Dial Books.

Aliki. (1993). *My Visit to the Aquarium.* New York:
HarperCollins.

Arnosky, Jim. (1993). *Crinkleroot's 25 Fish Every
Child Should Know.* New York: Simon &
Schuster.

Bailey, Donna. (1990). *Fishing.* Austin, TX:
Raintree/Steck Vaughn.

Barner, Bob. (2000). *Fish Wish.* New York:
Holiday House.

Boyle, Doe. (1997). *Coral Reef Hideaway: The
Story of a Clown Anemonefish.* Illus. by
Steven James Petruccio. Norwalk, CT:
Soundprints.

Carney, Margaret and Janet Wilson. (2001).
The Biggest Fish in the Lake. Illus. by Janet
Wilson. Toronto, Ontario, Canada: Kids
Can Press.

Clark, Elizabeth. (1990). *Fish.* Illus. by
John Yates. Minneapolis, MN:
Carolrhoda Books.

Cole, Joanna. (1997). *Magic School Bus Goes Upstream: A Book about Salmon on Migration.* Illus. by Bruce Degen. New York: Scholastic. (Pbk.)

Dunphy, Madeleine. (1998). *Here Is the Coral Reef.* Illus. by Tom Leonard. New York: Hyperion.

Ehlert, Lois. (1990). *Fish Eyes: A Book You Can Count On.* New York: Harcourt Brace.

Evans, Mark. (1993). *Fish: Practical Guide to Caring for Your Fish.* New York: Dorling Kindersley.

Fowler, Allan. (1995). *The Best Way to See a Shark.* Chicago: Children's Press.

Gibbons, Gail. (1992). *Sharks.* New York: Holiday House.

Holmes, Kevin J. (1998). *Sharks.* Chicago: Children's Press.

Johnston, Tony. (1996). *Fishing Sunday.* Illus. by Barry Root. New York: William Morrow.

Jonas, Anne. (1995). *Splash!* New York: Greenwillow.

Ling, Mary. (1991). *Amazing Fish.* Photos by Jerry Young. New York: Knopf.

McKissack, Patricia. (1992). *A Million Fish . . . More or Less.* Illus. by Dena Schutzer. New York: Knopf.

Morley, Christine et al. (1997). *Me and My Pet Fish.* Chicago: World Book.

Pfeffer, Wendy. (1996). *What's It Like to Be a Fish?* Illus. by Holly Keller. New York: HarperCollins.

Pfister, Marcus. (1992). *The Rainbow Fish.* Translated by J. Alison James. New York: North South Books.

Pfister, Marcus. (1995). *Rainbow Fish to the Rescue.* Translated by J. Alison James. New York: North South Books.

Pfister, Marcus. (2000). *The Adventures of Rainbow Fish.* New York: North South Books.

Rohmann, Eric. (2005). *Clara and Asha.* New Milford, CT: Roaring Brook Press.

Ryder, Joanne. (1997). *Shark in the Sea.* Illus. by Michael Rothman. New York: William Morrow.

Rylant, Cynthia and Arthur Howard. (2001). *Mr. Putter and Tabby Feed the Fish.* Illus. by Arthur Howard. San Diego, CA: Harcourt Brace.

Samson, Suzanne. (1995). *Sea Dragons and Rainbow Runners: Exploring Fish with Children.* (1995). Illus. by Preston Neel. Niwot, CO: Roberts Rinehart.

Sharp, N. L. (1993). *Today I'm Going Fishing with My Dad.* Illus. by Chris L. Demarest. Honesdale, PA: Boyds Mills Press.

Van Laan, Nancy. (1998). *Little Fish, Lost.* Illus. by Jane Conteh-Morgan. New York: Simon & Schuster.

Wallace, Karen. (1993). *Think of an Eel.* Illus. by Mike Bostock. Cambridge, MA: Candlewick Press.

Wood, Jakki. (1998). *Across the Big Blue Sea: An Ocean Wildlife Book.* Washington, DC: National Geographic.

Multimedia

The following multimedia products can be used to complement this theme:

Eastman, David. *What Is a Fish?* [video]. (1993). Northbrook, IL: Film Ideas.

Exploring the World of Fish [video]. (1992). Troy, MI: Anchor Bay Entertainment.

Fish [video]. Eyewitness Videos. Available from Kimbo Educational, Long Branch, NJ.

Tell Me Why: Fish, Shellfish, Underwater Life. [video]. (1987). Marina del Rey, CA: Tell Me Why.

Wet & Wild: Under the Sea with OWL/TV [video]. (1994). Toronto, Ont.: Children's Group Inc.

World of Pets: Fish [video]. (1985). Washington, DC: National Geographic.

Recordings and Song Titles

The following recordings can be used to complement this theme:

"Down, Down Below." (1977). *Science in a Nutshell*. Long Branch, NJ: Kimbo Educational.

"Finger Fish." (1999). *Sift and Splash*. Long Branch, NJ: Kimbo Educational.

"Five Gray Sharks." (1990). *Musical Playtime Fun*. Long Branch, NJ: Kimbo Educational.

"I'm a Fish." (1995). *Piggyback Songs*. Long Branch, NJ: Kimbo Educational.

"Octopus' Garden." (1999). *Five Little Monkeys*. Long Branch, NJ: Kimbo Educational.

What's in the Sea? (1990). Long Branch, NJ: Kimbo Educational.

Containers

vases
pots
window boxes
planters

Plant Parts

petals
stem
leaves
roots
buds
seeds

Uses

beauty
decoration
perfume
dye for clothing
gifts
ceremonial
food

Flowers

Names

violet
tulip
carnation
rose
lilac
lily
sunflower
orchid
magnolia
petunia
marigold
pansy

Places

wild
soil
water
greenhouses
gardens
homes

Care

water
soil
sunshine
air
pollination (bees)

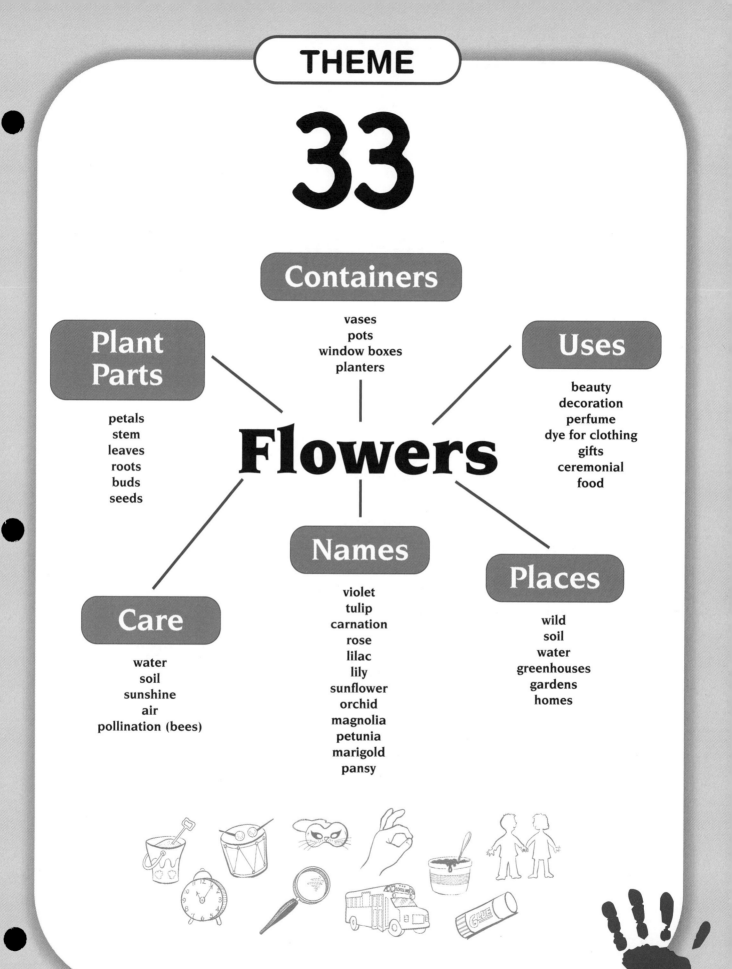

Theme Goals

Through participating in the experiences provided by this theme, the children may learn

1. Parts of the flower
2. Names of flowers
3. Places flowers grow
4. Uses of flowers
5. Containers that hold flowers
6. Care of flowers

Concepts for the Children to Learn

1. A flower is a plant.
2. Flowers add beauty to our world.
3. Flowers can be used for decoration.
4. Most flowers have a smell.
5. Vases, pots, window boxes, and planters are all flower containers.
6. Flowers need soil, water, sunshine, and air to grow.
7. Bees pollinate flowers.
8. Sometimes flowers are given to people for special reasons, such as holidays, birthdays, or if someone goes to the hospital.
9. Flowers are used at weddings.
10. Some flowers are used to make perfume.
11. Dye for clothing can be made from flowers.
12. There are many parts to flowers.
13. Seeds, roots, stem, leaves, buds, and petals are all parts of a flower.
14. Flowers need water to grow in the soil.
15. Flowers can be grown in the wild, in greenhouses, in gardens, and in homes.
16. Violets, tulips, carnations, roses, lilacs, lilies, sunflowers, orchids, magnolias, petunias, marigolds, and pansies are all names of flowers.

Vocabulary

1. **flower**—part of a plant that blossoms.
2. **greenhouse**—a glass house for growing plants.
3. **leaves**—growth from the stem.
4. **petal**—colored part of a flower.
5. **root**—the part of the plant that usually grows down into the soil.
6. **seed**—the part of the plant that produces a new plant.
7. **stem**—the trunk of the plant.

Bulletin Board

The purpose of this bulletin board is to develop visual discretion, problem-solving, and color-matching skills, as well as to foster the correspondence of sets to written numerals. Cut large numerals out of tagboard. Color each number a different color. Next, create tulips out of tagboard. The number will depend on the maturity of the children. Color each tulip the same color as its corresponding numeral: for example, three blue tulips for a blue numeral 3. The children can hang the appropriate number of tulips on the bulletin board next to each numeral. Moreover, the children can match the colored tulips to the corresponding colored numeral to make this activity self-correcting.

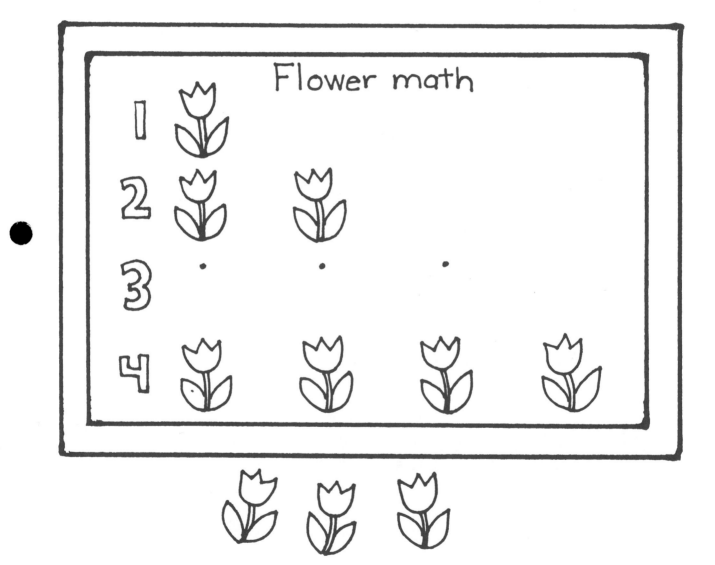

Family Letter

Dear Families,

Hello! As spring arrives and all the flowers begin to bloom, we will begin a unit on flowers. Through this unit the children will learn about the care, uses, and parts of a flowering plant. They will also learn about places where flowers are grown as well as the names of flowers and their containers.

AT SCHOOL

Some of the learning experiences planned to help the children make discoveries about flowers include:

- listening to the story *Dandelion,* by Ladislav Svatos
- observing and measuring the growth of various flowers
- visiting a floral shop
- playing a flower beanbag toss game
- reciting fingerplays
- planting seeds

AT HOME

You can integrate the concepts included in this unit into your home in many ways. If you are planning to plant a garden in your yard this spring, let your child help you. It might even be fun to section off a small part of your garden for your child to grow flowers and care for them. Another activity would be to examine the plants and flowers you have growing in your house. Also, let your child send flowers to someone special.

To develop language skills, we will be learning this fingerplay in school. Let your child teach it to you.

Daisies

One, two, three, four, five
(pop up fingers, one at a time)
Yellow daisies all alive.
Here they are all in a row.
(point to fingers standing)
The sun and the rain will help them grow.
(make a circle with fingers,
flutter fingers for rain)

Enjoy your child!

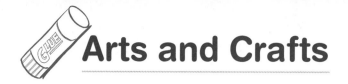

Arts and Crafts

1. Muffin Cup Flowers

For younger children, prepare shapes of flowers and leaves. The older children may be able to do this themselves. Attach the stems and leaves to muffin tin liners. Add a small amount of perfume to the flower for interest.

2. Easel

Cut easel paper into flower shapes.

3. Seed Collages

Place a pan containing a variety of seeds in the middle of the art table. In addition, supply glue and paper for the children to form a collage.

4. Egg Carton Flowers

Cut the sections of an egg container apart. Attach chenille stems for stems and decorate with watercolor markers.

5. Flower Mobile

Bring in a tree branch and hang from the classroom ceiling. Let the children make flowers and hang them on the branch for decoration.

6. Paper Plate Flowers

Provide snack-sized paper plates, markers, crayons, and colored construction paper. The children may use these materials to create a flower.

Children learn science concepts by growing flowers.

Cooking

1. Fruit Candy

Fruit grows on trees and plants. A flower blossom grows on the trees or plants. The flowers produce fruit.

1 pound dried figs
1 pound dried apricots
1/2 pound dates
2 cups oats
1/2 cup raisins

Put fruit and 2 cups of oats through a food grinder. Press into a buttered 9-inch × 13-inch pan. Chill and enjoy!

2. Pudding Fruit Salad

2 boxes sugar free instant vanilla pudding
3 bananas, slice into 1/4-inch pieces
2 oranges peeled and sectioned
1 - 30 ounce can fruit cocktail
1 - 11 ounce can mandarin oranges

Combine all of the ingredients and mix until the pudding is dissolved. As the pudding absorbs the juices from the canned fruit, it will thicken. Cool two hours before serving.

Dramatic Play

Fingerplays

1. Garden

Aprons, small garden tools, a tin of soil, seeds, watering cans, pots, and vases can all be provided. Pictures of flowers with names on them can be hung in the classroom.

2. Gardener

Gather materials for a gardener prop box. Include gloves, seed packets, sun hat, hand-held spade or hoe, stakes for marking, watering cans, etc.

3. Flower Shop

In the dramatic play area, set up a flower shop complete with plastic flowers, boxes, containers, watering cans, misting bottle, and cash register. Artificial corsages would also be a fun addition.

4. Flower Arranging

Artificial flowers and containers can be placed in the dramatic play area. The children can make centerpieces for the lunch table. Also, a centerpiece can be made for the science table, the lobby, and the secretary, director, or principal.

Field Trips/ Resource People

1. Florist

Arrange to visit a local floral shop. Observe the different kinds of flowers. Then watch the florist design a bouquet or corsage.

2. Walk

Walk around the neighborhood observing different types and colors of flowers.

My Garden

This is my garden
  (extend one hand forward, palm up)
I'll rake it with care
  (raking motion with fingers)
And then some flower seeds
  (planting motion)
I'll plant in right there.
The sun will shine
  (make circle with hands)
And the rain will fall
  (let fingers flutter down to lap)
And my garden will blossom
  (cup hands together, extend upward slowly)
And grow straight and tall.

Daisies

One, two, three, four, five
  (pop up fingers, one at a time)
Yellow daisies all alive.
Here they are all in a row.
  (point to fingers standing)
The sun and the rain will help them grow.
  (make a circle with fingers, flutter fingers for rain)

Flower Play

If I were a little flower
Sleeping underneath the ground,
  (curl up)
I'd raise my head and grow and grow
  (raise head and begin to grow)
And stretch my arms and grow and grow
  (stretch arms)
And nod my head and say,
  (nod head)
"I'm glad to see you all today."

Group Time

(Games, Language)

● **Hide the Flower**

Choose one child to look for the flower. Ask him or her to cover his or her eyes. Ask another child to hide a flower. After the flower is hidden and the child returns to the group, instruct the first child to uncover his or her eyes and find the flower. Clues can be provided. For example, if the child aproaches the area where the flower is hidden, the remainder of the children can clap their hands.

Math

1. **Flower Growth**

   Prepare sequence cards representing flowers at various stages of growth. Encourage the children to sequence them.

2. **Flower Match**

   Cut pictures of flowers from magazines or seed catalogs. If desired, mount the pictures. The children can match them by kind, size, color, and shape.

3. **Measuring Seed Growth**

   Plant several types of seeds. At determined intervals, measure the growth of various plants and flowers. Maintain a chart comparing the growth.

4. **Flower Petal Math**

   Make a flower stem and place a circle on it. Place a number in the circle. The children should glue the corresponding number of petals onto the circle to create a flower.

Music

"Flowers"

(*Sing to the tune of "Pop! Goes the Weasel"*)

All around the forest ground
There's flowers everywhere.
There's pink, yellow, and purple, too.
Here's one for you.

Science

1. **Flowers**

   Place a variety of flowers on the science table. Encourage the children to compare the color, shape, size, and smell of each flower.

2. **Planting Seeds**

   Plant flower seeds in a styrofoam cup. Save the seed packages and mount on a piece of tagboard. Place this directly behind the containers, on the science table. Encourage the children to compare their plants. When the plant starts growing, compare the seed packages to the plant growth.

3. **Carnation**

   Place a white carnation in a vase containing water with red food coloring added. Watch the tips of the carnation petals gradually change colors. Repeat the activity using other flowers and colors of water.

4. **Observing and Weighing Bulbs**

   Collect flower bulbs and place on the science table. Encourage the children to observe the similarities and differences. A balance scale can also be added.

5. **Microscopes**

   Place petals from a flower under a microscope for the children to observe.

Sensory

Additions to the Sensory Table

- Soil and plastic flowers
- Water and watering cans

Books

The following books can be used to complement this theme:

Barker, Cicely Mary. (1996). *Flower Fairies: The Meaning of Flowers*. New York: Frederick Warne.

Barker, Cicely Mary. (1998). *Flower Fairies of the Spring: A Celebration*. New York: Frederick Warne.

Bryant-Mole, Karen. (1996). *Flowers*. Austin, TX: Raintree/Steck Vaughn.

Bunting, Eve. (1994). *Flower Garden*. Illus. by Kathryn Hewitt. Orlando, FL: Harcourt Brace.

Burnie, David. (1992). *Flowers*. New York: Dorling Kindersley.

Cole, Henry. (1995). *Jack's Garden*. New York: Greenwillow.

Cole, Joanna. (1995). *The Magic School Bus Plants Seeds: A Book about How Living Things Grow*. Illus. by Bruce Degen. New York: Scholastic. (Pbk.)

De Paola, Tomie. (1994). *The Legend of the Poinsettia*. New York: G. P. Putnam.

Ehlert, Lois. (2003). *Planting a Rainbow*. San Diego: Harcourt. (1st Red Wagon Books edition.)

Fausch, Karen and Laura Jane Coats. (2001). *The Window Box Book*. Illus. by Laura Jane Coats. New York: Little Bookroom.

Ford, Miela. (1995). *Sunflower*. Illus. by Sally Noll. New York: Greenwillow.

Hickman, Pamela and Heather Collins. (2000). *Plant Book (Starting with Nature)*. Illus. by Heather Collins. Toronto, Ontario, Canada: Kids Can Press.

King, Elizabeth. (1993). *Backyard Sunflower*. New York: Dutton.

Lobel, Anita. (1990). *Alison's Zinnia*. New York: Greenwillow.

Lucht, Irmgard. (1995). *The Red Poppy*. Illus. by Frank Jacoby-Nelson. New York: Hyperion.

Marzollo, Jean. (1996). *I'm a Seed*. Madison, WI: Demco Media.

Pallotta, Jerry. (1990). *Flower Alphabet Book*. Illus. by Leslie Evans. Watertown, MA: Charlesbridge.

Pomeroy, Diana. (1997). *Wildflower ABC: An Alphabet of Potato Prints*. Orlando, FL: Harcourt Brace.

Robbins, Ken. (1990). *A Flower Grows*. New York: Dial Books.

Samson, Suzanne. (1994). *Fairy Dusters and Blazing Stars: Exploring Wildflowers with Children*. Illus. by Neel Preston. Niwot, CO: Roberts Rinehart.

Stoker, Joann and Gerald Stoker. (1999). *ABC Book of Flowers for Young Gardeners*. Columbia, SC: Summerhouse Press.

Sun, Chyng-Feng. (1996). *Cat and Cat-Face*. Illus. by Lesley Liu. Boston: Houghton Mifflin.

Wellington, Monica. (2005). *Zinnia's Flower Garden*. New York: Dutton Children's Books.

Multimedia

The following multimedia products can be used to complement this theme:

Flowers & Seeds [video]. (1994). Princeton, NJ: Films for the Humanities.

Flowers, Plants & Trees [video]. (1987). *Tell Me Why* series. Marina Del Rey, CA: Penguin Productions.

Raffi. *Spring Flowers* on Bananaphone [compact disc]. (1994). Cambridge, MA: Shoreline. Available from Kimbo Educational, Long Branch, NJ.

Recordings and Song Titles

The following recordings can be used to complement this theme:

"Dandelion Seed," "I'm Going to Plant a Garden." (1977). *Science in a Nutshell*. Long Branch, NJ: Kimbo Educational.

"Flower Garden." (1995). *Piggyback Songs*. Long Branch, NJ: Kimbo Educational.

"Gardener at Home," "The Seed Song." (1999). *On the Farm with* RONNO. Long Branch, NJ: Kimbo Educational.

"In Grandma's Garden." (1988). *Rainbow of Songs*. Long Branch, NJ: Kimbo Educational.

"Mary, Mary, Quite Contrary." (1986). *Singable Nursery Rhymes*. Long Branch, NJ: Kimbo Educational.

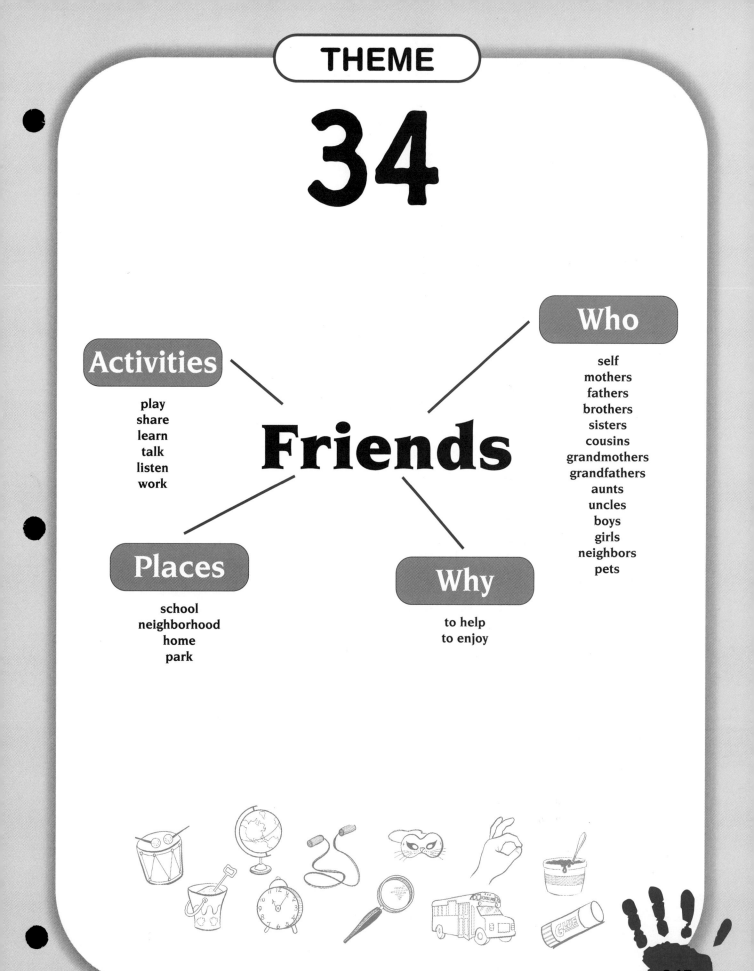

Activities

play
share
learn
talk
listen
work

Friends

Who

self
mothers
fathers
brothers
sisters
cousins
grandmothers
grandfathers
aunts
uncles
boys
girls
neighbors
pets

Places

school
neighborhood
home
park

Why

to help
to enjoy

Theme Goals

Through participating in the experiences provided by this theme, the children may learn

1. Who friends are
2. Why we have friends
3. Activities we can do with our friends
4. Places we can make friends

Concepts for the Children to Learn

1. A friend is someone who I like and who likes me.
2. My friends are special to me.
3. We can have friends at school, in our neighborhood, in our homes, and at the park.
4. Our brothers and sisters can be our friends.
5. Friends can help us with our work.
6. We enjoy playing with our friends.
7. We share and learn with friends.
8. Friends talk and listen to us.
9. A pet can be a friend.
10. Friends can be boys or girls.
11. Mothers, fathers, grandmothers, grandfathers, aunts, uncles, and cousins can be our friends.

Vocabulary

1. **cooperating**—working together to help someone.
2. **friend**—a person we enjoy.
3. **giving**—sharing something of your own with others.
4. **like**—feeling good about someone or something.
5. **pal or buddy**—other words for friend.
6. **sharing**—giving and taking turns.
7. **togetherness**—being with one another and sharing a good feeling.

Scrapbook of Teacher Made Materials

1 2 3 4 5 6 7 8 9 10

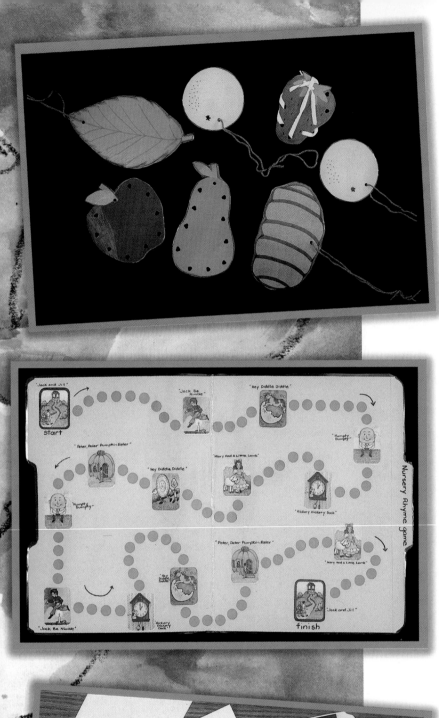

ACTIVITY 1
Lacing Cards

Construction Materials:
Construction paper or tagboard, yarn, or shoe strings, and a colored felt-tip marker.

Related Themes
Fruits and Vegetables, Health

ACTIVITY 2
Nursery Rhyme Folder Game

Construction Materials:
File folder, nursery rhyme stickers, circle stickers, and a colored felt-tip marker.

Related Themes:
Nursery Rhymes, Friends

ACTIVITY 3
Peek-a-Boo Cards

Construction Materials:
File folders and magazine pictures.

Related Themes:
Birds, Cats, Dogs, Zoo Animals, Pets, Mice, Scissors

ACTIVITY 4
Caramel Apple Match

Construction Materials:
Tongue depressors, brown tagboard, cupcake liners, small circles, and felt-tip markers.

Related Themes:
Apples, Numbers, Health, Fruits and Vegetables, Circus

ACTIVITY 5
Felt Frogs on a Log

Construction Materials:
Log, green felt pieces, craft eggs, polyester filling, and a felt-tip marker.

Related Themes:
Water, Camping, Summer, Nursery Rhymes, Creative Movement, Frogs

ACTIVITY 6
Pepperoni Pizza

Construction Materials:
Cardboard circle, red construction paper, yellow and white yarn, and green felt pieces.

Related Themes:
Numbers, Health, Families, Friends, Occupations

ACTIVITY 7
Valentine Number Cards

Construction Materials:
Pink and white construction paper and red tagboard.

Related Themes:
Valentine's Day Shapes, Numbers, Red, Mail Carrier, Communication, Feelings, Friends

ACTIVITY 8
Tongue Depressor Puzzles

Construction Materials:
Two tongue depressors for each puzzle and a set of felt-tip markers.

Related Themes:
Fruits and Vegetables, Gardens, Breads, Health, Doctors and Nurses, Plants

ACTIVITY 9
Snowmen Match

Construction Materials:
Stickers or wrapping figures and tagboard for mounting.

Related Themes:
Winter, Clothing, Numbers, Shapes, Hats

ACTIVITY 10
"This Old Man" Cue Cards

Construction Materials:
Ten tagboard rectangles and felt-tip markers.

Related Themes:
Nursery Rhymes, Music, Communication, Numbers

ACTIVITY 11
Spring Words Chart

Construction Materials:
Large sheet of colored tagboard, set of colored felt-tip markers, manuscript strips, or lined paper, and white construction paper.

Related Themes:
Spring, Communication, Flowers, Pets, Clothing, Farm Animals, Water

ACTIVITY 12
Our Favorite Ice Cream Graph

Construction Materials:
Large sheet of tagboard, colored construction paper, and felt-tip markers.

Related Themes:
Dairy Products, Health, Friends, Summer, Circus, Camping, Numbers

ACTIVITY 13
Bakery Dramatic Play Chart

Construction Materials:
Sheet of colored tagboard, construction paper, and felt-tip markers.

Related Themes:
Breads, Health, Occupations

ACTIVITY 14
Sensory Bottles

Construction Materials:
Plastic soda bottle with cap, mineral oil, food coloring, and objects such as beads, glitter, dice or sequins.

Related Themes:
Containers, Bubbles, Water, Blue, Red, Yellow, Purple, Creative Movement

ACTIVITY 15
Paper Cup Sort Palette

Construction Materials:
Colored tagboard, paper cups, construction paper, crayons or other objects to sort by color.

Related Themes:
Art, Blue, Red, Yellow, Purple, Numbers

ACTIVITY 16
Felt-Mitten Duck Puppets

Construction Materials:
Colored felt, colored tagboard, and a felt-tip marker.

Related Themes:
Birds, Puppets, Communication, Nursery Rhymes, Easter, Farm Animals, Pets, Yellow, Spring

ACTIVITY 17
Bookworm Bookstore Dramatic Play Sign

Construction Materials:
Green and yellow tagboard, felt-tip markers, and string to hang sign.

Related Themes:
Nursery Rhymes, Communication, Families, Friends, Occupations

ACTIVITY 18
Humpty Dumpty

Construction Materials:
Cardboard blocks, white pillowcase, black and pink felt pieces, polyester filling, and a black felt-tip marker.

Related Themes:
Eggs, Nursery Rhymes, Communication

ACTIVITY 19
Transportation Mat

Construction Materials:
Plastic tablecloth, set of colored felt-tip markers, and small wheeled toys.

Related Themes:
Cars, Trucks and Buses, Wheels, Occupations

ACTIVITY 20
Goldilocks and the Three Bears Props

Construction Materials:
Tagboard, markers, scissors, string or yarn, hole punch, lamination paper.

Related Themes:
Books, Bears, Storytelling, Make Believe, Communication

ACTIVITY 21
Farmer in the Dell Game Pieces

Construction Materials:
White tagboard, colored felt-tip markers, scissors, yarn, paper punch, lamination paper.

Related Themes:
Farms, Occupations, Games, Music, Friends

ACTIVITY 22
Heart Bingo Game

Construction Materials:
Construction paper or tagboard, permanent markers, scissors (craft scissors optional), ruler, lamination paper.

Related Themes:
Valentine's Day, Games, Numbers, Red, Letters, Friends

ACTIVITY 23
Who Took the Cookies from the Cookie Jar Chart?

Construction Materials:
Tagboard, black felt-tip marker, brown construction paper or tagboard, scissors, lamination paper.

Related Themes:
Breads, Communication, Containers, Friends

ACTIVITY 24
"Finding Colors" Song

Construction Materials:
Tagboard, construction paper or sentence strips, markers, glue or glue stick, scissors (craft scissors optional), tape, lamination paper.

Related Themes:
Colors, Music, School

ACTIVITY 25
Make a Rainbow Chain

Construction Materials:
One sheet of tagboard (22" × 28"), colored felt-tip markers, lamination paper.

Related Themes:
Colors, Patterns, Seasons, Rainbows, Holidays, Paper

ACTIVITY 26
Baseball and Glove Match

Construction Materials:
Brown and white tagboard, paper punch, glue or glue stick, black watercolor marker, scissors, lamination paper.

Related Themes:
Balls, Summer, Sports, Gloves

"Finding Colors"

Oh, can you find the color _____
The color _____, the color _____?
Oh, can you find the color _____,
Somewhere in this room?

Make a Rainbow Chain.

1.
2.
3.
4.
5.
6.

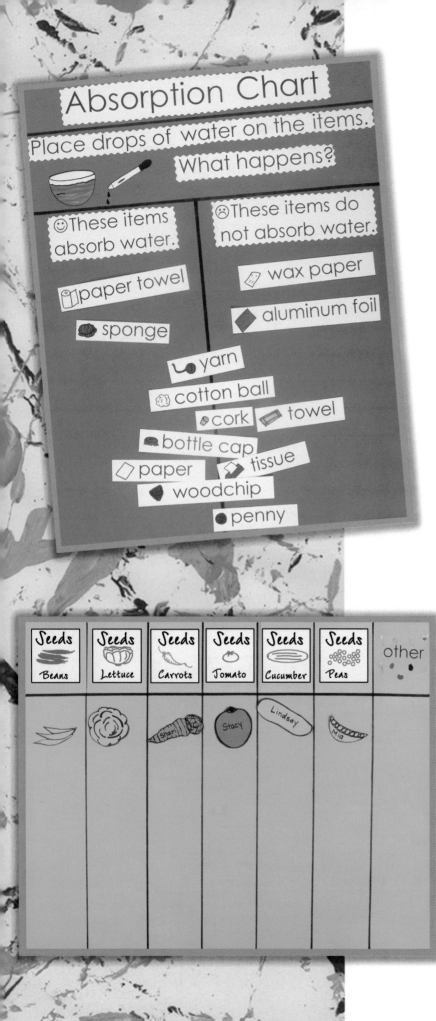

Absorption Chart

Place drops of water on the items. What happens?

☺ These items absorb water.	☹ These items do not absorb water.
🧻 paper towel	📄 wax paper
🧽 sponge	◆ aluminum foil
	🧶 yarn
	⊛ cotton ball
	▱ cork · towel
	⬮ bottle cap
	▱ paper · tissue
	⬟ woodchip
	● penny

ACTIVITY 27
Absorption Chart

Construction Materials:
White tagboard, tagboard or construction paper pieces (10" × 2-1/2"), markers, ruler, lamination paper.

Related Themes:
Water, Science

Seeds Beans	Seeds Lettuce	Seeds Carrots	Seeds Tomato	Seeds Cucumber	Seeds Peas	other
		Shari	Stacy	Lindsay	Mia	

ACTIVITY 28
What's Your Favorite Vegetable?

Construction Materials:
Tagboard, construction paper, six packages of vegetable seed, markers, scissors, glue or glue stick, ruler or straightedge, tape, lamination paper.

Related Themes:
Vegetables, Summer, Gardens, Plants, Seeds, Colors

ACTIVITY 29
Match the Blocks

Construction Materials:
Dark tagboard (red, blue, or green), white construction paper, markers, scissors, glue or glue stick, unit blocks, lamination paper.

Related Themes:
Blocks, Shapes, School, Construction

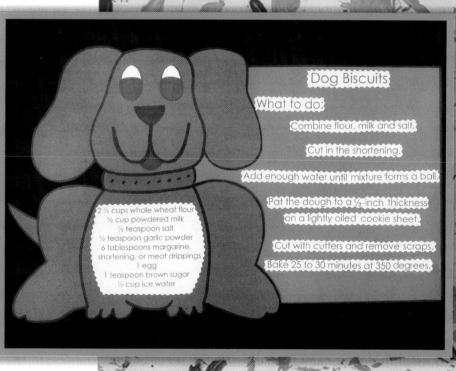

ACTIVITY 30
Recipe for Dog Biscuits

Construction Materials:
Tagboard, construction paper or sentence strips, scissors, glue or glue stick, markers, lamination paper.

Related Themes:
Dogs, Pets, Cooking, Family, Friends

Dog Biscuits

What to do:

Combine flour, milk and salt.

Cut in the shortening.

Add enough water until mixture forms a ball.

Pat the dough to a ½-inch thickness on a lightly oiled cookie sheet.

Cut with cutters and remove scraps.

Bake 25 to 30 minutes at 350 degrees.

2 ½ cups whole wheat flour
½ cup powdered milk
½ teaspoon salt
½ teaspoon garlic powder
6 tablespoons margarine, shortening, or meat drippings
1 egg
1 teaspoon brown sugar
½ cup ice water

Lightest to Darkest

	Lightest		Lightest	Lightest	Lightest	Lightest	Lightest
Darkest		Darkest	Darkest	Darkest	Darkest	Darkest

ACTIVITY 31
Shades of Colors Chart

Construction Materials:
White tagboard, construction paper or sentence strips, markers, ruler or straightedge, scissors, paint chip sample cards of various colors, glue or glue stick, lamination paper.

Related Themes:
Colors, Art, Sense of Sight

Toothpaste

Place 2 tablespoons of **SALT** in electric blender.

Run at high speed until salt is fine.

Add ½ cup plus 2 ounces of water.

Add one 16-ounce box of **BAKING SODA**

Blend until all is mixed.

ACTIVITY 32
Toothpaste

Construction Materials:
Tagboard (22" × 28"), watercolor markers, label from a container of salt, front panel of baking soda box, glue or glue stick, lamination paper.

Related Themes:
Health, Dentist, Teeth, Brushes, My Body

ACTIVITY 33
Worm Farm

Construction Materials:
Tagboard, construction materials, watercolor markers, scissors, glue or glue stick, lamination paper.

Related Themes:
Soil, Gardens, Plants, Animals

Worm Farm

1. Fill a glass or see-through container with soil.

2. Place 6 to 12 worms in the container.

3. Wrap black paper around the container.

4. Sprinkle corn meal or grated carrots on top of the soil.

ACTIVITY 34
Birthday Packages

Construction Materials:
12 sheets of construction, craft of wrapping paper (12" × 18"), black felt-tip marker, watercolor markers, scissors (craft scissors optional), lamination paper

Related Themes:
Birthdays, Special Days, Self-concept, Alphabet Letters, Symbols, Numerals

January   February   March

Bubble Prints

In a cup mix these ingredients:

½ cup   2 tbsp.   1 tbsp.

Place a straw in the cup.

Blow bubbles until they begin to overflow.

Remove straw and place paper over the bubbles.

Remove the paper from the bubbles.

ACTIVITY 35
Bubble Prints

Construction Materials:
One sheet of white tagboard, colored felt-tip markers, black construction paper, lamination paper.

Related Themes:
Water, Bubbles, Air, Colors, Sight, Our World

Crayon and Marker Bundles

To make a crayon or marker bundle you need:

or   and a

Wrap a few crayons or markers with a rubber band.

Color with the bundles to make a design.

ACTIVITY 36
Crayon and Marker Bundles

Construction Materials:
One sheet of tagboard, construction paper or sentence strips, markers, scissors, glue or glue stick, lamination paper.

Related Themes:
Colors, Art, Tools, Communication, Crayons

Bulletin Board

The purpose of this bulletin board is to call attention to print. It will help the children recognize their own and their friends' names. The bulletin board can also be used by the teacher as an attendance check. Prepare the board by constructing name cards for each child as illustrated. Then laminate and punch holes in each card. When the children arrive at school, they can attach their name cards to the bulletin board with pushpins.

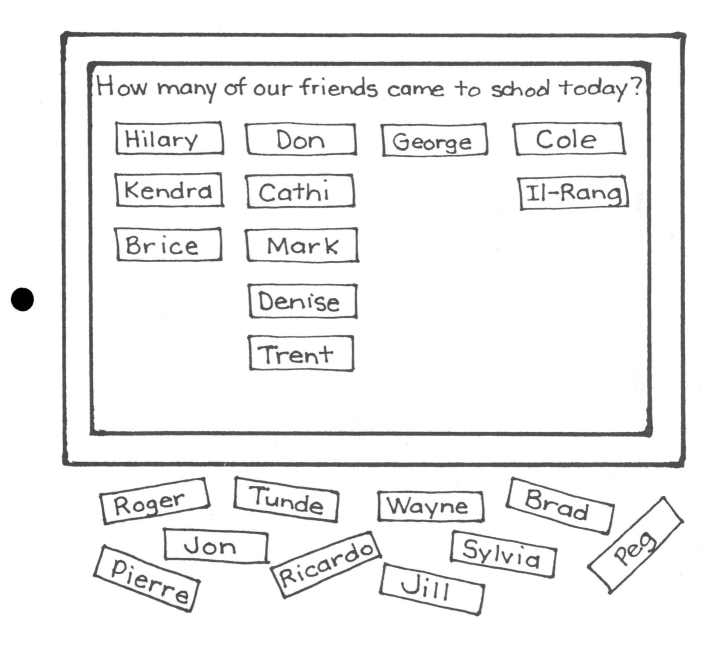

Family Letter

Dear Families,

We will be starting a curriculum unit on friends, which will include discovering people of all ages and even animal friends. The children have made many new friends at school, with whom they are learning to take turns, cooperate, work, and play. Through this unit, the children will become more aware of what a friend is and activities friends can do together. Moreover, they will learn the importance of prosocial behavior.

AT SCHOOL

Highlights of the learning experiences in this unit include:

- making cookies for our friends
- sending notes to pen pals
- creating a friendship chain with strips of paper
- looking at pictures of our friends at school in our classroom photo album
- reciting fingerplays related to friendships
- singing songs related to friendships

AT HOME

Your child may enjoy looking at photo albums of family and friends. Perhaps a friend could be invited to come and play with your child. We will be learning a poem about friends to promote an enjoyment of language and poetry.

Friends

I like my friends,
So when we are at play,
I try to be very kind,
and nice in every way.

Be your child's best friend!

Tina is my best friend!

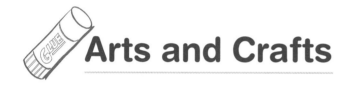 # Arts and Crafts

 # Cooking

1. **Friendship Chain**

   Provide strips of paper for the older children to print their names on. For those children who are not interested or unable, print their names for them. When all the names are on the strips of paper, the children can connect them to make a chain. The chain can symbolize that everyone in the class is a friend.

2. **Friendship Exchange Art**

   Provide each child with a piece of construction paper with "To: _____" printed in the upper-left corner and "From: _____" printed on the bottom. The teacher assists the children in printing their names on the bottom and the name of the person to their right on the top of the paper. Using paper scraps, tissue paper squares, fabric scraps, and glue, each child will construct a picture for a friend. When finished, have each child pass the paper to the friend for whom it was made.

Pound Cake Brownies

3/4 cup butter or margarine, softened
1 cup sugar
3 eggs
2 1-ounce squares unsweetened chocolate, melted and cooled
1 teaspoon vanilla
1 1/4 cups all-purpose flour
1/2 teaspoon baking powder
1/4 teaspoon salt

Cream butter and sugar; beat in eggs. Blend in chocolate and vanilla. Stir flour with baking powder and salt. Add to creamed mixture. Mix well. Spread in a greased 9- × 9- × 2-inch baking pan. Bake at 350 degrees for 25 to 30 minutes. Cool. If desired, sift powdered sugar over the top. Cut into bars. Yields 24 bars.

Dramatic Play

1. Puppet Show

Set up a puppet stage with various types of puppets. The children can share puppets and act out friendships using the puppets in various situations.

2. A Tea Party

Provide dress-up clothes, play dishes, and water in the dramatic play area.

Field Trips/ Resource People

1. The Zoo

Take a trip to the zoo to observe animals.

2. The Nursing Home

Visit a nursing home, allowing the children to interact with elderly friends.

3. Resource People

Invite the following community helpers into the classroom:

- police officer
- trash collector
- janitor/custodian
- firefighter
- doctor, nurse, dentist
- principal or director

Fingerplays

Friends

I like my friends.
So when we are at play,

I try to be very kind
and nice in every way.

Five Little Friends

(hold up five fingers; subtract one with each action)

Five little friends playing on the floor,
One got tired and then there were four.
Four little friends climbing in a tree,
One jumped down and then there were three.
Three little friends skipping to the zoo,
One went for lunch and then there were two.
Two little friends swimming in the sun,
One went home and then there was one.
One little friend going for a run,
Decided to take a nap and then there were none.

Large Muscle

1. Double Balance Beam

Place two balance beams side by side and encourage two children to hold hands and cross together.

2. Bowling Game

Set up pins or plastic bottles. With a ball, have the children take turns knocking down the pins.

3. Outdoor Obstacle Course

Design an obstacle course outdoors that is specifically designed for two children to go through at one time. Use balance beams, climbers, slides, etc. Short and simple obstacle courses seem to work the best.

Math

1. Group Pictures

Take pictures of the children in groups of 2, 3, 4, etc. Make separate corresponding number cards. The children then can match the correct numeral to the picture card.

352

Transition Activities

CLEAN UP

"Do You Know What Time It Is?"
(Sing to the tune of "The Muffin Man")

Oh, do you know what time it is,
What time it is, what time it is?
Oh, do you know what time it is?
It's almost clean-up time.
   (Or, It's time to clean up.)

"Clean-up Time"
(Sing to the tune of "London Bridge")

Clean-up time is already here,
Already here, already here.
Clean-up time is already here,
Already here.

"This Is the Way"
(Sing to the tune of "Mulberry Bush")

This is the way we pick up
   our toys,
Pick up our toys, pick up
   our toys.
This is the way we pick up
   our toys,
At clean-up time each day.

"Oh, It's Clean-up Time"
(Sing to the tune of "Oh, My Darling Clementine")

Oh, it's clean-up time,
Oh, it's clean-up time,
Oh, it's clean-up time right now.
It's time to put the toys away,
It is clean-up time right now.

"A Helper I Will Be"
(Sing to the tune of "The Farmer in the Dell")

A helper I will be.
A helper I will be.
I'll pick up the toys and put
   them away.
A helper I will be.

"We're Cleaning Up Our Room"
(Sing to the tune of "The Farmer in the Dell")

We're cleaning up our room.
We're cleaning up our room.
We're putting all the toys away.
We're cleaning up our room.

"It's Clean-up Time"
(Sing to the chorus of "Looby Loo")

It's clean-up time at school.
It's time for boys and girls
To stop what they are doing
And put away their toys.

"Time to Clean Up"
(Sing to the tune of "Are You Sleeping?")

Time to clean up.
Time to clean up.
Everybody help.
Everybody help.
Put the toys away, put the
   toys away.
Then sit down. (Or, Then
   come here.)

Specific toys can be mentioned in place of "toys."

"Clean-up Time"
(Sing to the tune of "Hot Cross Buns")

Clean-up time.
Clean-up time.
Put all of the toys away.
It's clean-up time.

ROUTINES

"Passing Around"
(Sing to the tune of "Skip to My Loo")

Brad, take a napkin and pass
   them to Sara.
Sara, take a napkin and pass
   them to Tina.
Tina, take a napkin and pass
   them to Eric,
Passing around the napkins.

Fill in appropriate child's name and substitute the napkin for any object that needs to be passed at mealtime.

"Put Your Coat On"
(Sing to the tune of "Oh, My Darling Clementine")

Put your coat on.
Put your coat on.
Put your winter coat on now.
We are going to play outside.
Put your coat on right now.

Change coat to any article of clothing.

"Time to Go Outside"
(Sing to the tune of "When Johnny Comes Marching Home")

When it's time for us to go
   outside
To play, to play,
We find a place to put our toys
Away, away.
We'll march so quietly to
   the door.
We know exactly what's in store
When we go outside to play for a
   little while.

(continued)

FRIENDS

Transition Activities *(continued)*

"We're Going on a Walk"
(*Sing to the tune of* "The Farmer in the Dell")

We're going for a walk.
We're going for a walk.
Hi-ho, the dairy-o,
We're going for a walk.

Additional verses:
What will we wear?
What will we see?
How will we go?
Who knows the way?

"Find a Partner"
(*Sing to the tune of* "Oh, My Darling Clementine")

Find a partner, find a partner,
Find a partner right now.

We are going for a walk.
Find a partner right now.

"Walk Along"
(*Sing to the tune of* "Clap Your Hands")

Walk, walk, walk along,
Walk along to the bathroom.
_____ and _____ walk along,
Walk along to the bathroom.

Change walk to any other types of movement— jump, hop, skip, crawl.

"We're Going . . ."
(*Sing to the tune of* "Go in and out the Window")

We're going to the bathroom,
We're going to the bathroom,

We're going to the bathroom,
And then we'll wash our hands.

"It's Time to Change"
(*Sing to the tune of* "Hello, Everybody")

It's time to change, yes indeed,
Yes indeed, yes indeed.
It's time to change, yes indeed
Time to change groups.
     (Or, Time to go outside.)

---

2. **Friend Charts**

   Take individual pictures of the children and chart them according to hair color, eye color, etc. Encourage the children to compare their looks to the characteristics of their friends.

 # Music

1. **"Do You Know This Friend of Mine?"**
   (*Sing to the tune of* "The Muffin Man")

   Do you know this friend of mine,
   This friend of mine,
   This friend of mine?
   Do you know this friend of mine?
   His name is _____.

   Yes, we know this friend of yours,
   This friend of yours,
   This friend of yours.
   Yes, we know this friend of yours.
   His name is _____.

2. **"The More We Are Together"**
   (*Sing to the tune of* "Have You Ever Seen a Lassie?")

   The more we are together, together, together,
   The more we are together, the happier we'll be.
   For your friends are my friends, and my friends
        are your friends.
   The more we are together the happier we'll be.
   We're all in school together, together, together,
   We're all in school together, and happy we'll be.
   There's Ali and Keisha and Jenny and Ben,
   There's _____ and _____ and _____ and _____.
   We're all in school together and happy we'll be.

   Insert names of children in your classroom.

3. **"Beth Met a Friend"**
   (*Sing to the tune of* "The Farmer in the Dell")

   Beth met a friend,
   Beth met a friend,
   When she came to school today,
   Beth met a friend.

   Insert names of children in your classroom for each verse.

4. The More We Get Together

The more we get together,
Together, together.
The more we get together,
The happier we'll be.
For your friends are my friends,
And my friends are your friends.
The more we get together,
The happier we'll be.

Science

1. Comparing Heartbeats

Provide stethoscopes for the children to listen to their friends' heartbeats.

2. Fingerprints

Ink pads and white paper can be provided for the children to make fingerprints. Also, a microscope can be provided to encourage the children to compare their fingerprints.

3. Friends' Voices

Tape the children's voices throughout the course of the day. The following day, leave the tape recorder at the science table. The children can listen to the tape and try to guess which classmate is talking.

4. Animal Friends

Prepare signs for the animal cages listing the animals' daily food intake and care.

Sensory

The sensory table is an area where two to four children can make new friends and share. Materials that can be added to the sensory table include:

- shaving cream
- play dough
- sand with toys
- water with boats
- wood shavings
- Silly Putty
- dry pasta with scoops and a balance scale
- goop

Mix equal parts of white glue and liquid starch. Food coloring can be added for color. Store in an airtight container.

Mix water and cornstarch. Add cornstarch to the water until you get the consistency that you want.

Caution: Carefully supervise children while playing with sensory materials.

Social Studies

Friends Bulletin Board

Ask the children to bring pictures of their friends into the classroom. Set up a bulletin board in the classroom where these pictures can be hung for all to see. Remind the children that friends can be family members and animals too.

Books

The following books can be used to complement this theme:

Agee, Jon (2005). *Terrific*. New York: Hyperion Books for Children.

Aliki. (1995). *Best Friends Together Again*. New York: Greenwillow.

Barnes, Emilie, Buchanan, Anne Christian, and Michal Spark. (1999). *My Best Friends and Me*. Illus. by Michal Spark. Eugene, OR: Harvest House.

Bruna, Dick. (2001). *Dick Bruna's 1st Picture Books: Miffy's Animal Friends*. New York: Kodansha International.

Carlson, Nancy L. (1994). *How to Lose All Your Friends*. New York: Viking.

Caseley, Judith. (1991). *Harry and Willy and Carrothead*. New York: Greenwillow.

Champion, Joyce. (1993). *Emily and Alice*. Illus. by Sucie Stevenson. Orlando, FL: Harcourt Brace.

Cohn, Aden and Dan Sullivan. (1999). *Friends of a Feather*. Illus. by Dan Sulllivan. Denver, CO: Accord Publishing Ltd.

Cote, Nancy. (1993). *Palm Trees*. New York: Four Winds.

Dugan, Barbara. (1992). *Loop the Loop*. Illus. by James Stevenson. New York: Greenwillow.

Egan, Tim. (1996). *Metropolitan Cow*. Boston: Houghton Mifflin.

Fuchs, Diane Marcial. (1995). *A Bear for All Seasons*. Illus. by Kathryn Brown. New York: Holt.

Gomi, Taro. (1990). *My Friends*. San Francisco: Chronicle Books.

Gorbachev, Valeri. (2005). *That's What Friends Are For*. New York: Philomel Books.

Haville, Juanita. (1993). *Jamaica and Brianna*. Illus. by Anne Sibley O'Brien. Boston: Houghton Mifflin.

Hoban, Russell. (1994). *Best Friends for Frances*. Illus. by Lillian Hoban. New York: HarperCollins.

Hutchins, Pat. (1993). *My Best Friend*. New York: Greenwillow.

Hutchins, Pat. (1996). *Titch and Daisy*. New York: Greenwillow.

Kroll, Virginia. (2005). *Forgiving a Friend*. Illus. by Paige Billin-Frye. Morton Grove, IL: Albert Whitman.

Leedy, Loreen. (1996). *How Humans Make Friends*. New York: Holiday House.

Mavor, Salley. (1997). *You and Me: Poems of Friendship*. New York: Orchard Books.

Miller, J. Phillip and Greene, Sheppard. (2001). *We All Sing With the Same Voice*. Illus. by Paul Meisel. New York: HarperCollins.

Monson, A. M. (1997). *Wanted: Best Friend*. Illus. by Lynn Munsinger. New York: Dial Books.

Morris, Ann. (1990). *Loving*. Photos by Ken Heyman. New York: Lothrop, Lee & Shepard.

Naylor, Phyllis Reynolds. (1991). *King of the Playground*. Illus. by Nola Langner Malone. Colchester, CT: Atheneum.

Polacco, Patricia. (1992). *Chicken Sunday*. New York: Philomel Books.

Polacco, Patricia. (1992). *Mrs. Katz and Tush*. New York: Bantam.

Raschka, Chris. (1993). *Yo! Yes?* New York: Orchard Books.

Reiser, Lynn. (1993). *Margaret and Margarita/ Margarita y Margaret*. New York: Greenwillow.

Reiser, Lynn. (1997). *Best Friends Think Alike*. New York: Greenwillow.

Seeger, Pete and Jacobs, Paul DuBois. (2005). *Some Friends to Feed: the Story of Stone Soup*. Illus.by Michael Hays. New York: G.P. Putnam's Sons.

Spohn, Kate. (1996). *Dog and Cat Shake a Leg*. New York: Viking.

Valckx, Catharina. (2005). *Lizette's Green Sock*. New York: Clarion Books. (First American edition.)

Waber, Bernard. (1995). *Gina*. Boston: Houghton Mifflin.

Weeks, Sarah. (2001). *Noisy Friends*. Pleasantville, NY: Reader's Digest Children's Books. (*Fisher Price Step by Step* Books.)

Multimedia

The following multimedia products can be used to complement this theme:

Berenstain Bears Get in a Fight [CD-ROM]. (1995). Random House/Broderbund.

Brown, Marc. *Arthur's Birthday* [CD-ROM]. (1994). Random House/Broderbund.

Hartmann, Jack. *Make a Friend, Be a Friend: Songs for Growing Up and Growing Together with Friends* [sound cassette]. (1990). Educational Activities.

Recordings and Song Titles

The following recordings can be used to complement this theme:

"A Friend in Need." (1994). *Get Up and Grow.* Long Branch, NJ: Kimbo Educational.

"Friends." (1997). Nelson Gill / *Friends.* Long Branch, NJ: Kimbo Educational.

"I Like Friends." (n.d.) *Tony Chestnut (The Learning Station).* Long Branch, NJ: Kimbo Educational.

"We Go Together." (2000). *Bean Bag Rock & Roll.* Long Branch, NJ: Kimbo Educational.

35

Colors

green
brown

Foods

insects
earthworms
spiders
minnows

Frogs

Life Stages

egg
tadpole
adult frog

Body Parts

eyes
mouth
tongue
skin
legs

Movement

swim
jump
walk
climb

Places

water
trees
ground

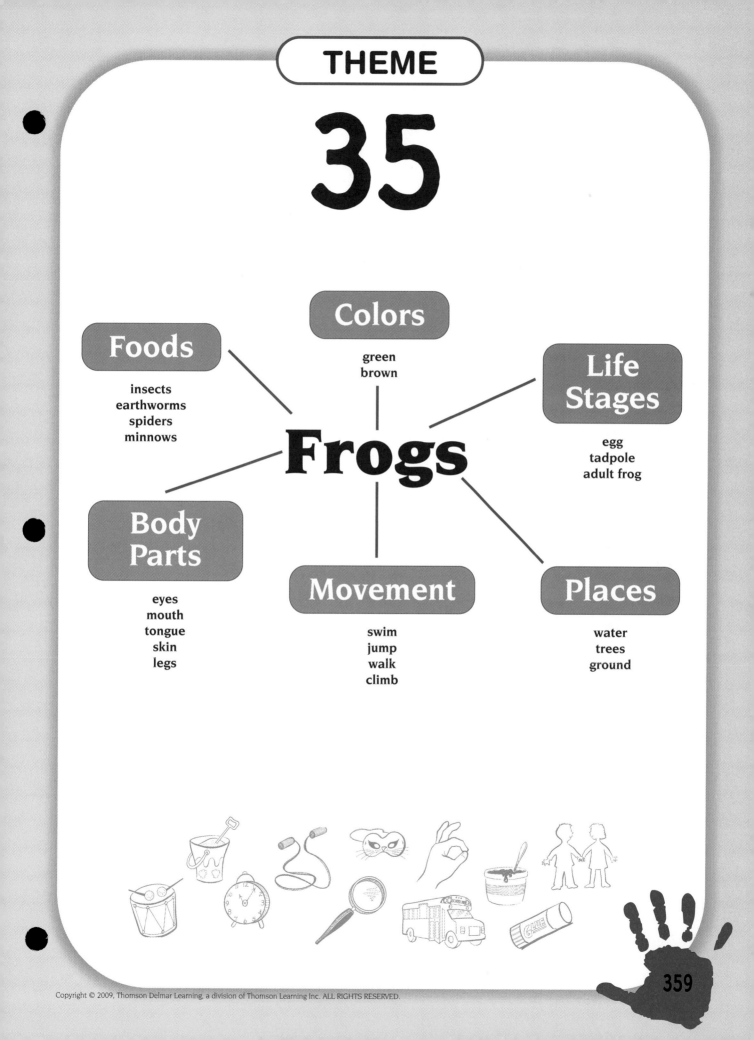

359

Theme Goals

Through participating in the experiences provided by this theme, the children may learn

1. Life stages of frog development
2. Body parts of frog development
3. Ways frogs move
4. Places frogs live
5. Foods frogs eat
6. Colors of frogs

Concepts for the Children to Learn

1. Frogs have eyes, a mouth, a tongue, legs, and skin covering their body.
2. Frogs may live in many places.
3. Frogs can live in water, trees, and on the ground.
4. Frogs can swim, climb, walk, and jump.
5. Frogs eat insects, earthworms, spiders, and minnows.
6. Frogs are colored green and brown.
7. The three life stages of a frog are egg, tadpole, and adult frog.

Vocabulary

1. **amphibian**—an animal that begins its life in the water, and then grows to live on land.
2. **frog**—a small animal with bulging eyes and long back legs.
3. **metamorphosis**—change, such as when a tadpole changes into a frog.
4. **tadpole**—tiny, fishlike baby frog.

Bulletin Board

The purpose of this bulletin board is to foster a positive self-concept as well as name-recognition skills. Construct a frug and lily pad shape out of tagboard for each child in your class. Print a child's name on each frog. Laminate all pieces. Staple the lily pads to the board. Punch a hole in the top of each frog piece with a paper punch. Attach a pushpin several inches above each lily pad. The children can hang their own frogs on the bulletin board as they arrive each day.

Family Letter

Dear Families,

What is usually green, has four legs, and jumps? You've guessed it—a frog! As we head into spring, we will begin a unit to discover many fascinating things about frogs. As you know, a frog is an amphibian, which means it spends part of its life in water and part on land. Frogs are related to toads but they are not the same animal. The children will learn the life stages, body parts, and movements of a frog.

AT SCHOOL

A few of the week's learning experiences include:

- watching tadpoles! Mr. Larson (Scott's dad) has volunteered to bring in some tadpoles, which we will place in an unused aquarium for maximum viewing. We will be able to observe the tadpoles' growth and development into frogs. Stop in our classroom and take a look!

- listening to books about frogs, including *Jump, Frog, Jump!* by Robert Kalan and *The Wide-Mouthed Frog* by Keith Faulkner

- playing leapfrog—a jumping game

AT HOME

You can foster the concepts of this unit at home by going to the library with your child and checking out books about frogs. Also, when you are near a lake or pond with your child, look for frogs or frog habitats.

Have a hoppin' good week!

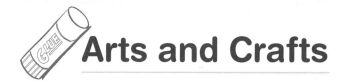

Arts and Crafts

1. Lily Pads

Cut large lily pad shapes out of construction paper. Children can decorate the shapes with green crayons, markers, tempera paint, or watercolor paint. A small, white flower shape can be added, if desired.

2. Frog Sponge Painting

Cut new sponges into simple frog and lily pad shapes. Children can use the sponges to dip in green paint and press on construction paper to create designs.

3. Green Play Dough Frogs

Use a play dough recipe in this book to make green play dough. Encourage the children to make frog shapes. If desired, the frog shapes can be set out to dry, creating a permanent object.

4. Egg Carton Frog

Collect cardboard egg cartons, construction paper, markers, small pompons, and paint. Cut egg carton cups apart. Children can then use the materials as desired to create a frog, using the pompons to represent eyes.

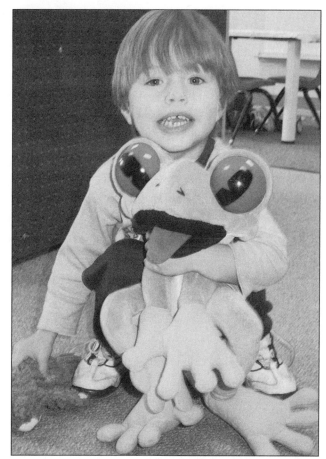

Stuffed toys can help stimulate interest in a theme and encourage play.

Cooking

1. Frog Cookies

With the children, prepare a batch of sugar cookie dough. Demonstrate how to roll three balls (one large, two smaller) and place on a cookie sheet so that they will resemble a frog head with two large eyes when baked. The frog cookies can be decorated with green frosting, chocolate chips, and string licorice.

2. Frog Floats

lime sherbet
mini marshmallows
lemon-lime soda

Place a scoop of sherbet in a clear cup or bowl. Pour a small amount of soda in a cup. Add two small marshmallows on top of sherbet to resemble eyes of a frog. Enjoy!

Dramatic Play

Frogs

Use green tagboard, markers, scissors, and 1-inch-wide elastic to create frog masks. Cut a large lily pad shape out of green tagboard, butcher paper, or fabric. Place items in the dramatic play area. The children can pretend to be frogs in a pond or act out favorite frog songs and fingerplays.

Field Trips

1. **Zoo**

   Visit the amphibian section of a zoo. Observe many kinds of colors of frogs. How are they the same? How are they different?

2. **Pond**

   If available, visit a pond area in the spring or summer. Look for tadpoles and frog habitat.

Fingerplays

Mr. Bullfrog

Here's Mr. Bullfrog,
   (left hand in fist position, thumb upright)
Sitting on a rock.
Along comes a little boy (or girl),
   (walking motion with fingers of right hand)
Mr. Bullfrog jumps, kerplop!

Little Frog

A little frog in a pond am I,
   (make fist with hand)
Hippity, hippity, hop.
   (move fist up and down)
And I can jump in the air so high,
   (raise fist into the air)
Hippity, hippity, hop.
   (move fist up and down)

Five Little Frogs

Five little frogs sitting on a log.
   (extend fingers on one hand)
This little frog is still a pollywog.
   (point to thumb)
This little frog wears a happy grin.
   (point to index finger)
This little frog is tall and thin.
   (point to middle finger)
This little frog can jump very high.
   (point to ring finger)
This little frog wants to fly.
   (point to little finger)

So he calls out, "Ribbit!" and a bird flies by,
And takes him for a ride way up to the sky!
   (make wings with both hands)

Little Green Frog

A little green frog once lived in a pool.
   (hold up fist)
The sun was hot and the water cool.
He sat in the pool the whole day long,
And sang a dear little, funny little song.
"Jaggery do, quaggery dee,
No one was ever as happy as me!"

Ten Little Froggies

Ten little froggies sitting on a lily pad.
   (all fingers up)
The first one said, "Let's catch a fly."
   (right pinkie down)
The second one said, "Let's go hide."
   (right ring finger down)
The third one said, "Let's go for a swim."
   (right middle finger down)
The fourth one said, "Look, I'm in!"
   (right pointer down)
The fifth one said, "Let's dive."
   (right thumb down)
The sixth one said, "There went five!"
   (left thumb down)
The seventh one said, "Where did they go?"
   (left pointer down)
The eighth one said, "Ho, ho."
   (left middle finger down)
The ninth one said, "I need a friend."
   (left ring finger down)
The tenth one said, "This is the end."
   (left pinkie down)

Tadpole, Tadpole

Tadpole, tadpole, swimming all around.
   (Use hands to make swimming motion.)
Swishing your tail without a sound.
   (Continue using hands to make swimming motion.)
Soon you will change into a little frog.
   (Make one hand into a tight fist to represent frog.)
Tadpole, tadpole, little polliwog.
   (Maintain hand in the tight fist.)

Group Time
(Games, Language)

● **Who Is the Frog?**

The purpose of this game is to promote the development of listening skills. The children sit in a circle formation. Begin by choosing one child to sit in the middle with his or her eyes closed. Another child is silently chosen to be the "frog" and say the word "ribbit" three times. Afterward, the child in the middle tries to identify who the "frog" is. Continue playing the game until all children have had a turn to play or until the group begins to lose interest.

Large Muscle

Leapfrog

Have each child find a partner. Child number one squats down on his or her hands and knees, while child number two straddles and jumps over the first child. Then, the children switch roles and the action continues!

Math

1. **Sets of Frogs**

   Cut out frog shapes from green tagboard or felt. Children can use the frog shapes for counting activities or frog-counting songs.

2. **Frogs—Biggest to Smallest**

   Cut out frog shapes of various sizes from construction paper, tagboard, or felt. The children can place the pieces in order from largest to smallest and then from smallest to largest.

3. **Frog Board Game**

   Cut out lily pads from green construction paper and arrange in a row on a piece of tagboard. Decorate remaining tagboard to resemble a pond (cattails, grass, etc.). Have children roll a die and make the frog "hop" on the corresponding number of lily pads. The game is over when a frog reaches the last lily pad.

Music

1. **"Ten Little Froggies"**
   (*Sing to the tune of* "*Ten Little Indians*")

   One little, two little, three little froggies.
   Four little, five little, six little froggies.
   Seven little, eight little, nine little froggies.
   Ten frogs in the pond.

2. **"Five Green Speckled Frogs"**

   Five green speckled frogs
   Sitting on a speckled log,
   Eating the most delicious bugs. Yum! Yum!

   One jumped into the pool,
   Where it was nice and cool.
   Now there are four green speckled frogs.
     (continue with additional verses, counting
     down to zero/none)

3. **"Jumping Frogs"**
   (*Sing to the tune of* "*Jingle Bells*")

   Jumping frogs, jumping frogs, jumping all around
   Looking for worms and bugs to eat,
   They make a croaking sound. Oh!
   Jumping frogs, jumping frogs, in the pond they go,
   Splishing, splashing, and swimming around,
   Moving to and fro.

Science

1. **Observing Tadpoles**

   In the spring, carefully collect tadpoles from a pond or lake area. Place tadpoles in a clean acquarium filled with water obtained from the pond or lake. The aquarium can be placed on the science table for the children to observe. Occasionally, add fresh pond or lake water.

FROGS

When the tadpoles begin to grow legs, place a piece of wood in the aquarium. (The young frogs will soon need a place to rest out of the water.) Eventually, return the frogs to their habitat.

2. Metamorphosis

Draw or collect pictures from children's science magazines that depict the life cycle of a frog. Pictures should include frog eggs, tadpole, tadpole with tail shrinking and legs sprouting, and frog. Discuss the word *metamorphosis*. Check the library for books that show frogs at various stages of development.

3. African Dwarf Frogs

Place African dwarf frogs in an aquarium that is filled with water. These frogs are swimmers and do not need time out of the water. Place magnifying glasses near the aquarium and encourage children to observe the characteristics of the frogs.

Sensory

1. Plastic Frogs

Place purchased plastic frogs in a water-filled sensory table. Add small strainers and nets.

2. Cork Frogs

Using permanent markers, color several corks green. Insert a green chenille stem in the center of each cork and bend it to resemble frog legs. Add details to frogs using markers. Place frogs in a sensory table that has been filled with water. If desired, attach a string to the cork frogs so they can be pulled around in the water.

Books

The following books can be used to complement this theme:

Bentley, Dawn and Salina Yoon. (1999). *The Icky Sticky Frog*. Santa Monica, CA: Piggy Toes Press.

Calmenseon, Stephanie and Denise Brunkus. (2001). *The Frog Principal*. New York: Scholastic.

Faulkner, Keith. (1996). *The Wide-Mouthed Frog*. Illus. by Jonathan Lambert. New York: Dial.

Fowler, Allan. (1992). *Frogs and Toads and Tadpoles, Too*. Chicago: Children's Press.

Kalan, Robert. (1981). *Jump, Frog, Jump!* Illus. by Byron Barton. New York: Greenwillow.

Lobel, Arnold. (1979). *Frog and Toad Are Friends*. New York: HarperTrophy. (Pbk.)

Lobel, Arnold. (1979). *Frog and Toad Together*. New York: HarperTrophy. (Pbk.)

Lobel, Arnold. (1984). *Days with Frog and Toad*. New York: HarperTrophy. (25th Anniversary Edition.)

Lobel, Arnold. (1984). *Frog and Toad All Year*. New York: HarperTrophy. (Pbk.)

London, Jonathon and Frank Remkiewicz. (2000). *Froggy Bakes a Cake*. New York: Grosset & Dunlap.

London, Jonathon and Frank Remkiewicz. (2000). *Froggy's Best Christmas*. New York: Viking.

London, Jonathon and Frank Remkiewicz. (2000). *Froggy's First Kiss*. New York: Puffin.

London, Jonathon and Frank Remkiewicz. (2000). *Froggy Goes to Bed*. New York: Viking.

London, Jonathon and Frank Remkiewicz. (2001). *Froggy Eats Out*. New York: Viking.

London, Jonathon and Frank Remkiewicz. (2001). *Froggy's Halloween*. New York: Puffin.

London, Jonathon and Frank Remkiewicz. (2001). *Froggy Plays Soccer*. New York: Puffin.

Riches, Sara. (2000). *Fat Frogs on a Skinny Log*. New York: Scholastic.

Talley, Linda and Itoko Maeno. (2001). *Toad in Town*. Kansas City, MO: MarshMedia.

Yolen, Jane and Bruce Degen. (1996). *Commander Toad and the Planet of the Grapes*. New York: Putnam & Grosset Group.

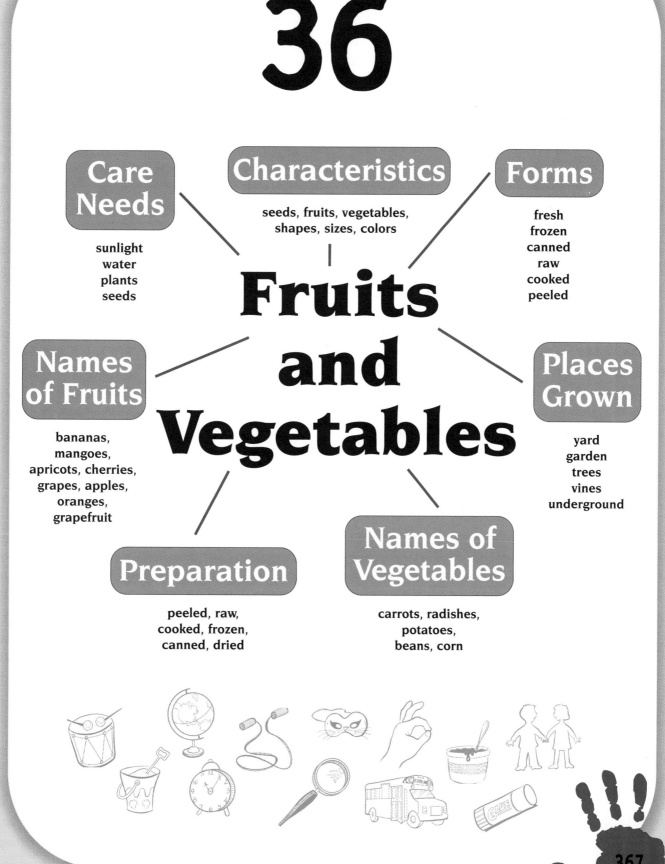

THEME

36

Care Needs
sunlight
water
plants
seeds

Characteristics
seeds, fruits, vegetables,
shapes, sizes, colors

Forms
fresh
frozen
canned
raw
cooked
peeled

Fruits and Vegetables

Names of Fruits
bananas,
mangoes,
apricots, cherries,
grapes, apples,
oranges,
grapefruit

Places Grown
yard
garden
trees
vines
underground

Preparation
peeled, raw,
cooked, frozen,
canned, dried

Names of Vegetables
carrots, radishes,
potatoes,
beans, corn

Theme Goals

Through participating in the experiences provided by this theme, the children may learn

1. Names of common fruits and vegetables
2. Care needs of fruits and vegetables
3. Places fruits and vegetables are grown
4. Preparation of fruits and vegetables
5. Forms in which fruits and vegetables can be served
6. Fruit or vegetable seeds
7. Characteristics of fruits and vegetables

Concepts for the Children to Learn

1. There are many kinds of fruits and vegetables.
2. Fruits and vegetables are grown from seeds and plants.
3. Fruits and vegetables come in many shapes, sizes, and colors.
4. Fruits and vegetables need sunlight and water to grow.
5. Apples, apricots, oranges, grapefruit, cherries, and mangoes are grown on trees.
6. Grapes are grown on vines.
7. Bananas are grown on trees.
8. Carrots, radishes, and potatoes are grown in the ground.
9. Beans and corn are grown on plants.
10. Fruits and vegetables can be bought fresh, frozen, or canned.
11. Some people grow fruits and vegetables in home gardens.
12. Fruits and vegetables have different names.
13. Most fruits and vegetables can be eaten raw or cooked.
14. We eat some fruits and vegetables with their skin; some we need to peel first.
15. Some fruits have seeds.

Vocabulary

1. **cook**—to prepare food by heating.
2. **frozen**—chilled or refrigerated to make solid.
3. **fruit**—usually a sweet-tasting part of a plant.
4. **garden**—ground used to grow plants.
5. **produce**—agriculture products such as fruits and vegetables.
6. **ripe**—ready to be picked and eaten.

7. **roots**—parts of a plant that grow downward into the soil and are edible in some plants (potatoes, turnips, radishes, onions, and carrots).

8. **seeds**—part of a plant used for growing a new crop and edible in some plants (sunflower, pumpkin).

9. **soil**—portion of earth; dirt used for growing.

10. **sprout**—to begin to grow.

11. **stems**—part of a plant used for transporting food and water and edible in some plants (celery).

12. **vegetable**—part of a plant that can be eaten.

13. **vine**—plant with a long, slender stem.

Bulletin Board

The purpose of this bulletin board is to observe the growth of a lima bean seed. Prepare by placing a moist paper towel in a small plastic bag, along with a lima bean (seed). Sprouting will occur faster if the seeds have been presoaked overnight. Staple each bag to the bulletin board as illustrated and place a child's name beside each one. Additional watering may be needed throughout this unit.

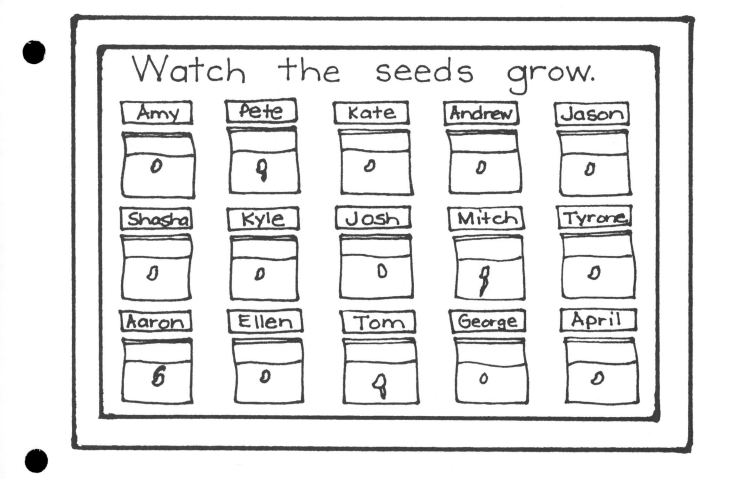

Family Letter

Dear Families,

Hello again! We hope that everyone in your family is healthy and happy. Speaking of health, we are starting a new curriculum unit on fruits and vegetables. Through the experiences planned for this unit, the children will learn the names of many fruits and vegetables, their forms, and places they are grown. Also, they will discover ways many different fruits and vegetables can be prepared and how they taste.

AT SCHOOL

Some of the many fun-filled learning activities scheduled for this unit include:

- planting lima beans (seeds) to sprout. Take a look at our bulletin board this week.
- playing the role of a gardener/farmer in the dramatic play area
- matching pictures of vegetables to where they are grown (trees, vines, underground, etc.)
- having a fruit and vegetable tasting party during snack
- visiting a produce section at the grocery store
- listening to a story called *What Was It before It Was Orange Juice?* by Jane Belk Moncure

AT HOME

There are many ways you can integrate this unit's concepts into your family life. To help develop memory and language skills, ask your child which vegetables or fruits he or she tried during the week. Then let your child help you prepare them at home. Cooking often tempts a child to try new foods. Also, here is a great dip recipe we will be making for snack on Tuesday that you may want to make at home.

Vegetable Dip

1 cup yogurt
1 cup mayonnaise

1 tablespoon dill weed
1 teaspoon seasoned salt

Mix all ingredients and chill. Serve with fresh raw vegetables.

We still need two more helpers to assist us with our field trip on Thursday to the grocery store. Let me know if you are available. The children enjoy having parents join in our activities.

Enjoy your child!

370

THEME 36

My favorite vegetable:			My favorite fruit is:		
Kenny M.		pumpkin	Kenny M.		pear
Shawn		corn	Shawn		strawberry
Robert		radishes	Robert		lemon
Jennifer M.		corn	Jennifer M.		apple
Tracy		peas	Tracy		peach
Angela		potato	Rhonda		strawberry
Ayman		carrots	Jennifer B.		cherries
Jennifer B.		peas	Angela		plums
Tricia		carrots	Ayman		pear
Andrea		carrots	Tricia		strawberry
Rhonda		carrots	Andrea		strawberry
Crystal		cucumber	Crystal		lemon
Jennifer H.		carrots	Jennifer H.		strawberry
Jeremiah		pumpkin	Jeremiah		plums
Eric		corn	Eric		strawberry

Charts can be prepared to record the children's favorite vegetables and fruit.

Arts and Crafts

1. Seeds

Save several seeds from fruits and vegetables for the children to make a seed collage. When seeds are securely glued, children can also paint them if desired. The collage can be secured to a bulletin board.

2. Cutting Vegetable and Fruit Shapes

Cut easel paper into a different shape of fruit or vegetable every day. Dry Kool-aid mix can be added to the paint to give it a "fruity" smell.

3. Mold with Play Dough

The children can mold and create fruits and vegetables out of clay and play dough. Another option would be to color and scent the play dough. Examples might include orange-scented orange, lemon-scented yellow, banana-scented yellow.

4. Potato Prints

Cut potatoes in half. The children can dip them in paints and stamp the potatoes on a large sheet of paper.

5. Paint with Celery Leaves

Mix some thin tempera paint. Use celery leaves as a painting tool.

6. Lemon Play Dough

2 cups water
3 teaspoons liquid food coloring
2 tablespoons cooking oil
2 1/2 cups flour
5 tablespoons cream of tartar
2 or 3 drops lemon oil

In a large pot, combine water, food coloring, and oil. Add flour, salt, and cream of tartar. Over medium heat, cook and stir for about five minutes, until a ball of dough forms. Cool the dough for five minutes and then knead it with your hands until smooth. Add additional flour if necessary. Store in an airtight container in the refrigerator when not using.

Cooking Vocabulary

The following vocabulary words can be introduced through cooking experiences:

bake	cube	garnish	measure	roll	sprinkle
beat	cut	grate	mince	scrape	squeeze
boil	dice	grease	mix	scrub	stir
broil	dip	grill	pare	shake	strain
brown	drain	grind	peel	shred	stuff
chop	freeze	heat	pit	sift	tear
cool	frost	knead	pour	simmer	toast
core	fry	marinate	roast	spread	whip
cream					

Cooking

1. Vegetable Dip

1 cup plain yogurt
1 cup mayonnaise
1 tablespoon dill weed
1 teaspoon seasoned salt

Mix all the ingredients together and chill. Serve with fresh, raw vegetables.

2. Ants on a Log

Cut celery into pieces and spread with cream cheese. Top with raisins, coconut, or grated carrots. (Celery is difficult for younger children to chew.)

3. Applesauce

4 apples
1 tablespoon water
2 tablespoons brown sugar or honey

Wash the apples and cut into small pieces. Dip the pieces into water and roll in brown sugar or honey. Serves eight.

4. Banana Rounds

4 medium bananas
1/2 cup yogurt
3 tablespoons honey

1/8 teaspoon nutmeg
1/8 teaspoon cinnamon
1/4 cup wheat germ

The children can participate by peeling the bananas and slicing them into "rounds." Measure the spices, wheat germ, and honey. Blend this mixture with yogurt and bananas. Chill before serving. Serves eight.

5. Finnish Strawberry Shake

20 fresh strawberries
4 cups milk
3 tablespoons sugar

Wash strawberries and remove stems. Cut strawberries into small pieces. Combine milk, sugar, and strawberries in a large mixing bowl or blender. Beat with an eggbeater or blend for 2 minutes. Pour strawberry shakes into individual glasses. Makes four to eight servings.

Variation: Raspberries or other sweet fruit may be used instead.

6. Banana Sandwiches

1/2 or 1 banana per child
honey

Peel the bananas and slice them in half lengthwise. Spread honey on one half of the banana and top with the other half.

Dramatic Play

Grocery Store

Plan a grocery store containing many plastic fruits and vegetables, a cash register, grocery bags, and play money if available. The children can take turns being a produce clerk, cashier, and price tagger.

Field Trips

1. Grocery Store

Take a trip to the grocery store to visit the produce department. Ask the clerk to show the children how the food is delivered.

2. Visiting a Farm

Visit a farm. Ask the farmer to show the children the fruits and vegetables grown on the farm.

3. Visit a Farmers' Market

Visit a farmers' market. Purchase fruits and vegetables that can be used for snacks.

4. Visit an Orchard

Visit an apple or fruit orchard. Observe how the fruit is grown. If possible, pick some fruit to bring back to the classroom.

Fingerplays

My Garden

This is my garden
   (extend one hand forward, palm up)
I'll rake it with care
   (make raking motion on palm with three
   fingers of other hand)
And then some seeds
   (planting motion)
I'll plant in there.

The sun will shine
   (make circle with arms)
And the rain will fall
   (let fingers flutter down to lap)
And my garden will blossom
   (cup hand together, extend upward slowly)
And grow straight and tall.

Dig a Little Hole

Dig a little hole.
   (dig)
Plant a little seed.
   (drop seed)
Pour a little water.
   (pour)
Pull a little weed.
   (pull and throw)
Chase a little bug.
   (chasing motion with hands)
Heigh-ho, there he goes.
   (shade eyes)
Give a little sunshine
   (circle arms over head)
Grow a little bean!
   (hands grow upward)

Apple Tree

Way up high in the apple tree
   (hold arms up high)
Two little apples smiled at me.
   (look at two hands up high)
I shook that tree as hard as I could.
   (shake arms)
Down came the apples,
   (arms fall)
Mmm, were they good!
   (rub tummy)

Bananas

Bananas are my favorite fruit.
   (make fists as if holding banana)
I eat one every day.
   (hold up one finger)
I always take one with me
   (act as if putting one in pocket)
When I go out to play.
   (wave good-bye)
It gives me lots of energy
   (make a muscle)

To jump around and run.
   (move arms as if running)
Bananas are my favorite fruit.
   (rub tummy)
To me they're so much fun!
   (point to self and smile)

Vegetables and Fruits

The food we like to eat that grows
On vines and bushes and trees
Are vegetables and fruits, my friends,
Like cherries, grapes, and peas.
Apples and oranges and peaches are fruits
And so are tangerines,
Lettuce and carrots are vegetables,
Like squash and beans.

Group Time

(Games, Language)

1. **Carrot, Carrot, Corn**

   Play Duck, Duck, Goose, but substitute "Carrot, Carrot, Corn."

2. **Hot Potato**

   The children sit in a circle and the teacher gives one child a potato. Teacher then plays lively music and the children pass the potato around the circle. When the music suddenly stops, the child with the potato must stand up and say the name of a fruit or vegetable. Encourage children to think of a fruit or vegetable that hasn't been named yet.

Large Muscle

Place child-sized plastic hoes, shovels, rakes, and watering cans around the outdoor sand area.

Math

1. **Fruit and Vegetable Match**

   Cut out various fruits and vegetables from a magazine. Trace their shapes onto tagboard. Have children match the fruit or vegetable to the correct shape on the tagboard.

2. **Seriation**

   Make five sizes of each vegetable or fruit you want to use. Have children place in order from smallest to largest, or largest to smallest.

3. **Measuring**

   The children can measure their bean sprouts. Maintain a small chart of their measurements.

4. **Parts and Wholes**

   Cut apples in half at snack time to introduce the concepts of parts and whole.

5. **Grouping Pictures**

   Cut pictures of fruits and vegetables for the children to sort according to color, size, and shape.

Music

1. **"The Vegetable Garden"**
   (*Sing to the tune of* "*Mulberry Bush*")

   Here we go 'round the vegetable garden,
   The vegetable garden, the vegetable garden,
   Here we go 'round the vegetable garden,
   So early in the morning.

   Other verses:
   This is the way we pull the weeds . . .
   This is the way we water the plants . . .
   This is the way we eat the vegetables . . .

2. "Vegetables"

(*Sing to the tune of "Mary Had a Little Lamb"*)

I'm a tomato, red and round,
Red and round, red and round.
I'm a tomato, red and round,
Seated on the ground.

I'm a corn stalk, tall and straight,
Tall and straight, tall and straight.
I'm a corn stalk, tall and straight
And I taste just great.

Science

1. Cut and Draw

Cut out or draw many different fruits and vegetables from tagboard or construction paper scraps. Also make a tree, a vine, and some soil. Have children classify the fruit by where it's grown—on a tree, on a vine, or underground.

2. Tasting Center

Cut small pieces of various fruits and set up a tasting center. Encourage the children to taste and compare different fruits and vegetables.

3. Tasting Party

Plan a vegetable-tasting party. Cut small pieces of vegetables. Also, have children taste raw vegetables and compare them to the same vegetable cooked.

4. Identify by Smelling

Place one each of several fruits and vegetables in small cups and cover with aluminum foil. Punch a small hole in the top of the aluminum foil. Then have the children smell the cups and try to identify each fruit or vegetable.

5. Carrot Tops in Water

Cut off the top of a carrot and place it in a shallow dish of water. Observe what happens day to day. Given time, the top of the carrot should sprout.

6. Colored Celery Stalks

Place celery stalks into water colored with food coloring. Observe what happens to the leaves of celery.

7. Fruit Dehydration

Provide plastic knives and a variety of fruit for the children to slice. Discuss with children how the fruit looks and feels. Place in dehydrator. Dry fruit overnight. The next day, invite the children to discuss the differences in how the fruit looks and feels. Introduce the concept of dehydration (taking the liquid out). Strawberries, bananas, pineapple, apples, and grapes usually have a significant change after dehydrating.

Sensory

1. Preparing Fruits and Vegetables

Wash vegetables and fruits to prepare for eating at snack time.

2. Fruit and Vegetable Scrub

Place play fruits and vegetables in the sensory table. Provide scrub brushes for the children to clean and scrub the fruits and vegetables.

Social Studies

1. Field Trip to a Garden

Plan a field trip to a large garden. Point out different fruits and vegetables. If possible, have the children pull radishes and carrots.

2. Hang Pictures

On a bulletin board in the classroom, hang pictures of fruits and vegetables.

3. Fruit and Vegetable Book

The children can make a fruit and vegetable book. Possible titles include "My Favorite Fruit Is," "My Favorite Vegetable Is," "I Would Like to Grow," and "I Would Most Like to Cook." The children can paste pictures or adhere stickers to the individual pages.

Books

The following books can be used to complement this theme:

Banks, Kate. (1988). *Alphabet Soup*. New York: Knopf: Distributed by Random House.

Brown, Laurene Krasny. (1995). *The Vegetable Show*. Boston: Little, Brown.

Caseley, Judith. (1990). *Grandpa's Garden Lunch*. New York: Greenwillow.

Chandler, Lynda E. (2001). *Fruits and Vegetables*. New York: Dover Publishers.

Charles, N. N. (1994). *What Am I? Looking through Shapes at Apples and Grapes*. Illus. by Leo and Diane Dillon. New York: Scholastic.

Ehlert, Lois. (1994). *Eating the Alphabet: Fruits & Vegetables from A to Z*. Orlando, FL: Harcourt Brace.

Fowler, Allan. (1995). *Corn—On and Off the Cob*. Chicago: Children's Press. (Pbk.)

Fowler, Allan. (1996). *It's a Fruit, It's a Vegetable, It's a Pumpkin*. Illus. by Robert L. Hillerich. Chicago: Children's Press.

French, Vivian. (1995). *Oliver's Vegetables*. Illus. by Alison Bartlett. New York: Orchard Books.

Gershator, Phillis. (1996). *Sweet, Sweet Fig Banana*. Illus. by Fritz Millvoix. Niles, IL: Albert Whitman.

Gordon, Elizabeth and M. T. Ross. (2000). *Mother Earth's Children: The Frolics of the Fruits and Vegetables*. Illus. by M. T. Ross. New York: Derrydale Books.

Greenstein, Elaine. (1996). *Mrs. Rose's Garden*. New York: Simon & Schuster.

Hall, Zoe. (1996). *The Apple Pie Tree*. Illus. by Shari Halpern. New York: Scholastic.

Hoban, Tana. (1995). *Animal, Vegetable, or Mineral?* New York: Greenwillow.

Maestro, Betsy C. (1992). *How Do Apples Grow?* Illus. by Giulio Maestro. New York: HarperCollins.

Patent, Dorothy Hinshaw. (1991). *Where Food Comes From*. Illus. by William Munoz. New York: Holiday House.

Powell, Jillian. (1997). *Fruit*. Austin, TX: Raintree/Steck Vaughn.

Robinson, Fay. (1994). *Vegetables, Vegetables*. Chicago: Children's Press.

Robson, Pam. (1998). *Banana*. Chicago: Children's Press.

Robson, Pam. (1998). *Corn*. Chicago: Children's Press.

Rylant, Cynthia. (1995). *Mr. Putter and Tabby Pick the Pears*. Orlando, FL: Harcourt Brace.

Schuette, Sarah. (2003). *An Alphabet Salad: Fruits and Vegetables from A to Z*. Mankato, MN: A+ Books.

Seabrook, Elizabeth. (1997). *Cabbages and Kings*. Illus. by Jamie Wyeth. New York: Viking.

Sekido, Isamu. (1993). *Fruits, Roots, and Fungi: Plants We Eat*. Minneapolis, MN: Lerner.

Wiesner, David. (1992). *June 29, 1999*. New York: Clarion Books.

Multimedia

The following multimedia products can be used to complement this theme:

5-a-Day Adventures [CD-ROM]. (1994). San Mateo, CA: Dole Food Company.

Bingham, Bing. "Goober Peas" on *A Rainbow of Songs* [cassette]. Available from Kimbo Educational, Long Branch, NJ.

Cranberry Bounce [video]. (1991). DeBeck Educational Video.

Fruit: Close Up and Very Personal [video]. (1995). Geneva, IL: Stage Fright Productions.

Scelsa, Greg and Steve Millang. "I Like Potatoes" on *We All Live Together—Volume 5* [cassette or CD]. Available from Kimbo Educational, Long Branch, NJ.

Recordings and Song Titles

The following recordings can be used to complement this theme:

"All Kinds of Farms," "Hello Harvest Moon," "Gardener at Home." (1999). *On the Farm with RONNO.* Long Branch, NJ: Kimbo Educational.

"Apples and Bananas," "Aikendrum." (1999). *Five Little Monkeys.* Long Branch, NJ: Kimbo Educational.

"Apples and Bananas," "Peanut Butter Song." (1996). *Where Is Thumbkin?* Long Branch, NJ: Kimbo Educational.

"Apple Pickin'." (1993). *Pre-K Hooray.* Long Branch, NJ: Kimbo Educational.

"Corn Dance." *Authentic Indian Dance.* Long Branch, NJ: Kimbo Educational.

"Do You Like Fruit?," "Do You Like Meat?" (1974). *Songs about Me.* Long Branch, NJ: Kimbo Educational.

"Do You Like Vegetables?," "Do You Like Dessert?" (1974). *More Songs About Me.* Long Branch, NJ: Kimbo Educational.

"Food for My Family." (1994). *Songs About Native Americans.* Long Branch, NJ: Kimbo Educational.

"I Always Eat What's on My Plate," "I Eat with My Mouth Closed." (1979). *Self Help Skills.* Long Branch, NJ: Kimbo Educational.

"Let's Sing About Food." (1994). *Get Up and Grow.* Long Branch, NJ: Kimbo Educational.

"Snack Time." (1990). *Musical Playtime Fun.* Long Branch, NJ: Kimbo Educational.

"The Food Song," "Caribbean Mango Song." (1993). *Joining Hands in Other Lands.* Long Branch, NJ: Kimbo Educational.

"Vegetable Soup Song," "Vegetables." (1995). *Piggyback Songs.* Long Branch, NJ: Kimbo Educational.

"Veggie Power." (1994). *Fun 'n' Friendly* (RONNO). Long Branch, NJ: Kimbo Educational.

"Vixen Who Makes Vegetable Soup." (1994). *A to Z, the Animals and Me.* Long Branch, NJ: Kimbo Educational.

Type

rock
vegetable
flower
terrarium

Purpose

food
beauty
hobby

Place

window box
indoor
community
rooftop

Gardens

Tools

hoe
rake
spade
hose
watering can

Care

sunshine
water
fertilizer
warmth
soil

Plants

bulbs
seeds
plants
roots

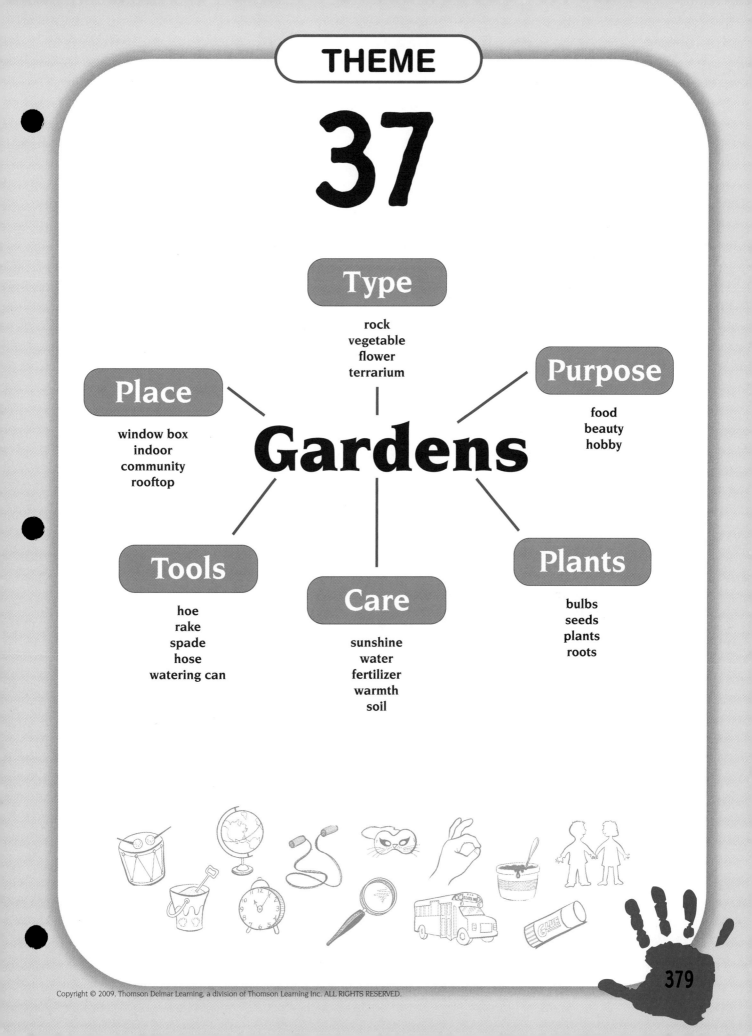

Theme Goals

Through participating in the experiences provided by this theme, the children may learn

1. Purposes of gardens
2. Places of gardens
3. Tools used for gardening
4. Care of gardens
5. Types of plants grown in a garden
6. Types of gardens

Concepts for the Children to Learn

1. Plants are living things.
2. Plants need sunshine, water, soil, fertilizer, and warmth to grow.
3. Gardens produce vegetables, fruits, and beautiful flowers.
4. Some people garden for a hobby.
5. We plant gardens by placing bulbs, seeds, plants, and/or roots in the ground.
6. Fruits, vegetables, and flowers can be planted in our gardens.
7. Many tools are needed for gardening.
8. A water can or hose can be used for watering gardens.
9. A hoe, rake, and spade are gardening tools.
10. There are many places gardens can be planted.
11. Gardens can be housed on rooftops, in window boxes, and in terrariums.
12. Rock, flower, vegetable, and terrarium are types of gardens.

Vocabulary

1. **bulb**—a type of seed.
2. **flower**—part of the plant that has colored petals.
3. **garden**—a place to grow plants.
4. **greenhouse**—building for growing plants and flowers.
5. **leaf**—flat, green part of a plant.
6. **rake**—a tool with teeth or prongs.
7. **root**—part of the plant that grows into the ground.
8. **seed**—part of the plant from which a new plant will grow.
9. **soil**—top of the ground.
10. **stem**—part of the plant that holds the leaves and flowers.
11. **vegetable**—a plant that can be eaten.
12. **weed**—a plant that is not needed.

Bulletin Board

The purpose of this bulletin board is to foster visual discrimination skills. To prepare the bulletin board, construct five or six watering cans out of tagboard. Color each one a different color with felt-tip markers and hang on the bulletin board. Attach a string to each watering can. Next, construct the same number of small rakes out of tagboard. Color each one using the same colors you used for the watering cans. Attach a pushpin to the top of each rake. The children can match each watering can to the corresponding colored rake by winding the string around the correct pushpin.

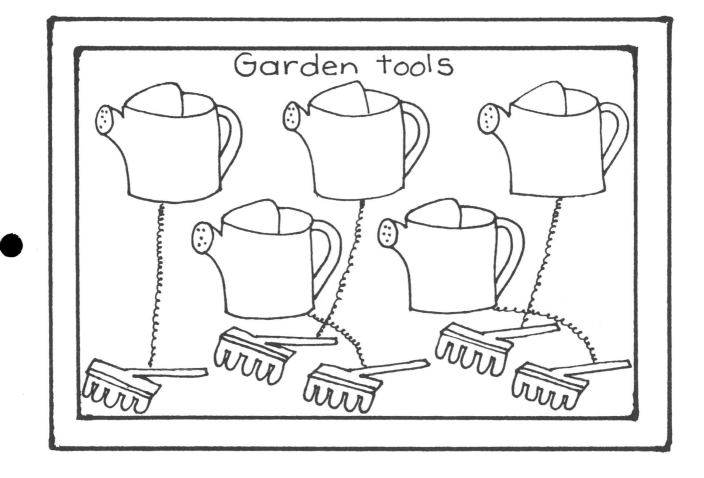

Family Letter

Dear Families,

"Mary, Mary, quite contrary, how does your garden grow?" That familiar nursery rhyme sums up our next curriculum unit—gardens! We will be exploring the purposes, types, and places for flower and vegetable gardens. We will also learn the names of garden tools and the care gardens need.

AT SCHOOL

Some of the learning experiences planned to foster concepts related to gardens include:

- enjoying a flower shop set up in the dramatic play area
- dramatizing the story of *The Big Turnip*
- preparing a section of our play yard for a garden. The children will help decide which seeds to plant.
- playing with mud in the sensory table

AT HOME

If you have a garden, ask your child to help you water, weed, and care for it. If you don't have a garden, take a walk and observe how many plants you can find that are cared for by people. What are the plants? What colors are they? How are they cared for?

Cut the tops of carrots off 1/4 inch from the stem to make a carrot-top garden. Place carrot tops in a shallow pie tin and pour 1/4 inch of water in the tin. Soon roots will appear, the greens will grow, and your child will be able to observe the growth.

Enjoy your child!

Watching a garden grow is a long-term science experience.

 # Arts and Crafts

1. **Leaf Rubbings**

   Take the children on a leaf walk. The children choose a couple of large leaves to bring back to school. Place the leaves between two sheets of paper and rub with flat, large crayons across the top sheet of paper.

2. **Stencils**

   Cut stencils out of tagboard of various-shaped leaves or vegetables (see patterns). Laminate the stencils. The children can use crayons, pencils, or marking pens to make the leaf or vegetable outlines. These stencils can be used as the front of the "soup and salad" party invitations listed under social studies activities.

3. **Decorating Vases**

   Collect tin cans or milk cartons for the children to use as vases. If cans are used, file the sharp edges or cover them with masking tape. The children can decorate the containers with colored paper, gift wrapping paper, or wallpaper. Greeting cards may also be useful for this activity.

4. **Root Painting**

   Dig up old plants (non-toxic) and save the roots and stems. Put paint in containers and take children, roots, paper, and paint outside to create a painting. The children will use the roots as "paintbrushes."

 # Cooking

1. **Vegetable Soup**

   Begin with consommé or soup base. Add whatever vegetables—beans, etc.—children want to add and can help to prepare. Make soup a day ahead so that all of the vegetables will be cooked thoroughly.

2. Indian—Cucumbers and Tomatoes with Yogurt

2 medium cucumbers
2 green onions with tops, chopped
1 teaspoon salt
2 tomatoes chopped
1/2 clove garlic, finely chopped
2 tablespoons snipped parsley
1/2 teaspoon ground cumin
1/8 teaspoon pepper
1 cup unflavored yogurt

Cut cucumbers lengthwise into halves. Scoop out seeds. Chop cucumbers. Mix cucumbers, green onions, and salt. Let stand 10 minutes. Add tomatoes. Mix remaining ingredients except yogurt. Toss with cucumber mixture. Cover and refrigerate at least 1 hour. Drain thoroughly. Just before serving, fold in yogurt. Makes 6 servings.

Note: From *Betty Crocker's International Cookbook*, 1980, New York: Random House.

3. Lettuce or Spinach Roll-ups

On clean lettuce or spinach leaves, spread softened cream cheese or cottage cheese. If desired, sprinkle with grated carrots. Roll them up. Chill and serve.

4. Carrot Cookies

1/2 cup honey
1 egg
1/2 cup margarine
1 cup whole-wheat flour
1 1/4 teaspoons baking powder
1/4 teaspoon salt
1/2 cup rolled oats
1/2 cup wheat germ
1/2 cup grated raw carrots
1/2 cup raisins
1 teaspoon vanilla

Mix all ingredients in a bowl. Drop mixture by spoonfuls onto a lightly greased cookie sheet. Flatten each ball slightly. Bake in a 350-degree oven for approximately 12 minutes.

Dramatic Play

1. Flower Shop

Create a flower shop by gathering plastic flowers and plants. If desired, flowers can be made from tissue paper and chenille stems. Collect different kinds of vases and also styrofoam or sponge blocks so the children can make flower arrangements. A cash register, aprons, money, and sacks can also be provided to encourage play.

2. Gardening Center

Gather tools, gloves, hats, seeds, and plastic flowers or plants. The children can pretend to plant and grow seeds. Provide seed catalogs and order blanks for children to choose seeds to order.

3. Fruit Stand

Set up a fruit stand by using plastic fruits and vegetables. Aprons, a cash register, market baskets or bags, and play money can also be used to encourage play. The children can take turns being the owner and the shopper.

4. Sandbox

The children can experiment with gardening tools in the sandbox.

Field Trips/ Resource People

1. Field Trips

Take a field trip to the following places:

- a flower garden
- a vegetable garden
- a flower shop

- a farmers' market
- a greenhouse
- a conservatory
- a park
- the produce section of a grocery store
- a natural food store

2. **Resource People**
   - gardeners
   - florist to demonstrate flower arranging

Fingerplays

Seeds

Some little seeds have parachutes
To carry them around
   (cup hand downward)
The wind blows them swish, swish, swish.
   (flip fingers outward from parachute)
Then gently lays them on the ground.
   (let hand gently float down and rest on lap)

Relaxing Flowers

Five little flowers standing in the sun
   (hold up five fingers)
See their heads nodding, bowing one by one?
   (bend fingers several times)
Down, down, down comes the gentle rain
   (raise hands, wiggle fingers, and lower arms to
   simulate falling rain)
And the five little flowers lift their heads up
again!
   (hold up five fingers)

How It Happens

A muddy hump,
   (make a fist using both hands)
A small green lump,
   (poke up thumbs together as one)
Two leaves and then
Two leaves again
   (raise forefinger of each hand from fist, then
   middle fingers)

And shooting up, a stem and cup.
   (put elbows, forearms, and hands together,
   fingers slightly curved)
One last shower,
   (rain movements with spread arms and
   fingers)
Then a flower.
   (elbows, forearms together with hands wide
   apart, palms up)

Little Flowers

The sun comes out and shines so bright
   (join hands over head in circle)
Then we have a shower.
   (wiggle fingers coming down)
The little bud pushes with all its might
   (one hand in fist; other hand clasped over,
   move hands up slowly)
And soon we have a flower.
   (join thumbs and spread fingers for flower)

Mr. Carrot

Nice Mr. Carrot
Makes curly hair.
   (hand on head)
His head grows underneath the ground,
   (bob head)
His feet up in the air.
   (raise feet)
And early in the morning
I find him in his bed
   (close eyes, lay head on hands)
And give his feet a great big pull
   (stretch legs out)
And out comes his head.

Group Time
(Games, Language)

Huckle Buckle Bean Stalk

A small object such as a plastic flower or acorn may be used for hiding. All the players cover their eyes, except the one who hides the object. After it is hidden, the players stand up and begin to look for it. When one locates it, he or she doesn't let others know the placement.

Instead he or she quietly takes a seat, saying, "Huckle buckle bean stalk." The game continues until all players have located the object. The first child to find the object usually hides it the next time. This game is appropriate for older children.

Large Muscle

Leaf Jumping

This is an active skill game that can be played indoors or outdoors. Cut out large cardboard leaves and arrange them in an irregular line, as they might appear on a stem. The closer they are together, the harder the game will be. Beginning at one end, each player tries to jump over the leaves without touching them. Older children may try to skip or hop over the leaves.

Math

1. **Sorting Beans**

   Mix together several shapes and colors of large, dried beans. The children can sort the beans by size and color.

2. **Inchworm Measuring**

   A good introduction for this activity is the story *Inch by Inch* by Leo Lionni. Cut two or three dozen inchworms out of felt. Then cut out flowers of various heights—with long or short stems. Encourage the children to place worms along each stem from bottom to top of the flower. How many inchworms tall is each flower? After this, have the children count the inchworms.

Music

"A Little Seed"

(*Sing to the tune of "I'm a Little Teapot"*)

Here's a little seed in the dark, dark ground.
Out comes the warm sun, yellow and round.
Down comes the rain, wet and slow.
Up comes the little seed, grow, grow, grow!

Science

1. **Growing Grass**

   Germinate grass seeds by placing a damp sponge in a pie tin of water and sprinkling seeds on the sponge. The children will notice tiny sprouts after a few days. Experiment by putting one sponge in the freezer, one near a heat source, and one in a dark closet. Discuss what happens to each group of seeds.

2. **Plants Contain Water**

   Cut off 1/4 inch from the bottom of a celery stalk. Fill a clear vase with water containing food coloring. Place the celery stalk in the vase. Encourage the children to observe color changes in the celery stalk. This activity can be repeated using a white carnation.

3. **Planting Seeds**

   Purchase bean and radish seeds. If space permits, plant outdoors. Otherwise, place soil in planters indoors. Plant the seeds with the children. Identify the plants by pasting the seed packages on the planters. This will help the children to recognize the plants as they emerge from the soil.

4. **The Science Table**

   Place a magnifying glass with different types of seeds and bulbs on the science table. During the week, add fresh flowers, plant leaves, and dried plants.

5. Rooting an Organically Grown Sweet Potato

To root an organically grown sweet potato in water, push toothpicks halfway into the potato. Then place the potato in a glass of water with the toothpicks resting on the top rim. Make sure the end of the potato is immersed in water. Place the glass where it will receive adequate light. Maintain the water level so that the bottom of the potato is always immersed. Note that in a few weeks roots will grow out of the sides and bottom of the potato, and leaves will grow out of the top. The plant can be left in the water or replanted in soil. This activity provides the children an opportunity to observe root growth.

6. Worm Farm

Collect the following materials: large clear jar with a wide mouth, soil, earthworms, gravel, food for worms (lettuce, cornmeal, cereals). Place gravel and soil in the jar. Add the worms. Add food on the top of the dirt and keep the soil moist, but not wet. Tape black construction paper around outside of jar. The paper can be temporarily removed to observe the worms and see their tunnels.

7. Sunflower Seeds

Place a sunflower seed in a damp napkin and place in a Ziploc bag. Hang in a window. After a few days, you will see roots and eventually a sprout. Invite the children to look at the bags daily and observe any changes.

Sensory

1. Place the following items in the sensory table:

- soil
- seeds
- plastic plants
- beans
- measuring cups
- balance scales
- worms

- miniature garden tools
- cut grass or hay

2. Fill and Guess

After showing and discussing several kinds of fruits or vegetables with the children, place the fruits or vegetables in a bag. Individually let children reach in and touch one item. See if they can guess what it is before pulling it out of the bag. Older children may also be able to describe the item.

Social Studies

1. Salad and Soup Party

The children can plan and participate in a salad and soup party for their parents. The groceries will need to be purchased, cleaned, and prepared.

2. Plant Hunt

Go on a hunt to discover how many non-flowering plants, such as algae, fungi, lichens, mosses, and ferns, are found in the school yard. Make a display. How are these plants different from garden plants?

Books

The following books can be used to complement this theme:

Brorstrom, Gay Bishop and Kathy Geotzel. (2000). A Class Trip to Miss Hallberg's Butterfly Garden. Illus. by Kathy Geotzel. Sebastopol, CA: Pipevine Press.

Bunting, Eve. (1994). Flower Garden. Illus. by Kathryn Hewitt. Orlando, FL: Harcourt Brace.

Carle, Eric. (1990). The Tiny Seed. Saxonville, MA: Picture Book Studio.

Cole, Henry. (1995). Jack's Garden. New York: Greenwillow.

Cutler, Jane. (1996). *Mr. Carey's Garden.* Illus. by G. Brian Karas. Boston: Houghton Mifflin.

Delaney, A. (1997). *Pearl's First Prize Plant.* New York: HarperCollins.

Dyjak, Elisabeth. (1995). *Bertha's Garden.* Illus. by Janet Wilkins. Boston: Houghton Mifflin.

Ehlert, Lois. (2003). *Planting a Rainbow.* San Diego: Harcourt. (1st Red Wagon Books edition.)

Florian, Douglas. (1991). *Vegetable Garden.* New York: Harcourt Brace.

Glaser, Linda. (1996). *Compost! Growing Gardens from Your Garbage.* Illus. by Anca Hariton. Brookfield, CT: Millbrook Press.

Godkin, Celia. (1998). *What About Ladybugs?* Boston: Little, Brown. (Pbk.)

Gordon, Elizabeth and M. T. Ross. (2000). *Flower Children: The Little Cousins of the Field and Garden.* Illus. by M. T. Ross. New York: Derrydale Books.

Greenstein, Elaine. (1996). *Mrs. Rose's Garden.* New York: Simon & Schuster.

Hall, Zoe. (1994). *It's Pumpkin Time!* Illus. by Shari Halpern. New York: Scholastic.

Hines, Anna Grossnickle. (1997). *Miss Emma's Wild Garden.* New York: Greenwillow.

Joyce, William. (1996). *The Leaf Men: And the Brave Good Bugs.* New York: HarperCollins.

Lionni, Leo. (1995). *Inch by Inch.* New York: Mulberry Books.

Llewellyn, Claire. (1991). *First Look at Growing Food.* Milwaukee, MN: Gareth Stevens.

Moore, Elaine. (1994). *Grandma's Garden.* Illus. by Dan Andreasen. New York: Lothrop, Lee & Shepard.

Perkins, Lynne Rae. (1995). *Home Lovely.* New York: Greenwillow.

Ryder, Joanne. (1994). *My Father's Hands.* New York: William Morrow.

Rylant, Cynthia. (1993). *Everyday Garden.* New York: Simon & Schuster. (Board book.)

Seabrook, Elizabeth. (1997). *Cabbages and Kings.* Illus. by Jamie Wyeth. New York: Viking.

Shannon, George. (1994). *Seeds.* Illus. by Steve Bjorkman. Boston: Houghton Mifflin.

Shories, Pat. (1996). *Over Under in the Garden: An Alphabet Book.* New York: Farrar, Straus & Giroux.

Stewart, Sarah. (1997). *The Gardener.* Illus. by David Small. New York: Farrar, Straus & Giroux.

Tamar, Erika. (1996). *The Garden of Happiness.* Illus. by Barbara Lambase. Orlando, FL: Harcourt Brace.

Wellington, Monica. (2005). *Zinnia's Flower Garden.* New York: Dutton Children's Books.

Multimedia

The following multimedia products can be used to complement this theme:

"I'm Going to Plant a Garden" on *Science in a Nutshell* [cassette]. Available from Kimbo Educational, Long Branch, NJ.

"In Grandma's Garden." (2006). *We've Got Harmony* [CD]. Available from Kimbo Educational, Long Branch, NJ.

Palmer, Hap. *Walter the Waltzing Worm* [cassette or CD]. Available from Kimbo Educational, Long Branch, NJ.

38

Symbols

jack-o'-lantern
(pumpkin),
witch, ghost,
skeleton,
black cat

Colors

orange
black

Halloween

Activities

trick-or-treating
bobbing for apples
parties
costume parades
making costumes
wearing makeup
safety

Costumes and Masks

goblin
witch
ghost
television character
clown
animal
gypsy
cartoon character
funny people

Theme Goals

Through participating in the experiences provided by this theme, the children may learn

1. Halloween colors
2. Halloween costumes and masks
3. Halloween activities
4. Halloween symbols

Concepts for the Children to Learn

1. Orange and black are Halloween colors.
2. Costumes and masks are worn on Halloween.
3. Some children make their costumes and wear makeup.
4. A costume is clothing put on for pretending.
5. A mask is a covering we put over our face.
6. Sometimes people wear makeup instead of a mask.
7. A pumpkin can be cut to look like a face.
8. Ghosts, goblins, pumpkins, skeletons, black cats, and witches are symbols of Halloween.
9. People go trick-or-treating on Halloween.
10. A costume parade is a march with many children who are dressed in costumes.
11. Bobbing for apples is an activity at Halloween parties.
12. People often dress in costumes, such as goblins, witches, ghosts, or gypsies, on Halloween.
13. Funny people such as clowns are often seen on Halloween.
14. Costumes that are like cartoon, movie, and television characters are often seen on Halloween.

Vocabulary

1. **costume**—clothing worn to pretend.
2. **ghost**—a make-believe being who wears all white.
3. **goblin**—a Halloween character.
4. **Halloween**—a day when children dress in costumes and go trick-or-treating.
5. **jack-o'-lantern**—a pumpkin cut to look like a face.
6. **mask**—face covering worn when pretending.
7. **pretending**—acting like something or someone else.
8. **trick-or-treat**—walking from house to house to ask for candy or treats.
9. **witch**—a make-believe being who wears black.

390

THEME 38

Bulletin Board

The purpose of this bulletin board is to have the children practice visual discrimination, problem-solving, and hand-eye coordination skills. To prepare the bulletin board, construct pumpkins out of orange-colored tagboard. The number prepared will be dependent on the developmental appropriateness for the group of children. An alternative would be to use white tagboard colored orange with paint or markers. Divide the pumpkins into pairs. Draw a different kind of face for each pair of pumpkins. Hang one pumpkin from each pair on the left side of the bulletin board as illustrated. Attach an orange string to each pumpkin. On the right side of the bulletin board, hang the matching pumpkins. See illustration. Attach a pushpin to each of these pumpkins. The child can match the faces on the pumpkins by winding the correct string around the correct pushpin.

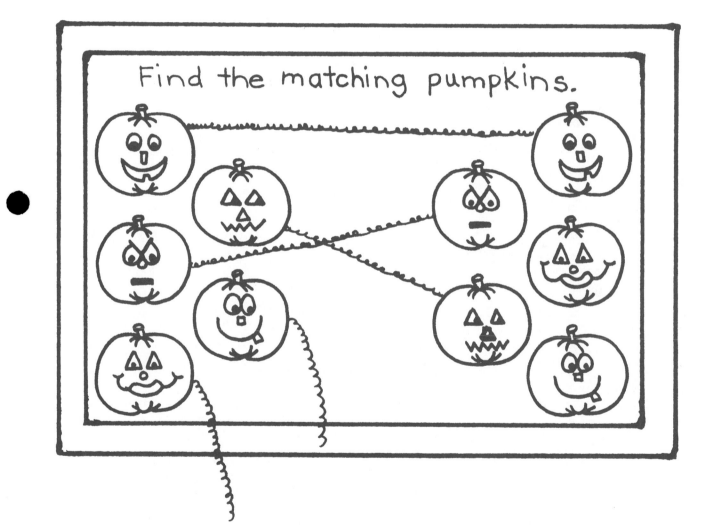

Family Letter

Dear Families,

The month of October has a special holiday for children—Halloween! Therefore, our next theme will center on Halloween. Many learning experiences have been planned to promote an awareness of colors that are associated with Halloween, as well as symbols that represent Halloween such as costumes, pumpkins, black cats, bats, and witches. Perhaps not all children and families in our program celebrate this holiday, but we feel it is very important for children to learn about and respect others' beliefs. A general understanding of other cultures is also interesting and fun. However, if you wish that your child not participate in this theme, please let us know.

AT SCHOOL

Some of the Halloween activities planned include:

- discussing Halloween safety procedures, especially while trick-or-treating
- carving a jack-o'-lantern for the classroom
- roasting pumpkin seeds and baking a pumpkin pie
- trying on a variety of costumes in the dramatic play area
- creating designs with pumpkin seeds and glue on paper

HALLOWEEN PARTY!

We will be having a Halloween party on Friday. You are welcome to send a costume to school with your child that day. The costume can be simple. A funny hat, a pair of silly glasses, a wig, or a little makeup would be fine Halloween attire. We would appreciate it if you could send the costume and accessories in a bag that is labeled with your child's name. This will prevent a mix-up of belongings. We will dress in our costumes at about 2:00 p.m. Then we will have a small party and parade around in our costumes. It should be a fun day. Join us!

AT HOME

To get into the spirit of Halloween and to help your child develop language skills, practice the following Halloween rhyme:

"Five Little Pumpkins"

Five little pumpkins sitting on a gate.
The first one said, "Oh my, it's getting late."
The second one said, "There are witches in the air."
The third one said, "But we don't care."
The fourth one said, "Let's run. Let's run."
The fifth one said, "It's Halloween fun!"
"Wooooooooo," went the wind,
And out went the lights.
And the five little pumpkins rolled out of sight.

To ensure a safe Halloween:

- Check to see if your child's costume is flame resistant or at least flame retardant.
- Children can easily trip in long garments. Be sure the hemline is several inches off the ground.
- Masks and hoods can slip and make it difficult for your child to see. If a mask is worn, be sure it is secure and that the holes for the eyes are properly positioned. An alternative to wearing a mask is to use makeup.
- Finally, check the batteries in the flashlight!

Have a safe and happy Halloween.

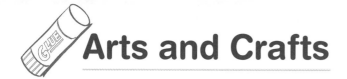

Arts and Crafts

1. Spooky Easel

Provide orange and black paint at the paint easels.

2. Pumpkin Seed Pictures

Dye pumpkin seeds many colors. Place the seeds with paste and paper on a table in the art area. The children then can create their own pictures.

3. Crayon Wash

On the art table, place paper, light-colored crayons, tempera paint, and brushes. The children can draw on paper with light-colored crayons. After this, they can paint over the entire picture.

4. Masks

Yarn, paper plates, felt-tip markers, and any other accessories needed to make interesting masks can be placed on a table in the art area. If desired, yarn can be used as hair on the mask.

Cooking

Masks and pumpkins are symbols of Halloween.

1. Pumpkin Pie

1 unbaked pie shell
2 cups (16–17 ounces) pumpkin
1 can sweetened condensed milk
1 egg
1/2 teaspoon salt
2 teaspoons pumpkin pie spice

Blend all of the ingredients in a large mixing bowl. Pour the mixture into the pie shell. Bake the pie in an oven preheated to 375 degrees for 50 to 55 minutes or until a sharp knife blade inserted near center of pie is clean when removed. Cool and refrigerate the pie for 1 hour before serving. Top with whipped cream if desired.

2. Pumpkin Patch Muffins

3 cups flour
1 cup sugar

4 teaspoons baking powder
1 teaspoon salt
1 teaspoon pumpkin pie spice
1 cup milk
1 cup canned pumpkin
1/2 cup (1 stick) butter or margarine, melted
2 eggs, beaten

Sift the flour, sugar, baking powder, salt, and pumpkin pie spice into a large mixing bowl. Add the milk, pumpkin, melted butter, and eggs. Mix with a wooden spoon just until flour is moist. (Batter will be lumpy.) Place paper liners in the muffin tins and fill 2/3 full with batter. Bake in a preheated 400-degree oven 20 minutes or until muffins are golden. Cool in muffin tins 10 minutes on a wire rack. Remove muffins from muffin tins and finish cooling on wire racks. Pile into serving baskets and serve warm for snack.

3. Witches' Brew

5 cups cranberry juice
5 cups apple cider
1 or 2 cinnamon sticks
1/4 teaspoon ground nutmeg

Place ingredients in a large saucepan. Cover, heat, and simmer for 10 minutes. Serve warm.

4. Roasted Pumpkin Seeds

Soak pumpkin seeds for 24 hours in saltwater (1/4 cup salt to 1 cup water). Spread on cloth-covered cookie sheet and roast at 100 degrees for 2 hours. Turn oven off and leave seeds overnight.

5. Non-bake Pumpkin Pie

1 can prepared pumpkin pie filling
1 package vanilla instant pudding
1 cup milk

Mix and pour into baked pie shell or graham cracker pie shell.

Dramatic Play

Costumes

Add Halloween costumes to the dramatic play area. (Some teachers purchase these at thrift stores or sales. From year to year they are stored in a Halloween prop box.)

Field Trips/ Resource People

1. Pumpkin Patch

Visit a pumpkin patch. During the tour, point out various-sized pumpkins. Discuss how the pumpkins grow, as well as their shapes, sizes, etc.

2. Halloween Safety

A police officer can be invited to talk with the children about Halloween safety.

Fingerplays

Jack-O'-Lantern

I am a pumpkin, big and round.
  (show size with arms)
Once upon a time, I grew on the ground.
  (point to ground)
Now I have a mouth, two eyes, and a nose.
  (point to each)
What are they for, do you suppose?
  (point to forehead and "think")
Why—I'll be a jack-o'-lantern on Halloween night.

Five Little Witches

Five little witches standing by the door.
  (hold up five fingers)
One flew out and then there were four.
  (flying motion with hand)
Four little witches standing by a tree.
  (four fingers)
One went to pick a pumpkin and then there were three.
  (picking motion, then three fingers)
Three little witches stirring their brew.
  (stir)
One fell in and then there were two.
  (two fingers)
Two little witches went for a run.
  (run with fingers)
One got lost and then there was one.
  (one finger)
One little witch, yes, only one.
  (one finger)
She cast a spell and now there are none.
  (make motions as if to cast spell and then put hands in lap)

Halloween Fun

Goblins and witches in high pointed hats,
  (hands above head to form hat)
Riding on broomsticks and chasing black cats.
  (ride broomstick)
Children in costumes might well give a fright.
  (look frightened)
Get things in order for Halloween night.
We like our treats
  (nod head)
And we'll play no mean pranks.
  (shake head)
We'll do you no harm and we'll only say, "Thanks!"

The Jack-O'-Lantern

Three little pumpkins growing on a vine.
  (three fingers)
Sitting in the sunlight, looking just fine.
  (arms up like sun)
Along came a ghost who picked just one
  (one finger)
To take on home for some Halloween fun.
  (smile)
He gave him two eyes to see where he goes.
  (paint two eyes)
He gave him a mouth and a big handsome nose.
  (point to mouth and nose)
Then he put a candle in.
  (pretend to put in candle)
Now see how he glows.
  (wiggle fingers from center of body out until arms are extended)

I've a Jack-O'-Lantern

I've a jack-o'-lantern
  (make a ball with open fist, thumb at top)
With a great big grin.
  (grin)
I've got a jack-o'-lantern
With a candle in.
  (insert other index finger up through bottom of first)

Halloween Witches

One little, two little, three little witches,
  (hold up one hand, nod fingers at each count)
Fly over the haystacks
  (fly hand in up-and-down motion)
Fly over ditches
Slide down moonbeams without any hitches
  (glide hand downward)
Heigh-ho! Halloween's here!

The Friendly Ghost

I'm a friendly ghost—almost!
  (point to self)
And I chase you, too!
  (point to child)
I'll just cover me with a sheet
  (pretend to cover self ending with hands covering face)
And then call "scat" to you.
  (uncover face quickly and call out "scat")

Witches' Cat

I am the witches' cat.
  (make a fist with two fingers extended for cat)
Meoow. Meoow.
  (stroke fist with other hand)
My fur is black as darkest night.

(continued)

Decorating a Pumpkin

While carving or decorating a pumpkin with the children, you can discuss:

- the physical properties of pumpkins—color, texture, size, shape (both outside and inside).

- food category to which pumpkins belong.

- what other forms pumpkins can be made into after the shell is scooped out.

- where pumpkins grow (plant some of the seeds).

- what size and shape to make the features of the pumpkin, including eyes, nose, and mouth, and what kind of expression to make.

Accessories:

1 bunch parsley (hair)
1 carrot (nose)
2 string beans (eyebrows)
2 radishes (eyes)
1 green pepper (ears)
1 stalk celery (teeth)
1 large pumpkin (head)

Prepare the pumpkin in the usual manner; that is, cut off the cap and scoop out the seeds inside. Save the seeds for roasting. If desired, individual vegetable pieces may be attached by carving or inserting toothpicks.

My eyes are glaring green and bright.
   (circle eyes with thumb and forefingers)
I am the witches' cat.
   (make a fist again with two fingers extended
   and stroke fist with other hand)

My Pumpkin

See my pumpkin round and fat.
   (make circle with hands, fingers spread wide,
   touching)
See my pumpkin yellow.
   (make a smaller circle)
Watch him grin on Halloween.
   (point to mouth, which is grinning wide)
He is a very funny fellow.

Group Time

(Games, Language)

1. **Thank-you Note**

   Write a thank-you note to any resource person.
   Encourage all of the children to participate by
   sharing what they liked or saw.

2. **Costume Parade**

   On Halloween day, the children can dress up
   in costumes and march around the room and
   throughout the school to music. If available, a
   walk to a local nursing home may be enjoyed
   by the children as well as the elderly.

Large Muscle

Ghost, Ghost, Witch

This game is played like Duck, Duck, Goose.
Form a circle and kneel. Choose one child to be
"it" and to walk around the outside of the circle
chanting, "Ghost, ghost, ghost." When the child
taps another child and says "witch," the tapped
child chases the initiator around the circle,
attempting to tag "it." If the child who is "it"
returns to the empty child's spot before being
tagged, he can sit in the circle. If not, the child

continues walking around the circle, repeating
the same procedure.

Math

1. **Counting Pumpkin Seeds**

   Cut circles from construction paper. The number
   needed will depend on the developmental level
   of the children. Write a numeral on each paper
   circle and place each into a pie tin. The children
   may count enough pumpkin seeds into each tin
   to match the numeral on the circle.

2. **Weighing Pumpkin Seeds**

   In the math area, place a scale and pumpkin
   seeds. The children may elect to experiment by
   balancing the scale with the pumpkin seeds.

Music

1. **"Flying Witches"**
   (*Sing to the tune of* "*When the Saints Come Marching In*")

   Oh, when the witches
   Come flying by.
   Oh, when the witches come flying by,
   It will be Halloween night,
   When the witches come flying by.

2. **"One Little, Two Little,
   Three Little Pumpkins"**
   (*Sing to the tune of* "*One Little, Two Little, Three Little
   Indians*")

   One little, two little, three little pumpkins,
   Four little, five little, six little pumpkins,
   Seven little, eight little, nine little pumpkins,
   Ready for Halloween night!

3. **"Have You Made a Jack-O'-Lantern?"**
   (*Sing to the tune of* "*Muffin Man*")

   Have you made a jack-o'-lantern,
   A jack-o'-lantern, a jack-o'-lantern?
   Have you made a jack-o'-lantern
   For Halloween night?

Science

1. Carve Pumpkins

Purchase several pumpkins. Carve them and save the seeds for roasting. An alternative activity would be to use a black felt-tip marker to draw facial features on the pumpkin. Pumpkins can also have added accessories. For example, a large carrot can be used for a nose, parsley for hair, cut green peppers for ears, radishes for eyes, and a small green onion can be placed in a cut mouth for teeth.

2. Roasting Pumpkin Seeds

Wash and dry pumpkin seeds. Then spread the seeds out on a cookie sheet to dry. Bake the seeds in a preheated oven at 350 degrees until brown. Salt, cool, and eat at snack time.

3. Plant Pumpkin Seeds

Purchase a packet of pumpkin seeds. Plant the pumpkin seeds in small paper cups. Set the paper cups with the pumpkin seeds in a sunny place. Water as needed. Observe daily to see if there is growth.

Sensory

1. Measuring Seeds

Pumpkin seeds and measuring cups can be added to the sensory table. The children will enjoy feeling and pouring seeds.

2. Goop

Add dry cornstarch to the sensory table. Slowly add enough water to make it a "goopy" consistency. If desired, add coloring to make it black or orange.

Books

The following books can be used to complement this theme:

Andrews, Sylvia. (1995). *Rattlebone Rock*. Illus. by Jennifer Plecas. New York: HarperCollins.

Capucilli, Alyssa Satin and Pat Schories. (1999). *Happy Halloween, Biscuit!* Illus. by Pat Schories. New York: HarperFestival.

Carlstrom, Nancy White. (1995). *Who Said Boo? Halloween Poems for the Very Young*. Illus. by R. W. Alley. New York: Simon & Schuster.

Caseley, Judith. (1996). *Witch Mama*. New York: Greenwillow.

Dillon, Jana. (1992). *Jeb Scarecrow's Pumpkin Patch*. Boston: Houghton Mifflin.

Enderle, Judith Ross. (1992). *Six Creepy Sheep*. Illus. by John O'Brien. Honesdale, PA: Boyds Mills Press.

Fleming, Denise. (2001). *Pumpkin Eve*. New York: Holt.

Gibbons, Gail. (1999). *The Pumpkin Book*. New York: Holiday House.

Gordon, Lynn and Karen Johnson. (2000). *52 Tricks and Treats for Halloween*. Illus. by Karen Johnson. New York: Chronicle Books.

Hall, Zoe. (1994). *It's Pumpkin Time!* Illus. by Shari Halpern. New York: Scholastic.

Heinz, Brian J. (1996). *The Monsters' Test*. Illus. by Sal Murdocca. Brookfield, CT: Millbrook Press.

Johnston, Tony. (1990). *The Soup Bone*. Illus. by Margot Tomes. Orlando, FL: Harcourt Brace.

Johnston, Tony. (1995). *Very Scary*. Illus. by Douglas Florian. Orlando, FL: Harcourt Brace.

Joyce, William. (2001). *Rolie Polie Olie Stick or Treat: A Sticker Story Book*. Seattle, WA: Disney Press.

Lachner, Dorothea. (1997). *Meredith: The Witch Who Wasn't*. Illus. by Christa Unzner. New York: North South Books.

Levine, Abby. (1997). *This Is the Pumpkin*. Niles, IL: Albert Whitman.

Martin, Bill. (1993). *Old Devil Wind*. Illus. by Barry Root. Orlando, FL: Harcourt Brace.

McCann, Jesse Leon. (1999). *Scooby-Doo and the Halloween Hotel Haunt: A Glow in the Dark Mystery*. New York: Scholastic.

Meddaugh, Susan. (1994). *Witches Supermarket*. Madison, WI: Demco Media.

Meddaugh, Susan. (2005). *The Witch's Walking Stick*. Boston, MA: Houghton Mifflin Co.

Moler, Robert E. (2000). *If I Were a Halloween Monster: a Mirror-Mask Book with Pop-Up Surprises!* Boston: Little, Brown.

Nikola-Lisa, W. (1997). *Shake Dem Halloween Bones*. Boston: Houghton Mifflin.

Pilkey, Dav. (1995). *Hallo-Wiener*. New York: Scholastic.

Roberts, Bethany. (1995). *Halloween Mice!* Illus. by Doug Cushman. New York: Clarion Books.

Shaw, Nancy. (1997). *Sheep Trick or Treat*. Boston: Houghton Mifflin.

Sierra, Judy. (1995). *The House That Drac Built*. Illus. by Will Hillenbrand. Orlando, FL: Harcourt Brace.

Silverman, Erica. (1992). *Big Pumpkin*. Illus. by S. D. Schindler. New York: Macmillan.

Stock, Catherine. (1990). *Halloween Monster*. New York: Simon & Schuster.

Stutson, Caroline. (1993). *By the Light of the Halloween Moon*. Illus. by Kevin Hawkes. New York: Lothrop, Lee & Shepard.

Van Rynbach, Iris. (1995). *Five Little Pumpkins*. Honesdale, PA: Boyds Mills Press.

Wolff, Ferida. (1994). *On Halloween Night*. Illus. by Dolores Avendano. New York: Tambourine Books.

Multimedia

The following multimedia products can be used to complement this theme:

Gold, Andrew. *Andrew Gold's Halloween Howls* [compact disc]. (1996). Redway, CA: Music for Little People.

Halloween [video]. (1993). Niles, IL: United Learning.

Holidays for Children: Halloween [video]. Schlessinger Media.

Lavender, Cheryl. *Moans, Groans and Skeleton Bones* [compact disc]. (1993). Milwaukee, WI: Hal Leonard.

Palmer, Hap. "Have a Good Halloween Night" on *Holiday Songs and Rhythms* [compact disc]. (1997). Freeport, NY: Educational Activities.

Skiera-Zucek, Lois. *Halloween Fun* [cassette]. (1989). Long Branch, NJ: Kimbo Educational.

Recordings and Song Titles

The following recordings can be used to complement this theme:

"Halloween Song," "Halloween Is Here," "Pumpkin Song." (1998). *Holiday Piggyback Songs*. Long Branch, NJ: Kimbo Educational.

Halloween Fun. (1989). Long Branch, NJ: Kimbo Educational.

"Monster Mash." (2001). *Dance Party Fun*. Long Branch, NJ: Kimbo Educational.

"Ten Little Goblins." (1985). *Toddlers on Parade*. Long Branch, NJ: Kimbo Educational.

"Ten Little Pumpkins." (1988). *Preschool Action Time*. Long Branch, NJ: Kimbo Educational.

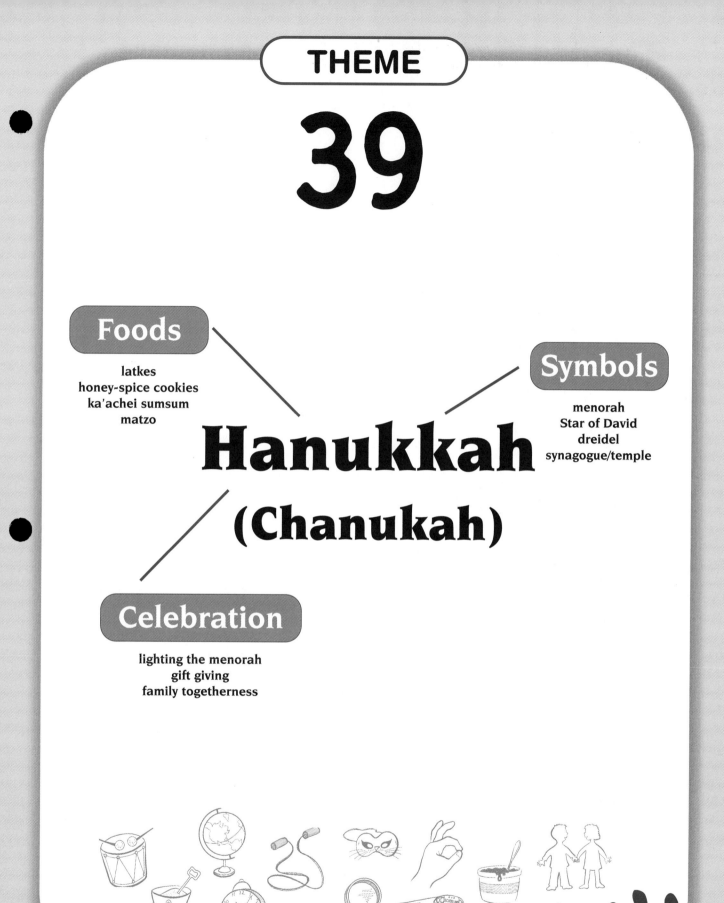

Foods

latkes
honey-spice cookies
ka'achei sumsum
matzo

Symbols

menorah
Star of David
dreidel
synagogue/temple

Hanukkah
(Chanukah)

Celebration

lighting the menorah
gift giving
family togetherness

Theme Goals

Through participating in the experiences provided by this theme, the children may learn

1. Foods eaten during Hanukkah
2. Symbols of Hanukkah
3. Hanukkah celebrations

Concepts for the Children to Learn

1. Hanukkah is a Jewish holiday celebrated for eight days.
2. Families celebrate together during Hanukkah.
3. Families attend their synagogue or temple during Hanukkah.
4. Hanukkah is a time for giving and sharing with others.
5. The menorah and the dreidel are symbols of Hanukkah.
6. Some foods eaten during Hanukkah include latkes, honey-spice cookies, ka'achei sumsum, and matzo.

Vocabulary

1. **dreidel**—four-sided toy that spins like a top.
2. **Hanukkah**—eight-day Jewish festival of lights. A celebration of the Jewish people's fight long ago to keep the right to practice their religion. One candle on the menorah is lighted each day.
3. **latkes**—potato pancakes eaten during Hanukkah.
4. **menorah**—eight-branched candlestick. The middle or ninth candle is taller than the other eight and is called the shammash.
5. **Star of David**—a six-pointed star that is a Jewish symbol.

Bulletin Board

The purpose of this bulletin board is to develop an awareness of the passage of time as well as the math concept of sets. This bulletin board starts out with the base of the menorah. Each day of Hanukkah the children work together to construct a candle and a flame to add to the menorah. Candles and flames are most interesting when made using a wide variety of mediums: sequins, feathers, cut construction paper, yarn, etc.

The festival of lights.

Family Letter

Dear Family,

For the next eight days, we will be celebrating Hanukkah. Hanukkah commemorates the victory of the Jews over the Syrians. Hanukkah, also known as the Festival of Lights, is celebrated for eight days in either November or December. In 175 B.C. a Syrian King, Antiochus, ordered the Jewish Temple defiled. After the Syrians desecrated the Temple, Judah Maccabee formed a small but powerful army to defend the Jews. The Maccabees rebuilt the Temple and the legend states that when it was time to light the Temple lamp for rededication, there was only enough sacred oil to burn for one day. Miraculously, it burned for eight days!

Hanukkah is celebrated by the lighting of a special candelabra called a menorah. On the menorah there is one holder for each of the eight nights and one for the shammash. Shammash means "helper" in Hebrew; this is the candle that is used to light the others. The candles are lit beginning on the right side and moving to the left.

Each night, after the lighting of the menorah, the children are given small gifts. Traditionally this gift was "gelt": money to be used while playing the dreidel game.

Unlike most Jewish holidays, work and schooling continues during the eight-day celebration. Perhaps not all children and families in our program celebrate this holiday, but we feel it is very important for children to learn about and respect others' beliefs. A general understanding of other cultures is also interesting and fun. However, if you wish that your child not participate in this theme, please let us know.

AT SCHOOL

Some of the learning experiences the children will participate in include:

- playing a game with a dreidel, which is similar to a toy top
- preparing latkes (potato pancakes) for snack
- creating wax-resist drawings at the art table

Happy Hanukkah!

Learning about Hanukkah and other religious holidays is an important social studies activity.

 **Arts and Crafts**

1. Star of David

Provide the children with triangles cut from blue construction paper. Demonstrate to the children how to invert one triangle over the other to form a star. The stars may be glued to construction paper.

2. Potato Art

Slice potatoes in half. The children may dip the potato halves in shallow pans containing various colors of tempera paint and then create designs on construction paper.

3. Hanukkah Handprints

Provide the children with construction paper, brushes, and tempera paint in shallow pans. Paint each of the children's hands with a brush that has been dipped in tempera paint. The children then may place their hands on the construction paper, creating handprints.

4. Dreidel

Collect and wash out 1/2-pint milk containers. Tape the top down so that the carton forms a square. Provide construction paper squares for the children to paste to the sides of the milk carton. The children may decorate with crayons or felt-tip markers. Upon completion, punch an unsharpened pencil through the milk container so that the children may spin it like a top.

 **Cooking**

1. Latkes

6 medium-sized potatoes washed, pared, and grated
1 egg
3 tablespoons flour
1/2 teaspoon baking powder

In a large bowl, mix the egg and the grated potatoes. Add the flour and baking powder. Drop by spoonfuls into hot cooking oil in a frying pan. Brown on both sides. Drain on paper towel. Latkes may be served with a spoonful of applesauce or sour cream.

2. Hanukkah Honey and Spice Cookies

1/2 cup (1 stick) margarine, softened
1/2 cup firmly packed dark brown sugar
1/2 cup honey
1 egg
2 1/2 cups unsifted flour
2 teaspoons ground ginger
1 teaspoon baking soda
1 teaspoon ground cinnamon
1 teaspoon ground nutmeg
1/2 teaspoon salt
1/4 teaspoon ground cloves

In a large mixing bowl, cream margarine and sugar. Beat in honey and egg until well combined. In a small bowl, combine flour, ginger, baking soda, cinnamon, nutmeg, salt, and cloves. Add to honey mixture. Beat on low speed until well blended. Cover dough and chill at least 1 hour or up to 3 days. Heat oven to 350 degrees. Grease cookie sheets. Set aside. Working quickly with 1/4 of the dough at a time, roll out on floured surface to 1/4-inch thickness. Cut into desired shapes, including a dreidel, menorah, or star. Using a spatula, place cookies on prepared cookie sheets 1 inch apart. Reroll scraps. Bake for 7 minutes. Transfer to wire racks to cool. Makes about 4 dozen cookies.

3. Ka'achei Sumsum—Bagel Cookies

4 cups flour
1 cup margarine
1 teaspoon salt
3 tablespoons cake-form yeast
1 egg
1 cup lukewarm water
1/4 teaspoon sugar

Place yeast and sugar in a bowl. Pour over lukewarm water. Put in a warm place for 10 minutes or until yeast rises. Prepare a dough from the flour, margarine, salt, and dissolved yeast mixture. Cover dough with a towel, put in a warm place for

2 hours. When dough rises, take small pieces and roll into strips about 4 inches long. Join the ends to form a bagel. Brush each one with beaten egg and place on a greased baking sheet. Bake in a 350-degree oven for 20 to 30 minutes.

Note: From Nahoum, Aldo (Ed.), (1970), *The Art of Israeli Cooking*, New York: Holt, Rinehart and Winston.

4. K'naidlach Soup

3 eggs
3 1/2 cups matzo meal
1/2 chicken bouillon cube
1 teaspoon celery leaves, chopped
nutmeg
juice of 1/2 lemon
salt
pepper

Beat eggs well. Add bouillon cube, salt, pepper, and a pinch of nutmeg. Add lemon juice and celery leaves. Continue to beat. Slowly add matzo meal, using a wooden spoon to stir. When matzo meal thickens, knead by hand. After matzo meal has been thoroughly kneaded, form small balls (1 inch). Arrange in a deep dish and leave in refrigerator for at least 3 hours. Prepare a clear chicken soup and when it reaches boiling, drop in matzo balls. Let cook for 10 to 12 minutes. Serve 3 to 4 balls per bowl of soup. Add lemon juice to taste.

Note: From Nahoum, Aldo (Ed.), (1970), *The Art of Israeli Cooking*, New York: Holt, Rinehart and Winston.

Dramatic Play

1. Family Celebration

Collect materials for a special family meal. These may include dresses, hats, coats, plates, cups, plastic food, napkins, etc. The children can have a holiday meal.

2. Gift Wrapping Center

Collect various-sized boxes, wrapping paper, tape, and ribbon. The children can wrap presents for Hanukkah.

Fingerplays

The Menorah Candle

I'm a menorah candle
    (stand, point at self)
Growing shorter you can see
    (bend down slowly)
Melting all my wax
    (go down more)
Until there's nothing left to see.
    (sit down)

Hanukkah Lights

One light, two lights, three lights, and four
    (hold up four fingers, one at a time)
Five lights, six lights, and three more,
    (hold up five fingers on other hand)
Twinkle, twinkle nine pretty lights,
    (move fingers)
In a golden menorah bright!
    (make cup with palm of hand)

My Dreidel

I have a little dreidel.
    (cup hands to form a square)
I made it out of clay.
    (move fingers in a molding motion)
And when it's dry and ready
    (flatten hands as if to hold in hand—palm up,
    pinkies together)
Then with it I will play.
    (pretend to spin dreidel on the floor)

Group Time

(Games, Language)

1. Hot Potato

Ask the children to sit in a circle. Provide one child with a real potato, a plastic potato, or a potato constructed from tagboard. Play music. As the music is playing, the children pass the potato around the circle until the music stops. The one holding the potato is out of the circle. The game continues until one child is left or the children no longer wish to play.

2. Dreidel Game

Each player starts with 10 to 15 pennies, nuts, or raisins. Each player places an object in the center of the circle. The dreidel is spun by one of the players, while the following verse is chanted:

I have a little dreidel.
I made it out of clay.
And when it's dry and ready.
Then with it I will play.

Whether the spinning player wins or loses depends on which side of the dreidel lands upward when it falls. The following may be used as a guide:

Nun (N) means nothing: player receives nothing
    from the pot.
Gimmel (G) means all: player receives everything
    from the pot.
Hay (H) means half: player takes 1/2 of the pot.
Shin (S) means put in: player adds two objects
    to the pot.

When one player has won all of the objects, the game is completed.

3. Gelt Hunt

Make a silver coin by cutting out a 4-inch round piece of cardboard and covering it with aluminum foil. Hide the coin (gelt) in the classroom and play a hide-and-seek game. For younger children hide the gelt in an obvious place.

    (Gelt is the Yiddish word for money. Traditionally, small amounts of gelt are given to children each night of Hanukkah.)

Large Muscle

1. Dreidel Dance

The children can dance the dreidel dance by standing in a circle and spinning as they sing this song to the tune of "Row, Row, Row Your Boat."

Dreidel, dreidel, dreidel,
A-spinning I will go.
Speed it up and slow it down,
And on the ground I'll go!

2. Frying Donuts—Dramatic Play

Children can act out frying donuts as they sing this song to the tune of "I Have a Little Turtle."

I have a little donut,
It is so nice and light,
And when it's all done cooking,
I'm going to take a bite!

Frying donuts usually pop up and out of the frying oil when they are finished cooking. The children can act out these motions. The oil used in frying the donuts is significant in the Hanukkah celebration. It signifies the oil burned in the Temple lamp.

Math

1. Sort the Stars

Provide children with various-colored stars. The children can match the colors. A variation would be to have stars of various sizes. The children could sequence the stars from largest to smallest.

2. Hanukkah Puzzles

Mount pictures of a menorah and the Star of David on tagboard. Cut into pieces. Laminate. The number of pieces will depend on the children's developmental age.

3. Candle Holder and Candle Match

Have a variety of candle holders set out with candles. The children will have to match the candles to the correct-sized candle holder.

Music

"Menorah Candles"

(*Sing to the tune of* "*Twinkle, Twinkle, Little Star*")

Twinkle, twinkle candles in the night,
Standing on the menorah bright,
Burning slow we all know,
Burning bright to give us light.

Twinkle, twinkle candles in the night,
Standing on the menorah bright.

Resource People

Invite a rabbi or parent of the Jewish faith to come and talk about Hanukkah and how it is celebrated.

Science

1. Potato Sprouts

Provide each child with a clear plastic cup. Fill the plastic cup half-full with water. Place a potato part-way in the water supported by toothpicks to keep it from dropping into the jar. Put the end with tubers into the water. The other end should stick out of the water. Refill with fresh water as it evaporates and watch the roots begin to grow and leaves start to sprout.

2. Light

Light a flashlight. Discuss other sources of light. (Examples: sun, lamp, candle, traffic lights, etc.)

3. Sunlight Power

Fill two glasses half-full of warm water. Stir some flour into one glass. In the other, dissolve a little yeast in the water, then add flour. Now set them both in a warm place for an hour and watch the results.

Sensory

Sand Temples

Fill the sensory table with sand and moisten until the sand is wet enough to form shapes. The children may pack sand into cans to mold into desired shapes and build sand temples from the molded forms.

Social Studies

1. Menorah

Glue eight wooden or styrofoam spools of equal size to a piece of wood, leaving a space in the middle. Glue a larger spool in the middle, thus making four smaller spools on each side. Spray with gold or silver paint. The menorah can be lit during the eight days of Hanukkah during group time. Explain the meaning of the menorah to the group as well.

2. Hanukkah Celebration

Display pictures at the children's eye level of the Hanukkah celebration. Examples would include such pictures as lighting the menorah, a family meal, etc.

3. Human Menorah

The children can make a human menorah by positioning themselves to resemble a menorah. A menorah is a lamp with nine flames that is used to celebrate Hanukkah. Two children can lie head-to-toe on the floor to form the base. Have nine children stand behind the base to form the candles. The tallest child can stand in the middle and be the shammash. The shammash is the center candle that lights the other candles. The children can make pretend flames out of construction paper for the candles to hold as if they were lit.

Books

The following books can be used to complement this theme:

Adler, David A. (1995). *One Yellow Daffodil: A Hanukkah Story*. Illus. by Lloyd Bloom. San Diego, CA: Gulliver Books.

Adler, David A. (1997). *Chanukah in Chelm*. Illus. by Kevin O'Malley. New York: Lothrop, Lee & Shepard.

Conway, Diana Cohen. (1994). *Northern Lights: A Hanukkah Story*. Rockville, MD: Kar-Ben Copies.

Jaffe, Nina. (1992). *In the Month of Kislev: A Story for Hanukkah*. Illus. by Louise August. New York: Viking.

Kimmel, Eric A. (1996). *The Magic Dreidels: A Hanukkah Story*. Illus. by Katya Krenina. New York: Holiday House.

Kuskin, Karla. (1995). *A Great Miracle Happened There: A Chanukah Story*. Madison, WI: Demco Media.

Nahoum, Aldo, ed. (1970). *The Art of Israeli Cooking*. New York: Holt, Rinehart and Winston.

Oberman, Sheldon. (1997). *By the Hanukkah Light*. Illus. by Neil Waldman. Honesdale, PA: Boyds Mills Press.

Penn, Malka. (1994). *The Miracle of the Potato Latkes: A Hanukkah Story*. Illus. by Giora Carmi. New York: Holiday House.

Polacco, Patricia. (1996). *Trees of the Dancing Goats*. New York: Simon & Schuster.

Rosen, Michael J. (1992). *Elijah's Angel: A Story for Chanukah and Christmas*. Illus. by Aminah B. L. Robinson. Orlando, FL: Harcourt Brace.

Schnur, Steven. (1995). *The Tie Man's Miracle: A Chanukah Story*. Illus. by Stephen Johnson. New York: William Morrow.

Schotter, Roni. (1993). *Hanukkah!* Illus. by Marylin Hafner. Madison, WI: Demco Media.

Schwartz, Linda and Beverly Armstrong. (1998). *The Hanukkah Happenings*. Illus. by Beverly Armstrong. Santa Barbara, CA: Learning Works.

Smith, Dian G. (2001). *Hanukkah Lights*. Illus. by JoAnn Kitchel. San Francisco, CA: Chronicle Books.

Wax, Wendy, ed. (1993). *Hanukkah, Oh Hanukkah!: A Treasury of Stories, Songs, and Games to Share*. Illus. by John Speirs. New York: Bantam Doubleday.

Multimedia

The following multimedia products can be used to complement this theme:

Chanukah at Home [cassette]. (1988). Cambridge, MA: Rounder Records.

Holidays for Children: Hanukkah/Passover [video]. Schlessinger Media.

Lewis, Shari. *Lamb Chop's Special Chanukah!* [video]. (1995). Cypress, CA: Youngheart Music.

Palmer, Hap. "Hanukkah" on *Holiday Songs and Rhythms* [compact disc]. (1997). Baldwin, NY: Educational Activities.

Rosenthal, Margie. *Just in Time for Chanukah!* [compact disc]. (1987). Portland, OR: Sheera Recordings.

Recordings and Song Titles

The following recordings can be used to complement this theme:

"Dreidel, Dreidel, Dreidel." (2001). *Seasonal Songs in Motion.* Long Branch, NJ: Kimbo Educational.

"Hanukkah, Hanukkah," "Hanukkah Menorah," "Dreidel Song," "The Latkes Are Frying in the Pan." (1998). *Holiday Piggyback Songs.* Long Branch, NJ: Kimbo Educational.

"Hanukkah, Oh Hanukkah," "Dreidel," "How Many Candles?" (2001). *Sing 'N Sign Holiday Time (Gaia).* Long Branch, NJ: Kimbo Educational.

"The Dreidel Song." (1991). *Children of the World.* Long Branch, NJ: Kimbo Educational.

40

Parts

crown
brim

Materials

felt, plastic,
canvas, wool,
fur, yarn,
leather,
straw

Hats

Sizes

small
medium
large

Uses

ceremonial
occupational
protection
identification
decoration
religious
fraternal

Types

baseball hat,
top hat,
hard hat,
bonnet,
stocking cap,
ski hat,
cowboy hat,
sombrero,
helmet,
hood, derby,
graduation,
birthday,
yarmulka,
headdress,
veil, turban

Colors

red
blue
yellow
green
white
brown
purple
black
pink

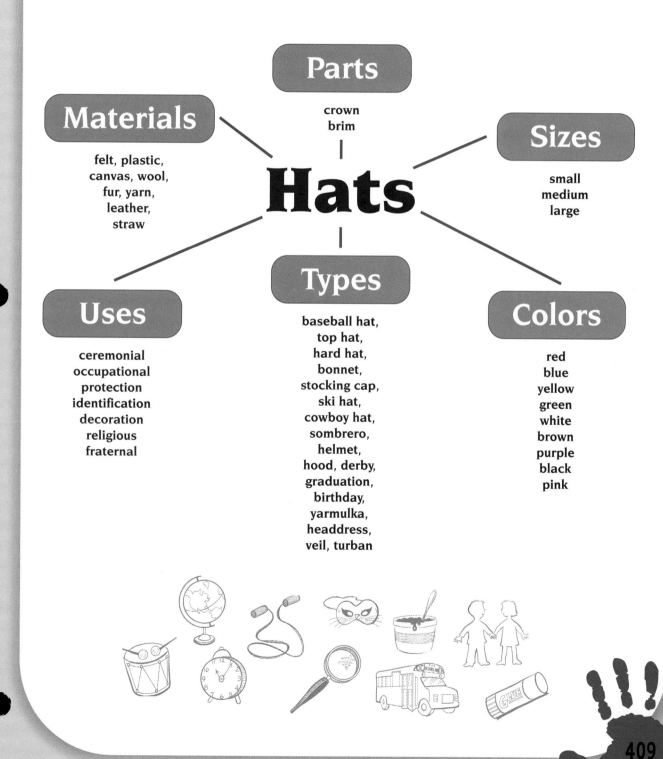

409

Theme Goals

Through participating in the experiences provided by this theme, the children may learn

1. Types of hats
2. Uses for hats
3. Materials used to make hats
4. Parts of a hat
5. Colors of hats
6. Sizes of hats

Concepts for the Children to Learn

1. Hats are coverings worn on our heads for protection, warmth, and identification.
2. Stocking and ski hats keep us warm.
3. Felt, plastic, wool, fur, straw, leather, cloth, and yarn are all materials used to make hats.
4. Hats come in many different sizes.
5. Hats come in different colors.
6. Hats can be red, blue, green, yellow, pink, brown, purple, or black.
7. Some hats have special names.
8. Some hats can keep us cool.
9. Hats can be worn for fun.
10. Some people wear hats when they are working.
11. Most hats have a crown and a brim.
12. Baseball hats can be worn for decoration and protection.
13. Motorcyclists and people who ride bicycles should wear helmets for protection.
14. Construction workers and firefighters should wear hard hats for protection.
15. Police officers, conductors, and airplane pilots wear hats for identification.
16. Brides often wear a headdress or veil at a wedding ceremony.
17. Cowboys wear cowboy hats for protection from the sun.
18. Bonnets can be worn for decoration.

Vocabulary

1. **brim**—the part of a hat that surrounds the crown.
2. **crown**—top part of the hat.
3. **hat**—a covering for the head.

Bulletin Board

The purpose of this bulletin board is to have the children match the colored pieces to their corresponding shadow, thereby promoting the development of visual discrimination, hand-eye coordination, and problem-solving skills. To construct the bulletin board, draw different types of hats on white tagboard. Color the hats with watercolor markers and cut them out. Trace the cut-out hats onto black construction paper to create shadows. Then cut the shadows out and attach to the bulletin board. A magnet piece or a pushpin can be fastened to the shadow. A magnet piece or a hole can be applied to the colored hats.

HATS

Family Letter

Dear Families,

Hats will be the focus of our next curriculum unit. Through this theme the children will become familiar with types, colors, and sizes of hats. They will also learn the materials used to construct hats, and the uses of hats, such as for protection, decoration, and identification.

AT SCHOOL

Some of the learning activities planned include:

- playing in the Hat Store located in the dramatic play area
- making paper plate hats at the art table
- listening to and dramatizing the story *Caps for Sale*, by Esphyr Slobodkina

SPECIAL REQUEST!

On Friday we will have a Hat Day. The children will show and wear hats that they have brought from home. If your child wishes to share a special hat, please label it and send it to school with your child in a paper bag. This will help us to keep track of which hat belongs to each child. Thank you for your help.

AT HOME

Ask your child to help you search the closets of your home for hats. To develop classification skills, discuss the colors and types of hats with your child. Are there more seasonal hats or sports hats? What are the hats made from? Why were those materials used?

Hats off to a fun unit!

Hats serve many different functions and come in many sizes and colors.

Arts and Crafts

1. Easel Ideas

- top hat–shaped paper
- baseball cap–shaped paper
- football helmet–shaped paper
- graduation cap–shaped paper

2. Paper Plate Hats

Decorate paper plates with many different kinds of scraps, glitter, construction paper, and crepe paper. Punch a hole, using a paper punch, on each side of the hat. Attach strings so that the hat can be tied on and fastened under the chin.

Cooking

The children may enjoy wearing baker's hats for the cooking experiences! Ask a bakery or fast-food restaurant to donate several for classroom use.

1. Cheese Crunchies

1/2 cup butter or margarine
1 cup all-purpose flour
1 cup shredded cheddar cheese
pinch of salt
1 cup rice cereal bits

Cut the butter into six or eight slices and mix together with the flour, cheese, and salt. Use fingers or fork to mix. Knead in the cereal bits and then roll the dough into small balls or snakes. Press them down flat and place onto an ungreased cookie sheet. Bake at 325 degrees for approximately 10 minutes. Cool and serve for snack.

2. Hamantaschen from Israel

Children in Israel eat hamantaschen on the holiday of Purim. A hamantaschen is a pastry that represents the hat worn by the evil Haman, who plotted against the ancient Jews. Today, Israeli children dress in costumes, parade in the streets, and have parties on Purim.

7 tablespoons butter or margarine
1/3 cup sugar
2 eggs

2 1/2 cups flour
1/4 cup orange juice
1 teaspoon lemon juice
1 jar prune or plum jam

Cream the butter or margarine and sugar together in a large mixing bowl. Separate the eggs. Discard the whites. Add the yolk to the mixture and stir. Add the flour and juices to the mixture and mix to form dough. On a floured board, roll the dough to about 1/8-inch thickness. Use a cookie cutter to cut into 4-inch circles. Spoon a tablespoon of jam into the center of each circle and fold up three edges to create a triangle shape. Leave a small opening at the center. (Other fillings, such as poppy seeds or apricot jam, can be used.) Place the shaped dough on a cookie sheet and bake for 20 minutes in a 350-degree preheated oven. Serve for snack.

Dramatic Play

1. **Sports Hats**

   Provide football helmets and jerseys, baseball hats, batters' helmets, and uniforms. Encourage the children to pretend they are football and baseball players.

2. **Construction Site**

   Provide the children with toy tools, blocks, and construction hard hats.

3. **Hat Store**

   Firefighter hats, bonnets, top hats, hard hats, bridesmaids' hats, baby hats, and so on can all be made available in the hat store. Encourage the children to buy and sell hats using a cash register and play money.

Field Trips

1. **Hat Store**

   Visit a hat store or hat department of a store. Examine the different kinds, sizes, and colors of hats.

2. **Sports Store**

   Visit a sporting goods store. Locate the hat section. Observe the types of hats used for different sports.

Group Time

(Games, Language)

1. **"My Favorite Hat Day"**

   Encourage the children to share their favorite hats with the class on a specific day. Talk about each hat and ask where it was bought or found. Colors, sizes, and shapes can also be discussed.

2. **Dramatization**

   Read the story, *Caps for Sale*. After the children are familiar with the storyline, they may enjoy acting out the story.

Large Muscle

Hat Beanbag Toss

Lay several large hats on the floor. Encourage the children to stand about 2 feet from the hats and try to throw the beanbags into the hats.

Math

1. **Hat Match**

   Construct pairs of hat puzzles out of tagboard. On each pair, draw a different pattern. Encourage the children to mix the hats up and sort them by design.

2. **Hat Seriation**

   Collect a variety of hats. The children can arrange them from smallest to largest and largest to smallest. Also, they can classify the hats by colors and uses.

Music

"My Hat"

(traditional song)

My hat it has three corners.
    (point to head, hold up three fingers)
Three corners has my hat.
    (hold up three fingers, point to head)
And had it not three corners
    (hold up three fingers)
It wouldn't be my hat.
    (shake head, point to head)

Variation: Make three-cornered paper hats to wear while acting out this song.

Science

What's It Made Of?

Hats representing a variety of styles and materials can be placed on the science table. Magnifying glasses can also be provided to allow the children to explore. They can look at, feel, and try on the hats.

- Before letting the children try on the hats, make sure the children do not have head lice.

Social Studies

Many of these activities lend themselves to group time situations.

1. **"Weather" or Not to Wear a Hat**

   Discuss the different kinds of hats that are worn in cold weather. Ask questions such as, "What parts of our body does a hat keep warm?" "What kinds of hats do we wear when it is warm outside?" "How does a hat help to keep us cool?"

2. **Sports Hats**

   Make an arrangement of different sports hats. Place a mirror close by. The children can try on the hats.

3. **Community Helpers**

   Many people in our community wear hats as part of their uniform. Collect several of these hats, such as firefighter, police officer, mail carrier, baker, and so on, and place in a bag for a small group activity. Identify one child at a time to pull a hat out of the bag. Once the hat is removed, the children can identify the worker. Older children may be able to describe the activities of the identified worker.

Hats

A variety of hats can be collected for use in the dramatic play area. Some examples are:

firefighter	party (birthday)	hard hats	bicycle helmet
police officer	nurse's cap	ski caps	pillbox
visor	railroad engineer	berets	sports:
sunbonnets	motorcycle helmet	top hat	football
sombrero	cloche	cowboy	baseball
straw hats	chef	stocking cap	skiing
mantilla	sailor	mail carrier	

Books

The following books can be used to complement this theme:

Adams, Pam. (2000). *Mrs. Honey's Hat: Giant Lap Book*. Auburn, ME: Child's Play.

Bancroft, Catherine. (1993). *Felix's Hat*. Illus. by Hannah Coale Gruenberg. New York: Simon & Schuster.

Berenstain, Stan and Jan Berenstain. (1999). *Old Hat, New Hat: The Berenstain Bears*. Illus. by Jan Berenstain. New York: Random House.

Bogdanowicz, Basia. (1999). *Yellow Hat, Red Hat*. Brookfield, CT: Millbrook Press.

Brett, Jan. (1997). *The Hat*. New York: G. P. Putnam.

Carlson, Laurie. (1998). *Boss of the Plains: The Hat That Won the West*. Illus. by Holly Meade. New York: Dorling Kindersley.

Gardella, Tricia. (1997). *Casey's New Hat*. Illus. by Margot Apple. Boston: Houghton Mifflin.

Geringer, Laura. (1987). *A Three Hat Day*. Illus. by Arnold Lobel. New York: HarperCollins.

Hanel, Wolfram. (1995). *The Extraordinary Adventures of an Ordinary Hat*. Illus. by Christa Unzner-Fischer. New York: North South Books. (Pbk.)

Howard, Elizabeth Fitzgerald. (1991). *Aunt Flossie's Hats (and Crab Cakes Later)*. Illus. by James Ransome. New York: Clarion Books.

Kalman, Bobbie. (1998). *Bandanas, Chaps, and Ten-Gallon Hats*. New York: Crabtree.

Keller, Holly. (1995). *Rosata*. New York: Greenwillow.

Koeppel, R. (1999). *Elmo's World: Shoes, Hats, and Jackets (Sesame Street)*. New York: CTW Books.

Malka, Lucy. (1995). *Fun with Hats*. Illus. by Melinda Levine. Greenvale, NY: Mondo. (Pbk.)

Milich, Melissa. (1997). *Miz Fannie Mae's Fine New Easter Hat*. Illus. by Yong Chen. Boston: Little, Brown.

Miller, Margaret. (1988). *Whose Hat?* New York: William Morrow.

Morris, Ann. (1989). *Hats, Hats, Hats*. Photos by Ken Heyman. New York: Lothrop, Lee & Shepard.

Oborne, Martine. (1997). *Juice the Pig*. Illus. by Axel Scheffler. New York: Holt.

Pearson, Tracey Campbell. (1997). *The Purple Hat*. New York: Farrar, Straus & Giroux.

Pratt, Pierre. (1992). *Follow That Hat!* Willowdale, Ontario, Canada: Annick Press.

Reed, Lynn Rowe. (1995). *Pedro, His Perro, and the Alphabet Sombrero*. New York: Hyperion.

Slobodkina, Esphyr. (1947). *Caps for Sale*. New York: W. R. Scott.

Smath, Jerry. (1995). *A Hat So Simple*. Mahwah, NJ: Troll. (Pbk.)

Stoeke, Janet Morgan. (1994). *A Hat for Minerva Louise*. New York: Dutton.

Recordings and Song Titles

The following recording can be used to complement this theme:

"I Got a Hat." (2001). *Seasonal Songs in Motion*. Long Branch, NJ: Kimbo Educational.

41

Health

Occupations

doctors
dentists
nurses

Exercise

running
aerobics
walking
bicycling
swimming
skiing

Exercise Clothing

shorts
sweatshirts
rubber-soled shoes
swimming suits
T-shirts

Foods

fruits
vegetables
meats
dairy products
beans
legumes
breads
cereal

Personal Habits

taking baths
brushing teeth
washing hair
taking naps
night sleep

Tools and Supplies

hairbrushes
toothbrushes
shampoo
soap
toothpaste
vitamins

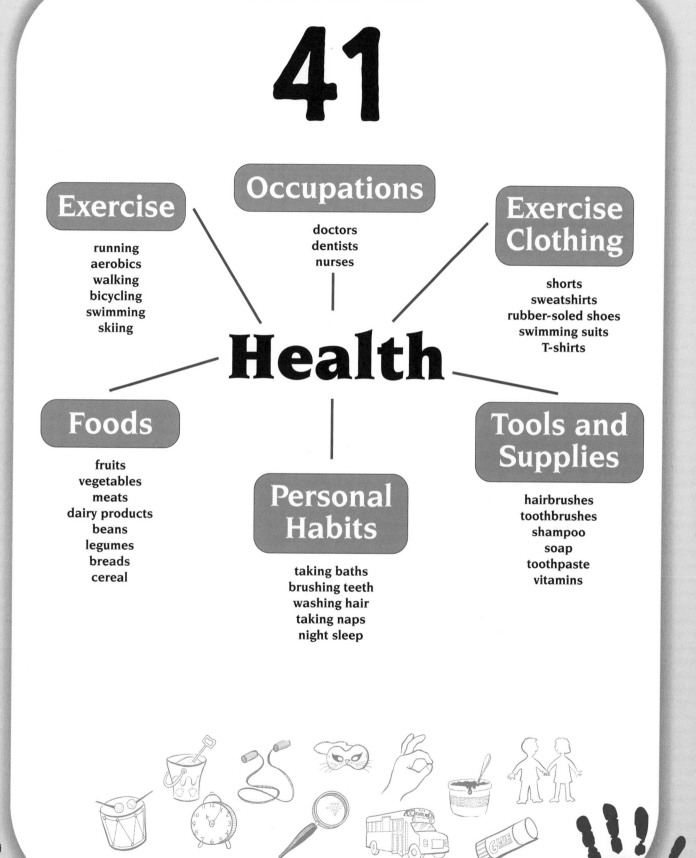

Theme Goals

Through participating in the experiences provided by this theme, the children may learn

1. Importance of good health
2. Healthy foods
3. Exercise clothes
4. Health tools and supplies
5. Personal habits related to health
6. Health occupations

Concepts for the Children to Learn

1. We need to take good care of our bodies to keep healthy.
2. Vitamins, shampoo, soap, and toothpaste are health aids.
3. Doctors, nurses, and dentists provide health checkups.
4. Running, aerobics, and walking are all forms of exercise.
5. Bicycling, swimming, and skiing are other forms of exercise.
6. Fruits, vegetables, dairy products, beans, legumes, meat, breads, and cereals keep our bodies healthy.
7. Our bodies need rest.
8. Different types of clothing are worn during exercise.
9. Shorts, sweatshirts, T-shirts, swimming suits, and rubber-soled shoes are exercise clothing.
10. Brushing teeth, washing hair, and bathing are ways to keep our bodies clean.
11. Hairbrushes and toothbrushes are health tools.
12. Taking naps, sleeping, and eating good foods are ways to have healthy bodies.

Vocabulary

1. **checkup**—a visit to a doctor to make sure you are healthy.
2. **cleanliness**—keeping our body parts free from dirt.
3. **diet**—the food we eat.
4. **exercise**—moving body parts.
5. **health**—feeling good.
6. **nutrition**—eating foods that are good for our body.

Bulletin Board

The purpose of this bulletin board is to have the children develop visual discrimination, hand-eye coordination, and problem-solving skills by matching the health aids to their corresponding shadow. Construct the health aid pieces from white tagboard. Include a toothbrush, toothpaste, comb, brush, and soap. Color the objects with colored felt-tip markers and laminate. Trace each of the health aids onto black construction paper to construct shadows as illustrated. Staple the shadow aids on the bulletin board either by affixing magnets or using pushpins. Punch a hole in each of the health aid pieces, allowing the children to hang them on the appropriate shadow.

Family Letter

Dear Families,

We will be starting a unit on health. This unit will include many aspects of health. We will be discussing foods that are good for us, important personal habits, and exercise. Through this unit the children will develop an awareness of the importance of keeping their bodies healthy and ways to do so.

AT SCHOOL

Some of the learning experiences planned for the week include:

- tracing our bodies at the art center
- visiting Dr. Thomas, the dentist, at her office
- having a visit by an aerobics instructor
- creating healthy snacks
- weighing and measuring ourselves

FIELD TRIP

Arrangements have been made to visit Dr. Thomas's office on Thursday of this week. Dr. Thomas will give us a tour of the dental clinic and show us various pieces of dental equipment. We will walk to her office, leaving school at 10:00 a.m., and return just in time for lunch. Please have your child at school by 10:00 a.m. if he or she wishes to participate. Parents, please feel free to join us.

JUST A REMINDER

If your child's toothbrush at school is missing, please send another one. We teach the importance of dental hygiene by brushing our teeth after all meals and snacks at school.

AT HOME

Cotton swabs may be used instead of brushes for painting. They may also be used to dot paper with different colors. Painting is a valuable sensory experience for a child. It provides an opportunity to experiment with color.

Teach your child healthy habits today!

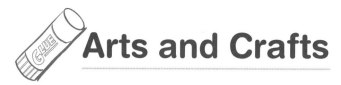

Arts and Crafts

1. Paper Plate Meals

Magazines for the children to cut food pictures from the five food groups should be provided. The pictures can be pasted on a paper plate to represent a balanced meal. Plates from microwave dinners, if thoroughly cleaned, work well, too.

2. Body Tracing

Instruct each child to lie on a large piece of paper. Trace the child's body and let him or her take the tracing home and decorate it with his or her family. After this, it can be returned to school for display. This activity should help the children become aware of individual uniqueness and fosters parent-child interaction.

Clean hands can prevent the spread of germs.

Cooking

Fruit Tree Salad

On a plate, place a lettuce leaf. On the lettuce, place a pineapple slice. Peel and slice a banana horizontally into 2-inch pieces, and place them on the pineapple. Drain 1 small can of fruit cocktail. Spoon the fruit over the bananas.

Dramatic Play

1. Health Club

Mats, fake weights (made from large tinker toys), headbands, and music to represent a health club can be placed in the dramatic play area.

2. Doctor's Office (Hospital)

White clothing, stethoscopes, strip thermometers, magazines, bandages, cots, sheets, and plastic syringes without needles can be placed in the dramatic play area to represent a hospital.

3. Restaurant

Tables, tablecloths, menus, and tablets for taking orders can be placed in the dramatic play area. Paste pictures of food on the menus. A sign for the area could be "Eating for Health."

Field Trips/ Resource People

1. Take a field trip to the following places:
   - hospital
   - health care facility
   - doctor's office
   - dentist's office
   - beauty shop
   - health club
   - drugstore

HEALTH

2. Invite the following resource people to visit the classroom:

- doctor
- nurse
- dentist
- dietician
- aerobics instructor
- beautician

Fingerplays

Brushing Teeth

I jiggle the toothbrush again and again.
(pretend to brush teeth)
I scrub all my teeth for awhile.
I swish the water to rinse them and then
(puff out cheeks to swish)
I look at myself and I smile.
(smile at one another)

Group Time

(Games, Language)

Tasting Party

Prepare for a tasting party. Collect a wide variety of foods. For example, the children could experiment by dipping bananas in honey and then rolling in wheat germ. To extend this activity, charts can be prepared listing the children's favorite foods.

Large Muscle

1. Weight Awareness

The object of this activity is to become aware of weight and to feel the difference between heavy and light. To do this, the child should experiment with body force. Exercise in the following ways: lift arms slowly and gently, stomp on the floor, walk on tiptoes, kick out one leg as hard as possible, very smoothly and lightly slide one foot along the floor. Music can be added to imitate aerobics.

2. Mini-Olympics

Set up various areas for jumping jacks, jogging, relays, and a "beanbag launch." For the "launch" put a beanbag on the top edge of a child's foot and launch by kicking. Observe the distance each beanbag goes.

Math

1. Food Group Sorting

Create a food group display. To do this, encourage the children to bring empty food containers. The food containers can be sorted into food groups. This could be a small group activity or a choice during the self-selected play period.

2. Height and Weight Chart

Weigh and measure each of the children at various times throughout the year. Record the data on a chart. This chart can be posted in the classroom.

Music

1. "Brush Your Teeth"
by Raffi on *Get Up and Grow*

2. "My Body"
(*Sing to the tune of "Where Is Thumbkin?"*)

This is my body.
This is my body.
It's the only one I've got.
It's the only one I've got.
I'm going to take good care of it.
I'm going to take good care of it.
Yes I am. Yes I am.

3. "Miss Polly Had a Dolly"

Miss Polly had a dolly
Who was sick, sick, sick,
So she called for the doctor
To be quick, quick, quick.
The doctor came
With his bag and his hat,
And he knocked at the door
With a rat-a-tat-tat.
He looked at the dolly
And he shook his head,
And he said, "Miss Polly,
Put her straight to bed."
He wrote out a paper
For a pill, pill, pill,
That'll make her better,
Yes it will, will, will!

Science

Soap Pieces

Add different kinds of soaps and a magnifying glass to the science area. Talk about what each one is used for.

Sensory

Add shampoo or dish detergent to the sensory table.

Books

The following books can be used to complement this theme:

Aliki. (1992). *I'm Growing*. New York: HarperCollins.

Barner, Bob. (1996). *Dem Bones*. New York: Chronicle Books.

Berger, Melvin. (1995). *Germs Make Me Sick*. Rev. ed. Illus. by Marylin Hafner. New York: HarperCollins.

Brown, Laurene Krasny and Marc Tolon Brown. (1990). *Dinosaurs Alive and Well! A Guide to Good Health*. Boston: Little, Brown.

Butterfield, Moira, Peter Utton and Karen Fung. (2000). *Let's Go Potty*. Illus. by Peter Utton. Hauppauge, NY: Barron Juveniles.

Caffey, Donna. (1998). *Yikes—Lice!* Illus. by Patrick Girouard. Niles, IL: Albert Whitman.

Dooley, Virginia. (1996). *Tubes in My Ears: My Trip to the Hospital*. Illus. by Miriam Katin. Greenvale, NY: Mondo Pub.

Edwards, Pamela Duncan. (2003). *Miss Polly Has a Dolly*. Illus. by Elicia Castaldi. New York: Putnam's.

Gosselin, Kim. (1998). *Taking Diabetes to School*. 2nd ed. Illus. by Moss Freedman. Manchester, MO: JayJo Books.

Hopman, Ellen and Evert and Steven Foster (Photographer). (2000). *Walking the World in Wonder: A Children's Herbal*. Rochester, VT: Healing Arts Press.

Janovitz, Marilyn. (1994). *Is It Time?* New York: North South Books.

Leedy, Loreen. (1994). *The Edible Pyramid: Good Eating Every Day*. New York: Holiday House.

London, Jonathan. (1992). *The Lion Who Had Asthma*. Illus. by Nadine B. Westcott. Beaver Dam, WI: Concept Books.

Newcome, Zita. (1997). *Toddlerobics*. New York: Candlewick Press.

Owen, Ann. (2004). *Keeping You Healthy: a Book About Doctors*. Illus. by Eric Thomas. Minneapolis, MN: Picture Window Books.

Powell, Jillian. (1997). *Exercise Matters*. Austin, TX: Raintree/Steck Vaughn. (*Health Matters* series.)

Powell, Jillian. (1997). *Food and Your Health*. Austin, TX: Raintree/Steck Vaughn. (*Health Matters* series.)

Powell, Jillian. (1997). *Hygiene and Your Health*. Austin, TX: Raintree/Steck Vaughn. (*Health Matters* series.)

Ratnett, Michael, June Goulding and Iain Smyth. (1998). *Dracula Steps Out: A Pop-Up Book (Venture Health & the Human Body)*. Illus. by June Goulding. New York: Orchard Books.

Rockwell, Harlow. (1992). *My Doctor*. New York: Macmillan.

Showers, Paul. (1991). *How Many Teeth?* Newly illus. by True Kelley. New York: HarperCollins.

Showers, Paul. (1997). *Sleep Is for Everyone*. Illus. by Wendy Watson. New York: HarperCollins.

Teague, Mark. (1994). *Pigsty*. New York: Scholastic.

Thompson, Carol. (1997). *Piggy Washes Up*. New York: Candlewick Press.

Van Cleave, Janice. (1998). *Janice Van Cleave's Play and Find Out about the Human Body*. New York: Wiley.

Whitford, Rebecca and Martina Selway. (2005). *Little Yoga: a Toddlers First Book of Yoga*. New York: Henry Holt and Co.

Multimedia

The following multimedia products can be used to complement this theme:

Raffi. "Bathtime" on *Raffi in Concert with the Rise and Shine Band* [video]. (1988). Hollywood, CA: Troubadour Records.

Chef Combo's Fantastic Adventures in Tasting and Nutrition [kit]. (1996). Rosemont, IL: National Dairy Council.

Come See What the Doctor Sees [video]. (1994). Half Moon Bay, CA: Visual Mentor.

Goofy over Dental Health [video]. (1991). Disney Educational Productions.

K-6 Classroom Gallery [CD-ROM]. (1997). Lancaster, PA: Classroom Connect.

Preschool Power! Jacket Flips and Other Tips [video]. (1991). Concept Associates.

Rock 'n' Roll Fitness Fun [compact disc or cassette]. (1989). Long Branch, NJ: Kimbo Educational.

Stewart, Georgiana. *Good Morning Exercises for Kids* [cassette]. (1987). Long Branch, NJ: Kimbo Educational.

Recordings and Song Titles

The following recordings can be used to complement this theme:

"Brush Your Teeth," "I'm in the Tub," "Let's Sing about Food." (1994). *Get Up and Grow*. Long Branch, NJ: Kimbo Educational.

"Doctor, Doctor." (1994). *People in Our Neighborhood*. Long Branch, NJ: Kimbo Educational.

"Good Grooming." (1995). *Piggyback Songs*. Long Branch, NJ: Kimbo Educational.

"Hygiene," "Respiration." (1977). *Science in a Nutshell*. Long Branch, NJ: Kimbo Educational.

"Physical Ed," "Twelve Days of Gym Class." (2000). *Physical Ed*. Long Branch, NJ: Kimbo Educational.

"Say No to Drugs," "Please Don't Smoke." (1989). *Make the Right Choice*. Long Branch, NJ: Kimbo Educational.

"Sticky, Sticky." (1994). *Positively Singable Songs*. Long Branch, NJ: Kimbo Educational.

Rooms

living room
kitchen
bathroom
bedroom
den
dining room
closet
family room
office/study
garage
basement

Sizes

many

Homes

Workers

carpenters
architects
painters
plumbers
electricians
masons
cabinet makers

Parts

roof
garage
basement
toilets
stairs
ceiling
floors
walls
doors
windows
cupboards
sinks
bathtubs

Materials

adobe
brick
straw
stone
wood
cement

Kinds

shelters/halfway houses
apartments
houseboats
trailers
houses
condominiums
duplexes
cabins
tents
huts
townhouses
solar

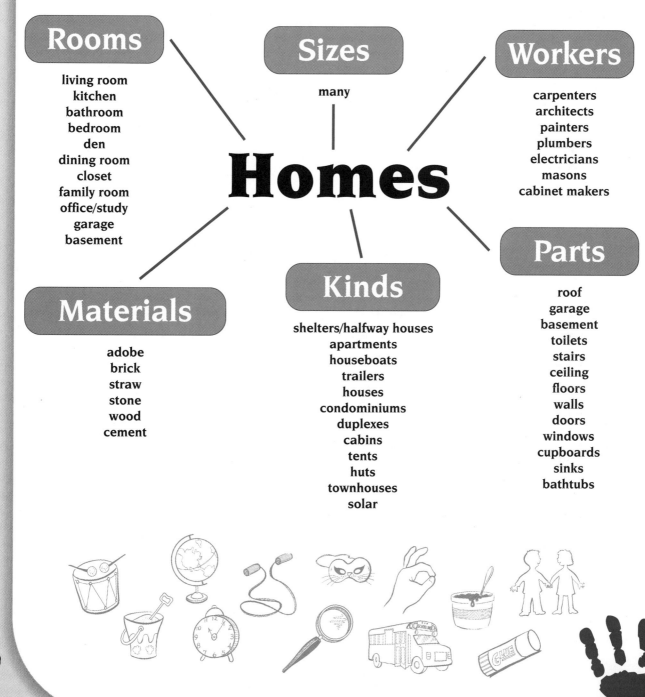

Theme Goals

Through participating in the experiences provided by this theme, the children may learn about

1. Home workers
2. Parts of a home
3. Rooms in a home
4. Kinds of homes
5. Materials for building a home

Concepts for the Children to Learn

1. A home is a place to live.
2. Apartments, condominiums, townhouses, duplexes, trailers, and houses are all kinds of homes.
3. Cabins, huts, tents, and houseboats are other types of homes.
4. Most homes have a kitchen, bedroom, bathroom, living room, and closets.
5. Some homes have a dining room, den, family room, and an office/study.
6. Homes come in many sizes.
7. Homes can be built from brick, stone, wood, and/or cement.
8. The ceiling, floor, roof, windows, doors, walls, and stairs are parts of a home.
9. Construction workers build houses.
10. Homes can be decorated many ways.

Vocabulary

1. **apartment**—a building including many homes.
2. **architect**—a person who designs homes.
3. **bedroom**—a room for sleeping.
4. **construction worker**—a person who builds.
5. **duplex**—a house divided into two separate homes.
6. **house**—a place to live.
7. **kitchen**—a room for cooking.

Bulletin Board

The purpose of this bulletin board is to promote the development of classification skills. Begin by drawing an unfurnished model of a home on a large sheet of tagboard as illustrated. Include the basic rooms such as kitchen, bedroom, and living room. Draw and cut furnishings to add to the home. Laminate home and furnishings. The children can place the furnishings in the proper room by using "fun tack" or magnetic strips on the furnishings.

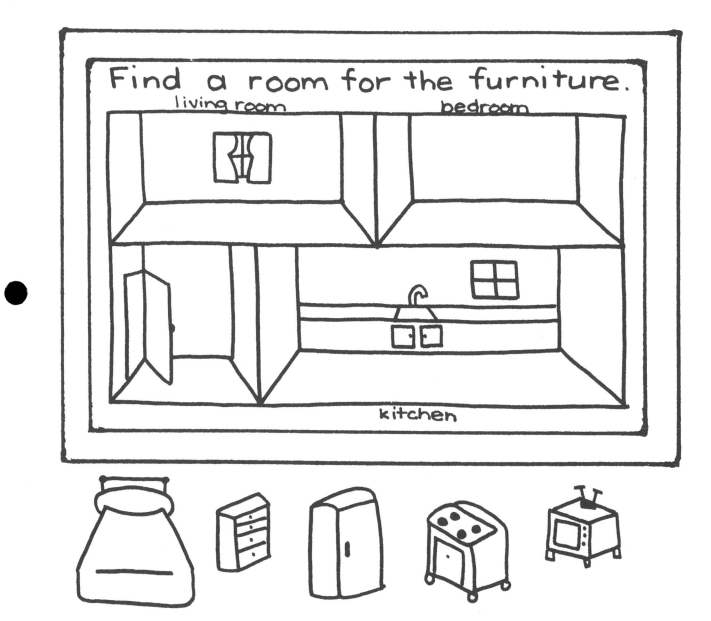

Family Letter

Dear Families,

Homes will be the focus of our next curricular theme. Since everyone's home is unique, we will be discussing how homes differ. We will also be discussing home workers, materials for building a home, and the rooms in our homes.

AT SCHOOL

Some of our activities will include:

- constructing homes out of cardboard boxes and paper in the art area
- acting out the story of *The Three Little Pigs* in the dramatic play area
- building at the workbench

A special activity will include making placemats, but we need your help. For our placemats we will need a few pictures of your family, home, or both. These will be glued to construction paper and laminated during our project. They will not be returned in their original form. Thank you!

This week we will also be taking a neighborhood tour to observe the various types of homes in the area. We will be taking our walk at 10:00 a.m. on Thursday. Please feel free to join us!

AT HOME

To develop observation skills, take your child on a walk around your neighborhood to look at the houses in your area. Talk about the different colors and sizes of dwellings.

Enjoy the time you spend with your child!

Playing house is an activity where everyone can share the "chores."

Arts and Crafts

1. Shape Homes

An assortment of construction paper shapes such as squares, triangles, rectangles, and circles should be placed on a table in the art area. Glue and large pieces of paper should also be provided.

2. Tile Painting

Ask building companies to donate cracked, chipped, or discontinued tiles. The children can paint the tiles.

3. Household Tracings

Several household items such as a spatula, wooden spoon, or cookie cutter can be placed on the art table. Also include paper, scissors, and crayons. These items can be traced. Some of the older children may color and cut their tracings.

Cooking

Individual Pizza

English muffins
grated mozzarella cheese
pizza sauce

Spread a tablespoon of sauce on each muffin half. Sprinkle the top with grated cheese. Bake in a preheated oven at 375 degrees until cheese melts.

Dramatic Play

1. Tent Living

A small tent can be set up indoors or outdoors depending upon weather and space. Accessories such as sleeping bags, flashlights, rope, cooking utensils, and backpacks should also be provided if available.

2. **Cardboard Houses**

Collect large cardboard boxes. Place outdoors or in an open classroom area. The children may build their own homes. If desired, tempera paint can be used for painting the homes. Wallpaper may also be provided.

3. **Cleaning House**

Housecleaning tools such as a vacuum cleaner, dusting cloth, sponges, mops, and brooms can be placed in the dramatic play area. During the self-selected play periods the children may choose to participate in cleaning.

Field Trips/ Resource People

1. **Neighborhood Walk**

Walk around the neighborhood. Observe the construction workers' actions and tools.

2. **Construction Site**

If available visit a local construction site. Discuss the role of the construction worker.

3. **Resource People**

The following resource people could be invited to the classroom:

- builder
- architect
- plumber
- painter
- electrician

Fingerplays

My House

I'm going to build a little house
(fingers make roof)

With windows big and bright
(stand with arms in air)
Drifting out of sight.
In winter when the snowflakes fall
(hands flutter down)
Or when I hear a storm
(hand cupped to ear)
I'll go sit in my little house
(sit down)
Where I'll be snug and warm.
(cross arms over chest)

Where Should I Live?

Where should I live?
In a castle with towers and a moat?
(make a point with arms over head)
Or on a river in a houseboat?
(make wavelike motions)
A winter igloo made of ice may be just the thing
(pretend to pack snow)
But what would happen when it turned to spring?
(pretend to think)
I like tall apartments and houses made of stone,
(stretch up tall)
But I'd also like to live in a blue mobile home.
(shorten up)
A cave or cabin in the woods would give me lots of space
(stretch out wide)
But I guess my home is the best place!
(point to self)

Knocking

Look at _____ knocking on our door.
(knock)
Look at _____ knocking on our door.
(knock)
Come on in out of the cold
(shiver)
Into our nice, warm home.
(rub hands together to get warm)

My Chores

In my home, I wash the dishes
(pretend to wash)
Vacuum the floor
(push vacuum)
And dust the furniture.
(dust)

Outside my home, I rake the leaves
  (rake)
Plant the flowers
  (plant)
And play hard all day.
  (wipe sweat from forehead)
When the day is over
  I eat my supper,
  (eat)
Read a story
  (read)
And go to sleep.
  (put head on hands)

Group Time

(Games, Language)

Construct a "My home is special because . . ." chart. Encourage the children to name a special thing about their homes. Display the chart at the children's eye level in the classroom for the week.

Large Muscle

Roofing Nails

Collect building materials such as soft pine scraps and styrofoam for the workbench. Provide safety goggles, a child-sized hammer, and roofing nails. **Caution:** Adult supervision is always required with this activity.

Math

My House

Construct a "My House" book for each child. On the pages write things like

My house has _____ steps.
My house is the color _____.
My house has _____ windows.
There are _____ doors in my house.
My house has _____ keyholes.

Other ideas could include the number of beds, people, pets, etc. Send this home with the child to complete with family.

Music

"This Is the Way We Build Our House"
(*Sing to the tune of* "Here We Go 'Round the Mulberry Bush")

This is the way we build our house,
Build our house, build our house.
This is the way we build our house,
So early in the morning.

Other suggestions:
This is the way we paint the house.
This is the way we wash the car.
This is the way we rake the leaves.

Science

Building Materials

Building materials and magnifying glasses should be placed in the science area. The children may observe and examine materials. Included may be wood, brick, canvas, tar paper, shingles, etc.

Sensory

1. Identifying Sounds

Record several sounds found in the home such as a vacuum cleaner, television, water running, and a toilet flushing. Encourage children to name sounds. For older children, this could also be played as a lotto game. Make cards containing pictures of sounds and vary pictures from card to card. When a sound is heard, cover the corresponding picture with a chip.

2. Sand Castles

Add wet sand to the sensory table. Provide forms to create buildings, homes, etc.
Note: Examples may include empty cans, milk cartons, plastic containers, etc.

Social Studies

Room Match

Collect several boxes. On one box print "kitchen"; on another print "bathroom"; on another print "living room"; and on another print "bedroom." Cut objects related to each of these rooms from catalogs. The children may sort objects by placing them in the appropriate boxes. For example, dishes, silverware, and a coffeepot would be placed in the box labeled "kitchen."

Books

The following books can be used to complement this theme:

Ackerman, Karen. (1992). *I Know a Place*. Illus. by Deborah Kogan Ray. Boston: Houghton Mifflin.

Ackerman, Karen. (1995). *The Sleeping Porch*. Illus. by Elizabeth Sayles. New York: William Morrow.

Ballard, Robin. (1994). *Good-Bye House*. New York: Greenwillow.

Brown, Richard Eric. (1988). *100 Words about My House*. Orlando, FL: Harcourt Brace.

Bunting, Eve. (1991). *Fly Away Home*. Illus. by Ronald Himler. New York: Clarion Books.

Carle, Hermit. (2005). *A House for Hermit Crab*. New York: Alladdin Paperbacks.

Cooner, Donna D., Guy Davis and Jane Valentine-Ruppe. (1998). *Barney's Animal Homes: A Lift & Peek Book*. Illus. by Jane Valentine-Ruppe. Austin, TX: Barney.

Cowley, Joy and Elizabeth Fuller. (2005). *Mrs. Wishy-Washy's Scrubbing Machine*. New York: Philomel Books.

Delafosse, Claude, ed. (1998). *Houses*. New York: Scholastic.

Dorros, Arthur. (1992). *This Is My House*. New York: Scholastic.

Forest, Heather. (1996). *A Big Quiet House: a Yiddish Folktale from Eastern Europe*. Little Rock, AK: August House LittleFolk.

Gibbons, Gail. (1990). *How a House Is Built*. New York: Holiday House.

Grimshaw, Caroline. (2000). *Our Homes*. London: Two-Can.

Hill, Elizabeth Starr. (1991). *Evan's Corner*. Revised and newly illus. by D. Brodie. New York: Viking.

Jackson, Mike. (1999). *Houses & Homes*. London: Evans Brothers.

Kalman, Bobbie. (1994). *Homes around the World*. New York: Crabtree.

Kuklin, Susan. (1992). *How My Family Lives in America*. Minneapolis, MN: Bradbury Press.

McDonald, Megan. (1996). *My House Has Stars*. Illus. by Peter Catalanotto. New York: Orchard Books.

McGovern, Ann. (1997). *The Lady in the Box*. Illus. by Marni Backer. New York: Turtle Books.

Morris, Ann. (1992). *Houses and Homes*. Photos by Ken Heyman. New York: Lothrop, Lee & Shepard.

Rosen, Michael, ed. (1992). *Home*. New York: HarperCollins.

Rosen, Michael. (1996). *This Is Our House*. Illus. by Bob Graham. Cambridge, MA: Candlewick Press.

Rounds, Glen. (1996). *Sod Houses on the Great Plains*. New York: Holiday House.

Rylant, Cynthia. (1993). *Everyday House*. New York: Simon & Schuster. (Board book.)

Saul, Carol P. (1995). *Someplace Else*. Illus. by Barry Root. New York: Simon & Schuster.

Shelby, Anne. (1996). *The Someday House*. Illus. by Rosanne Litzinger. New York: Orchard Books.

Williams, John. (1997). *Houses and Homes*. Austin, TX: Raintree/Steck Vaughn.

Wood, Audrey. (2004). *The Napping House*. Illus. by Don Wood. Orlando, FL: Harcourt, Inc. (1st Harcourt book-and-musical CD edition).

Zweibel, Alan. (2005). *Our Tree Named Steve*. New York: G.P. Putnam's Sons.

Multimedia

The following multimedia products can be used to complement this theme:

Community Construction Kit [CD-ROM]. (1998). Watertown, MA: Tom Snyder Productions.

Dig Hole, Build House [video]. (1994). Gig Harbor, WA: Real World Video.

Gryphon Bricks [CD-ROM]. (1996). San Diego, CA: Gryphon Software Corp.

Let's Build a House [video]. (1996). San Diego, CA: Video Connections.

A Silly, Noisy House [CD-ROM]. (1991). Santa Monica, CA: Voyager Company.

Recordings and Song Titles

The following recording can be used to complement this theme:

"Hungry Caterpillar," (2001). *Seasonal Songs in Motion*. Melbourne, FL: The Learning Station.

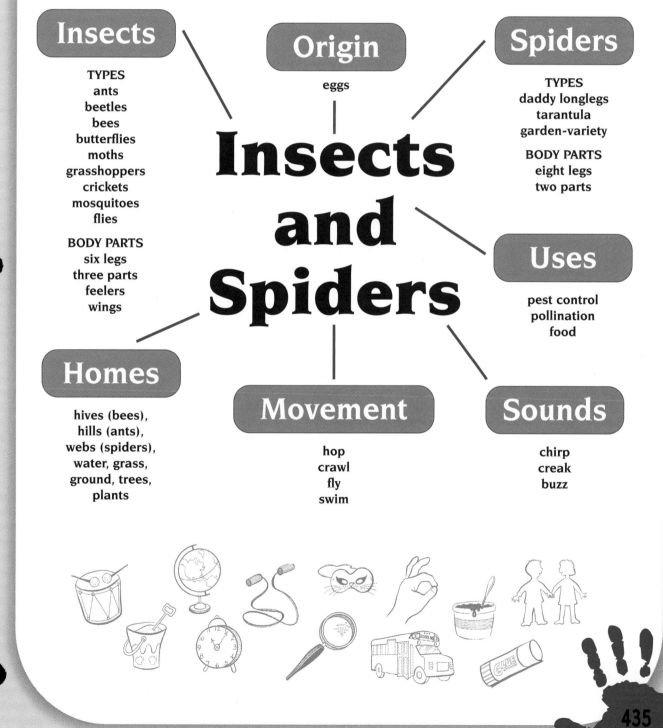

Insects

TYPES
ants
beetles
bees
butterflies
moths
grasshoppers
crickets
mosquitoes
flies

BODY PARTS
six legs
three parts
feelers
wings

Origin

eggs

Insects and Spiders

Spiders

TYPES
daddy longlegs
tarantula
garden-variety

BODY PARTS
eight legs
two parts

Uses

pest control
pollination
food

Homes

hives (bees),
hills (ants),
webs (spiders),
water, grass,
ground, trees,
plants

Movement

hop
crawl
fly
swim

Sounds

chirp
creak
buzz

Theme Goals

Through participating in the experiences provided by this theme, the children may learn

1. Types and body parts of insects and spiders
2. Homes for insects and spiders
3. Movements of insects and spiders
4. Uses for insects and spiders
5. Sounds of insects and spiders
6. The origins of insects and spiders

Concepts for the Children to Learn

1. There are many kinds of insects and spiders.
2. Ants, beetles, bees, butterflies, moths, grasshoppers, crickets, mosquitoes, and fleas are all insects.
3. Insects are different in many ways: size, shape, color, eyes, mouths, and number of wings.
4. Insects have six legs (three pairs) and, if winged, four wings.
5. Spiders have eight legs (four pairs) and no wings.
6. Spiders have two parts to their bodies.
7. Insects and spiders come from eggs.
8. Insects can help us by making honey and pollinating flowers for fruit and vegetables.
9. Spiders can help us by eating insect pests.
10. Types of spiders include daddy longlegs, tarantulas, and garden-variety.
11. Most spiders spin a web.
12. Some insects fly, others walk.
13. Spiders spin a web to catch insects to eat.
14. Spiders and insects can chirp, creak, and/or buzz.
15. Insects and spiders live in different places.
16. Some insects and spiders may live in water, grass, the ground, trees, or plants.

Vocabulary

1. **antennae**—feelers on an insect that stick out from the head.
2. **caterpillar**—the wormlike larva of a butterfly or moth.
3. **cricket**—small leaping insect known for its chirping.
4. **insect**—small animal with six legs.
5. **moth**—night-flying insect with four wings, related to the butterfly.
6. **pollinate**—the way insects help flowers to grow.
7. **pupa**—intermediate stage of an insect; chrysalis.
8. **spider**—small animal with eight legs. Spiders have no wings. Spiders are not insects.
9. **spiderling**—a baby spider.
10. **wasp**—winged insect with a poisonous sting.

Bulletin Board

The purpose of this bulletin board is to develop visual discrimination as well as to promote problem-solving, matching, and hand-eye coordination skills. Construct several butterflies, each of a different shape, out of tagboard. Trace the butterfly figures onto black construction paper to create shadows. Cut out and laminate the butterfly figures and shadows. Staple shadow butterflies to bulletin board. Punch holes in colored butterflies for children to hang on the pushpin of the corresponding shadow butterfly.

Family Letter

Dear Families,

We are continuing our study of animals. We are introducing a new category—insects and spiders. The children will become aware of the difference between insects and spiders and the ways that those creatures are helpful. Do you know the difference between insects and spiders? Most insects have three body parts and six legs. Spiders have two body parts and eight legs.

AT SCHOOL

Some of the learning experiences planned include:

- singing and acting out the song "One Elephant Went Out to Play." It's about an elephant that plays on a spider web!
- listening to a flannel board version of the story *The Very Hungry Caterpillar* by Eric Carle
- watching and observing an ant farm set up in the science area
- creating spiders and insects out of a variety of materials in the art area

AT HOME

There are many ways to bring this unit into your home. Take a walk with your child and see how many spiders and insects you can find. Avoid touching unknown types of insects or spiders with your fingers. Instead, use a clear jar with a lid to observe the creature close up. Release the insect or spider after the observation.

We will be having a snack this week called ants on a log. Let your child make some for you! Spread cream cheese on pieces of celery. Top with raisins. Enjoy!

Enjoy your child!

Arts and Crafts

1. Make insects and spiders out of clay. Use toothpicks, straws, and chenille stem segments for the appendages.

2. Make insects and spiders with thumbprints. Children can draw crayon legs to make prints look like insects and spiders.

3. Egg carton caterpillars. Cut egg cartons in half, lengthwise. Each child paints a carton half. When dry, children can make a face on the end of the carton and insert chenille stems or straws for feelers.

4. Have children make spiders from black construction paper—one large black circle for a body and eight strips for legs. Children can paste on two yellow circles for eyes. Hang by a string around the room.

5. Make ladybug shapes out of red and orange construction paper. Have children sponge paint dots and legs on the bugs.

6. Sprinkle crayon shavings between two pieces of waxed paper and iron. Put a butterfly template over the waxed paper and glue it on. A pretty butterfly will be the final product!

7. Tissue paper butterflies. Have children lightly paint white tissue paper or use colored tissue paper. Fasten a chenille stem around the middle. Add circles on the ends for antennae.

8. Balloon bugs. Blow up several long balloons. Cover them with strips of paper dipped in wallpaper paste. Put on three to four layers of this sticky paper. Let dry for 2 to 3 days. Then paint your own giant bug!

Children enjoy observing bugs.

Cooking

1. **Ants on a Log**
   (*traditional*)

   Cut celery pieces into 3-inch strips. Fill the cavity of the celery stick with cream cheese. Garnish with raisins. (As with all recipes calling for celery, this might be more appropriate for older children.)

2. **Spider Snacks**

   Use chow-mein noodles to place eight "spider legs" into a prune.

Dramatic Play

1. **Scientist**

   The children can dress up in white lab coats and observe spiders and insects with magnifying glasses.

2. **Spider Web**

   Tie together a big piece of rope to resemble a spider web. Have children pretend they are spiders playing on their web. **Caution:** Closely supervise this activity.

3. Spider Sac

Tape a 10-foot by 25-foot piece of plastic together on the sides. Blow it up with a fan to make a big bubble. Make a slit in the plastic for the entrance. The children can pretend to be baby spiders coming out of the spider sac when they are hatching. **Caution:** Closely supervise this activity.

4.

The children can act out "Little Miss Muffet."

Field Trips/ Resource People

1. Go on a walk to a nearby park to find bugs. Look under rocks, in cracks in sidewalks, in bushes, etc.

2. Have someone who has a butterfly collection come in.

3. Visit a pet store. Ask them to show you what kind of insects they feed to the animals in the store. Do they sell any insects?

4. Invite a zoologist to come in and talk about insects and how important they are.

5. Invite an individual who raises bees to talk to the children. Ask him or her to bring in a honeycomb for the children to taste.

Fingerplays

Ants

Once I saw an anthill, with no ants about.
So I said "Little ants, won't you please come out?"
Then, as if they heard my call, one, two, three, four, five came out.
And that was all!

Bumblebee

Brightly colored bumblebee
Looking for some honey.
Flap your wings and fly away
While it still is sunny.

The Caterpillar

A caterpillar crawled to the top of a tree.
   (index finger of left hand moves up right arm)
"I think I'll take a nap," said he.
So under a leaf, he began to creep
   (wrap right hand over left fist)
To spin his chrysalis and he fell asleep.
All winter long he slept in his chrysalis bed,
   (keep right hand over left fist)
Till spring came along one day, and said,
"Wake up, wake up little sleepy head."
   (shake left fist with right hand).
"Wake up, it's time to get out of bed!"
So, he opened his eyes that sunshiny day
   (shake fingers and look into hand)
Lo—he was a butterfly and flew away!
   (move hand into flying motion)

Little Miss Muffet

Little Miss Muffet
Sat on a tuffet
Eating her curds and whey.
Along came a spider
And sat down beside her
And frightened Miss Muffet away!

Spiders can be prepared in the art area.

On a Spider Web

On a spider web that once I saw.
Ten little spiders did creep and crawl.
   (show ten fingers)
They crawled and they crawled and they crawled around.
   (wiggle fingers)
Then one little spider fell down, down, down.
   (put one finger down)

Repeat, reducing the number of spiders by one each time.

Group Time
(Games, Language)

1. **Matching Insects**

Divide children into two groups. For each group hand out pictures of different spiders and insects that match pictures in the other group. Point to a child from one group and have that child act out his or her insect in some way (movement or noises). The child that has the same insect from the other group must go and meet the first child in the middle and act out the insect also.

2. Have many pictures of insects and spiders on display. Talk about a different insect or spider every day. Include where it lives, how it walks, what it might eat, etc.

Large Muscle

1. Have children pretend to walk as different insects when in transition from one activity to another.

2. Explain to the children how bats eat insects. Play a version of "tag" where one child is the "bat" trying to catch the "insects." Make a bat headband out of black construction paper for the "bat" to wear.

Math

1. **Butterfly Match**

   Make several triangles of different colors. On one triangle put the numbers 1 to 10; on the other make dots to correspond to the numbers 1 to 10. Have the children match the dots to the numbers and clip the triangles together with a clothespin to form a butterfly.

2. **Ladybug Houses**

   Paint several 1/2-pint milk cartons red. Write the numerals 1 to 10 on each. Make 50 small ladybugs, dotting 5 sets of 1 to 10. Have children put ladybugs in their correct houses by matching dots to numerals.

3. **Numeral Caterpillar**

   Make a caterpillar with 10 body segments and a head. Have the children put the numbers in order to complete the caterpillar's body.

4. Sing the song "The Ants Go Marching One by One," and have the children act out the song using their fingers as numbers.

5. Make an insect and spider lotto or concentration game with stickers for children to play.

Music

1. **"The Eensy Weensy Spider"**
   (*traditional*)

   The eensy weensy spider crawled up the
       water spout.
       (walk fingers of one hand up other hand)
   Down came the rain and washed the spider out.
       (lower hands to make rain, wash out spider by
       placing hands together in front and extending
       out to either side)
   Out came the sun and dried up all the rain,
       (form sun with arms in circle over head)
   And the eensy weensy spider went up the
       spout again.
       (walk fingers up other arm)

2. **"The Elephant Song"**
   (*chant*)

   One elephant went out to play
   On a spider's web one day.
   He had such enormous fun,
   That he called for another elephant to come.

   Elephant! Elephant! Come out to play!
   Elephant! Elephant! Come out to play!

   Two elephants . . .

3. **"The Insects and Spiders"**
   (*Sing to the tune of* "The Wheels on the Bus")

   The bugs in the air fly up and down,
   up and down, up and down.
   The bugs in the air fly up and down all through
       the day.

   The spiders on the bush spin a web.
   The crickets in the field hop up and down.
   The bees in their hive go buzz, buzz, buzz.

4. "The Bees Are Buzzing All Around"
(*tune: The Ants Go Marching*)

The bees are buzzing all around,
buzz, buzz, buzz, buzz.
The bees are buzzing all around,
buzz, buzz, buzz, buzz.
The bees are buzzing all around,
they're buzzing up and buzzing down.
Oh, the bees are buzzing all around.
Buzz, buzz, buzz.

5. "Shoo Fly"

Shoo fly, don't bother me,
(walk in a circle to the left)
Shoo fly, don't bother me,
(walk in a circle to the right)
Shoo fly, don't bother me,
(walk in a circle to the left)
For I belong to somebody.
(place hands on hips and shake head no)

Flies in the buttermilk,
(walk around shooing flies)
Shoo fly, shoo,
Flies in the buttermilk,
Shoo fly, shoo,
Flies in the buttermilk,
Shoo fly, shoo,
Please just go away.
(place hands on hips and shake head no)

Shoo fly, don't bother me,
(walk to the left in a circle)
Shoo fly, don't bother me.
(walk to the right in a circle)
Shoo fly, don't bother me,
(walk to the left in a circle)
Come back another day.
(wave good-bye)

Science

1. Observe an Ant Farm

The children can watch the ants dig tunnels, build roads and rooms, eat and store food, etc. (Ant farms are available in some commercial play catalogs.)

2. Go outside and observe anthills in the playground area.

3. Observe deceased flies and ants under a microscope.

4. Observe insects and spiders in a caged bug keeper or plastic jars with holes in the lids.

5. Listen to a cricket during quiet time.

6. Capture a caterpillar and watch it spin a chrysalis and turn into a butterfly.

Sensory

1. Add soil and plastic insects to the sensory table.

2. Secret Smells

Discuss with children how bees use their sense of smell to find nectar. Prepare "secret smells" by placing cotton balls inside empty film canisters. Add a variety of fruit extracts to each canister. Use enough to soak the cotton ball. Ask the children to guess the flavor of the smell.

Social Studies

1. Take the children on an insect hunt near your school. When the children are finished, have everyone show the rest of the class what they found. Talk about where they found the insects (on a tree, under a log, etc.).

2. Have children make homes for all the insects they found. They can put dirt, grass, twigs, and small rocks in plastic jars and cans.

3. Discuss what it is like to be a member of a family. Ask the children if each member of their family has a certain job. Then focus on ant colonies as families. Ants live together

much like people do, except that ants live in a larger community. Each ant has a certain task within the community. Some of the jobs are

- nurse: to look after the young
- soldier: defend colony and attack enemies
- others: search for food; enlarge and clean the nest (house)

Books

The following books can be used to complement this theme:

Allen, Judy and Tudor Humphries. (2001). *Are You a Bee*? Illus. by Tudor Humphries. New York: Larousse Kingfisher Chambers.

Arnosky, Jim. (1996). *Crinkleroot's Guide to Knowing Butterflies and Moths*. New York: Simon & Schuster.

Banks, Kate. (1997). *Spider, Spider*. Illus. by Georg Hallensleben. New York: Farrar, Straus & Giroux.

Blum, Mark. (1998). *Bugs in 3-D*. San Francisco: Chronicle Books.

Carle, Eric. (1984). *The Very Busy Spider*. New York: Philomel Books.

Carle, Eric. (1999). *The Very Clumsy Click Beetle*. New York: Philomel Books.

Carle, Eric. (1969). *The Very Hungry Caterpillar*. Harlow, NY: Longman.

Carle, Eric. (1995). *The Very Lonely Firefly*. New York: Philomel Books.

Carle, Eric. (1990). *The Very Quiet Cricket*. New York: Philomel Books.

Carter, David A. (1998). *Bed Bugs: A Pop-Up Bedtime Book*. New York: Little Simon.

Cassie, Brian and Jerry Pallotta. (1995). *The Butterfly Alphabet Book*. Illus. by Mark Astrella. Watertown, MA: Charlesbridge Publishers.

Cole, Joanna. (1995). *Spider's Lunch: All about Garden Spiders*. Illus. by Ron Broda. New York: Grosset & Dunlap. (Pbk.)

Cole, Joanna. (1996). *The Magic School Bus Inside a Beehive*. Illus. by Bruce Degen. New York: Scholastic.

Cole, Joanna. (1997). *The Magic School Bus Spins a Web*: A *Book about Spiders*. Illus. by Bruce Degen. New York: Scholastic. (Pbk.)

Crewe, Sabrina. (1997). *The Bee*. Austin, TX: Raintree/Steck Vaughn.

Fowler, Allan. (1997). *It Could Still Be a Butterfly*. Chicago: Children's Press.

Gerholdt, James E. (1996). *Black Widow Spiders*. Minneapolis, MN: Abdo & Daughters.

Gerholdt, James E. (1996). *Jumping Spiders*. Austin, TX: Raintree/Steck Vaughn.

Gerholdt, James E. (1996). *Trapdoor Spiders*. Minneapolis, MN: Abdo & Daughters.

Gerholdt, James E. (1996). *Wolf Spiders*. Minneapolis, MN: Abdo & Daughters.

Gibbons, Gail. (1993). *Spiders*. New York: Holiday House.

Gibbons, Gail. (1997). *The Honey Makers*. New York: William Morrow.

Greenberg, David T. (1997). *Bugs!* Illus. by Lynn Munsinger. Boston: Little, Brown.

Hariton, Anca. (1995). *Butterfly Story*. New York: Dutton.

Heiligman, Deborah. (1996). *From Caterpillar to Butterfly*. Illus. by Bari Weissman. New York: HarperCollins.

Hill, Frances. (2002). *The Bug Cemetery*. Illus. by Vera Rosenberry. New York: Henry Holt and Co.

Hillyard, P. D. (1993). *Insects and Spiders*. New York: Dorling Kindersley.

Jeunesse, Gallimard. (1997). *Bees*. New York: Scholastic.

Jeunesse, Gallimard. (1997). *Butterflies*. New York: Scholastic.

Krulik, Nancy E. and Joanna Cole. (1996). *The Magic School Bus: Butterfly and the Bog Beast*: A *Book about Butterfly Camouflage*. Illus. by Dana and Del Thompson. New York: Scholastic. (Pbk.)

Laughlin, Robin Kittrell. (1996). *Backyard Bugs*. Illus. by Sue Hubbell. New York: Chronicle Books.

Ling, Mary. (1992). *Butterfly*. Photos by Kim Taylor. New York: Dorling Kindersley.

MacDonald, Amy. (1996). *The Spider Who Created the World*. Illus. by G. Brian Karas. New York: Orchard Books.

MacQuitty, Miranda. (1996). *Amazing Bugs*. New York: Dorling Kindersley.

McDonald, Megan. (1995). *Insects Are My Life*. Illus. by Paul Brett Johnson. New York: Orchard Books.

Oppenheim, Joanne. (1998). *Have You Seen Bugs?* Illus. by Ron Broda. New York: Scholastic.

Pallotta, Jerry. (1993). *The Icky Bug Alphabet Book*. Illus. by Ralph Masiello. Watertown, MA: Charlesbridge Books.

Pinczes, Elinor. (1995). *A Remainder of One*. Illus. by Bonnie MacKain. Boston: Houghton Mifflin.

Polacco, Patricia. (1993). *The Bee Tree*. New York: Philomel Books.

Porte, Barbara Ann. "*Leave That Cricket Be, Alan Lee.*" Illus. by Donna Ruff. New York: Greenwillow.

Ring, Elizabeth. (1994). *Night Flier*. Photos by Dwight Kuhn. Brookfield, CT: Millbrook Press.

Ryden, Hope. (1996). *ABC of Crawlers and Flyers*. New York: Clarion Books.

Ryder, Joanne. (1994). *My Father's Hands*. Illus. by Mark Graham. New York: William Morrow.

Savage, Stephen. (1995). *Butterfly*. Cincinnati, OH: Thomson Learning.

Savage, Stephen. (1995). *Spider*. Illus. by Phil Weare. Cincinnati, OH: Thomson Learning.

Sayre, April Pulley. (2005). *The Bumblebee Queen*. Illus. by Patricia J. Wynne. Watertown, MA: Charlesbridge.

Sill, Cathryn. (2000). *About Insects: a Guide for Children*. Illus. by John Sill. Atlanta, GA: Peachtree.

Sturges, Philemon. (2005). *I Love Bugs!* Illus. by Shari Halpern. New York: HarperCollins.

Thompson, Mary. (1996). *Gran's Bees*. Illus. by Donna Peterson. Brookfield, CT: Millbrook Press.

Trapani, Iza. (1993). *The Itsy Bitsy Spider*. Dallas, TX: Whispering Coyote Press.

Waber, Bernard. (1999). *A Firefly Named Torchy*. Boston: Houghton Mifflin.

Wechsler, Doug. (1995). *Bizarre Bugs*. New York: Cobblehill.

Wells, Rosemary. (1998). *The Itsy-Bitsy Spider*. New York: Scholastic Press.

Multimedia

The following multimedia products can be used to complement this theme:

Griffith, Joelene. (1993). *We Like Bugs* [cassette and book]. East Wenatchee, WA: Learning Workshop.

Insects and Spiders [video]. (©1993). New York: Sony Kids' Video.

The Multimedia Bug Book [CD-Rom]. (©1995). New York: Workman Publishing Co.

Murphy, Jane Lawliss. (1993). *Songs about Insects, Bugs and Squiggly Things* [cassette]. Long Branch, NJ: Kimbo Educational.

Tell Me Why: Insects [video]. (1987). Marina del Rey, CA: Tell Me Why.

Recordings and Song Titles

The following recordings can be used to complement this theme:

"Butterfly." (1982). *It's Toddler Time*. Long Branch, NJ: Kimbo Educational.

"Caterpillar–Cocoon–Butterfly." (1987). *Animal Walks*. Long Branch, NJ: Kimbo Educational.

"Eensy Weensy Spider," "Be My Little Baby Bumblebee/Bringing Home a Baby Bumblebee," "Shoo! Fly, Don't Bother Me." (2001). *Four Baby Bumblebees*. Long Branch, NJ: Kimbo Educational.

"Fuzzy Wuzzy Caterpillar." (1990). *Musical Play Fun*. Long Branch, NJ: Kimbo Educational.

"I Got a Mosquito." (1986). *Singing, Moving and Fun* (*The Learning Station*). Long Branch, NJ: Kimbo Educational.

Songs about Insects, Bugs and Squiggly Things. (1993). Long Branch, NJ: Kimbo Educational.

44

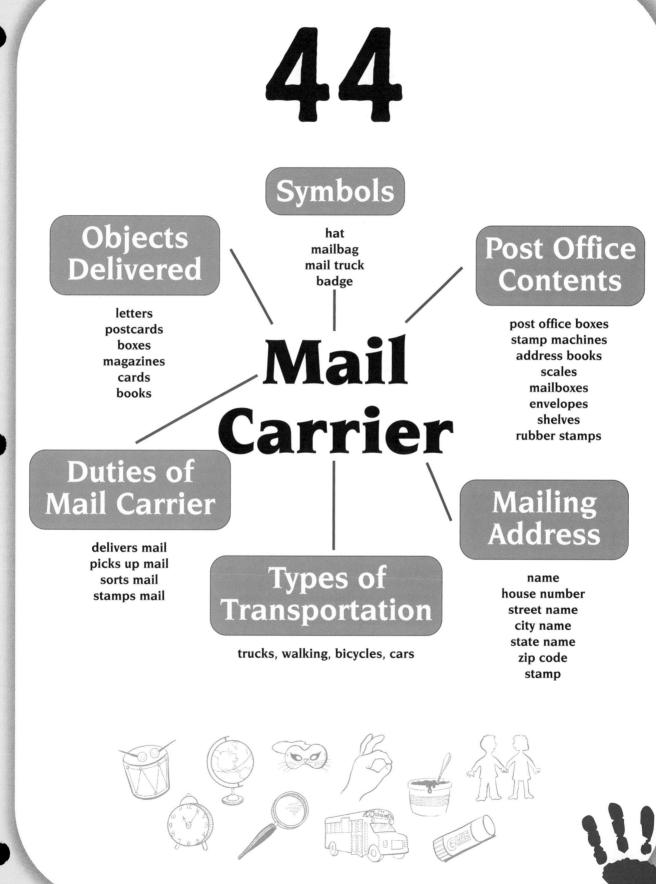

Symbols

hat
mailbag
mail truck
badge

Objects Delivered

letters
postcards
boxes
magazines
cards
books

Post Office Contents

post office boxes
stamp machines
address books
scales
mailboxes
envelopes
shelves
rubber stamps

Mail Carrier

Duties of Mail Carrier

delivers mail
picks up mail
sorts mail
stamps mail

Types of Transportation

trucks, walking, bicycles, cars

Mailing Address

name
house number
street name
city name
state name
zip code
stamp

Theme Goals

Through participating in the experiences provided by this theme, the children may learn

1. Duties of a mail carrier
2. Symbols identifying a mail carrier
3. Contents found in a post office
4. Parts of a mailing address
5. Types of transportation
6. Objects delivered by mail carriers

Concepts for the Children to Learn

1. A man or woman who delivers mail is a mail carrier.
2. The mail carrier usually wears a badge and a hat.
3. A mail carrier either walks, rides a bicycle, or drives a car or truck to deliver mail.
4. Mail carriers deliver cards, letters, postcards, boxes, books, and magazines.
5. Mail carriers sort, stamp, pick up, and deliver mail.
6. Stamps are placed on objects for mailing.
7. Names, house numbers, street names, city names, state names, and zip codes are on mailing labels.
8. A post office has stamp machines, address books, mailboxes, and envelopes.
9. Scales are used to weigh mail.
10. Some mail carriers use mailbags to carry the mail.

Vocabulary

1. **address**—directions for the mail carrier.
2. **envelope**—a cover for a letter.
3. **letter**—a printed message. A letter contains alphabet letters.
4. **mail**—letters, cards, postcards, and packages.
5. **mailbag**—bag that holds letters and postcards.
6. **mail carrier**—person who delivers mail.
7. **post office**—place where mail is sorted.
8. **stamp**—a sticker put on mail.
9. **zip code**—the last numbers on a mailing address.

Bulletin Board

The purpose of this bulletin board is to reinforce the mathematical skill of matching a set to its written numeral. Construct mailboxes out of tagboard. Each mailbox should include a red flag and contain a numeral. The number will depend on developmental appropriateness. A set of dots, corresponding to the numeral on the flag, should be placed on the mailbox. Hang the mailboxes on the bulletin board. Next, construct letters by using small cards with sets of dots on them. The children can match the dots on the cards to the dots and numerals on the mailboxes. If desired, magnet pieces can be attached to both the mailboxes and the cards.

Family Letter

Dear Families,

During the past several weeks, we have been busy discussing the roles of a variety of community helpers. Next, we will focus the curriculum on the role of the mail carrier. The children will learn about letters, stamps, and addresses, and will be able to identify objects found in a post office. They will also become aware of what needs to be included on a letter or package before it is delivered. Moreover, they will learn the types of transportation used for delivering.

AT SCHOOL

Some of the many learning activities scheduled include:

- listening to the story *Adventures of a Letter* by G. Warren Schloat
- playing in a post office set up in the classroom
- making mailboxes and postcards
- weighing letters and packages
- delivering mail to our friends in our room

AT HOME

Let your children help or watch you open the mail. Give your child the "junk mail" to play with. Show your child where your address is on your house and mailbox. You may also enjoy having your children dictate a letter to a grandparent, favorite aunt, or cousin. As you write the letter, show your child the printed alphabet letters to develop an awareness of alphabet letters. After you finish the letter, address an envelope. Let your child show the proper placement of the stamp. Then it's off to the post office!

Enjoy your child!

Arts and Crafts

1. **Postcards**

   Have children make postcards at school to send to family and friends. Provide index cards. Let the children design the postcards.

2. **Mailboxes**

   Make mailboxes out of old shoeboxes. Each child can decorate his or her own box. Names can be added by the child or teacher. Include a home address for older children.

3. **Mail Truck**

   Construct a mail truck out of a large cardboard box. Provide paint for the children to decorate it. When dried, place chairs and, if available, a steering wheel inside for the children to use.

4. **Stamps**

   Collect assorted stamps or stickers. Cancelled stamps can be reglued. The children can make a stamp collage.

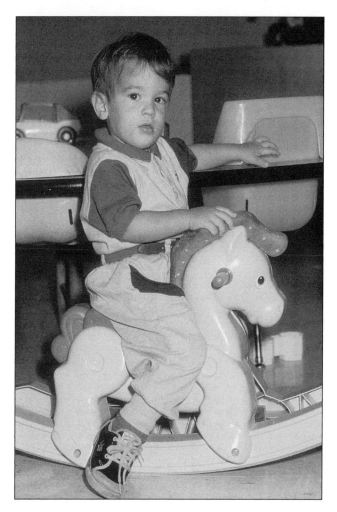

The mail used to be delivered by pony!

Cooking

Zip Code Special

1 1/2 cups nonfat dry milk
2 cups fresh or frozen berries
1 teaspoon vanilla
1 cup water
1 tray ice cubes

Blend all ingredients in a blender. Serve and enjoy.

Dramatic Play

1. **Post Office**

   Develop the dramatic play area into a post office. Provide a mailbox, mail carrier hats, mailbag, stamps, cash register, rubber date stamps, and a letter scale. The children may enjoy acting out the role of a mail carrier or a post office worker.

2. **Letters**

   Provide a variety of writing materials. Include different colors of paper, writing tools, and envelopes. The children can dictate a letter to a friend or a family member. After all interested children have completed dictation, apply stamps and walk to the nearest mailbox or post office. (Contact a local printer, office supply store, or card shop and ask for discontinued samples or misprinted envelopes.)

Field Trips/ Resource People

1. Post Office

Plan a field trip to the local post office. Observe the mailboxes, stamp machines, address books, scales, and rubber stamps with the children. Mail a postcard back to the center. Count the number of days it takes to arrive.

2. Mail Carrier

Invite the mail carrier who delivers mail or the local postmaster to your center or school to visit in the classroom. Ask the mail carrier to show his or her mailbag, hat, and so on, to the children.

Fingerplays

Little Mail Carrier

I am a little mail carrier
(point to self)
Who can do nothing better.
I walk.
(walk in place)
I run.
(run in place)
I hop to your house.
(hop in place)
To deliver your letter.

Five Little Letters

Five little letters lying on a tray.
(extend fingers of right hand)
Mommy came and took the first one away.
(bend down thumb)
Daddy said, "This one's for me!"
I counted them twice, now there are three.
(bend down pointer finger)
Brother Bill asked, "Did I get any mail?"
He found one and cried, "A letter from Gail."
(bend down middle finger)

My sister Jane took the next to the last
And ran upstairs to open it fast.
(bend down ring finger)
As I can't read, I am not able to see,
Whom the last one is for, but I hope it's for me!
(wiggle last finger, clap hands)

The Mail Carrier

I come from the post office
(walk from post office)
My mail sack on my back.
(pretend to carry sack on back)
I go to all the houses
(pretend to go up to a house)
Leaving letters from my pack.
(pretend to drop letters into mailbox)
One, two, three, four
(hold up fingers as you count)
What are these letters for?
(pretend to hold letters as you count)
One for John. One for Lou.
(pretend to hand out letters)
One for Tom and one for you!
(pretend to hand out letters to others)

Letter to Grandma

Lick them, stamp them
(make licking and stamping motions)
Put them in a box.
(extend arms outward)
Hope that Grandma
Loves them a lot!
(hug self)

Group Time
(Games, Language)

Thank You

Write a thank-you note to the postmaster or mail carrier after visiting.

Math

The number of items and numerals used in these activities needs to be adjusted to reflect children's level of development.

1. **Dominoes**

   Create dominoes out of envelopes. Have the children match the numbers and dots.

2. **How Many Stamps?**

   Write an individual numeral on an envelope. Make or collect many stamps. The children can place the correct number of stamps in the envelope with the corresponding numeral. A variation of this activity is to make mailboxes from shoeboxes. Again, write a numeral on each box. Make or collect many different envelopes. The children can put the correct number of letters in the corresponding mailboxes.

3. **Package Seriation**

   Prepare several packages and letters of different sizes. The children can place the letters and packages in order from largest to smallest or smallest to largest.

Music

1. **"Mailing Letters"**
   (*Sing to the tune of* "The Mulberry Bush")

   This is the way we mail a letter,
   Mail a letter, mail a letter.
   This is the way we mail a letter,
   So early in the morning.

2. **"Let's Pretend"**
   (*Sing to the tune of* "Here We Are Together" *and* "Did You Ever See a Lassie?")

   Let's pretend that we are mail carriers,
   Are mail carriers, are mail carriers.
   Let's pretend that we are mail carriers,
   We'll have so much fun.
   We'll carry the letters and put them in boxes.

Let's pretend that we are mail carriers,
We'll have so much fun.

Science

1. **Dress the Mail Carrier**

   Place flannel board pieces representing seasonal clothing for a mail carrier. Let the children select the appropriate clothing for the weather. This may be an interesting activity to introduce daily during group time.

2. **Weighing Mail**

   A variety of letters, boxes, stamps, and a scale can be placed in the science area. The children can weigh letters and packages. This activity can be extended by placing materials in the boxes and weighing them, noting the difference.

3. **How Does the Mail Feel?**

   Place different types of envelopes and stationery on the sensory table for the children to explore. Include airmail paper, onionskin, bond paper, computer paper, and different kinds of stationery. Also, provide a magnifying glass.

Social Studies

Mailboxes

Plan a walk around the neighborhood. Observe the different types of mailboxes and addresses.

Books

The following books can be used to complement this theme:

Cuneo, Mary Louise and Pamela Paparone. (2000). *Mail for Husher Town*. Illus. by Pamela Paparone. New York: Greenwillow.

Flanagan, Alice K. and Christine Osinski (Photographer). (1999). *Here Comes Mr. Eventoff with the Mail (Our Neighborhood)*. New York: Children's Press.

Gibbons, Gail. (1987). *The Post Office Book: Mail and How It Moves*. New York: HarperCollins.

Henkes, Kevin. (1995). *Good-Bye, Curtis*. Illus. by Marisabina Russo. New York: Greenwillow.

Keats, Ezra Jack. (1998). *A Letter to Amy*. Reprint edition. New York: Viking.

Kottke, Jan. (2000). *A Day with a Mail Carrier (Hard Work)*. New York: Children's Press.

Lakin, Pat. (1995). *Red-Letter Day*. Illus. by Doug Cushman. Austin, TX: Raintree/ Steck Vaughn.

Landstrom, Olof and Lena Landstrom. (1994). *Will Goes to the Post Office*. New York: Farrar, Straus & Giroux.

Levinson, Nancy Smiler. (1992). *Snowshoe Thompson*. Illus. by Joan Sandin. New York: HarperCollins.

Lillegard, Dee. (1997). *Tortoise Brings the Mail*. Illus. by Jillian Lund. New York: Dutton.

Miller, Robert H. (1994). *The Story of "Stagecoach" Mary Fields*. Illus. by Cheryl Hanna. Englewood Cliffs, NJ: Silver Press.

Rylant, Cynthia. (1989, 1993). *Mr. Griggs' Work*. Illus. by Julie Downing. New York: Orchard Books.

Schaefer, Lola M. (1999). *We Need Mail Carriers*. Mankato, MN: Pebble Books.

Schloat, G. Warren. (1949). *Adventures of a Letter*. New York: Scribner.

Scott, Ann Herbert. (1994). *Hi*. Illus. by Glo Coalson. New York: Philomel Books.

Skurzynksi, Gloria. (1992). *Here Comes the Mail*. New York: Macmillan.

Multimedia

The following multimedia products can be used to complement this theme:

At the Post Office [video]. (1995). Tallahassee, FL: Dogwood Video.

Post Office [video]. (1991). Washington, DC: National Geographic.

Postal Station [video]. (1991). TV Ontario/ distributed by Films for the Humanities.

There Goes the Mail [video]. (1997). New York: KidVision.

Recordings and Song Titles

The following recording can be used to complement this theme:

"The Community Helper Hop." (1996). *People in Our Neighborhood*. Long Branch, NJ: Kimbo Educational.

45

Foods

insects, leaves,
roots, seeds,
leather, fruits,
nuts, cheese,
plants

Size

small

Homes

barns
attics
basements
fields
nests

Types

house
American harvest
grasshopper
deer

Mice

Noises

squeaking
scratching
chattering

Needs

food
water
shelter

Enemies

people, dogs,
hawks, foxes,
snakes, owls, rats,
other mice, cats

Body Parts

head, body, tail,
ears, eyes, mouth,
whiskers

Colors

white
black
brown

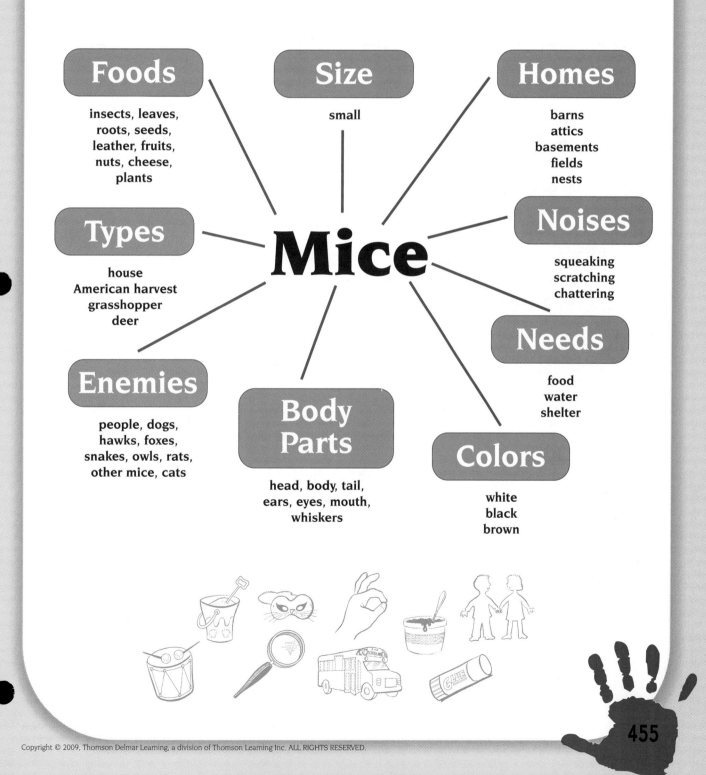

Theme Goals

Through participating in the experiences provided by this theme, the children may learn

1. Body parts of mice
2. Size of mice
3. Needs of mice
4. Color of mice
5. Noises mice make
6. Foods mice eat
7. Homes mice make
8. Enemies of mice
9. Types of mice

Concepts for the Children to Learn

1. A mouse is a small animal.
2. Mice is the word to use when you refer to more than one mouse.
3. There are four main types of mice: house, American harvest, grasshopper, and deer.
4. The body of a mouse is 2 1/2 to 3 1/2 inches long. The tail is almost as long as the body.
5. The body of a mouse is covered with fur.
6. Mice may have white-, brown-, or black-colored fur.
7. Mice need water, food, and shelter to live.
8. Mice eat plants, insects, leaves, roots, seeds, leather, fruits, cheese, and nuts.
9. Barns, attics, basements, fields, and nests are homes for mice.
10. Mice live where they can find food and shelter.
11. Mice have good hearing but poor sight.
12. Mice have strong, sharp front teeth that keep growing.
13. Mice have a head, body, tail, ears, eyes, mouth, and whiskers.
14. A house mouse has a brown back and white belly.
15. People can sometimes hear mice squeaking and scratching.
16. House mice are good climbers. People sometimes hear them running inside the walls of their homes.
17. Mice are sometimes used for pets and for health-care discoveries.
18. People, cats, dogs, hawks, foxes, snakes, owls, rats, and other mice can be enemies of mice.

Vocabulary

1. **mouse**—a small furry animal that has a head, ears, eyes, a mouth, whiskers, four legs, a body, and a tail.
2. **scratching**—a noise a mouse makes by rubbing its nails against a surface.
3. **squeaking**—a clear, sharp sound made by a mouse.

Bulletin Board

The purpose of this bulletin board is to promote the identification of written numerals as well as matching a set to a written numeral. Construct cheese and mice shapes out of construction paper or tagboard. Draw a set of dots on each piece of cheese. The number of dots used should correspond to the developmental level of the children. Print a corresponding numeral on each mouse. Staple the cheese pieces to the bulletin board along the side edges and the bottom, creating a pocket. The children should be encouraged to match the written numeral of each mouse to the corresponding set of dots on the cheese pieces and place the mice in the pockets.

Help the mice find their cheese.

Family Letter

Dear Families,

Squeak! Squeak! Squeak! We will be enjoying a new theme that will provide us with discoveries about small animals called mice. The children will be learning about types, colors, care, needs, and enemies of mice. They will also learn about foods mice eat and the homes they make.

AT SCHOOL

Learning experiences planned for this unit include:

- visiting the pet store to observe mice
- pretending to be mice in the dramatic play area
- listening to the stories titled *Mouse Paint* and *Mouse Count* by Lois Ehlert

AT HOME

Go to the library and check out some children's books about mice. Some titles to look for include:

- *If You Give a Mouse a Cookie* by Laura Numeroff
- *Mouse Poems* by John Foster

Enjoy the following fingerplay titled, "Where Are the Baby Mice?" with your child.

> Where are the baby mice?
> (Hide fists behind back)
> Squeak, squeak, squeak.
> I cannot see them.
> Peek, peek, peek.
> (show fists)
> Here they come out of their hole in the wall.
> One, two, three, four, five and that is all!
> (show fingers one at a time)

Have a nice week!

Can you squeak like a mouse?

Arts and Crafts

1. **Mouse Sponge Painting**

   Cut sponges into mice shapes. Place on the art table with paper and a shallow pan of thick tempera paint. The children can make designs by pressing the sponge into the paint and then on a piece of paper.

2. **Seed Collage**

   Place a variety of seeds, glue, and paper on a table in the art area. The children can create designs with the materials.

Cooking

1. **Macaroni and Cheese**

   Purchase prepackaged macaroni and cheese. Prepare following the directions provided on the container. Compare the flavor to the recipe that follows.

   3–3 1/2 cups cooked macaroni
   1/4 cup butter or margarine
   1/4 cup chopped onion (optional)
   1/2 teaspoon salt
   1/2 teaspoon pepper
   1/4 cup flour
   1 1/2 cups milk
   1/2 pound of Swiss or American cheese cut into small cubes

   Combine butter, onion, salt, and pepper in a saucepan; cook over medium heat until onion is tender. Blend in the flour. Lower heat and stir constantly until the mixture is smooth and bubbly. Add milk and heat to boiling, stirring constantly. Stir and boil one minute. Remove from heat. Add cheese and stir until melted.

   Place macaroni in ungreased 1 1/2 quart casserole. Stir cheese sauce into the macaroni. Bake in an oven heated to 375 degrees for 30 minutes. (Makes five servings.)

2. **Mouse Cookies**

   With the children, prepare a batch of drop cookie dough according to the recipe. Demonstrate how to drop three spoonfuls of dough onto a cookie sheet so that it will resemble a mouse head with two ears when baked. The mouse cookies can be frosted or details can be added with raisins, chocolate chips, and string licorice.

Dramatic Play

1. Mouse House

The children can pretend to be mice! Construct mouse ears out of fabric or construction paper and attach to headbands. Provide large cardboard boxes to represent houses for the mice.

2. Pet Store

Arrange the dramatic play area as a pet store. Provide props such as a cash register, play money, stuffed animals, animal cages, animal toys, and empty pet food boxes. Display posters of pets, including mice.

Field Trips

1. Pet Store

Visit a pet store to observe the colors of pet mice and animal accessories. Photographs can be taken during the trip and later displayed in the classroom.

2. Mouse Walk

Take a walk around your school and look for places mice might live.

Fingerplays

Where Are the Baby Mice?

Where are the baby mice?
  (hide fists behind back)
Squeak, squeak, squeak!
I cannot see them.
Peek, peek, peek.
  (show fist)
Here they come out of their hole in the wall.
One, two, three, four, five, and that is all!
  (show fingers one at a time)

Five Little Baby Mice

Five little mice on the kitchen floor.
  (hold up five fingers)
This little mouse peeked behind the door.
  (point to thumb)
This little mouse nibbled at the cake.
  (point to index finger)
This little mouse not a sound did he make.
  (point to middle finger)
This little mouse took a bite of cheese.
  (point to ring finger)
This little mouse heard the kitten sneeze.
  (point to pinky)
"Ah-choo!" sneezed the kitten,
And "squeak" they cried.
As they found a hole and ran inside.
  (move hand behind back)

Little Mouse

See the little mousie,
  (place index and middle finger on thumb to
  represent a mouse)
Creeping up the stair,
  (creep mouse slowly up the forearm)
Looking for a warm rest.
There—Oh! There!
  (spring mouse into an elbow corner)

Hickory Dickory Dock

Hickory, dickory, dock.
  (bend arm at elbow; hold up and open palm)
The mouse ran up the clock.
  (run fingers up the arm)
The clock struck one,
  (hold up index finger)
The mouse ran down,
  (run fingers down arm)
Hickory, dickory, dock.

Mouse

Here is a mouse with ears so funny,
  (place index and middle finger on thumb to
  represent a mouse)
And here is a hole in the ground.
  (make a hole with the other fist)
When a noise he hears, he pricks up his ears.
And runs to his hole in the ground.
  (jump mouse into hole in other fist)

Group Time

(Games, Language)

1. **"Mouse, Mouse, Where's Your Cheese?"**

   This game is played in a circle formation. Arrange the chairs and place one in the center of the circle. Place a block to represent the cheese under the chair. Select one child, the "mouse," to sit on the chair and close his or her eyes. Then point to another child. This child must try to remove the cheese without making a sound. After the child returns to his or her chair in the circle, instruct all of the children to place their hands behind their backs. Then, in unison, the children say, "Mouse, Mouse, where is your cheese?" The mouse then opens his or her eyes and tries to guess who is holding the cheese.

2. **Language Chart**

   Across the top of a piece of tagboard, print the question, "Where would you like to live if you were a mouse?" During group time introduce the chart and record the children's responses. Display the chart in the classroom.

Music

1. **"Ten Little Mice"**
   (*Sing to the tune of "Ten Little Indians"*)

   One little, two little, three little mice.
   Four little, five little, six little mice.
   Seven little, eight little, nine little mice.

2. **"Two Little Brown Mice"**
   (*Sing to the tune of "Two Little Blackbirds" or "Baa Baa Black Sheep"*)

   Two little brown mice,
   Scampering through the hall.
   One named Sarah.
   One named Paul.

   Run away, Sarah.
   Run away, Paul.

   Come back, Sarah.
   Come back, Paul.

   Two little brown mice,
   Scampering through the hall.
   One named Sarah.
   One named Paul.

3. **"Find the Mouse"**
   (*Sing to the tune of "The Muffin Man"*)

   Oh, can you find the little mouse,
   The little mouse, the little mouse.
   Can you find the little mouse,
   He's somewhere in the house.

4. **"One Little Mouse"**
   (*Sing to the tune of "Six Little Ducks"*)

   One little brown and whiskery mouse
   Lived in a hole in a cozy house.
   When the cat came along to
   Take a little peek,
   The mouse ran away with a "Squeak,
       squeak, squeak."
   "Squeak, squeak, squeak."
   "Squeak, squeak, squeak."
   "The mouse ran away with a "Squeak,
       squeak, squeak."

5. **"Three Brown Mice"**
   (*Sing to the tune of "Three Blind Mice"*)

   Three brown mice, three brown mice.
   See how they run. See how they run.
   They were chased through the house by the big
       black cat.
   Lucky for them, she was lazy and fat.
   Did you ever see such a sight as that?
   Three brown mice, three brown mice.

Science

Mice

Purchase or borrow mice from a pet store to keep as classroom pets. Place the cage on the science table for the children to observe. Allow the children to assist in caring for the animals.

Sensory

Additions to the Sensory Table

- grains with scoops, cups, and spoons
- seeds with pails and shovels
- clean cedar chips (animal bedding) with measuring cups, scoops, and pails

Books

The following books can be used to complement this theme:

Brett, Jan. (1994). *Town Mouse, Country Mouse.* New York: G. P. Putnam.

Carlson, Nancy L. (1999). *Look Out Kindergarten, Here I Come!* New York: Viking.

Cousins, Lucy. (1998). *Maisy on the Farm.* Cambridge, MA: Candlewick Press.

Cowley, Joy. (1995). *Mouse Bride.* Illus. by David Christiana. New York: Scholastic.

Craig, Helen. (1993). *Angelina's Ice Skates.* Illus. by Katharine Holabird. New York: C. N. Potter.

De Paola, Tomie. (1997). *Mice Squeak, We Speak.* New York: Putnam. (Poem by Arnold Shapiro.)

Duke, Kate. (1992). *Isabelle Tells a Good One.* New York: Dutton.

Edwards, Pamela Duncan. (1996). *Livingstone Mouse.* Illus. by Henry Cole. New York: HarperCollins.

Farris, Pamela J. (1996). *Young Mouse and Elephant: An East African Folktale.* Illus. by Valeri Gorbachev. Boston: Houghton Mifflin.

Fleming, Denise. (1992). *Lunch.* New York: Henry Holt and Co.

Galvin, Laura Gates et al. (1998). *Deer Mouse at Old Farm Road.* Illus. Katy Bratun. Norwalk, CT: Soundprints.

Goodall, John S. (1999). *Naughty Nancy Goes to School.* New York: Margaret McElderry.

King-Smith, Dick and Jon Goodell. (1999). *A Mouse Called Wolf.* Illus. by Jon Goodell. New York: Knopf.

Krensky, Stephen. (1995). *Three Blind Mice Mystery.* Illus. by Lynn Munsinger. New York: Delacorte.

McBratney, Sam. (1996). *The Dark at the Top of the Stairs.* Illus. by Ivan Bates. Cambridge, MA: Candlewick Press.

McMillan, Bruce. (1993). *Mouse Views: What the Class Pet Saw.* New York: Holiday House.

Monson, A. M. (1997). *Wanted: Best Friend.* Illus. by Lynn Munsinger. New York: Dial.

Palazzo-Craig, Janet. (1995). *Max and Maggie in Spring.* Illus. by Paul Meisel. Mahwah, NJ: Troll.

Reiser, Lynn. (1995). *Two Mice in Three Fables.* New York: Greenwillow.

Riley, Linnea Asplind. (1997). *Mouse Mess.* New York: Blue Sky Press.

Ring, Elizabeth. (1995). *Lucky Mouse.* Illus. by Dwight Kuhn. Brookfield, CT: Millbrook Press.

Roth, Susan. (1997). *My Love for You.* New York: Dial.

Ryan, Pam Munoz and Joe Cepeda. (2001). *Mice and Beans.* Illus. by Joe Cepeda. New York: Scholastic.

Sathre, Vivian. (1995). *Mouse Chase.* Illus. by Ward Schumaker. Orlando, FL: Harcourt Brace.

Scarry, Richard. (2001). *Is this the House of Mistress Mouse?* New York: Golden Books.

Schindel, John. (1994). *What's for Lunch?* Illus. by Kevin O'Malley. New York: Lothrop, Lee & Shepard.

Summers, Kate. (1997). *Milly and Tilly: The Story of a Town Mouse and a Country Mouse.* Illus. by Maggie Kneen. New York: Dutton.

Waber, Bernard. (1995). *Do You See a Mouse?* Boston: Houghton Mifflin.

Walsh, Ellen Stoll. (1995). *Mouse Count.* Orlando, FL: Harcourt.

Walsh, Ellen Stoll. (1995). *Mouse Paint*. Orlando, FL: Harcourt.

Walsh, Ellen Stoll. (1996). *Samantha*. Orlando, FL: Harcourt Brace.

Young, Ed. (1992). *Seven Blind Mice*. New York: Philomel Books.

Multimedia

The following multimedia products can be used to complement this theme:

If You Give a Mouse a Cookie [CD-ROM]. (1995). New York: HarperCollins Interactive.

Lionni, Leo. "Frederick" on *Five Lionni Classics* [video]. (1987). New York: Random House Home Video.

Palmer, Hap. "The Mice Go Marching" on *Rhythms on Parade*. [compact disc]. (1995). Baldwin, NY: Educational Activities.

Sharon, Lois and Bram. "Three Blind Mice" and "Hickory, Dickory, Dock" on *Mainly Mother Goose* [compact disc]. (1984). Toronto, Ont.: Elephant Records.

46

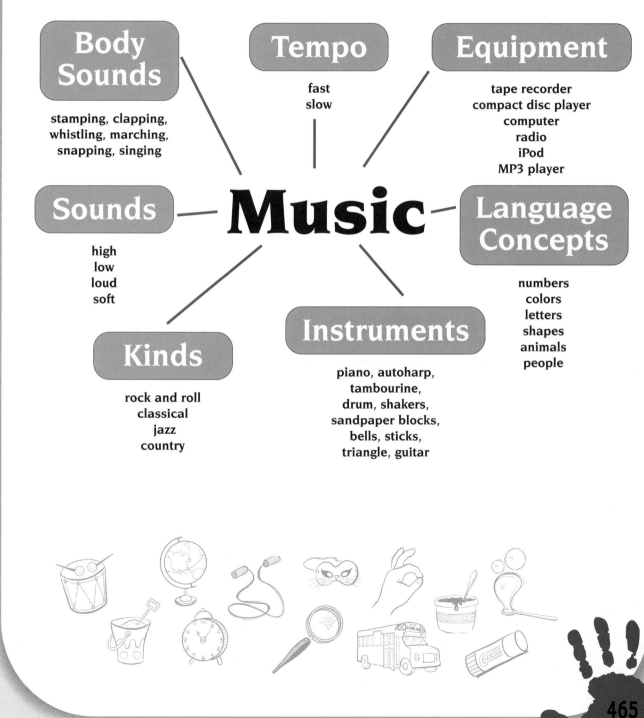

Music

Body Sounds

stamping, clapping, whistling, marching, snapping, singing

Tempo

fast
slow

Equipment

tape recorder
compact disc player
computer
radio
iPod
MP3 player

Sounds

high
low
loud
soft

Language Concepts

numbers
colors
letters
shapes
animals
people

Kinds

rock and roll
classical
jazz
country

Instruments

piano, autoharp, tambourine, drum, shakers, sandpaper blocks, bells, sticks, triangle, guitar

Theme Goals

Through participating in the experiences provided by this theme, the children may learn

1. Kinds of music
2. Music tempos
3. Language concepts
4. Different sounds
5. Names of many musical instruments
6. Body sounds
7. Equipment used for playing and recording music

Concepts for the Children to Learn

1. Music is a language.
2. Music is a way of expressing ideas and feelings.
3. There are many types of instruments.
4. The piano, autoharp, tambourine, drum, shakers, sandpaper blocks, bells, sticks, triangle, and guitar are all musical instruments.
5. Each instrument has its own sound.
6. Music sounds can be high, low, loud, and soft.
7. Music can express different moods.
8. Music can be played in different rhythms.
9. Songs can tell stories.
10. Our bodies are musical instruments that can make sounds.
11. Our hands can clap.
12. Our feet can stamp and march.
13. Our fingers can snap.
14. Our mouths can whistle and sing.
15. The piano, autoharp, and guitar are played with our fingers.
16. Sticks are used on the triangle, drum, xylophone, and bells.
17. We shake bells, shakers, and tambourines.
18. We rub sandpaper blocks.
19. There are many kinds of music.
20. We can tape music with a recorder.
21. Rock and roll, classical, jazz, and country are kinds of music.
22. We can play music with a tape recorder, compact disc player, computer, radio, iPod, and MP3 player.

Vocabulary

1. **body sounds**—sounds made by moving one or more body parts.
2. **instrument**—makes musical sounds.
3. **mallets**—special sticks used to play the xylophone and bells.
4. **music**—a way of expressing ideas and feelings through sound.
5. **tempo**—the speed of music.

Bulletin Board

The purpose of this bulletin board is to develop visual discrimination and visual memory skills. Create a musical bulletin board by drawing musical instruments on tagboard as illustrated. Color the instruments with markers, cut out, and laminate. Trace these pieces onto black construction paper. Cut out the pieces and attach to the bulletin board. A magnet strip should be attached to both the colored pieces and the black shadow pieces. The children can match the appropriately shaped instrument piece to its shadow on the bulletin board.

Family Letter

Dear Families,

We will be singing and playing instruments during our curriculum unit on music. Music is a universal language. It is a way of communicating and expressing oneself. For young children, singing is not that much different from talking—as I'm sure you've noticed from observing the children! Throughout the unit the children will make interesting discoveries about the many sounds that we can make with our voices, body parts, and musical instruments.

AT SCHOOL

A few highlights of our scheduled musical learning activities include:

- making musical instruments
- painting at the easel while listening to music with headphones
- trying on band uniforms (courtesy of Mead School) in the dramatic play area
- forming a rhythm band outside in the play yard

FAMILY INVOLVEMENT

If you enjoy any special cultural or ethnic music or instruments, we invite you to share them with our class. Please contact me so a time for your visit can be arranged. The children, especially your own, will enjoy having you visit our class and learning more about music.

AT HOME

To stimulate creativity and language, create verses with your child for this song to the tune of "Old MacDonald Had a Farm":

Mr. Roberts had a band,
E-I-E-I-O.
And in his band he had a drum
E-I-E-I-O.
With a boom, boom here, and a boom, boom, there,
Here a boom, there a boom,
Everywhere a boom, boom.
Mr. Roberts had a band,
E-I-E-I-O.

And in his band he had a horn . . .

Continue adding instruments that your child can think of.

Provide materials for your child to make simple musical instruments. A drum can be made using an empty oatmeal carton or coffee can. Your child can personalize the instrument by decorating the outside of the container with paper, crayons, and markers. A kazoo can also be made with a cardboard tube and a small piece of waxed paper attached to the end of the tube with a rubber band. Poke a small hole in the waxed paper and your child will be ready to blow up a storm! Compare the sounds produced by the different instruments to develop auditory discrimination skills.

Keep a song in your heart!

Children enjoy listening to and creating their own music.

# Arts and Crafts

1. Drums

Create drums out of empty coffee cans with plastic lids, plastic ice cream pails, or oatmeal boxes. The children can decorate as desired with paper, paint, felt-tip markers, or crayons.

2. Shakers

Collect a variety of egg-shaped panty hose containers. Fill each egg with varying amounts of sand, peas, or rice, and securely tape or glue them shut. To compare sounds, empty film containers can also be filled.

3. Cymbals

Make cymbals out of old tinfoil pans. Attach a string for the handles.

4. Tambourines

Two paper plates can be made into a tambourine. Begin by placing pop bottle caps or small stones between the plates. Staple the paper plates together. Shake to produce sound.

5. Musical Painting

On a table in the art area, place a tape recorder with headphones. The children can listen to music as they paint.

6. Kazoos

Kazoos can be made with empty paper towel rolls and waxed paper. The children can decorate the outside of the kazoos with colored felt-tip markers. After this, place a piece of waxed paper over one end of the roll and secure it with a rubber band. Poke two or three small holes into the waxed paper, allowing sound to be produced.

7. Rhythm Sticks

Two wooden dowels should be given to each interested child. The sticks can be decorated with paint or colored felt-tip markers.

MUSIC

Cooking

Popcorn

Make popcorn and have the children listen to the sounds of the oil and corn popping. **Caution:** Supervise this activity closely because the corn popper will become hot. This activity is most appropriate for older children—younger children may choke on popcorn.

Dramatic Play

1. **Band**

   Collect materials for a band prop box, which may include band uniforms, a baton, music stand, cassette or CD player, and CDs or tapes with marching music. The children can experiment with instruments.

2. **Dramatizing**

   Add a cassette recorder and a small microphone to the dramatic play area. The children may enjoy using it for singing and recording their voices.

3. **Disc Jockey**

   In the music area, provide a tape recorder and cassettes or a CD player and CDs for the children.

Field Trips/ Resource People

1. **Band Director**

   Visit a school band director. Observe the different instruments available to students. Listen to their sounds.

2. **Who Can Play?**

   Invite parents, grandparents, brothers, sisters, relatives, friends, and so on, to visit the classroom and demonstrate their talent.

3. **Radio Station**

   Visit a local radio station.

4. **Taping**

   Use a digital recorder to record the children singing and using rhythm instruments. Replay the video for the children. Save this for a future open house, parent meeting, or holiday celebration.

Fingerplays

I Want to Lead a Band

I want to lead a band
With a baton in my hand.
   (wave baton in air)
I want to make sweet music high and low.
Now first I'll beat the drum
   (drum-beating motion)
With a rhythmic tum-tum-tum,
And then I'll play the bells
A-ting-a-ling-a-ling,
   (bell-playing motion)
And next I'll blow the flute
With a cheery toot-a-toot.
   (flute-playing motion)
Then I'll make the violin sweetly sing.
   (violin-playing motion)
Now I'm leading a band
With a baton in my hand.
   (wave baton in air again)

If I Could Play

If I could play the piano
This is the way I would play.
   (move fingers like playing a piano)

If I had a guitar
I would strum the strings this way.
   (hold guitar and strum)

If I had a trumpet
I'd toot to make a tune.
   (play trumpet)

But if I had a drum
I'd go boom, boom, boom.
   (pretend to play a drum)

Musical Instruments

This is how a horn sounds
Toot! Toot! Toot!
  (play imaginary horn)

This is how guitars sound
Vrrroom, vrrroom, vrrroom
  (strum imaginary guitar)

This is how the piano sounds
Tinkle, grumble, brring.
  (run fingers over imaginary keyboard)

This is how the drum sounds
Rat-a-tat, grumble, brring.
  (strike drum, include cymbal)

Jack-in-the-Box

Jack-in-the-box all shut up tight
  (fingers wrapped around thumb)
Not a breath of air, not a ray of light.
  (other hand covers fist)
How tired he must be all down in a heap.
  (lift off)
I'll open the lid and up he will leap!
  (thumbs pop out)

Large Muscle

1. Body Movement Rhythms

Introduce a simple body movement. Then have the children repeat it until they develop a rhythm. Examples include:

- stamp foot, clap hands, stamp foot, clap hands
- clap, clap, stamp, stamp
- clap, stamp, clap, stamp
- clap, clap, snap fingers
- clap, snap, stamp, clap, snap, stamp
- clap, clap, stamp, clap, clap, stamp

2. Body Percussion

Instruct the children to stand in a circle. Repeat the following rhythmic speech:

We walk and we walk and we stop (rest)
We walk and we walk and we stop (rest)

We walk and we walk and we walk and we walk
We walk and we walk and we stop. (stop)

3. March

Play different rhythm beats on a piano or another instrument. Examples include hopping, skipping, gliding, walking, running, tiptoeing, galloping, etc. The children can move to the rhythm.

4. Scarf Dancing

Give each child a scarf and play a variety of music. Encourage the children to move the scarf fast or slow according to the music.

5. Musical Freeze

Arrange children in a circle. Pass around a beanbag as you play music. When the music stops, whoever is holding the beanbag "freezes" with it. When the music restarts, the child begins passing it again.

Math

1. Colors, Shapes, and Numbers

Sing the song, "Colors, Shapes, and Numbers," mentioned in the Shapes unit or make up a song about shapes. Hold up different colors, shapes, and numbers while you sing the song for the children to identify.

2. Number Rhyme

Say the following song to reinforce numbers:

One, two, three, four
Come right in and shut the door.
Five, six, seven, eight
Come right in. It's getting late.
Nine, ten, eleven, twelve
Put your books upon the shelves.
Will you count along with me?
It's as easy as can be!

3. Ten in the Bed

Chant the following words to reinforce numbers:

There were 10 in the bed and the little one said,
"Roll over, roll over."
So they all rolled over and one fell out.

There were nine in the bed and the little one said,
"Roll over, roll over."
So they all rolled over and one fell out.

Continue until there is only one left. The last line will be ". . . and the little one said, "Good night!"

4. **Music Calendar**

Design a calendar for the month of your music unit. The different days of the week can be made out of musical notes and different instruments.

5. **Drum Beats**

Arrange children in a circle and ask them to close their eyes. Have them listen for the number of times you beat the drum. (If it is too difficult for them to count in their heads, count out loud as you beat the drum.) Whoever names the correct number gets to beat the drum next.

Miscellaneous

Instrument of the Day

Focus on a different instrument each day. Talk about its construction and demonstrate the instrument's sound.

Music

Music for this unit should consist of the children's favorite and well-known songs. The children will enjoy singing these songs, and you will be able to focus on the sound of the music. Here are some suggestions of traditional songs that most children enjoy:

1. "Old MacDonald Had a Farm"
2. "Five Green Speckled Frogs"
3. "The Farmer in the Dell"
4. "Row, Row, Row Your Boat"
5. "Mary Had a Little Lamb"

6. "Hickory Dickory Dock"
7. "If You're Happy and You Know It"
8. "ABC Song"
9. "The Little White Duck"
10. "Six Little Ducks"
11. "Do Your Ears Hang Low?"
12. "Old King Cole"
13. "Head, Shoulders, Knees, and Toes"

Science

1. **Water Music**

Fill four identically sized crystal glasses each with a different amount of water. Supervise the children tracing their wet finger around the rim of each glass. Each glass will have a different tune. Older children may enjoy reordering the glasses from the highest to the lowest tone.

2. **Pop Bottle Music**

Fill six 12-ounce pop bottles, each with a different amount of water. For effect, in each bottle place a drop of food coloring, providing six different colors. Younger children can tap the bottles with a spoon as they listen for the sound. Older children may try blowing directly into the opening for sound production.

3. **Throats**

Show the children how to place their hands across their throat. Then have them whisper, talk, shout, and sing while feeling the differences in vibration.

4. **Jumping Seeds**

Set seeds or other small objects on top of a drum. Then beat the drum. What happens? Why? This activity can be extended by having the children jump to the drum beat.

5. **Identifying Instruments**

Prepare a CD or tape recording of classroom musical instruments. Play the CD or tape,

472

encouraging the children to identify the correct instrument related to each sound.

6. Matching Sounds

Collect 12 containers, such as film canisters, milk cartons, or covered potato chip cans, that would be safe to use with the children. Fill two containers with rice, two cans with beans, two cans with pebbles, two cans with water, and the remaining cans with dry pasta. Coins, such as pennies, could be substituted. Color code each pair of containers on the bottom. Let the children shake the containers, listening to the sounds, in an attempt to find the matching pairs.

7. Musical Vibrations

Tie two pieces of string to a wire hanger near both ends. Hold the strings to your ears and swing the hanger on the back of a chair or table. The vibration from the metal hanger will travel up the strings. Discuss with children the musical instruments that also make a vibration (triangles, drums, tone blocks, etc.). (**Note:** Supervise the children carefully when they are using hangers.)

Sensory

1. Rainstick

Ask the children to close their eyes as you slowly turn a rainstick upside down. Ask the children to try to identify the sound they hear. Once they have guessed the correct sound, see if they can name the instrument. Allow time for children to experiment with the rainstick. (Rainsticks can easily be made with any cardboard roll and pebbles. Be sure to securely cap both ends before giving the rainstick to children).

2. Bubble Wrap

Give each child a piece of bubble wrap. Let them experiment with making it pop. Sing "Pop Goes the Weasel" and ask the children to try to keep a beat or pop a bubble when the word "pop" is sung in the song.

Social Studies

1. Our Own Songs

Encourage the children to help you write a song about a common class experience. Substitute the words into a melody that everyone knows ("Twinkle, Twinkle, Little Star" or "The Mulberry Bush").

2. Pictures

Put up pictures of instruments and band players in the room to add interest and stimulate discussion.

3. Sound Tapes

Make a special tape or CD of sounds heard in a home. Homes are full of different sounds. The following may be included:

- people knocking on doors
- wind chimes
- telephone ringing
- teakettle whistling
- clock ticking
- toilet flushing
- popcorn popping
- vacuum cleaner
- doorbell
- running water
- car horn

Play the tape or CD and have the children listen carefully to identify the sounds.

Books

The following books can be used to complement this theme:

Bartlett, T. C. (1997). *Tuba Lessons*. Illus. by Monique Felix. Orlando, FL: Harcourt Brace.

Brett, Jan. (1991). *Berlioz the Bear*. New York: G. P. Putnam.

(*continued*)

Multicultural Songs

Children's Folk Dances
By Georgiana Stewart

1. Polly Wolly Doodle
2. Walking Song
3. Go Round and Round the Village
4. Jump Jim Jo
5. Mi Jachol Lassim
6. Sma Grodorna
7. Unite Unite/Hobby Horse Parade
8. The French Musician
9. Where, Oh Where
10. Schottische
11. Troika
12. Everyone Likes Calypso
13. Ulili E
14. Cielito Lindo
15. Goodbye, Mrs. Durkin
16. Sur Le Pont D'Avignon
17. Die Hammerschiedsgesellen
18. Tarantella Doll
19. Carousel
20. Fado
21. Tant Hessie

Multicultural Rhythm Stick Fun
By Georgiana Stewart

1. Puerto Rico ("Ambos a Dos")
2. Caribbean ("Calypso")
3. Ireland ("Piper Piper")
4. Israel ("Zum Gali Gali")
5. Greece ("Children's Song")
6. Germany ("Hansel and Gretel Polka")
7. Span ("Espana Cani")
8. Australia ("Waltzing Matilda")
9. India ("Daysie")
10. Puerto Rico (Instrumental)
11. Caribbean (Instrumental)
12. Israel (Instrumental)
13. West Africa ("Kourilengay")

14. Mexico ("La Cucaracha")
15. China ("Show Ha Mo")
16. Japan ("Haru Ga Kita")
17. Italy ("Tarantella")
18. Russia ("Trepak — Nutcracker")
19. Brazil ("Tico Tico")
20. France ("Alouette")
21. Vietnam ("Chu Ech On")
22. Italy (Instrumental)
23. Russia (Instrumental)

Joining Hands with Other Lands
Kimbo Educational

1. Joining Hands with Other Lands
2. Mi Casa, My House
3. Sasha and Natasha
4. You Are Super the Way You Are
5. The Yodeling Song
6. How Do YOU Say Yes?
7. Many Ways to Say Hello
8. The Friendship Game
9. The Food Song
10. Let's Have a Party
11. The Caribbean Mango Song
12. Chinese New Year
13. Lady of the Light
14. Birthdays Around the World
15. Uno, Uno, Dos, Dos
16. Native American Names

Folk Dance Fun
By Georgiana Stewart

Tracks 1–9
(*Vocals and Music*)

1. Hi To You
2. Mexican Hat Dance
3. Irish Jig
4. German Clapping Dance
5. Hawaiian Hukilau Dance (Hukilau Song)

6. Italian Tarantella

7. American Virginia Reel (Pop Goes the Weasel)

8. Greek Zorba Dance

9. So Long, Farewell (*The Sound of Music*)

Tracks 10–18
(*Music Only*)

10. Hi To You

11. Mexican Hat Dance

12. Irish Jig

13. German Clapping Dance

14. Hawaiian Hukilau Dance (Hukilau Song)

15. Italian Tarantella

16. American Virginia Reel (Pop Goes the Weasel)

17. Greek Zorba Dance

18. So Long, Farewell (*The Sound of Music*)

Children of the World
By Georgiana Stewart

1. Children of the World

2. Brazilian Carnival

3. A Visit to My Friend

4. Yolanda

5. The Wonders of the World

6. Haitian Alphabet Song

7. The Dreidel Song

8. Lullabies Around the World

9. Polka Party

10. Funiculi, Funicula

11. Pata Pata

12. Wonderful Copenhagen

13. Love Makes the World Go Round

14. It's a Small World

15. I'd Like to Teach the World to

16. Sing Somewhere Out There

Songs About Native Americans
By Lois Skiera-Zucek

1. America Honors You

2. The Circle of Life

3. Indians Live Today

4. Sun and Rain

5. Food for My Family

6. The Tepee

7. Beautiful Music

8. Wake, Little Children

9. A Work of Art

10. Cradleboard Lullaby

11. An Indian Village

12. A Place Called Home

13. Many, Many Tribes

Buck, Nola. (1996). *Sid and Sam*. Illus. by G. Brian Karas. New York: HarperCollins.

Davis, Wendy. (1997). *From Metal to Music: A Photo Essay*. Chicago: Children's Press.

Drew, Helen. (1993). *My First Music Book*. New York: Dorling Kindersley.

Eversole, Robyn. (1995). *Flute Player/La Flautista*. Illus. by G. Brian Karas. New York: Orchard Books.

Fleming, Candace. (1997). *Gabriella's Song*. Illus. by Giselle Potter. Colchester, CT: Atheneum.

Hayes, Ann. (1995). *Meet the Marching Smithereens*. Illus. by Karmen Thompson. Orlando, FL: Harcourt Brace.

Hayes, Ann. (1995). *Meet the Orchestra*. Illus. by Karmen Thompson. Orlando, FL: Harcourt Brace.

Hewitt, Sally. (1994). *Pluck and Scrape*. Illus. by Peter Millard. Chicago: Children's Press.

Imai, Miko. (1995). *Sebastian's Trumpet*. Cambridge, MA: Candlewick Press.

Kalman, Bobbie. (1997). *Musical Instruments from A to Z*. New York: Crabtree Publishing.

Livo, Norma J. (1996). *J. Troubadour's Storybag: Musical Folktales of the World*. Golden, CO: Fulcrum.

Millman, Isaac. (1998). *Moses Goes to a Concert*. New York: Farrar, Straus & Giroux.

Moss, Lloyd. (2000). *Zin! Zin! A Violin: A Violin.* Illus. by Margorie Priceman. New York: Alladin Paperbacks.

Petty, Kate and Jennie Maizels. (1999). *The Amazing Pop-Up Music Book.* Illus. by Jennie Maizels. New York: Dutton Books.

Pinkney, J. Brian. (1994). *Max Found Two Sticks.* New York: Simon & Schuster.

Raschka, Chris. (1992). *Charlie Parker Played Bebop.* New York: Orchard Books.

Raschka, Chris. (1997). *Mysterious Thelonious.* New York: Orchard Books.

Rachlin, Ann. (1992). *Bach.* Illus. by Susan Hellard. Hauppage, NY: Barrons Educational Series. (*Famous Children* series.) (Pbk.)

Rachlin, Ann. (1994). *Beethoven.* Illus. by Susan Hellard. Hauppage, NY: Barrons Educational Series. (*Famous Children* series.) (Pbk.)

Rachlin, Ann. (1993). *Brahms.* Illus. by Susan Hellard. Hauppage, NY: Barrons Educational Series. (*Famous Children* series.) (Pbk.)

Rachlin, Ann. (1993). *Chopin.* Illus. by Susan Hellard. Hauppage, NY: Barrons Educational Series. (*Famous Children* series.) (Pbk.)

Rachlin, Ann. (1992). *Handel.* Illus. by Susan Hellard. Hauppage, NY: Barrons Educational Series. (*Famous Children* series.) (Pbk.)

Rachlin, Ann. (1992). *Haydn.* Illus. by Susan Hellard. Hauppage, NY: Barrons Educational Series. (*Famous Children* series.) (Pbk.)

Rachlin, Ann. (1992). *Mozart.* Illus. by Susan Hellard. Hauppage, NY: Barrons Educational Series. (*Famous Children* series.) (Pbk.)

Rachlin, Ann. (1994). *Schubert.* Illus. by Susan Hellard. Hauppage, NY: Barrons Educational Series. (*Famous Children* series.) (Pbk.)

Rachlin, Ann. (1993). *Schumann.* Illus. by Susan Hellard. Hauppage, NY: Barrons Educational Series. (*Famous Children* series.) (Pbk.)

Rachlin, Ann. (1993). *Tchaikovsky.* Illus. by Susan Hellard. Hauppage, NY: Barrons Educational Series. (*Famous Children* series.) (Pbk.)

Reynolds, Marilynn, Laura Fernandez and Rick Jacobson. (2001). *The Magnificent Piano Recital.* Illus. by Laura Fernandez and Rick Jacobson. Custer, WA: Orca Book Publishers.

Shields, Carol Diggory and Svjetlan Junakovic. (2000). *Animagicals: Music.* Illus. by Svjetlan Junakovic. Brooklyn, NY: Handprint Books.

Multimedia

The following multimedia products can be used to complement this theme:

Child's Celebration of Showtunes [cassette]. (1992). Music for Little People.

Grunsky, Jack. *Playground* [compact disc]. (2001). Jack Grunsky Productions.

Jenkins, Ella. *This is Rhythm* [compact disc]. (1994). Smithsonian/Folkways.

Jenkins, Ella. *Rhythm and Game Songs for the Little Ones* [cassette]. (1990). Smithsonian/Folkways.

Louchard, Ric. *Hey, Ludwig! Classical Piano Solos for Playful Times* [compact disc]. (1993). Music for Little People.

Meter [video]. (1994). Films for the Humanities & Sciences.

Pitch [video]. (1994). Films for the Humanities & Sciences.

Songs About America. [compact disc]. (2003). Long Branch, NJ: Kimbo Educational.

Stanley, Leotha. *Be a Friend: The Story of African American Music in Song, Words and Pictures* [book and cassette]. (1994). Illus. by Henry Hawkins. Zino Press.

Stewart, Georgiana. *Multicultural Rhythm Stick Fun* [compact disc]. (1992). Kimbo Educational.

"Twist! Stop! Hop!," "I Can Dance," "I Like Me," "Pelican Polka," "My Chance to Dance." (2002). *Jump-Start Action.* Long Branch, NJ: Kimbo Educational.

47

Names

symbol

Sources

clocks
rulers
telephones
calendars
games

Numbers

Uses

communication
identification
time
age
address
telephone number

Recording Tools

calculator
pens
markers
pencils
computers
cash registers
phones
grocery/store scanners

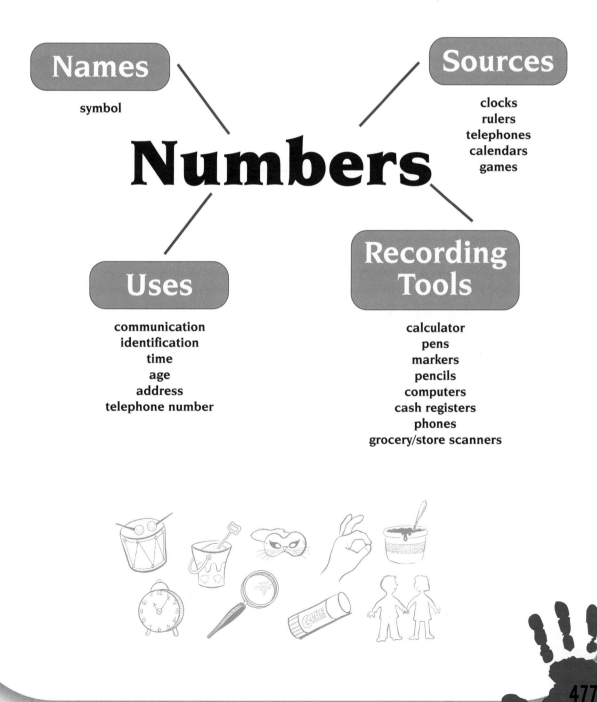

Theme Goals

Through participating in the experiences provided by this theme, the children may learn

1. Uses of numbers
2. Sources of numbers
3. Number names
4. Tools for recording numbers

Concepts for the Children to Learn

1. A number is a symbol that communicates an amount.
2. Each number symbol has a name.
3. Pencils and computers are tools used to make numbers.
4. Numbers can be found on clocks, rulers, telephones, calendars, and games.
5. Communication, identification, time, and age are uses for numbers.
6. Telephones, calculators, and cash registers have numerals.
7. Pens and markers can be used to make numbers.
8. Numbers are used to show where people live.
9. Numbers are on clocks to help us tell time.
10. Numbers are used in telephone numbers.

Vocabulary

1. **number**—a symbol used to represent an amount. A number tells how many.
2. **numeral**—a symbol that represents a number.

Bulletin Board

The objective of this bulletin board is for the children to match the numeral to the set by winding the string around the other pushpin next to the items. Construct the numerals out of tagboard. Construct objects familiar to the children and make one type of object correspond to each numeral. The number of objects and numerals should be developmentally appropriate for the group of children. Laminate. Staple the numbers down the left side of the bulletin board. Staple the sets of objects in random order down the right side of the bulletin board as illustrated. Affix a pushpin with an attached string of sufficient length next to each numeral. Affix a pushpin in front of each set row.

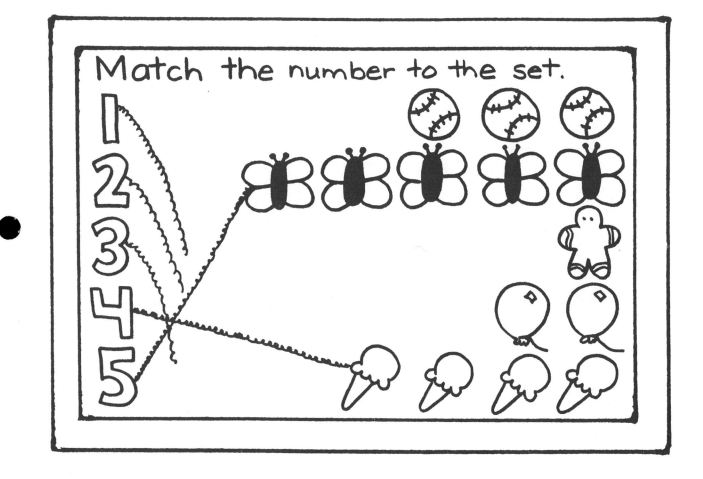

Family Letter

Dear Families,

Our next unit will focus on numbers. The children will be exposed to the uses and sources of numbers. They will learn number names and use tools for recording numbers.

AT SCHOOL

Some of the play-related activities include:

- measuring with scales and rulers at the science table
- charting our weight and height
- listening to the book titled *I Can Count* by Lynn Grundy
- using number cookie cutters with play dough
- bowling with numbered pins

Personnel from the telephone company will be visiting us Tuesday. They will show us a variety of phones. They will also stress the importance of knowing our telephone number. Feel free to join us for this activity.

AT HOME

Cooking provides a concrete foundation for mathematical concepts. It involves amounts, fractions, and measures. While you are cooking, have your child help. Count how many spoonfuls it takes to fill a 1-cup measurer.

Your child can help you make this simple no-bake recipe for rice crispy treats.

Rice Crispy Treats

6 1/2 crispy rice cereal
1 package miniature marshmallows
3 tablespoon butter or margarine
1 teaspoon vanilla

Pour the crispy rice cereal in a large bowl. Melt the butter and marshmallows in the microwave. Stir vanilla into the butter and marshmallows. Pour this mixture over the rice cereal. Mix and pat into a 9 × 12 pan. Cool before cutting and serving.

Enjoy counting with your child!

Developmentally appropriate software can be an effective way to teach children numbers.

Arts and Crafts

1. Marker Sets

Using rubber bands, bind two watercolor markers together. Repeat this procedure, making several sets. Set the markers, including an unbound set, on the art table. The children can use the bound marker sets for creating designs on paper.

2. Coupon Collage

Clipped coupons, paste, and paper can be placed on a table in the art area.

3. Ruler Design

Collect a variety of rulers that are of different colors, sizes, and types. Using paper and a marking tool, the children can create designs.

4. Numeral Cookie Cutter

Numeral cookie cutters should be provided with play dough.

Cooking

Rice Crispy Treats

6 1/2 crispy rice cereal
1 package miniature marshmallows
3 tablespoon butter or margarine
1 teaspoon vanilla

Pour the crispy rice cereal in a large bowl. Melt the butter and marshmallows in the microwave. Stir vanilla into the butter and marshmallows. Pour this mixture over the rice cereal. Mix and pat into a 9 × 12 pan. Cool before cutting and serving.

Dramatic Play

1. Grocery Store

In the dramatic play area, arrange a grocery store. To do this, collect a variety of empty boxes, paper bags, sales receipts, etc. Removable

NUMBERS

stickers can be used to indicate the grocery prices. A cash register and play money can also be added to create interest.

2. Clock Shop

Collect a variety of clocks for the children to explore. Using discarded clocks, with the glass face removed, is an interesting way to let the children explore numerals and internal mechanisms.

3. Telephoning

Prepare a classroom telephone book with all the children's names and telephone numbers. Contact your local telephone company to borrow the training system. The children can practice dialing their own numbers as well as their classmates'.

Fingerplays

I Can Even Count Some More

One, two, three, four
I can even count some more.
Five, six, seven, eight
All my fingers stand up straight
Nine, ten are my thumb men.

Five Little Monkeys Swinging from a Tree

Five little monkeys swinging from the tree,
Teasing Mr. Alligator, "You can't catch me."
Along comes Mr. Alligator as sneaky as can be . . .
SNAP
Four little monkeys swinging from the tree.
Three little monkeys swinging from the tree.
Two little monkeys swinging from the tree.
One little monkey swinging from the tree.
No more monkeys swinging from the tree!

Five Little Birds

Five little birds without any home.
   (hold up five fingers)
Five little trees in a row.
   (raise hands high over head)
Come build your nests in our branches tall.

(cup hands)
We'll rock them to and fro.

Ten Little Fingers

I have 10 little fingers and 10 little toes.
   (children point to portions of body as they repeat words)
Two little arms and one little nose.
One little mouth and two little ears.
Two little eyes for smiles and tears.
One little head and two little feet.
One little chin, that makes _____ complete.

Group Time

(Games, Language)

1. Squirrels in the Park

Choose five children to be squirrels. The children should sit in a row while one child pretends to go for a walk in the park carrying a bag of raisins and/or dried fruit. When the child who is walking approaches the squirrels, provide directions. These may include: feeding the first squirrel, the fifth, the third, etc.

2. Block Form Board

On a large piece of cardboard, trace around one of each of the shapes of the blocks in the block area. Let children match blocks to the shape on the board.

3. Match Them

Show the child several sets of identical picture cards, squares, objects, or flannel board pictures. Mix the items. Then have the children find matching pairs. One method of doing this is to hold up one item and have the children find the matching one.

4. Follow the Teacher

At group time, provide directions containing a number. For example, say: one jump, two hops, three leaps, four tiptoe steps, etc. The numbers used should be developmentally appropriate for the children.

482

THEME 47

Math

1. **Number Chain**

   Cut enough strips of paper to make a number chain for the days of the month. During group time each day, add a link to represent the passage of time. Another option is to use the chain as a countdown by removing a link per day until a special day. This is an interesting approach to an upcoming holiday.

2. **Silverware Set**

   Provide a silverware set. The children can sort the pieces according to sizes, shapes, and/or use.

3. **Constructing Numerals**

   Provide each interested child with a ball of play dough. Instruct children to form some numerals randomly. It is important for the teacher to monitor work and correct reversals. Then children can add the proper corresponding number of dots for the numeral just formed.

   An extension of this activity would be to make cards with numerals. The children roll their play dough into long ropes that can be placed over the lines of the numerals.

Music

1. **"Hickory Dickory Dock"**
   (*traditional*)

   Hickory dickory dock.
   The mouse ran up the clock.
   The clock struck one,
   The mouse ran down.
   Hickory dickory dock.

2. **"Two Little Blackbirds"**
   (*traditional*)

   Two little blackbirds sitting on a hill
   One named Jack,
   One named Jill.
   Fly away, Jack,
   Fly away, Jill.
   Come back, Jack,
   Come back, Jill.
   Two little blackbirds sitting on a hill
   One named Jack,
   One named Jill.

3. **"One Elephant"**

   One elephant went out to play
   Out on a spider's web one day.
   He had such enormous fun,
   He called for another elephant to come.

(*continued*)

Manipulatives for Math Activities

buttons	toothpicks	golf tees	cotton balls
beads	pennies	stickers	bottle caps
bobbins	checkers	fishing bobbers	poker chips
craft pompoms	crayons	keys	paper clips
spools	plastic caps from markers, milk containers, plastic bottles	small toy cars	clothespins
shells		plastic bread ties	erasers
seeds (corn, soybeans)		marbles	

Additional verses:

Two elephants went out to play . . .
Three elephants went out to play . . .
Four elephants went out to play . . .
Five elephants went out to play . . .

Science

1. Height and Weight Chart

Design a height and weight chart for the classroom. The children can help by measuring each other. Record the numbers. Later in the year, measure the children and record their progress. Note the differences.

2. Using a Scale

Collect a variety of small objects and place on the science table with a balancing scale. The children can measure with the scale, noting the differences.

3. Temperature

Place an outdoor thermometer on the playground. Encourage the children to examine the thermometer. Record the temperature. Mark the temperature on the thermometer with masking tape. Bring the thermometer into the classroom. Check the thermometer again in half an hour. Show the children the change in temperature.

Sensory

Add colored water and a variety of measuring tools to the sensory table.

Books

The following books can be used to complement this theme:

Anno, Mitsumasa. (1995). *Anno's Magic Seeds.* New York: G. P. Putnam.

Bates, Ivan. (2006). *Five Little Ducks.* Illus. by Ivan Bates. New York: Scholastic.

Big Fat Hen. (1994). Illus. by Keith Baker. Orlando, FL: Harcourt Brace.

Blackstone, Stella. (1996). *Grandma Went to Market: A Round-the-World Counting Rhyme.* Illus. by Bernard Lodge. Boston: Houghton Mifflin.

Brusca, Maria Christina. (1995). *Three Friends: A Counting Book/Tres Amigos: Un Cuento Para Contar.* New York: Holt.

Burmingham, John. (2000). *First Steps: Letters, Numbers, Colors, Opposites.* Cambridge, MA: Candlewick Press.

Carle, Eric. (2005). *10 Little Rubber Ducks.* New York: HarperCollins.

Carlstrom, Nancy White. (1996). *Let's Count It Out, Jesse Bear.* Illus. by Bruce Degen. New York: Simon & Schuster.

Challoner, Jack. (1992). *Science Book of Numbers.* Orlando, FL: Harcourt Brace.

Cole, Norma. (1994). *Blast Off! A Space Counting Book.* Illus. by Marshall Peck III. Watertown, MA: Charlesbridge.

Dale, Penny. (1994). *Ten Out of Bed.* Cambridge, MA: Candlewick Press.

Davis, Rebecca Fjelland. (2007). *10, 9, 8 Polar Animals! A Counting Backward Book.* Mankato, MN: Capstone Press.

Five Little Ducks: An Old Rhyme. (1995). Illus. by Pamela Paparone. New York: North South Books.

Fleming, Denise. (1992). *Count!* New York: Holt.

Geisert, Arthur. (1992). *Pigs from 1 to 10*. Boston: Houghton Mifflin.

Geisert, Arthur. (1996). *Roman Numerals I to MM*. Boston: Houghton Mifflin.

Giganti, Paul. (1992). *Each Orange Had 8 Slices*: A *Counting Book*. Illus. by Donald Crews. New York: Greenwillow.

Goennel, Heidi. (1994). *Odds and Evens*: A *Numbers Book*. New York: Tambourine Books.

Harley, Bill. (1996). *Sitting Down to Eat*. Illus. by Kitty Harvill. Little Rock, AR: August House LittleFolk.

Henderson, Kathy. (1996). *Counting Farm*. Cambridge, MA: Shaw's Candlewick Press.

Hoban, Tina. (1999). *Let's Count*. New York: Greenwillow Books.

Jandl, Ernst and Norman Junge. (2003). *Next Please*. New York: G.P. Putnam's Sons.

Jonas, Ann. (1995). *Splash!* New York: Greenwillow.

Lee, Kate, Caroline Repchuk, and Derek Matthews. (1998). *Snappy Little Numbers*: *Count the Numbers from 1 to 10*. Brookfield, CT: Millbrook Press.

Martin, Bill Jr. and Michael Sampson. (2004). *Chick, Chicka, 1, 2, 3*. Illus. by Lois Ehlert. New York: Simon & Schuster Books for Young Readers.

Mazzola, Frank. (1997). *Counting Is for the Birds*. Watertown, MA: Charlesbridge.

Moerbck, Kees. (2001). *Numbers*. Swindon, Wiltshire: Child's Play International.

Noll, Sally. (1997). *Surprise!* New York: Greenwillow.

Ong, Cristina and Watty Piper. (1999). *The Little Engine That Could Numbers*: *Numbers* (*Board Books*). New York: Platt & Munk.

Root, Phyllis. (1998). *One Duck Stuck*. Illus. by Jane Chapman. Cambridge, MA: Candlewick Press.

Ryan, Pam Munoz. (1996). *Crayon Counting Book*. Illus. by Frank Mazzola, Jr. Watertown, MA: Charlesbridge.

Schlein, Miriam. (1996). *More Than One*. Illus. by Donald Crews. New York: Greenwillow.

Sturges, Philemon. (1995). *Ten Flashing Fireflies*. Illus. by Anna Vojtech. New York: North South Books.

Wadsworth, Olive. (2002). *Over in the Meadow*: A *Counting Rhyme*. Illus. by Anna Vojtech. New York: North-South Books.

Wells, Robert E. (1993). *Is a Blue Whale the Biggest Thing There Is?* Niles, IL: Albert Whitman.

Yektai, Niki. (1996). *Bears at the Beach*: *Counting 10–20*. Brookfield, CT: Millbrook Press.

Multimedia

The following multimedia products can be used to complement this theme:

Counting and Sorting [CD-ROM]. (1997). DK Multimedia.

How Much Is a Million? [video]. (1997). Hosted by LeVar Burton. GPN/WNED-TV 120.

Introduction to Letters and Numerals [video]. (1985). SRA/McGraw-Hill.

Jenkins, Ella. *Counting Games and Rhythms for the Little Ones*, Vol. 1 [cassette]. (1990). Smithsonian Folkways.

Millie's Math House [CD-ROM]. (1992). Edmark.

Palmer, Hap. *Learning Basic Skills* [video]. (1986). Educational Activities.

Palmer, Hap. *Math Readiness—Vocabulary and Concepts* [cassette]. Educational Activities.

Reader Rabbit's Preschool [CD-ROM]. (1997). Learning Company.

Recordings and Song Titles

The following recordings can be used to complement this theme:

"Counting Together." (n.d.). *Children Love to Sing and Dance* (*The Learning Station*). Long Branch, NJ: Kimbo Educational.

"Count My Fingers." (1974). *Songs about Me.* Long Branch, NJ: Kimbo Educational.

"Count the Stars." (1999). *Moving with Mozart.* Long Branch, NJ: Kimbo Educational.

"Count to Three," "One Blue Square." (1995). *Piggyback Songs.* Long Branch, NJ: Kimbo Educational.

"Count Your Money." (1988). A *Rainbow of Songs.* Long Branch, NJ: Kimbo Educational.

"Five Gray Sharks." (1990). *Musical Playtime Fun.* Long Branch, NJ: Kimbo Educational.

"Five Little Monkeys," "Six Little Ducks." (1990). *Car Songs.* Long Branch, NJ: Kimbo Educational.

"Let's Count the Animals." (1993). *Toddlerific.* Long Branch, NJ: Kimbo Educational.

"Numba Rhumba." (1998). *Sing, Dance 'N Sing (Gaia).* Long Branch, NJ: Kimbo Educational.

"One Potato, Two Potato." (1987). *Baby Games.* Long Branch, NJ: Kimbo Educational.

"One, Two, Buckle My Shoe," "Five Green and Speckled Frogs," "Four Leaf Clover," "Five Little Monkeys." (1999). *Five Little Monkeys.* Long Branch, NJ: Kimbo Educational.

"One, Two, Buckle My Shoe," "Five Little Monkeys." (1997). *Tony Chestnut (The Learning Station).* Long Branch, NJ: Kimbo Educational.

"One, Two, Buckle My Shoe," "Three Little Kittens." (1986). *Singable Nursery Rhymes.* Long Branch, NJ: Kimbo Educational.

"Roll Over," "Three Little Monkeys," "Five Little Ducks." (1996). *Where Is Thumbkin?* Long Branch, NJ: Kimbo Educational.

"Ten Little Goblins." (1985). *Toddlers on Parade.* Long Branch, NJ: Kimbo Educational.

"Ten Little Indians." (1985). *Diaper Gym.* Long Branch, NJ: Kimbo Educational.

"There are Seven Days in the Week," "My Five Senses." (2004). *Circle Time Activities.* Long Branch, NJ: Kimbo Educational.

"This Old Man," "Five Little Monkeys," "Six Little Ducks." (1997). *Six Little Ducks.* Long Branch, NJ: Kimbo Educational.

"We Are All Counting Today." (1974). *Put Your Finger in the Air.* Long Branch, NJ: Kimbo Educational.

48

Uses

enjoyment
learning words
learning numbers
bedtime rituals

Forms

written
spoken
sung

Nursery Rhymes

Characters

animals
people

Favorites

Little Bo Peep
Mary Had a Little
    Lamb
Old Mother Hubbard
Hey, Diddle Diddle
Little Miss Muffet
Humpty Dumpty
Jack and Jill
Mary Mary Quite
    Contrary

Jack Be Nimble
Rub-a-Dub-Dub
The Muffin Man
Little Jack Horner
Old MacDonald Had
    a Farm
Two Little Blackbirds
Hickory Dickory Dock
Three Kittens' Mittens

Theme Goals

Through participating in the experiences provided by this theme, the children may learn

1. Favorite nursery rhymes
2. Uses of nursery rhymes
3. Forms of nursery rhymes
4. Characters portrayed in nursery rhymes

Concepts for the Children to Learn

1. Nursery rhymes are short, simple poems or rhymes.
2. Nursery rhymes are fun to listen to and say.
3. Nursery rhymes help us learn new words.
4. Nursery rhymes can be bedtime rituals.
5. Nursery rhymes can be written, spoken, or sung.
6. Nursery rhymes can contain real or pretend words.
7. Nursery rhymes can be about animals, people, or objects.
8. Some nursery rhymes help us learn numbers and counting.
9. Some nursery rhymes teach us about different people.
10. There are many favorite nursery rhymes.
11. "Little Bo Peep," "Mary Had a Little Lamb," "Old Mother Hubbard," and "Hey, Diddle Diddle" are favorite nursery rhymes.
12. "Little Miss Muffett," "Humpty Dumpty," "Jack and Jill," "Mary Mary Quite Contrary," and "Jack Be Nimble" are favorite nursery rhymes.
13. "Rub-a-Dub-Dub," "The Muffin Man," "Little Jack Horner," and "Old MacDonald Had a Farm" are favorite nursery rhymes.
14. "Two Little Black Birds," "Hickory Dickory Dock," and "Three Kittens' Mittens" are favorite nursery rhymes.

Vocabulary

nursery rhyme—short, simple poem or rhyme.

Bulletin Board

The purpose of this bulletin board is to promote visual discrimination skills, name recognition, and call attention to the printed word. This can be used as an attendance bulletin board. Each child should be provided a bulletin board piece with his or her name printed on it. When the children arrive each morning at school, they should be encouraged to hang their name on the bulletin board. To create a "Find Your Mitten" bulletin board, cut a mitten out of tagboard for each child in the class. Use a paper punch to cut a hole in the top of each mitten. Three kittens can be constructed and attached to the bulletin board to represent the three little kittens who lost their mittens. Hang pushpins on the bulletin board for the children to hang their mittens.

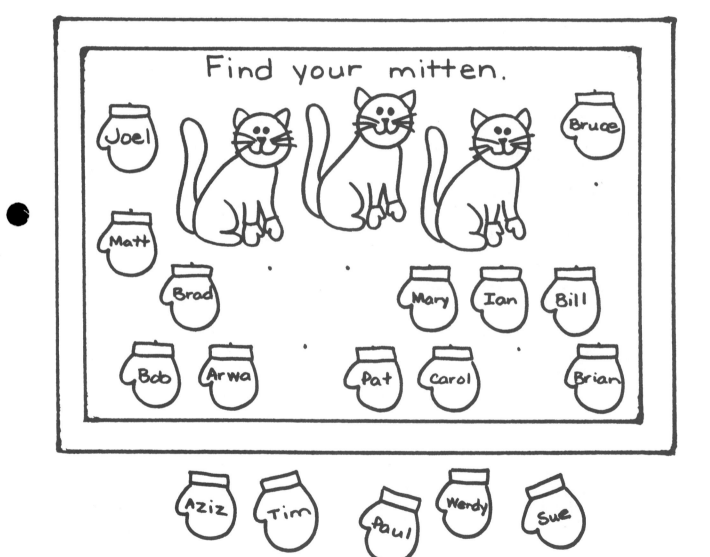

NURSERY RHYMES

Family Letter

Dear Families,

Nursery rhymes will be the focus of our next theme. These rhymes can serve as a bridge between the home and school. I'm sure many of you have shared favorite nursery rhymes with your child at home. Nursery rhymes are an easy introduction to poetry, as well as to the concept of rhyming words.

AT SCHOOL

We have a fun-filled curriculum planned for our unit on nursery rhymes. A few highlights include:

- acting out various rhymes with puppets that represent different characters from familiar nursery rhymes
- unraveling the riddle of the "Humpty Dumpty" nursery rhyme. (Why couldn't Humpty be put back together? Because Humpty was an egg!)
- creating "Little Miss Muffet" spiders in the art area
- taking turns being nimble and quick as we jump over a candlestick to dramatize the rhyme of "Jack Be Nimble"

AT HOME

To foster concepts of the unit at home, try the following:

- Let your child help you crack eggs open to make scrambled eggs. Children like to feel that they have accomplished a grown-up task when they crack the eggs.
- Sing or recite some of the many rhymes your child already knows such as "Jack and Jill" and "Mary Had a Little Lamb." These also develop an enjoyment of music and singing.

Share a nursery rhyme with your child today!

THEME 48

Reciting nursery rhymes can be a group activity.

 # Arts and Crafts

1. Spiders

Add black tempera paint to a play dough mixture. In addition to the play dough, provide black chenille stems or yarn. Using these materials, spiders or other objects can be created.

2. Spider Webs

Cut circles of black paper to fit in the bottom of a pie tin. Mix thin silver or white tempera paint. Place a marble and two teaspoons of paint on the paper. Gently tilt the pie tin, allowing the marble to roll through the paint, creating a spider web design.

3. Twinkle, Twinkle Little Stars

The children can decorate stars with glitter and sequins. The stars can be hung from the ceiling. During group time sing "Twinkle, Twinkle, Little Star."

 # Cooking

1. Bran Muffins
(Use with the "Muffin Man" rhyme)

3 cups whole-wheat bran cereal
1 cup boiling water
1/2 cup shortening or oil
2 eggs
2 1/2 cups unbleached flour
1 1/2 cups sugar
2 1/2 teaspoons baking soda
2 cups buttermilk

Preheat the oven to 400 degrees. Line the muffin tins with paper baking cups. In a large bowl combine the cereal and boiling water. Stir in the shortening and eggs. Add the remaining ingredients. Blend well. Spoon the batter into cups about 3/4 full. Bake at 400 degrees for 18 to 22 minutes or until golden brown. Eat at snack and sing the "Muffin Man" song.

2. Cottage Cheese

2 quarts pasteurized skim milk (to make 1 to 3/4 pounds of cottage cheese)
salt
liquid rennet or a junket tablet

Heat the water to 80 degrees Fahrenheit in the bottom part of a double boiler. Use a thermometer to determine the water temperature. Do not guess.

Pour the skim milk into the top of the double boiler. Dilute 1 or 2 drops of liquid rennet in a tablespoon of cold water and stir it into the milk. If rennet is not available, add 1/8 of a junket tablet to a tablespoon of water and add it to the milk. Allow the milk to remain at 80 degrees until it curdles, about 12 to 18 hours. During this period no special attention is necessary. If desired, the milk may be placed in a warm oven overnight. Place the curd in a cheese cloth over a container to drain the whey. Occasionally, pour out the whey that collects in the container so that the draining will continue. In 15 to 20 minutes, the curd will become mushy and will drain more slowly. When it is almost firm and the whey has nearly ceased to flow, the cheese is ready for salting and eating. Salt the cheese to taste. The cottage cheese can be spread on crackers for a snack.

Note: This activity is time-consuming. It may be more appropriate for older children.

3. Miss Muffet's Curds and Whey

2 cups whole milk
1 teaspoon vinegar

Heat the milk to lukewarm and add vinegar. Stir as curds separate from the whey. Curds are the milk solids and the whey is the liquid that is poured off. You can let your children taste the whey but they probably will not be thrilled by it. Strain the curds from the whey, and then dump the curds onto a paper towel and gently press the curds with more towels to get out the liquid. Sprinkle with salt and refrigerate. Eat as cottage cheese. You can also serve the curds at room temperature. Stir them until they are smooth. Add different flavorings (such as cinnamon, orange flavoring, vanilla, etc.). Use as a spread on crackers. Serves 12 (two crackers each).

Dramatic Play

1. Baker

Baking props such as hats, aprons, cookie cutters, baking pans, rolling pins, mixers, spoons, and bowls can be placed in the dramatic play area.

2. Puppets

A puppet theater can be placed in the dramatic play area for the duration of the unit. To add variety, each day a different set of puppets can be added for the children.

Field Trips/ Resource People

1. Candlemaking

Invite a resource person to demonstrate candle-making, or take a field trip to a craft center so that the children can view candles being made.

2. Greenhouse

Visit a florist or greenhouse to observe flowers and plants.

Fingerplays

Little Jack Horner

Little Jack Horner
Sat in a corner
Eating a Christmas pie.
  (pretend you're eating)
He put in his thumb,
  (thumb down)
And pulled out a plum
  (thumb up)
And said, "What a good boy am I!"
  (say out loud)

Pat-a-Cake

Pat-a-cake, pat-a-cake, baker's man.
Bake me a cake as fast as you can!
  (clap hands together lightly)
Roll it
  (roll hands)
And pat it
  (touch hands together lightly)
And mark it with a "B"
  (write "B" in the air)
And put it in the oven for baby and me.
  (point to baby and to yourself)

Wee Willie Winkle

Wee Willie Winkle runs through the town
  (pretend to run)
Upstairs, downstairs in his nightgown,
  (point up, point down, then point to clothes)
Rapping at the window, crying through the lock
  (knock in the air, peek through a hole)
"Are the children all in bed, for now it's eight
    o'clock!"
  (shake finger)

Old King Cole

Old King Cole was a merry old soul
  (lift elbows up and down)
And a merry old soul was he.
  (nod head)
He called for his pipe.
  (clap two times)
He called for his bowl.
  (clap two times)
And he called for his fiddlers three.
  (clap two times then pretend to play violin)

Hickory Dickory Dock

Hickory dickory dock
  (swing arms back and forth together,
  bent down low)
The mouse ran up the clock.
  (run fingers up your arm)
The clock struck one
  (clap, and then hold up one finger)
The mouse ran down.
  (run fingers down your arm)
Hickory dickory dock.
  (swing arms back and forth together, bent
  down low)

Group Time
(Games, Language)

**Old Mother Hubbard's
Doggie Bone Game**

Save a bone or construct one from tagboard.
Ask one child to volunteer to be the doggie.
Seat the children in a circle with the doggie
in the center and the bone in front of him or
her. The doggie closes his or her eyes. A child
from the circle quietly comes and steals the
bone. When the child is reseated with the
bone out of sight, the children will call,

"Doggie, doggie, where's your bone?
Someone took it from your home!"

The doggie gets three chances to guess who
has the bone. If he or she guesses correctly,
the child who took the bone becomes
the doggie.

Large Muscle

1. Jack Be Nimble's Candlestick

Make a candlestick out of an old paper towel
holder and tissue paper for the flame. Repeat
the rhyme by substituting each child's name.

Jack be nimble. Jack be quick.
Jack jump over the candlestick.

2. Hey, Diddle Diddle Jump

Make cow headbands for the children to wear.
Create a large moon and tape it to the floor.
Encourage children to jump over the moon
while saying the rhyme.

Hey, Diddle Diddle,
the cat and the fiddle.
The cow jumped over the moon.
The little dog laughed to see such a sport,
And the dish ran away with the spoon.

3. Wall Building

Encourage the children to create a large wall out of blocks for Humpty Dumpty. Act out the rhyme.

4. London Bridge

Play London Bridge game while chanting the rhyme:

London Bridge is falling down,
falling down, falling down.
London Bridge is falling down,
my fair lady.

Shake her up with sticks and stones,
sticks and stones, sticks and stones.
Shake her up with sticks and stones,
my fair lady.

Math

1. Puzzles

Draw or cut out several pictures of different nursery rhymes ("Jack and Jill," "Jack Be Nimble," etc.) and mount on tagboard. Laminate and cut each picture into five to seven pieces. The children can match nursery rhyme puzzle pieces.

2. Rote Counting

Say or sing the following nursery rhyme to help the children with rote counting.

1, 2 buckle my shoe
3, 4 shut the door
5, 6 pick up sticks
7, 8 lay them straight
9, 10 a big fat hen.

3. Matching

Draw from 1 to 10 simple figures from a nursery rhyme (mittens, candlesticks, pails, etc.) on the left side of a sheet of tagboard and the corresponding numeral on the right side. Laminate the pieces and cut each in half creating different-shaped puzzle pieces. The children can match the number of figures to the corresponding numeral.

4. Mitten Match

Collect several matching pairs of mittens. Mix them up and have children match the pairs.

5. Muffin Man Math Game

Place several empty muffin tins on the table. Place one large die on the table. Each child takes turns rolling the die and placing the corresponding number of chips into the muffin tin. The game is over when one player has filled his or her muffin tin.

6. Humpty Dumpty Egg Match

Paint the eggs in a deviled egg dish. Place Easter eggs in matching egg slot of the dish.

7. Little Bo Peep Sheep

Make sheep cutouts. Place a numeral on each sheep and have children glue the corresponding number of cotton balls on the sheep.

8. Twinkle, Twinkle Star Count

Write numerals 1–10 on cutout stars. Have children arrange the stars in the correct order. Dots may also be placed beneath the numeral if more appropriate.

Music

1. "Hickory Dickory Dock"
(*traditional*)

Hickory dickory dock
The mouse ran up the clock.
The clock struck one, the mouse ran down,
Hickory dickory dock.

2. "The Muffin Man"
(*traditional*)

Oh, do you know the muffin man,
The muffin man, the muffin man?
Oh, do you know the muffin man
Who lives on Drury Lane?

Yes, I know the muffin man . . .

3. "Two Little Blackbirds"

(*traditional*)

Two little blackbirds sitting on a hill
One named Jack. One named Jill.
Fly away, Jack. Fly away, Jill.
Come back, Jack. Come back, Jill.
Two little blackbirds sitting on a hill.
One named Jack. One named Jill.

4. "Jack and Jill"

(*traditional*)

Jack and Jill went up a hill
To fetch a pail of water.
Jack fell down and broke his crown
And Jill fell tumbling after.

5. "A Peanut Sat on a Railroad Track"

A peanut sat on a railroad track,
His heart was all a-flutter,
Round the bend came number ten.
Toot! Toot! Peanut butter!
SQUISH!

6. "Jack Be Nimble"

Jack be nimble,
Jack be quick;
Jack jump over
The candlestick.

Additional verses:

Jack be nimble,
Jack be late;
Jack jump over
The dinner plate.

Jack be nimble,
Jack be soon;
Jack jump over
The sliver spoon.

Jack be nimble,
Jack be up;
Jack jump over
The sippy cup.

7. "Little Bo-Peep"

Little Bo-Peep has lost her sheep,
And can't tell where to find them;
Leave them alone, and they'll come home,
Wagging their tails behind them.

Little Bo-Peep fell fast asleep,
And dreamt she heard them bleating;
But when she awoke, she found it a joke,
For they were still a-fleeting.

Then up she took her little crook,
Determined for to find them;
She found them indeed, but it made her
    heart bleed,
For they left all their tails behind them.

8. "Little Miss Muffet"

Little Miss Muffet sat on her tuffet,
Eating her curds and whey.
Along came a spider,
And sat down beside her,
And frightened Miss Muffet away.

9. "London Bridge Is Falling Down"

London Bridge is falling down,
Falling down, falling down.
London Bridge is falling down,
My fair lady.

Build it up with needles and pins,
Needles and pins, needles and pins.
Build it up with needles and pins,
My fair lady.

Pins and needles rust and bend,
Rust and bend, rust and bend.
Pins and needles rust and bend,
My fair lady.

Build it up with silver and gold . . .
Gold and silver I've not got . . .
Here's a prisoner I have got . . .
Take the key and lock her up . . .

10. "Looby Loo"

Here we go Looby-Loo
Here we go Looby-Light
Here we go Looby-Loo
All on a Saturday night.

You put your right hand in,
You put your right hand out,
You give your hand a shake, shake, shake,
And turn yourself about.

(*continued*)

NURSERY RHYMES

Chorus:

Here we go Looby-Loo
Here we go Looby-Light
Here we go Looby-Loo
All on a Saturday night.

You put your left hand in . . .
You put your right foot in . . .
You put your left foot in . . .
You put your whole self in . . .

11. "Miss Polly Had a Dolly"

Miss Polly had a dolly
Who was sick, sick, sick,
So she called for the doctor
To be quick, quick, quick.

The doctor came
With his bag and his hat,
And he knocked at the door
With a rat-a-tat-tat.

He looked at the dolly
And he shook his head,
And he said, "Miss Polly,
Put her straight to bed."

He wrote out a paper
For a pill, pill, pill,
That'll make her better,
Yes it will, will, will!

12. "Mary Had a Little Lamb"

Mary had a little lamb,
Little lamb, little lamb,
Mary had a little lamb,
Its fleece was white as snow.

And everywhere that Mary went,
Mary went, Mary went,
And everywhere that Mary went
The lamb was sure to go.

It followed her to school one day,
School one day, school one day,
It followed her to school one day,
Which was against the rules.

It made the children laugh and play,
Laugh and play, laugh and play,
It made the children laugh and play,
To see a lamb at school.

"Why does the lamb love Mary so?
Love Mary so? Love Mary so?"

"Why does the lamb love Mary so?"
The eager children cry.

"Why, Mary loves the lamb, you know.
Loves the lamb, you know. Loves the lamb,
  you know."
"Why, Mary loves the lamb, you know."
The teacher did reply.

13. "Old King Cole"

Old King Cole was a merry old soul,
And a merry old soul was he.
He called for his pipe,
And he called for his bowl,
And he called for his fiddlers three.
Evr'y fiddler had a fiddle,
And a very fine fiddle had he.
Tweedle dee, tweedle dee,
Tweedle dee, tweedle dee,
Tweedle dee, tweedle dee,
Went the fiddlers three,
Oh, there's none so rare
As can compare,
With King Cole and his fiddlers three.

14. "Open, Shut Them"

Open, shut them.
  (hold hands up and open and close fingers)
Open, shut them.
Give a little clap.
  (clap)
Open, shut them.
  (hold hands up and open and close fingers)
Open, shut them.
Put them in our lap.
  (place hand in lap)
Walk them, walk them,
  (walk fingers up chest to chin)
Walk them, walk them.
Way up to your chin.
Walk them, walk them,
  (walk fingers around face, but not into mouth)
Walk them, walk them,
But don't let them walk in.

15. "Pat-a-Cake"

Pat-a-cake, pat-a-cake, baker's man.
  (clap hands together)
Bake me a cake as fast as you can.

Roll it,
     (roll hands over each other)
And pat it,
     (pat hands together)
And mark it with B,
     (draw B in the air)
And put it in the oven for baby and me.
     (point to a child or tickle child's tummy)

16. "Pop! Goes the Weasel"

All around the cobbler's bench
The monkey chased the weasel.
Then monkey thought 'twas all in fun . . .
Pop! Goes the weasel.

Johnny has the whooping cough,
Mary has the measles.
That's the way the money goes . . .
Pop! Goes the weasel.

A penny for a spool of thread
A penny for a needle.
That's the way the money goes . . .
Pop! Goes the weasel.

All around the mulberry bush,
The monkey chased the weasel.
That's the way the money goes . . .
Pop! Goes the weasel.

17. "Rock-a-Bye Baby"

Rock-a-bye, baby,
In the tree top,
When the wind blows,
The cradle will rock.
When the bough breaks,
The cradle will fall,
And down will come baby,
Cradle and all.

18. "Row, Row, Row Your Boat"

Row, row, row your boat
Gently down the stream.
Merrily, merrily, merrily, merrily,
Life is but a dream.

19. "Teddy Bear, Teddy Bear"

Teddy bear, teddy bear,
Turn around.
Teddy bear, teddy bear,
Touch the ground.

Teddy bear, teddy bear,
Touch your shoes.
Teddy bear, teddy bear,
Say how-di-do.
Teddy bear, teddy bear,
Go up the stairs.
Teddy bear, teddy bear,
Say your prayers.
Turn out the light.
Say good night.

20. "There Was an Old Woman"

There was an old woman,
Who lived in a shoe.
She had so many children,
She didn't know what to do.
She gave them some broth,
With butter and bread,
Then kissed them all sweetly,
And sent them to bed.

21. "This Old Man"

This old man, he played one.
     (hold up one finger)
He played knick-knack on my thumb.
     (pretend to knock on thumb)

Chorus:

With a knick-knack paddy whack give a dog
     a bone.
     (knock on head, clap twice, pretend to throw
     a bone over your shoulder)
This old man came rolling home.
     (roll hand over hand)

This old man, he played two.
     (hold up two fingers)
He played knick-knack on my shoe.
     (knock on shoe)

(Chorus)

This old man, he played three.
     (hold up three fingers)
He played knick-knack on my knee.
     (knock on knee)

(Chorus)

This old man, he played four.
     (hold up four fingers)
He played knick-knack on the door.
     (pretend to knock on the door)

(Chorus)

This old man, he played five.
   (hold up five fingers)
He played knick-knack on a hive.
   (pretend to knock on a hive)

(Chorus)

. . . six . . . sticks
   (continue hand motions)
. . . seven . . . heaven
. . . eight . . . gate
. . . nine . . . line
. . . ten . . . over again!

22. "Are You Sleeping?"

Are you sleeping?
Are you sleeping?
Brother John, Brother John?
Morning bells are ringing,
Morning bells are ringing.
Ding! Dong! Ding!
Ding! Dong! Ding!

23. "Where Is Thumbkin?"

Where is Thumbkin?
   (hands behind back)
Where is Thumbkin?
Here I am. Here I am.
   (bring out right thumb, then left)
How are you today, sir?
   (bend right thumb)
Very well, I thank you.
   (bend left thumb)
Run away. Run away.
   (put right thumb behind back, then left thumb
   behind back)

Other verses:

Where is Pointer?
Where is Middle One?
Where is Ring Finger?
Where is Pinky?
Where are all of them?

24. "Hey, Diddle Diddle"

Hey, diddle diddle,
The cat and the fiddle,
The cow jumped over the moon.
The little dog laughed to
See such a sport,
And the dish ran away with the spoon.

Science

1. Mary's Garden

A styrofoam cup with the child's name printed on it and a scoop of soil should be provided. Let everyone choose a flower seed. Be sure to save the seed packages. The children can plant their seed, water, and care for it. When the plant begins to grow, try to identify the names of the plants by comparing them to pictures on the seed packages.

2. Hickory Dickory Dock Clock

Draw and cut a large Hickory Dickory Dock clock from cardboard. Move the hands of the clock and see if the children can identify the numeral.

3. Wool

Pieces of wool fabric mounted on cardboard can be matched with samples.

4. Pumpkin Tasters

Plan a Peter, Peter, Pumpkin Eater pumpkin-tasting party.

5. Jack and Jill's Pail

See what objects will sink or float in Jack and Jill's pail.

Sensory

Water and Pails

Add water, pails, and scoopers to the sensory table.

Social Studies

1. Table Setting

On a sheet of tagboard, trace the outline of a plate, cup, knife, fork, spoon, and napkin. Laminate. The children can match the silverware and dishes to the outline on the placemat in preparation for snack or meals. This activity can be extended by having the children turn the place-mat over and arrange the place setting without the aid of an outline.

2. Shoe House

Create a large boot or shoe out of tagboard. Print digital photographs of each child. Invite the children to take turns gluing their picture onto the shoe. (**Note:** If photographs are not available, have each child draw his/her picture on the shoe.)

Books

The following books can be used to complement this theme:

Adams, Pam and Child's Play. (2000). *There Was an Old Woman Who Swallowed a Fly*. Illus. by Pam Adams. Auburn, ME: Child's Play International.

Aylesworth, Jim. (1992). *The Cat and the Fiddle and More*. New York: Macmillan.

Aylesworth, Jim. (1994). *My Son John*. Illus. by David Frampton. New York: Holt.

Benjamin, Floella, ed. (1995). *Skip across the Ocean: Nursery Rhymes from around the World*. Illus. by Sheila Moxley. New York: Orchard Books.

Big Fat Hen. (1994). Illus. by Keith Baker. Orlando, FL: Harcourt Brace.

Bornstein, Harry et al. (1992). *Nursery Rhymes from Mother Goose: Told in Signed English*. Washington, DC: Kendall Green.

Chorao, Kay. (1994). *Mother Goose Magic*. New York: Dutton.

Christelow, Eileen. (1998). *Five Little Monkeys Jumping on the Bed*. Boston: Houghton Mifflin.

Cravath, Lynne Woodcock and Steven Carpenter. (2000). *My First Action Rhymes*. Illus. by Lynne Woodcock Cravath & Steven Carpenter. New York: HarperFestival.

Degen, Bruce. (1991). *Jamberry*. Albany, NY: Delmar Publishers.

Dyer, Jane. (1996). *Animal Crackers: A Delectable Collection of Pictures, Poems, and Lullabies for the Very Young*. Boston: Little, Brown.

Eagle, Kin. (1994). *It's Raining, It's Pouring*. Illus. by Robert Gilbert. Dallas, TX: Whispering Coyote Press.

Five Little Ducks: An Old Rhyme. (1995). Illus. by Pamela Paparone. New York: North South Books.

Hale, Sara. (1995). *Mary Had a Little Lamb*. Illus. by Salley Mavor. New York: Orchard Books.

Heller, Nicholas. (1997). *This Little Piggy*. Illus. by Sonja Lamut. New York: Greenwillow.

Joyce, William and Kerry Milliron, ed. (2001). *William Joyce's Mother Goose*. New York: Random House.

Keats, Ezra Jack. (1999). *Over in the Meadow (Picture Book)*. New York: Viking.

Kroll, Virginia L. (1995). *Jaha and Jamil Go Down the Hill: An African Mother Goose*. Illus. by Katherine Roundtree. Watertown, MA: Charlesbridge.

Lansky, Bruce. (1993). *New Adventures of Mother Goose: Gentle Rhymes for Happy Times*. Illus. by Stephen Carpenter. New York: Simon & Schuster.

Little Robin Redbreast: A Mother Goose Rhyme. (1994). Illus. by Shari Halpern. New York: North South Books.

Lobel, Arnold. (1997). *Arnold Lobel Book of Mother Goose*. New York: Random House.

Manson, Christopher. (1993). *Tree in the Wood: An Old Nursery Song*. New York: North South Books.

Marks, Alan. (1991). *Ring-A-Ling o' Roses and A Ding, Dong, Bell: A Book of Nursery Rhymes*. New York: North South Books.

Marks, Alan. (1993). *Over the Hills and Far Away: A Book of Nursery Rhymes*. New York: North South Books.

Miranda, Anne. (1997). *To Market, to Market*. Illus. by Janet Stevens. Orlando, FL: Harcourt Brace.

Old Mother Hubbard and Her Wonderful Dog. (1991). Illus. by James Marshall. New York: Farrar, Straus & Giroux.

Opie, Iona Archibald, ed. *My Very First Mother Goose*. (1996). Illus. by Rosemary Wells. Cambridge, MA: Candlewick Press.

Opie, Iona Archibald. (1997). *Humpty Dumpty and Other Rhymes*. Cambridge, MA: Candlewick Press. (Board book.)

Opie, Iona Archibald. (1997). *Pussycat Pussycat and Other Rhymes*. Cambridge, MA: Candlewick Press. (Board book.)

Opie, Iona Archibald. (1997). *Wee Willie Winkie and Other Rhymes*. Cambridge, MA: Candlewick Press. (Board book.)

Pearson, Tracey Campbell. (2005). *Little Miss Muffet*. New York: Farrar Straus Giroux.

Polacco, Patricia. (1995). *Babushka's Mother Goose*. New York: Philomel.

Scieszka, Jon. (1994). *The Book That Jack Wrote*. Illus. by Daniel Adel. New York: Viking.

Slier, Debby. (1993). *Real Mother Goose Book of American Rhymes*. Illus. by Patty McCloskey-Padgett et al. New York: Scholastic.

Sweet, Melissa. (1992). *Fiddle-i-ee: A Farmyard Song for the Very Young*. Boston: Little, Brown.

Thompson, Jennifer (Ed.). and Joseph Levack (Photographer). (1999). *Picture Me Three Little Kittens*. Akron, OH: Picture Me Books.

Van Rynbach, Iris. (1995). *Five Little Pumpkins*. Honesdale, PA: Boyds Mills Press.

Whatley, Bruce. (1999). *My First Nursery Rhymes*. New York: HarperFestival.

Multimedia

The following multimedia products can be used to complement this theme:

Children's Treasury II: Rhymes, Poems, Stories [CD-ROM]. (1994). Fairfield, CT: Queue Inc.

Mixed-Up Mother Goose [CD-ROM]. (1995). Bellevue, WA: Sierra On-Line.

Nursery Songs and Rhymes [video]. (1993). Sandy, UT: Waterford Institute.

Olde Mother Goose [paperback and cassette]. (1993). Performed by the Hubbards. Illus. by Blanche Fisher Wright. August House Audio.

Palmer, Hap. *Hap Palmer Sings Classic Nursery Rhymes* [cassette]. (1991). Freeport, NY: Educational Activities.

Rusty and Rosy Nursery Songs and Rhymes [video]. (1993). Sandy, UT: Waterford Institute.

Recordings and Song Titles

The following recordings can be used to complement this theme:

"Pop Goes the Weasel," "Hickory Dickory Dock." (2001). *Four Baby Bumblebees*. Long Branch, NJ: Kimbo Educational.

"Rock 'n' Roll Nursery Rhymes." (1997). *Rock 'n' Roll Songs That Teach (The Learning Station)*. Long Branch, NJ: Kimbo Educational.

"Simon Says." (2001). *Dance Party Fun*. Long Branch, NJ: Kimbo Educational.

Singable Nursery Rhymes. (1986). Long Branch, NJ: Kimbo Educational.

Community Helpers

police officer
firefighter
mail carrier
judge

Transportation

taxi driver, bus driver,
car salesperson, pilot,
ambulance driver, truck driver,
gas station attendant, astronaut

Production

farmer, cook/chef,
baker, miner,
factory worker, artist

Occupations

Health

doctor
nurse
dentist
hygienist
paramedic
child care

Sports

announcer, umpire,
coach, athlete,
hockey players,
baseball players,
golfers, tennis players,
soccer players

Other

homemaker
seasonal
part-time
self-employed
shift
cottage

Service Workers

teacher, librarian, waitress/waiter,
banker, cashier, custodian, secretary,
auto mechanic, butcher, clerk,
sanitation engineer

Communications

computer operator,
television reporter,
newspaper reporter, actor

Construction

carpenter, plumber,
cabinetmaker, architect,
electrician

Theme Goals

Through participating in the experiences provided by this theme, the children may learn

1. Occupations of community helpers
2. Sports figure occupations
3. Health occupations
4. Transportation occupations
5. Communications occupations
6. Construction occupations
7. Production occupations
8. Service occupations
9. Community helpers
10. Other types of occupations

Concepts for the Children to Learn

1. An occupation is a job a person performs.
2. There are many different kinds of occupations.
3. Truck drivers, gas station attendants, and astronauts are in transportation occupations.
4. Taxi drivers, bus drivers, pilots, and ambulance drivers are in transportation occupations.
5. Doctors, nurses, hygienists, paramedics, child care workers, and dentists are in health occupations.
6. A community helper is someone who helps us.
7. Police officers, firefighters, mail carriers, and judges are community helpers.
8. Teachers, librarians, and custodians are in service occupations.
9. Farmers, cooks, chefs, and factory workers are in production occupations.
10. Hockey players, golfers, tennis players, and soccer players are in sports occupations.
11. Announcers, umpires, and coaches are also in sports occupations.
12. Football and baseball players are in sports occupations.
13. Television and newspaper reporters are in communications occupations.
14. Carpenters, plumbers, cabinetmakers, and electricians are occupations in construction.
15. Builders and architects are in construction occupations.

Vocabulary

1. **job**—type of work that someone has to do.
2. **occupation**—the job a person performs to earn money.
3. **service**—helping people.

Bulletin Board

The purpose of this bulletin board is to learn about gender. Both men and women can be doctors, farmers, construction workers, teachers, judges, etc. In addition, visual discrimination, hand-eye coordination, and problem-solving skills are promoted. To prepare the bulletin board, construct a boy and girl out of tagboard. Design several occupational outfits that may be worn by either sex. Color and laminate the pieces. Magnet pieces or pushpins and holes should be provided to affix clothing on the children.

Dress us for work.

Family Letter

Dear Families,

Hello! We will explore a new unit on occupations. Through experiences provided by this theme, the children will become aware of a great number of occupations and the way these workers help us today. Transportation, health care, sports, community helpers, communication, production, construction, and service workers will all be included.

AT SCHOOL

Some learning experiences include:

- listening to books and recordings about people in our neighborhoods
- making occupation hats
- visiting a police station on Wednesday at 2:00 p.m. Join us if you can!
- observing an ambulance and talking with a paramedic
- designing a job chart for our classroom

AT HOME

Page through magazines with your child. Discuss equipment and materials that are used in various occupations. Questions such as the following can be asked to stimulate thinking skills: Who might use a computer to perform a job? What occupations involve the use of a cash register? Your child might be interested in visiting your place of employment!

Enjoy your child!

James likes to dress up as a mail carrier.

Arts and Crafts

1. Mail Truck

Cut out mail truck parts including one rectangle, one square, and two circles. The children can paste the pieces together and decorate. This activity is most appropriate for older children.

2. Occupation Vests

Cut a circle out of the bottom of a large paper grocery bag. Then, from the circle, cut a slit down the center of the bag. Cut out armholes. Provide felt-tip colored markers for the children to decorate the vests. They may elect to be a pilot, police officer, mail carrier, baker, flight attendant, doctor, firefighter, etc.

3. Mail Pouch

Cut the top half off a large grocery bag. Use the cutaway piece to make a shoulder strap. Staple it to the bag. The children can decorate the bag with crayons or markers.

Dramatic Play

1. Hat Shop

Police officer hats, firefighter hats, construction worker hats, businessperson hats, and other occupation-related hats should be placed in the dramatic play area.

2. Classroom Cafe

Cover the table in the dramatic play area with a tablecloth. Provide menus, a tablet for the waitress to write on, a space for a cook, etc. A cash register and play money may also be added to encourage play.

3. Hairstylist

Collect empty shampoo bottles, combs, barrettes, ribbons, hair spray containers, and magazines. Cut the cord off a discarded hair dryer and curling iron and place in the dramatic play area.

OCCUPATIONS

4. Our Library

Books on a shelf, a desk for the librarian, stamper and ink pad to check out books should be placed in the dramatic play area. A small table for children to sit and read their books would also add interest.

5. Workbench

A hammer, nails, saws, vises, a carpenter's apron, and so forth should be added to the workbench. Eye goggles for the children's safety should also be included. **Caution:** Constant supervision is needed for this activity.

6. An Airplane

Create an airplane out of a large cardboard refrigerator box. If desired, the children can paint the airplane.

7. Post Office

A mailbox, letters, envelopes, stamps, and mail carrier bags can be set up in the dramatic play or art area.

8. Fast-Food Restaurant

Collect bags, containers, and hats to set up a fast-food restaurant.

9. A Construction Site

Hard hats, nails, a hammer, large blocks, and scrap wood can be provided for outdoor play. Cardboard boxes and masking tape should also be made available.

10. Prop Boxes

The following prop boxes can be made by collecting the materials listed.

Police Officer

- badge
- hat
- uniform
- whistle
- walkie-talkie

Mail Carrier

- letter bag
- letter/stamps
- uniform
- mailbox
- wrapped cardboard boxes
- paper
- pencil
- rubber stamp
- ink pad
- envelopes

Firefighter

- boots
- helmet
- hose
- uniform
- gloves
- raincoat
- suspenders
- goggles

Doctor

- stethoscope
- medicine bottles
- adhesive tape
- cotton balls
- Red Cross armband
- chart holder

Field Trips/ Resource People

1. Take field trips to the following:
   - bank
   - library
   - grocery store
   - police station
   - doctor/dentist office
   - beauty salon/barber
   - television/radio station
   - courthouse
   - airport
   - farm
   - restaurant

2. Invite the following resource people to school:
   - police officer with squad car
   - firefighter with truck
   - ambulance driver with ambulance
   - truck driver with truck
   - taxi driver with cab
   - librarian with books

Fingerplays

Farm Chores

Five little farmers woke up with the sun.
 (hold up hand, palm forward)
It was early morning and the chores must be done.
The first little farmer went out to milk the cow.
 (hold up hand, point to thumb)
The second little farmer thought he'd better plow.
 (hold up hand, point to index finger)
The third little farmer cultivated weeds.
 (point to middle finger)
The fourth little farmer planted more seeds.
 (point to fourth finger)
The fifth little farmer drove his tractor round.
 (point to last finger)
Five little farmers, the best that can be found.
 (hold up hand)

Traffic Policeman

The traffic policeman holds up his hand.
 (hold up hand, palm forward)
He blows the whistle,
 (pretend to blow whistle)
He gives the command.
 (hold up hand again)
When the cars are stopped
 (hold up hand again)
He waves at me.

Then I may cross the street, you see.
 (wave hand as if indicating for someone to go)

The Carpenter

This is the way he saws the wood
 (right hand saws left palm)
Sawing, sawing, sawing.
This is the way he nails a nail
 (pound right fist on left palm)
Nailing, nailing, nailing.
This is the way he paints the house
 (right hand paints left palm)
Painting, painting, painting.

Group Time
(Games, Language)

1. **Brushes as Tools**

Collect all types of brushes and place in a bag. The children can reach into the bag and feel one. Before removing it, the child describes the kind of brush. When using with younger children, limit the number of brushes. Also, before placing the brushes in the bag, show the children each brush and discuss its use.

Excursions

Special excursions and events in an early childhood program give opportunities for widening the young child's horizons by providing exciting direct experiences. The following places or people are some suggestions:

train station	offices	hospital	shoe repair shop
dentist office	animal hospital	meat market	print shop
post office	fire station	library	artist's studio
grocery store	tree farm	apple orchard	bowling alley
zoo	car wash	farm	department store
dairy	children's houses	airport	windows
family garden	garage mechanic	riding stable	potter's studio
poultry house	television studio	barber shop	teacher's house
construction site	drugstore	college dormitory	street repair site
beauty shop	bakery		

2. Machines as Helpers Chart

Machines and tools help people work and play. Ask the children to think of all of the machines they or their parents use around the house. As they name a machine, list it on a chart and discuss how it is used.

3. Mail It

Play a variation of Duck, Duck, Goose. The children can sit in a circle. One child holds an envelope and walks around the circle saying, "letter," and taps each child on the head. When he or she gets to the one he or she wants to chase him or her, have the child drop the letter and say, "Mail it!" Then both children run around the circle until they return to the letter. The chaser gets to "mail" the letter by walking around and repeating the game.

Large Muscle

Cut large cardboard boxes to make squad cars. Take the boxes and spray paint them either blue or white. Emblems can be constructed for the sides.

Music

1. "Do You Know the Muffin Man?"

Do You Know the Muffin Man?
Oh, do you know the muffin man,
The muffin man, the muffin man?
Oh, do you know the muffin man
Who lives on Drury Lane?
Oh, yes, I know the muffin man,
The muffin man, the muffin man.
Oh, yes, I know the muffin man
Who lives on Drury Lane.

2. "What Is My Job?"
(*Sing to the tune of "Are You Sleeping?"*)

What is my job? What is my job?
Can you guess? Can you guess?
I keep your body healthy, I keep your body healthy.
Who am I? Who am I?

Variations in song:

I keep your pets healthy: Veterinarian.
I deliver letters: Mail carrier.
I keep your teeth healthy: Dentist.
I keep your building clean: Custodian.
I put out the fires: Firefighter.

Sensory

The following materials can be added to the sensory table:

- sponge hair rollers with water
- wood shavings with scoops and scales
- sand with toy cars, trucks, airplanes
- pipes with water

Social Studies

1. Occupation Pictures

Pin occupation pictures on classroom bulletin boards and walls.

2. A Job Chart

Make a chart containing classroom jobs. Include tasks such as feeding the class pet, watering plants, sweeping the floor, wiping tables, etc.

Books

The following books can be used to complement this theme:

Brandenberg, Alexa. (1996). *I Am Me*. Orlando, FL: Harcourt Brace.

Chapman, Jane. (2003). *Let's Build*. Cambridge, MA: Candlewick Press.

Cordsen, Carol Foskett. (2005). *The Milkman*. Illus. by Douglas B. Jones. New York: Dutton Children's Books.

Cousins, Lucy. (2005). *Maisy Goes to the Library*. Cambridge, MA: Candlewick Press.

Davis, Kate and Kate Endle. (2000). *What Do You Want to Be?* Illus. by Kate Endle. Norwalk, CT: Innovative Kids.

Duvall, Jill D. (1997). *Chef Ki Is Serving Our Dinner*. San Francisco: Children's Book Press. (*Our Neighborhood* series.)

Duvall, Jill D. (1997). *Meet Rory Hohenstein, a Professional Dancer*. San Francisco: Children's Book Press. (*Our Neighborhood* series.)

Duvall, Jill D. (1997). *Mr. Duvall Reports the News*. San Francisco: Children's Book Press. (*Our Neighborhood* series.)

Duvall, Jill D. (1997). *Ms. Moja Makes Beautiful Clothes*. San Francisco: Children's Book Press. (*Our Neighborhood* series.)

Duvall, Jill D. (1997). *Who Keeps the Water Clean?: Ms. Schindler!* San Francisco: Children's Book Press. (*Our Neighborhood* series.)

Flanagan, Alice K. (1996). *A Busy Day at Mr. Kang's Grocery Store*. San Francisco: Children's Book Press. (*Our Neighborhood* series.)

Flanagan, Alice K. (1996). *The Wilsons, a House-Painting Team*. San Francisco: Children's Book Press. (*Our Neighborhood* series.)

Flanagan, Alice K. (1997). *A Day in Court with Mrs. Trinh*. San Francisco: Children's Book Press. (*Our Neighborhood* series.)

Flanagan, Alice K. (1997). *Ask Nurse Pfaff, She'll Help You*. San Francisco: Children's Book Press. (*Our Neighborhood* series.)

Flanagan, Alice K. (1997). *Mrs. Murphy Fights Fires*. San Francisco: Children's Book Press. (*Our Neighborhood* series.)

Florian Douglas. (1992). *A Chef*. New York: Greenwillow. (*How We Work* series.)

Florian Douglas. (1992). *A Fisher* New York: Greenwillow. (*How We Work* series.)

Florian Douglas. (1993). *A Painter*. New York: Greenwillow. (*How We Work* series.)

Florian Douglas. (1994). *An Auto Mechanic*. New York: Greenwillow. (*How We Work* series.)

Gibbons, Gail. (1992). *Say Woof!: The Day of a Country Veterinarian*. New York: Macmillan.

Grossman, Patricia. (1991). *The Night Ones*. Illus. by Lydia Dabcovich. Orlando, FL: Harcourt Brace.

Henkes, Kevin. (1995). *Good-Bye, Curtis*. Illus. by Marisabina Russo. New York: Greenwillow.

Isaacs, Gwynne. (1991). *While You Are Asleep*. Illus. by Cathi Hepworth. New York: Walker.

Kalman, Maira. (1993). *Chicken Soup, Boots*. New York: Viking.

Kunhardt, Edith. (1995). A *Fire Fighter*. New York: Scholastic. (*I'm Going to Be* series.) (Pbk.)

Kunhardt, Edith. (1995). A *Police Officer*. New York: Scholastic. (*I'm Going to Be* series.) (Pbk.)

Kunhardt, Edith. (1996). A *Vet*. New York: Scholastic. (*I'm Going to Be* series.) (Pbk.)

Lenski, Lois and Heidi Kilgras, ed. (2001). *Policeman Small*. New York: Random House.

MacKinnon, Debbie. (1996). *What Am I?* Illus. by Anthea Sieveking. New York: Dial Books.

Markes, Julie. (2005). *Shhhhhh! Everybody's Sleeping*. Illus. by David Parkins. New York: HarperCollins.

Maynard, Christopher. (1997). *Jobs People Do*. New York: DK Publishing.

McMullan, Kate and Jim. (2002). I *Stink!* New York: Joanne Cotler Books.

Miller, Margaret. (1990). *Who Uses This?* New York: Greenwillow.

Miller, Margaret. (1994). *Guess Who?* New York: Greenwillow.

Miller, Margaret. (1997). *Whose Hat?* New York: Greenwillow.

Moses, Amy. (1997). *Doctors Help People*. Mankato, MN: Child's World.

Paulsen, Gary. (1997). *Worksong*. Illus. by Ruth Wright Paulsen. Orlando, FL: Harcourt Brace.

Radford, Derek. (1995). *Harry at the Garage*. Cambridge, MA: Candlewick Press.

Ready, Dee. (1997). *Doctors*. San Francisco: Children's Book Press. (*Community Helpers* series.)

Ready, Dee. (1997). *Farmers*. San Francisco: Children's Book Press. (*Community Helpers* series.)

Ready, Dee. (1997). *Fire Fighters*. San Francisco: Children's Book Press. (*Community Helpers* series.)

Ready, Dee. (1997). *Police Officers*. San Francisco: Children's Book Press. (*Community Helpers* series.)

Ready, Dee. (1997). *Veterinarians*. San Francisco: Children's Book Press. (*Community Helpers* series.)

Ready, Dee. (1998). *Astronauts*. San Francisco: Children's Book Press. (*Community Helpers* series.)

Ready, Dee. (1998). *Bakers*. San Francisco: Children's Book Press. (*Community Helpers* series.)

Ready, Dee. (1998). *Construction*. San Francisco: Children's Book Press. (*Community Helpers* series.)

Ready, Dee. (1998). *Garbage Collectors*. San Francisco: Children's Book Press. (*Community Helpers* series.)

Ready, Dee. (1998). *Nurses*. San Francisco: Children's Book Press. (*Community Helpers* series.)

Ready, Dee. (1998). *Teacher*. San Francisco: Children's Book Press. (*Community Helpers* series.)

Ready, Dee. (1998). *Zoo Keeper*. San Francisco: Children's Book Press. (*Community Helpers* series.)

Rey, Margaret and H.A. (2003). *Curious George Visits the Library*. Illus. in the style of H.A. Rey by Martha Weston. Boston, MA: Houghton Mifflin.

Rylant, Cynthia. (1993). *Mr. Griggs' Work*. Illus. by Julie Downing. New York: Orchard Books.

Schaefer, Lola M. (2001). *Zoo* (*Who Works Here?*). Chicago, IL: Heinemann Library.

Thomas, Mark. (2001). *A Day with a Plumber*. New York: Children's Press.

Winne, Joanne. (2001). *A Day with a Mechanic*. New York: Children's Press.

Multimedia

The following multimedia products can be used to complement this theme:

Big Job [CD-ROM]. (1995). Discovery Channel Multimedia.

Harriet's Magic Hats IV series [video]. (1986). Edmonton, AB: Access Network, Alberta Educational Communication Corp. 25 videos. 15 min. Primary level.

Dog Trainer	*Rodeo Cowboy*
Hotel Manager	*Sheep Farmer*
Hat Maker	*Ski Instructor*
Librarian	*Telephone Installer*
Museum Curator	*Toy Tester*
Naturalist	*Vegetable Processor*
Newspaper Reporter	*Veterinarian*
Paleontologist	*Water Treatment Engineer*
Pasta Maker	
Photographer	*Weather Forecaster*
Potter	*Welder*
Puppeteer	*Zookeeper*

Body Covering

fur
feathers
scales
shell

Movement

swimming
walking
flying
hopping
running
crawling

Pets

Sounds

barking
meowing
squeaking
chirping
hissing

Care

food
water
loving care
air
exercise
grooming
shelter

Kinds

HOUSE		FARM
dogs	rabbits	pig
cats	snakes	horse
hamsters	lizards	sheep
gerbils	spiders	goat
turtles	mice	cow
guinea pigs	ferrets	
fish	chinchillas	
birds		

People

breeders
trainers
groomers
owners
veterinarians

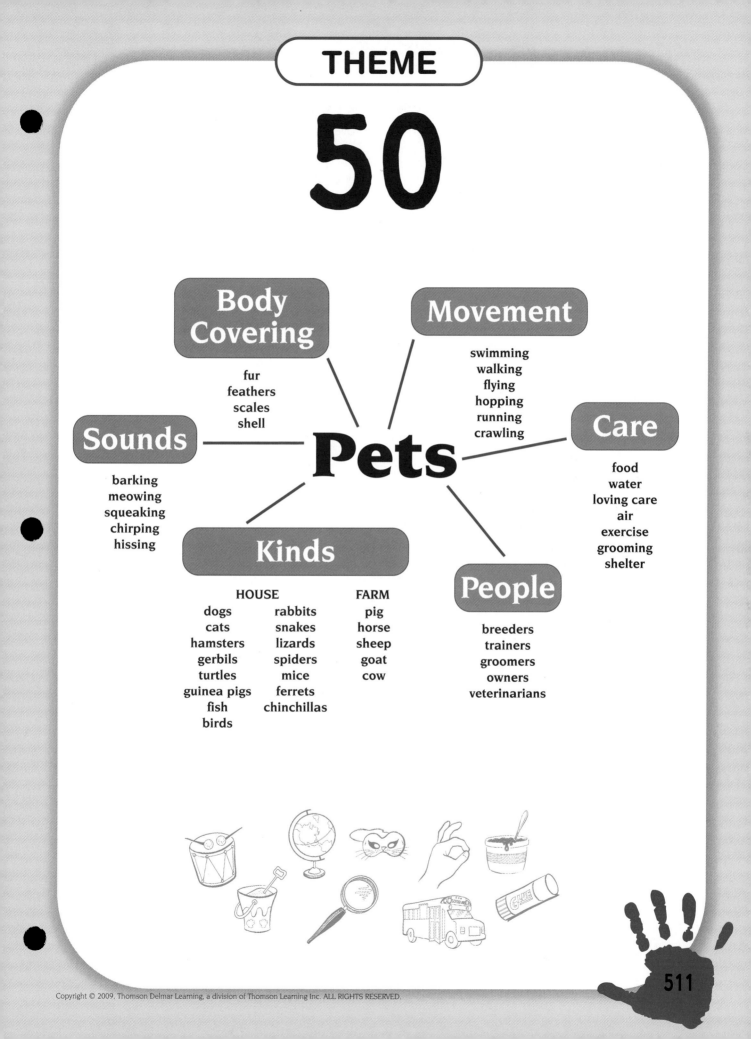

511

Theme Goals

Through participating in the experiences provided by this theme, the children may learn

1. People who work with pets
2. Pet care
3. Kinds of pets
4. Body coverings of pets
5. Sounds of pets
6. Movements of pets

Concepts for the Children to Learn

1. An animal kept for pleasure is called a pet.
2. Dogs, cats, fish, hamsters, gerbils, turtles, and birds can all be house pets.
3. Rabbits, snakes, lizards, spiders, mice, and chinchillas can also be house pets.
4. Pigs, ponies, horses, sheep, goats, and cows can be pets on a farm.
5. Pets need food, water, shelter, exercise, and loving care.
6. Some pets need to be groomed.
7. Barking, meowing, squeaking, and chirping are pet sounds.
8. To move, pets may swim, walk, fly, hop, run, or crawl.
9. The care of a pet depends on the type of animal.
10. Body coverings on pets differ.
11. Body coverings can be fur, feathers, scales, or a shell.
12. A veterinarian is an animal doctor.
13. Breeders and trainers also work with pets.
14. Groomers wash, brush, and care for animals.

Vocabulary

1. **collar**—a band worn around an animal's neck.
2. **feathers**—skin covering of birds.
3. **fur**—hairy coating covering the skin of some animals.
4. **leash**—a cord that attaches to a collar.
5. **pet**—animal that is kept for pleasure. Cats and dogs are pets.
6. **scales**—skin covering of fish and reptiles.
7. **veterinarian**—an animal doctor.
8. **whiskers**—stiff hair growing around the animal's nose, mouth, and eyes.

Bulletin Board

The purpose of this bulletin board is to encourage the development of mathematical, visual discrimination, hand-eye coordination, and problem-solving skills. To prepare the bulletin board, construct fishbowls out of white tagboard or construction paper. Write a numeral beginning with one on each fishbowl and the corresponding number of dots. Hang the fishbowls on the bulletin board. Next, construct pieces as illustrated that will fit on top of the fishbowl to represent water in the bowl. Draw fish to match the numerals in each bowl. The pieces can be attached to each other to hang on the bulletin board by using magnet pieces, or pushpins and a paper punch. The children should count the fish in each water piece and match it to the corresponding numbered fishbowl.

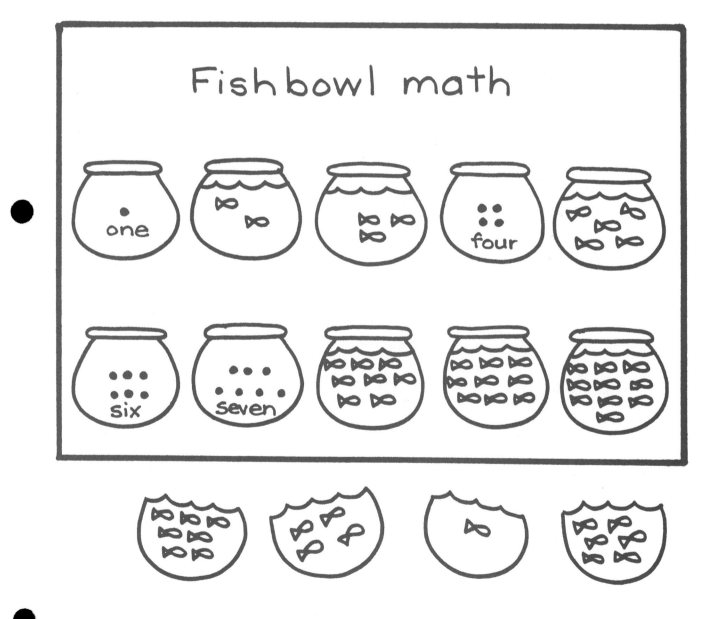

Family Letter

Dear Families,

Children are naturally curious about animals. To build on their interests, we are starting a curriculum unit on pets, and I'm sure that we'll be busy! The children will discover the kinds of animals most people keep as pets. They will also learn sounds, care, body coverings, and movements of pets. Also, the children will learn the occupations of people who work with pets.

AT SCHOOL

The following are some of the learning experiences in which your child will participate during our pet unit:

- making a special treat for Greta, our classroom gerbil
- creating a large doghouse out of an appliance box for the dramatic play area
- interacting with a variety of pets. Dani and Donny will bring their rabbit on Tuesday, and Cindy will bring her bird on Wednesday. If you are willing to bring your family pet to school to show the children, we welcome you. Contact me and we can arrange a time that would be convenient for you (and your pet).
- listening to the story *Clifford, the Big Red Dog*, by Norman Birdwell

AT HOME

Is your family considering adding a pet to your household? If so, there are many variables to take into consideration because not all households are meant to include pets. Allergies, fears, and lifestyles are three things that need to be considered. Also, you need to consider your child's readiness for a pet.

To develop fine motor skills, provide magazines and newspapers for your child to cut or tear out pictures of animals. These can be used to create an animal alphabet book or a collage to hang in your child's bedroom.

Enjoy your child!

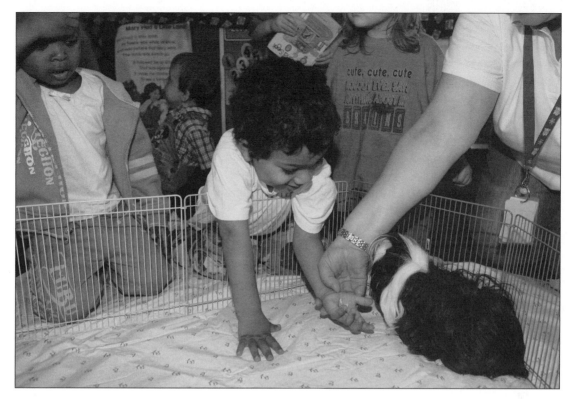

Children enjoy learning about and caring for all kinds of pets.

 ## Arts and Crafts

1. **Pet Sponge Painting**

   Cut sponges into a variety of pet shapes. Place on the art table with paper and a shallow pan of tempera paint.

2. **Doghouse**

   Provide an old, large cardboard box for the children to make a doghouse with adult supervision. They can cut holes, paint, and decorate it. When dry, the doghouse can be moved into the dramatic play area or to the outdoor play yard.

3. **Cookie Cutters and Play Dough**

   Pet-shaped cookie cutters and play dough can be placed on the art table.

 ## Cooking

Animal Cookies

1 1/2 cups powdered sugar
1 cup butter or margarine
1 egg
1 teaspoon vanilla extract
2 1/2 cups flour
1 teaspoon baking soda
1 teaspoon cream of tartar

Mix powdered sugar, margarine, egg, and vanilla extract. Mix in flour, baking soda, and cream of tartar. Cover and refrigerate for 2 hours. Preheat oven to 375 degrees. Divide dough into halves. Roll out 1/2-inch thick on a lightly floured, cloth-covered board. Cut the dough into animal shapes with cookie cutters or let children cut. Place on lightly greased cookie sheet. Bake 7 to 10 minutes. Serve for snack.

Dramatic Play

1. Pet Store

The children can all bring in their stuffed animals to set up a pet store. A counter, a cash register, and several empty pet food containers should be provided to stimulate play.

2. Veterinarian Prop Box

Collect materials for a veterinarian prop box. Include a stethoscope, empty pill bottles, fabric cut as bandages, splints, and stuffed animals.

Field Trips/ Resource People

1. Pet Show

Plan a pet show. Each child who wants to show a pet should sign up for a time and day. If children can all bring in a pet the same day, have a big pet show. Award prizes for longest tail, longest ears, biggest, smallest, best groomed, loudest barker, most obedient, etc. Children who do not have a pet or cannot arrange to bring it to school can bring a stuffed toy.

2. Veterinarian

Invite a veterinarian to talk to the children about how a veterinarian helps pets and animals. Pet care can also be addressed.

3. Pet Store

Visit a pet store to observe types of pets, their toys, and other accessories. Pictures can be taken on the trip and later placed on the bulletin board of the classroom.

4. Pet Groomer

Visit a pet groomer. Observe how the pet is bathed and groomed.

Fingerplays

My Puppy

I like to pet my puppy.
  (pet puppy)
He has such nice soft fur.
  (pet puppy)
And if I don't pull his tail
  (pull tail)
He won't say "Grr!"
  (make face)

If I Were

If I were a dog
I'd have four legs to run and play.
  (down on all four hands and feet)
If I were a fish
I'd have fins to swim all day.
  (hands at side fluttering like fins)
If I were a bird
I could spread my wings out wide.
And fly all over the countryside.
  (arms out from sides fluttering like wings)
But I'm just me.
I have two legs, don't you see?
And I'm just as happy as can be.

The Bunny

Once there was a bunny
  (fist with two fingers tall)
And a green, green cabbage head.
  (fist of other hand)
"I think I'll have some breakfast," this little
  bunny said.
So he nibbled and he cocked his ears to say,
"I think it's time that I be on my way."

Sammy

Sammy is a super snake.
  (wave finger on opposite palm)
He sleeps on the shore of a silver lake.
  (curl finger to indicate sleep)
He squirms and squiggles to snatch a snack
  (wave finger and pounce)
And snoozes and snores till his hunger is back.
  (curl finger on palm)

516

THEME 50

Not Say a Single Word

We'll hop, hop, hop like a bunny
    (make hopping motion with hand)
And run, run, run like a dog.
    (make running motion with fingers)
We'll walk, walk, walk like an elephant
    (make walking motion with arms)
And jump, jump, jump like a frog.
    (make jumping motions with arms)
We'll swim, swim, swim like a goldfish
    (make swimming motion with hand)
And fly, fly, fly like a bird.
    (make flying motion with arms)
We'll sit right down and fold our hands
    (fold hands in lap)
And not say a single word!

Music

1. **"Rags"**
(*Sing this song to one of the children's favorite tunes*)

I have a dog and his name is Rags.
    (point to self)
He eats so much that his tummy sags.
    (hold tummy)
His ears flip-flop and his tail wig-wags.
    (flip hands by ears and wag hands at back)
And when he walks he zigs and zags.
    (put hands together and zig-zag them)

Flip-flop
Wiggle-waggle
Zig-zag   (Repeat the same actions)
Flip-flop
Wiggle-waggle
Zig-zag

2. **"Six Little Pets"**
(*Sing to the tune of "Six Little Ducks,"
a traditional early childhood song*)

Six little gerbils I once knew, fat ones, skinny ones, fair ones, too. But the one little gerbil was so much fun. He would play until the day was done.

Six little dogs that I once knew, fat ones, skinny ones, fair ones, too. But the one little dog with the brown curly fur, he led the others with a grr, grr, grr.

Six little fish that I once knew, fat ones, skinny ones, fair ones, too. But the one little fish who was the leader of the crowd, he led the others around and around.

Six little birds that I once knew, fat ones, skinny ones, fair ones, too. But the one little bird with the pretty little beak, he led the others with a tweet, tweet, tweet.

Six little cats that I once knew, fat ones, skinny ones, fair ones, too. But the one little cat who was as fluffy as a ball, he was the prettiest one of all.

3. **"Have You Ever Seen a Rabbit?"**
(*Sing to the tune of "Have You Ever Seen a Lassie?"*)

Have you ever seen a rabbit, a rabbit, a rabbit?
Have you ever seen a rabbit go hopping around?
Go hopping, go hopping, go hopping, go hopping
Have you ever seen a rabbit go hopping around?

Science

1. **Pet Foods**

Cut pictures of pets and pet foods and place on the science table. Include different foods such as meat, fish, carrots, lettuce, nuts, and acorns. The children can match the food to a picture of the animal that would eat each type of food.

2. **Bird Feathers**

Bird feathers with a magnifying glass can be placed on the science table for the children to examine.

Sensory

1. **Minnows**

Fill the sensory table with cold water. Place minnows purchased from a bait store into the water. The children will attempt to catch the minnows. Teachers should stress the importance of being gentle with the fish and follow through with limits set for the activity. After participating in this activity, the children should wash their hands.

2. Texture Rubbings

Cut out sandpaper "footprints" representing a variety of animals (cat, dog, birds, etc.). Tape the prints on the table and have children place a piece of paper over the print. Rub the side of a crayon over the sandpaper to form a print. Have the children guess what kind of pet made each print.

Social Studies

1. Animal Sounds

Tape several animal sounds and play them back for the children to identify.

2. Feeding Chart

Design and prepare a feeding chart for the classroom pets.

3. Weekend Visitor

Let children take turns bringing class pets home on weekends. Prepare a card for each animal's cage outlining feeding and behavioral expectations.

Books

The following books can be used to complement this theme:

Baker, Karen Lee. (1997). *Seneca*. New York: Greenwillow.

Birdwell, Norman. (1992). *Clifford, the Big Red Dog*. Torrence, CA: Frank Schafer Publications.

Caseley, Judith. (1995). *Mr. Green Peas*. New York: Greenwillow.

Evans, Mark. (1993). *Fish: A Practical Guide to Caring for Your Fish*. New York: Dorling Kindersley.

Evans, Mark. (1993). *Hamster: A Practical Guide to Caring for Your Hamster*. New York: Dorling Kindersley.

Flanagan, Alice K. (1996). *Talking Birds*. San Francisco: Children's Book Press.

Gibbons, Gail. (1992). *Say Woof: The Day of a Country Veterinarian*. New York: Macmillan.

Greenwood, Pamela D. (1993). *What About My Goldfish*? Illus. by Jennifer Plecas. New York: Clarion Books.

Giffith, Helen V. (1992). *"Mine Will," Said John*. Newly illus. edition by Jos. A. Smith. New York: Greenwillow.

Johnson, Angela. (1993). *The Girl Who Wore Snakes*. Illus. by James Ransome. New York: Orchard Books.

Johnson, Angela. (1993). *Julius*. Illus. by Dav Pilkey. New York: Orchard Books.

Joose, Barbara M. (1997). *Nugget and Darling*. Illus. by Sue Truesdell. New York: Clarion Books.

Kasza, Keiko. (2005). *The Dog Who Cried Wolf*. New York: G.P. Putnam's Sons.

King-Smith, Dick. (1995). *I Love Guinea Pigs*. Illus. by Anita Jeram. Cambridge, MA: Candlewick Press.

Kristine, Spangard. (1997). *My Pet Rabbit*. Photos by Andy King. Minneapolis, MN: Lerner.

L'Engle, Madeleine and Christine Davenier. (2001). *The Other Dog*. Illus. by Christine Davenier. New York: Seastar.

McDonald, Megan and Nancy Poydar. (2000). *Beezy & Funnybone*. Illus. by Nancy Poydar. New York: Orchard Books.

Nichols, Grace. (1997). *Asana and the Animals: A Book of Pet Poems*. Illus. by Sarah Adams. Cambridge, MA: Candlewick Press.

Petersen-Fleming, Judy et al. (1996). *Kitten Training and Critters, Too!* New York: Tambourine Books.

Petersen-Fleming, Judy et al. (1996). *Puppy Training and Critters, Too!* New York: Tambourine Books.

Pfeffer, Wendy and Holly Keller. (1996). *What's It Like to Be a Fish*? Illus. by Holly Keller. New York: HarperCollins.

Reiser, Lynn W. (1992). *Any Kind of Dog*. New York: Greenwillow.

Ross, Michael Elsohn et al. (1998). *Ladybugology*. Illus. by Brian Grogan. Minneapolis, MN: Lerner.

Rylant, Cynthia. (1993). *Everyday Pets*. Little Simon. (Board book.)

Rylant, Cynthia. (1997). *Mr. Putter and Tabby Row the Boat*. Illus. by Arthur Howard. Orlando, FL: Harcourt Brace.

Scruton, Clive. (1999). *Where Are Mary's Pets: A Flip-Flap Book*. Cambridge, MA: Candlewick Press.

Smith, Lane. (1991). *The Big Pets*. New York: Viking.

Sovak, Jan. (2001). *Learning about Farm Animals*. New York: Dover.

Stevens, Janet and Susan Stevens Crummel. (1999). *My Big Dog*. New York: Golden Books.

Wolf, Jake. (1996). *Daddy, Could I Have an Elephant?* Illus. by Marylin Hafner. New York: Greenwillow.

Ziefert, Harriet. (1996). *Let's Get a Pet*. Illus. by Mavis Smith. New York: Puffin Books. (Pbk.)

Zolotow, Charlotte. (1995). *The Old Dog* (Rev. ed.). Revised and newly illus. by James Ransome. New York: HarperCollins.

Multimedia

The following multimedia products can be used to complement this theme:

Bourgeois, Paulette. *Franklin Wants a Pet* [cassette and book]. (1995). New York: Scholastic.

Cats [video]. (1985). National Geographic.

Dogs [video]. (1985). National Geographic.

Fish [video]. (1985). National Geographic.

Keats, Ezra Jack. *Pet Show* [video]. (1987). Weston Woods.

Pets: See How They Grow [video]. Sony Video.

Recordings and Song Titles

The following recording can be used to complement this theme:

"Love Your Pet." (1989). *Make the Right Choice*. Long Branch, NJ: Kimbo Educational.

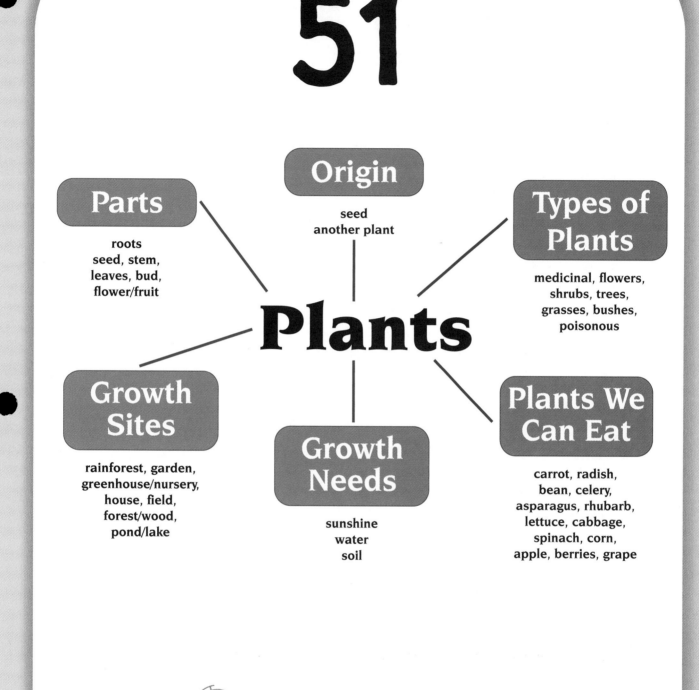

Origin

seed
another plant

Parts

roots
seed, stem,
leaves, bud,
flower/fruit

Types of Plants

medicinal, flowers,
shrubs, trees,
grasses, bushes,
poisonous

Plants

Growth Sites

rainforest, garden,
greenhouse/nursery,
house, field,
forest/wood,
pond/lake

Growth Needs

sunshine
water
soil

Plants We Can Eat

carrot, radish,
bean, celery,
asparagus, rhubarb,
lettuce, cabbage,
spinach, corn,
apple, berries, grape

Theme Goals

Through participating in the experiences provided by this theme, the children may learn

1. Types of plants
2. Growth needs of plants
3. The parts of a plant
4. Plant growth sites
5. Edible plants
6. Origin of plants

Concepts for the Children to Learn

1. Plants are living things, usually green, that grow and change.
2. There are many kinds of plants.
3. Flowers, shrubs, trees, grasses, and bushes are all plants.
4. Some plants grow from seeds.
5. Some plants grow from another plant.
6. Plants need water, sunlight, and soil to grow.
7. People and animals eat some types of plants.
8. The parts of a plant are the stem, roots, leaves, flower/fruit, and seeds.
9. Carrots, radishes, beans, celery, asparagus, and rhubarb are plants.
10. Lettuce, cabbage, spinach, corn, berries, and grapes are all plants.
11. There are different sizes, colors, and shapes of seeds.
12. Plants grow in the garden, greenhouses, nurseries, fields, forests, and the woods.
13. Plants grow in a pond or lake.

Vocabulary

1. **flower**—a colored plant part that contains seeds.
2. **fruit**—edible plant product that has seeds. Oranges, apples, and strawberries are fruits.
3. **garden**—ground for growing plants.
4. **leaf**—part of the plant that grows on the stem.
5. **plant**—living thing, usually green, that grows and changes. Bushes, flowers, grass, and trees are all plants.
6. **root**—part of the plant that grows into the soil.
7. **seed**—part of plant that can grow into a new plant.
8. **sprout**—first sign of growth.
9. **stem**—part of the plant that supports the leaves and grows upward.
10. **vegetable**—a plant grown for food. Beans, carrots, and corn are vegetables.

Bulletin Board

The purpose of this bulletin board is to promote visual discrimination, hand-eye coordination, problem-solving, and numeral-recognition skills. To prepare the bulletin board, construct flowerpots out of construction paper. Color each pot and draw dots on it as illustrated. Hang the pots on the bulletin board. Next, construct the same number of flowers with stems as pots. In the center of each flower, write a numeral. The children can place each flower in the flowerpot with the corresponding number of dots.

Family Letter

Dear Families,

Plants will be the focus of our next unit. Through the unit, the children will become aware of the origin and parts of a plant. They will also discover where plants can be grown and what plants can be eaten. They will be exposed to the parts of plants, plant growth sites, as well as foods that are edible plants.

AT SCHOOL

Some of the learning experiences related to plants will include:

- listening to the story *The Plant Sitter* by Gene Zion
- sprouting alfalfa seeds to add to a salad
- walking around our play yard to collect plants
- playing hopscotch in the shape of a flower

AT HOME

There are many ways to foster the concepts of this unit at home. If you have plants, let your child help water them. If you are planning to start a garden, section off a small portion for your child to grow plants.

At mealtimes, identify various parts of plants that are eaten. For example, we eat the leaves of lettuce, the stems of celery, the root of a carrot, and so on.

Plant some flower seeds with your child! Or, perhaps you could root a vegetable. To do this, place a potato or carrot in a jar, root end down so that one-third is covered by water. A potato can be held upright by inserting toothpicks or small nails at three points so that the vegetable can be rested on the rim of the jar. Encourage your child to water the vegetable as needed. Label the plant. Roots should grow out from the bottom of the vegetable. Likewise, shoots will grow from the top.

Enjoy your child!

Arts and Crafts

1. **Grass Hair**

   Save 1/2-pint milk cartons. The children can decorate the outside of the carton like a face. Place soil in the cartons and add grass seeds. After approximately 7 days the grass will start to grow, and it will look like hair. If the grass becomes too long, have the child give it a haircut.

2. **Flower Collage**

   Collect flowers and weeds. Press the flowers and weeds between paper and books. Old telephone directories can be used. Dry them for 7 to 10 days. The children can use the pressed foliage to create their own collages on paper plates or construction paper.

3. **Nature Tree**

   Cut a branch off a tree and place in a pail of plaster of Paris. The children can decorate the tree with a ribbon and different forms of plant life that they have collected or made. Included may be flowers, plants, fruits, vegetables, and seeds.

4. **Leaf Rubbings**

   Place a thin piece of paper over a leaf. Rub gently with the long side of a crayon.

5. **Easel Ideas**

   Cut easel paper into different shapes, such as:

   - leaves
   - flowers
   - flowerpots
   - fruits and vegetables

6. **Egg Carton Flowers**

   Use egg cartons and chenille stems to make flowers. To make the flower stand up, place a chenille stem into the egg carton as well as a Styrofoam block.

7. **Hand and Foot Flowers**

   Create a flower by using the child's hands and feet. Trace and cut two left and right hands and one set of left and right feet. Put one set of

What does a flower look like inside?

hands together to form the top of the flower and the other set (facing down) to form the bottom side. Add a circle to the middle. Cut a stem from green paper and add the green feet, as leaves. This makes a cute Mother's Day idea. Mount on white paper.

Cooking

1. **Vegetable-Tasting Party**

   Prepare raw vegetables for a tasting party. Discuss the color, texture, and flavor of each vegetable.

2. **Sprouts**

   Provide each interested child with a small jar. Fill the bottom with alfalfa seeds. Fill the jar with warm water and cover with cheesecloth and a rubberband. Each day, rinse and fill the jar with fresh warm water. In three or four days the

PLANTS

seeds will sprout. The sprouts may be used on sandwiches or salads at lunchtime.

3. **Latkes (Potato Pancakes)**

2 potatoes, peeled and grated
1 egg, slightly beaten
1/4 cup flour
1 teaspoon salt
cooking oil

Mix the ingredients in a bowl. Drop the mixture by tablespoons into hot oil in an electric skillet. Brown on both sides. Drain on paper towels. **Caution:** This activity must be carefully supervised.

Dramatic Play

1. **Greenhouse**

Provide materials for a greenhouse. Include window space, pots, soil, water, watering cans, seeds, plants, posters, work aprons, garden gloves, a terrarium, and seed packages to mount on sticks.

2. **Jack and the Beanstalk**

Act out the story *Jack and the Beanstalk*. The children can dramatize a beanstalk growing.

3. **Vegetable-Fruit Stand**

Display plastic fruits and vegetables. Set up a shopping area with carts, cash registers, and play money. Provide a balance scale for children to weigh the produce.

4. **Garden Planting**

Plant a small garden outdoors. Provide seeds, watering cans, garden tools, gloves, and garden hats.

Field Trips

1. **Greenhouse**

Visit a greenhouse or a tree nursery to observe the different plants and trees and inquire about their care.

2. **Farm**

Plan a visit to a farm. While there, observe the various forms of plant life.

3. **Florist**

Visit a florist. Observe the different colors, types, and sizes of flowering plants.

Fingerplays

My Garden

This is my garden.
   (extend one hand forward, palm up)
I'll rake it with care
   (make raking motion on palm with other hand)
And then some flower seeds
   (make planting motion with thumb and index fingers)
I'll plant in there.
The sun will shine
   (make circle above head)
And the rain will fall
   (let fingers flutter down to lap)
And my garden will blossom
   (cup hands together, extend upward slowly until fingers stand straight)
And grow straight and tall.

Plants

Plants need care to help them grow
   (make fist with hand)
Just like boys and girls you know.
Good soil, water, sunshine bright.
Then watch them pop overnight.
   (extend fingers from fist)

Group Time
(Games, Language)

Feltboard Fun

Construct felt pieces representing the stages of a flower's growth. Include a bulb, seed, cuttings, root, stem, leaves, and a flower. During group

526

THEME 51

time, review the name and purpose of each part with the children. The children can take turns coming up to the flannel board and adding the pieces. After group time, the felt pieces should be left out so that the child can reconstruct the growth during self-selected activity periods.

Large Muscle

1. **Leaf Jumping**

   Cut out eight large leaves from tagboard. Arrange the leaves in a pattern on the floor. Encourage the children to jump from one leaf to another. This game could also be played outdoors by drawing the leaves on the sidewalk with chalk.

2. **Flower Hopscotch**

   Design a hopscotch in the form of a flower. Chalk can be used on a sidewalk outdoors or masking tape can be used indoors to make the form.

3. **Vegetable, Vegetable, Plant**

   Play "Vegetable, Vegetable, Plant" as a variation of "Duck, Duck, Goose."

4. **Raking and Hoeing**

   Provide the children with plastic child-sized hoes and rakes to tend to the play yard.

Math

1. **Charting Growth**

   The children can observe the growth of a small plant by keeping a chart of its growth. Record the date of the observation and the height. For convenience, place the chart near the plant table.

2. **Flowerpot Match Game**

   Construct flowerpots. The number constructed will depend on the developmental appropriateness. Write a numeral on each, beginning with the numeral one. Make the same number of flowers, with the petals varying from one to the

total number of flowerpots constructed. The children match the flowerpot to the flower with the same number of petals.

3. **Counting and Classifying Seeds**

   Place a variety of seeds on a table. Encourage the children to count and classify them into groups. To assist in counting and classifying, an egg carton with each section given a number from 1 to 12 may be helpful. Encourage the children to observe the numeral and place a corresponding number of seeds in each section.

4. **Plant Growth Seriation**

   Construct pictures of plants through stages of growth. Begin with a seed, followed by the seed sprouting. The third picture should be the stem erupting from the soil surface. Next, a stem with leaves can be constructed. Finally, flowers can be added to the last picture. This could also be made into a bulletin board.

5. **Seed Match**

   Collect a variety of seeds such as corn, pumpkin, orange, apple, lima bean, watermelon, pea, and peach. Cut several rectangles out of white tagboard. On the top half of each rectangle, glue one of the seed types you have collected. Encourage the children to sort the seeds, matching them to those seeds glued on the individual cards.

Music

1. **"The Seed Cycle"**
   (*Sing to the tune of "The Farmer in the Dell"*)

   The farmer sows his seeds.
   The farmer sows his seeds.
   Hi-ho the dairy-o
   The farmer sows his seeds.

   Other verses:
   The wind begins to blow . . .
   The rain begins to fall . . .
   The sun begins to shine . . .
   The seeds begin to grow . . .
   The plants grow big and tall . . .
   The farmer cuts his corn . . .

PLANTS

He puts it in his barns . . .
And now the harvest is in . . .

Children can dramatize the parts for each verse.

2. **"This Is the Way We Rake the Garden"**
(*Sing to the tune of "Here We Go Round the Mulberry Bush"*)

This is the way we rake the garden,
Rake the garden, rake the garden.
This is the way we rake the garden,
So early in the morning.

Other verses:
This is the way we plant the seeds . . .
This is the way the rain comes down . . .
This is the way we hoe the weeds . . .
This is the way the garden grows . . .
This is the way we pick the vegetables . . .
This is the way we eat the vegetables . . .

3. **"The Farmer in the Dell"**
(*traditional*)

Science

1. **Watch Seeds Grow**

Two identical plastic transparent plates and blotting paper are needed for this activity. Moisten the blotting paper. Lay the wet paper on one of the plates. On the top of the paper plate place various seeds—corn, peas, squash, bean, etc. Place the other plate over the seeds to serve as a cover. Tie the plates together tightly. Stand the plate on its edge in a pan containing 1/2-inch water. Watch the seeds sprout and grow.

2. **Colored Celery**

In clear containers place several celery stalks with leaves. In each container add 3 inches of water and drop a different color of food coloring. The leaves of the celery should turn colors in a few hours. Try splitting a celery stalk in half, but do not split the stalk all the way up to the top. Put one half of the stalk in red water, and the other half in blue water. Watch what happens to the leaves.

3. **Sunlight Experiment**

Place seeds in two jars with a half-inch of soil. Place one jar in a dark place such as a closet or cupboard and avoid watering it. Keep the other jar in a sunny area and water it frequently. Which one grew? Why?

4. **Growing Bean Plants**

Each child can grow a bean plant.

5. **Tasting Plants**

Various fruits and vegetables grown from plants should be provided for the children to taste and smell.

6. **Feely Box**

In the feely box, place different parts of a plant such as root, stem, leaves, flowers, fruit, and buds. The children can feel and verbally identify the part of the plant before looking at it.

7. **Root a Vegetable**

Place a potato or carrot in a jar, root end down so that one-third is covered by water. A potato can be held upright by inserting toothpicks or nails at three points. This can be rested on the rim of the jar. The children can water as needed. Roots should grow out from the bottom and shoots from the top. Plant the root in soil for an attractive plant.

8. **Beans**

Soak dry navy beans in a jar of water overnight. The next day compare soaked beans with dry beans. Note the difference in texture and color. Open some beans that were soaked. A tiny plant should be inside the bean. These can be placed under a microscope for closer observation.

9. **Budding Branches**

Place a branch that has buds ready to bloom in a jar of water on the science table. Let the children observe the buds bloom. Notice that after all the stored food of the plant is used the plant will die.

Social Studies

1. Plant Walk

Walk around the neighborhood and try to identify as many plants as you can.

2. Play Yard Plants

Make a map of the play yard. The children can collect a part of each plant located in the playground. The plant samples can be mounted on the map.

3. Planting Trees

Plant a tree on your playground. Discuss the care needed for trees.

4. Family Tree

Make a Family Tree by mounting a bunch of branches in a pail of dirt. Each child can bring in a family picture to be placed on a leaf shape and hung on the tree branches.

Books

The following books can be used to complement this theme:

Ardley, Neil. (1991). *The Science Book of Things That Grow*. Orlando, FL: Harcourt Brace.

Batten, Mary and Paul Mirocha. (2000). *Hungry Plants*. Illus. by Paul Mirocha. New York: Golden Book Family Entertainment.

Berger, Melvin. (1994). *All About Seeds*. Reprint edition. New York: Scholastic.

Charman, Andrew. (1997). *I Wonder Why Trees Have Leaves and Other Questions About Plants*. Stanwood, WA: Kingfisher.

Christensen, Bonnie. (1994). *An Edible Alphabet*. New York: Dial.

Dorros, Arthur. (1990). *Rain Forest Secrets*. New York: Scholastic.

Dunphy, Madeleine. (1994). *Here Is the Tropical Rain Forest*. Illus. by Michael Rothman. New York: Hyperion.

Fowler, Allan. (1998). *Good Mushrooms and Bad Toadstools*. Chicago: Children's Press.

Ganeri, Anita. (1995). *What's Inside Plants?* New York: Peter Bedrick Books.

Gibbons, Gail. (1991). *From Seed to Plant*. New York: Holiday House.

Gill, Jamie Spaht, Kris Cox, Mike Cox, Dan Wasserman (Ed.), and Bob Reese. (1997). *Flowers (Ten Word Book)*. Illus. by Bob Reese. Ramsey, NJ: Aro.

Guiberson, Brenda Z. (1991). *Cactus Hotel*. Illus. by Megan Lloyd. New York: Holt.

Jordan, Helene J. (1992). *How a Seed Grows*. Rev. ed. Illus. by Loretta Krupinski. New York: HarperCollins.

Krauss, Ruth. (2005). *The Carrot Seed*. Illus. by Crockett, Johnson. New York: HarperCollins Publishers. (60th Anniversary Edition.)

Luchts, Irmgard. (1995). *Red Poppy*. Translated by Frank Jacoby-Nelson. New York: Hyperion.

Maestro, Betsy. (1992). *How Do Apples Grow?* Illus. by Giulio Maestro. New York: HarperCollins.

Maestro, Betsy. (1994). *Why Do Leaves Change Color?* Illus. by Loretta Krupinski. New York: HarperCollins.

Marzollo, Jean. (1996). *It's a Seed*. Illus. by Judith Moffatt. New York: Scholastic.

Morgan, Sally. (1996). *Flowers, Trees, and Fruits*. Stanwood, WA: Kingfisher.

Nielsen, Nancy J. (1992). *Carnivorous Plants*. New York: Franklin Watts.

Robbins, Ken. (1990). *A Flower Grows*. New York: Dial.

Sekido, Isamu. (1993). *Fruits, Roots, and Fungi: Plants We Eat*. Minneapolis, MN: Lerner.

Visual Dictionary of Plants. (1992). New York: Dorling Kindersley.

What's Inside? Plants. (1992). New York: Dorling Kindersley.

Yolen, Jane. (1993). *Welcome to the Green House*. Illus. by Laura Regan. New York: G. P. Putnam.

Multimedia

The following multimedia products can be used to complement this theme:

Let's Explore the Jungle with Buzzy the Knowledge Bug [CD-ROM]. (1995). Woodinville, WA: Humongous Entertainment.

Tell Me Why Vol. 3: Flowers, Plants and Trees [video]. (1987). Marina Del Rey, CA: Tell Me Why.

Wonders of Growing Plants [video]. (1992). 3rd ed. Churchill Media/SVE.

Recordings and Song Titles

The following recordings can be used to complement this theme:

"I'm Going to Plant a Garden." (1997). *Science in a Nutshell*. Long Branch, NJ: Kimbo Educational.

Save the Animals, Save the Earth. (1991). Long Branch, NJ: Kimbo Educational.

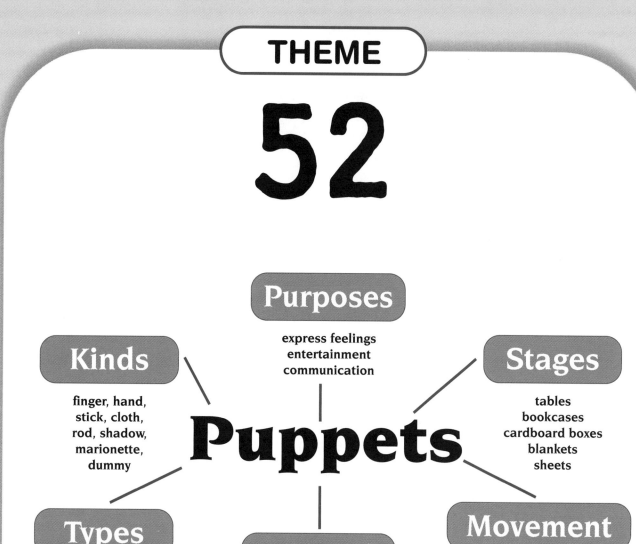

Purposes

express feelings
entertainment
communication

Kinds

finger, hand,
stick, cloth,
rod, shadow,
marionette,
dummy

Puppets

Stages

tables
bookcases
cardboard boxes
blankets
sheets

Types

animals
people
pretend creatures

Materials

paper/paper bags,
novelty sticks,
cloth, socks,
wooden spoons,
string, felt,
coat hangers,
pot holders,
mittens, gloves,
paper plates,
flyswatters

Movement

string
wire
rods
hands
fingers

Theme Goals

Through participating in the experiences provided by this theme, the children may learn

1. The purpose of using puppets
2. Kinds of puppets
3. Types of puppets
4. Materials used to make puppets
5. Ways of moving puppets
6. Types of puppet stages

Concepts for the Children to Learn

1. A puppet is a toy that can be moved by the hand or finger.
2. There are many kinds of puppets.
3. Our hands and fingers can be puppets.
4. Rod, shadow, marionette, and dummy are types of puppets.
5. Puppets can be fun.
6. Puppets can be used for communication and entertainment.
7. We can use puppets to express feelings.
8. People talk for puppets.
9. Puppets can be made from paper bags, socks, wooden spoons, cloth, or even wood.
10. Puppets can also be made from coat hangers, pot holders, mittens, gloves, paper plates, and flyswatters.
11. Puppets can be made to look like animals, people, or pretend creatures.
12. Some puppets can be moved with strings, wires, or rods.
13. Large boxes, cardboard, tables, bookcases, blankets, and sheets can be used for puppet stages.

Vocabulary

1. **entertainment**—things we enjoy seeing and listening to.
2. **imaginary**—something that is not real.
3. **marionette**—a puppet with strings for movement.
4. **puppet**—a toy that is moved by the hand, fingers, strings, wires, or rods.
6. **puppet show**—a story told with puppets.
5. **puppeteer**—a person who makes a puppet move and speak.
7. **puppet stage**—a place for puppets to act.

532

THEME 52

Bulletin Board

The purpose of this bulletin board is to expose the children to a variety of puppets. The children's expressive language skills will be stimulated by interacting with the puppets. Design the bulletin board by constructing about five or six simple puppets for the children to take off the bulletin board to play with. Include a flyswatter puppet, a paper bag puppet, hand puppet, sock puppet, and a wooden spoon puppet. Hooks or pushpins can be used to attach the puppets to the bulletin board.

Family Letter

Dear Families,

Our new curriculum unit will focus on puppets. They are magical and motivating to young children. Sometimes a child will respond or talk to a puppet in a situation when he or she might not talk to an adult or another child. Through learning experiences involving puppets, the children will become aware of the different types, kinds, and movements of puppets. They will also learn materials that can be used to make puppets. Through using puppets in their play, they will learn to express themselves creatively and imaginatively.

AT SCHOOL

Some of the activities related to puppets include:

- creating our own puppets with a variety of materials
- using the puppet stage throughout the week, putting on puppet shows for one and all
- exploring various types of puppets, including finger, hand, stick, shadow, and marionette puppets

AT HOME

The children enjoy retelling familiar stories and making up original stories for puppet characters. To stimulate this type of play, you and your child can make simple puppets at home with objects found around the house.

Paper Bag Puppets—Using small paper lunch bags, children can use crayons or markers to create a puppet. The fold in the bag can be used as the mouth. After the child's hand is in the bag, the puppet can talk. Yarn scraps can easily be glued on for hair and construction paper scraps can add a decorative touch.

Sock Puppets—I'm sure you have a couple of socks around the house that seem to have lost their mates. (Does your dryer eat socks, too?) Depending on your child's skills and how much supervision you can provide, you can sew or glue on the eyes, a nose, and hair made from a variety of materials (yarn, buttons, fabric). Insert your hand and your puppet is ready!

Stick Puppets—Make story characters' faces or bodies on heavy paper or on cardboard with crayons, markers, or paint. Cut the figures out and attach them with strong glue or tape to a ruler, craft stick, tongue depressor, or any stick that can be used to hold the puppet and move it. A large box or table can serve as the puppet stage.

Enjoy your child!

Young children become engrossed in puppet shows.

 # Arts and Crafts

1. Making Puppets

Puppets can be made from almost any material. Some suggestions are listed here.

- cotton covered with cloth attached to a tongue depressor
- paper sacks stuffed with newspaper
- a cork for a head with a hole in it for a finger
- socks
- cardboard colored with crayon attached to a tongue depressor
- wooden spoon
- flyswatter
- oatmeal box attached to a dowel
- panty hose stretched over a hanger bent into an oval shape
- empty toilet paper and paper towel rolls

2. Puppet Stages

Puppet stages can be made from the following materials:

- boxes, including tempera paint and markers for decorating
- large paper bags
- half-gallon milk carton
- towel draped over an arm
- towel draped over the back of a chair
- blanket covering a card table

 # Cooking

1. Puppet Faces

Make open-faced sandwiches using jelly or cream cheese spread onto a slice of bread or a bun. Carrot curls can be used to represent hair. Raisins and green or purple grape halves can be used for the eyes, nose, and mouth.

2. Dog Puppet Salad

Place a pear half onto a plate. Two apple slices can be added to resemble a dog's ears hanging down. Raisins or grape halves can be used to represent the eyes and nose of a dog.

Dramatic Play

1. Puppet Show

A puppet stage should be available throughout the entire unit in the dramatic play area. Change or add the puppets on a regular basis using as many different kinds of puppets as possible.

2. Puppet Shop

A variety of materials should be provided for the children to construct puppets. Include items such as buttons, bows, felt, paper bags, cloth pieces, socks, tongue depressors, etc.

Field Trips/ Resource People

1. Puppet Show

Place puppets by the puppet stage to encourage the children to put on puppet shows.

2. Puppeteer

Invite a puppeteer to visit the classroom and show the children the many uses of puppets.

Fingerplays

Speckled Frogs

Five green-speckled frogs
Sitting on a speckled log
Eating the most delicious bugs,
Yum, yum!
   (rub tummy)

One jumped into the pool
Where it was nice and cool
Now there are four green-speckled frogs.

Repeat until there are no green-speckled frogs.

This fingerplay can be told using puppets made from felt or tagboard.

Chickadees

Five little chickadees sitting in a door
   (hold up hand)
One flew away and then there were four.
   (put down one finger at a time)
Four little chickadees sitting in a tree
One flew away and then there were three.
Three little chickadees looking at you
One flew away and then there were two.
Two little chickadees sitting in the sun
One flew away and then there was one.
One little chickadee sitting all alone
He flew away and then there were none.

This fingerplay can be told using puppets made from felt or tagboard.

Two Little Puppets

Two little puppets,
   (hold up both hands)
One on each hand.
   (wave hands)
Isn't she pretty?
   (look at right hand, wave fingers)
Isn't he grand?
   (look at left hand, wave fingers)
Her name is Bella.
   (wave right hand fingers)
His name is Beau.
   (wave left hand fingers)
Hear her say, "Good morning."
   (bend right hand)
Hear him say, "Hello!"
   (bend left hand)

Group Time
(Games, Language)

Puppet Show

Using your favorite classroom stories, put on a puppet show. The children can volunteer to be the various characters. Pretape the story so that the children can listen to it while they practice. This might be a good activity to invite parents to attend.

Large Muscle

1. Creative Movement

Demonstrate how to manipulate a marionette. Then have the children pretend that they are marionettes and that they have strings attached to their arms and legs. Say, "Someone is pulling up the string that is attached to your arm; what would happen to your arm?" Allow the children to make that movement. Continue with other movements.

2. Large Puppets

Large puppets such as stick or rod puppets can provide the children with a lot of large muscle movement.

3. Pin the Nose on the Puppet

This game is a variation of the traditional "Pin the Tail on the Donkey." (This game would be more appropriate for five-, six-, seven-, and eight-year-old children.)

Math

1. Examine a Puppet

With the children, examine a puppet and count all of its various parts. Count its eyes, legs, arms, stripes on its shirt, etc. Discuss how it was constructed.

2. Puppet Dot-to-Dot

Draw a large puppet on a sheet of tagboard. Laminate or cover the tagboard sheet with clear adhesive paper. A grease pencil or felt-tip water-color marker should be provided for the children for drawing. Also, felt scraps should be available to remove grease markings. Otherwise, a damp cloth or paper towel should be available.

Music

"Eensy Weensy Spider"
(*traditional*)

Science

1. Classify Puppets

During group time, let the children classify the various puppets into special categories such as animals, people, insects, imaginary things, etc.

2. Button Box

A large box of buttons should be provided. The children can sort the buttons according to color, size, or shape into a muffin tin or egg carton.

Sensory

Sensory Table

During this unit, add to the sensory table all of the various materials that puppets are made of.

- string
- buttons
- felt
- toilet paper rolls
- cardboard
- paper
- sticks
- wood shavings

Social Studies

Occupation Puppets

Introduce various types of occupation puppets. Ask the children to describe each.

Books

The following books can be used to complement this theme:

Babbitt, Natalie. (1989). *Nellie: A Cat on Her Own*. New York: Farrar, Straus & Giroux.

Bulloch, Ivan. (1997). *I Want to Be a Puppeteer*. Illus. by Diane James. Chicago, IL: World Book.

Collodi, Carlo. (1996). *Pinocchio*. Illus. by Ed Young. New York: Philomel Books.

Hoyt-Goldsmith, Diane. (1991). *Pueblo Storyteller*. Illus. by Lawrence Migdale. New York: Holiday House.

Jean Claverie's Fairy Tale Theater: Pop-Up Book with Puppets. (1996). Illus. by Jean Claverie. Hauppauge, NY: Barron's Educational Series.

Keats, Ezra Jack. (1983). *Louie*. New York: William Morrow.

Little Red Riding Hood. (1997). Illus. by Peter Stevenson. St. Paul, MN: Cartwheel Books. (Finger Puppet Theater.)

Wallis, Mary. (1994). *I Can Make Puppets*. Buffalo, NY: Firefly Books.

Weiss, George David and Bob Thiele. (1994). *What a Wonderful World*. Illus. by Ashley Bryan. New York: Simon & Schuster.

Wood, David and Richard Fowler. (2000). *The Toy Cupboard*. London: Pavilion Books.

Multimedia

The following multimedia products can be used to complement this theme:

Adventures of Pinocchio [video]. (1994). Charlotte, NC: United American Video (UAV Corp.).

Introduction to Puppet Making [video]. (1996). Jim Gamble Puppet Productions. Available from Library Video.

Johnson, Laura. "Puppet Pals" on *Homemade Games and Activities: Make Your Own Rhythm Band!* [cassette]. (1987). Long Branch, NJ: Kimbo Educational.

Foods

grapes
eggplant
cabbage

Flowers

violet
iris
lilac

Purple

Shades

lavender (pale purple)
violet (bluish purple)

Color Mixing

red + blue = purple
purple + white = lavender

Theme Goals

Through participating in the experiences provided by this theme, the children may learn

1. Color mixing to make the color purple
2. Shades of purple
3. Purple flowers
4. Foods that are purple

Concepts for the Children to Learn

1. Purple is the name of a color.
2. Mixing the color red with the color blue makes purple.
3. There are light and dark shades of purple.
4. Many objects are purple in color.
5. Grapes, eggplant, and cabbage are foods that are purple in color.
6. Violets, irises, and lilacs are purple colors.
7. Lavendar is a pale purple color.
8. Violet is a bluish purple color.

Vocabulary

1. **purple**—a color created by mixing red and blue.
2. **shade**—lightness or darkness of color.
3. **tint**—variety of a color produced by mixing it with white.

540
THEME 53

Bulletin Board

The purpose of this bulletin board is to promote name recognition and call attention to the printed word. Interaction promotes the development of visual discrimination, problem-solving, and hand-eye coordination skills. This bulletin board can also be used to check attendance. Trace and cut a crayon for each child in the class from purple tagboard. Then print each child's name on a crayon. Laminate and cut out the crayon pieces. Use a paper punch to cut a hole in the top of each crayon. Hang pushpins on the bulletin board for the children to hang their crayons.

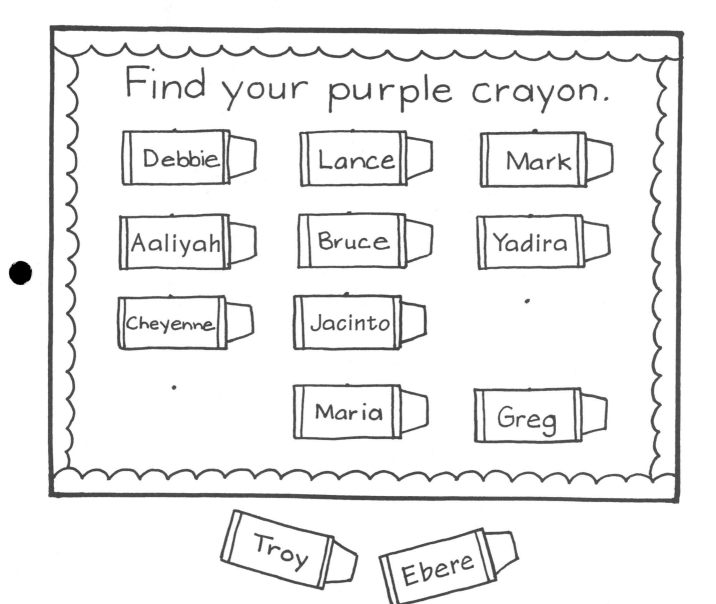

PURPLE

Family Letter

Dear Families,

What color is made when blue is mixed with red? The popular color PURPLE! This week at school we will explore aspects of the royal color purple. The children will learn how purple is made and find out about items that are purple.

AT SCHOOL

A few of this week's learning experiences include:

- creating designs and drawings in the art area with purple crayons, paints, markers, yarn, tissue paper, pom-poms, and glitter

- listening to the story *Harold and the Purple Crayon* by Crockett Johnson. Afterward, we will each make a page to create a classroom purple crayon book. Look for it in the book area by the end of the week!

- looking at various items that are purple. Could you help your child find an object that is purple and bring it to school on Wednesday? Thank you for your help!

AT HOME

The theme of purple can be explored at home as well. Feel free to try the following purple activities:

- preparing purple foods with your child for meals or snacks such as grapes, purple cabbage, gelatin, grape juice, or jelly

- making grape popsicles by freezing grape juice or grape-flavored fruit drink

- creating a purple collage by cutting out purple pictures and letters from magazines. Glue pictures on a purple sheet of construction paper.

Have a good week!

542

THEME 53

Children love painting with the color purple.

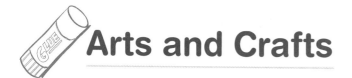

Arts and Crafts

1. Marble Painting

For each child, place a 9-inch × 12-inch piece of white construction paper in a dishpan. Squeeze a few teaspoons of purple liquid tempera paint onto the paper. Place two or three marbles on the paper. Designs are created by holding the pan and tilting it back and forth, allowing the marbles to slide through the paint.

2. Grape Prints

Wrap a piece of masking tape around three toilet paper tubes to create a stamp to make designs of grapes. The children can then dip the end of the stamp into a shallow tray of purple paint, and then press it down on white construction paper to print bunches of grapes. After paint is dry, crayons or markers can be used to add stems or leaves.

3. Purple Glitter Dough

Make purple play dough using your favorite recipe (or combine 1 cup flour, 1/2 cup of salt, 1 cup of water, 1 tablespoon of vegetable oil, 2 teaspoons cream of tartar, and red and blue food coloring). Cook for 3 minutes, stirring frequently until the mixture thickens and pulls away from the pan. Cool play dough. Give each child a lump of play dough and sprinkle a small amount of purple glitter on the tabletop. The children can work the glitter into the dough. **Caution:** Supervision is required with glitter activities.

4. Wacky Watercolors

Combine 1 1/2 tablespoons corn syrup and 3 tablespoons cornstarch. Add 3 tablespoons baking soda and 3 tablespoons vinegar. Mix and watch it foam! Add food coloring of choice (red and blue to make purple). Pour mixture into shallow paint cups and allow to dry for two days. Use watercolors to create designs on paper.

5. Purple Play Dough Grapes

Make a batch of red play dough and a batch of blue play dough using your favorite play dough recipe. Give each child a small lump of the two play dough colors. The children can squeeze the lumps together to create purple. Then, small balls of play dough can be rolled to represent grapes. Allow to dry if desired.

Cooking

1. Purple Pops

1 3-ounce package grape-flavored gelatin
1 cup boiling water
1 6-ounce can frozen grape juice concentrate
3 cups water
15 3-ounce paper cups
15 wooden sticks

In a medium bowl, dissolve gelatin in boiling water. Add frozen juice concentrate and stir until melted. Add water and stir. Pour about 1/3 cup of juice mixture into each paper cup. Cover each cup with foil. Insert a stick through the foil into the juice mixture. Freeze overnight or until firm. To serve, peel paper cups off pops.

2. Purple Popcorn

10 cups popped popcorn (remove all unpopped kernels)
1 cup butter or margarine
3/4 cups sugar
1 3-ounce package grape-flavored gelatin
3 tablespoons water
1 tablespoon light corn syrup

Place the popcorn in a greased 17×12×2-inch baking dish. Keep popcorn warm in a 300-degree oven while making syrup mixture. In a heavy 2-quart saucepan, combine butter, sugar, gelatin, water, and corn syrup. Cook mixture over medium heat until it boils, stirring constantly. Clip a candy thermometer to the side of the pan. Continue cooking over medium heat, stirring constantly, until the thermometer reaches 255 degrees (hardball stage).

Pour syrup mixture over popcorn and stir gently to coat popcorn. Bake in a 300-degree oven for 5 minutes. Stir once and bake 5 minutes longer. Place popcorn mixture onto a large piece of foil. Cool completely. Break popcorn mixture into clusters. Store in an airtight container. Serves 14–16 children.

3. Purple Pudding

Spoon vanilla pudding into small paper cups. Add a few drops of red and blue food coloring to each cup. Children can stir their pudding with spoons to observe what happens.

4. Purple Cow

Pour 1 quart of milk into a blender. Add one 6-ounce can of frozen grape juice concentrate. Blend until ingredients are well mixed. Pour into cups and serve. Serves six.

5. Purple Coleslaw

6 cups shredded purple cabbage
1 cup sliced purple grapes
1 cup mayonnaise
3 tablespoons lemon juice
2 tablespoons sugar
1 teaspoon salt

Combine mayonnaise, lemon juice, sugar, and salt. Stir in cabbage and grapes. Cover and chill until ready to eat.

Dramatic Play

Flower Shop

Collect artificial flowers, focusing on the color purple if possible, to create a flower shop in the dramatic play area. Additional props for the area could include vases, flower pots, small garden tools, sheets of tissue paper, pictures and posters of flowers, and a cash register. Books on flowers and mail-order catalogs or bulbs and flowers can also be displayed.

Field Trips/ Resource People

1. Art or Paint Store

Visit an art supply or paint store. Observe the many shades of purple paints and papers.

2. Flower and Garden Shop

Make arrangements to tour a greenhouse or flower shop. Take note of the varieties of purple-colored flowers and plant leaves.

Fingerplays

Purple Lollipop

Here is a purple, sweet lollipop.
   (make fist pretending to hold a stick of
   lollipop)
I bought it today at a candy shop.
One lick, mmm, it tastes so good.
   (pretend to lick)
Two licks, oh, I knew it would.
Three licks, yes, I like the taste.
Four licks, now I will not waste.
Five licks, keep on and on.
Six licks, oh! It's nearly gone!
Seven licks, it's getting small.
Eight licks and still not all.
Nine licks, my tongue goes fast.
Ten licks and that's the last!

One Grape and One Grape

One grape and one grape, that makes two.
   (hold up two fingers)
But you have three friends, now what do you do?
   (shrug shoulders and hold hands up)
Go to the store and buy a few more.
Then you'll have a whole bunch.
   (hold out arms to create circle shapes)
They're great with your lunch!

Group Time
(Games, Language)

1. Game: "I Spy"

Have the children glance around the room. Begin game by saying, "I spy with my little eye something *purple*." Have the children try to guess what the object is. When a player guesses correctly, he or she is the next "spy."

2. Purple Color Bag or Box

Use purple fabric to make a drawstring bag for "Purple Day" or cover a box and lid with purple wrapping paper. Fill the bag or box with small purple items. At circle time, each child in turn can describe an item from the bag or box for others to identify. Repeat the activity throughout the week.

3. Purple Shapes "Hokey Pokey"

Cut a set of geometric shapes from purple construction paper for each child to use for this game. Game is played in circle formation.

"Purple Hokey Pokey"
(*Sing to the tune of "Hokey Pokey"*)

Put your purple (shape name) in,
Put your purple (shape name) out,
Put your purple (shape name) in,
And shake it all about.

Do the hokey pokey,
And turn yourself around.
That's what it's all about.

Large Muscle

Purple Shape March

Using purple construction paper, cut large geometric shapes and tape them to the floor. Play music as the children walk, march, hop, and so forth, across the shapes.

Math

1. Purple Chain

Provide 8-inch × 1 1/2-inch strips of purple, lilac, and white construction paper. If necessary, demonstrate to children how to create a paper chain using tape or glue to fasten strips. Encourage children to create a pattern with the colored strips. Display chains in the classroom.

2. Shades of Purple Sort

Collect purple paint color strips from a hardware, paint, or building supply store. Have children assist in cutting the color strips apart. The paint chips can be used for sorting activities (light purple, dark purple, etc.) or for counting activities.

PURPLE

Music

1. "A Lilac, a Lilac"
(Sing to the tune of "A Tisket, a Tasket")

A lilac, a lilac, a pretty purple lilac.
There's a lilac bush on the way to school.
And on the way I picked some,
I picked some, I picked some.
And on the way I picked some.
There's a lilac bush on the way to school.
And on the way I picked some.

2. "Purple Things"
(Sing to the tune of "Mary Had a Little Lamb")

Many things are colored purple,
Colored purple, colored purple.
Many things are colored purple,
Can you think of some?

3. "Here's a Grape"
(Sing to the tune of "Hot Cross Buns")

Here's a grape,
A purple grape.
What a yummy little fruit,
A purple grape.

Science

1. Purple Bubble Prints

In a small plastic bowl or cup, mix one tablespoon purple liquid tempera paint with two tablespoons liquid dishwashing detergent and gently stir in a small amount of water. One child at a time can put a straw in the paint mixture and blow until bubbles rise above the rim of the bowl or cup. Remove straw and lay a piece of white paper on top of the bubbles. As the bubbles pop, they will leave prints on the paper. Supervise activity closely.

2. Purple Carnation

Insert a white carnation into a clear glass or vase of water. To the water, add drops of red and blue food coloring to create a dark purple. In a few days, the children should be able to observe the petals of the flower turning purple.

3. Purple Glasses

Help the children view the world through purple-tinted eyeglasses. For each child, cut frame shapes out of tagboard. Assist the children in gluing purple cellophane squares over the eye holes. Attach chenille stems to the sides of the frames and bend them to fit over the children's ears.

4. Making Raisins

Purchase 1 or 2 pounds of purple grapes. Wash them thoroughly. Spread grapes in a single layer on baking sheets. Dry by placing in a sunny windowsill for several days or bake in a slow oven. To bake, turn the oven to 165 degrees and let fruit dry for eight hours. Turn off the oven and leave the fruit in it overnight.

Sensory

1. Purple Water

Add red and blue food coloring to 3 inches of water in the sensory table. Add water toys (look for purple ones!) as tools to explore the properties of water.

2. Purple Shaving Cream

Spray the contents of one or two cans of shaving cream in a sensory table. Color the shaving cream purple by mixing in drops of red and blue food coloring.

3. Purple Goop

In a sensory table or dishpan, combine two cups of cornstarch, two cups of water, and red and blue food coloring.

Social Studies

Occupation: Painter

Invite a local house painter to come to the classroom and talk about his or her job. If possible, perhaps painting tools and supplies could be shown and demonstrated.

Books

The following books can be used to complement this theme:

Adams, Jean Ekman. (2000). *Clarence Goes Out West and Meets a Purple Horse*. Flagstaff, AZ: Rising Moon.

Atwood, Margaret. (1995). *Princess Prunella and the Purple Peanut*. Illus. by Maryann Kowalski. New York: Workman.

Burrowes, Adjoa J. (2000). *Grandma's Purple Flowers*. New York: Lee & Low Books.

Henkes, Kevin. (1996). *Lilly's Purple Plastic Purse*. New York: Greenwillow.

Hest, Amy. (1986). *The Purple Coat*. Illus. by Amy Schwartz. New York: Four Winds Press.

Johnson, Crockett. (1987). *Harold and the Purple Crayon*. New York: HarperCollins.

Kessler, Leonard P. (2000). *Mr. Pine's Purple House*. Keller, TX: Purple House Press.

Martin, Bill Jr. (1992). *Brown Bear, Brown Bear, What Do You See?* Illus. by Eric Carle. New York: H. Holt.

Mayer, Mercer. (1996). *Purple Pickle Juice*. New York: Random House.

Munsch, Robert N. (1992). *Purple, Green, and Yellow*. Illus. by Helene Desputeaux. Willowdale, Ontario, Canada: Annick Press.

Pearson, Tracey Campbell. (1997). *The Purple Hat*. New York: Farrar, Straus & Giroux.

Prelutsky, Jack. (1986). *Ride a Purple Pelican*. New York: William Morrow.

Williams, Rozanne Lanczak and Mary Grandpre. (2000). *The Purple Snerd*. Illus. by Mary Grandpre. San Diego, CA: Harcourt Brace.

Effects

rainbow
puddles
mud
floods

Origins

clouds

Uses

WATERING
plants
crops
grass

FILLING
creeks
ponds
lakes
rivers
ocean

DRINKING
AND BATHING
people
animals

Clothing

rainhat
raincoat
rain shoes
umbrella

Rain

Measurements

gauge

Forms

drizzle,
shower,
snow, dew, hail

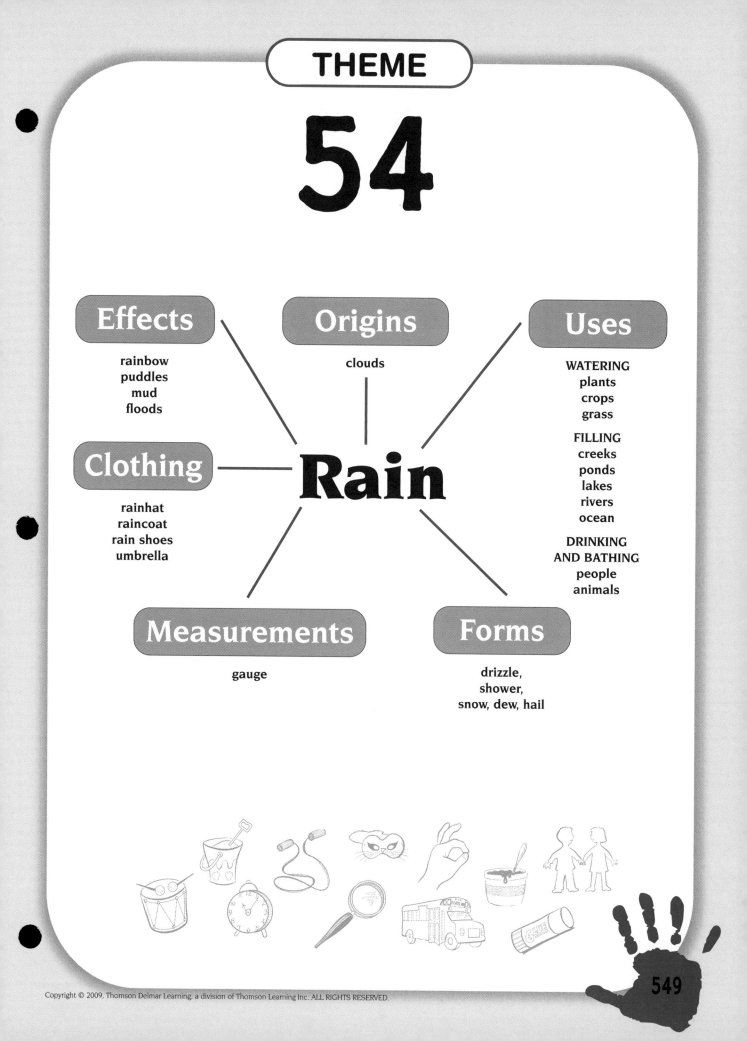

Theme Goals

Through participating in the experiences provided by this theme, the children may learn

1. Uses of rain
2. Effects of rain
3. Clothing worn for protection from the rain
4. Forms of rain
5. Origin of rain
6. The tool used for the measurement of rain

Concepts for the Children to Learn

1. Rain falls as a liquid from the clouds.
2. Rain can fall in the form of drizzle, dew, hail, snow, or a shower.
3. Rain can be used for watering lawns, plants, crops, and grass.
4. Rain fills ponds, creeks, rivers, and oceans.
5. A rainbow sometimes appears when it rains while the sun is shining.
6. A rainbow is colorful.
7. An umbrella is used in the rain to keep us dry.
8. Raincoats, hats, and rubber shoes are rain clothing.
9. Puddles can form during a rainfall.
10. The amount of rain can be measured in a water gauge.
11. Farmers need rain to water the crops.
12. Rain waters people's outdoor plants and grass.
13. People and animals can use rainwater for drinking and bathing.

Vocabulary

1. **gauge**—a tool for measuring rain.
2. **puddle**—rain collection on the ground.
3. **rain**—drops of water that fall from the clouds.
4. **rainbow**—a colorful arc of many colors formed when the sun is reflected in rain drops, spray, or mist.
5. **snow**—frozen drops of water. Snow comes from the clouds during winter.
6. **umbrella**—a shade for protection against rain.

Bulletin Board

The purpose of this bulletin board is to develop an awareness of sets, as well as to identify written numerals. Interaction with the board will also promote visual discrimination, problem-solving, and hand-eye coordination skills. Construct clouds out of gray tagboard. Write a numeral on each cloud. Cut out and laminate. Next, trace and cut cloud shadows from construction paper. Attach the shadows to the bulletin board. A set of raindrops, from 1 to 10, should be attached underneath each cloud shadow. Magnet pieces or pushpins and holes in the cloud piece can be used for the children to match each cloud to a corresponding shadow, using the raindrops as a clue.

RAIN

Family Letter

Dear Families,

"Rain, rain, go away. Come again some other day," is a familiar nursery rhyme. It is one that we may often hear as a unit on rain begins. Through the experiences provided, the children will become aware of the origins, effects, uses, and forms of rain as well as how rainbows are created. They will become aware of the clothing worn in the rain.

AT SCHOOL

The following activities are just a few that have been planned for the rain unit:

- a visit by TV 8's weatherman. Tom Hector will come at 2:00 p.m. on Tuesday to show us a video made for preschoolers that depicts various weather conditions.
- finding out about evaporation by setting out a shallow pan of water and marking the water level each day
- creating a rainbow on a sunny day outdoors with a garden hose

AT HOME

To develop language skills practice this rain poem with your child:

> Rain on the green grass
> And rain on trees.
> Rain on the rooftops,
> But not on me!!

Use an empty can or jar to make a rain gauge. Place the container outdoors to measure rainfall. Several gauges could be placed in various places in your yard.

Enjoy your child!

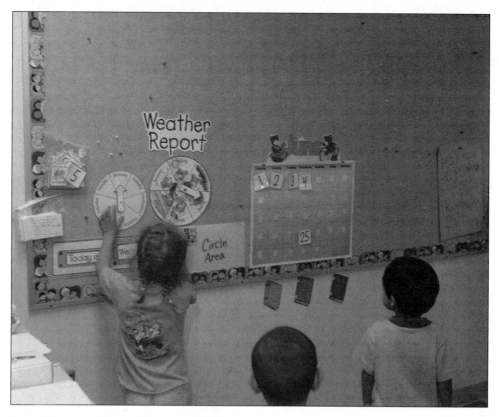

A weather report helps us be prepared if it is going to rain.

Arts and Crafts

1. Eyedropper Painting

Use eyedroppers filled with colored water as applicators.

2. Waxed Paper Rainbows

Cut waxed paper in the shape of large rainbows. Then prepare red, yellow, green, and blue crayon shavings. After this, the children can sprinkle the crayon shavings on one sheet of waxed paper. Place another sheet of waxed paper on the top of the sheet with sprinkled crayon. Finally, the teacher should place a towel over the top of the waxed paper sheets. A warm iron should be applied to melt the two pieces together. Cool and attach a string. Hang from the window. **Caution:** This activity needs constant adult supervision.

3. Rainbow Yarn Collage

Using rainbow-shaped paper and rainbow-colored yarn, the children can make rainbow yarn collages.

4. Thunder Painting

Tape-record a rain or thunderstorm. Leave this tape, with a tape recorder and earphones, at the easel. Gray, black, and white paint can be provided. Let the children listen to the rainstorm and paint to it. Ask the children how the music makes them feel.

5. Rainbow Mobiles

Precut rainbow arcs. On these, the children can paste Styrofoam packing pieces. After this, they can paint the pieces. Display the mobiles in the room.

Cooking

Rainbow Fruits

Serve a different colored snack each day to correspond with the colors of the rainbow.

- strawberries
- grapes or blackberries

RAIN

- oranges
- lettuce salad
- lemon finger gelatin
  (see a gelatin box for recipe)
- blueberries added to yogurt
- grape juice

Dramatic Play

1. Rainy Day Clothing

Umbrellas, raincoats, hats, rain shoes, and a tape containing rain sounds should be added to the dramatic play area. **Caution:** Be careful when selecting umbrellas for this activity. Some open quickly and can be dangerous.

2. Weather Station

A map, pointer, adult clothing, and pretend microphone should be placed in the dramatic play area. The children can play weather person. Pictures depicting different weather conditions can be included.

Field Trips/ Resource People

1. Reflection

Take a walk after it rains. Enjoy the puddles, overflowing gutters, and swirls of water caught by sewers. Look in the puddles. Does anyone see a reflection? Look up in the sky. Do you see any clouds, the sun, or a rainbow? What colors are in a rainbow?

2. The Weather Person

Take a field trip to a television station and see what equipment a weather person uses.

Fingerplays

Little Raindrop

This is the sun, high up in the sky.
  (hold hands in circle above head)
A dark cloud suddenly comes sailing by.
  (slide hands to side)
These are the raindrops,
  (make raining motion with fingers)
Pitter patter down,
Watering the flowers,
  (pouring motion)
Growing on the ground.
  (hands pat the ground)

Rainy Day Fun

Slip on your raincoat.
  (pretend to put coat on)
Pull up your galoshes.
  (pretend to pull up galoshes)
Wade in puddles,
Make splishes and sploshes.
  (make stomping motions)

Thunderstorm

Boom, bang, boom, bang!
  (clap hands)
Rumpety, lumpety, bump!
  (stomp feet)
Zoom, zam, zoom, zam!
  (swish hands together)
Rustles and bustles
  (pat thighs)
And swishes and zings!
  (pat thighs)
What wonderful noises
A thunderstorm brings.

Rain

From big black clouds
  (hold up arms)
The raindrop fell.
  (pull finger down in air)
Drip, drip, drip one day,
  (hit one finger on palm of hand)

Until the bright sunlight changed them
Into a rainbow gay!
   (make a rainbow with hands)

Note: First four fingerplays from Wilmes, Dick and Liz. *Everyday Circle Times.* (1983). Mt. Rainier, MD: Distributed by Gryphon House.

The Rain

I sit before the window now
   (seat yourself, if possible)
And I look out at the rain.
   (shade your eyes and look around)
It means no play outside today
   (shake head, shrug)
So inside I remain.
   (rest chin on fist, look sorrowful)
I watch the water dribble down
   (follow up-to-down movements with eyes)
And turn the brown grass green.
   (sit up, take notice)
And after a while I start to smile
At Nature's washing machine.
   (smile, lean back, relax)

Note: From Cromwell, Hibner, & Faitel. *Finger Frolics—Finger Plays for Young Children.*

Group Time
(Games, Language)

Jump in Puddles

This game is played like "Musical Chairs." The puddles are made from circles on the floor with one child in each and one fewer circle than children so one child is not in a circle. On the signal, "Jump in the puddles," the children have to switch puddles. The child who was out has a chance to get in a puddle. The child who does not get into a puddle waits until the next round. This can be played indoors or outdoors. Hula hoops could also be used in small groups of four children using three hoops. (This activity is most appropriate for older children.)

Large Muscle

Worm Wiggle

The purpose of this game is to imitate worm motions. Show the children how to lie on their stomachs, holding their arms in at their sides. The children should try to move forward without using their hands or elbows like a worm would wiggle.

Math

Rainbow Match

Fabrics of all the colors of the rainbow can be cut into pieces. The children can sort these and group them into different colors, textures, and sizes.

Music

1. **"Rainy"**

   There was a day when we got wet
   and rainy was the weather
   R-A-I-N-Y, R-A-I-N-Y, R-A-I-N-Y
   and rainy was the weather.

   Repeat each verse, eliminating a letter and substituting it with a clap until the last chorus is all claps to the same beat.

2. **"Rain, Rain, Go Away"**

   Rain, rain, go away.
   Come again another day.
   Clouds, clouds, go away.
   Little children want to play.
   Thunder, thunder, go away.
   Little children want to play.
   Rain, rain, come back soon.
   Little flowers want to bloom.

Science

1. Tasting Water

Collect tap water, soda water, mineral water, and distilled water. Pour the different types of water into paper cups and let children taste them. Discuss the differences.

2. Evaporation

The children can pour water into a clear, plastic jar. Mark a line at the water level. Place the jar on a window ledge and check it every day. The disappearance is called evaporation.

3. Catching Water

If it rains one day during your unit, place a bucket outside to catch the rain. Return the bucket to your science table. Place a bucket of tap water next to the rainwater and compare.

4. Color Mixing

Using water and food coloring or tempera, mix the primary colors. Discuss the colors of the rainbow.

Sensory

Additions to the Sensory Table

- water with scoops, cups, and spoons
- sand and water (Make puddles in the sand.)
- rainbow-colored sand, rice, and pasta
- rainwater

Books

The following books can be used to complement this theme:

Base, Graeme. (2001). *The Water Hole*. New York: Harry N. Abrams.

Baxter, Nicola. (1998). *Rain, Wind, and Storm*. Austin, TX: Raintree/Steck Vaughn.

Beecham, Caroline. (1996). *Rainbow*. New York: Random House.

Bogacki, Tomek. (1997). *Cat and Mouse in the Rain*. New York: Farrar, Straus & Giroux.

Branley, Franklyn M. (1997). *Down Comes the Rain*. New York: HarperCollins.

Buchanan, Ken and Debby Buchanan. (1994). *It Rained in the Desert Today*. Illus. by Libba Tracey. Flagstaff, AZ: Northland.

Calhoun, Mary. (1997). *Flood*. Illus. by Erick Ingraham. New York: William Morrow.

Canizares, Susan and Betsey Chessen. (1997). *Storms*. New York: Scholastic.

Carlstrom, Nancy White. (1993). *What Does the Rain Play*? New York: Macmillan.

Davies, Kay and Wendy Oldfield. (1995). *Rain*. Photos by Robert Pickett. Austin, TX: Raintree/Steck Vaughn.

Deming, Alhambra G. (1994). *Who Is Tapping at My Window*? Illus. by Monica Wellington. New York: Penguin.

Germein, Katrina and Bronwyn Bancroft. (1999). *Big Rain Coming*. New York: Clarion Books.

Godfrey, Jan. (1994). *Why Is It Raining*? Illus. by D'Reen Neeves. Minneapolis, MN: Augsburg Fortress.

Hesse, Karen and Jon J. Muth. (1999). *Come on, Rain*! Illus. by Jon J. Muth. New York: Scholastic.

Hest, Amy. (1995). *In the Rain with Baby Duck*. Illus. by Jill Barton. Cambridge, MA: Candlewick Press.

Johnson, Angela. (1994). *Rain Feet*. Illus. by Rhonda Mitchell. New York: Orchard Books. (Board book.)

Kuskin, Karla. (1995). *James and the Rain*. Illus. by Reg Cartwright. New York: Simon & Schuster.

Laser, Michael. (1997). *The Rain*. Illus. by Jeffrey Green. New York: Simon & Schuster.

Llewellyn, Claire and Anthony Lewis. (1995). *Wind and Rain*. Hauppauge, NY: Barron's Educational Series.

London, Jonathan. (1997). *Puddles*. Illus. by G. Brian Karas. New York: Viking.

Lynn, Sara and Diane James. (1998). *Rain and Shine*. Illus. by Joe Wright. Chicago: World Book.

Markle, Sandra. (1993). *A Rainy Day*. Illus. by Cathy Johnson. New York: Orchard Books.

May, Garelick. (1997). *Where Does the Butterfly Go When It Rains?* Illus. by Nicholas Wilton. Greenvale, NY: Mondo.

McPhail, David M. (1998). *The Puddle*. New York: Farrar, Straus & Giroux.

Merk, Ann and Jim Merk. (1994). *Rain, Snow and Ice*. Vero Beach, FL: Rourke.

Nikola-Lisa, W. (1993). *Storm*. Illus. by Michael Hays. Colchester, CT: Atheneum.

Polacco, Patricia. (1990). *Thunder Cake*. New York: Philomel Books.

Ray, Mary Lyn. (1996). *Mud*. Illus. by Lauren Stringer. New York: Harcourt Brace.

Reay, Joanne. (1995). *Bumpa Rumpus and the Rainy Day*. Illus. by Adriano Gon. Boston: Houghton Mifflin.

Schaefer, Lola M. and Jane Wattenberg. (2001). *This Is the Rain*. Illus. by Jane Wattenberg. New York: Greenwillow.

Shannon, George. (1995). *April Showers*. Illus. by Jose Aruego and Ariane Dewey. New York: Greenwillow.

Simon, Norma. (1995). *Wet World*. Illus. by Alexi Natchev. Cambridge, MA: Candlewick Press.

Stallone, Linda. (1992). *The Flood That Came to Grandma's House*. Illus. by Joan Schooley. Dallas, PA: Upshur Press.

Stevenson, James. (1997). *Heat Wave at Mud Flat*. New York: Greenwillow.

Cleaver, Mary. "Rain Is Falling Down" and "The Incey Wincey Spider" on *Songs and Fingerplays for Little Ones* [video]. (1993). Cleaver Productions.

"On a Rainy Day" on *A Rainbow of Songs* [cassette]. Long Branch, NJ: Kimbo Educational.

"Why Does It Rain?" on *Our Earth* [CD-ROM]. (1992). Washington, DC: National Geographic.

Recordings and Song Titles

The following recordings can be used to complement this theme:

"On a Rainy Day." (1998). *A Rainbow of Songs*. Long Branch, NJ: Kimbo Educational.

"Raindrop Song." (1996). *Where Is Thumbkin?* Long Branch, NJ: Kimbo Educational.

"Rain Song." (1995). *Piggyback Songs*. Long Branch, NJ: Kimbo Educational.

"Singing in the Rain." (1997). *Rock 'n' Roll Songs That Teach (The Learning Station)*. Long Branch, NJ: Kimbo Educational.

"Sun and Rain." (1994). *Songs about Native Americans*. Long Branch, NJ: Kimbo Educational.

Multimedia

The following multimedia products can be used to complement this theme:

"Clean Rain" on *Evergreen Everblue* [compact disc]. (1990). Shoreline Records.

Red

Food

apples
strawberries
raspberries
cherries
tomatoes
beets
radishes

Flowers

roses
tulips
carnations

Signs

stop/danger
traffic light
fire trucks (some)
fire hydrants (some)

Color Mixing

red + yellow = orange
red + blue = purple
red + white = pink

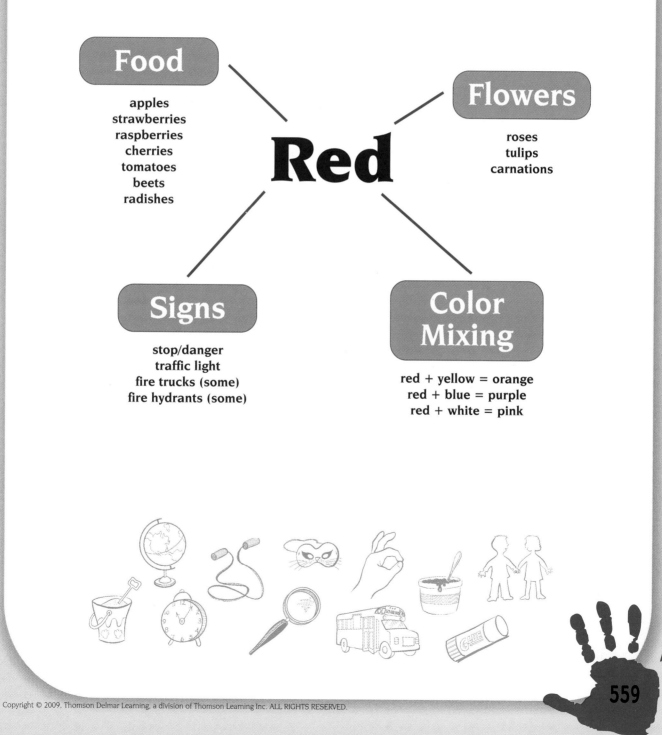

Theme Goals

Through participating in the experiences provided by this theme, the children may learn

1. Red can be mixed with other colors to make different colors
2. Some foods are red
3. Some flowers are colored red
4. Red signs

Concepts for the Children to Learn

1. Red is a primary color.
2. Some foods, such as apples, tomatoes, beets, radishes, raspberries, cherries, and strawberries, are red.
3. Some flowers are colored red.
4. Red and yellow mixed together make orange.
5. Red and blue mixed together make purple.
6. Red and white mixed together make pink.
7. Some fire trucks and fire hydrants are red.
8. Red signs warn us of danger.
9. A stop sign is colored red.
10. Some roses, tulips, and carnations are red.

Vocabulary

1. **primary colors**—red, yellow, and blue.
2. **red**—a primary color.

Bulletin Board

The purpose of this bulletin board is to reinforce the mathematical skills of matching sets of objects to a written numeral. Green produce baskets or other small baskets can be hung on the bulletin board for a strawberry-counting bulletin board. Attach baskets to the bulletin boards using staples or pushpins. Collect small plastic strawberries, or make strawberries out of tagboard. On each basket mark a numeral. The children can place the appropriate number of strawberries into each basket.

RED

Family Letter

Dear Families,

Colors are everywhere, and they make our world beautiful. That's why we'll focus on a specific color during our next curriculum theme: the color red! It's a popular color with young children and many objects in our world are red. The experiences provided will also help the children become aware of colors that are formed when mixed with red.

AT SCHOOL

A few of the curriculum experiences include:

- mixing the color red with yellow and blue to make orange and purple
- setting up an art store in the dramatic play area where the children can act out the buying and selling of art supplies
- exploring red-colored crayons, markers, pencils, chalk, paint, and paper
- filling the sensory table with red goop
- listening to stories related to the color red

AT HOME

To reinforce the concepts in this unit, try the following activities at home with your child:

- To develop observation skills, look around your house with your child for red items. How many red objects can you find in each room?
- Prepare meals using red foods such as apples, strawberries, tomatoes, and jam.
- Prepare red ice cubes to cool your drinks. To do this, just add a few drops of red food coloring to the water before freezing it.

Enjoy making colorful discoveries with your child.

THEME 55

Arts and Crafts

1. Red Paint

Red and white paint can be provided at the easels. By mixing these colors, children can discover shades of red.

2. Red Crayon Rubbings

Red crayons, red paper, or both can be used to do this activity. Place an object such as a penny, button, or leaf under paper. Use the flat edge of a crayon to color over the item. An image of the object will appear on the paper.

3. Paint Blots

Fold a piece of paper in half. Open up and place a spoonful of red paint on the inside of the paper. Refold paper and press flat. Reopen and observe the design. Add two colors such as blue and yellow and repeat process to show color mixing.

4. Paint over Design

Paint over a crayon picture with watery red paint. Observe how the paint will not cover the crayon marks.

5. Glitter Pictures

The children make a design using glue on a piece of paper. Shake red glitter onto the glue. Shake the excess glitter into a pan. **Caution:** Carefully supervise this activity.

6. Red Fingerpaint

Red fingerpaint and foil should be placed on an art table. Yellow and blue paint can be added to explore color mixing.

Cooking

Raspberry Slush

Thaw and cook four 10-ounce packages of frozen raspberries for 10 minutes. Use a wooden spoon to rub the cooked raspberries through a strainer. Cool. Add one can (6 ounces) of frozen

Sponges and red paint can make interesting designs.

lemonade concentrate, thawed. Just before serving, stir in 2 quarts of ginger ale, chilled. Makes 24 servings, about 1/2 cup each.

Dramatic Play

1. Art Store

Set up an art supply store. Include paints, crayons, markers, paper, chalk, brushes, money, and cash register.

2. Fire Station

Firefighter hats can be added to the dramatic play area.

3. Colored Hats

After reading *Caps for Sale* by Esphyr Slobodkina, set out colored hats for children to use to retell the story.

RED

Field Trips/ Resource People

1. Art Store

Visit an art store. Observe all the red items for sale.

2. Take a Walk

Take a walk around the neighborhood and look for red objects.

3. Floral Shop

Visit a floral shop and specifically observe red flowers.

4. Fire Station

Visit a fire station. Note the color of the engine, hats, sirens, etc.

5. Resource People

Invite the following resource people to the classroom:

- artist
- gardener
- firefighter

Fingerplays

Tulips

Five little tulips—red and bright
(hold up hand)
Let us water them every day.
(make sprinkle motion with other hand)
Watch them open in the bright sunlight.
(cup hand, then open)
Watch them close when it is night.
(close hand again).

My Apple

Look at my apple, it's red and round.
(make ball shape with hands)

It fell from a tree down to the ground.
(make downward motion)
Come let me share my apple, please do!
(beckoning motion)
My mother can cut it right in two—
(make slicing motion)
One half for me and one half for you.
(hold out two hands, sharing halves)

Five Red Apples

Five red apples in a grocery store.
(hold up five fingers)
Bobby bought one, and then there were four.
(bend down one finger)
Four red apples on an apple tree.
Susie ate one, and then there were three.
(bend down one finger)
Three red apples. What did Alice do?
Why, she ate one, and then there were two.
(bend down one finger)
Two red apples ripening in the sun.
Timmy ate one, and then there was one.
(bend down one finger)
One red apple and now we are done.
I ate the last one, and now there are none.
(bend down last finger)

Group Time

(Games, Language)

1. Colored Jars

Collect five large clear jars. Fill three with red water, one with yellow water, and one with blue water. Show children the three red jars. Discuss the color red. Discuss that it can make other colors too. Show them the yellow jar. Add yellow to red. What happens? Add blue water to other red jar. What happens? Discuss color mixing.

2. Play "Red Light, Green Light"

Pick one child to be your traffic light. Place the "traffic light" about 30 feet away from the other children facing away from children who have formed a long line. With back to children, the traffic light says, "green light." Children try to creep toward the traffic light. Traffic light may then say,

564

THEME 55

"red light," and turn toward the children. Children must freeze. If the traffic light sees a child move, he/she needs to go back to the starting line. The game continues with "green light." The first child to reach the traffic light becomes the new light.

Large Muscle

1. Ribbon Dance

Attach strips of red crepe paper to short wooden dowels or unsharpened pencils to make ribbons. The children can use the ribbons to move to their favorite songs.

2. Red Bird, Red Bird

The children should form a circle by holding hands. Choose a child to be a bird and start the game. Children chant:

Red bird, red bird through my window
Red bird, red bird through my window
Red bird, red bird through my window
Oh!

The bird goes in and out, under the children's arms. The bird stops on the word "Oh" and bows to the child facing him. This child becomes the new bird. The color of the bird can be determined by the color of the clothing of each child picked to be the bird.

Math

1. Color Cards

Construct color cards that start with white and gradually become cherry red. The children can sequence the cards from white to red or red to white. Discontinued sample color cards could be obtained from a paint store.

2. Bead Stringing

Yarn and a variety of colored beads should be available to the children. After initial exploration, the children can make patterns with beads, such as red, yellow, red, yellow, red.

3. Colored Bags

Place three bags labeled red, yellow, and blue and a variety of blocks on a table. The children can sort the blocks by placing them in the matching colored bag.

4. Color Sort

Obtain paint color sample cards and cut apart. Tape each color onto a container. Provide objects for the children to sort into each container.

Science

Mixing Colors

Place two or three ice cube trays and cups filled with red-, yellow-, and blue-colored water on the science table. Using an eyedropper, the children can experiment mixing colors in the ice cube trays. Smocks should be provided to prevent stained clothing.

Sensory

1. Red Water

Fill the sensory table with water and red food coloring. The children can add coloring and observe the changes.

2. Red Shaving Cream

Shaving cream with red food coloring added can be placed in the sensory table. During self-selected play the children can explore the shaving cream.

3. Red Goop

Mix together red food coloring, 1 cup cornstarch, and 1 cup water in sensory table.

4. Red Funny Putty

Mix together red food coloring, 1 cup liquid starch, and 2 cups white glue. This mixture usually needs to be stirred continuously for an extended period of time before it jells.

RED

Social Studies

1. Discussion about Colors

During group time discuss colors and how they make us feel. Hold up a color card and ask a child how it makes him or her feel.

2. Color Chart

Construct a "My Favorite Color Is . . ." chart. Encourage each child to name his or her favorite color. After each child's name, print his or her favorite color with a colored marker. Display the chart in the classroom.

3. Colored Balloons

Each child should be provided with a balloon. The balloons should be the colors of the rainbow: red, orange, yellow, green, blue, and purple. Arrange the children in the formation of a rainbow. Children with red balloons should stand together, etc. Take a picture of the class. Place the picture on the bulletin board. **Caution:** This activity needs to be carefully supervised.

Books

The following books can be used to complement this theme:

Bailey, Carolyn Sherwin, Jacqueline Rogers, and Monique Z. Stephens, eds. (2001). *The Little Rabbit Who Wanted Red Wings*. Illus. by Jacqueline Rogers. Los Angeles, CA: Price Stern Sloan.

Barton, Byron. (1993). *The Little Red Hen*. New York: HarperCollins.

Bazilian, Barbara. (1997). *The Red Shoes*. Dallas, TX: Whispering Coyote Press.

Carle, Eric. (2001). *Hello, Red Fox*. New York: Alladin Paperbacks.

Carroll, Kathleen S. (1994). *One Red Rooster*. Illus. by Suzette Barbier. Boston: Sandpiper.

Casey, Mike. (1996). *Red Lace, Yellow Lace: Learn to Tie Your Shoe!* Hauppauge, NY: Barron's Educational Series.

Horacek, Petr. (2001). *Strawberries Are Red*. Cambridge, MA: Candlewick Press. (First U.S. edition.)

Johnson, Stephen T. (2000). *My Little Red Toolbox*. San Diego, CA: Harcourt Brace.

Lucht, Irmgard. (1995). *The Red Poppy*. New York: Hyperion.

Martin, Bill Jr. (1992). *Brown Bear, Brown Bear, What Do You See?* Illus. by Eric Carle. New York: H. Holt.

Peek, Merle. (1998). *Mary Wore Her Red Dress, and Henry Wore His Green Sneakers*. Boston: Houghton Mifflin.

Price, Mathew and Steve Augarde. (2000). *Little Red Car Plays Taxi*. Illus. by Steve Augarde. New York: Abbeville Press.

Serfozo, Mary. (1992). *Who Said Red?* New York: Maxwell Macmillan.

Slobodkina, Esphyr. (1985). *Caps for Sale*. New York: Harper & Row.

Walsh, Ellen Stoll. (1989). *Mouse Paint*. Orlando, FL: Harcourt Brace.

Whitman, Candace. (1998). *Ready for Red*. New York: Abbeville.

Woolfitt, Gabrielle. (1992). *Red*. Minneapolis, MN: Carolrhoda Books.

Multimedia

The following multimedia products can be used to complement this theme:

Colors, Shapes, and Size [CD-ROM]. (1995). StarPress Multimedia.

JumpStart Preschool [CD-ROM]. (1996). Glendale, CA: Knowledge Adventure.

"Little Red Caboose" on *Toddler Favorites* [cassette]. (1998). Redway, CA: Music for Little People.

Rock 'n' Learn Colors, Shapes, and Counting [video]. (1997). Conroe, TX: Rock 'n' Learn.

Indoors

walking
scissors care
fire drills
metal detectors
rules

Field Trips

rules

Safety

Vehicles

traffic signs
seat belts
rules
airbags

People

police officers
firefighters
doctors
nurses
ambulance drivers
strangers

Outdoors

rules
animals
street
bicycle
helmets

Theme Goals

Through participating in the experiences provided by this theme, the children may learn

1. Indoor safety precautions
2. Outdoor safety
3. People who keep us safe
4. Field trip safety
5. Vehicle safety

Concepts for the Children to Learn

1. Safety means freedom from danger.
2. We walk indoors.
3. Play yard rules help keep us safe.
4. Rules are the way we are to act.
5. We have special rules for field trips.
6. Fire drills prepare us for emergencies.
7. Scissors need to be handled carefully.
8. Wearing a seat belt is practicing car safety.
9. Wearing a helmet when riding a bicycle is practicing safety.
10. Traffic signs help prevent accidents.
11. Police officers, firefighters, doctors, nurses, and ambulance drivers help keep us safe.
12. Talk only to people you know, not to strangers.
13. Pet only friendly animals you know.

Vocabulary

1. **fire drill**—practicing leaving the building in case of a fire.
2. **rule**—the way we are to act. A rule tells what we should do and not do.
3. **safety**—freedom from danger or harm.
4. **seat belt**—strap that holds a person in a vehicle.
5. **sign**—a lettered board that tells you what to do and not do.

Bulletin Board

The purpose of this bulletin board is to help the children recognize safety signs. To prepare this bulletin board, construct six safety signs out of tagboard, each a different shape. Color appropriately and laminate. Trace the outline of these signs onto black construction paper to create shadow signs as illustrated. Staple the shadow signs to the bulletin board. Punch holes in the safety signs using a hole punch. The children can match the shape of the safety signs to the shadow signs by hanging them on the appropriate pushpins.

Family Letter

Dear Families,

Safety will be the focus of our next unit. We will be learning about safety at school, at home, and outdoors. Through this unit the children will also become more aware of traffic signs and their importance.

AT SCHOOL

A few of the activities planned for this unit include:

- taking a safety walk to practice crossing streets

- counting the number of traffic signs that are in our school neighborhood

- visiting the fire station on Tuesday morning. We will be leaving at 9:30 and should return to school by 11:00.

AT HOME

One of the songs we will learn follows. It will help your child become aware of the purpose and colors of a traffic light. You may enjoy singing the song at home with your child. The song is sung to the tune of "Twinkle, Twinkle, Little Star." The words are as follows:

Twinkle, twinkle, traffic light,
Standing on the corner bright.
When it's green it's time to go.
When it's red it's stop, you know.
Twinkle, twinkle, traffic light,
Standing on the corner bright.

During your daily routines, share safety tips with your child.

Understanding and recognizing traffic signs helps prevent accidents.

 # Arts and Crafts

 # Cooking

1. **Firefighter Hats**

   Cut firefighter hats out of large sheets of red construction paper for the children to wear.

2. **Easel Painting**

   On the easel, place cutout shapes of fire hats or boots.

3. **Traffic Lights**

   Construct stop and go lights out of shoeboxes. Tape the lid to the bottom of the box. Cover with black construction paper and have children place green, yellow, and red circles in correct order on the box. The red circle should be placed on the top, yellow in the middle, and green on the bottom.

4. **Officer Hats and Badges**

   Police officer hats and badges can be constructed out of paper and colored with crayons or felt-tip watercolor markers.

1. **Banana Rounds**

   4 medium bananas
   1/2 tablespoon honey
   1/8 teaspoon nutmeg
   1/8 teaspoon cinnamon
   1/4 cup wheat germ

   The children can peel the bananas and then slice them with a plastic knife. Measure the spices, wheat germ, and honey. Finally, mix them with the bananas. Chill. Serves eight.

2. **Stop Signs**

   eight-sided crackers
   cream cheese
   jelly

   Spread a thin layer of cream cheese or jelly on each cracker.

3. Yield Signs

triangle crackers
yellow cheese

Cut yellow cheese into triangles. Put the cheese on the crackers.

Dramatic Play

1. Fire Engine

A large cardboard box can be decorated by the children as a fire engine with yellow or red tempera paint. When the fire engine is dry, place it in the dramatic play area with short hoses and firefighter hats. This prop could also be placed outdoors, weather permitting.

2. Prop Boxes

Develop prop boxes such as:

Firefighter	Police Officer
bell	hat
jacket/uniform	badges
boots	handcuffs
whistle	stop sign (for holding)
hose	
oxygen mask	
hat	

3. Firefighter Jackets

Construct firefighter jackets out of large paper bags. Begin by cutting three holes. One hole is used for the child's head at the top of the bag. Then cut two large holes for arms. These props may encourage the children to dramatize the roles of the firefighters.

4. Seat Belts

Collect child-sized car seats. Place them around like chairs and let the children adjust them for themselves or their dolls.

Field Trips/ Resource People

1. Firefighter

Invite a firefighter to the classroom. Ask him or her to bring firefighter clothing and equipment and to discuss each item.

2. Police Car

Invite a police officer to visit the classroom. Ask him or her to bring a police car to show the children.

Fingerplays

Silly Teddy Bear

Silly little teddy bear
Stood up in a rocking chair.
   (make rocking movement)
Now he has to stay in bed
   (lay head on hands)
With a bandage round his head.
   (circular movement of hand around head)

Crossing Streets

At the curb before I cross
I stop my running feet
   (point to feet)
And look both ways to left and right
   (look left and right)
Before I cross the street.
Lest autos running quietly
Might come as a surprise.
I don't just listen with my ears
   (point to ears)
But look with both my eyes.
   (point to eyes)

Red Light

Red light, red light, what do you say?
I say, "Stop and stop right away!"
   (hold palms of both hands up)
Yellow light, yellow light, what do you say?
I say, "Wait till the light turns green."
   (hold one palm of hand up)
Green light, green light, what do you say?
I say "Go, but look each way."
   (circle arm in forward motion and turn head
   to the right and left)
Thank you, thank you, red, yellow, green
Now I know what the traffic light means.

Five Police Officers

Five strong police officers standing by a store.
   (hold up the one hand)
One became a traffic cop, then there were four.
   (hold up four fingers)
Four strong police officers watching over me.
One took a lost boy home, then there were three.
   (hold up three fingers)
Three strong police officers all dressed in blue.
One stopped a speeding car and then there
   were two.
   (hold up two fingers)
Two strong police officers, how fast they can run.
One caught a bad man and then there was one.
   (hold up one finger)
One strong police officer saw some smoke
   one day.
He called a firefighter who put it out right away.

The Crossing Guard

The crossing guard keeps us safe
As he works from day to day.
He holds the stop sign high in the air.
   (hold palm of hand up)
For the traffic to obey.
And when the cars have completely stopped
And it's as safe as can be,
He signals us to walk across
   (make a beckoning motion)
The street very carefully.

Group Time

(Games, Language)

Toy Safety

Collect a variety of unsafe toys that may have sharp edges, such as a broken wagon, etc. During group time discuss the dangers of each toy. As soon as group activity is finished, remove the toys from the classroom.

Large Muscle

1. Safety Walk

Take a safety walk. Practice observing traffic lights when crossing the street. Point out special hazards to the children.

2. Stop, Drop, and Roll

Practice "Stop, Drop, and Roll" with the children. This will be valuable to them if they are ever involved in a fire and their clothes happen to catch on fire. Usually a firefighter will teach them this technique while they are visiting the fire station.

3. Traffic Light

Cut a green circle and red circle from construction paper. Choose one child to be the officer. Give other children toy vehicles to "drive" on the floor. The other children should line up horizontally away from the officer. When the officer shows the green light, the children "drive" toward him/her. When the officer shows the red light, the children should stop.

Math

1. Sequencing Hats

Draw pictures of three police hats. Make each picture identical except design three different sizes. The children can sequence the objects from largest to smallest or smallest to largest. Discuss the sizes and ask which is largest, smallest, middle.

2. Safety Items

Walk around the school and observe the number of safety items. Included may be exit signs, fire drill posters, fire extinguishers, sprinkler systems, fire alarm/drill bells, etc.

Music

1. "Twinkle, Twinkle, Traffic Light"
(*Sing to the tune of "Twinkle, Twinkle, Little Star"*)

Twinkle, twinkle, traffic light,
Standing on the corner bright.
When it's green it's time to go.
When it's red it's stop, you know.
Twinkle, twinkle, traffic light,
Standing on the corner bright.

2. "Do You Know the Police Officer?"
(*Sing to the tune of "The Muffin Man"*)

Oh, do you know the police officer,
The police officer, the police officer?
Oh, do you know the police officer
Who helps me cross the street?

This song can be extended. For example, the song can be continued substituting "who helps me when I'm lost" or "who helps one cross the street."

Science

1. Sorting for Safety

Collect and thoroughly wash empty household product containers. Include safe and dangerous items such as cleaning supplies, orange juice containers, etc. Place all the items in one large box. The children can separate the containers into "safe" and "dangerous" categories. Younger children may be able to separate the containers into edible and nonedible categories.

2. All About Me

On a table place identification items. Prepare a separate card for each child. Record the following information on the cards:

- height
- weight
- color hair
- color eyes
- fingerprint
- signature (if child can or a teacher can help)

Sensory

1. Pumps and Hoses

Water pumps, hoses, and water can be placed in the sensory table.

2. Trucks

Small toy fire trucks and police cars can be placed in the sensory table with sand.

Social Studies

1. **Safety Pictures and Signs**

   Post safety pictures and signs around the room.

2. **Stop and Go Light**

   Draw a large stop and go light on a piece of tagboard. Color with felt-tip markers. Print the following across from the corresponding colors:

   Green means go we all know
   Yellow means wait even if you're late,
   Red means stop!

3. **Safety Signs**

   Take a walk and watch for safety signs. Discuss the colors and letters on each sign.

Books

The following books can be used to complement this theme:

Arnosky, Jim. (1990). *Crinkleroot's Guide to Walking in Wild Places*. New York: Simon & Schuster.

Berenstain, Stan and Jan Berenstain. (1999). *My Trusty Car Seat: Buckling Up for Safety*. New York: Random House.

Boelts, Maribeth. (1997). *A Kid's Guide to Staying Safe Around Water*. New York: Rosen.

Brown, Marc Tolon and Stephen Krensky. *Dinosaurs, Beware: A Safety Guide*. Boston: Little, Brown.

Butler, Daphne. (1996). *What Happens When Fire Burns?* Austin, TX: Raintree/Steck Vaughn.

Givon, Hannah Gelman. (1996). *We Shake in a Quake*. Illus. by David Uttal. Berkeley, CA: Tricycle Press.

Gordon, Wendy and Paul Gordon. (1999). *I'm Safe, On My Bike*. Illus. by Paul Gordon. Camden, ME: Backyard Books.

Kuklin, Susan. (1999). *Fighting Fires*. New York: Alladin Paperbacks.

Lakin, Patricia. (1995). *Aware and Alert*. Photos by Doub Cushman. Austin, TX: Raintree/Steck Vaughn.

Loewen, Nancy. (1996). *Bicycle Safety*. Illus. by Penny Danny. Mankato, MN: Child's World.

Loewen, Nancy. (1996). *Traffic Safety*. Illus. by Penny Danny. Mankato, MN: Child's World.

Marzollo, Jean. (1996). *I Am Fire*. Illus. by Judith Moffatt. New York: Scholastic.

Rand, Gloria. (1996). *Willie Takes a Hike*. Illus. by Ted Rand. Orlando, FL: Harcourt Brace.

Rathmann, Peggy. (1995). *Officer Buckle and Gloria*. New York: G. P. Putnam.

Schulson, Rachel. (1997). *Guns—What You Should Know*. Illus. by Mary Jones. Niles, IL: Albert Whitman.

Spelman, Cornelia. (1997). *Your Body Belongs to You*. Illus. by Teri Weidner. Niles, IL: Albert Whitman.

Wheatley, K. C. and Marianne Hallock. (1998). *Kids Keeping Kids Safe*. Illus. by Marianne Hallock. Eugene, OR: Leading Edge.

Multimedia

The following multimedia products can be used to complement this theme:

Child Safety Outdoors [video]. (1994). Chino Hills, CA: KidSafety of America.

K.C.'s First Bus Ride. [video]. (1994). Chino Hills, CA: KidSafety of America.

Play It Safe [kit includes books, sound cassettes, video, etc.]. (1995). Bothell, WA: Wright Group.

Safety on Wheels [video]. (1994). Films for the Humanities & Sciences.

Seat Belts Are for Kids Too [video]. (1987). AIMS Media.

Recordings and Song Titles

The following recordings can be used to complement this theme:

"Are You Ready for Halloween?" (1989). *Halloween Fun*. Long Branch, NJ: Kimbo Educational.

"Child Abuse Won't Do," "Don't Talk To Strangers," "Don't Drink and Drive," "Buckle Up." (1989). *Make the Right Choice*. Long Branch, NJ: Kimbo Educational.

"Safety Pros Know." (1996). *People in Our Neighborhood* (RONNO). Long Branch, NJ: Kimbo Educational.

"Say No (To Strangers)." (1986). *Singing, Moving, and Fun (The Learning Station)*. Long Branch, NJ: Kimbo Educational.

"Signs and Signals." (1997). *Cars, Trucks, and Trains*. Long Branch, NJ: Kimbo Educational.

"Stop at the Red Light." (1993). *Pre-K Hooray*. Long Branch, NJ: Kimbo Educational.

Construction

plastic
metal

Care

cleaning
storing
handling
sharpening

Types

left-handed
paper
pinking
cloth
cuticle
shears
haircutting
electric
toenail
kitchen
children's

Scissors

**Materials
to Cut**

paper
cardboard
fabric
hair
fingernails
toenails
yarn/thread
pastry

Parts

handle
blade

Purpose

cutting tool
trimming tool

Users

barber
hairstylist
tailor/dressmaker
sheep shearer
cook/chef
animal groomer
adult
child

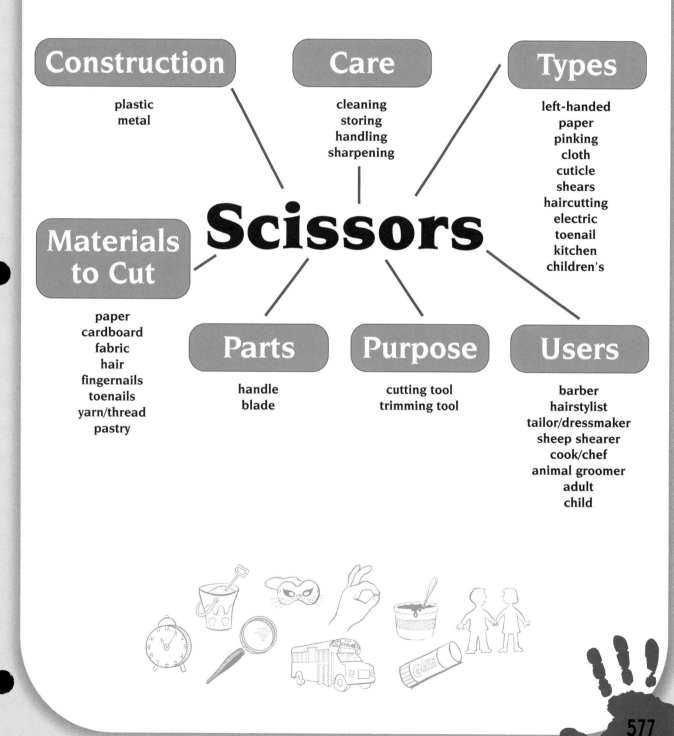

Theme Goals

Through participating in the experiences provided by this theme, the children may learn

1. Parts of scissors
2. Users of scissors
3. Materials that can be cut with scissors
4. Care of scissors
5. Scissor construction
6. Purposes of scissors
7. Types of scissors

Concepts for the Children to Learn

1. Scissors are tools for cutting and trimming.
2. A blade and handle are the two parts of a scissors.
3. Scissors help us do our work.
4. Scissors can be made from plastic or metal.
5. Scissors cut paper, fingernails, hair, and material.
6. Paper, pinking, cloth, cuticle, and shears are names for scissors.
7. Toenail, kitchen, and children's are other names for scissors.
8. Some people need scissors for their job.
9. Barbers, hairstylists, tailors, dressmakers, cooks, chefs, and animal groomers use scissors.
10. Adults and children use scissors.
11. Hand motions make scissors cut.
12. Scissors need to be handled carefully.
13. Scissors need care.
14. Scissors need to be cleaned and sharpened.
15. Scissors can cut many materials.
16. Paper, cardboard, fabric, and hair can be cut with scissors.
17. Fingernails, toenails, yarn, thread, and pastry can be cut with scissors.

Vocabulary

1. **blade**—cutting edge of scissors.
2. **pinking shears**—sewing scissors.
3. **scissors**—a tool for cutting or trimming.
4. **shears**—large scissors.

578

Bulletin Board

The purpose of this bulletin board is to have the children match the colored scissors to the corresponding colored skein of yarn. To prepare the bulletin board, construct six scissors out of tagboard. With felt-tip markers, color each scissor a different color and laminate. Fasten the scissors to the top of the bulletin board. Next, construct six skeins of yarn out of tagboard. Color each skein a different color to correspond with the scissors. Attach the skeins to the bottom part of the bulletin board. Fasten a string to each of the scissors and a pushpin to each of the skeins of yarn.

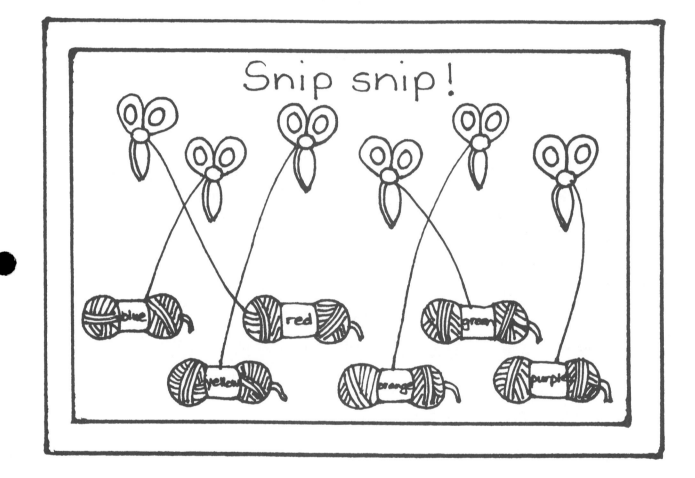

Family Letter

Dear Families,

Snip, snip, snip! This sound will be heard frequently in the classroom as we start a curriculum unit focusing on scissors. Through the experiences provided, the children will be introduced to various kinds and uses of scissors. They will also learn the proper care and safety precautions to consider when handling and using scissors.

AT SCHOOL

Some activities related to scissors will include:

- discussing safety and proper uses of scissors
- experimenting cutting with different kinds of scissors
- cutting a variety of materials such as yarn, fabric, paper, wallpaper, and aluminum foil
- visiting Tom's Barber Shop on Wednesday morning. We will leave at 10:00 a.m. and expect to watch a haircut demonstration. Also, we will observe the tools and equipment used by a barber.
- listening to the story "Michael's New Hair Cut"

AT HOME

Children need many experiences working with scissors before they are able to master cutting skills. Each child will learn this skill at his or her own rate. To assist your child, save scraps of paper and junk mail. Allow your child to practice cutting the paper using child-sized scissors. Once the cutting skills have been mastered, your child may enjoy cutting coupons out of newspaper sections or magazines.

Have fun with your child!

Some children need left-handed scissors; others can use right-handed scissors.

Arts and Crafts

1. Scissor Snip

Strips of paper with scissors can be provided for snipping.

2. Cutting

For experimentation, a wide variety of materials and types of scissors can be added to the art area for the children.

Cooking

Pretzels

1 1/2 cups warm water
1 envelope yeast
4 cups flour
1 teaspoon salt
1 tablespoon sugar
coarse salt
egg

Mix the warm water, yeast, and sugar together. Set this mixture aside for 5 minutes. Pour salt and flour into a bowl. Add the yeast mixture to make dough. Roll the dough into a long snake form. Cut the dough into smaller sections using scissors. The children can then form individual shapes with dough. Brush egg on the shapes with pastry brush and sprinkle with salt. Preheat the oven and bake pretzels at 425 degrees for 12 minutes.

Dramatic Play

1. Beauty Shop

Set up a beauty shop in the dramatic play area. Include items such as curling irons, hair dryers, combs, and wigs. Also include a chair, plastic covering, and Beauty Shop sign. A cash register and money can be added to encourage play. **Caution:** For safety purposes, cut the cords off the hair dryer and curling irons.

2. Tailor/Dressmaking Shop

Materials that are easy to cut should be provided. Likewise, a variety of scissors should be placed next to the material. Older children may want to make doll clothes.

Pastes

Bookmaker's Paste

1 teaspoon flour
2 teaspoons cornstarch
1/4 teaspoon powdered alum
3 ounces water

Mix dry ingredients. Add water slowly, stirring out all lumps. Cook over slow fire (preferably in a double boiler), stirring constantly. Remove when paste begins to thicken. It will thicken more as it cools. Keep in covered jars. Thin with water if necessary.

Cooked Flour Paste

1 cup boiling water
1 tablespoon powdered alum
1 pint cold water
1 pint flour

1 heaping teaspoon oil of cloves
oil of wintergreen
 (optional)

To 1 cup boiling water add powdered alum. Mix flour and fold in water until smooth; pour mixture gradually into boiling alum water. Cook until it has a bluish cast, stirring all the time. Remove from fire, add oil of cloves, and stir well. Keep in airtight jars. Thin when necessary by adding water. A drop or two of oil of wintergreen may be added to give the paste a pleasing aroma.

Colored Salt Paste

Mix 2 parts salt to 1 part flour. Add powdered paint and

enough water to make a smooth heavy paste. Keep in airtight container.

Crepe Paper Paste

Cut or tear 2 tablespoons crepe paper of a single color. The finer the paper is cut, the smoother the paste will be. Add 1/2 tablespoon flour, 1/2 tablespoon salt, and enough water to make a paste. Stir and squash the mixture until it is as smooth as possible. Store in airtight container.

---

3. Bake Shop

Play dough, scissors, and other cooking tools can be placed on a table. If desired, make paper baker hats and a sign.

4. Dog Groomer

A dog grooming area can be set up in the dramatic play corner with stuffed animals, brushes, and combs. If available, cut off the cord of an electric dog shaver and provide for the children.

Field Trips/ Resource People

1. Hairstylist

Visit a hairstylist. While there, observe a person's hair being cut. Notice the different scissors that are used and how they are used.

2. Pet Groomer

Invite a pet groomer to class. If possible, arrange for a dog to be groomed.

 Fingerplays

Open, Shut Them

Open, shut them, open, shut them.
 (use index and middle finger to make scissors motion)
Give a little snip, snip, snip.
 (three quick snips with fingers)
Open, shut them, open, shut them.
 (repeat scissors motion)
Make another clip.
 (make another scissors motion)

Group Time

(Games, Language)

Scissors Safety

Discuss safety while using scissors. The children can help make a list titled "How we use our scissors safely." Display chart in room.

Math

Shape Sort

Cut out different-colored shapes. Place the shapes on a table for the children to sort by color, shape, and size.

Science

1. **Scissor Show**

   Place a variety of scissors on an overhead projector. Encourage the children to describe each by naming it and explaining its use.

2. **Shadow Profiles**

   Tape a piece of paper on a wall or bulletin board. Stand a child in front of the paper. Shine a light source to create a shadow of the head. Trace the outline of each child's shadow. Provide scissors for the children to use to cut out their own shadows.

3. **Weighing Scissors**

   On the science table, place a variety of scissors and a scale. The children should be encouraged to note the differences in weight.

Sensory

Play Dough

Scissors can be placed next to the play dough in the sensory area.

Books

The following books can be used to complement this theme:

Birch, Barbara and Beverly Lewis. (1995). *Katie and the Haircut Mistake*. Illus. by Taia Morley. Minneapolis, MN: Augsburg Fortress.

Klinting, Lars. (1996). *Bruno the Tailor*. New York: Holt.

Landstrom, Olof et al. (1993). *Will Gets a Haircut*. Stockholm, NY: R&S Book.

Moore, Eva. (1997). *The Day of the Bad Haircut*. Illus. by Meredith Johnson. St. Paul, MN: Cartwheel Books. (Pbk)

Robins, Joan. (1993). *Addie's Bad Day*. Illus. by Sue Truesdell. New York: HarperCollins.

Ruediger, Beth. (1997). *The Barber of Bingo*. Illus. by John McPherson. Kansas City, KS: Andrews McMeel.

Strickland, Michael R. and Keaf Holliday. (1998). *Haircuts at Sleepy Sam's*. Illus. by Keaf Holliday. Honesdale, PA: Boyds Mills.

Tusca, Tricia. (1991). *Camilla's New Hairdo*. New York: Farrar, Straus and Giroux.

Names

circle
triangle
rectangle
square
oval

Shapes

Construction

lines
round
four sides
three sides

Theme Goals

Through participating in the experiences provided by this theme, the children may learn

1. The names of basic shapes
2. Identification of basic shapes
3. Objects have shapes

Concepts for the Children to Learn

1. The shape is the way something looks.
2. There are many shapes of different sizes and colors in our world.
3. Some shapes have names.
4. Circles, triangles, rectangles, squares, and ovals are all shapes.
5. A circle is round.
6. Triangles have three sides.
7. A rectangle is a shape with four sides.
8. An oval is shaped like an egg.
9. A square has four sides all the same size.
10. All objects contain one or more shapes.
11. We can draw lines to make shapes.

Vocabulary

1. **circle**—a shape that is round.
2. **line**—a mark made with a pencil, crayon, and so on, to make a shape.
3. **oval**—shaped like an egg.
4. **rectangle**—a shape with four sides.
5. **shape**—the way something looks.
6. **square**—a shape with four sides of equal length.
7. **triangle**—a shape with three sides.

THEME 58

Bulletin Board

The purpose of this bulletin board is to develop visual discrimination, hand-eye coordination, and problem-solving skills by making a shape train. To prepare the bulletin board use the model shown to construct a train using basic shapes. Color the shapes, cut them out, and laminate. Trace laminated shapes onto black construction paper to construct shadow shapes. Cut out the shadow shapes. Staple the shadow shapes onto the board in a train pattern. The children can affix the colored shape pieces to the shadows by using magnets.

SHAPES

Family Letter

Dear Families,

Hello again! Shapes are the focus of our new curriculum unit. Our world consists of shapes. The children will become aware of this on an introductory walk around the block. They also will become familiar with the names of shapes and will classify objects according to their shapes. Consequently, the children will be more aware of all the shapes in our world. In addition, the children who are developmentally ready will practice drawing some of the basic shapes.

AT SCHOOL

Some of the fun-filled learning activities scheduled for this unit include:

- playing a game called "Shape Basket Upset"
- listening to the story *Shapes and Things*, by Tana Hoban
- feeling and identifying objects by shape in a feely box
- making and baking cookies of various shapes

AT HOME

You can reinforce the activities included in this curriculum unit at home by observing shaped objects in your house. Each day at school we will have a special shape theme. Your child can bring in an object from home to fit the shape of the day. I will send home the shape the night before so you and your child will have time to look for an object. The following fingerplay can be recited to foster language and memory skills.

Circle and Square

Close my eyes, shut them tight.
(close eyes)
Make a circle with my one hand.
(make a circle with one hand)
Keep them shut; make it fair.
(keep eyes shut)
With my other hand, make a square.
(make a square with other hand)

Enjoy your child!

What can you make with these shapes?

 # Arts and Crafts

1. Sponge Painting

Cut sponges into the four basic shapes. The children can hold the sponges with a clothespin. The sponge can be dipped in paint and printed on the paper. Make several designs and shapes.

2. Shape Mobiles

Trace shapes of various sizes on colored construction paper. If appropriate, encourage the children to cut the shapes from the paper and punch a hole at the top of each shape. Next, put a piece of string through the hole and tie onto a hanger. The mobiles can be hung in the classroom for decoration.

3. Easel Ideas

Feature a different shape of easel paper each day at the easel.

4. Shape Collage

Provide different-colored paper shapes and glue for the children to create collages from shapes.

5. My Shape Book

Stickers, catalogs, and magazines should be placed on the art table. Also, prepare booklets cut into the basic shapes. Encourage the children to find, cut, and glue the objects in each shape book.

6. Shape Stamps

Collect jar lids and pieces of thick cardboard. Cut the cardboard into shapes and glue them to jar lids. The children can dip them in paint and stamp them onto paper.

 # Cooking

1. Shaped Bread

The children can cut bread with different-shaped cookie cutters. Spread soft cheese, cream cheese, or other toppings on the bread.

2. Fruit Cutouts

1/2 cup sugar
4 envelopes unflavored gelatin
2 1/2 cups pineapple juice, apple juice, orange juice, grape juice, or fruit drink

In a mixing bowl, stir the sugar and gelatin with rubber scraper until well mixed. Pour fruit juice into a 1-quart saucepan. Put the pan on the burner. Turn the burner to high heat. Cook until the juice boils. Turn burner off. Pour boiling fruit juice over sugar mixture. Stir with a rubber scraper until all the gelatin is dissolved. Pour into a 13-inch × 9-inch × 2-inch pan. Place in the refrigerator and chill until firm. Cookie cutters can be used to make shapes. Enjoy! **Caution:** This activity requires close supervision.

3. **Shape Snacks**

Spread cheese onto variously shaped crackers and serve.

Serve cheese cut into circles, triangles, squares, and rectangles.

Serve vegetable circles—cucumbers, carrots, zucchini.

Cut fruit snacks into circles—bananas, grapefruit wedges, apple slices, grapes—serve.

4. **Nachos**

4 flour tortillas
3/4 cup grated cheese
1/3 cup chopped green pepper (optional)

With clean kitchen scissors, cut each tortilla into 4 or 6 triangle wedges. Place on a cookie sheet and sprinkle the tortilla wedges with the cheese. Garnish with green pepper if desired. Bake in a 350-degree oven for 4 to 6 minutes or until the cheese melts. Makes 16 to 20 nachos.

5. **Swedish Pancakes**

3 eggs
1 cup milk
1 1/2 cups flour
1 tablespoon sugar
1/2 teaspoon salt
4 tablespoons butter
1 cup heavy cream
2 tablespoons confectioner's sugar or a
    12-ounce jar of fruit jelly

Using a fork or whisk, beat the eggs lightly in a large mixing bowl. Add half the milk. Fold in the flour, sugar, and salt. Melt the butter and add it, the cream, and the remaining milk to the mixture. Stir well. Lightly grease a frying pan or griddle, and place it over medium-high heat on a hot

plate or stove. Carefully pour small amounts of the mixture onto the frying pan or griddle. Cook until the pancakes are golden around the edges and bubbly on top. Turn the pancakes over with a spatula and cook until the other sides are golden around the edges. Remove to a covered plate. Repeat until all the mixture is used. Sprinkle pancakes lightly with confectioner's sugar, or spread jelly over them. Makes 3 dozen pancakes.

Dramatic Play

1. **Baker**

Provide play dough, cake pans, and cookie cutters.

2. **Puppets**

A puppet prop box should be placed in the dramatic play area. A puppet stage should be added if available. Otherwise a puppet stage can be made from cardboard.

Field Trips

Shape Walk

Walk around the school neighborhood. During the walk, observe the shapes of the traffic signs and houses. After returning to the school, record the shapes observed on a chart.

Fingerplays

Right Circle, Left Square

Close my eyes, shut them tight.
    (close eyes)
Make a circle with my one hand.
    (make circle with one hand)
Keep them shut; make it fair.
    (keep eyes shut)
With my other hand, make a square.
    (make square with other hand)

590

THEME 58

Lines

One straight finger makes a line.
    (hold up one index finger)
Two straight lines make one "t" sign.
    (cross index fingers)
Three lines made a triangle there
    (form triangle with index fingers touching and
    thumbs touching)
And one more line will make a square.
    (form square with hands)

Draw a Square

Draw a square, draw a square
Shaped like a tile floor.
Draw a square, draw a square
All with corners four.

A Circle

Around in a circle we will go.
    (walk in a circle as a group)
Little tiny baby steps make us go very slow.
    (walk in a circle with little steps)
And then we'll take some great giant steps,
    (walk in a circle with big steps)
as big as they can be.
Then in a circle we'll stand quietly.
    (stand in a circle)

Draw a Triangle

Draw a triangle, draw a triangle
With corners three.
Draw a triangle, draw a triangle
Draw it just for me.

Draw a Circle

Draw a circle, draw a circle
Made very round.
Draw a circle, draw a circle
No corners can be found.

What Am I Making?

This is a circle.
    (draw circle in the air)
This is a square.
    (draw square in the air)
Who can tell me
What I'm making there?
    (draw another shape in the air)

Group Time

(Games, Language)

1. **Shape Hunt**

    Throughout the classroom hide colorful shapes. Each of the children can find a shape.

2. **Twister**

    On a large old bed sheet, secure many shapes of different colors, or draw the shapes on with magic markers. Make a spinner. Have children place parts of their bodies on the different shapes.

3. **Shape Day**

    Each day highlight a different shape. Collect related items that resemble the shape of the day and display throughout the classroom. During group time, have each child find an object in the classroom that is the same shape as the shape of the day.

Large Muscle

1. **Walk and Balance**

    Using masking tape, outline the four basic shapes on the floor. The children can walk and balance on the shapes. Older children may walk forward, backward, and sideways.

2. **Hopscotch**

    Draw a hopscotch board with chalk on the sidewalk outdoors. Masking tape can be used to form the grid on the floor indoors.

Math

1. **Wallpaper Shape Match**

    From scraps of old wallpaper, cut out two sets of basic shapes. Mix all of the pieces. The children can match the sets by pattern and shape.

To Teach Math Concepts

Before a child can learn the more abstract concepts of arithmetic, he or she must be visually, physically, and kinesthetically aware of basic quantitative concepts. Included could be

Form Discrimination	Vocabulary			
circle	big	top	all	more
square	little	bottom	none	less
triangle	small	long	some	through
rectangle	smaller	short	first	around
	large	tall	last	fast
	larger	high	middle	slow
	heavy	low	near	up
	light	thick	far	down
	in	thin	above	most
	out	front	below	least
	over	back	many	
	under	behind	few	

2. Shape Completion

On several pieces of white tagboard draw a shape, leaving one side, or part of a circle, unfinished or dotted. Laminate the tagboard. The children can complete the shape by drawing with watercolor markers or grease pencils. Erase with a damp cloth.

Music

The following songs can be found in Butler, Talmadge, Kirkland, Terry, & Leach. (1975). *Music for Today's Children*. Broadman Press.

1. **"Colors, Shapes, and Numbers"**
2. **"Different Shapes"**
3. **"Twinkle, Twinkle, Little Star"**

   Twinkle, twinkle, little star,
   How I wonder what you are.
   Up above the world so high,
   Like a diamond in the sky.

Twinkle, twinkle, little star.
How I wonder what you are.
When the blazing sun is set,
And the grass with dew is wet,
Then you show your little light,
Twinkle, twinkle, all the night.

Science

1. Feely Box

Cut many shapes out of different materials such as felt, cardboard, wallpaper, carpet, etc. Place the shapes into a feely box. The children can be encouraged to reach in and identify the shape by feeling it before removing it from the box.

2. Evaporation

Pour equal amounts of water into a large round and a small square cake pan. Mark the water level with a grease pencil. Allow the

water to stand for a week. Observe the
amount of evaporation.

3. **Classifying Objects**

   Collect four small boxes. Mark a different shape
   on each box. Include a circle, triangle, square,
   and rectangle. Cut shapes out of magazines.
   The children can sort the objects by placing
   them in the corresponding boxes.

4. **What Shape Is It?**

   Place objects with distinct shapes, such as
   marbles, dice, pyramid, deck of cards, book, ball,
   button, and so on, in the feely box. Encourage
   the children to reach in and identify the shape of
   the object they are feeling before they pull it out.

Sensory

Add the following items to the sensory table:

1. marbles and water
2. different-shaped sponges and water
3. colored water
4. scented water
5. soapy water

Books

The following books can be used to
complement this theme:

Aigner-Clark, Julie and Nadeem Zaidi. (2001).
See and Spy Shapes (*Baby Einstein Books*).
Illus. by Nadeem Zaidi. New York:
Hyperion Press.

Dillon, Leo et al. (1994). *What Am I? Looking
Through Shapes at Apples and Grapes.*
New York: Scholastic.

Ehlert, Lois. (1989). *Color Zoo.* New York:
Lippincott.

Ehlert, Lois. (1990). *Color Farm.* New York:
Lippincott.

Grover, Max. (1996). *Circles and Squares Everywhere.*
Orlando, FL: Harcourt Brace.

Hoban, Tana. (1986). *Shapes, Shapes, Shapes.*
New York: William Morrow.

Hoban, Tana. (1992). *Spirals, Curves, Fanshapes &
Lines.* New York: Greenwillow.

MacDonald, Suse. (1994). *Sea Shapes.* Orlando,
FL: Harcourt Brace.

Morgan, Sally. (1994). *Circles and Spheres.*
Cincinnati, OH: Thomson Learning.
(*World of Shapes* series)

Morgan, Sally. (1994). *Squares and Cubes.*
Cincinnati, OH: Thomson Learning.
(*World of Shapes* series)

Morgan, Sally. (1995). *Spirals.* Cincinnati,
OH: Thomson Learning. (*World of
Shapes* series)

Morgan, Sally. (1995). *Triangles and Pyramids.*
Cincinnati, OH: Thomson Learning.
(*World of Shapes* series)

Serfozo, Mary. (1996). *There's a Square: A Book
about Shapes.* Illus. by David A. Carter.
New York: Scholastic.

Sharman, Lydia. (1994). *The Amazing Book of
Shapes.* New York: Dorling Kindersley.

Shaw, Charles Green. (1947). *It Looked Like Spilt
Milk.* New York: Harper.

Thong, Roseanne and Grace Lin. (2000). *Round
Is a Mooncake: A Book of Shapes.* Illus. by
Grace Lin. San Francisco, CA:
Chronicle Books.

Tomczyk, Mary and Loretta Trezzo Braren.
(1999). *Shapes, Sizes, & More Surprises:
A Little Hands Early Learning Book.*
Charlotte, VT: Williamson.

Touch and Feel Shapes. (2000). New York: Dorling
Kindersley.

Multimedia

The following multimedia products can be
used to complement this theme:

Colors, Shapes & Size [CD-ROM]. (1995). San
Francisco, CA: Star Press Multimedia.

Jumpstart Preschool [CD-ROM]. (1996). Glendale,
CA: Knowledge Adventure.

Let's Start Learning [CD-ROM]. (1996).
Freemont, CA: The Learning Co.

SHAPES

Rock 'n' Learn Colors, Shapes & Counting [video]. (1997). Conroe, TX: Rock 'n' Learn.

Shape Up! [CD-ROM]. (1995). Cupertino, CA: Sunburst Communications.

Traugh, Steven et al. "Shapes" on *Music and Movement* [cassette]. (1993). Cypress, CA: Creative Teaching Press.

Participants

spectators, players, coaches,
umpires, scorekeepers,
announcers

Clothing

uniforms, swimsuits,
shorts, jerseys,
sweatshirts,
sweatpants,
hats, ski clothing,
jacket, gloves,
pants, goggles

Sports

Types

baseball, basketball,
football, soccer,
rugby, swimming,
tennis, volleyball,
skiing, biking,
bowling, skating,
track/running,
fishing, golf, hockey

Places
Indoors & Outdoors

yards, fields,
swimming pools,
tennis courts,
roads, gyms,
golf courses,
bowling alleys,
ski slopes, lakes

Equipment

balls, bats, shoulder pads,
rackets, bikes, skis,
boots, poles, gloves,
special shoes,
helmets, golf clubs, skates

Theme Goals

Through participating in the experiences provided by this theme, the children may learn

1. Places used for sports participation
2. Types of sports people play
3. Equipment used for sports
4. Kinds of clothing worn for sports participation
5. There are many people who participate in sports.

Concepts for the Children to Learn

1. Sports are activities played for fun and exercise.
2. Swimming pools, playing fields, tennis courts, roads, gyms, golf courses, backyards, bowling alleys, lakes, and ski slopes are all places that are used for sports.
3. Spectators, players, and coaches are all sports participants.
4. Umpires, scorekeepers, and announcers work at sporting activities.
5. Baseball, biking, hockey, football, and golf are all types of sports.
6. Soccer, rugby, swimming, and volleyball are sports.
7. Balls, bikes, and golf clubs are sports equipment.
8. Uniforms are worn when playing some sports.
9. Football and basketball players wear uniforms and helmets.
10. Some sports are played indoors, others outdoors.
11. There are individual and team sports.
12. Skating, track/running, and fishing are also sports.
13. Baseball players have bats, baseballs, and gloves for equipment.
14. Skiers have skis, boots, gloves, poles, hats, ski suits, and sometimes goggles.
15. Golfers have golf clubs, golf balls, and special shoes.
16. Swimsuits, shorts, jerseys, sweatshirts, and sweatpants are clothing worn in some sports.

Vocabulary

1. **ball**—equipment used for sports.
2. **sport**—an activity played for fun.
3. **team**—a group of people who play together.
4. **uniform**—clothing worn for some sports.

596

Bulletin Board

The purpose of this bulletin board is to encourage the children to hang each ball with a numeral on the glove that has the corresponding number of dots. To prepare the bulletin board, construct baseball mitts out of brown tagboard. Cut out the mitts and attach dots starting with one on each of the gloves. The number of gloves prepared and dots will depend on the developmental maturity of the children. Hang the gloves on the bulletin board. Next construct white baseballs. Write a numeral, starting with 1, on each of the balls.

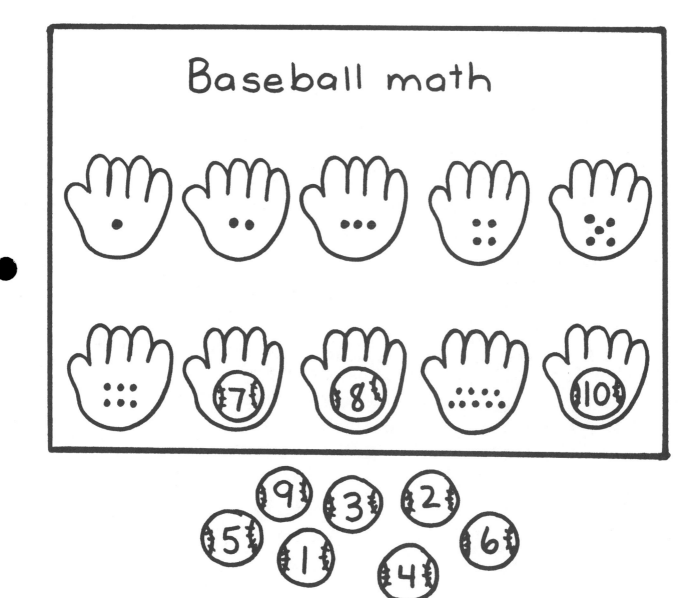

SPORTS

Family Letter

Dear Families,

Sports are the focus of our next unit. Through the experiences provided, the children will become familiar with types of sports equipment and clothing, and people who participate in sports. They will also recognize sports as a form of exercise.

AT SCHOOL

Activities planned to foster sports concepts include:

- exploring balls used in different sports and classifying them into groups by size, color, and ability to bounce and roll

- trying on a variety of clothing used in different sports, including a swim cap, goggles, shoulder and leg/knee pads, helmets, gloves, and uniforms

- skating in the room by wrapping squares of waxed paper around our feet and attaching them with rubber bands around our ankles. Our feet will then easily glide over the carpet!

AT HOME

You can incorporate sports concepts at home by

- looking through sports magazines with your child and pointing out the equipment that is used or the clothing that is worn. This will develop your child's observation skills.

- observing a sporting event with your child, such as basketball, baseball, or football. Likewise, let your child watch you participate in a sport!

- participating in a sport together. Your child will enjoy spending special time with you!

Enjoy your child!

Soccer is a good physical activity.

Arts and Crafts

1. Easel Ideas

Cut easel paper in various sports shapes.

- baseball glove
- baseball diamond
- tennis racket
- bike
- tennis shoe
- football
- baseball cap
- football helmet
- different sizes of balls

2. Team Pennants

Prepare triangular pennants using a variety of colors of construction paper or fun foam. Allow the children to use sequins, pom-poms, etc. to decorate the pennant.

3. Ball Collages

Balls used in various sports come in all different sizes. Using construction paper or wallpaper, cut the paper in various round shapes, as well as football shapes. Encourage the children to paste them on a large piece of construction paper and decorate.

4. Golf Ball Painting

Place a piece of paper in a shallow tray or pie tin. Spoon 2 or 3 teaspoons of thin paint onto the paper. Next, put a golf ball or ping-pong ball in the tray and tilt the pan in several directions, allowing the ball to make designs in the paint.

Cooking

Cheese Balls

8 ounces cream cheese, softened
1 stick of butter, softened

2 cups grated cheddar cheese
1/2 package of onion soup mix

Blend all of the ingredients together. Shape the mixture into small balls.

Dramatic Play

1. **Baseball**

   Baseball caps, plastic balls, uniforms, catcher's mask, and gloves can be placed in the dramatic play area.

2. **Football**

   Balls, shoulder pads, uniforms, and helmets can be provided for the children to use outdoors.

3. **Tennis**

   Tennis rackets, balls, visors, sunglasses, and shorts for the children can be placed outdoors. A variation would be to use balloons for balls and hangers with pantyhose pulled around them for rackets.

4. **Skiing**

   Ski boots and skis can be provided for the children to try on.

5. **Skating**

   Waxed paper squares for children to wrap around their feet and ankles can be provided. The children can attach the waxed paper with rubber bands around their ankles. Encourage the children to slide across the carpeting.

Field Trips

Suggested trips include:

1. a football field
2. a baseball field
3. tennis court
4. health (fitness) club
5. stadium
6. a swimming pool
7. the sports facilities of a local high school or college

Fingerplays

Here Is a Ball

Here's a ball
  (make a circle with your thumb and
  pointer finger)
And here's a ball
  (make a bigger circle with two thumbs and
  pointers)
And a great big ball I see.
  (make a large circle with arms)
Now let's count the balls we've made,
One, two, three.
  (repeat)

Football Players

Five big football players standing in the locker
  room door.
One had a sore knee
And then there were four.

Four big football players down on their knees.
One made a touchdown
And then there were three.

Three big football players looking up at you.
One made a tackle
And then there were two.

Two big football players running in the sun.
One was offsides
And then there was one.

One big football player standing all alone.
He decided to go home
And then there were none.

600

THEME 59

Group Time

(Games, Language)

"What's Missing?"

Provide a large group of children with a tray of sports equipment such as a ball, baseball glove, golf ball, sunglasses, goggles, etc. Let the children examine the tray of items. Then have the children close their eyes and place their heads in their laps. Remove one item from the tray and see if the children can guess what is missing. This activity will be more successful if the numbers are related to the age of the child. For example, with two-year-old children, use only two items. Three-year-olds may be successful with an additional item. If not, remove one.

Large Muscle

1. **Going Fishing**

   Use a large wooden rocking boat or a large box that two to three children can sit in. Make fish out of construction paper or tagboard, and attach paper clips to the top. Tie a magnet to a string and pole. The magnet will attract the fish.

2. **Kickball**

   Many sports involve kicking a ball. Discuss these sports with the children. Then provide the children with a variety of balls to kick. Let the children discover which balls go the farthest and which are the easiest to kick.

3. **Sports Charades**

   Dramatize various sports, including swimming, golfing, tennis, and bike riding.

4. **Golfing**

   Using a child-sized putter and regular golf balls, the children hit golf balls. This is an outdoor activity that requires a lot of teacher supervision.

5. **Beach Volleyball**

   Use a large beach ball and a rope or net in a central spot outdoors. Let the children volley the beach ball to one another.

Math

1. **Ball Sort**

   Sort various balls by size, texture, and color.

2. **Hat Sorting**

   Sort hats such as baseball cap, football helmet, biking helmet, visor, and others, by color, size, texture, and shape.

3. **Soccer Ball Pattern**

   Cut large balls from white construction paper. Cut out small octagons from black construction paper. Encourage the children to glue the black octagons on the white ball to create a pattern. Help the children identify a black-white-black-white pattern to create a soccer ball.

Science

1. **Feely Box**

   Place a softball, baseball, golf ball, and tennis ball in a feely box. The children can reach into the box, feel, and try to guess the type of ball.

2. **Ball Bounces**

   Observe the way different balls move. Check to see if footballs, basketballs, and soccer balls can be bounced. Observe to see if some go higher than others. Also repeat using smaller balls such as tennis balls, baseballs, and golf balls.

3. Wheels

Observe the wheels on a bicycle. If possible, bring a bike to the classroom and demonstrate how peddling makes the wheels move.

4. Examining Balls

Observe the composition of different balls. Ask the children to identify each. Then place the balls in water. Observe to see which ones float and which ones sink.

5. Types of Grass

Place real grass and artificial turf on the science table. The children can feel both types of grass and describe differences in texture.

6. Stethoscopes

Place stethoscopes on the science shelf. Show children how to listen to their heart rate. Have children run in place for 30 seconds and again listen to their heartbeats. What did they notice?

Note: Be certain the stethoscope earplugs are cleaned after each use.

Sensory

1. Swimming

Add water to the sensory table with dolls or small people figures.

2. Weighing Balls

Fill the sensory table with small balls, such as golf balls, foam balls, Wiffle balls, or tennis balls. Add a balance scale so that the children can weigh the balls.

3. Measuring Mud and Sand

Add a mud and sand mixture to the sensory table with scoops and spoons.

4. Feeling Turf

Line the bottom of the sensory table with artificial turf.

Books

The following books can be used to complement this theme:

Adler, David A. (1997). *Lou Gehrig: The Luckiest Man*. Illus. by Terry Widener. Orlando, FL: Harcourt Brace.

Blackstone, Margaret. (1993). *This Is Baseball*. Illus. by John O'Brien. New York: Holt.

Borden, Louise. (1993). *Albie the Lifeguard*. Illus. by Elizabeth Sayles. New York: Scholastic.

Brown, Mark Tolon. (1993). *D. W. Rides Again!* Boston: Little, Brown.

Carrier, Roch. (1993). *The Longest Home Run*. Illus. by Sheldon Cohen. Plattsburgh, NY: Tundra Books.

Christopher, Matt and Daniel Vasconcellos. (2000). *Hat Trick*. Illus. by Daniel Vasconcellos. Boston: Little, Brown.

Dragonwagon, Crescent. (1993). *Annie Flies the Birthday Bike*. Illus. by Emily Arnold McCully. Colchester, CT: Atheneum.

Drake, Jane, Ann Love, and Heather Collins. (1998). *The Kids' Campfire Book*. Illus. by Heather Collins. Toronto, Ontario, Canada: Kids Can Press.

Florian, Douglas. (1994). *A Fisher*. New York: Greenwillow.

Gibbons, Gail. (1995). *Bicycle Book*. New York: Holiday House.

Hest, Amy. (1994). *Rosie's Fishing Trip*. Illus. by Paul Howard. Cambridge, MA: Candlewick Press.

Jakob, Donna. (1994). *My Bike*. Illus. by Nelle Davis. New York: Hyperion.

Johnston, Tony. (1996). *Fishing Sunday*. Illus. by Barry Root. New York: William Morrow.

Kessler, Leonard. (1988). *Old Turtle's Soccer Team*. New York: Greenwillow.

Kessler, Leonard. (1996). *Kick, Pass, and Run*. Orlando, FL: HarperCollins.

Lewis, Maggie and Michael Chesworth. (1999). *Morgy Makes His Move*. Illus. by Michael Chesworth. Boston: Houghton Mifflin.

Loewen, Nancy. (1996). *Bicycle Safety*. Illus. by
Penny Danny. Mankato, MN: Child's World.

London, Jonathan. (1994). *Let's Go Froggy!* Illus.
by Frank Remkiewicz. New York: Viking.

London, Jonathan. (1995). *Froggy Learns to Swim*.
Illus. by Frank Remkiewicz. New York: Viking.

Martin, Bill and Michael Sampson. (1997).
Swish. Illus. by Michael Chesworth.
New York: Holt.

McKissack, Patricia C. (1996). *A Million Fish . . .
More or Less*. Illus. by Dena Schutzer.
New York: Random House.

Moran, George. (1994). *Imagine Me on a
Sit-Ski!* Illus. by Nadine Bernard Westcott.
Beaver Dam, WI: Concept Books.

Norworth, Jack and Alec Gillman. (1999). *Take
Me Out to the Ballgame*. Illus. by Alec
Gillman. New York: Scholastic Trade.

Parish, Peggy. (1996). *Play Ball, Amelia Bedelia*.
Illus. by Wallace Tripp. New York:
HarperCollins.

Pulver, Robin. (1997). *Alicia's Tutu*. Illus. by Mark
Graham. New York: Dial Books.

Rex, Michael. (2005). *Dunk Skunk*. New York:
G.P. Putnam's Sons.

Rice, Eve. (1996). *Swim!* Illus. by Marisabina
Russo. New York: Greenwillow.

Sampson, Michael. (1996). *The Football That
Won . . .* Illus. by Ted Rand. New York: Holt.

Teague, Mark. (1992). *The Field Beyond the
Outfield*. New York: Scholastic.

Tryon, Leslie. (1996). *Albert's Ball Game*.
Colchester, CT: Atheneum.

Welch, Willy. (1995). *Playing Right Field*. Illus. by
Marc Simont. New York: Scholastic.

Wells, Rosemary. (1995). *Edward in Deep Water*.
New York: Dial Books.

Weston, Martha. (1995). *Tuck in the Pool*.
New York: Clarion Books.

Wolff, Ashley. (1993). *Stella and Roy*.
New York: Dutton.

Multimedia

The following multimedia products can be
used to complement this theme:

Brown, Marc Tolon. *Arthur Makes the Team*
[cassette and book]. (1998). Old
Greenwich, CT: Listening Library.

"Take Me Out to the Ballgame" on *Six Little
Ducks* [compact disc]. (1997). Long
Branch, NJ: Kimbo Educational.

Recordings and Song Titles

The following recordings can be used to
complement this theme:

"Take Me Out to the Ballgame." (1997). *Six
Little Ducks*. Long Branch, NJ: Kimbo
Educational.

"There's a Game Today." (1996). *People in Our
Neighborhood*. Long Branch, NJ: Kimbo
Educational.

Spring

Activities

flying kites
gardening
fishing
baseball
picnics
golf
tennis
camping
walking
bicycling

Plants

flowers
dandelions
grass
tree buds

Colors

green
white
yellow
pastels

Weather

rain
wind
warmer
thunderstorms

Animals

chicks
lambs
birds
calves
robins

Holidays

St. Patrick's Day
Mother's Day
Arbor Day
May Day
Memorial Day
Passover
Easter

Insects

caterpillars
butterflies
ants

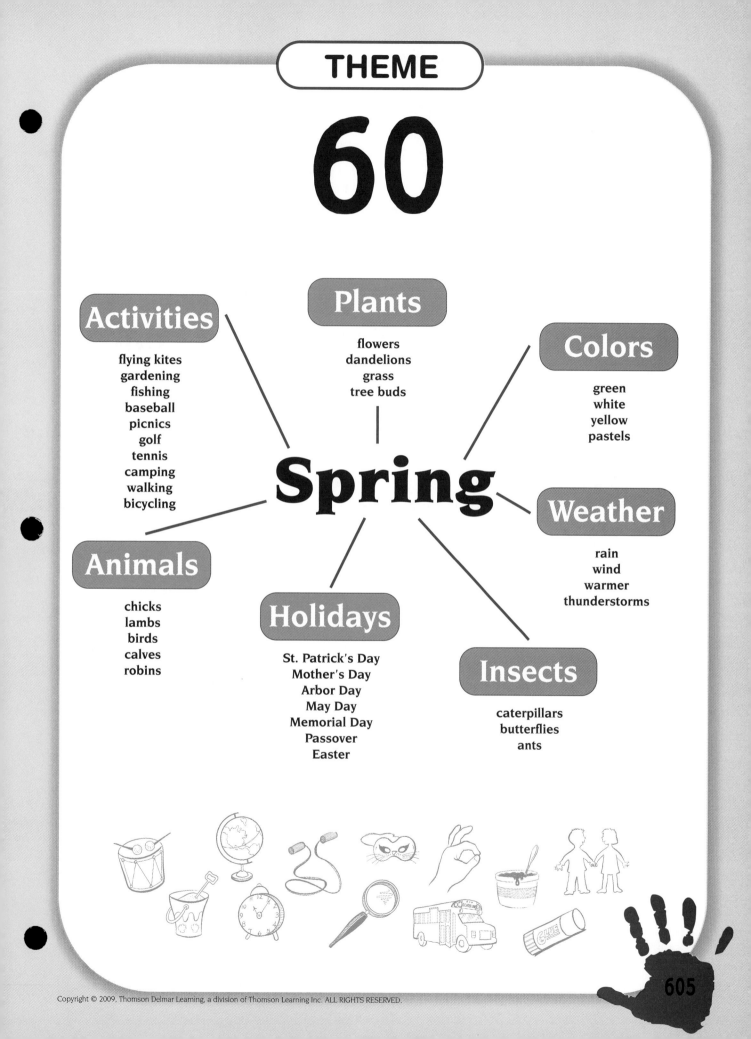

605

Theme Goals

Through participating in the experiences provided by this theme, the children may learn

1. Spring colors
2. Spring weather
3. Plants that grow in the spring
4. Insects seen during the spring
5. Springtime holidays
6. Spring animals
7. Spring activities

Concepts for the Children to Learn

1. Spring is a season that comes after winter and before summer.
2. It rains in the spring and there can be thunderstorms and wind.
3. Spring is usually warmer than winter.
4. Light colors are seen during the spring.
5. Green, white, and yellow are spring colors.
6. Caterpillars, butterflies, spiders, and ants are insects seen in the spring.
7. Some holidays are celebrated in the spring: Mother's Day, Passover, Easter, St. Patrick's Day, May Day, Arbor Day, and Memorial Day.
8. Chicks, lambs, calves, and robins are springtime animals.
9. Some people go on picnics, to baseball games, fishing, and golfing in the spring.
10. Picnics, camping, walking, and flying kites are spring activities.
11. Many gardens are planted in the spring.
12. Flowers, dandelions, and grass are spring plants.
13. Gardens are often planted in the spring.

Vocabulary

1. **garden**—a place where plants and flowers are grown.
2. **rain**—water from the clouds.
3. **spring**—the season that comes after winter and before summer.

Bulletin Board

The purpose of this bulletin board is to have the children place the proper number of ribbons on each kite tail. To do this, they need to count the number of dots on the kite. Construct kites and print the numerals beginning with 1 and the corresponding number of dots on each. Construct ribbons for the tails of the kites as illustrated. Color the kites and tails and laminate. Staple kites to bulletin board. Affix magnetic strips to each kite as the string. Affix a magnetic piece in the middle of each ribbon.

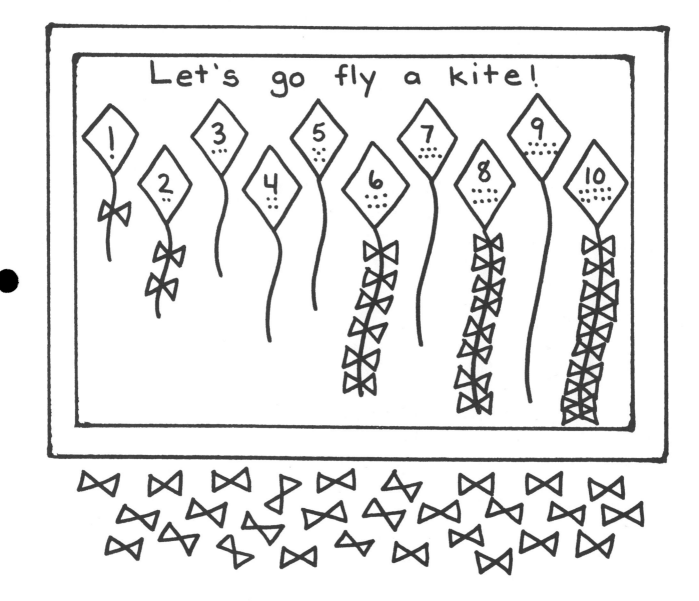

Family Letter

Dear Families,

The temperature is slowly rising, and there are patches of green grass on the playground. In other words, spring is here! And spring is the subject we will explore at school. Throughout the week, the children will become more aware of the many changes that take place during this season, as well as common spring activities. They will be exposed to spring holidays, and plants, animals, and insects will be highlighted.

Our goals for the theme include spring colors, weather, plants, insects, and animals. We will also talk about spring holidays and activities.

AT SCHOOL

Some of the learning experiences for this curriculum unit include:

- finding a suitable place on the playground to plant flowers
- taking a walk around the neighborhood to observe signs of spring
- planting grass seed in eggshells at the science table
- creating pictures and designs with pastel watercolor markers in the art area

AT HOME

To foster concepts of spring at home, save seeds from fruits such as oranges and apples. Assist your child in planting the seeds. Your child can also sort the seeds by color, size, or type to develop classification skills. The seeds could also be used for counting. Happy seed collecting!

Enjoy your child as you explore concepts related to spring.

Flower gardens are often planted in the spring.

 # Arts and Crafts

1. Butterfly Wings

Fold a sheet of light-colored paper in half. Show the children how to paint on only one side of the paper. The paper can be folded again and pressed. The result will be a symmetrical painting. Antennae can be added using crayons and markers to make butterflies.

2. Pussy Willow Fingerprints

Trace around a tongue depressor with a colored marker. Then, using ink pads or fingerpaint, the children can press a finger on the ink pad and transfer the fingerprint to the paper. This will produce pussy willow buds.

3. Caterpillars

Cut egg cartons in half lengthwise. Place the long rows on the art table with short pieces of chenille stems, markers, and crayons. From these materials, the children can make caterpillars.

4. Kites

Provide diamond-shaped construction paper, string, hole punch, crepe paper, glue, glitter, and markers. For older children, provide the paper with a diamond already traced. This provides them an opportunity to practice finger motor skills by cutting out the shapes. Using the triangle shapes, the children can create kites, and use them outdoors.

 # Cooking

1. Lemonade

1 lemon
2 to 3 tablespoons sugar
1 1/4 cups water
2 ice cubes

Squeeze lemon juice out of lemon. Add the sugar and water. Stir to dissolve the sugar. This makes one serving. Adjust the recipe to accommodate your class size.

2. Watermelon Popsicles

Remove the seeds and rind from a watermelon. Puree the melon in a blender or food processor. Pour into small paper cups. Insert popsicle sticks and freeze. These fruit popsicles can be served at snack time.

Dramatic Play

1. Fishing

Using short dowels, prepare fishing poles with a string taped to one end. Attach a magnet piece to the loose end of the string. Construct fish from tagboard and attach a paper clip to each fish. The magnet will attract the paper clip, allowing the children to catch the fish. Add a tackle box, canteen, hats, and life jackets for interest.

2. Garden

A small plastic hoe, rake, and garden shovel can be placed outdoors to encourage gardening. A watering can, flower pots, seed packages, and sun hats will also stimulate interest.

3. Flower Shop

Collect plastic flowers, vases, wrapping paper, seed packages, and catalogs and place in the dramatic play area. A cash register and play money can be added.

4. Spring Cleaning

Small mops, brooms, feather dusters, and empty pails can be placed in the dramatic play area. A spray bottle filled with blue water, which can be used to wash designated windows, can also be provided.

Field Trips

1. Nature Walk

Walk around your neighborhood, looking for signs of spring. Robins and other birds are often early signs of spring and can usually be observed in most areas of the country.

2. Farm

Arrange a field trip to a farm. It is an interesting place to visit during the spring. Ask the farmer to show you the farm equipment, buildings, crops, and animals.

Fingerplays

See, See, See

See, see, see
   (shade eyes with hands)
Three birds are in a tree.
   (hold up three fingers)
One can chirp
   (point to thumb)
And one can sing.
   (point to index finger)
One is just a tiny thing.
   (point to middle finger, then rock baby bird in arms)
See, see, see
Three birds are in a tree
   (hold up three fingers)

Look, look, look
   (shade eyes)
Three ducks are in a brook.
   (hold up three fingers)
One is white, and one is brown.
One is swimming upside down.
   (point to a finger each time)
Look, look, look
Three ducks are in a brook.
   (hold up three fingers)

This Little Calf

(extend fingers, push each down in succession)

This little calf eats grass.
This little calf eats hay.
This little calf drinks water.
This little calf runs away.
This little calf does nothing
But just lies down all day.
   (rest last finger in palm of hand)

610

THEME 60

Raindrops

Rain is falling down.
Rain is falling down.
  (raise arm, flutter fingers to ground, tapping the floor)
Pitter-patter
Pitter-patter
Rain is falling down.

Creepy Crawly Caterpillar

A creepy crawly caterpiller that I see
  (shade eyes)
Makes a chrysalis in the big oak tree.
  (make body into a ball)
He stays there and I know why
  (slowly stand up)
Because soon he will be a butterfly.
  (flap arms)

My Garden

This is my garden.
  (extend one hand forward, palm up)
I'll rake it with care
  (make raking motion on palm with three other fingers)
And then some flower seeds
I'll plant there.
  (planting motion)
The sun will shine
  (make circle with hands)
And the rain will fall.
  (let fingers flutter down to lap)
And my garden will blossom
And grow straight and tall.
  (cup hands together, extend upwards slowly)

Caterpillar

The caterpillar crawled from a plant, you see.
  (left hand crawls up and down right arm)
"I think I'll take a nap," said he.
So over the ground he began to creep
  (right hand crawls over left arm)
To spin a chrysalis, and he fell asleep.
  (cover right fist with left hand)
All winter he slept in his bed
Till spring came along and he said,
"Wake up, it's time to get out of bed!"
  (shake fist and pointer finger)

So he opened his eyes that sunny spring day.
  (spread fingers and look into hand)
"Look I'm a butterfly!" . . . and he flew away.
  (interlock thumbs and fly hands away)

Group Time

(Games, Language)

1. **What's Inside?**

Inside a large box, place many spring items. Include a kite, an umbrella, a hat, a fishing pole, etc. Select an item without showing the children. Describe the object and give clues about how the item can be used. The children should try to identify the item.

2. **Insect Movement**

During transition time, ask the children to move like the following insects: worm, grasshopper, caterpillar, butterfly, bumblebee, etc.

Large Muscle

1. **Windmills**

The children can stand up, swing their arms from side to side, and pretend to be windmills. A fan can be added to the classroom for added interest. Sing the song "Let's Be Windmills," which is listed under music.

2. **Puddles**

Construct puddles out of tagboard and cover with aluminum foil. Place the puddles on the floor. The children can jump from puddle to puddle. A variation would be to do this activity outside, using chalk to mark puddles on the ground.

3. **Caterpillar Crawl**

During a transition time, the children can imitate caterpillar movements.

Math

1. Seed Counting

On an index card, mark a numeral. The number of cards prepared will depend on the developmental appropriateness for the children. The children are to glue the appropriate number of seeds onto the card.

2. Insect Seriation

Construct flannel board pieces representing a ladybug, an ant, a caterpillar, a butterfly, etc. The children can arrange them on the flannel board from smallest to largest.

Music

1. "Catch One If You Can"
(*Sing to the tune of* "*Skip to My Lou*")

Butterflies are flying. Won't you try and catch one?
Butterflies are flying. Won't you try and catch one?
Butterflies are flying. Won't you try and catch one?
Catch one if you can.

Raindrops are falling. Won't you try and catch one?
Raindrops are falling. Won't you try and catch one?
Raindrops are falling. Won't you try and catch one?
Catch one if you can.

2. "Signs of Spring"
(*Sing to the tune of* "*Muffin Man*")

Do you see a sign of spring,
A sign of spring, a sign of spring?
Do you see a sign of spring?
Tell us what you see.

3. "Let's Be Windmills"
(*Sing to the tune of* "*If I Were a Lassie*")

Oh I wish I were a windmill, a windmill, a windmill.
Oh I wish I were a windmill. I know what I'd do.
I'd swing this way and that way, and this way
   and that way.
Oh I wish I were a windmill, when the wind blew.

Science

1. Alfalfa Sprouts

Each child who wishes to participate should be provided with a small paper cup, soil, and a few alfalfa seeds. The seeds and soil can be placed in the cup and watered. Place the cups in the sun and watch the sprouts grow. The sprouts can be eaten for snack. A variation is to plant the sprouts in eggshells as an Easter activity.

2. Weather Chart

A weather chart can be constructed that depicts weather conditions such as sunny, rainy, warm, cold, windy, etc. Attach at least two arrows to the center of the chart so that the children can point the arrow at the appropriate weather conditions.

3. Thermometers

On the science table, place a variety of outdoor thermometers. Also, post a thermometer outside a window, at a low position, so the children can read it.

4. Sprouting Carrots

Cut the large end off a fresh carrot and place it in a small cup of water. In a few days, a green top will begin to sprout.

5. Nesting Materials

Place string, cotton, yarn, and other small items outside on the ground. Birds will collect these items to use in their nest building.

6. Grass Growing

Grass seeds can be sprinkled on a wet sponge. Within a few days the seeds will begin to sprout.

7. Ant Farm

An ant farm can by made by using a large jar with a cover. Fill the jar 2/3 full with sand and soil, and add ants. Punch a few air holes in the cover of the jar, and secure the cover to the top of the jar. The children can watch the ants build tunnels.

THEME 60

Science Activities

Twenty-five other interesting science activities include:

1. Observe **food forms** such as potatoes in the raw, shredded, or sliced form. Fruits can be juiced, sliced, or sectioned.

2. **Prepare tomatoes** in several ways, such as sliced, juiced, stewed, baked, and pureed.

3. **Show corn** in all forms, including on the cob, popcorn, fresh cooked, and canned.

4. **Sort** picture cards into piles, living and nonliving.

5. **Tape record voices.** Encourage the children to recognize each others' voices.

6. **Tape record familiar sounds** from their environment. Include a ticking clock, telephone ringing, doorbell, toilet flushing, horn beeping, etc.

7. Take the children on a **sensory walk**. Fill dishpan-sized containers with different items. Foam, sand, leaves, pebbles, mud, cold and warm water, and grains can be used. Have the children remove their shoes and socks to walk through the items.

8. **Enjoy a nature walk.** Provide each child with a grocery bag and instructions to collect leaves, rocks, soil, insects, etc.

9. Provide the children with **bubbles**. To make the solution, mix 2 quarts of water, 3/4 cup liquid soap, and 1/4 cup glycerine (available from a local druggist). Dip plastic berry baskets and plastic six-pack holders into the solution. Wave to produce bubbles.

10. Show the children how to feel their **heartbeat** after a vigorous activity.

11. Observe **popcorn** popping.

12. Record **body weights and heights**.

13. Prepare **hair and eye color charts**. This information can be made into bar graphs.

14. If climate permits, **freeze water outdoors**. Return it to the class and observe the effects of heat.

15. **Introduce water absorption** by providing containers with water. Allow the children to experiment with coffee filters, paper towels, newspaper, sponges, dishcloths, waxed paper, aluminum foil, and plastic wrap.

16. Explore **magnets**. Provide magnets of assorted sizes, shapes, and strengths. With the magnets, place paper clips, nuts, bolts, aluminum foil, copper pennies, metal spoons, jar lids, feathers, etc.

17. Plan a **seed party**. Provide the children with dried beans, sunflower seeds, flower seeds, and coconuts. Observe the different sizes, shapes, textures, and flavors.

18. Make a **desk garden**. Cut carrots, turnips, and a pine-apple 1 1/2 inches from the stem. Place the stem in a shallow pan of water.

19. Create a **worm farm**. Place gravel and soil in a clear, large-mouth jar. Add worms and keep soil moist. Place lettuce, corn, or cereal on top of the soil. Tape black construction paper around the outside of the jar. Remove the paper temporarily and see the tunnels.

20. Place a **celery stalk** with leaves in a clear container of water. Add blue or red food coloring. Observe the plant's absorption of the colored water. A similar experiment can be introduced with a white carnation.

21. Make a **rainbow** with a garden hose on a sunny day. Spray water across the sun rays. The rays of the sun contain all of the colors, but the water, acting as a prism, separates the colors.

(continued)

Science Activities *(continued)*

22. Make **shadows**. In a darkened room, use a flashlight. Place a hand or object in front of the light source, making a shadow.

23. Produce **static electricity** by rubbing wool fabric over inflated balloons. (**Note:** Supervise the use of balloons.)

24. Install a **birdfeeder** outside the classroom window.

25. During large group, play the **What's Missing? game**. Provide children with a variety of small familiar items. Tell them to cover their eyes or put their heads down. Remove one item. Then tell the children to uncover. Ask them what is missing. As children gain skill, remove a second and a third item.

Sensory

The following items can be added to the sensory table:

- string, hay, sticks, and yarn to make birds' nests
- tadpoles and water
- dirt with worms
- seeds
- water and boats
- ice cubes to watch them melt

Social Studies

1. Animal Babies

Collect pictures of animals and their young. Place the adult animal pictures in one basket and the pictures of the baby animals in another basket. The children can match adult animals to their offspring.

2. Dressing for Spring

Flannel board figures with clothing items should be provided. The children can dress the figures for different kinds of spring weather.

3. Spring Clothing

Collect several pieces of spring clothing such as a jacket, hat, galoshes, and short-sleeved shirts. Add these to the dramatic play area.

Books

The following books can be used to complement this theme:

Agell, Charlotte. (1994). *Mud Makes Me Dance in the Spring*. Gardner, ME: Tilbury House.

Albee, Sarah and Carol Niklaus. (2001). *Spring Fever*. Illus. by Carol Niklaus. New York: Random House.

Baxter, Nicola. (1997). *Spring*. Illus. by Kim Woolley. Chicago: Children's Press.

Brown, Craig. (1994). *In the Spring*. New York: Greenwillow.

De Coteau Orie, Sandra. (1995). *Did You Hear Wind Sing Your Name?: An Oneida Song of Spring*. Illus. by Christopher Canyon. New York: Walker.

Emberley, Michael. (1993). *Welcome Back, Sun*. Boston: Little, Brown.

Fleming, Denise. (1993). *In the Small, Small, Pond*. New York: H. Holt.

Janovitz, Marilyn. (1996). *Can I Help?* New York: North South Books.

Kinsey-Warnock, Natalia. (1993). *When Spring Comes.* Illus. by Stacey Schuett. New York: Dutton.

Kroll, Virginia L. (1993). *Naomi Knows It's Springtime.* Illus. by Jill Kastner. Honesdale, PA: Boyds Mills Press.

Maass, Robert. (1996). *When Spring Comes.* Madison, WI: Demco Media. (Rebound)

Rau, Dana Meachen. (1995). *Robin at Hickory Street.* Illus. by Joel Snyder. Norwalk, CT: Soundprints.

Ray, Mary Lyn. (1996). *Mud.* Illus. by Lauren Stringer. Orlando, FL: Harcourt Brace.

Richardson, Judith Benet. (1996). *Old Winter.* Illus. by R. W. Alley. New York: Orchard Books.

Rockwell, Anne F. (1996). *My Spring Robin.* Madison, WI: Demco Media.

Saldain, Dawn. (2001). *Disney's Winnie the Pooh: Spring Has Sprung.* New York: Random House.

Shannon, George. (1996). *Spring: A Haiku Story.* Illus. By Malcah Zeldis. New York: Greenwillow.

Stevenson, James. (1999). *Mud Flat Spring.* New York: Greenwillow.

Walters, Catherine. (1998). *When Will It Be Spring?* New York: Dutton.

Multimedia

The following multimedia products can be used to complement this theme:

Let's Find Out About Spring [video]. (1991). Hightstown, NJ: American School Publishers.

Through the Seasons with Birds: Spring [video]. (1994). Evanston, IL: Altschul Group Corp.

Recordings and Song Titles

The following recordings can be used to complement this theme:

"April." (1984). *Singing Calendar.* Long Branch, NJ: Kimbo Educational.

"Spring Is Here." (2001). *Seasonal Songs in Motion.* Long Branch, NJ: Kimbo Educational.

"Spring Morning," "Season Song." (1995). *Piggyback Songs.* Long Branch, NJ: Kimbo Educational.

61

Weather

warm
sunny
rainy
humid

Activities

vacationing
swimming
biking
boating
water sports
baseball
camping
golfing
picnics

Summer

Holidays

Bastille Day
Memorial Day
Labor Day
Fourth of July
Father's Day
Grandparents' Day

Clothing

shorts
swimsuits
sunglasses
sundresses
lightweight fabrics

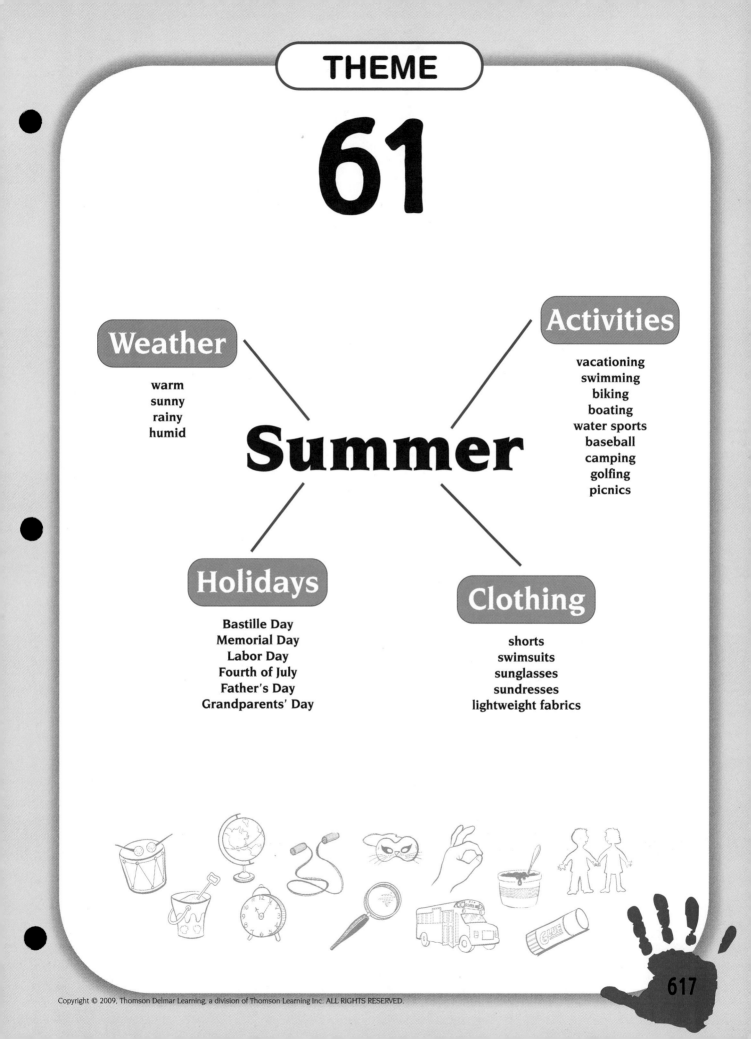

Theme Goals

Through participating in the experiences provided by this theme, the children may learn

1. Summer holidays
2. Types of weather
3. Summer clothing needs
4. Summer activities

Concepts for the Children to Learn

1. Summer is one of four seasons.
2. Summer comes after spring and before fall.
3. Summer is usually the warmest season.
4. Summer months are usually warm and sunny.
5. It can rain and become humid in the summer.
6. Lightweight clothing is worn in the summer.
7. Shorts, swimsuits, and sundresses are summer clothing.
8. Shade trees protect us from the sun during the summer.
9. Memorial Day, Father's Day, Grandparents' Day, the Fourth of July, Bastille Day, and Labor Day are all summer holidays.
10. There are many summer activities.
11. Swimming, biking, and camping are all summer activities.
12. Baseball, golfing, and picnics are also summer activities.
13. Many people take vacations during the summer.

Vocabulary

1. **beach**—a sandy place used for sunbathing and playing.
2. **hot**—a warm temperature experienced during summer months.
3. **shade**—the shadow of something.
4. **shorts**—short pants worn in warm weather.
5. **summer**—one of the four seasons. Summer comes after spring and before fall.
6. **swimming**—a water sport usually enjoyed by many people during the summer months.

Bulletin Board

The purpose of this bulletin board is to promote the identification of written numerals as well as matching sets of objects to a written numeral. Pairs of pails are constructed out of various scraps of tagboard. Using a black marker, print a different numeral on each pail. The number of pairs made and numerals used should depend on the developmental level of the children. Cut seashells out of tagboard and decorate as desired. Laminate all pieces. Attach pails to the bulletin board by stapling them along the side and bottom edges, leaving the tops of the pails open. The children should place the corresponding sets of shells in each pail.

Family Letter

Dear Families,

Summer is the favorite season of most children. As summer approaches, we will start a unit on the season. Through this unit, the children will become more aware of summer weather, activities, holidays, and clothing.

AT SCHOOL

Learning experiences planned to highlight summer concepts include:

- exploring the outside and inside of a watermelon and then eating it!
- trying on shorts, sunglasses, and sandals in the dramatic play area
- preparing fruit juice Popsicles
- eating a picnic lunch on Wednesday. We will walk to Wilson Park at 11:45. Please feel free to pack a lunch and meet us there!

AT HOME

To reinforce summer concepts at home, try the following:

- Plan a family picnic and allow your child to help plan what food and items will be needed.
- Take part in or observe any summer activity such as boating, fishing, camping, or taking a bike ride.

Have a good summer!

Summer means a lot of outdoor activities.

Arts and Crafts

1. Outdoor Painting

An easel can be placed outside. The children can choose to use the easel during outdoor playtime. If the sun is shining, encourage the children to observe how quickly the paint dries.

2. Chalk Drawings

Large pieces of chalk should be provided for the children to draw on the sidewalks outdoors. Small plastic berry baskets make handy chalk containers.

3. Foot Painting

This may be used as an outdoor activity. The children can dip their feet in a thick tempera paint mixture and make prints by stepping on large sheets of paper. Sponges and pans of soapy water should be available for cleanup.

4. Shake Painting

Tape a large piece of butcher paper on a fence or wall outdoors. Let the children dip their brushes in paint and stand 2 feet from the paper. Then show them how to shake the brush, allowing the paint to fly onto the paper.

5. Sailboats

Color Styrofoam meat trays with markers. Stick a chenille stem in the center of the tray and secure it by bending the end underneath the carton. Prepare a sail and glue to the chenille stem.

Cooking

1. Popsicles

pineapple juice
grape juice
cranapple juice
craft sticks
small paper cups

If frozen juice is used, mix according to the directions on the can. Fill the paper cups 3/4 full of juice. Place the cups in the freezer. When the juice begins to freeze, insert a craft stick in the middle of each cup. When frozen, peel away the cup and serve.

2. Watermelon Popsicles

Remove the seeds and rind from watermelon. Puree the melon in a blender. Follow the recipe for Popsicles.

3. Zippy Drink

2 ripe bananas
2 cups orange juice
2 cups orange sherbet
ice cubes
orange slices

Peel the bananas, place in a bowl, and mash with a fork. Add orange juice and sherbet and beat with a rotary beater or whisk until smooth. Pour into pitcher. Add ice cubes and orange slices.

4. Indian Yogurt Dessert

8 ounces plain yogurt
1 can sweetened condensed milk
1 can evaporated milk
4 cardamoms crushed or 1 teaspoon cardamom
1/4 teaspoon nutmeg
1 pinch cinnamon
1/2 cup raisins

Blend first 6 ingredients and pour into a baking dish. Bake at 275 degrees for 1 hour. After first 1/2 hour, add raisins by sprinkling over the top. Continue to bake for another 30 minutes. This recipe serves six children and will need to be adjusted to group size if served for snack.

5. Sand Dollar Cookies

1 cup butter
1 cup oil
1 cup sugar
2 eggs
1 teaspoon Vanilla
4 1/4 cups flour
1 teaspoon salt
1 teaspoon baking soda
1 teaspoon cream of tartar
Dried fruit bits or sunflower seeds

Make balls and press into cookies. Place 5 sunflower seeds or pieces of dried fruit in middle of cookie to resemble a sand dollar. Bake 8–10 minutes in 350-degree oven.

 # Dramatic Play

1. Juice Stand

Set up a lemonade or orange juice stand. Use real oranges and lemons. Let the children squeeze the fruit and make the drinks. The juice or lemonade can be served at snack time.

2. Ice Cream Stand

Trace and cut ice cream cones from brown construction paper. Cotton balls or small yarn pompoms can be used to represent ice cream. The addition of ice cream buckets and ice cream scoopers can make this activity more inviting during self-selected play periods.

3. Indoors or Outdoors Picnic

A blanket, picnic basket, plastic foods, purses, small cooler, paper plates, plastic silverware, napkins, and so on, can be placed in the classroom to stimulate play.

4. The Beach

In the dramatic play area, place beach blankets, lawn chairs, buckets, sunglasses, beach balls, magazines, and books. If the activity is used outdoors, a sun umbrella can be added to stimulate interest in play.

5. Camping Fun

A small freestanding tent can be set up indoors, if room permits, or outdoors. Sleeping bags can also be provided. Blocks or logs could represent a campfire.

6. Traveling by Air

Place a telephone, tickets, travel brochures, and suitcases in the dramatic play area.

Field Trips/ Resource People

1. Picnic at the Park

A picnic lunch can be prepared and eaten at a park or in the play yard.

2. Resource People

The following resource people may be invited to the classroom:

- A lifeguard can talk about water safety.
- A camp counselor can talk to the children about camping and sing some camp songs with the children.

Fingerplays

Here Is the Beehive

Here is the beehive. Where are the bees?
 (make a fist)
They're hiding away so nobody sees.
Soon they're coming creeping out of their hive,
1, 2, 3, 4, 5. Buzz-z-z-z-z-z.
 (draw fingers out of fist on each count)

Green Leaf

Here's a green leaf
 (show hand)
And here's a green leaf.
 (show other hand)
That, you see, makes two.

Here's a bud
 (cup hands together)
That makes a flower.
Watch it bloom for you!
 (open cupped hands gradually)

A Roly-Poly Caterpillar

Roly-poly caterpillar
Into a corner crept.
Spun around himself a blanket
 (spin around)

Then for a long time slept.
 (place head on folded hands)

Roly-poly caterpillar
Wakened by and by.
 (stretch)
Found himself with beautiful wings
Changed into a butterfly.
 (flutter arms like wings)

Group Time

(Games, Language)

1. Exploring a Watermelon

Serve watermelon for snack. Talk about the color of the outside, which is called the rind. Next, cut the watermelon into pieces. Give each child a piece to examine carefully. "What color is the inside? Are there seeds? Do we eat the seeds? What can we do with them?" The children can remove all the seeds from their piece of watermelon. They also may eat the watermelon. Collect all the seeds. After circle time, wash the seeds. When dry, they can be used for a collage.

2. Puppet Show

Weather permitting, bring puppets and a puppet stage outdoors and have an outdoor puppet show.

Large Muscle

1. Barefoot Walk

Check the playground to ensure that it is free of debris. Sprinkle part of the grass and sandbox with water. Go on a barefoot walk.

2. Balls

In the outdoor play yard, place a variety of large balls.

3. Catching Balloons

Balloons can be used indoors and outdoors. Close supervision is required. **Caution:** If a balloon breaks, all its pieces must be immediately discarded.

4. Parachute Play

Use a real parachute or a sheet to represent one. The children should hold onto the edges. Say a number and then have the children count and wave the parachute in the air that number of times.

5. Balloon Racket Ball

Bend coat hangers into diamond shapes. Bend the handles closed and tape them for safety. Pull nylon stockings over the diamond shapes to form swatters. The children can use the swatters to keep the balloons up in the air by hitting them. **Caution:** If a balloon breaks, all its pieces must be discarded immediately.

Math

1. Sand Numbers and Shapes

During outdoor play, informally make shapes and numbers in the sand and let children identify the shape or number.

2. Kites

Make a kite out of construction paper. Write a numeral on the kite. Children can glue the appropriate number of ties onto the string.

Music

1. "Summer Clothing"
(*Sing to the tune of "The Farmer in the Dell"*)

Oh, if you are wearing shorts,
If you are wearing shorts,
You may walk right to the door,
If you are wearing shorts.

Also include stripes, sandals, tennis shoes, flowers, a sundress, blue jeans, belt, barrettes, etc.

This song can be used during transition times to point out children's summer clothing.

2. "Summer Activities"
(*Sing to the tune of "Skip to My Lou"*)

Swim, swim, swim in a circle.
Swim, swim, swim in a circle.
Swim, swim, swim in a circle.
Swim in a circle now.

Also include jump, hop, skip, run, walk, etc.

Use this song as a transition song to introduce summer activities.

3. "Oh, The Sun Is Shining Brightly"
(*Sing to the tune of "She'll Be Coming Around the Mountain"*)

Oh, the sun is shining brightly in the sky!
Oh, the sun is shining brightly in the sky!
Oh, the sun is far away,
but shines down all through the day.
Oh, the sun is shining brightly in the sky!

Science

1. Science Table

Add the following items to the science table:

- all kinds of sunglasses with different-colored shades
- grass seeds planted in small cups of dirt for the children to water daily
- dirt and grass with magnifying glasses
- sand with scales and magnifying glasses
- pinwheels (children use their own wind to make them move)
- bubbles to blow outdoors

2. Water and Air Make Bubbles

Bubble Solution Recipe

3/4 cup liquid soap
1/4 cup glycerine (obtain at a drugstore)
2 quarts water

Place mixed solution in a shallow pan and let children place the bubble makers in the solution.

Bubble makers can be successfully made from the following:

- plastic six-pack drink holder
- straws
- bent wire with no sharp edges
- funnels

3. **Flying Kites**

On a windy day, make and fly kites.

4. **Making Rainbows**

If you have a hose available, the children can spray the hose into the sun. The rays of the sun contain all the colors mixed together. The water acts as a prism and separates the water into colors, creating a rainbow.

Sensory

1. **Sensory Table**

The following items can be added to the sensory table:

- sand with toys
- colored sand
- sand and water
- water with toy boats
- shells
- small rocks and pebbles
- grass and hay

2. **Kool-Aid Smell**

Purchase several different kinds of Kool-Aid or powdered drink mix. Pour each packet into a container. Give children a spray bottle to spray water over the powdered Kool-Aid. Ask them to smell each kind and try to identify the flavor.

Social Studies

1. **Making Floats**

To celebrate the Fourth of July, decorate trikes, wagons, and scooters with crepe paper, streamers, balloons, etc. Parade around the school or neighborhood.

2. **Summer at School**

Take pictures or slides of community summer activities. Construction workers, parades, children playing, sports activities, people swimming, library hours, picnics, band concerts, and people driving are examples. Show the slides and discuss them during group time.

3. **Summer Fun Book**

Magazines should be provided for the children to find pictures of summer activities. The pictures can be pasted on a sheet of paper. Bind the pages by stapling them together to make a book.

Books

The following books can be used to complement this theme:

Agell, Charlotte. (1994). *I Wear Long Green Hair in Summer.* Gardner, ME: Tilbury House.

Aliki. (1996). *Those Summers.* New York: HarperCollins.

Appel, Karel. (1996). *Watermelon Day.* Illus. by Dale Gottlieb. New York: Holt.

Armstrong, Debbie, Kelly Terrill, and George Starks, compilers. (2000). *Summer Dailies.* Salt Lake City, UT: Rainbow Bridge.

Baxter, Nicola. (1997). *Summer.* Illus. by Kim Woolley. Chicago: Children's Press.

Crews, Nina. (1995). *One Hot Summer Day.* New York: Greenwillow.

Fleming, Denise. (1991). *In the Tall, Tall Grass*. New York: H. Holt.

George, Lindsay Barrett. (1996). *Around the Pond: Who's Been Here?* New York: Greenwillow.

Giovanni, Nikki. (1994). *Knoxville, Tennessee*. Illus. by Larry Johnson. New York: Scholastic.

Jessup, Harley. (1999). *Grandma Summer*. New York: Viking.

Low, Alice and Roy McKie. (2001). *Summer*. Illus. by Roy McKie. New York: Beginniner Books.

Maass, Robert. (1995). *When Summer Comes*. New York: Holt.

Rylant, Cynthia. (1997). *Mr. Putter and Tabby Row the Boat*. Illus. by Arthur Howard. Orlando, FL: Harcourt Brace.

Van Leeuwen, Jean. (1997). *Touch the Sky Summer*. Illus. by Dan Andreasen. New York: Dial Books.

Wonderful World Macmillan Early Skills Program. (1985). New York: Macmillan Educational Company.

Yolen, Jane. (1993). *Jane Yolen's Songs of Summer*. Illus. by Cyd Moore. Honesdale, PA: Boyds Mills Press.

Yolen, Jane. (1995). *Before the Storm*. Illus. by Georgia Pugh. Honesdale, PA: Boyds Mills Press.

Multimedia

The following multimedia product can be used to complement this theme:

Let's Find Out About Summer [video]. Hightstown, NJ: American School Publishers.

Recordings and Song Titles

The following recordings can be used to complement this theme:

"Seasons." (2004). *Circle Time Activities*. Long Branch, NJ: Kimbo Educational.

"Summer Fun." (1990). *Musical Playtime Fun*. Long Branch, NJ: Kimbo Educational.

"Summertime, Summertime." (2000). *Bean Bag Rock and Roll*. Long Branch, NJ: Kimbo Educational.

"Sunscreen." (2001). *Seasonal Songs in Motion*. Long Branch, NJ: Kimbo Educational.

Symbols

Native Americans, harvest, turkey, cornucopia, fruits/vegetables, Pilgrims

Traditions

family celebrations giving thanks

Thanksgiving

Foods

turkey
dressing
potatoes and gravy
corn
squash
cornbread
cranberries
pumpkin pie

Giving Thanks

our health
our friends
our families

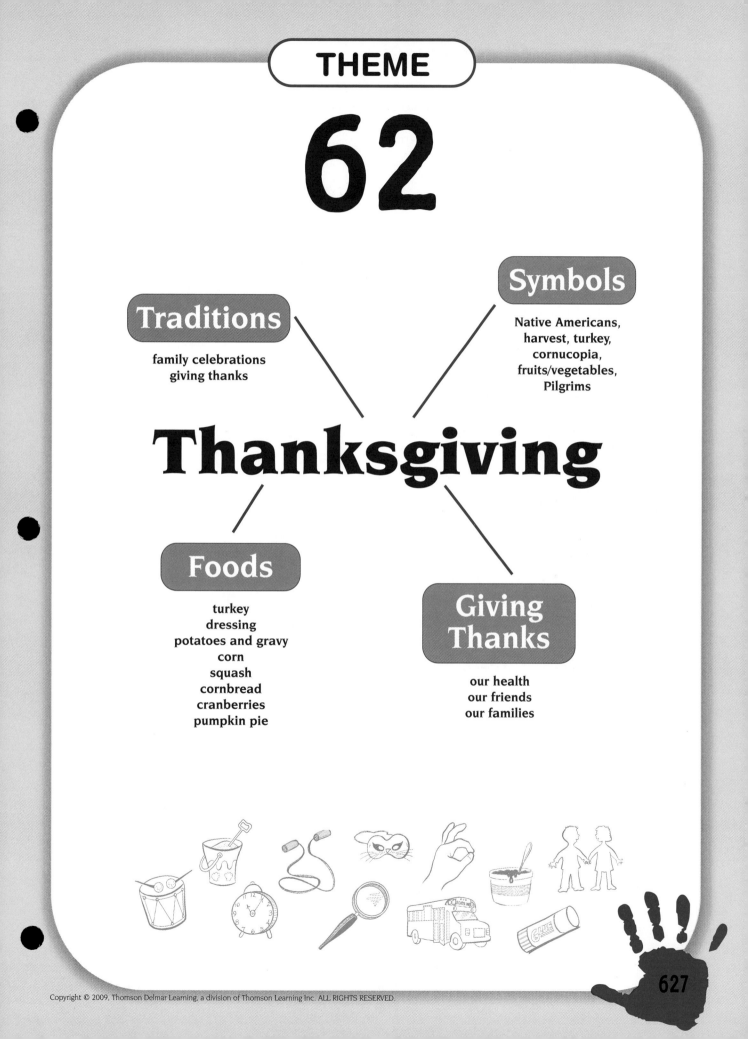

Theme Goals

Through participating in the experiences provided by this theme, the children may learn

1. The purpose of Thanksgiving
2. Thanksgiving traditions
3. Thanksgiving foods
4. Thanksgiving symbols

Concepts for the Children to Learn

1. Thanksgiving is a holiday.
2. Thanksgiving is a time for giving thanks.
3. Families and friends celebrate together on Thanksgiving.
4. Turkey, dressing, potatoes, gravy, corn, squash, cranberries, and pumpkin pie are eaten on Thanksgiving by many families.
5. A turkey, cornucopia, Pilgrims, and Native Americans are Thanksgiving symbols.

Vocabulary

1. **cornucopia**—a horn-shaped container with fruits, vegetables, and flowers.
2. **Native Americans**—natives who lived in America when the Pilgrims first arrived.
3. **Pilgrims**—early settlers who sailed to America.
4. **thankful**—expressing thanks.
5. **Thanksgiving**—a holiday in November.
6. **turkey**—large bird that is cooked for Thanksgiving.

Bulletin Board

The purpose of this bulletin board is to have the children hang the color-coded card with the printed word onto the corresponding colored feather. Construct a large turkey out of tagboard. Color each feather a different color. Hang the turkey on the bulletin board. Next, hang a pushpin in each feather. On small index cards, make a circle of each color and write the color name above it as illustrated. Use a hole punch to make a hole in each card.

THANKSGIVING

Family Letter

Dear Families,

During the month of November each year, we celebrate Thanksgiving. To coincide with this holiday at school, we will focus our curriculum on Thanksgiving. Through the activities provided, the children will develop an understanding of Thanksgiving symbols and foods. They will also become more aware of the many people and things for which we are thankful.

AT SCHOOL

Planned learning experiences related to Thanksgiving include:

- popping corn
- creating hand turkeys
- visiting a turkey farm
- exploring various types of corn with scales and magnifying glasses

AT HOME

There are many ways for you to incorporate Thanksgiving concepts at home. Talk with your child about the special ways your family celebrates Thanksgiving. Involve your child in the preparation of a traditional Thanksgiving dish. Also, emphasize things and people for which you are thankful.

REMINDER

There will be no school on Thursday, November 27 and Friday, November 28. For those of you who are traveling during the Thanksgiving weekend, drive safely!

Happy Thanksgiving from the staff!

Families like to celebrate Thanksgiving.

Arts and Crafts

1. Thanksgiving Collage

Place magazines on the art table so the children can cut out things for which they are thankful. After the pictures are cut, they can be pasted on paper to form a collage.

2. Cornmeal Play Dough

Make cornmeal play dough. Mix 2 1/2 cups flour with 1 cup cornmeal. Add 1 tablespoon oil and 1 cup water. Additional water can be added to make desired texture. The dough should have a grainy texture. Cookie cutters and rolling pins can extend this activity.

3. Popcorn Collage

Place popped popcorn and dried tempera paint into small sealable bags. Have children shake bags to color the popcorn. Have them create designs and pictures by gluing the popcorn onto the paper. You can also use unpopped colored popcorn. **Caution:** Make sure the children do not eat any of the popcorn after it has been mixed with paint.

4. Hand Turkey

Paper, crayons, or pencils are needed. Begin by instructing the children to place a hand on a piece of paper. Next, tell them to spread their fingers. If possible, have the children trace their own fingers. Otherwise, you need to trace them. The hand can be decorated to create a turkey. Eyes, a beak, and a wattle can be added to the outline of the thumb. The fingers can be colored to represent the turkey's feathers. Legs can be added below the outline of the palm.

5. Pumpkin Pie Play Dough

This smells great, so remind small children that it is not for eating.

6 1/2 cups flour
2 cups salt
9 teaspoons cream of tarter
3/4 cup vegetable oil
1 (1 1/2 ounce) container pumpkin pie spice
Orange food coloring (4 drops yellow, 2 drops red)
4 1/2 cups water

Combine all of the ingredients. Over medium heat, cook and stir until all lumps disappear.

Knead the dough on a floured surface, and add additional flour if necessary, until it is smooth. Store in an airtight container.

Cooking

1. Fu Fu—West Africa

3 or 4 yams
water
1/2 teaspoon salt
Optional: 3 tablespoons honey or sugar

Wash and peel yams and cut into 1/2-inch slices. Place slices in a large saucepan and add water to cover them. Bring to a boil over a hot plate or stove. Reduce heat, cover saucepan, and simmer for 20 to 25 minutes, until yams are soft enough to mash. Remove saucepan from stove and drain off liquid into a small bowl. Let yams cool for 15 minutes. Place yam slices in a medium-sized mixing bowl, mash with a fork, add salt, and mash again until smooth. Roll mixture into small, walnut-sized balls. If mixture is too dry, moisten it with a tablespoon of the reserved yam liquid. For sweeter Fu Fu, roll yam balls in a dish of honey or sugar. Makes 24 balls.

2. Muffins

1 egg
3/4 cup milk
1/2 cup vegetable oil
2 cups all-purpose flour
1/3 cup sugar
3 tablespoons baking powder
1 teaspoon salt

Heat oven to 400 degrees. Grease bottoms only of 12 medium muffin cups. Beat egg. Stir in milk and oil. Stir in remaining ingredients all at once, just until flour is moistened. Batter will be lumpy. Fill muffin cups about 3/4 full. Bake until golden brown about 20 minutes.

For pumpkin muffins: stir in 1/2 cup pumpkin and 1/2 cup raisins with the milk and 2 teaspoons pumpkin pie spice with the flour.

For cranberry-orange muffins: stir in 1 cup cranberry halves and 1 tablespoon grated orange peel with milk.

3. Cranberry Freeze

16-ounce can (2 cups) whole cranberry sauce
8-ounce can (1 cup) crushed pineapple, drained
1 cup sour cream or yogurt

In a medium bowl, combine all the ingredients and mix well. Pour the mixture into an 8-inch-square pan or an ice cube tray. Freeze 2 hours or until firm. To serve, cut into squares or pop out of the ice cube tray.

Dramatic Play

Shopping

Set up a grocery store in the dramatic play area. To stimulate play, provide a cash register, shopping bags, and empty food containers such as boxes, packages, and plastic bottles.

Field Trips

Turkey Farm

Visit a turkey farm. The children can observe the behavior of the turkeys as well as the food they eat.

Fingerplays

Thanksgiving Dinner

Every day we eat our dinner.
Our table is very small.
    (palms of hands close together)
There's room for father, mother, sister, brother,
    and me—that's all.
    (point to each finger)
But when it's Thanksgiving Day and the
    company comes,
You'd scarcely believe your eyes.
    (rub eyes)
For that very same reason, the table stretches
    until it is just this size!
    (stretch arms wide)

THEME 62

Gobble, Gobble

The turkey is a funny bird,
His head goes wobble wobble.
   (place hands together and go back and forth)
And all he knows is just one word,
Gobble, gobble, gobble.

The Big Turkey

The big turkey on the farm is so very proud.
   (form fist)
He spreads his tail like a fan
   (spread fingers of other hand behind fist)
And struts through the animal crowd.
   (move two fingers of fist as walking)
If you talk to him as he wobbles along
He'll answer back with a gobbling song.
"Gobble, gobble, gobble."
   (open and close hand)

Little Turkey

I saw a little turkey
   (use hands to show the little)
Standing by a tree.
It gobbled and wobbled.
   (use hands to show gobbling and wobbling)
Then it ran away from me.

Oh, turkey, turkey, turkey.
Please come back out and play!
   (use hands to motion come)
I promise I will not eat you.
On Thanksgiving Day.

Group Time

(Games, Language)

1. Turkey Chase

Have the children sit in a circle formation. The game requires two balls of different colors. Vary the size, depending on the age of the children. Generally, the younger the child, the larger the ball size. Begin by explaining that the first ball passed is the "turkey." The second ball is the "turkey farmer." The first ball should be passed from child to child around the circle. Shortly after, pass the second ball in the same direction. The game ends when the turkey farmer, the second ball, catches up to the turkey, the first ball. This game is played like Hot Potato.

2. Feast

Place several kinds of food on a plate in the middle of the circle. Tell the children to cover their eyes. Choose one child to take something from the plate to eat. The child hides one item, and the others open their eyes and try to guess which food item the child has eaten! The number of items included in this activity should be determined by the children's developmental age. It may be advisable to begin with only two food items.

3. Turkey Keeper

To play this game, you need a turkey cut from cardboard or a small plastic replica. Instruct one child to cover his or her eyes. Quietly hide the turkey in the classroom. Next, instruct the child to open his or her eyes and look for the turkey. When the child begins walking in the direction of the turkey, the rest of the children quietly provide a clue by saying, "gobble gobble." As the child approaches the turkey, the children's voices serve as a clue by becoming louder. Once the turkey is located, another child becomes the turkey keeper.

4. Drop the Wishbone

Tell the children to sit in a circle formation. Choose one child to walk around the outside of the circle and drop a wishbone behind another child. (If a real wishbone is unavailable, a wishbone can be cut from cardboard.) The child who had the wishbone dropped behind him or her must pick it up and chase the first child. If the first child is tagged before he or she runs around the circle and sits in the second child's place, he or she is "it" again. If not, the second child is "it." This is a variation of Drop the Handkerchief.

5. Turkey Waddle

Provide the children with verbal and visual clues to waddle like turkeys. The following terms may be used:

- big turkey
- little turkey
- fast turkey
- slow turkey
- tired turkey
- happy turkey
- proud turkey
- sad turkey
- hungry turkey
- full turkey

Large Muscle

Popping Corn

Pretend to be popping corn. Begin by demonstrating how to curl down on the floor, explaining that everyone is a kernel of corn. Then plug in the popcorn popper and listen to the sounds. Upon hearing popping sounds, jump up and down to the sounds.

Math

1. **Turkey Shapes**

   Give children several geometric shapes to create their own turkeys with circles, squares, and triangles. Have children identify the shapes and colors as they create their turkeys.

2. **Colored Popcorn**

   Provide the children with colored popcorn seeds. Place corresponding colored circles in the bottom of muffin tins or egg cartons. Encourage the children to sort the seeds by color.

Music

1. **"Popcorn Song"**
   (*Sing to the tune of "I'm a Little Teapot"*)

   I'm a little popcorn in a pot.
   Heat me up and watch me pop.
   When I get all fat and white, then I'm done.
   Popping corn is lots of fun.

2. **"If You're Thankful"**
   (*Sing to the tune of "If You're Happy"*)

   If you're thankful and you know it, clap your hands.
   If you're thankful and you know it, clap your hands.
   If you're thankful and you know it, then your face
      will surely show it,
   If you're thankful and you know it, clap your hands.

   Additional verses could include stamp your feet, tap your head, turn around, shout hooray, etc.

Science

1. **Corn**

   Display several types of corn on the science table. Include field corn, popcorn, and popped popcorn.

2. **Wishbone**

   Bring in a wishbone from a turkey and place it in a bottle. Pour some vinegar in the bottle to cover the wishbone. Leave the wishbone in the bottle for 24 hours. Remove it and feel it. It will feel and bend like rubber.

Sensory

The following items can be placed in the sensory area for the children to discover:

- unpopped or popped popcorn
- pinecones
- cornmeal and measuring cups

Books

The following books can be used to complement this theme:

Accorsi, William. (1992). *Friendship's First Thanksgiving*. New York: Holiday House.

Alden, Laura. (1993). *Thanksgiving*. Illus. by Susan Lexa-Senning. Chicago: Children's Press.

Bauer, Caroline Feller. (1994). *Thanksgiving; Stories and Poems*. Illus. by Nadine B. Westcott. New York: HarperCollins.

Behrens, June. (1996). *Thanksgiving Feast: The First American Holiday*. Illus. by Joann Rounds. Newport Beach, CA: York House.

Boynton, Alice B. (1996). *Priscilla Alden and the First Thanksgiving*. Morristown, NJ: Silver Burdett Press. (Pbk.)

Bruchac, Joseph. (1996). *Circle of Thanks: Native American Poems and Songs of Thanksgiving*. Illus. by Murv Jacob. Moraga, CA: Bridgewater Books.

Capote, Truman. (1996). *Thanksgiving Visitor*. Illus. by Beth Peck. New York: Knopf.

Cowley, Joy. (1996). *Gracias, the Thanksgiving Turkey*. Illus. by Joe Cepeda. New York: Scholastic.

DeRubertis, Barbara. (1996). *Thanksgiving Day: Let's Meet the Wampanoags and the Pilgrims*. Illus. by Thomas Sperling. New York: Kane Press. (Pbk.)

Dubowski, Cathy E. (1997). *Squanto: First Friend to the Pilgrims*. Illus. by Steven Peruccio. Milwaukee: Gareth Stevens.

Hallinan, P. K. (1993). *Today Is Thanksgiving*. Lake Forest, IL: Forest House.

Hintz, Martin and Kate Hintz. (1998). *Thanksgiving*. Chicago: Children's Press.

Huelin, Jodi and Kelly Asbury. (2000). *Turkey Time*. Illus. by Kelly Asbury. Los Angeles, CA: Price Stern Sloan.

Jackson, Alison et al. (1997). *I Know an Old Lady Who Swallowed a Pie*. Illus. by Byron Schachner. New York: Dutton.

MacMillan, Dianne M. (1997). *Thanksgiving Day*. Springfield, NJ: Enslow.

Pinkwater, Jill and Daniel Manus Pinkwater. (1999). *The Hoboken Chicken Emergency*. Illus. by Jill Pinkwater. New York: Alladin Paperbacks.

Ross, Katharine. (1995). *The Story of the Pilgrims*. Illus. by Carolyn Cross. New York: Random House.

Stewart, Pat. (2001). *Learning about Thanksgiving*. New York: Dover.

Tryon, Leslie. (1994). *Albert's Thanksgiving*. New York: Simon & Schuster.

Wing, Natasha and Tammie Lyon. (2001). *The Night before Thanksgiving*. Illus. by Tammie Lyon. New York: Grosset & Dunlap.

Woods, Andrew. (1996). *Young Squanto: The First Thanksgiving*. Illus. by Chris Powers. Mahwah, NJ: Troll.

Multimedia

The following multimedia products can be used to complement this theme:

Gallina, Jill. *Holiday Songs for All Occasions* [cassette]. Long Branch, NJ: Kimbo Educational.

Holiday Action Songs [cassette]. Long Branch, NJ: Kimbo Educational.

Squanto and the First Thanksgiving [video]. (1993). Rabbit Ears Productions.

Thanksgiving [video]. (1994). Schlessinger Video Productions.

Recordings and Song Titles

The following recordings can be used to complement this theme:

"Five Fat Turkeys Are We." (1996). *Where Is Thumbkin?* Long Branch, NJ: Kimbo Educational.

"Hello Mr. Turkey," "We Are Thankful." (1998). *Holiday Piggyback Songs*. Long Branch, NJ: Kimbo Educational.

"November." (1984). *Singing Calendar*. Long Branch, NJ: Kimbo Educational.

"The Pilgrims," "Come Let's All Pray Together," "The Indians," "The Strutting Turkey," "The Chick in the Yard." (n.d.) *Holiday Action Songs*. Long Branch, NJ: Kimbo Educational.

"The Turkey Wobble." (1978). *Holiday Songs for All Occasions*. Long Branch, NJ: Kimbo Educational.

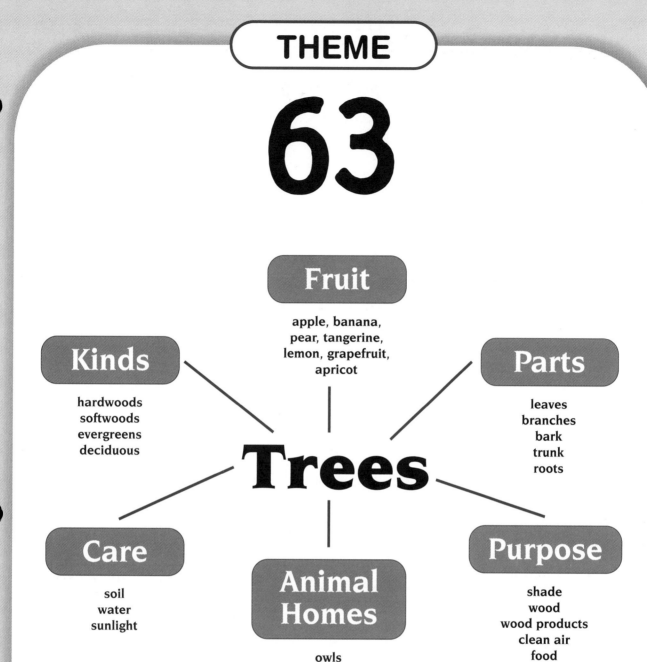

Fruit

apple, banana,
pear, tangerine,
lemon, grapefruit,
apricot

Kinds

hardwoods
softwoods
evergreens
deciduous

Parts

leaves
branches
bark
trunk
roots

Trees

Care

soil
water
sunlight

Animal Homes

owls
squirrels
birds
chipmunks

Purpose

shade
wood
wood products
clean air
food
animal homes

Theme Goals

Through participating in the experiences provided by this theme, the children may learn

1. Parts of a tree
2. Kinds of trees
3. Care of trees
4. The purpose of trees
5. Types of fruit trees
6. Animal homes in trees

Concepts for the Children to Learn

1. A tree is a large plant.
2. There are many kinds of trees, including hardwoods and softwoods.
3. A tree has many parts: buds, leaves, branches, bark, trunk, and roots.
4. The leaves of some trees are like needles.
5. The trunk is the stem of the tree and is covered with bark.
6. The roots of a tree are underground.
7. Roots help the tree stand; they also get water and nutrients from the soil.
8. Sap is a liquid that supplies food to the tree.
9. Trees need soil, water, and sunlight to grow.
10. Trees provide us with wood.
11. Many items are made from wood, such as houses, chairs, tables, some toys, doors, fences, paper, and paper products.
12. Some trees provide us with food.
13. Some fruits grow on trees.
14. Apples, bananas, pears, lemons, and grapefruits grow on trees.
15. Trees provide homes for many animals.
16. Owls, squirrels, birds, and chipmunks live in trees.
17. Trees provide us with shade to keep us cool and protect us from the sun.

Vocabulary

1. **bark**—the tough, outer covering of a tree.
2. **root**—the underground part of a plant.
3. **sap**—the fluid part of a tree.
4. **tree**—a large plant.
5. **trunk**—the main stem and largest part of a tree.

Bulletin Board

The purpose of this bulletin board is to provide numeral identification as well as matching sets of objects to numerals. To prepare the bulletin board, construct tree trunks out of brown tagboard. Print a numeral on each trunk. Next, construct treetops out of green tagboard. Draw leaves on each treetop. Trace and cut out treetop shadows from black construction paper. Using the illustration as a guide, attach the shadows and tree trunks to the bulletin board. Adhesive magnet pieces or map tacks can be used by the children to match each tree trunk to the corresponding treetop.

Family Letter

Dear Families,

Did you ever stop to think about what our world would be like without trees? Trees serve many purposes; consequently, we will explore a theme on trees beginning this week. Through the experiences provided in this curriculum unit, the children will become aware of the parts of a tree, kinds of trees, and, of course, the importance of trees.

AT SCHOOL

We will use wood to build houses, schools, chairs, tables, and several other objects. We will make paper. We will talk about foods that grow on trees. The foods served at snack time will be foods that grow on trees. Some of the week's activities will include:

- creating leaf and bark rubbings in the art area
- going on a "tree walk" and recording the number and kinds of trees we see
- cooking with foods we get from trees
- creating our own books in the writing center
- planting citrus fruit seeds and an avocado seed
- listening to stories related to trees

AT HOME

Walk around your home and find all the things that are made from wood. Which room contains the most wood items?

Polish your furniture with your child. Show him or her how to care for fine wood products.

Try preparing the following recipe with your child:

Apple Bake

Core an apple and place it in a dish with a tablespoon or two of water. Sprinkle with cinnamon and a dash of sugar, if desired. Cover and bake at 350 degrees for 20 minutes. If you prefer microwaving, cover with plastic wrap and cook on "high" for 5 minutes.

Enjoy your child!

There are many kinds of trees, with many kinds of leaves.

Arts and Crafts

1. Tree Rubbing

Use crayons or chalk to create rubbings of various tree parts. Place leaves under a single sheet of newsprint. Rub the crayon over the top of the paper until the imprint of the leaf appears. Try making additional rubbings using bark and maple seeds.

2. Twig Painting

Twigs from trees can be used as painting tools. Provide the children with trays of tempera paint of a thick consistency and construction paper to create designs. The children may also enjoy experimenting with the twig as a writing tool.

3. Pine Needle Brushes

Cut branches from a pine needle tree. Place the branches at the easel so that the children can use them as brushes to apply paint.

4. Decorating Pinecones

Collect pinecones of different sizes. Place them on the art table with trays of thick, colored tempera paints, glitter, glue, yarn, sequins, and strips of paper for the children to decorate the pinecones.

5. Sawdust Play Dough

Combine 2 cups of sawdust, 3 cups of flour, and 1 cup of salt. Add water as needed to make a pliable dough. (Sawdust can be obtained, usually at no cost, from a local lumber company.)

6. Textured Paint

Add sawdust to prepared paints for use at the art table or easel.

7. Make a Tree

Collect paper towel and toilet paper rolls. The children can paint or cover them with construction paper to resemble tree trunks. Branches and leaves can be fabricated from chenille stems and construction paper. The branches and leaves can then be attached to the trunk.

Cooking

1. Guacamole Dip

1 medium avocado
2 tablespoons chopped onion
1/4 teaspoon chili powder
1/4 teaspoon garlic salt
2 tablespoons mayonnaise or salad dressing

Peel and cut the avocado into pieces and process at medium speed in a blender. Add remaining ingredients and blend. Serve the dip with tortilla or corn chips.

2. Orange Raisin Cookies

1 cup sugar
3/4 cup softened butter or margarine
1/4 cup milk
1 teaspoon vanilla
1 egg
2 cups flour

1/2 cup raisins
2 tablespoons grated orange peel
1 teaspoon baking powder
3/4 teaspoon salt

Combine sugar, butter, milk, vanilla, and egg in a large mixing bowl. Add remaining ingredients and blend well. Drop by rounded teaspoonfuls onto ungreased cookie sheets. Bake for 9–12 minutes or until lightly browned in a 370-degree oven. Remove cookies from sheet and cool.

3. Prepare recipes that include:

apples	figs	nutmeg
apricots	grapefruit	olives
avocados	lemons	oranges
cherries	limes	peaches
cinnamon	maple syrup	pears
cloves	nectarines	prunes
dates		

Caution: Beware of the potential of children choking on fruit seeds. Remove seeds such as avocado, cherry, apricot, peach, and olive pits when using in recipes for young children. Also, check for children's allergies before food experiences.

4. **Broccoli Trees**

Use broccoli florets to resemble trees and eat as a healthy snack.

 **Dramatic Play**

1. **Construction Site**

Design a construction site in the dramatic play area. Provide props such as hard hats, blueprints, floor plans, rulers, tape measures, lumber scraps, wooden blocks, and cardboard boxes.

2. **Birds**

Trace and cut bird masks and wings from tagboard for the children to wear. Display pictures of trees and birds. Play a tape of bird songs. A variation would be to decorate a climber with green crepe paper to resemble a tree.

 **Field Trips/ Resource People**

The following sources can be contacted for more information:

- area forest industries such as paper mills and logging companies
- Department of Natural Resources
- university or county extension offices
- national, state, and local parks
- nature centers
- university departments of biology, botany, construction, forestry, and horticulture

 **Fingerplays**

The Apple Tree

Way up high in the apple tree
    (raise arms over head)
Two little apples smiled at me.
    (make fists or circles with hands)
I shook that tree as hard as I could
    (move hands as if shaking something)
Down came the apples
    (falling motion with fists)
Mmmmmmmmm—were they good!
    (rub tummy)

Orange Tree

This is the orange tree with leaves so green
    (raise arms over head, making a circle)
Here are the oranges that hang in between.
    (make fists)
When the wind blows the oranges will fall.
Here is the basket to gather them all.
    (make circle with arms in front of body)

I Am a Tall Tree

I am a tall tree.
I reach toward the sky
    (reach upward with both hands)

Where the bright stars twinkle
And white clouds float by.
   (sway arms above head)
My branches toss high
As the wild winds blow.
   (wave arms rapidly)
Now they bend forward
Loaded with snow.
   (arms out front swaying)
I like it best
When I rock birds to sleep in their nest.
   (place hands at the side of head and close eyes)

The Wind

Who has seen the wind?
Neither I nor you;
But when the leaves hang trembling,
   (hold hands downward and wiggle fingers)
The wind is passing through.

Who has seen the wind?
Neither you nor I;
But when the trees bow down their heads,
   (move head downward)
The wind is passing by.

Group Time

(Games, Language)

1. Tree Chart

On a large piece of tagboard, print the title "Things Made from Trees." During group time, present the chart and record the children's responses. Display the completed chart and refer to it throughout the theme.

2. Movement Activity—"Happy Leaves"

Cut leaves out of various colors of construction paper. During group time, give each child one leaf. When the children hear the color of their leaf in the following rhyme, they may stand up and move like leaves:

Little red leaves are glad today,
For the wind is blowing them off and away,

They are flying here, they are flying there.
Oh, little red leaves, you are everywhere.

Repeat the rhyme and insert additional color words.

Large Muscle

1. Wooden Climber

If available, set up a wooden climber on the playground or in the classroom so the children can practice their climbing skills.

2. Wooden Balance Beam

If available, set up a wooden balance beam in an open area of the classroom. Suggest ways for the children to cross the beam: walking heel to toe, walking sideways, crawling, and walking holding an object. Older children may be able to walk backward.

Math

1. Trace Walk

Record the number of trees observed on a walk. If appropriate, the trees might also be classified as "broadleaf" or "evergreen" or by the type of tree, such as maple, oak, pine, etc.

2. Sorting and Counting Activities

The following items can be collected and used for various sorting and counting activities:

- acorns
- small pinecones
- apple seeds
- citrus fruit seeds

3. Items Made from Trees

Collect items from the classroom for children to sort and then classify those made from trees as "wooden items" and others as "non-wooden items." Label and provide boxes or similar containers for the children to place the items. If appropriate, the children can count the number of items in each category and record the results.

Music

1. "Little Leaves"
(*Sing to the tune of "Ten Little Indians"*)

One little, two little, three little leaves.
Four little, five little, six little leaves.
Seven little, eight little, nine little leaves.
Ten little leaves fall down.

2. "Foods That Grow on Trees"
(*Sing to the tune of "The Farmer in the Dell"*)

Foods that grow on trees.
Foods that grow on trees.
Let's sing a song about
Foods that grow on trees.

Apples grow on trees.
Apples grow on trees.
Pick them, red and sweet.
Apples grow on trees.

Bananas grow on trees.
Bananas grow on trees.
Pick them, yellow and long.
Bananas grow on trees.

Oranges grow on trees.
Oranges grow on trees.
Pick them, sweet and juicy.
Oranges grow on trees.

Walnuts grow on trees.
Walnuts grow on trees.
Pick them, brown and crunchy.
Walnuts grow on trees.

Science

1. Weighing Items from Trees

Provide a balance scale and acorns, pinecones, or seed pods at the science table.

2. Planting Seeds

Collect and plant seeds from fruits that grow on trees such as apples and citrus fruits. Make and record predictions about when the plants will sprout.

3. Grow an Avocado Tree

Remove a seed from an avocado. Peel the brown outer covering of the seed. Poke three toothpicks into the avocado seed at equal distances from one another. Place the seed in a glass of lukewarm water with the largest end submerged. Replace the water once a week. Sprouts will appear in about three weeks. When the stem and roots are several inches long, transplant the avocado into a pot that is about 1 inch wider than the avocado.

4. Leaf Book

Collect leaves from various trees. Mount each leaf on a piece of construction paper or tagboard. Then print the name of the tree the leaf represents. Gather the pages and bind with loose-leaf rings. Place the book in the science area for the children to review.

5. Shade Versus Sun

Place an outdoor thermometer in direct sunlight and another beneath the shade of a tree. Compare results. A chart could also be made for this activity and results could be compared for several days.

6. Pinecone Bird Feeders

Collect pinecones. Attach a piece of yarn or string to the stem. Use a plastic knife to spread shortening, lard, or soft butter over the pinecone and then roll in birdseed. Hang the feeder outside.

7. Make Paper

Cut a piece of screen 7 inches × 11 inches and frame with wood. Tear construction paper or tissues into 1-inch pieces. Place the shredded paper pieces in a blender. Add enough water to cover and blend the paper into pulp. Pour the pulp into a 9-inch × 13-inch tray. Use the framed screen to pan the pulp, moving it to get an even layer of pulp. Lift the screen out of the pan in a straight, upward direction. Place the screen on a stack of newspapers. Roll with a rolling pin to squeeze out water. Lift off the newspaper and gently peel the homemade paper from the screen; allow it to dry on paper towels or newspaper.

Sensory

1. Wood Shavings

Obtain wood shavings from a local lumber company. Place them in the sensory table along with scoops and pails.

2. Pinecones

Collect pinecones of various sizes and place them in the sensory table. Small boxes, pails, and scoops can be added.

3. Acorns

Collect acorns and allow them to dry thoroughly before placing in the sensory table. Add accessories to encourage participation such as pails, small paper bags, scoops, and spoons.

Social Studies

Family Tree

Cut a tree trunk out of brown tagboard. Cut a treetop out of green tagboard. Attach the trunk and treetop to a bulletin board and display on a wall. Ask the children to bring family photographs that can be displayed on the tree.

Books

The following books can be used to complement this theme:

Aldridge, Josephine Haskell. (1993). *A Possible Tree*. Illus. by Daniel San Souci. New York: Simon & Schuster.

Arnosky, Jim. (1992). *Crinkleroot's Guide to Knowing the Trees*. New York: Simon & Schuster.

Bunting, Eve. (1993). *Someday a Tree*. Illus. by Ronald Himler. New York: Houghton Mifflin.

Burns, Diane L. (1990). *Sugaring Season: Making Maple Syrup*. Illus. by Cheryl Walsh Bellville. Minneapolis, MN: Carolrhoda Books.

Carrier, Lark. (1996). *A Tree's Tale*. New York: Dial Books.

DePalma, Mary Newell. (2005). *A Grand Old Tree*. New York: A.A. Levine Books.

Dorros, Arthur. (1997). *A Tree Is Growing*. Illus. by S. D. Schindler. New York: Scholastic.

Drawson, Blair. (1996). *Mary Margaret's Tree*. New York: Orchard Books.

Edwards, Richard. (1993). *Ten Tall Oaktrees*. Illus. by Caroline Crossland. New York: William Morrow.

Ehlert, Lois. (1991). *Red Leaf, Yellow Leaf*. Orlando, FL: Harcourt Brace.

Gackenbach, Dick. (1992). *Mighty Tree*. Orlando, FL: Harcourt Brace.

Green, Jen. (1999). *A Dead Log*. New York: Crabtree.

Hall, Zoe. (1996). *The Apple Tree*. Illus. by Shari Halpern. New York: Scholastic.

Hayes, Geoffrey. (1999). *Patrick's Christmas Tree*. New York: Random House.

Jaspersohn, William. (1996). *Timber*. Boston: Little, Brown.

Levine, Ellen. (1995). *The Tree That Would Not Die*. Illus. by Ted Rand. New York: Scholastic.

Manson, Christopher. (1993). *The Tree in the Wood: An Old Nursery Song*. New York: North South Books.

Maestro, Betsy. (1994). *Why Do Leaves Change Color?* Illus. by Loretta Krupinski. New York: HarperCollins.

Martin, Bill Jr. and Michael Archambault. (1989). *Chicka, Chicka Boom Boom*. Illus. by Lois Ehlert. New York: Simon & Schuster Books for Young Readers.

Oppenheim, Joanne. (1995). *Have You Seen Trees?* Illus. by Jean and Mou-Sien Tseng. New York: Scholastic.

Pluckrose, Henry Arthur. (1990). *Trees*. Illus. by Joy Friedman. Chicago: Children's Press.

Polacco, Patricia. (2000). *The Trees of the Dancing Goats*. New York: Alladin.

Reed-Jones, Carol. (1995). *The Tree in the Ancient Forest*. Illus. by Christopher Canyon. Nevada City, CA: Dawn.

Sanders, Scott R. (1996). *Meeting Trees*. Illus. by Robert Hynes. Washington, DC: National Geographic Society.

Suzuki, David and Yvonne Cathcart. (1998). *The Tree Suitcase*. Illus. by Yvonne Cathcart. Toronto, Ontario, Canada: Somerville House.

Tresselt, Alvin. (1992). *The Gift of the Tree*. Illus. by Henri Sorenson. New York: Lothrop, Lee & Shepard.

Ward, Helen and Wayne Anderson. (2001). *The Tin Forest*. New York: Dutton.

Zalben, Jane Breskin. (1995). *Pearl Plants a Tree*. New York: Simon & Schuster.

Zweibel, Alan. (2005). *Our Tree Named Steve*. New York: G.P. Putnam's Sons.

Multimedia

The following multimedia products can be used to complement this theme:

Bean, Norman and Sandy Bean. A *First Look at Trees* [video]. (©1992). Van Nuys, CA: AIMS Media.

Cole, Joanna. *Goes the Seed* [video]. (1995). NY: KidVision. (*Magic School Bus* series)

Cutting, Michael. *The Little Crooked Christmas Tree* [video]. (1990). Stamford, CT: ABC Video.

Tell Me Why: *Flowers, Plants and Trees* [video]. (1987). Marina del Rey, CA: Tell Me Why.

What Is a Leaf? [video]. (1991). Washington, DC: National Geographic.

Purpose

share feelings
show love

Colors

red
pink
white

Valentine's Day

Symbols

hearts
Cupid
cards
candy
arrows
flowers

Activities

parties
card giving
flowers
gifts

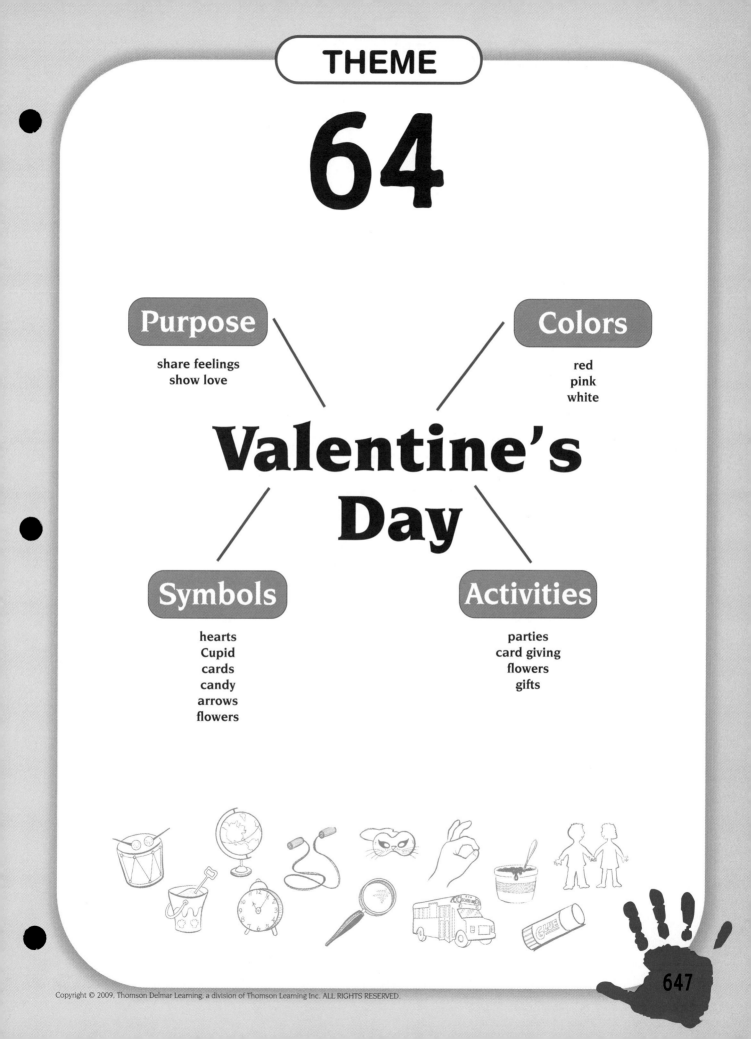

Theme Goals

Through participating in the experiences provided by this theme, the children may learn

1. Valentine's Day colors
2. Valentine's Day activities
3. Symbols of Valentine's Day
4. Purpose of Valentine's Day

Concepts for the Children to Learn

1. On Valentine's Day, we share our love with others.
2. Red, pink, and white are Valentine's Day colors.
3. Hearts, Cupids, candy, arrows, and flowers are symbols of Valentine's Day.
4. People send cards on Valentine's Day.
5. Valentine cards share our feelings and show our love.
6. Some people attend or give parties on Valentine's Day.
7. Flowers and gifts are given to special people on Valentine's Day.

Vocabulary

1. **card**—a decorative paper with a written message.
2. **Cupid**—a symbol of Valentine's Day, usually a baby boy with a bow and arrows.
3. **heart**—a symbol of love.
4. **Valentine**—a card designed for someone special.
5. **Valentine's Day**—a special day when we share our love with others

Bulletin Board

The purpose of this bulletin board is to promote numeral recognition, visual discrimination, hand-eye coordination, and problem-solving skills by having the children place the correct number of hearts into the corresponding numbered box. Using decorated boxes as illustrated, a Valentine's Day bulletin board can be created. The bottom of each box should be cut, so it can be taped shut while putting hearts in and easily opened to release the hearts. Mark each box with a numeral and a corresponding number of hearts, as illustrated. The number of numerals will depend on developmental appropriateness. Attach the boxes to the bulletin board using pushpins or staples. Next, construct many small hearts.

Family Letter

Dear Families,

Valentine's Day is a special day, so this unit celebrates Valentine's Day. It is a day when we share our positive feelings about special people. This day also provides an opportunity to talk about the importance of sharing, giving, loving, and friendship. The children will also learn the purpose, symbols, colors, and activities related to Valentine's Day.

Perhaps not all children and families celebrate this holiday, but we feel it is very important for children to learn about and respect others' beliefs. A general understanding of other cultures is also interesting and fun. However, if you wish that your child not participate in this theme, please let us know.

AT SCHOOL

Some of the activities related to Valentine's Day will include:

- having a post office in the dramatic play area to mail valentines to friends
- constructing valentine mobiles to decorate our room
- constructing a "What a Friend Is . . ." chart to hang in our room
- sending and receiving valentines
- watching the video *Valentine's Day*
- inviting special people at school, including the custodian and secretary, to a party
- listening to Valentine's stories and poems

AT HOME

Try to set aside time to have a heart-to-heart chat with your child. To develop self-esteem, talk to your child about feelings and why you are proud of him or her. Also, help your child make a valentine for a grandparent, aunt, uncle, or other person. A special note could be dictated by your child and written by you.

Have a Happy Valentine's Day!

THEME 64

Arts and Crafts

1. Easel Painting

Mix red, white, and pink paint and place at the easel.

2. Chalk Drawings

White chalk and red and pink construction paper can be used to make chalk drawings.

3. Classroom Valentine

Cut out one large paper heart. Encourage all children to decorate and sign it. The valentine can be hung in the classroom or be given to a classroom friend. The classroom friend may be the cook, custodian, center director, or principal.

4. Heart Prints

On the art table, place white paper and various heart-shaped cookie cutters. Mix pink and red tempera paint and pour into shallow pans. The children can print hearts on white construction paper using the cookie cutters as a tool and then paint them.

5. Heart Materials

The children can cut hearts out of construction paper and decorate them with lace scraps, yarn, and glitter to make original Valentine's Day cards. Precut hearts should be available for children who have not mastered the skill. For other children who have cutting skills, a heart shape can be traced on paper for them to cut.

Cooking

1. Valentine Cookies

2/3 cup shortening
1 egg
3/4 cup sugar
1 teaspoon vanilla
1 1/2 cups flour
1 1/2 teaspoons baking powder
4 teaspoons milk
1/4 teaspoon salt

Individual bags can be made to hold valentines.

Mix all of the ingredients together. If time permits, refrigerate the dough. Roll out dough. Use heart-shaped cookie cutters. Bake at 375 degrees for 12 minutes. Frost. The children can make two cookies, one for themselves, and one to give to a friend.

2. Heart-Shaped Sandwiches

1 loaf bread
heart-shaped cookie cutters
strawberry jam or jelly

Give each child one or two pieces of bread (depending on size of cutter). Cut out two heart shapes from bread. Spread on jam or jelly to make a sandwich. Eat at snack time.

3. Valentine Mints

2 8-ounce packages of cream cheese at room temperature
2 teaspoons of peppermint extract
10 drops of red food coloring
8–9 cups of powdered sugar

Combine the first three ingredients in a mixing bowl. Gradually add the powdered sugar, mixing at a low speed until well blended. Next, place the dough on a pastry cloth; keep kneading and adding additional powdered sugar until the dough is very stiff. Roll out the dough. Use a heart-shaped cookie cutter to make the candy hearts. Chill overnight to harden.

Dramatic Play

1. **Mailboxes**

Construct an individual mailbox for each child using shoeboxes, empty milk cartons, paper bags, or partitioned boxes. Print each child's name on the box or encourage the child to

Materials to Collect for the Art Center

aluminum foil	eyelets	paper dishes	spools
ball bearings	fabrics	paper doilies	stockings
barrel hoops	felt	paper napkins	sweaters
beads	felt hats	paper tissue	tacks
belts	flannel	paper towels	tape
bottles	floor covering	paper tubes	thread
bracelets	glass	paper wrapping	tiles
braiding	gourds	phonograph	tin cans
brass	hat boxes	records	tin foil
buckles	hooks	photographs	tongue depressors
burlap	inner tubes	picture frames	towels
buttons	jars	pinecones	tubes
candles	jugs	pins	twine
canvas	lacing	plastic board	wallpaper
cartons	lampshades	plastic paint	wax
cellophane	leather remnants	pocket books	window shades
chains	linoleum	reeds	wire
chalk	marbles	ribbon	wire eyelets
chamois	masonite	rings	wire hairpins
chenille stems	metal foil	rope	wire hooks
clay	mirrors	rubber bands	wire mesh
cloth	muslin	rug yarn	wire paper clips
colored pictures	nails	safety pins	wire screen
confetti	necklaces	sand	wire staples
containers	neckties	sandpaper	wooden beads
copper foil	newspaper	seashells	wooden blocks
cord	oilcloth	seeds	wooden clothespins
cornhusks	ornaments	sheepskin	wooden sticks
cornstalks	pans	shoelaces	wool
costume jewelry	paper bags	shoe polish	yarn
crayon pieces	paper boxes	snaps	zippers
crystals	paper cardboard	soap	
emery cloth	paper, corrugated	sponges	

652

THEME 64

do so. The children can sort mail, letters, and small packages into the boxes.

2. **Florist**

Plastic flowers, vases, Styrofoam pieces, tissue paper, ribbons, candy boxes, a cash register, and play money can be used to make a flower shop.

3. **Card Shop**

Stencils, paper, markers, scraps, stickers, and so forth can be provided to make a card-making shop.

Field Trips

1. **Visit a Post Office**

Visit the local post office. Valentine's Day cards made in the classroom can be mailed.

2. **Visit a Floral Shop**

Visit a flower store. Observe the different valentine arrangements. Call attention to the beautiful color of the flowers, arrangements, and containers.

Fingerplays

Five Little Valentines

Five little valentines were having a race.
The first little valentine was frilly with lace.
  (hold up one finger)
The second little valentine had a funny face.
  (hold up two fingers)
The third little valentine said, "I love you."
  (hold up three fingers)
The fourth little valentine said, "I do too."
  (hold up four fingers)
The fifth little valentine was sly as a fox.
He ran the fastest to the valentine box.
  (make five fingers run behind back)

Group Time
(Games, Language)

Valentine March

Place large fabric or paper hearts with numerals on them on the floor. Include one valentine per child. Play a marching song and encourage children to march from heart to heart. When the music stops, so do the children. Each child then tells the numeral on which he or she is standing. To make the activity developmentally appropriate for young children, use symbols. Examples might include a ball, car, truck, glass, cup, door, etc.

Large Muscle

1. **Hug Tag**

One child is "it" and tries to tag another child. Once tagged, the child is "frozen" until another child gently hugs him or her to "unfreeze" him or her.

2. **Balloon Ball**

Blow up two or three red, pink, or white balloons. Using nylon paddles made by stretching nylon pantyhose over bent coat hangers, the children can hit the balloons to each other. The object is to try to keep the balloon off the floor or ground. This activity needs to be carefully supervised. **Caution:** If a balloon breaks, all its pieces must be discarded immediately.

Math

1. **Broken Hearts**

Cut heart shapes out of red and pink tagboard. Print a numeral on one side and a number set of heart stickers or drawings on the other side. Cut the hearts in half as a puzzle. The children can match the puzzle pieces.

2. Heart Seriation

Cut various-sized hearts from pink, red, and white construction paper. The children can sequence the heart shapes from small to big or vice versa.

3. Sorting Hearts

Cut out red, white, and pink hearts of varying sizes (small, medium and large). Provide containers for the children to sort the hearts according to their size or color.

Music

1. "My Valentine"
(*Sing to the tune of* "*The Muffin Man*")

Oh, do you know my valentine,
My valentine, my valentine?
Oh, do you know my valentine?
His name is _____.

Chosen valentine then picks another child.

2. "Ten Little Valentines"
(*Sing to the tune of* "*Ten Little Indians*")

One little, two little, three little valentines.
Four little, five little, six little valentines.
Seven little, eight little, nine little valentines.
Ten little valentines here!

3. "Two Little Cupids"
(*Sing to the tune of* "*Two Little Blackbirds*")

Two little cupids sitting on a heart.
    (hold hands behind back)
One named _____. One named _____.
    (bring out one pointer for each name)
Fly away, _____. Fly away, _____.
    (place one pointer behind back for
    each name)
Come back, _____. Come back, _____.
    (bring out pointers one at a time again)
Two little cupids sitting on a heart.
    (hold up two fingers)
One named _____. One named _____.
    (wiggle each pointer separately)

For each _____ insert a child's name.

4. "Will You Be My Valentine?"

Will you be my V-A-L-E-N-T-I-N-E?
If you will, you know how very happy I will be.

(Children will try to guess who you are thinking of. The child who guesses correctly gets to choose the next person for others to guess.)

Science

1. Valentine's Day Flowers

In the science area, place various flowers and magnifying glasses. The children can observe and explore the various parts of the flowers.

2. Valentine's Day Colors

Mixing red and white tempera paint, the children can make various shades of red or pink.

Sensory

Soap

Mix dish soap, water, and red food coloring in the sensory table. Provide egg beaters for children to make bubbles.

Social Studies

1. Sorting Feelings

Cut pictures of happy and sad people out of magazines. On the outside of two boxes, draw a smiling face on one and a sad face on the other. The children can sort the pictures into the corresponding boxes.

2. Sign Language

Show the children how to say, "I love you," in sign language. They can practice with each other. When the parents arrive, the children can share with them.

I   point to self

love   cross arms over chest

you   point outward

Books

The following books can be used to complement this theme:

Bauer, Caroline Feller. (1993). *Valentine's Day: Stories and Poems.* Illus. by Blanche Sims. New York: HarperCollins.

Capucilli, Alyssa Satin and Pat Schories. (2001). *Biscuit's Valentine's Day.* Illus. by Pat Schories. New York: HarperFestival.

Carrick, Carol. (1995). *Valentine.* Illus. by Paddy Bouma. Boston: Houghton Mifflin.

Davies, Simon, Serena Feneziani, and A. J. Wood. (2000). *Pucker Up, Buttercup!* Illus. by Serena Feneziani. Brookfield, CT: Millbrook Press.

Devlin, Wende and Harry Devlin. (1991). *Cramberry Valentine.* New York: Simon & Schuster.

Hoban, Lillian. (1997). *Silly Tilly's Valentine.* New York: HarperCollins.

Hopkins, Lee Bennett. (1992). *Good Morning to You, Valentine.* Illus. by Tomie De Paola. Honesdale, PA: Boyds Mills Press.

Hurd, Thacher. (1990). *Little Mouse's Big Valentine.* New York: HarperCollins.

Inches, Alison and Alison Winfield. (2001). *Be My Valentine (Raggedy Ann and Andy).* Illus. by Alison Winfield. New York: Little Simon.

Katz, Karen. (2001). *Counting Kisses.* New York: Margaret McElderry.

London, Jonathan. (1997). *Froggy's First Kiss.* Illus. by Frank Remkiewicz. New York: Viking.

Nerlove, Miriam. (1992). *Valentine's Day.* Niles, IL: Albert Whitman.

Sabuda, Robert. (1992). *Saint Valentine.* New York: Simon & Schuster.

Shannon, George. (1995). *Heart to Heart.* Boston: Houghton Mifflin.

Sharmat, Marjorie Weinman. (1994). *Nate the Great and the Mushy Valentine.* Illus. by Marc Simont. New York: Dell.

Watson, Wendy. (1993). *A Valentine for You.* Boston: Houghton Mifflin. (Pbk.)

Multimedia

The following multimedia products can be used to complement this theme:

Coleman, Warren. *Valentine's Day* [video]. (1993). United Learning.

Valentine's Day [video]. (1994). Schlessinger Video Productions.

Recordings and Song Titles

The following recordings can be used to complement this theme:

"February." (1984). *Singing Calendar.* Long Branch, NJ: Kimbo Educational.

"On Valentine's Day." (1978). *Holiday Songs for All Occasions.* Long Branch, NJ: Kimbo Educational.

"Special Friend," "Lacey Hearts," "I'm a Valentine for You," "H-E-A-R-T." (1998). *Holiday Piggyback Songs.* Long Branch, NJ: Kimbo Educational.

65

Purposes

drinking
cleaning
energy
recreation

Forms

liquid
solid
vapor

Water

Uses

soak
dilute
spray
sprinkle
flood
moisten

Reaction

mix
absorb

Sports

swimming
fishing
skiing
boating
skating

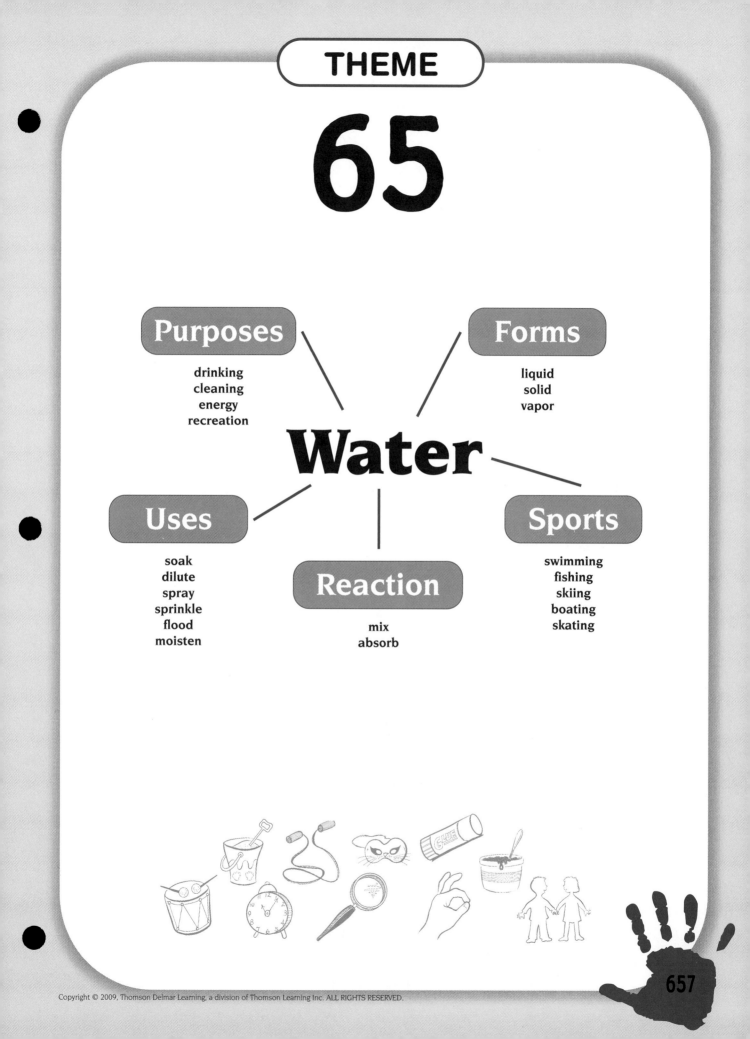

Theme Goals

Through participating in the experiences provided by this theme, the children may learn

1. Uses of water
2. Forms of water
3. Water sports
4. Purposes of water
5. Reactions of water

Concepts for the Children to Learn

1. Water is clear and colorless.
2. Water is tasteless and has no smell.
3. All living things need water.
4. Water takes three forms: liquid, vapor, and solid.
5. Ice is a solid form of water.
6. Steam is a vapor form of water.
7. Some things mix with water, others do not.
8. Some things absorb water, others do not.
9. Some things float when placed on water.
10. Some animals and plants live in bodies of water.
11. Animals, people, and plants need water.
12. Water can be used to soak, dilute, spray, sprinkle, flood, and moisten.
13. There are many water sports.
14. Swimming, fishing, skiing, and boating are water sports.

Vocabulary

1. **cloud**—water droplets formed in the sky.
2. **float**—to rest on top of a liquid.
3. **freeze**—hardened liquid.
4. **ice**—water that has frozen.
5. **lake**—a large body of water surrounded by land.
6. **liquid**—substance that can be poured.
7. **melt**—to change from a solid to a liquid.
8. **ocean**—body of salt water.
9. **rain**—water that falls from clouds.
10. **sink**—to drop to the bottom of a liquid.
11. **snow**—water that freezes and falls from the sky.
12. **swimming**—moving yourself through water with body movements.
13. **water**—a clear, colorless, odorless, tasteless liquid.

Bulletin Board

The purpose of this bulletin board is to develop visual discrimination, problem-solving, and matching skills. Construct and color four or five pictures of swimming and water-related items from tagboard. Laminate. Trace these pictures on black construction paper to make shadows. Staple the shadows on the bulletin board. Encourage the children to hang the colored picture over the correct shadow.

Family Letter

Dear Families,

Did you know all living things have something in common? They all need water to survive. Water will be the theme that we explore with our next curriculum unit. The children will become familiar with the purpose, forms, uses, and reaction of water, as well as sports that require water.

AT SCHOOL

Some of the learning experiences planned to include water concepts are

- placing celery stalks in colored water to observe plants' use of water
- experimenting with objects that sink or float when placed in water
- washing doll clothes in the sensory table
- observing ice with magnifying glasses and watching it change from a solid to a liquid
- watching a video titled *Let's Explore Water*
- looking at books about water

AT HOME

There are many ways that you can reinforce water concepts at home. Try any of the following with your child:

- Allow your child to assist in washing dishes after a meal. This will give your child a sense of responsibility and will develop self-esteem.
- Provide water and large paintbrushes for your child to paint sidewalks and fences outdoors.
- Bubbles made with an eggbeater in a container of soapy water are fun for children of all ages!

Enjoy your child!

Arts and Crafts

1. Liquid Painting

Paper, straws, thin tempera, and spoons can be placed on the art table. Spoon a small amount of paint onto paper. Using a straw, blow paint on the paper to make a design.

2. Bubble Prints

Collect the following materials: 1/2 cup water, 1/2 cup liquid soap, food coloring, straws, and light-colored construction paper. Mix together the water, soap, and food coloring in a container. Place a straw in the solution and blow until the bubbles reach about 1 inch to 2 inches over the top of the container. Remove the straw and place a piece of paper over the jar. The bubbles will pop as they touch the paper, leaving a print.

3. Wet Chalk Drawings

Chalk, paper, and water in a shallow pan are needed for this activity. The children can dip chalk into water and then draw on paper. Encourage children to note the difference between wet and dry chalk.

Cooking

1. Fruit Ice

Mix 1/2 can partially thawed juice concentrate with 2 cups of crushed ice in the blender. Liquify until the contents become snowy. Serve immediately.

2. Floating Cake—Philippines

2 cups sweet rice flour
1 cup water
1/2 to 3/4 cup sugar
1/2 cup toasted sesame seeds, hulled
1 cup grated coconut

Mix rice flour and water. Form into 10 to 20 small balls. Flatten each ball into a round or elongated shape and drop into 8 to 10 cups boiling water. As each cake floats to the surface, remove from

A water table can be used for science activities.

water with a slotted spoon. Roll in grated coconut and coat with sugar and sesame seeds. Adult supervision is required. Makes four servings.

Dramatic Play

1. Firefighter

Place hoses, hats, coats, and boots in the dramatic play area.

2. Doll Baths

Fill the dramatic play sink with water. Children can wash dishes or give dolls baths.

3. The Beach

Provide towels, sunglasses, umbrellas, pails, shovels, and beach toys for the children to use indoors or outdoors.

4. Canoeing

Bring a canoe into the classroom or onto the play yard. Provide paddles and life vests for the children to wear.

Fingerplays

Five Little Ducks

Five little ducks
   (hold up five fingers)
Swimming in the lake.
   (make swimming motions)
The first duck said,
   (hold up one finger)
"Watch the waves I make."
   (make waves motions)
The second duck said,
   (hold up two fingers)
"Swimming is such fun."
   (smile)
The third duck said,
   (hold up three fingers)
"I'd rather sit in the sun."
   (turn face to sun)
The fourth duck said,
   (hold up four fingers)
"Let's swim away."
   (swimming motions)
The fifth duck said,
   (hold up five fingers)
"Oh, let's stay."
Then along came a motorboat.
With a Pop! Pop! Pop!
   (clap three times)
And five little ducks
Swam away from the spot.
   (put five fingers behind back)

Swimming

I can dive.
   (make diving motion with hands)
I can swim.
   (swimming motion)
I can float.
   (hands outstretched with head back)
I can fetch.
But dog paddle
   (paddle like dog)
Is the stroke I do best.

Five Little Fishes

Five little fishes swimming in a pond.
   (wiggle five fingers)

The first one said, "I'm tired," as he yawned.
   (yawn)
The second one said, "Well, let's take a nap."
   (put hands together on side of face)
The third one said, "Put on your sleeping cap."
   (pretend to pull on hat)
The fourth one said, "Wake up! Don't sleep."
   (shake finger)
The fifth one said, "Let's swim where it's deep."
   (point down and say with a low voice)
So, the five little fishes swam away.
   (wiggle fingers and put behind back)
But they came back the very next day.
   (wiggle fingers out front again)

The Rain

I sit before the window now
   (sit down)
And look out at the rain.
   (shade eyes and look around)
It means no play outside today,
   (shake head)
So inside I remain.
   (rest chin on fist; look sad)

I watch the water dribble down
   (look up and down)
As it turns the brown grass green.
And after a while I start to smile
At Nature's washing machine.
   (smile and lean back)

Group Time
(Games, Language)

Water Fun

Discuss the various recreational uses of water. Included may be swimming, boating, ice fishing, ice skating, fishing, and canoeing. Also discuss water safety issues, such as wearing a life vest. Encourage the children to name their favorite water activities. Prepare a chart using each child's name and favorite water activity, along with a small picture of that activity. Display in the room.

Large Muscle

Catch Me

Children form a circle with one child in the middle. While walking in a circle they chant:

_____ over the water.
_____ over the sea.
_____ caught a tunafish.
But he can't catch me!

(Insert child's name.)

On "me," all the children stoop quickly. If the child in the middle touches another child, the fish, before he or she stoops, that child is it. Likewise, he or she now goes into the middle. This game is for older children.

Math

1. Measuring

Assorted measuring cups in a variety of sizes can be added to the sensory table or sandbox.

2. Clipping Raindrops

Cut raindrops in a variety of sizes from construction paper. Tie a small string to the bottom of two chair legs and have the children use clothespins to clip the raindrops in order from smallest to largest. (The children will need to sit on the floor for this activity).

3. Drops of Water

Count the number of drops of water you can put into a marker cap before it overflows. (Be sure to cover the table with a towel.) Invite the children to guess how many drops it will hold before it overflows.

4. Sliding Drops

Cover a piece of cardboard with aluminum foil and prop up one end. Color water and begin to drop water on the top of the board with an eyedropper. Count how many drops it takes before the water begins to "slide" down the ramp.

5. Counting Raindrops

Place large, blue beads into a bucket. Provide a sand shovel for the children to scoop out the "raindrops" and count how many they have. Type or write a rain poem and glue it to the bucket so the children can say it as they scoop out the raindrops. (Rain, Rain, Go Away.)

Music

1. "Raindrops"
(*Sing to the tune of* "*London Bridge*")

Raindrops falling from the sky,
From the sky, from the sky.
Raindrops falling from the sky
On my umbrella.

2. "Raindrops Falling"
(*Tune:* "*Twinkle, Twinkle*")

I see raindrops falling down.
Falling down upon the ground.
See them falling in the air.
See them falling everywhere.
I see raindrops falling down.
Falling down upon the ground.

Science

1. Painting Sidewalks

On a sunny day, allow children to paint sidewalks with water. To do this, provide various paintbrushes and buckets of water. Call attention to the water evaporation.

2. Measuring Rainfall

During spring, place a bucket outside with a plastic ruler set vertically by securing to the bottom. Check the height of the water after each rainfall. With older children, make a chart to record rainfall.

3. Testing Volume

Containers that hold the same amounts of liquid are needed. Try to include containers that are tall, skinny, short, and flat. Ask the children, "Do they hold the same amount?" Encourage them to experiment by pouring liquids from one container to another.

4. Freezing Water

Freeze a container of water. Periodically, observe the changes. In colder climates, the water can be frozen outdoors. The addition of food coloring may add interest.

5. Musical Scale

Make unique musical tone jars by pouring various levels of water into glass bottles or jars. Color each bottle of water differently. Provide the children with spoons, encouraging them to experiment with sounds by tapping each bottle. **Caution:** Supervise this activity carefully.

6. Plants Use Water

Place celery stalks in colored water. Observe how water is absorbed in their veins.

7. Chase the Pepper

Collect the following materials: water, pepper, shallow pan, piece of soap, and sugar. Fill the pan with water and shake the pepper on the water. Take a piece of wet soap and dip it into the water. What happens? (The pepper moves away from the soapy water to the clear water.) The surface of water pulls, and on soapy water the pull is weak. On clear water, it is strong and pulls the pepper. Now take some sugar and shake it into the soapy water. What happens? Sugar gives the surface a stronger pull.

8. Warm Water/Cold Water

Collect the following materials: a small aquarium, a small bottle, food coloring, and water. First fill the aquarium with very warm water. Fill the small bottle with colored cold water. Put your thumb on the mouth of the bottle. Hold the bottle sideways and lower it into the warm water. Take away your thumb. What happens? (The cold water sinks to the bottom of the tank. The cold water is heavier than the warm water.) Now fill the tank with cold

water and fill the small bottle with colored warm water. What do you predict will happen when you repeat the procedure?

9. Wave Machine

Collect the following materials: mineral oil, water, food coloring, and a transparent jar. Fill the jar 1/2 to 2/3 full with water. Add a few drops of food coloring. Add mineral oil to completely fill the jar. Secure the lid on the jar. Tilt the jar slowly from side to side to make waves. Notice that the oil and water have separate layers and do not stay mixed after the jar is shaken.

10. Water and Vinegar Fun

Collect the following materials: two small plastic jars with lids, water, and white vinegar. Pour water into one jar and an equal amount of vinegar into the other jar. Replace caps. Let the children explore the jars of liquids and discuss the similarities, and then let the children smell each jar.

11. Color Mixing

Mix water and food coloring to make a variety of colors. Place a different color of water in a separate place on a muffin tin. Give children an eyedropper and an empty muffin tin to experiment with mixing the colors of water to make a new color.

Sensory

1. Colored Ice

Fill the sensory table with colored ice cubes for the children to explore.

2. Sink and Float

Fill the sensory table with water. Provide the children with a variety of items that will sink and float. Let them experiment. A chart may be prepared listing items that sink and float.

3. Boating

Fill the water table. Let the children add blue food coloring. Provide a variety of boats for them to play with.

Water Play and Sensory Experiences

Sensory experiences are especially appealing to young children. They delight in feeling, listening, smelling, tasting, and seeing. They also love to manipulate objects by pulling, placing, pouring, tipping, shoving, as well as dipping. As they interact, they learn new concepts and solutions to old problems. When accompanied by other children, these experiences lead to cooperative, social interactions. As a result, the child's egocentricity is reduced, allowing him or her to become less self-centered.

Containers

Begin planning sensory experiences by choosing an appropriate container. Remember that it should be large enough so that several children may participate at any given time. If you select a dishpan, due to its size, you may want to use several. Other containers that may be used include a commercially made sensory/water table, baby bathtub, wash tub, pail, wading pool, sink, or bathtub.

Things to Add to Water

A variety of substances can be added to water to make it more inviting. Food coloring is one example. Start by individually choosing and adding one primary color. Later soaps can be added. These may be in liquid or flake form. Baking soda, cornstarch, and salt will affect the feel of the water. Baby and vegetable oil may leave a residue on the child's hand. Extracts add

another dimension. Lemon, pine oil, peppermint, anise, and orange all provide a variety for the child. On the other hand, ice cubes allow the child to experience an extreme touch.

Tools and Utensils

A wide variety of household tools can be used in the water play table. Measuring cups, small pitchers, small pots and pans, and film canisters can all be used for pouring. Scoops, spoons, turkey basters, small squeeze bottles, and funnels can be used for transferring the liquid from one container to another. Pipes, rubber hoses, sponges, wire whisks, and eggbeaters all can be used for observing water in motion. Plastic toys, corks, spools, strainers, boots, and so forth also encourage exploration.

Other Sensory Experiences

There are wide varieties of other materials that can be used in the sensory table. Natural materials such as sand, gravel, rocks, grain, mud, wood chips, clay, corn, and birdseed can be used. Children also enjoy having minnows and worms in the table. They delight in visually tracking the minnow and worm movement. As they attempt to pick them up, eye-hand coordination skills are practiced. Styrofoam pieces and shavings are attractive materials that can lend variety.

A strange mixture called goop is a fun material to play with. To

prepare goop, empty 1 box of cornstarch into a dishpan or similar container. Sprinkle a few drops of food coloring on the cornstarch. Add small amounts of water (about 1/2 cup) at a time and mix with a spoon or with fingers. (This is a unique sensory experience!) The mixture feels hard when you touch it on the surface, yet melts in your hands when you pick some up! (This will keep for up to 1 week if kept covered when not in use. You will probably need to add water the next time you use it.)

Silly putty is just as easy to prepare as goop. This mixture is prepared by combining 1 part of liquid starch, 2 parts of white glue, and dry tempera paint for color. Begin by measuring the liquid starch first, as it will prevent the glue from sticking to the measuring cup. Mix with a spoon, adding single tablespoons of liquid starch to get the right consistency. Next, knead with hands. Store in an airtight container (such as a zipper-seal bag) in the refrigerator. You will be thrilled to find that it will keep for several weeks.

Enjoy yourself with the children, but always change the sensory experiences on a daily basis. In doing so, you stimulate the child's curiosity as well as provide a meaningful curriculum.

For health purposes, children should be encouraged to wash their hands after sensory play.

4. Moving Water

Provide the children with a variety of materials that move water. Include the following:

- sponges
- basters
- eye droppers
- squeeze bottles
- empty film canisters
- funnels
- pitchers
- plastic tubing
- measuring cups

5. Making Rain

Punch or cut out holes (vary the size and number) in the bottoms of containers (non-dairy whipped topping, yogurt, etc.). Place in sensory table with water and encourage children to scoop water into them and compare the amount of "rain" coming from each container.

Books

The following books can be used to complement this theme:

Arnold, Tedd. (1995). *No More Water in the Tub*. New York: Dial Books.

Asch, Frank. (1995). *Water*. San Diego, CA: Gulliver Books.

Baker, Sanna A. (1996). *Mississippi Going North*. Illus. by Bill Farnsworth. Niles, IL: Albert Whitman.

Base, Graeme. (2001). *The Water Hole*. New York: Harry N. Abrams.

Bittinger, Gayle. (1993). *Exploring Water and the Ocean*. Illus. by Gary Mohrmann. Alderwood Manor, WA: Warren.

Calhoun, Mary. (1997). *Flood*. Illus. by Erick Ingraham. New York: William Morrow.

Carlstrom, Nancy W. (1997). *Raven and River*. Illus. Jon Van Zyle. Boston: Little, Brown.

Cast, C. Vance. (1992). *Where Does Water Come From?* Illus. by Sue Wilkinson. Hauppauge, NY: Barron's Educational Series.

Challoner, Jack. (1996). *Wet and Dry*. Austin, TX: Raintree/Steck Vaughn.

Cowley, Joy and Fuller, Elizabeth. (2005). *Mrs. Wishy-Washy's Splishy-Sploshy*. New York: Philomel.

Dunphy, Madeline. (1998). *Here Is the Coral Reef*. Illus. by Tom Leonard. New York: Hyperion.

Fleming, Denise. (1993). *In the Small, Small Pond*. New York: Holt.

Fowler, Allan. (1995). *The Earth Is Mostly Ocean*. Chicago: Children's Press.

Fowler, Allan. (1997). *It Could Still Be a Lake*. Chicago: Children's Press.

Fowler, Allan. (1997). *Life in a Pond*. Chicago: Children's Press.

Gibbons, Gail. (1998). *Marshes and Swamps*. New York: Holiday House.

Gibson, Gary. (1995). *Making Things Float and Sink*. Illus. by Tony Kenyon. Brookfield, CT: Millbrook Press.

Gordon, Maria. (1995). *Float and Sink*. Illus. by Mike Gordon. Austin, TX: Raintree/Steck Vaughn.

Graham, Joan B. (1994). *Splish Splash*. Illus. By Steven M. Scott. New York: Ticknor and Fields.

Jarnow, Jill (Editor), and Elizabeth Hathon. (2000). *Splish! Splash! (All Aboard Books)*. Illus. by Elizabeth Hathon. New York: Grosset & Dunlap.

Jackson, Shelley. (1998). *The Old Woman and the Wave*. New York: Dorling Kindersley.

Kingsley, Charles and Jesse Willcox Smith. (1999). *The Water Babies (Book of Wonder)*. Illus. by Jesse Willcox Smith. London: Sebastian Kelly.

Llewellyn, Claire. (1995). *Rivers and Seas (Why Do We Have . . .)*. Illus. by Anthony Lewis. Hauppauge, NY: Barron's Educational Series.

Locker, Thomas. (1997). *Water Dance*. Orlando, FL: Harcourt Brace.

The Magic School Bus Wet All Over: A Book about the Water Cycle. (1996). New York: Scholastic.

Marshall, Janet Perry. (1998). *Banana Moon*. New York: Greenwillow.

Marzollo, Jean. (1996). *I Am Water*. Illus. by Judith Moffatt. New York: Scholastic. (Pbk.)

Murata, Michinori. (1993). *Water and Light; Looking Through Lenses*. Minneapolis, MN: Lerner.

Nielsen, Shelly and Julie Berg. (1993). *I Love Water*. Minneapolis, MN: Abda Daughters.

O'Mara, Anna. (1996). *Oceans*. Chicago: Children's Press.

Rauzon, Mark J. and Cynthia O. Bix. (1994). *Water, Water Everywhere*. San Francisco: Sierra Club.

Smee, Nicola. (1999). *Freddie Learns to Swim* (*Little Barron's Toddler Books*). Hauppage, NY: Barron Juveniles.

Speed, Toby. (1998). *Water Voices*. Illus. by Julie Downing. New York: G. P. Putnam.

Multimedia

The following multimedia products can be used to complement this theme:

Circle of Water [video]. (1995). Washington, DC: National Geographic.

Deep Sea Dive [video]. Washington, DC: National Geographic. Available from Kimbo Educational, Long Branch, NJ.

Oceans (*Science for You* series) [video]. (1992). Agency for Instructional Technology.

Let's Explore Water (*Science Is Elementary* series) [video]. (1993). Agency for Instructional Technology.

Wet and Wild: Under the Sea with OWL/TV [video]. (1994). Toronto: Children's Group, Inc.: BMG KIDZ.

What's in the Sea?: Songs about Marine Life and Ocean Ecology [cassette]. Long Branch, NJ: Kimbo Educational.

Recordings and Song Titles

The following recordings can be used to complement this theme:

"Friends in the Water," "Water Pump," "Splish Splash," "Float or Sink," "Dry Them Off." (1999). *Sift and Splash*. Long Branch, NJ: Kimbo Educational.

"Splish, Splash." (2000). *Bean Bag Rock and Roll*. Long Branch, NJ: Kimbo Educational.

What's in the Sea? (1993). Long Branch, NJ: Kimbo Educational.

Purpose

movement
transportation

Materials

rubber
plastic
wood
metal

Wheels

Sizes

small
medium
large

Uses

bicycles	carts
motorcycles	chairs
trikes	trailers
scooters	roller skates
cars	in-line skates
trucks	pulleys
buses	gears
planes	trains
unicycles	wheelchairs
wagons	pizza cutters
wheelbarrows	

Theme Goals

Through participating in the experiences provided by this theme, the children may learn

1. Sizes of wheels
2. Purposes of wheels
3. Materials used to make wheels
4. Uses of wheels

Concepts for the Children to Learn

1. Wheels are round.
2. Wheels can help us do our work.
3. Wheels help move people and things.
4. Cars, trains, trucks, buses, motorcycles, tricycles, and bicycles have wheels.
5. Wagons, wheelbarrows, carts, and trailers have wheels.
6. Some chairs have wheels.
7. Wheelchairs have wheels.
8. In-line skates and roller skates have wheels.
9. Pulleys and gears have wheels.
10. Wheels can be different sizes.
11. A unicycle is a one-wheeled cycle.
12. Wheels can be made of rubber, plastic, metal, or wood.

Vocabulary

1. **bicycle**—a two-wheeled vehicle.
2. **pulley**—a wheel that can be connected to a rope to move things.
3. **unicycle**—a vehicle with one wheel.
4. **wheel**—a form in the shape of a circle.
5. **wheelbarrow**—a vehicle used for moving small loads.
6. **wheelchair**—a chair on wheels.

Bulletin Board

The purpose of this bulletin board is to encourage the development of mathematical concepts. To prepare the bulletin board, draw pictures of a unicycle, bicycle, and tricycle on tagboard. Color, cut out, and post on the bulletin board. Next, construct the numerals 1, 2, and 3 out of tagboard. Hang the numerals on the top of the bulletin board. A corresponding set of dots can be placed below the numeral to assist children in counting. A string can be attached to each numeral by using a stapler. Have the children wind the string around a pushpin connected to the vehicle with the corresponding number of wheels.

WHEELS

Family Letter

Dear Families,

Wheels! Wheelchairs, wheelbarrows, tricycle wheels, bicycle wheels, and car wheels! Children see wheels almost every day of their lives. We are studying wheels. Through participating in the activities planned for this unit, the children will discover the purpose, uses, and sizes of wheels. They will also learn what materials are used to make wheels.

AT SCHOOL

We have many learning experiences planned for this unit, including:

- examining tire rubber at the science table
- painting with toy cars at the art table
- singing a song called "The Wheels on the Bus"

AT HOME

There are many ways that you can incorporate this unit in your home. Try any of these activities with your child:

- Walk around the neighborhood with your child. To develop observation skills, look for different wheels.
- Count the wheels on the different types of transportation. Semi-trucks have several, whereas a unicycle has only one.
- Recite the following fingerplay with your child to foster language and memory skills. We will learn it this week.

Wheels

Wheels big.
    (form big circles with fingers)
Wheels small.
    (form little circles with fingers)
Count them one by one.
Turning as they're pedaled
    (make pedaling motion with hands)
In the springtime sun!
1-2-3-4-5.
    (count fingers)

Enjoy your child!

Arts and Crafts

1. Car Painting

Provide small plastic cars, tempera paint, and paper. Place the tempera paint in a shallow pan. Car tracks can be created by dipping the car wheels in the tempera paint and rolling them across paper.

2. Wheel Collage

Provide magazines for the children to cut out pictures of wheels. The pictures can be pasted or glued onto sheets of paper.

3. Tracing Wheels

Provide sewing tracing wheels, pizza cutters, pastry wheels, carbon paper, and construction paper. The children can place the carbon paper on the construction paper and run one of the wheels over the carbon paper, making a design on the construction paper.

Children need real-life objects to associate them with their world.

Cooking

1. Cheese Wheels

Using a cookie cutter, cut cheese slices into circle shapes to represent wheels. Top the pieces with raisins or serve with crackers.

2. Pizza Rounds

Provide each child with a half an English muffin. Demonstrate how to spread pizza sauce on a muffin. Next, lay a few skinny strips of cheese across the top, making the cheese look like wheel spokes. Now let the children prepare their own. Bake in an oven at 350 degrees for 5 to 7 minutes or until the cheese melts. Cool slightly before serving.

Dramatic Play

1. Car Mechanic

Outdoors, place various wheels, tires, tools, overalls, and broken trikes. The children can experiment using tools.

2. Floats

Paper, tape, crepe paper, and balloons can be provided to decorate the wheels on the tricycles, wagons, and scooters.

Field Trips/ Resource People

Group Time

(Games, Language)

1. Cycle Shop

Visit a cycle shop. Observe the different sizes of wheels that are in the shop. Talk about the different materials that wheels can be made of.

2. Machine Shop

Visit a machine parts shop. Look at the different gears, pulleys, and wheels. Discuss their sizes, shapes, and possible uses.

3. Resource People

- cycle specialist
- mechanic
- machinist
- person who uses a wheelchair

Fingerplays

My Bicycle

One wheel, two wheels on the ground.
   (revolve hand in forward circle to form
   each wheel)
My feet make the pedals go round and round.
   (move feet in pedaling motion)
Handlebars help me steer so straight
   (pretend to steer bicycle)
Down the sidewalk, through the gate.

Wheels

Wheels big.
   (form big circles with fingers)
Wheels small.
   (form little circles with fingers)
Count them one by one
Turning as they're pedaled
   (make pedaling motion with hands)
In the springtime sun.
1-2-3-4-5.
   (count fingers)

Who Took the Wheel?

(Variation of "Who Took the Cookie from the Cookie Jar")

Who took the wheel off the car today?
_____ took the wheel off the car today.
  (fill _____ with a child's name)
Chosen child says, "Who me?"
Class responds, "Yes, you!"
Chosen child says, "Couldn't be!"
Class responds, "Well then, who?"

The chant continues as the chosen child picks another child. Continue repeating the chant using the children's names.

Large Muscle

1. Wheelbarrow

Place wheelbarrows in the play yard. Provide materials of varying weights for the children to move.

2. Wagons

Place wagons in the playground. Provide objects for the children to move.

Math

1. Wheel Sequence

Cut out various-sized circles from tagboard to represent wheels. The children can sequence the wheels from largest to smallest.

2. How Many Wheels?

Pictures of a unicycle, bicycle, tricycle, cars, scooters, and trucks of all sizes can be cut from magazines and catalogs. Mount the pictures on tagboard. Laminate. Sort the pictures according to the number of wheels.

Music

"The Wheels on the Bus"

The wheels on the bus go round and round,
Round and round, round and round.
The wheels on the bus go round and round
All through the town.

Other verses:

The wipers on the bus go swish, swish, swish.
The doors on the bus go open and shut.
The horn on the bus goes beep, beep, beep.
The driver on the bus says, "Move on back."
The people on the bus go up and down.

Science

1. **Tire Rubber**

   Cut off several pieces of rubber from old bicycle tires. Provide magnifying glasses. Encourage the children to observe similarities and differences.

2. **Pulley**

   Set up a pulley. Provide the children with blocks so they may lift a heavy load with the help of a wheel. Supervision may be necessary for this activity.

3. **Gears**

   Collect gears and place on the science table. The children can experiment, observing how the gears move. When appropriate, discuss their similar and different characteristics.

4. **Wheels and Axles**

   Set out a few wheels and axles. Discuss how they work as a lever to help lift heavy loads. Encourage the children to think about where they might find wheels and axles.

Sensory

Sensory Table

Add the following items to the sensory table:

- sand with wheel molds
- rubber from tires
- gravel and small toy cars and trucks

Social Studies

Wheelchair

Borrow a wheelchair (child-sized if possible) from a local hospital or pharmacy. During group time, discuss how wheelchairs help some people to move. Children can experience moving and pushing a wheelchair.

Books

The following books can be used to complement this theme:

Butler, Daphne. (1995). *What Happens When Wheels Turn?* Austin, TX: Raintree/Steck Vaughn.

Catiglione, Janice. (1999). *The Musical Wheels on the Bus.* Brooklyn, NY: Straight Edge.

Cowen-Fletcher, Jane. (1993). *Mamma Zooms.* New York: Scholastic.

Dahl, Michael. (1996). *Wheels and Axles.* Chicago: Children's Press.

Hayward, Linda et al. (1996). *Wheels.* New York: Random House.

Healey, Tim. (1993). *The Story of the Wheel.* Illus. by Nicholas Hewetson. Mahwah, NJ: Troll.

Hindley, Judy. (1994). *The Wheeling and Whirling-Around Book*. Illus. by Margaret Chamberlain. Cambridge, MA: Candlewick Press.

Kalman, Bobbie and Petrina Gentile. (1997). *Big Truck, Big Wheels*. New York: Crabtree.

Kovalski, Maryann. (1990). *The Wheels on the Bus*. Boston: Little, Brown. (Pbk.)

Marzollo, Jean and Walter Wick (Photography). (1998). *I Spy Little Wheels (I Spy)*. New York: Scholastic.

Mellentin, Kath. (1998). *The Wheels on the Bus*. Illus. by Jenny Tulip. Reistertown, MD: Flying Frog.

Miller, Margaret. (1997). *Wheels Go Round*. New York: Simon & Schuster.

Nikola-Lisa, W. (1994). *Wheels Go Round*. Illus. by Jane Conteh-Morgan. New York: Doubleday.

Raffi. (1998). *Wheels on the Bus*. New York: Crown Books.

Regan, Dana. (1996). *The Wheels on the Bus*. New York: Scholastic.

Rockwell, Anne. (2006). *Big Wheels*. New York: Walker & Co.

Rotner, Shelley. (1995). *Wheels Around*. Boston: Houghton Mifflin.

Rush, Caroline. (1997). *Wheels and Cogs*. Illus. by Mike Gordon. Austin, TX: Raintree/Steck Vaughn.

Scarry, Richard. (1997). *Richard Scarry's Pop-Up Wheels*. New York: Simon & Schuster.

Zelinsky, Paul O. (1990). *The Wheels on the Bus: With Pictures That Move*. New York: Dutton.

Multimedia

The following multimedia product can be used to complement this theme:

Fisher, Diana. *Wee Sing Wheels Sounds and Songs* [cassette]. (1996). New York: G. P. Putnam.

Recordings and Song Titles

The following recordings can be used to complement this theme:

Cars, Trucks, and Trains. (1997). Long Branch, NJ: Kimbo Educational.

"The Wheels on the Bus." (1997). *Six Little Ducks*. Long Branch, NJ: Kimbo Educational.

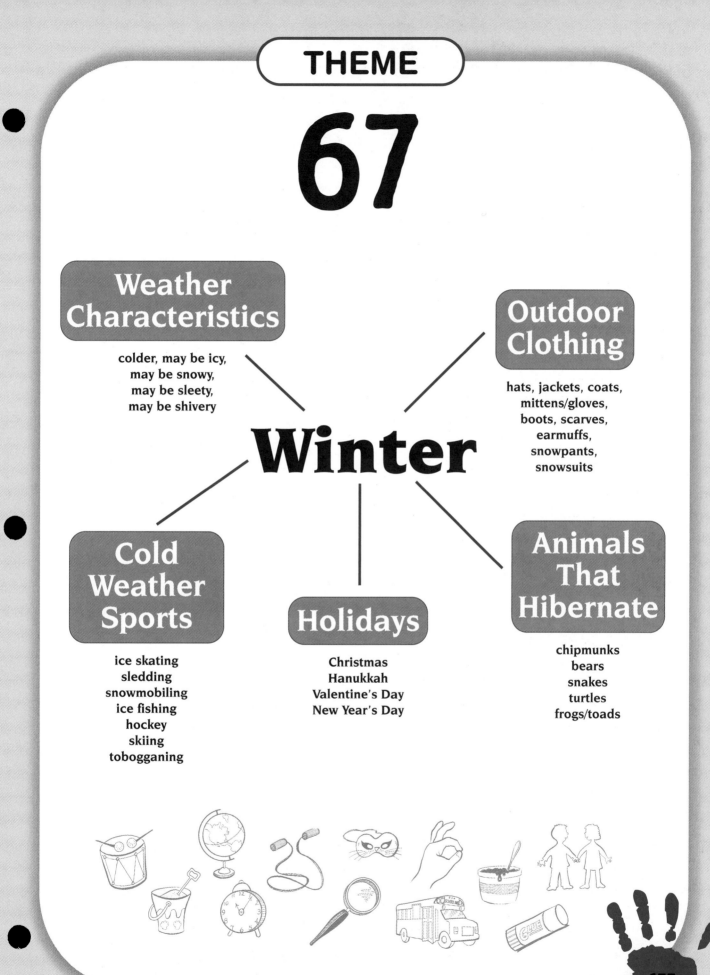

THEME

67

Weather Characteristics

colder, may be icy,
may be snowy,
may be sleety,
may be shivery

Outdoor Clothing

hats, jackets, coats,
mittens/gloves,
boots, scarves,
earmuffs,
snowpants,
snowsuits

Winter

Cold Weather Sports

ice skating
sledding
snowmobiling
ice fishing
hockey
skiing
tobogganing

Holidays

Christmas
Hanukkah
Valentine's Day
New Year's Day

Animals That Hibernate

chipmunks
bears
snakes
turtles
frogs/toads

Theme Goals

Through participating in the experiences provided by this theme, the children may learn

1. Winter holidays
2. Characteristics of winter weather
3. Winter sports
4. Winter outdoor clothing
5. Hibernating animals

Concepts for the Children to Learn

1. Winter is one of the four seasons.
2. Winter is usually the coldest season.
3. Winter comes after fall and before spring.
4. Ice, snow, and sleet are found during the winter in some places.
5. People wear warmer clothes in the winter.
6. Hats, jackets, coats, mittens, boots, scarves, earmuffs, snowpants, and snowsuits are worn during the winter.
7. Some animals hibernate in the winter.
8. Chipmunks, bears, snakes, turtles, and toads hibernate for the winter.
9. Trees may lose their leaves in the winter.
10. Lakes, ponds, and water may freeze in the winter.
11. Sledding, skiing, tobogganing, snowmobiling, ice fishing, hockey, and ice skating are winter sports in colder areas.
12. To remove snow, people shovel and plow.
13. December, January, and February are winter months.
14. Christmas, Hanukkah, Valentine's Day, and Christmas are winter holidays.

Vocabulary

1. **boots**—clothing worn on feet to keep them dry and warm.
2. **cold**—not warm.
3. **frost**—very small ice pieces.
4. **hibernate**—to sleep during the winter.
5. **ice**—frozen water.
6. **icicle**—a hanging piece of frozen ice.
7. **shiver**—to shake from cold or fear.
8. **ski**—a runner that moves over snow and ice.
9. **sled**—transportation for moving over snow and ice.
10. **sleet**—mixture of rain and snow.
11. **snow**—frozen particles of water that fall to the ground.
12. **snowperson**—snow shaped in the form of a person.
13. **temperature**—how hot or cold something is.
14. **winter**—one of four seasons. Winter comes after fall and before spring.

Bulletin Board

The purpose of this bulletin board is to provide the children with an opportunity to match patterns. Construct several pairs of mittens out of tagboard, each with a different pattern, as illustrated. Laminate the pieces. On the bulletin board, string one of each pair of the mittens through a rope or clothesline (one or two rows). Tie enough clothespins in place by putting the line through the wire spring of the clothespins so children can attach the matching mittens. (Tie a clothespin beside each mitten.) Children can match the mittens by hanging the second next to the first with a clothespin. This is mainly a small motor exercise for older children, unless you make the mittens with patterns or colors that are similar. More detailed patterns will increase the difficulty of the task.

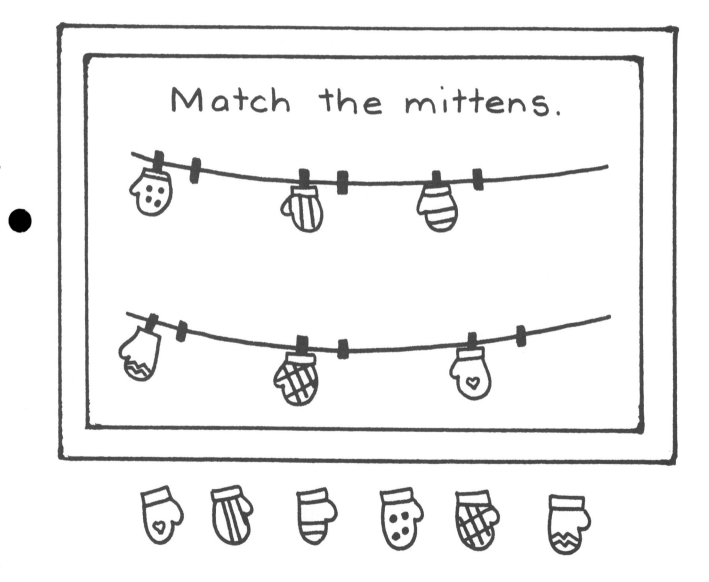

Match the mittens.

Family Letter

Dear Families,

We are beginning a curriculum unit on winter. The children will learn about the coldest season by taking a look at winter clothing, weather characteristics that occur during this season indoors and outdoors, and winter sports. Throughout the unit, the children will develop an awareness of winter activities. The children will also learn to identify the winter holidays and animals that hibernate during the winter.

AT SCHOOL

Some of our learning experiences related to winter include:

- creating cottonball snowpeople
- sorting mittens by size, shape, and color
- enjoying stories about winter
- setting up an ice-skating rink in the dramatic play area
- experiencing snow and ice in the sensory table

AT HOME [DELETE THIS PARAGRAPH IF SNOW IS UNAVAILABLE.]

To experience winter at home, try this activity—snow in the bathtub! Bring in some snow from outside and place in your bathtub. Also place some measuring cups, spoons, and scoops in the bathtub and let your child use mittens to play in the snow. In addition, a spray bottle filled with colored water (made with food coloring) will allow your child to make colorful sculptures. This is sure to keep your children busy and will develop an awareness of the senses.

Happy Winter from all of us!

Children wear warmer clothes in the winter but can still enjoy playing outdoors.

Arts and Crafts

1. Whipped Soap Painting

Mix 1 cup Ivory Snow flakes with 1/2 cup warm water in bowl. The children can beat with a hand eggbeater until mixture is fluffy. Apply mixture to dark construction paper with various tools (toothbrushes, rollers, tongue depressors, brushes, etc.). To create variety, food coloring can be added to paint mixture.

2. Cotton Ball Snowman

Cut a snowperson figure from dark construction paper. Provide the children with cotton balls and glue. They can decorate the snowperson by gluing on cotton balls.

3. Snowflakes

Cut different-sized squares out of white construction paper. Fold the squares in half, and then in half again. Demonstrate and encourage the children to cut and open their own designs. The snowflakes can be hung in the entry or classroom for decoration.

4. Ice Cube Art

Place a craft stick in each ice compartment of a tray and fill with water. Freeze. Sprinkle dry tempera paint on paper. To make their own design, the children can move an ice cube on the paper.

5. Frosted Pictures

Mix 1 part Epsom salts with 1 part boiling water. Let the mixture cool. Encourage the children to make a crayon design on paper. The mixture can be brushed over the picture. Observe how the crystals form as the mixture dries.

6. Winter Shape Printing

Cut sponges into various winter shapes such as boots, snowmen, mittens, snowflakes, fir trees, and stars. The children can use the sponges as a tool to print on different pieces of colored construction paper.

7. Easel Ideas

Feature white paint at the easel for snow pictures on colored paper. Or, cut easel paper into winter shapes: snowmen, hats, mittens, scarves, snowflakes, etc.

8. **Snow Drawings**

White chalk and dark construction paper can be placed in the art area.

9. **Snow Painting**

Using old spray bottles filled with colored water, let the children make pictures in the snow outside. This activity is limited to areas where snow is available.

Cooking

1. **Banana Snowpeople**

2 cups raisins
2 bananas
shredded coconut

Chop the bananas and raisins in a blender. Place them in a mixing bowl. Refrigerate until mixture is cool enough to be handled. Roll the mixture into balls and into shredded coconut. Stack three balls and fasten with toothpicks. **Caution:** Close supervision is needed when using toothpicks with young children.

2. **Hot Chocolate**

Add warm water or milk to instant hot chocolate and mix. Heat as needed.

3. **Snow Cones**

Crush ice and spoon into small paper cups. Pour a fruit juice over the ice. Serve.

Dramatic Play

1. **Ice-Skating Palace**

Make a masking tape border on a carpeted floor. Give each child two pieces of waxed paper. Show children how to fasten waxed paper to their ankles with rubber bands. Play instrumental music and encourage the children to skate around on the carpeted floor.

2. **Dress Up**

If available, put outdoor winter clothing such as coats, boots, hats, mittens, scarves, and ear-muffs in the dramatic play area of the classroom with a large mirror. The children may enjoy trying on a variety of clothing items.

Field Trips/ Resource People

1. Visit an ice-skating rink. Observe the ice and watch how it is cleaned.

2. Visit a sledding hill. Bring sleds and go sledding.

3. Invite a snowplow operator to school to talk to the children. After a snowfall, the children can observe the plowing.

4. Take the children to a grocery store and view the freezer area. Also, observe a refrigerated delivery truck.

Fingerplays

Five Little Snowpeople

Five little snowpeople standing in the door.
This one melted and then there were four.
   (hold up all five fingers, put down thumb)
Four little snowpeople underneath a tree.
This one melted and then there were three.
   (put down pointer finger)
Three little snowpeople with hats and mittens too.
This one melted and then there were two.
   (put down middle finger)
Two little snowpeople outside in the sun.
This one melted and then there was one.
   (put down ring finger)
One little snowperson trying hard to run.
He melted too, and then there were none.
   (put down pinky)

Variations:

- Make five little snowpeople finger puppets and remove them one by one.
- Make five stick puppets for children to hold and sit down one by one at appropriate times during fingerplay.

Making a Snowperson

Roll it, roll it, get a pile of snow.
  (make rolling motions with hands)
Rolling, rolling, rolling, rolling, rolling here we go.
Pat it, pat it, face it to the south.
  (patting motion)
Now my little snowperson's done, eyes
  and nose and mouth.
  (point to eyes, nose, and mouth)

Zippers

Three little zippers on my snowsuit,
  (hold up three fingers)
Fasten up as snug as snug can be
It's a very easy thing as you can see
Just zip, zip, zip!
  (do three zipping motions)
I work the zippers on my snowsuit.
Zippers really do save time for me
I can fasten them myself with one, two, three.
Just zip, zip, zip!
  (do three zipping motions)

The Snowperson and the Bunny

A chubby little snowperson
  (make a fist)
Had a carrot nose.
  (poke thumb out)
Along came a bunny
And what do you suppose?
  (other hand, make rabbit ears)
That hungry little bunny
Looking for his lunch
  (bunny hops around)
Ate that snowperson's carrot nose.
  (bunny nibbles at thumb)
Crunch, crunch, crunch.

Build a Snowperson

First you make a snowball,
  (rolling motion)
Big and fat and round.
  (extend arms in large circle)

Then you roll the snowball,
  (rolling motion)
All along the ground.
Then you build the snowperson
One-two-three!
  (place three pretend balls on top of each other)
Then you have a snowperson,
Don't you see?
  (point to eyes)
Then the sun shines all around and
Melts the snowperson to the ground.
  (drop to the ground in a melting motion)

Group Time

(Games, Language)

1. Who Has the Mitten?

Ask the children to sit in a circle. One child should sit in the middle. Make a very small mitten out of felt or construction paper. Tell the children to pass the mitten around the circle. All the children should imitate the passing actions even if they do not have the mitten in hand. When the verse starts, the child in the middle tries to guess who has the mitten. Chant the following verse while passing a mitten.

I pass the mitten from me to you to you,
I pass the mitten and that is what I do.

2. Hat Chart

Prepare a hat chart by listing all the types and colors of hats worn by the children in the classroom.

Large Muscle

1. Freeze

Play music and have the children walk around in a circle. When the music stops, the children freeze by standing still in a stooped position. Vary the activity by substituting other actions such as hopping, skipping, galloping, sliding, etc.

2. Snowperson

During outdoor play, make a snowperson. Decorate with radish eyes, carrot nose, scarf, hat, and holding a stick. Other novel accessories can be substituted by using the children's ideas.

3. Snowpeople

After a snowfall, have the children lie down in the snow and move their arms and legs to make shapes.

4. Snowball Target

Because children love throwing snowballs, set up a target outside for children to throw snowballs.

5. Shovel

Provide child-sized shovels for the children to help shovel a walk.

6. Balance

Make various tracks in the snow, such as a straight line, a zig-zag line, a circle, square, triangle, and rectangle.

Math

1. Shape Sequence

Cut three different-sized white circles from construction paper for each child to make a snowperson. Which is the largest? Smallest? How many do you have? What shape? Have children sequence the circles from largest to smallest and smallest to largest.

2. Winter Dominoes

Trace and cut 30 squares out of white tagboard. Section each square into four spaces diagonally. In each of the four spaces, draw different winter objects or stick on winter stickers. The children can match the pictures by playing dominoes.

3. Dot to Dot

Make a dot-to-dot snowperson. The children connect the dots in numerical order. You can also make dot-to-dot patterns of other winter objects such as hats, snowflakes, mittens, etc. This activity requires numeral recognition and order, so it is restricted to the school-aged child.

4. Puzzles

Mount winter pictures or posters on tagboard sheets. Cut into pieces. The number of pieces cut will depend on the children's developmental age. Place in the small manipulative area of the classroom for use during self-selected activity periods.

Music

1. "Snowperson"
(Sing to the tune of "Twinkle, Twinkle, Little Star")

Snowperson, snowperson, where did you go?
I built you yesterday out of snow.
I built you high and I built you fat.
I put on eyes and a nose and a hat.
Now you're gone all melted away
But it's sunny outside so I'll go and play.

2. "Winter Clothes"
(Sing to the tune of "Did You Ever See a Lassie?")

Children put your coats on, your coats on, your
   coats on.
Children put your coats on, one, two, and three.
   (hats, boots, mittens, etc.)

3. "Mitten Song"

Thumbs in the thumb place, fingers all together.
This is the song we sing in mitten weather.

Science

1. Weather Doll

Make a felt weather doll. Encourage the children to dress and undress the doll according to the weather.

2. Make Frost

Changes in temperature cause dew. When dew freezes it is called frost. Materials needed are a tin can with no lid, rock salt, and crushed ice. Measure and pour 2 cups of crushed ice and 1/2 cup rock salt in a can. Stir rapidly. Let the mixture sit for 30 minutes. After 30 minutes, the outside of the can will have dew on it. Wait longer and the dew will change to frost. To hasten the process, place in a freezer.

3. Make Birdfeeders

Roll pinecones in a shortening, lard, or softened butter and cornmeal mixture and then in birdseed. Attach a string to the pinecones and hang them outside. Encourage the children to check the birdfeeders frequently.

A birdfeeder can also be prepared from suet. To do this, wrap suet in a netting. Gather the edges up and tie together with a long string. Another method is to place suet in a net citrus fruit bag.

4. Snow

Bring a large container of snow into the classroom. After it is melted, add colored water and place the container outdoors. When frozen, bring a colored block of ice back into the classroom and watch it melt.

5. Examine Snowflakes

Examine snowflakes with a magnifying glass. Each is unique. For classrooms located in warmer climates, make a snow-like substance by crushing ice.

6. Catching Snowflakes

Cover a piece of cardboard with dark felt. Place the cardboard piece in the freezer. Go outside and let snowflakes land on the board. Snowflakes will last longer for examination.

7. Coloring Snow

Provide children with spray bottles containing colored water, preferably red, yellow, and blue. Allow them to spray the snow and mix colors.

8. Thermometers

Experiment with a thermometer. Begin introducing the concept by observing and discussing what happens when the thermometer is placed in a bowl of warm water and a bowl of cold water. Demonstrate to the children and encourage them to experiment under supervision during the self-selected activity period.

9. Signs and Sounds of Winter

On a winter walk in colder climates, have the children watch and listen for signs and sounds of winter. The signs of winter are: (1) weather: cold, ice, daylight is shorter, and darkness is earlier; (2) plants: all but evergreen trees are bare; and (3) people: we wear warmer clothes, we play inside more, we shovel snow, we play in the snow. Some of the sounds of winter are: boots crunching, rain splashing, wind howling, etc. (Adapt this activity to the signs of winter in your climate.)

Sensory

The following items can be placed in the sensory table:

- snow and ice (plain or colored with drops of food coloring)
- cottonballs with measuring/balancing scale
- pinecones
- ice cubes (colored or plain)
- snow and magnifying glasses

Social Studies

1. Travel

Discuss ways people travel in winter, such as sled, toboggan, snowmobile, snowshoes, skis, etc.

2. Winter Happenings

Display pictures of different winter happenings, for example, sports, clothing, snow, and so forth, around the room at the children's eye level.

3. Winter Book

Encourage the children to make a book about winter. Do one page a day. The following titles could be used:

- What I Wear in Winter
- What I Like to Do Outside in Winter
- What I like to Do Inside in Winter
- My Favorite Food During Winter
- My Favorite Thing About Winter

(This activity may be more appropriate for the school-aged child.)

4. Winter Clothing Match

Draw a large paper figure of a boy and of a girl. Design and cut winter clothing to fit each figure. The children can dress the figures for outdoor play.

Books

The following books can be used to complement this theme:

Agell, Charlotte. (1994). I *Slide Into the White of Winter*. Gardner, ME: Tilbury House.

Allue, Joseph M., M. E. Sole, N. C. Canals, and M. P. Pons. (2001). *100 Games for Winter*. Illus. by Joseph M. Allue, M. E. Sole, and M. P. Pons. Hauppage, NY: Barron Juveniles.

Bancroft, Henrietta and Richard G. Van Gelder. (1996). *Animals in Winter*. Newly illus. by Helen K. Davie. New York: HarperCollins.

Barasch, Lynne. (1993). A *Winter Walk*. New York: Tickor and Fields.

Berger, Melvin and Gilda Berger. (1995). *What Do Animals Do In Winter?* Illus. by Susan Harrison. Nashville, TN: Hambleton-Hill.

Bracken, Carolyn. (2001). *Bear in the Big Blue House: Bear's Winter Wonderland*. New York: Random House.

Capucilli, Alyssa Satin. (1995). *Peekaboo Bunny: Friend in the Snow*. Illus. by Mary Melcher. New York: Scholastic. (Peek-a-book.)

Carlstrom, Nancy White. (1993). *How Does the Wind Walk?* New York: Macmillan.

Chapman, Cheryl. (1994). *Snow on Snow on Snow*. Illus. by Synthia Saint James. New York: Dial Books.

Dunphy, Madeleine. (1993). *Here Is the Arctic Winter*. Illus. by Alan James Robinson. New York: Hyperion.

Ehlert, Lois. (1996). *Snowballs*. Orlando, FL: Harcourt Brace.

Evans, Lezlie. (1997). *Snow Dance*. Illus. by Cynthia Jabar. Boston: Houghton Mifflin.

Fain, Moria. (1996). *Snow Day*. New York: Walker.

Fleming, Denise. (2005). *The First Day of Winter*. New York: Henry Holt.

Fleming, Denise. (1996). *Time to Sleep*. New York: Henry Holt.

Galbraith, Kathryn Osebold. (1992). *Look! Snow!* Illus. by Nina Montezinos. New York: Simon & Schuster.

Gammell, Stephen. (1997). *Is That You, Winter?* Orlando, FL: Harcourt Brace.

George, Jean Craighead. (1993). *Dear Rebecca, Winter Is Here*. Illus. by Loretta Krupinski. New York: HarperCollins.

George, Lindsay Barrett. (1995). *In the Snow: Who's Been Here?* New York: Greenwillow.

Hiscock, Bruce. (1995). *When Will It Snow?* New York: Simon & Schuster.

Howard, Kim. (1994). *In Wintertime*. New York: Lothrop, Lee & Shepard.

Inches, Alison, David B. Levy, Traci Paige Johnson, and T. Kessler. (2000). *Blue's Snowy Day*. Illus. by David B. Levy. New York: Simon Spotlight.

Joosse, Barbara M. (1995). *Snow Day!* Illus. by Jennifer Plecas. Boston: Houghton Mifflin.

Lee, Huy-Voun. (1995). *In the Snow*. New York: H. Holt.

Lenski, Lois. (2000). *I Like Winter*. New York: Random House.

Lerner, Carol. (1994). *Backyard Birds of Winter*. New York: William Morrow.

London, Jonathan. (1992). *Froggy Gets Dressed*. Illus. by Frank Remkiewicz. New York: Viking.

Maass, Robert. (1993). *When Winter Comes*. New York: H. Holt.

Richardson, Judith Benet. (1996). *Old Winter*. Illus. by R. W. Alley. New York: Orchard Books.

Ryder, Joanne. (1997). *Winter White*. Illus. by Carol Lacey. New York: William Morrow.

Rylant, Cynthia. (2007). *Snow*. Illus. by Lauren Stringer. Orlando, FL: Harcourt.

Simon, Seymour. (1994). *Winter Across America*. New York: Hyperion Books.

Stoeke, Janet Morgan. (1994). *A Hat for Minerva Louise*. New York: Dutton.

Willard, Nancy. (1996). *A Starlit Somersault Downhill*. Illus. by Jerry Pinkney. Boston: Little, Brown. (Pbk.)

Multimedia

The following multimedia products can be used to complement this theme:

Keats, Ezra Jack. *The Snowy Day* [cassette, book]. Long Branch,NJ: Kimbo Records.

Let's Find Out About Winter [video]. (1991). American School Publishers.

Piggyback Songs: Singable Poems Set to Favorite Tunes [compact disc]. (1995). Includes 21 songs/poems for Fall/Winter. Long Branch,NJ: Kimbo Records.

Snowplows at Work [video]. (1994). Bill Aaron Productions.

Where Do Animals Go in Winter? [video]. (1995). Washinton, DC: National Geographic.

Recordings and Song Titles

The following recordings can be used to complement this theme:

"Jingle Bells." (1996). *Where Is Thumbkin?* Long Branch, NJ: Kimbo Educational.

"Sing a Song of Winter," "Snowflakes Falling from the Sky." (1991). *Piggyback Songs*. Long Branch, NJ: Kimbo Educational.

"Snow Fun." (1988). *Preschool Action Time*. Long Branch, NJ: Kimbo Educational.

68

Worms

Purpose

fishing bait
tunnels in soil

Earthworm enemies

birds
lizards
frogs
toads
turtles
moles
shrews

Places

soil/underground
oceans
ponds

Sizes

small
medium
large

Foods

dirt
rotting leaves
plants

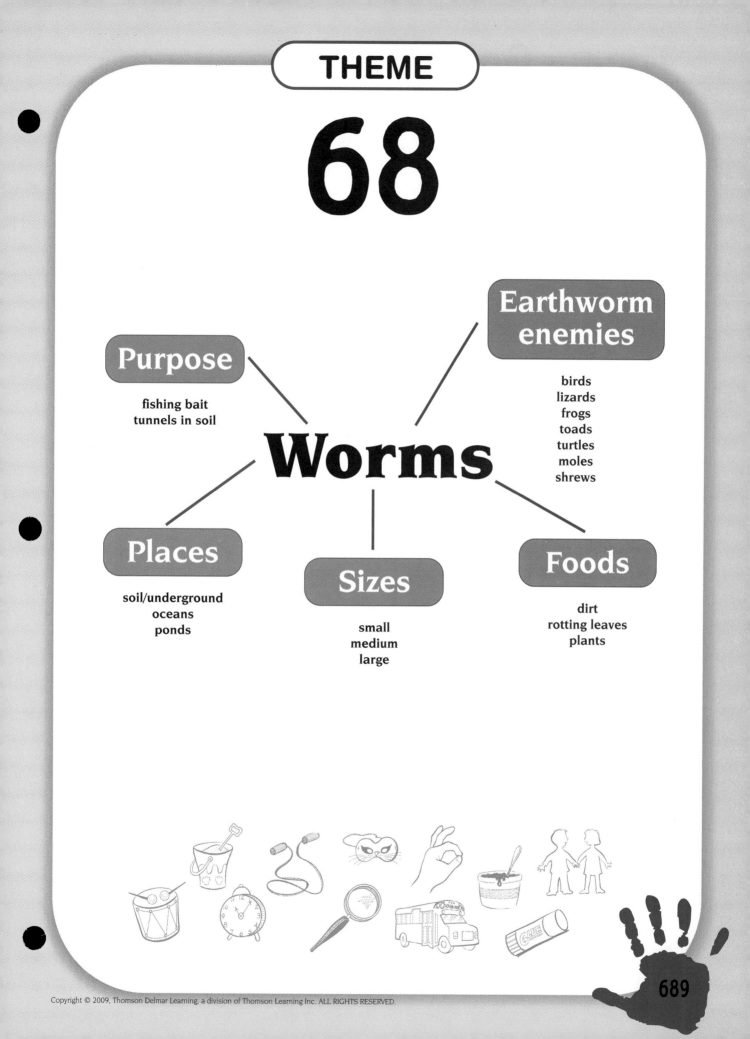

Theme Goals

Through participating in the experiences provided by this theme, the children may learn

1. Places worms live
2. Sizes of worms
3. Earthworm enemies
4. Foods worms eat
5. Purpose of earthworms

Concepts for the Children to Learn

1. Worms can be different sizes and lengths.
2. Earthworms live underground.
3. An earthworm moves by stretching itself thin and then pulling its body together.
4. Earthworms make tunnels in the soil.
5. Earthworms help keep soil healthy for plant growth.
6. Earthworms breathe through their skin.
7. Many insects at the caterpillar stage of growth are worms, such as apple worms, inchworms, and tomato worms.
8. Earthworms are food for many animals, including birds, lizards, frogs, toads, turtles, moles, and shrews.
9. Earthworms are sometimes used as fishing bait.

Vocabulary

1. **burrow**—a tunnel in the earth made by a worm.
2. **soil**—top layer of the earth in which plants grow.
3. **worm**—an animal that has a soft, slender body and no backbone or legs.

Bulletin Board

The purpose of this bulletin board is to identify written numerals, as well as match sets of objects to a written numeral. Construct bucket shapes out of tagboard. Print a different numeral on each bucket. (Numerals used should depend on the developmental level of the children.) Cut worms out of tagboard and decorate as desired. Laminate all pieces. Attach the buckets to the bulletin board by stapling them along the side and bottom edges, leaving the tops of the buckets open. The children are to place the corresponding number of worms in each bucket.

WORMS

Family Letter

Dear Families,

Did you know that there are thousands of kinds of worms? Worms are fascinating. They are any of several kinds of animals that have a soft, slender body, with no backbone or legs. The smallest worms cannot be seen without a microscope, and the largest can be many feet long. At school this week, we will focus on the common earthworm, which is a member of the segmented worm group. The children will learn the places worms live and the foods they eat.

AT SCHOOL

Some of this week's learning experiences include:

- creating a worm farm to place on the science table and observe worms
- sorting gummi worm candies by colors
- making pretzels in the shape of worms!
- playing with plastic worms and sand in the sensory table

AT HOME

After a rainfall, look for worms and worm holes with your child to reinforce concepts of this unit at home. Also, we will learn the following song. You may want to try it with your child.

"I'm a Little Worm"
(Sing to the tune of "I'm a Little Teapot")

I'm a little worm in the soft, cool ground.
I like to wiggle and squirm around.
When a bird comes near,
I scoot away.
Back into the ground is where I'll stay!

Have a good week!

THEME 68

Children enjoy feeling and watching worms.

Arts and Crafts

1. Worm Painting

Plastic fishing worms on string, paint, and paper are needed for this activity. Children dip a worm or string into paint and apply to the paper, moving it around the paper.

2. Package Worm Collages

Save Styrofoam package "worms" and place on the art table with paper, markers, and glue. The children can use materials to create designs of their choice.

Cooking

1. Mud Cake

1 1/2 cups flour
1 cup sugar
1/4 cup unsweetened cocoa powder
1 teaspoon baking soda
1/2 teaspoon salt
1/3 cup vegetable oil

1 tablespoon vinegar
1 teaspoon vanilla
1 cup water
gummi worm candies (for decoration)

Place dry ingredients in an 8-inch × 8-inch × 2-inch baking pan. Mix well. Using a fork, make a hole shape in the middle of the flour mixture. Pour liquid ingredients into the hole. Stir together all ingredients with a fork. Bake for 40 to 45 minutes in a 350-degree oven. Cool in pan. Decorate cake by gently pushing worm candies into each piece.

2. Worm Pretzels

Use frozen bread dough to make worm-shaped pretzels. Follow directions on the package for thawing and baking.

3. Worm and Dirt Cupcakes

1 package fudge brownie mix
1/2 cup shredded sweetened coconut
1/2 cup semisweet chocolate chips
2 teaspoons coconut extract

Preheat oven to the directions provided on the mix. Follow the directions for preparation of the mix. Stir in the extract, shredded coconut, and chocolate chips.

Divide the batter into a regular-size cupcake tin and bake according to the directions on the brownie mix. Recipe should make 12 cupcakes. (Depending on the size of the class, you may want to use more than one mix.)

4. **Dirty Worm Snack**

Prepare desired amount of chocolate pudding. Place in cups and add gummy worms.

Dramatic Play

Bait Shop

In the dramatic play area, place tackle boxes, plastic worms (in small containers), fishing lures (with the hooks removed), bobbers, nets, fishing poles, cash register, and play money. The children can pretend to be customers and bait shop workers.

Field Trips

1. **Bait Store**

Plan a trip to an area bait store. Ask to see the variety of worms that are sold. Also, look closely at worm bedding.

2. **Go Fishin'**

If appropriate and with plenty of adult supervision, arrange a fishing trip to a pond, lake, or fish farm. Bring along a picnic lunch and enjoy the day!

Fingerplays

A Robin

When a robin cocks his head
(tilt head to side)

Sideways in a flower bed,
He can hear the tiny sound
Of a worm beneath the ground.
(make crawling motion with fingers)

Little Worm

The little tiny wiggly worm
(move index finger)
Went crawling through the ground.
Down came the rain
(wiggle all fingers downward)
It was muddy all around.

Rain filled the tunnels
(make slow fist)
And out came the little worm.
(push index finger of one hand through fist of other)
So the puddles on the ground
Were the only place to squirm.
(move index finger)

Group Time
(Games, Language)

1. **Hide the Worm**

Ask several children to close or cover their eyes. Then hide a plastic worm in an observable place in the room. Children uncover their eyes and try to find the worm. The first child to find the worm hides it again, and the game continues until all have had a chance to look for the worm.

2. **Drop the Worm (a Variation of Drop the Handkerchief)**

To play this game, children stand in a circle formation. One child is chosen to hold a plastic worm and walk around the outside of the circle, dropping the worm behind another child. The child who has the worm dropped behind him or her must pick it up and chase the child who dropped it. The first child tries to return to the vacated space by running before he or she is tagged.

Large Muscle

Wiggle Worms

Encourage children to move like worms by wiggling on the floor. A "freeze" game could be played. Children wiggle while music plays and stop or "freeze" when the music stops.

Math

1. **Gummi Worm Candy Sort**

   As a group, sort a package of gummi worm candies by color. Count the number of each color. Count all gummi worms. If appropriate, record information on a graph.

2. **Set of Worms**

   Using plastic fishing worms and number cards, encourage children to count sets of worms to match written numbers.

3. **How Many Worms?**

   Create "inchworms" by drawing a worm (or pasting a clip art worm) in a strip of paper one inch long. Make one full sheet and photocopy for desired amount. Cut apart and give some to each child. Give children a variety of objects to "measure" by placing inchworms end to end.

   Variation: You could also make inchworm measuring cubes by taping inchworms to cubes that are approximately one inch long.

Music

1. **"I'm a Little Worm"**
   (*Sing to the tune of* "*I'm a Little Teapot*")

   I'm a little worm in the soft, cool ground.
   I like to wiggle and squirm around.

When a bird comes near,
I scoot away.
Back into the ground is where I'll stay!

2. **"Did You Ever See a Wiggly Worm?"**
   (*Sing to the tune of* "*Did You Ever See a Lassie?*")

   Did you ever see a wiggly worm,
   A wiggly worm, a wiggly worm?
   Did you ever see a wiggly worm,
   Move on the ground?

   It stretches and scrunches,
   And stretches and scrunches.
   Did you ever see a wiggly worm,
   Move on the ground?

3. **"Here's a Little Worm"**
   (*Sing to the tune of* "*Where Is Thumbkin?*")

   Here's a little worm, here's a little worm,
   Crawling around, in the ground.
   Making little tunnels, making little tunnels,
   Crawling around, in the ground.

4. **"Just a Little Worm"**
   (*Sing to the tune of* "*Mary Had a Little Lamb*")

   I am just a little worm,
   Little worm, little worm.
   I am just a little worm,
   In the nice cool ground.

   Wiggling is what I do,
   What I do, what I do.
   Wiggling is what I do,
   When I want to move around.

5. **"Wiggle, Wiggle, Little Worm"**
   (*Sing to the tune of* "*Twinkle, Twinkle*")

   Wiggle, wiggle, little worm.
   Wiggle, wiggle, jiggle, squirm.
   If a robin you should see,
   hide as quick as quick can be.
   Wiggle, wiggle, little worm.
   Wiggle, wiggle, jiggle, squirm.

Science

1. Worm Farm

Fill a large, clear jar with earthworm bedding or soil. Add a few worms to the jar. Poke holes in the cover and attach to the jar. Because worms prefer dark areas, cover the glass with black construction paper pieces. Remove periodically to observe the worms and their trails. Sprinkle cornmeal in the jar a few times a week.

2. Worm Hunt

After a rainfall, join the children in a worm hunt! Collect worms in buckets or similar containers. Use magnifying glasses to get a closer look at the worms. Return the worms to the soil (or a garden) on completion of the hunt.

Sensory

1. Plastic Worms

Place plastic fishing worms in the sensory table with sand, potting soil, or water. Add small nets, scoops, and bowls to add interest.

2. Package "Worms"

Collect Styrofoam packing "worms" and place in the sensory table with scoops and buckets.

Books

The following books can be used to complement this theme:

Bailey, Jill. (2001). *Worm*. Oxford: Heinemann Library.

Caple, Kathy. (2001). *Wow, It's Worm*. London: Walker.

Chanell, Jim. (1999). *Worms*. Austin, TX: Raintree/Steck-Vaughn. (*Minipets* series.)

Fowler, Allan. (1996). *It Could Still Be a Worm*. New York: Children's Press.

Freeman, Becky and Matthew Archambault. (2000). *The Worm Surprise*. Colorado Springs, CO: Chariot Victor.

Gill, Janie Spaht and Bob Reese. (1997). *Wonder Worm*: 10 *Words*. Provo, UT: Aro.

Glaser, Linda. (1992). *Wonderful Worms*. Illus. by Loretta Krupinski. Brookfield, CT: Millbrook Press.

Lauber, Patricia. (1994). *Earthworms*. Illus. by Todd Telander. New York: H. Holt.

Pinczes, Elinor J. and Randall Enos. (2000). *Inchworm and a half*. Boston: Houghton Mifflin.

O'Callahan, Jay and Laura O'Callahan. (1996). *Herman and Marguerite: An Earth Story*. Atlanta: Peachtree.

St. Pierre, Stephanie. (1999). *Slimey to the Moon*. New York: CTW Books.

Stone, Lynn M. (1995). *Worms*. Vero Beach, FL: Rourke.

Woods, Samuel G. (1999). *Sorting Out Worms and Other Invertebrates*. Woodbridge, CT: Blackbirch Press.

69

Animals

chicks
canary
cats

Traffic Signs

traffic light
yield signs

Color Mixing

yellow + blue = green
yellow + red = orange

Yellow

Flowers

daisy
dandelion
rose
daffodil

Foods

pineapple
banana
lemon
corn
grapefruit
cheese
egg yolk

Objects

sun
paint
cars
bikes
clothes

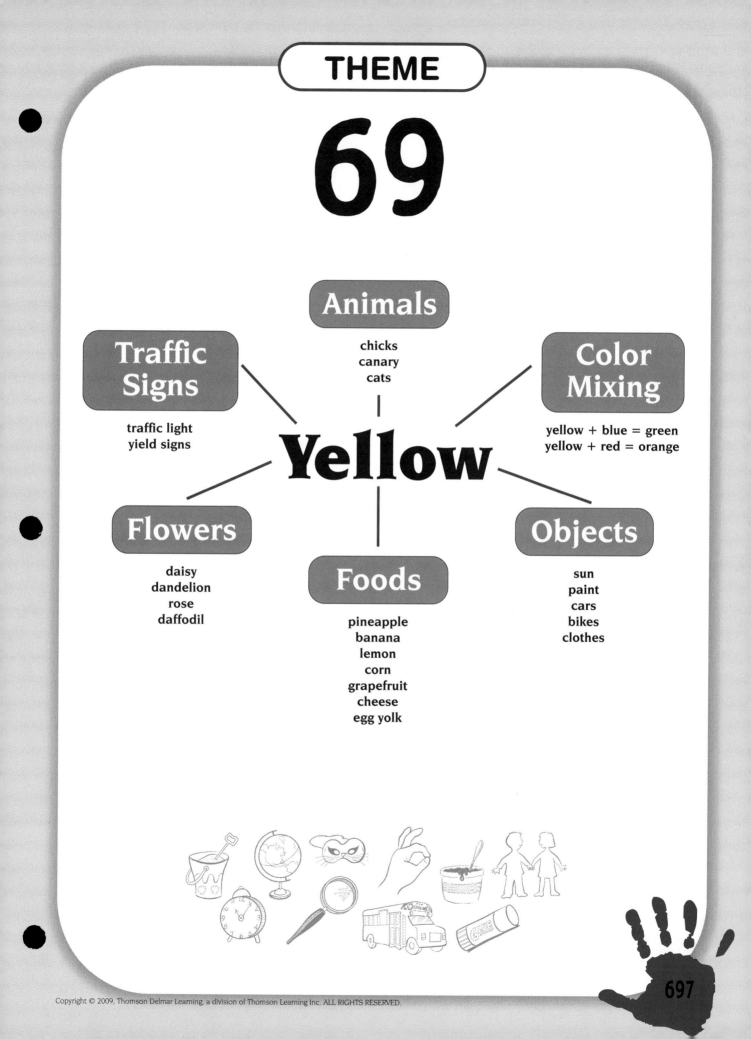

Theme Goals

Through participating in the experiences provided by this theme, the children may learn

1. Yellow-colored flowers
2. Yellow traffic signs
3. Yellow animals
4. Many objects that are colored yellow
5. Yellow objects
6. Colors formed by adding yellow

Concepts for the Children to Learn

1. Yellow is a primary color.
2. Yellow mixed with blue makes green.
3. Yellow mixed with red makes orange.
4. The sun is yellow.
5. The middle color on a traffic light is yellow.
6. Daisies, dandelions, and daffodils are yellow flowers.
7. A canary is a yellow bird.
8. Paints, cars, bikes, and clothing can be yellow.
9. Some flowers are yellow.
10. Pineapples, bananas, and corn are yellow foods.
11. Chicks and canaries are a yellow color.
12. Cats may be a yellow color.
13. There are yellow-colored foods.
14. Lemons, corn, and egg yolks are colored yellow.
15. Some grapefruit and cheeses are colored yellow.

Vocabulary

1. **primary colors**—red, blue, and yellow.
2. **yellow**—a primary color.

Bulletin Board

The purpose of this bulletin board is to have the children match the shapes, providing practice in visual discrimination and hand-eye coordination skills. To prepare the bulletin board, collect yellow tagboard, a black felt-tip marker, scissors, yellow string, and pushpins. Using yellow tagboard, draw sets of different-shaped balloons as illustrated. Outline with a black felt-tip marker and cut out. Take one balloon from each set and attach to the top of the bulletin board as illustrated. Staple a yellow string to hang from each balloon. Next, attach the remaining balloons on the bottom of the bulletin board. A pushpin can be fastened next to each balloon, and the children can match the balloons by shape.

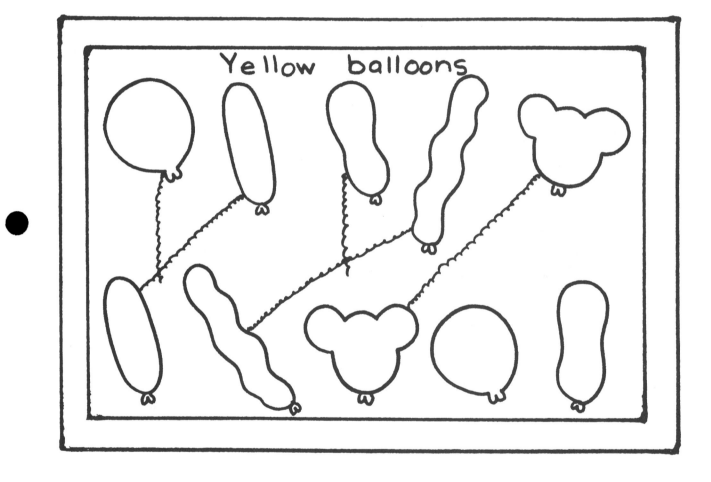

Family Letter

Dear Families,

Colors are such a big part of our world. Consequently, our new theme focuses on the color yellow. Throughout this week, the children will become aware of the color in their environment. It should be a bright time discovering the color yellow! They will learn to identify the signs, flowers, animals, foods, and objects that are colored yellow.

AT SCHOOL

Some learning experiences planned for the unit include:

- making scrambled eggs
- visiting a paint store
- learning the fingerplay "Six Yellow Chickadees"
- making yellow soap crayons
- playing with corn kernels in the sensory table

AT HOME

At school we will make yellow play dough. The children enjoy helping prepare the play dough and, of course, playing with it! It would be great fun for them to make it at home and they will be exposed to the mathematical concepts of amounts, fractions, and measurements. Here is the recipe:

2 cups flour
1 cup salt
1 cup water
2 tablespoons cooking oil
food coloring

Let your child assist in gathering and measuring the ingredients. Next, mix all the ingredients together. To encourage play, provide some tools for your child to use: rolling pins, cookie cutters, spatulas, or potato mashers. Have fun!

Enjoy your child!

Arts and Crafts

1. Yellow Paint

Provide yellow fingerpaint and yellow tempera paint in the art area.

2. Corncob Painting

Cover the bottom of a shallow pan with thick yellow tempera paint. Using a corncob as an applicator, apply paint to paper.

3. Popsicle Stick Prints

Cover the bottom of a shallow pan with thick yellow tempera paint. Apply the paint to paper using a Popsicle stick or craft stick as an applicator.

4. Yellow Play Dough

Combine 2 parts flour, 1 part salt, 1 part water, and 2 tablespoons cooking oil. Add yellow food coloring. Mix well. If prepared dough becomes sticky, add more flour.

5. Baker's Clay

Combine 4 cups flour, 1 cup salt, and 1 1/2 cups water. Mix the ingredients. The children can shape forms. Place the forms on a cookie sheet and bake at 350 degrees for about 1 hour. The next day the children can paint the objects yellow.

Cooking

1. Banana Bobs

Cut bananas into chunks and dip into honey. Next roll in wheat germ and use large toothpicks for serving. **Caution:** Close supervision is needed when using toothpicks with young children.

2. Carribbean Banana Salad

3 green (unripe) bananas, peeled
2 cups water
1 teaspoon salt
2 medium carrots, shredded
1 small cucumber, sliced

Bananas are yellow in color.

1 medium tomato, chopped
1 avocado, cubed
1 stalk celery, sliced
vinaigrette dressing

Heat bananas, water, and salt to boiling; reduce heat. Cover and simmer until bananas are tender, about 5 minutes. Drain and cool. Cut bananas crosswise into 1/2-inch slices. Toss bananas and remaining ingredients with vinaigrette dressing.

Note: From *Betty Crocker's International Cookbook,* 1980, New York: Random House. Reprinted with permission.

3. Corn Bread

1 cup flour
1 cup cornmeal
2 tablespoons sugar
4 teaspoons baking powder
1 teaspoon salt
1 cup milk
1/4 cup cooking oil or melted shortening
1 egg, slightly beaten

Preheat oven to 425 degrees. Grease (not oil) an 8- or 9-inch square pan. In medium mixing bowl, combine the dry ingredients. Stir in the remaining ingredients, beating by hand until just smooth. Pour batter into prepared pan. Bake for 20 to 25 minutes or until toothpick inserted in center comes out clean.

Dramatic Play

Paint Store

Set up a paint store by including paint caps, paintbrushes, pans, rollers, drop cloths, paint clothes, a cash register, and play money.

Field Trips

1. Paint Store

Visit a paint store and observe the different shades of yellow. Collect samples of paint for use in the art area. If possible, also observe the manager mixing yellow paint.

2. Yellow in Our World

Take a walk and look for yellow objects. Prepare a language experience chart when you return to the classroom.

3. Greenhouse

Visit a greenhouse and observe the different kinds of yellow flowers.

Fingerplays

Six Yellow Chickadees

(*Suit the actions to the words*)

Six yellow chickadees sitting by a hive.
One flew away and then there were five.
Five yellow chickadees sitting by the door.
One flew away and then there were four.

Four yellow chickadees sitting in a tree.
One flew away and then there were three.
Three yellow chickadees sitting by my shoe.
One flew away and then there were two.
Two yellow chickadees sitting by my thumb.
One flew away and then there was one.
One yellow chickadee flying around the sun.
She flew away and then there were none.

Ten Fluffy Chickens

Five eggs and five eggs
   (hold up two hands)
That makes ten.
Sitting on top is the mother hen.
   (fold one hand over the other)
Crackle, crackle, crackle
   (clap hands three times)
What do I see?
Ten fluffy chickens
   (hold up ten fingers)
As yellow as can be!

Group Time

(Games, Language)

Guessing Game: What's Missing?

Use any yellow familiar objects or toys that can be easily handled. The number will depend upon developmental appropriateness. For two-year-olds choose only two objects. On the other hand several objects can be used for five-year-olds. Spread them out on the floor and ask children to name each item. Then ask the group to close their eyes. Remove one item. When the group opens their eyes, ask them to tell you which item is missing.

Math

1. Sorting Shapes

Cut circles, triangles, and rectangles out of yellow tagboard. Place on the math table. The children can sort the yellow shapes into groups. For younger children, the objects can be cut from different colors. Then the objects can be sorted by color.

2. Block Patterning

Place a bucket of yellow and white cubes on the table. Encourage the children to make yellow-white-yellow-white patterns with the blocks. This activity can be extended by making pattern cards for the children to copy the pattern with the blocks.

Science

1. Paper Towel Dip

Fold a paper towel in half several times. Dip the towel into red water and then into yellow water. Open the towel carefully and allow it to dry. Orange designs will appear on the paper towel.

2. Carnation Coloring

Put a white carnation into a glass of water that has been dyed yellow with food coloring. Soon the carnation will show yellow streaks. During the summer other white garden flowers can be substituted.

3. Yellow Soap Crayons

Measure 1 cup of mild powdered laundry soap. Add 1 tablespoon of food coloring. Add water by the teaspoonful until the soap is in liquid form. Stir well. Pour the soap into ice cube trays. Set in a sunny, dry place until hard. Soap crayons are great for writing in the sink, tub, or sensory table.

Sensory

1. Shaving Cream Fun

Spray the contents of one can of shaving cream in the sensory table. Color the shaving cream by adding yellow food coloring.

2. Corn Kernels

Place corn kernels in the sensory table.

3. Yellow Goop

In the sensory table, mix 1 cup cornstarch, 1 cup water, and yellow food coloring. Mix together well.

4. Water Toys

Add yellow food coloring to 3 inches of water in the sensory table. Provide water toys as accessories to encourage play during self-selected play activites.

Social Studies

Tasting Party

Cut a banana, a pineapple, a lemon, and a piece of yellow cheese into small pieces. Let the children sample each during snack time. The concept of color, texture, and taste can all be discussed.

Books

The following books can be used to complement this theme:

Bang, Molly. (1991). *Yellow Ball*. New York: William Morrow.

Bogdanowicz, Basia. (1999). *Yellow Hat, Red Hat*. Brookfield, CT: Millbrook Press.

Cabrera, Jane. (1997). *Cat's Colors*. New York: Dial Books.

Carle, Eric. (1998). *Let's Paint a Rainbow*. New York: Scholastic.

Dodds, Dayle Ann. (1992). *The Color Box*. Illus. by Giles Laroche. Boston: Little, Brown.

Faulkner, Keith. (1995). *My Colors: Let's Learn About Colors*. New York: Simon & Schuster.

Heller, Ruth. (1995). *Color*. New York: G. P. Putnam.

Hoban, Tana. (1987). *Is It Red? Is It Yellow? Is It Blue?* New York: Greenwillow.

Hoban, Tana. (1995). *Colors Everywhere*. New York: Greenwillow.

Hunt, Janie Louise. (1997). *Red and Yellow.* Brookfield, CT: Millbrook Press.

Jackson, Ellen B. (1995). *Brown Cow, Green Grass, Yellow Mellow Sun, Vol. 1.* Illus. by Victoria Raymond. New York: Hyperion.

Lionni, Leo. (1994). *Little Blue and Little Yellow.* New York: William Morrow. (Pbk.)

Martin, Bill Jr. (1992). *Brown Bear, Brown Bear, What Do You See?* Illus. by Eric Carle. New York: H. Holt.

Munsch, Robert. (1992). *Purple, Green, and Yellow.* Illus. by Helene Desputeaux. Willowdale, ON: Annick Press.

Rogers, Alan. (1997). *Yellow Hippo.* Chicago: World Book.

Rotner, Shelley. (1996). *Colors Around Us.* New York: Simon & Schuster. (Lift-the-flap book.)

Sage, Angie. (1998). *Yellow Ice (Color Board Books).* Willowdale, Ontario, Canada: Firefly Books.

Seuss, Dr. (1996). *My Many Colored Days.* Illus. by Steve Johnston. New York: Knopf.

Walsh, Ellen Stoll. (1989). *Mouse Paint.* Orlando, FL: Harcourt Brace.

Multimedia

The following multimedia products can be used to complement this theme:

Big Yellow School Bus [sound cassette]. (1991). Alfred Publishing.

Bingham, Bing. "Primary Colors" from A *Rainbow of Songs* [sound cassette]. Kimbo Records.

Color, Shapes, and Size [computer file]. (1995). Star Press Multimedia.

Colors, Shapes, and Counting [video]. Kimbo Records.

My Silly CD of Colors [CD-ROM]. (1995). Discis Knowledge Research.

Peter's Colors Adventure [CD-ROM]. (1994). Arborescence.

"A Yell for Yellow" on *There's Music in the Colors* [cassette]. Kimbo Records.

Recordings and Song Titles

The following recordings can be used to complement this theme:

"Colors." (1995). *Piggyback Songs.* Long Branch, NJ: Kimbo Educational.

"The Color Song." (1996). *Where Is Thumbkin?* Long Branch, NJ: Kimbo Educational.

"Color Square." (1987). *Homemade Games.* Long Branch, NJ: Kimbo Educational.

"Color Wheel Dance." (1993). *Pre-K Hooray.* Long Branch, NJ: Kimbo Educational.

"Colour My World." (1984). *Let's Visit Lullaby Land.* Long Branch, NJ: Kimbo Educational.

"Draw a Circle." (1975). *I Like Myself.* Long Branch, NJ: Kimbo Educational.

"Everything Has a Color." (n.d.). *Children Love to Sing and Dance* (The Learning Station). Long Branch, NJ: Kimbo Educational.

"Primary Colors." (1988). *Rainbow of Songs.* Long Branch, NJ: Kimbo Educational.

There's Music in the Colors. (1976). Long Branch, NJ: Kimbo Educational.

70

Kinds

elephants
giraffes
monkeys
snakes
lions
bears
zebras
camels

Homes

cages
fences
water
trees

Zoo Animals

Needs

food
water
shelter
air

Caretakers

zookeeper
veterinarian

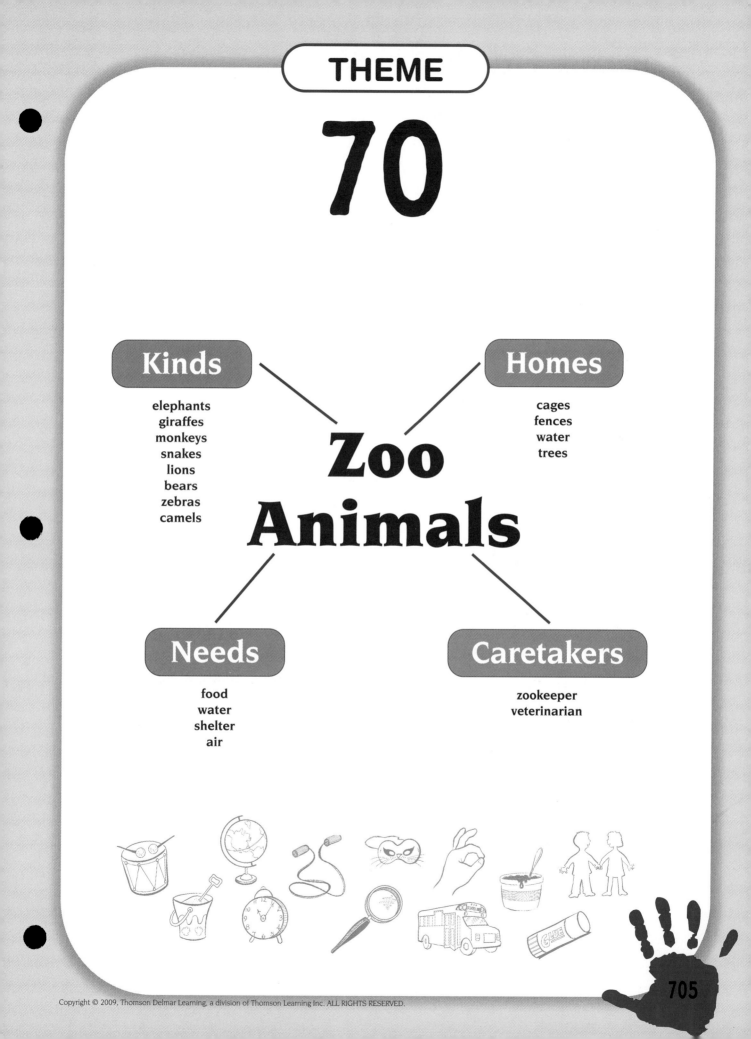

705

Theme Goals

Through participating in the experiences provided by this theme, the children may learn

1. Kinds of zoo animals
2. Needs of zoo animals
3. Types of animal homes
4. The caretakers of zoo animals

Concepts for the Children to Learn

1. A zoo is a place where animals are kept.
2. People go to the zoo to look at animals.
3. Zoo animals are housed in cages, fences, water, or in trees.
4. Elephants, giraffes, monkeys, snakes, lions, zebras, camels, and bears are zoo animals.
5. A zookeeper gives food and water to the animals.
6. Zoo animals need food, water, shelter, and air.
7. Veterinarians are doctors who care for animals.

Vocabulary

1. **cage**—a home for animals.
2. **veterinarian**—a doctor who cares for animals.
3. **zoo**—a place where animals are kept. People go to the zoo to look at animals.
4. **zookeeper**—a person who feeds the zoo animals.

Bulletin Board

The purpose of this bulletin board is to encourage the children to place the correct number of balls above each seal corresponding to the numeral on the drum. To prepare the bulletin board, construct seals sitting on a drum as illustrated. Place a numeral on each drum with the corresponding number of dots. Construct colored balls from tagboard. Laminate and cut out the pieces. Staple the seal figures and drums to bulletin board. Place a magnetic strip above each seal. Also adhere a magnetic strip to the back of each ball.

Family Letter

Dear Families,

Our new theme is called zoo animals. This is an appropriate theme to introduce to the children because they are fascinated by the zoo and the animals that live there. Through our study of zoo animals, the children will become familiar with the names, needs, and homes of many zoo animals. They will also be introduced to new occupations: the zookeeper and the veterinarian.

AT SCHOOL

Some of the experiences planned for the zoo animal unit include:

- looking at peek-a-boo pictures of zoo animals
- using zoo animal-shaped cookie cutters with play dough at the art table
- pretending to be caged zoo animals using boxes as cages in the dramatic play area

FIELD TRIP

Our class is taking a field trip to the Dunn County Reserve Park on Friday. There we can see some unusual animals. Please let me know by Wednesday if you are interested in accompanying the group. We will leave the center at 9:30 a.m. and return by 11:30 a.m.

AT HOME

To develop observation skills, you can show your child pictures of zoo animals from books or magazines. Plan a family trip to a zoo. Many opportunities for learning present themselves at the zoo. Children can actually see different kinds of animals and many times, such as at petting zoos, are able to touch and feed them. What a great way to develop an appreciation and respect for animal life!

Enjoy your child!

Can you roar like a leopard?

Arts and Crafts

1. **Paper Plate Lions**

   Collect paper plates, sandwich bags, and yellow cotton. Color the cotton balls by pouring powdered tempera paint into the sandwich bag and shaking. The children can trim the cut side of the paper plate with the yellow cotton to represent a mane. Facial features can also be added. This activity is for older children.

2. **Cookie Cutters**

   Play dough and zoo animal-shaped cookie cutters can be placed on a table in the art area.

Dramatic Play

1. **The Zoo**

   Collect large appliance boxes. Cut slits to resemble cages. Old fur coats or blankets can be added. The children may use the fur pieces while pretending to be animals in the zoo.

2. **Pet Store**

   Cages and many small stuffed animals can be added to the dramatic play area.

3. **Block Play**

   Set out many blocks and rubber, plastic, or wooden models of zoo animals.

Cooking

Animals on Grass

Take a graham cracker and spread green-tinted cream cheese on the top. Stand an animal cracker on the top of the graham cracker.

Field Trips

1. **Zoo**

   Visit a local zoo if available. Observe the animals that are of particular interest to the children such as the elephants, giraffes, bears, and monkeys.

2. **Reserve Park**

If your community has a reserve park, or an area where wild animals are secured in a natural environment, take the children to visit. Plan a picnic snack to take along.

Fingerplays

Lion

I knew a little lion who went roar, roar, roar.
(make sounds)
Who walked around on all fours.
(walk on both hands and feet)
He had a tail we could see behind the bars
(point to tail)
And when we visit we should stand back far.
(move backward)

Alligator

The alligator likes to swim.
(two hands flat on top of the other)
Sometimes his mouth opens wide.
(hands open and shut)
But when he sees me on the shore,
Down under the water he'll hide.

The Monkey

The monkey claps, claps, claps his hands.
(clap hands)
The monkey claps, claps, claps his hands.
(clap hands)
Monkey see, monkey do.
The monkey does the same as you.
(use pointer finger)
(change actions)

Three Little Monkeys

Three little monkeys jumping on the bed.
(hold up 3 fingers)
One fell off and bumped his head.
(touch head)

Mamma called the doctor and the doctor said,
No more monkeys jumping on the bed!
(shake pointer finger as if scolding)
As each monkey falls off, start the next verse with 2 monkeys, and then 1 monkey.

Zoo Animals

This is the way the elephant goes.
(clasp hands together, extend arms, move back and forth)
With a curly trunk instead of a nose.
The buffalo, all shaggy and fat.
Has two sharp horns in place of a hat.
(point to forehead)
The hippo with his mouth so wide—
Let's see what's inside.
(hands together and open wide and close them)
The wiggly snake upon the ground
Crawls along without a sound.
(weave hands back and forth)
But monkey see and monkey do is the funniest animal in the zoo.
(place thumbs in ears and wiggle fingers)

The Zoo

The zoo holds many animals inside
(make a circle with your hands and peer inside)
So unlatch the doors and open them wide.
(open your hands wide)
Elephants, tigers, zebras, and bears
(hold up one finger for each animal)
Are some of the animals you'll find there.

Group Time
(Games, Language)

What Am I?

Give the children verbal clues to describe an animal. Have the children guess which zoo animal you are describing. An example is, "I am very large, gray-colored, and have a long nose that looks like a hose. What zoo animal am I?"

Large Muscle

1. Walk Like the Animals

"Walk Like the Animals" is played like "Simon Says." Say, "The zookeeper says to walk like a giraffe." The children can walk as they believe that particular zoo animal would walk. Repeat using different animals such as monkeys, elephants, lions, tigers, bears, etc. This activity can also be used for transition.

2. Zookeeper, May I?

Designate one child to be the zookeeper. This child should stand about 6 feet in front of the remaining children. The zookeeper provides directions for the other children. To illustrate, they may say take three elephant steps, one kangaroo hop, two alligator glides, etc. Once the children reach the zookeeper, the zookeeper chooses a child to be his or her successor.

Math

1. Animal Sort

Collect pictures of elephants, lions, giraffes, monkeys, and other zoo animals from magazines, calendars, or coloring books. Encourage the children to sort the pictures into labeled baskets. For example, one basket may be for large animals and another for small animals.

2. Which Is Bigger?

Collect many toy models of zoo animals in various sizes. Encourage the children to order from smallest to biggest, etc.

3. Animal Sets

Cut and mount pictures of zoo animals. The children can classify the pictures by sorting. Examples might include birds, four-legged animals, furry animals, etc.

4. Zoo Sort Hula Hoops

Collect pictures of zoo animals that live on land or live on water. Place two hula hoops on the floor and place a picture of land inside one hoop and place a picture of water inside the other hoop. Have children sort animals into the appropriate hoop.

5. Giraffe Math

Make a giraffe cutout. Place a numeral on the giraffe and have the children place a corresponding number of black stickers on the giraffe.

6. Zebra Stripes

Make a zebra cutout and strips of black paper. Encourage children to glue the black strips of paper on the zebra to make a black-white-black-white pattern.

Music

1. "Zoo Animals"
(*Sing to the tune of* "*Muffin Man*")

Do you know the kangaroo
The kangaroo, the kangaroo?
Oh, do you know the kangaroo
That lives in the zoo?

(Adapt this song and use other zoo animals such as the monkey, elephant, giraffe, lion, turtle, bear, snake, etc.)

2. "One Elephant"

One elephant went out to play
On a spider web one day.
He had such enormous fun
That he called for another elephant to come.

(Makes a nice flannel board story, or choose one child to be an "elephant." Add another "elephant" with each verse.)

3. **"Animals at the Zoo"**
   (*Sing to the tune of "Frère Jacques"*)

   See the animals, see the animals
   At the zoo, at the zoo.
   Elephants and tigers, lions and seals
   Monkeys too, monkeys too.

4. **"The Bear Went Over the Mountain"**
   (*Sing to the tune of "For He's a Jolly Good Fellow"*)

   The bear went over the mountain,
   The bear went over the mountain,
   The bear went over the mountain
   To see what he could see.
   To see what he could see,
   To see what he could see.
   The bear went over the mountain
   To see what he could see.

5. **"Five Little Monkeys (jumping on the bed)"**

   Five little monkeys jumping on the bed.
   One fell off and bumped her head.
   Mamma called the doctor, and the doctor said,
   "No more monkeys jumping on the bed!"

   *Repeat, subtracting a monkey each time. Sing the
   rhyme using fingers or act it out.*

Science

1. **Animal Skins**

   Place a piece of snakeskin, a patch of animal
   hide, and animal fur out on the science table.
   The children can see and feel the differences.
   These skins can usually be borrowed from the
   Department of Natural Resources.

2. **Habitat**

   On the science table, place a bowl of water, a
   tray of dirt, and a pile of hay or grass. Also,
   include many small toy zoo animals. The
   children can place the animals in their correct
   habitat.

Sensory

Additions to the Sensory Table

- sand and zoo animal models
- seeds and measuring scoops
- corn and scales
- hay
- water

Social Studies

Helpful Zoo Animals

During large group, discuss how some animals
can be useful. Show the children pictures of various helping animals and discuss their uses.
Examples include:

- camel (transportation in some countries)
- elephant (often used to pull things)
- dogs (Seeing Eye dogs, sled dogs)
- goats (used for milk)

Books

The following books can be used to
complement this theme:

Aliki. (1997). *My Visit to the Zoo*. New York:
  HarperCollins.

Ancona, George and Mary Beth Ancona.
  (1991). *Handtalk Zoo*. New York: Simon
  & Schuster.

Arnold, Caroline. (1992). *Camel*. New York:
  William Morrow.

Arnold, Caroline. (1993). *Elephant*. New York:
  William Morrow.

Arnold, Caroline. (1993). *Lion*. New York: William Morrow.

Arnold, Caroline. (1993). *Monkey*. New York: William Morrow.

Barton, Byron. (1996). *Zoo Animals*. New York: HarperCollins. (Board book.)

Benjamin, Cynthia. (1995). *I Am a Zookeeper*. Illus. by Miriam Sagasti. Hauppauge, NY: Barron's Educational series. (Board book.)

Brenner, Barbara. (2003). *What the Elephant Told*. Illus. by Akemi Gutierrez. New York: Henry Holt.

Buehner, Caralyn and Mark Buehner. (1992). *The Escape of Marvin the Ape*. New York: Dial Books.

Denim, Sue and Dave Pilkey. (1996). *The Dumb Bunnies Go to the Zoo*. New York: Scholastic.

Finnegan, Evelyn and Margaret Bruno. (1998). *My Little Friend Goes to the Zoo*. Scituate, MA: Little Friend Press.

Ford, Miela. (1994). *Little Elephant*. Illus. by Tana Hoban. New York: Greenwillow.

Ford, Miela. (1995). *Bear Play*. New York: Greenwillow.

Ford, Miela. (1998). *Watch Us Play*. New York: Greenwillow.

Fowler, Allan. (1996). *The Biggest Animal on Land*. Chicago: Children's Press.

Hazelaar, Cor. (1997). *Zoo Dreams*. New York: Farrar, Straus & Giroux.

Hendrick, Mary Jean. (1993). *If Anything Goes Wrong at the Zoo*. Illus. by Jane Dyer. Orlando, FL: Harcourt Brace.

Hewett, Joan. (1993). *Tiger, Tiger Growing Up*. Illus. by Richard Hewett. New York: Clarion Books.

Hillenbrand, Will. (1999). *Down by the Station*. San Diego, CA: Harcourt Brace.

Hort, Lenny. (2000). *The Seals on the Bus*. Illus. by Karas, G. Brian. New York: Henry Holt.

Hosea Hilker, Cathryn. (1992). *A Cheetah Named Angel*. New York: Franklin Watts.

Kalman, Bobbie and Hannelore Sotzek. (1997). *A Koala Is Not a Bear*. New York: Crabtree.

Kasza, Keiko. (1990). *When the Elephant Walks*. New York: Putnam.

Kenny, David et al. (1995). *Klondike and Snow: The Denver Zoo's Remarkable Story of Raising Two Polar Bear Cubs*. Niwot, CO: Roberts Rinehart. (Pbk.)

Koebner, Linda. (1994). *Zoo Book*. New York: T. Doberty.

Lemmon, Tess. (1993). *Apes*. Illus. by John Butler. New York: Ticknor & Fields.

Maestro, Betsy. (1992). *Take a Look at Snakes*. New York: Scholastic.

Martin, Ann M. (1998). *Baby Animal Zoo*. Illus. by Charles Tang. New York: Scholastic. (Pbk.)

Martin, Bill. (1991). *Polar Bear, Polar Bear, What Do You Hear?* Illus. by Eric Carle. New York: H. Holt.

McMillan, Bruce. (1995). *The Baby Zoo*. New York: Scholastic. (Pbk.)

Menton, Jacqueline. (1998). *Zoo in the Sky: A Book of Animal Constellations*. Illus. by Christine Balit. Maps by Wil Tirion. Washington, DC: National Geographic Society.

Morozumi, Atsuko. (1998). *My Friend Gorilla*. New York: Farrar, Straus & Giroux.

Munari, Bruno. (2005). *Bruno Munari's Zoo*. San Francisco, CA: Chronicle Books.

Noble, Kate. (1994). *The Blue Elephant*. Illus. by Rachel Bass. Chicago: Silver Seahorse Press.

Ormerod, Jan. (1991). *When We Went to the Zoo*. New York: Lothrop, Lee & Shepard.

Oxenbury, Helen. (1991). *Monkey See, Monkey Do*. 2nd ed. New York: Dial Books. (Board book.)

Paxton, Tom. (1996). *Going to the Zoo*. Illus. by Karen Schmidt. New York: William Morrow.

Rathmann, Peggy. (1994). *Good Night, Gorilla*. New York: G. P. Putnam.

Robinson, Martha. (1995). *The Zoo at Night*. Illus. by Antonio Frasconi. New York: Simon & Schuster.

Rowan, James P. (1990). *I Can Be a Zoo Keeper*. Chicago: Children's Press. (Pbk.)

Ryder, Joanne. (2001). *Little Panda: The World Welcomes Hua Mei at the San Siego Zoo*. New York: Simon & Schuster.

Rylant, Cynthia. (2007). *Alligator Boy*. Illus. by Diane Goode. Orlando, FL: Harcourt.

Sierra, Judy and Barney Saltzberg. (2000). *There's a Zoo in Room 22*. Illus. by Barney Saltzberg. San Diego, CA: Harcourt Brace.

Simon, Seymour. (1992). *Snakes*. New York: HarperCollins.

Smith, Roland. (1992). *Cats in the Zoo*. Illus. by William Munoz. Brookfield, CT: Millbrook Press.

Tibbitts, Alison and Alan Roocraft. (1992). *Polar Bears*. New York: Capstone Press.

Waber, Bernard. (1996). *A Lion Named Shirley Williamson*. Boston: Houghton Mifflin.

Wolff, Ashley. (2004). *Me Baby, You Baby*. New York: Dutton Children's Books.

Multimedia

The following multimedia products can be used to complement this theme:

A Day at the Zoo [video]. Kimbo Records.

At Home with Zoo Animals [video]. (1992). Washington, DC: National Geographic Society.

At the Zoo [video]. Kimbo Records.

At the Zoo: 2 [video]. Kimbo Records.

Choo Choo to the Zoo [CD]. (2006). Kimbo Records.

Let's Go to the Zoo [video]. Kimbo Records.

National Zoo [videodisc]. (1989). Washington, DC: Smithsonian Institution.

Sharon, Lois, and Bram at the Zoo [video]. (1985). Golden Book Video.

Zoo Keeper [computer file]. (1992). Davidson & Associates.

Zoo Opolis [CD-ROM]. (1994). Compton's New Media.

Recordings and Song Titles

The following recordings can be used to complement this theme:

"Animal Acts," "Prancing Ponies." (1980). *Do It Yourself Kids' Circus*. Long Branch, NJ: Kimbo Educational.

Animal Walks. (1987). Long Branch, NJ: Kimbo Educational.

A to Z, the Animals and Me. (1994). Long Branch, NJ: Kimbo Educational.

Five Little Monkeys. (1999). Long Branch, NJ: Kimbo Educational.

"Going to the Zoo," "Five Little Monkeys." (1997). *Six Little Ducks*. Long Branch, NJ: Kimbo Educational.

"Let's All Be Giraffes." (1978). *Alphabet in Action*. Long Branch, NJ: Kimbo Educational.

"Monkey Town." (1988). *Preschool Action Time*. Long Branch, NJ: Kimbo Educational.

Save the Animals, Save the Earth. (1991). Long Branch, NJ: Kimbo Educational.

What's in the Sea? (1990). Long Branch, NJ: Kimbo Educational.

APPENDIX A

Multicultural Materials in the Early Childhood Classroom

Teaching children about diversity is an important role of an early childhood professional. The center materials, room décor, and books you select for the classroom can influence children's judgments, social attitudes, and behaviors. Teachers must carefully plan and examine all classroom materials so that they can positively and realistically introduce children to a variety of cultural backgrounds. The contents of this Appendix will help you choose books, music, and dramatic play props that can be used in the classroom to reflect a variety of cultures.

 ## Multicultural Musical Instruments

Using musical instruments is an excellent opportunity to expose children to a variety of cultures. Following is a list of instruments you might want to add to your music shelf for the children to experiment with:

- Agogo bells
- Chilean rainstick
- Ankle bells
- Steel drum
- Maracitos
- Samba whistles
- Casaba
- Vibra slap
- Tambourine
- Castanets
- Claves
- Maracas
- Bongos
- Guiro tone block
- Conga drum
- Tom tom drum

 ## Multicultural Books

Ada, Alma Flor (selected by). (2003). *Pio Peep!* Illus. by Vivi Escriva. New York: HarperCollins.

Agassi, Martine. (2002). *Hands Are Not for Hitting.* Illus. by Marieka Heinlen. Minneapolis, MN: Free Spirit Pub.

Ajmera, Maya and John D. Ivanko. (2002). *Animal Friends: A Global Celebration of Children and Animals.* Watertown, MA: Charlesbridge.

Ajmera, Maya and John D. Ivanko. (2004). *Be My Neighbor.* With words of wisdom from Fred Rogers. Washington, DC: Shakti for Children; Watertown, MA: Charlesbridge.

Ajmera, Maya and John D. Ivanko. (2004). *To Be a Kid.* Watertown, MA: Charlesbridge; Washington, DC: Shakti for Children.

Ajmera, Maya. (2004). *To Be An Artist.* Watertown, MA: Charlesbridge.

Bang, Molly. (1985). *Ten, Nine, Eight.* New York, NY: Puffin Books.

Bannerman, Helen. (1996). *The Story of Little Babaji.* Illus. by Fred Marcellino. New York: HarperCollins Publishers.

Barnwell, Ysaye M. (1998). *No Mirrors in My Nana's House.* Painting by Synthia Saint James. San Diego: Harcourt Brace.

Bloom, Suzanne. (2001). *The Bus for Us.* Honesdale, PA: Boyds Mills Press.

Brett, Jan. (2005). *Honey . . . Honey . . . Lion! A Story from Africa*. New York: G.P. Putnam's Sons.

Brown, Margaret Wise. (1996). *El gran granero rojo* (*The Big Red Barn*). Illus. by Felicia Bond. New York: Harper Arco Iris.

Carle, Eric. (1994). *La oruga muy hambrienta* (*The Very Hungry Caterpillar*). New York, NY: Philomel Books.

Carryl, Charles E. (2004). *The Camel's Lament*. Illus. by Charles Santore. New York: Random House.

Chamberlin, Mary and Rich. (2005). *Mama Panya's Pancakes: Village Tale From Kenya*. Illus. by Julia Cairns. Bath, ME: Barefoot Books.

Christelow, Eileen. (2005). *Cinco monitos brincando en la cama* (*Five little monkeys jumping on the bed*). New York, NY: Clarion Books.

Crews, Donald. (1985). *Freight Train*. New York, NY: Puffin Books.

Demarest, Chris L. (2000). *Firefighters A to Z*. New York: Margaret K. McElderry Books.

Demi. (1990). *The Empty Pot*. New York: H. Holt.

Dwight, Laura. (2005). *Brothers and Sisters*. New York: Star Bright Books.

Ehlert, Lois. (1996). *A sembrar sopa de verdures* (*Growing Vegetable Soup*). San Diego: Libros Viajeros.

Elya, Susan Middleton. (2005). *Cowboy José*. Illus. by Tim Raglin. New York: G. P. Putnam's Sons.

Emberley, Rebecca. (2002). *My animals = Mis animales*. Boston: Little, Brown and Co.

Emberley, Rebecca. (2005). *My city = Mi ciudad*. New York: Little, Brown and Co.

Emberley, Rebecca. (2000). *My colors = Mis colores*. Boston: Little, Brown and Co.

Emberley, Rebecca. (2002). *My food = Mi comida*. Boston: Little, Brown and Co.

Emberley, Rebecca. (2005). *My garden = Mi jardin*. New York: Little, Brown and Co.

Emberley, Rebecca. (2005). *My room = Mi cuarto*. New York: Little, Brown and Co.

Emberley, Rebecca. (2005). *My school = Mi escuela*. New York: Little, Brown and Co.

Flack, Marjorie and Kurt Wiese. (2000). *The Story About Ping*. New York: Grosset & Dunlap.

Fleming, Denise. (2000). *The Everything Book*. New York: Henry Holt.

Fleming, Denise. (2005). *The First Day of Winter*. New York: Henry Holt.

Fleming, Denise. (1993). *In the Small, Small Pond*. New York: Henry Holt.

Fleming, Denise. (1991). *In the Tall, Tall Grass*. New York: Henry Holt.

Freeman, Don. (1968). *Corduroy*. New York, Viking Press.

Frost, Helen. (1999). *Going to the Dentist*. Mankato, MN: Pebble Books.

Greenberg, Polly. (1968). *Oh Lord, I wish I was a Buzzard*. Illus. by Aliki. New York: Macmillan.

Greenfield, Eloise. (2003). *Honey, I Love*. Illus. by Jan Spivey Gilchrist. New York: HarperCollins.

Guy, Ginger Foglesong. (1996). *Fiesta!* Pictures by Rene King Moreno. New York: Greenwillow Books.

Guy, Ginger Foglesong. (2005). *Siesta*. Pictures by Rene King Moreno. New York: Greenwillow Books.

Heelan, Jamee Riggio. (2000). *Rolling Along: The Story of Taylor and His Wheelchair*. Illus. by Nicola Simmonds. Atlanta, GA: Peachtree.

Hester, Denia Lewis. (2005). *Grandma Lena's Big Ol' Turnip*. Illus. by Jackie Urbanovic. Morton Grove, IL: Albert Whitman & Co.

Hindley, Judy. (1999). *Eyes, Nose, Fingers, and Toes: A First Book All About You*. Illus. by Brita Granstrom. Cambridge, MA: Candlewick Press.

Holiday, Billie and Arthur Herzog Jr. (2004). *God Bless the Child*. Illus. by Jerry Pinkney. New York: HarperCollins/Amistad.

Hooks, Bell. (2001). *Happy to be Nappy*. Illus. by Chris Raschka. New York, NY: Jump at the Sun.

Howell, Theresa. (2003). *A Is for Airplane. A es para Avion*. Illus. by David Brooks. Flagstaff, AZ: Rising Moon.

Hubbell, Will. (2002). *Apples Here!* Illus. by Will Hubbell. Morton Grove, IL: Albert Whitman and Company.

Isadora, Rachel. (2002). *Peekaboo Morning*. New York: G.P. Putnam's Sons.

Jocelyn, Marthe and Tom Slaughter. (2005). ABC × 3. Plattsburgh, NY: Tundra Books.

Jones, Bill T. and Susan Kuklin. (1998). *Dance*. Photographed by Susan Kuklin. New York: Hyperion Books for Children.

Joosse, Barbara M. (2000). *Mama, Do You Love Me?* Illus. by Barbara Lavallee. San Francisco: Chronicle Books.

Keats, Ezra Jack. (1967). *The Snowy Day.* London, Sydney [etc.] Bodley Head.

Khan, Rukhsana. (2005). *Silly Chicken.* Pictures by Yunmee Kyong. New York: Viking.

Kroll, Virginia. (2005). *Forgiving a Friend.* Illus. by Paige Billin-Frye. Morton Grove, IL: Albert Whitman.

Lewis, E.B. (2005). *This Little Light of Mine.* New York: Simon & Schuster Books for Young Readers.

Lin, Grace. (2004). *Fortune Cookie Fortunes.* New York: Alfred A. Knopf.

Lindsay, Jeanne Warren. (1991). *Do I Have a Daddy?* A *Story about a Single Parent Child.* Illus. by Cheryl Boeller. Buena Park, CA: Morning Glory Press.

Lo, Ginnie. (2005). *Mahjong All Day Long.* Illus. by Beth Lo. New York: Walker & Co.

Lunge-Larsen, Lise and Margi Preus. (1999). *The Legend of the Lady Slipper: An Ojibwe Tale.* Illus. by Andrea Arroyo. Boston: Houghton Mifflin.

Manders, John. (2003). *Señor Don Gato: A Traditional Song.* Illus. by John Manders. Cambridge, MA: Candlewick Press.

Manning, Jane K. (2001). *My First Baby Games.* New York, NY: HarperFestival.

Markes, Julie. (2005). *Shhhhh! Everybody's Sleeping.* Illus. by David Parkins. New York: HarperCollins.

Martin, Bill. (1998). *Oso pardo, oso pardo, que ves ahí?* (*Brown Bear, Brown Bear, What Do You See?*) Illus. by Eric Carle. New York: Holt.

Martin, Bill and John Archambault. (1998). *Here Are My Hands.* Illus. by Ted Rand. New York: H. Holt.

Medearis, Angela Shelf. (2004). *Snug in Mama's Arms.* Illus. by John Sandford. Columbus, Ohio: Gingham Dog Press.

Miller, J. Philip and Sheppard M. Greene. (2001). *We All Sing with the Same Voice.* Illus. by Paul Meisel. New York: HarperCollins.

Morales, Yuyi. (2003). *Just a Minute: A Trickster Tale and Counting Book.* San Francisco: Chronicle Books.

Morris, Ann. (1993). *Bread Bread Bread.* Photographs by Ken Heyman. New York: Mulberry Books.

Morris, Ann. (2000). *Families.* New York: HaperCollins.

Morris, Ann. (1993). *Hats Hats Hats.* Photographs by Ken Heyman. New York: Mulberry Books.

Morris, Ann. (1992). *Houses and Homes.* Photographs by Ken Heyman. New York: Lothrop, Lee & Shepard Books.

Morris, Ann. (1995). *Weddings.* New York: Lothrop, Lee & Shepard Books.

Mosel, Arlene. (1989). *Tikki Tikki Tembo.* Illus. by Blair Lent. New York: Henry Holt and Co.

Nelson, Kadir. (2005). *He's Got the Whole World in His Hands.* New York: Dial Books for Young Readers.

Orozco, José-Luis (selected, arranged, and translated). (1994). *De Colores and Other Latin-America Folk Songs for Children.* Illus. by Elisa Kleven. New York: Dutton Children's Books.

Orozco, José-Luis (selected, arranged, and translated). (1997). *Diez Deditos/Ten Little Fingers and Other Play Rhymes.* Illus. by Elisa Kleven. New York: Dutton Children's Books.

Orozco, José-Luis and David Diaz. (2005). *Rin, Rin, Rin, Do, Re, Mi.* New York: Orchard Books.

Owen, Ann. (2004). *Keeping You Healthy: A Book About Doctors.* Illus. by Eric Thomas. Minneapolis, MN: Picture Window Books.

Oxenbury, Helen. (1987). *All Fall Down.* New York: Aladdin Books.

Oxenbury, Helen. (1987). *Clap Hands.* New York: Aladdin Books.

Oxenbury, Helen. (1987). *Tickle, Tickle.* New York: Aladdin Books.

Park, Linda Sue. (2005). *Bee-Bim Bop!* Illus. by Ho Baek Lee. New York: Clarion Books.

Parr, Todd. (1998). *Somewhere Today: A Book of Peace.* Photographs by Eric Futran. Morton Grove, IL: A. Whitman.

Pedersen, Janet. (2005). *Pino and the Signora's Pasta.* Cambridge, MA: Candlewick Press.

Pilobous. (2005). *The Human Alphabet.* Photographs by John Kane. Brookfield, CT: Roaring Brook Press.

Pinkney, Andrea Davis and Brian Pinkney. (1997). *I Smell Honey.* San Diego, CA: Harcourt Brace.

Pinkney, Andrea Davis and Brian Pinkney. (1997). *Pretty Brown Face.* San Diego, CA: Harcourt Brace.

Pinkney, Sandra L. (2000). *Shades of Black: A Celebration of Our Children.* Photographs by Myles Pinkney. New York: Scholastic.

Raschka, Christopher. (1992). *Charlie Parker Played Be Bop.* New York: Orchard Books.

Reiser, Lynn. (1998). *Tortillas and Lullabies*. Pictures by Corazones Valientes. Coordinated and translated by Rebecca Hart. New York: Greenwillow Books.

Rosa-Mendoza, Gladys. (2000). *My family and* I = *Mi familia y yo*. Illus. by Jackie Snider edited by Carolina Cifuentes. Wheaton, IL: Me+mi Pub.

Rylant, Cynthia. (2005). *The Stars Will Still Shine*. Illus. by Tiphanie Beeke. New York: HarperCollins.

Rylant, Cynthia. (1982). *When I Was Young in the Mountains*. Illus. by Diane Goode. New York: Dutton.

Sanger, Amy Wilson. (2001). *First Book of Sushi*. Berkeley, CA: Tricycle Press.

Sanger, Amy Wilson. (2002). *Hola! Jalapeno*. Berkeley, CA: Tricycle Press.

Sanger, Amy Wilson. (2002). *Let's Nosh!* Berkeley, CA: Tricycle Press.

Sanger, Amy Wilson. (2004). *A Little Bit of Soul Food*. Berkeley, CA: Tricycle Press.

Sanger, Amy Wilson. (2005). *Mangia! Mangia!* Berkeley, CA: Tricycle Press.

Sanger, Amy Wilson. (2003). *Yum Yum Dim Sum*. Berkeley, CA: Tricycle Press.

Scott, Ann Herbert. (1992). *On Mother's Lap*. Illus. by Glo Coalson. New York: Clarion Books.

Seeger, Pete. (2005). ABIYOYO. Illus. by Michael Hays. New York: Aladdin Paperbacks.

Senisi, Ellen B. (2002). *All Kinds of Friends, Even Green!* Photographed by Ellen B. Senisi. Bethesda, MD: Woodbine House.

Simon, Norma. (2003). *All Families Are Special*. Illus. by Teresa Flavin. Morton Grove, IL: A. Whitman & Co.

So, Meilo. (2004). *Gobble, Gobble, Slip, Slop*. New York: Alfred A. Knopf.

Sockabasin, Allen. (2005). *Thanks to the Animals*. Illus. by Rebekah Raye. Gardiner, ME: Tilbury House.

Spinelli, Eileen. (2005). *City Angel*. Illus. by Kyrsten Brooker. New York: Dial Books for Young Readers.

Spinellie, Eileen. (2000). *Night Shift Daddy*. Illus. by Melissa Iwai. New York: Hyperion Books for Children.

Sturges, Philemon. (2004). *I Love School!* Illus. by Shari Halpern. New York: HarperCollins.

Taback, Simms. (1999). *Joseph Had a Little Overcoat*. New York: Viking.

Tarpley, Natasha Anastasia. (1998). *I Love My Hair!* Illus. by E.B. Lewis. New York: Little, Brown.

Verdick, Elizabeth. (2004). *Feet Are Not for Kicking*. Illus. by Marieka Heinlen. Minneapolis, MN: Free Spirit Pub.

Verdick, Elizabeth. (2005). *Tails Are Not for Pulling*. Illus. by Marieka Heinlen. Minneapolis, MN: Free Spirit Pub.

Verdick, Elizabeth. (2003). *Teeth Are Not for Biting*. Illus. by Marieka Heinlen. Minneapolis, MN: Free Spirit Pub.

Verdick, Elizabeth. (2004). *Words Are Not for Hurting*. Illus. by Marieka Heinlen. Minneapolis, MN: Free Spirit Pub.

Williams, Sue. (2006). *Sali de paseo* (I Went Walking). Illus. by Julie Vivas. Orlando: Harcourt.

Williams, Vera B. (1982). *A Chair for My Mother*. New York: Greenwillow Books.

Williams, Vera B. (1990). *More More More, Said the Baby*. New York: Greenwillow Books.

Willis, Jeanne and Tony Ross. (2004). *Shhh!* New York: Hyperion Books for Children.

Winter, Jeanette. (2004). *The Librarian of Basra*. Orlando: Harcourt, Inc.

Winthrop, Elizabeth. (2005). *Squashed in the Middle*. Illus. by Pat Cummings. New York: Henry Holt.

Wolff, Ashley. (2003). *The Baby Chicks Are Singing* = *Los Pollitos Dicen*. Boston, MA: Little, Brown and Co.

Wolff, Ashley. (2003). *Oh, the Colors* = *De colores*. Boston: Little, Brown and Co.

Woodson, Jacqueline. (2001). *The Other Side*. Illus. by Earl B. Lewis. New York: Putnam's.

Woodson, Jacqueline. (2002). *Our Gracie Aunt*. Illus. by Jon J. Muth. New York: Hyperion Books for Children/Jump at the Sun.

Woodson, Jacqueline. (2002). *Visiting Day*. Illus. by James Ransome. New York: Scholastic Press.

Yashima, Taro. (1958). *Umbrella*. New York: Viking Press.

Multicultural Dramatic Play Ideas

Multicultural props should be included in the dramatic play area. These props can be authentic or teacher made. Following is a list of ideas for props that can be used in the dramatic play area.

Grocery Store: Use containers and boxes that include a variety of products that appeal to many cultures and both genders. Create ethnically diverse foods from clipart or play dough to display in the store. Some ideas for multicultural materials to include in this area could be:

- Taco or rice boxes
- Variety of spice containers
- Variety of plastic fruits and vegetables
- Play money (from other countries)

Restaurants: A variety of restaurants that reflect ethnically diverse foods can be set up in the dramatic play area. Include the cooking utensils, special dishes, and menus for the type of restaurant you choose (Mexican, Indian, Chinese, Korean, Italian, etc.). If the materials aren't available from a restaurant in your area, make them using clipart. Some ideas for multicultural materials to include in this area could be:

- Karahi or wok
- Chopsticks
- Floor mats (instead of chairs)
- Take-out containers
- Rice pot
- Wooden spoons

- Escobeta (Mexican cooking brush)
- Flan pan
- Bean masher

Department Store: Include a variety of clothing, hats, scarves, jewelry, or home décor that represents many cultures. Some ideas for multicultural materials to include in this area could be:

- Kimonos
- Turbans
- Stone/shell necklaces
- African beads
- Headband/headdress
- Various shades of nylons and tights
- Ceramics/pottery
- Woven baskets

Multicultural Music

Kimbo Educational. (1993). *Joining Hands with Other Lands*. Long Branch, NJ: Kimbo Educational.

Skiera-Zucek, Lois. (1994). *Songs About Native Americans*. Long Branch, NJ: Kimbo Educational.

Stewart, Georgiana Liccione. (1991). *Children of the World Multicultural Rhythmic Activities*. Long Branch, NJ: Kimbo Educational.

Stewart, Georgiana Liccione. (1998) *Children's Folk Dances*. Long Branch, NJ: Kimbo Educational.

Stewart, Georgiana Liccione. (1992). *Multicultural Rhythm Stick Fun*. Long Branch, NJ: Kimbo Educational.

APPENDIX B

International Holidays

When planning the curriculum, it is important to note international holidays. The exact date of the holiday may vary from year to year; consequently, it is important to check with parents or a reference librarian at a local library. International holidays for Buddhist, Christian, Eastern Orthodox, Hindu, Jewish, and Muslim people are as follows:

Buddhist

Nirvana Day (Mahayana Sect)—observes the passing of Sakyamuni into Nirvana. He obtained enlightment and became a Buddha.

Magna Puja (Theravada Sect)—one of the holiest Buddhist holidays; it marks the occasion when 1,250 of Buddha's disciples gathered spontaneously to hear him speak.

Buddha Day (Mahayana Sect)—this service commemorates the birth of Gautama in Lumbini Garden. Amida, the Buddha of Infinite Wisdom and Compassion, manifested himself among men in the person Gautama.

Versakha Piya (Theravada Sect)—the most sacred of the Buddhist days. It celebrates the birth, death, and enlightenment of Buddha.

Maharram—marks the beginning of Buddhist Lent, it is the anniversary of Buddha's sermon to the first five disciples.

Vassana (Theravada Sect)—the beginning of the three-month period when monks stay in their temple to study and meditate.

Bon (Mahayana Sect)—an occasion for rejoicing in the enlightenment offered by the Buddha; often referred to as a "Gathering of Joy." Buddha had saved the life of the mother Moggallana. The day is in remembrance of all those who have passed away.

Pavarana (Theravada Sect)—celebrates Buddha's return to earth after spending one Lent season preaching in heaven.

Bodhi Day (Mahayana Sect)—celebrates the enlightenment of Buddha.

Christian

Ash Wednesday—the first day of Lent.

Palm Sunday—the Sunday before Easter; commemorates the triumphant entry of Jesus into Jerusalem.

Holy Thursday—also known as Maundy Thursday; it is the Thursday of Holy Week.

Good Friday—commemorates the crucifixion of Jesus.

Easter—celebrates the resurrection of Jesus.

Christmas Day—commemorates the birth of Jesus.

Eastern Orthodox

Christmas—commemorates the birth of Jesus.

First Day of Lent—begins a period of fasting and penitence in preparation for Easter.

Easter Sunday—celebrates the resurrection of Jesus.

Ascension Day—the 40th day after Easter; commemorates the ascension of Jesus to heaven.

Pentecost—commemorates the descent of the Holy Spirit upon the Apostles, 50 days after Easter Sunday. Marks the beginning of the Christian Church.

Hindu

Pongal Sankrandi—a three-day harvest festival.

Vasanta Pachami—celebrated in honor of Saraswati, the charming and sophisticated goddess of scholars.

Shivarari—a solemn festival devoted to the worship of Shiva, the most powerful of deities of the Hindu pantheon.

Holi—celebrates the advent of spring.

Ganguar—celebrated in honor of Parvari, the consort of Lord Shiva.

Ram Navami—birthday of the God Rama.

Hanuman Jayanti—birthday of Monkey God Humumanji.

Meenakshi Kalyanam—the annual commemoration of the marriage of Meenakshi to Lord Shiva.

Teej—celebrates the arrival of the monsoon; Parvari is the presiding deity.

Jewish

Yom Kippur—the most holy day of the Jewish year, it is marked by fasting and prayer as Jews seek forgiveness from God and man.

Sukkot—commemorates the 40-year wandering of Israelites in the desert on the way to the Promised Land; expresses thanksgiving for the fall harvest.

Simchat Torah—celebrates the conclusion of the public reading of the Pentateuch and its beginning anew, thus affirming that the study of God's word is an unending process. Concludes the Sukkot Festival.

Hanukkah—the eight-day festival that celebrates the rededication of the Temple to the service of God. Commemorates the Maccabean victory over Antiochus, who sought to suppress freedom of worship.

Purim—marks the salvation of the Jews of ancient Persia, through the intervention of Queen Esther, from Haman's plot to exterminate them.

Passover—an eight-day festival marking ancient Israel's deliverance from Egyptian bondage.

Yom Hashoah—day of remembrance for victims of Nazi Holocaust.

Sahvout—celebrates the covenant established at Sinai between God and Israel and the revelation of the Ten Commandments.

Rosh Hashanah—the first of the High Holy Days marking the beginning of a ten-day period of penitence and spiritual renewal.

Muslim

Isra and Miraj—commemorates the anniversary of the night journey of the Prophet and his ascension to heaven.

Ramadan—the beginning of the month of fasting from sunrise to sunset.

Id al-Fitr—end of the month of fasting from sunrise to sunset; first day of pilgrimage to Mecca.

Hajj—the first day of pilgrimage to Mecca.

Day of Amfat—gathering of the pilgrims.

Id al-adha—commemorates the Feast of the Sacrifice.

Muharram—the Muslim New Year; marks the beginning of the Hedjra Year 1412.

Id al-Mawlid—commemorates the nativity and death of Prophet Muhammad and his flight from Mecca to Medina.

APPENDIX C

Early Childhood Commercial Suppliers

ABC School Supply, Inc.
3312 N. Berkely Lake Road
Duluth, Georgia 30096-9419
(800) 669-4222
http://www.abcschoolsupply.com

Childcraft Educational Corporation
20 Kilmer Road
P.O. Box 3081
Edison, New Jersey 08818-3081
(800) 631-5652
http://www.childcraft.com

Children's Press
5440 North Cumberland Avenue
Chicago, Illinois 60656
(800) 621-1115
http://www.scholasticlibrary.com

Constructive Playthings
1227 East 119th Street
Grandview, Missouri 64030-1117
(800) 832-0224
http://www.constplay.com

Corporate Express
1233 West County Road E
St. Paul, Minnesota 55112
(800) 338-SPBS (7727)
http://www.corporateexpress.com

Delmar Learning
Executive Woods, #5 Maxwell Drive
Clifton Park, New York 12065-2919
(800) 998-7498
http://www.earlychilded.delmar.com

Discount School Supply
P.O. Box 7636
Spreckels, California 93962-7636
(800) 627-2829
FAX: (800) 879-2829
http://www.discountschoolsupply.com

Environments, Inc.
P.O. Box 1348
Beaufort Industrial Park
Beaufort, South Carolina 29901-1348
(800) 342-4453
http://www.eichild.com

Gryphon House, Inc.
3706 Otis Street
Mt. Rainier, Maryland 20712
(800) 638-0928
http://www.gryphonhouse.com

The Highsmith Co., Inc.
W5527 Highway 106
P.O. Box 800
Fort Atkinson, Wisconsin 53538-0800
(800) 558-2110
http://www.highsmith.com

Kaplan School Supply Corporation
P.O. Box 609
Lewisville, North Carolina 27023-0609
(800) 334-2014
http://www.kaplanco.com

Kimbo Educational
10 North Third Avenue
Long Branch, New Jersey 07740
(800) 631-2187
http://www.kimboed.com

Lakeshore Learning Materials
2695 E. Dominguez Street
Carson, California 90749
(800) 421-5354
http://www.lakeshorelearning.com

School Specialty
9645 Gerwig Lane
Columbia, Maryland 21046-1503
(800) 631-5652
http://www.123ecd.com

The authors and Delmar Learning make every effort to ensure that all Internet resources are accurate at the time of printing. However, due to the fluid, time-sensitive nature of the Internet, we cannot guarantee that all URLs and Web site addresses will remain current for the duration of this edition.

APPENDIX D

Rainy Day Activities*

1. Get Acquainted Game	The children sit in a circle formation. The teacher begins the game by saying, "My name is _____ and I'm going to roll the ball to _____ ." Continue playing the game until every child has a turn. A variation of the game is to have the children stand in a circle and bounce the ball to each other. This game is a fun way for the children to learn each other's names.
2. Hide the Ball	Choose several children and ask them to cover their eyes. Then hide a small ball, or other object, in an observable place. Ask the children to uncover their eyes and try to find the ball. The first child to find the ball hides it again.
3. Which Ball Is Gone?	In the center of the circle, place six colored balls, cubes, beads, shapes, and so forth, in a row. Ask a child to close his or her eyes. Then ask another child to remove one of the objects and hide it behind him or her. The first child uncovers his or her eyes and tells which colored object is missing from the row. The game continues until all the selections have been made. When playing with older children, two objects may be removed at a time to further challenge their abilities.
4. What Sound Is That?	The purpose of this game is to promote the development of listening skills. Begin by asking the children to close their eyes. Make a familiar sound. Then ask a child to identify it. Sources of sound may include:

tearing paper	shaking a rattle	sweeping sound, such as a
sharpening a pencil	turning the lights on	brush or broom
walking, running,	knocking on a door	raising or lowering
shuffling feet	blowing a pitch pipe	window shades
clapping hands	dropping an object	leafing through book pages
sneezing, coughing	moving a desk or chair	cutting with scissors
tapping on glass, wood,	snapping fingers	snapping rubber bands
or metal	blowing nose	ringing a bell
jingling money	opening or closing drawer	clicking the tongue
opening a window	stirring paint in a jar	crumpling paper
pouring water	clearing the throat	opening a box
shuffling cards	splashing water	sighing
blowing a whistle	rubbing sandpaper	stamping feet
banging blocks	together	rubbing palms together
bouncing a ball	chattering teeth	rattling keys

A variation of this game could be played by having a child make a sound. Then the other children and the teacher close their eyes and attempt to identify the sound. For older children, this game can be varied with the production of two sounds. Begin by asking the children if the sounds are the same or different. Then have them identify the sounds.

*Carefully select games for young children. Most games are more appropriate for older four-, five-, six-, and seven-year old children.

5. Near or Far?

The purpose of this game is to locate sound. First, tell the children to close their eyes. Then play a sound recorded on a cassette tape. Ask the children to identify the sound as being near or far away.

6. Descriptions

The purpose of this game is to encourage expressive language skills. Begin by asking each child to describe himself or herself. Included with the description can be the color of his eyes, hair, and clothing. The teacher might prefer to use an imaginative introduction such as: "One by one, you may take turns sitting up here in Alfred's magic chair and describe yourself to Alfred." Another approach may be to say, "Pretend that you must meet somebody at a very crowded airport who has never seen you before. How would you describe yourself so that the person would be sure to know who you are?"

A variation for older children would be to have one of the children describe another child without revealing the name of the person he is describing. To illustrate, the teacher might say, "I'm thinking of someone with shiny red hair, blue eyes, many freckles, etc. . . ." The child being described should stand up.

7. Mirrored Movements

The purpose of this game is to encourage awareness of body parts through mirrored movements. Begin the activity by making movements. Encourage the children to mirror your movements. After the children understand the game, they may individually take the leader role.

8. Little Red Wagon Painted Red

As a prop for the game, cut a red wagon with wheels out of construction paper. Then cut rectangles the same size as the box of the red wagon. Include purple, blue, yellow, green, orange, brown, black, and pink colors.

Sing the song to the tune of **"Skip to My Lou."**

Little red wagon painted **red.**
Little red wagon painted **red.**
Little red wagon painted **red.**
What color would it be?

Give each child a turn to pick and name a color. As the song is sung, let the child change the wagon color.

9. Police Officer Game

Select one child to be the police officer. Ask him or her to find a lost child. Describe one of the children in the circle. The child who is the police officer will use the description as a clue to find the "missing child."

10. Mother Cats and Baby Kits

Choose one child to be the mother cat. Then ask the mother cat to go to sleep in the center of the circle, covering her eyes. Then choose several children to be kittens. The verse below is chanted as the kittens hide in different parts of the classroom. Following this, the mother cat hunts for them. When all of the kittens have been located, another mother cat may be selected. The number of times the game is repeated depends upon the children's interest and attention span.

Mother cat lies fast asleep.

To her side the kittens creep.

But the kittens like to play.

Softly now they creep away.

Mother cat wakes up to see.

No little kittens. Where can they be?

11. Memory Game

Collect common household items, a towel, and tray. Place the items on the tray. Show the tray containing the items. Cover with a towel. Then ask the children to recall the names of the items on the tray. To ensure success, begin the activity with only two or three objects for young children. Additional objects can be added depending upon the developmental maturity of the children.

12. Cobbler, Mend My Shoes

Sit the children in a circle formation. Then select one child to sit in the center. This child gives a shoe to a child in the circle, and then closes his or her eyes. The children in the circle pass the shoe around behind them while the rhyme is chanted. When the chant is finished, the shoe is no longer passed. The last child with the shoe in his or her hand holds the shoe behind his back. Then the child sitting in the center tries to guess who has the shoe.

Cobbler, cobbler, mend my shoe

Have it done by half past two

Stitch it up and stitch it down

Now see with whom the shoe is found.

13. Huckle Buckle Beanstalk

Ask the children to sit in a circle. Once seated, tell them to close their eyes. Then hide a small ball in an obvious place. Say, "Ready." Encourage all of the children to hunt for the object. Each child who spots it returns to a place in the circle and says, "Huckle buckle beanstalk." No one must tell where he or she has seen the ball until all the children have seen it.

14. What's Different?

Sit all of the children in a circle formation. Ask one child to sit in the center. The rest of the children are told to look closely at the child sitting in the center. Then the children are told to cover their eyes while you change some detail on the child in the center. For example, you may place a hat on the child, untie his or her shoe, remove a shoe, roll up one sleeve, etc. The children sitting in the circle act as detective to determine "what's different?"

15. Cookie Jar

Sit the children in a circle formation on the floor with their legs crossed. Together they repeat a rhythmic chant while using alternating leg-hand clap to emphasize the rhythm. The chant is as follows.

Someone took the cookies from the cookie jar.

Who took the cookies from the cookie jar?

Mary took the cookies from the cookie jar.

Mary took the cookies from the cookie jar?

Who, me? (Mary)

Yes, you. (all children)

Couldn't be. (Mary)

Then who? (all children)

_____ took the cookies from the cookie jar. (Mary names another child.)

Use each child's name.

16. Hide and Seek Tonal Matching

Sit the children in a circle formation. Ask one child to hide in the room while the other children cover their eyes. The children in the circle sing, "Where is _____ hiding?" The child who is hiding responds by singing back, "Here I am." With their eyes remaining closed, the children point in the direction of the hiding child. All open eyes and the child emerges from his or her hiding place.

17. Listening and Naming

This game is most successful with a small group of children. The children should take turns shutting their eyes and identifying sounds as you tap with a wooden dowel on an object such as glass, triangle, drum, wooden block, cardboard box, rubber ball, etc.

18. Funny Shapes

Ask each child to choose a partner. One partner must make a large shape with his body. The other partner must follow the directions of movement. Roles reverse for the second set of directions. Provide directions such as:

1. **Make a big shape.**
    *go **over***
    *go **under***
    *go **through***
    *go **around***

2. **Make a small shape.**
    *go **over***
    *go **under***
    *go **through***
    *go **around***

19. Drop the Handkerchief

Direct the children to stand in a circle formation. Ask one child to run around the outside of the circle, dropping a handkerchief behind another child. The child who has the handkerchief dropped behind him or her must pick it up and chase the child who dropped it. The first child tries to return to the vacated space by running before he or she is tagged.

20. If You Please

This game is a simple variation of "Simon Says." Ask the children to form a circle around a leader who gives directions, some of which are prefaced with "if you please." The children are to follow only the "if you please" directions, ignoring any that do not begin with "if you please." Directions to be used may include walking forward, hopping on one foot, bending forward, standing tall, etc. This game can be varied by having the children follow the directions when the leader says, "do this," and not when he or she says, "do that." Play only one version of this game on a single day. Too much variety will confuse the children.

21. Duck Duck Goose

Ask the children to squat in a circle formation. Then ask one child to walk around the outside of the circle, lightly touching each child's head and saying "Duck, Duck." When he or she touches another child and says "Goose," that child chases him or her around the circle. If the child who was "it" returns to the "goose's" place without being tagged, the tapped child becomes "it." This game is appropriate for older four-, five-, six-, and seven-year-old children.

22. Fruit Basket Upset

Ask the children to sit in a circle formation on chairs or on carpet squares. Then ask one child to sit in the middle of the circle as the chef. Hand pictures of various fruits to the rest of the children. Then to continue the game, ask the chef to call out the name of a fruit. The children holding that particular fruit exchange places. If the chef calls out, "fruit basket upset," all of the children must exchange places, including the chef. The child who doesn't find a place is the new chef. A variation of this game would be bread basket upset. For this game use pictures of breads, rolls, bagels, muffins, breadsticks, etc. This game is appropriate for older children.

23. Bear Hunt

This is a rhythmic chant that may easily be varied. Start by chanting each line, encouraging the children to repeat the line.

Teacher: *Let's go on a bear hunt.*
Children: (*Repeat. Imitate walk by slapping knees alternately.*)
Teacher: *I see a wheat field.*
Can't go over it;
Can't go under it.
Let's go through it.
(arms straight ahead like you're parting wheat)

I see a bridge.
Can't go over it;
Can't go under it.
Let's swim.
(arms in swimming motion)

I see a tree.
Can't go over it;
Can't go under it.
Let's go up it.
(climb and look)

I see a swamp.
Can't go over it;
Can't go under it.
Let's go through it.
(pull hands up and down slowly)

I see a cave.
Can't go over it;
Can't go under it.
Let's go in.
(walking motion)

I see two eyes. I see two ears.
I see a nose. I see a mouth.
It's a BEAR!!!
(Do all in reverse very fast)

24. Guess Who?	Individually tape the children's voices. Play the tape during group time, and let the children identify their classmates' voices.
25. Shadow Fun	Hang a bed sheet up in the classroom for use as a projection screen. Then place a light source such as a slide, filmstrip, or overhead projector a few feet behind the screen. Ask two of the children to stand behind the sheet. Then encourage one of the two children to walk in front of the projector light. When this happens, the children are to give the name of the person who is moving.
26. If This Is Red— Nod Your Head	Point to an object in the room and say, "If this is green, shake your hand. If this is yellow, touch your nose." If the object is not the color stated, children should not imitate the requested action.
27. Freeze	Encourage the children to imitate activities such as washing dishes, cleaning house, dancing, etc. Approximately every 10 to 20 seconds, call out "Freeze!" When this occurs, the children are to stop whatever they are doing and remain frozen until you say, "Thaw" or "Move." A variation of this activity would be to use music. When the music stops, the children freeze their movements.
28. Spy the Object	Designate a large area on the floor as home base. Then select an object and show it to the children. Ask the children to cover their eyes while you place the object in an observable place in the room. Then encourage the children to open their eyes and search for the object. As each child spies the object he or she quietly returns to the home base area without telling. The other children continue searching until all have found the object. After all the children are seated, they may share where the object is placed.
29. Who Is Gone	This game is played in a circle format. Begin by asking a child to close his or her eyes. Then point to a child to leave the circle and go to a spot where he or she can't be seen. The child with his or her eyes closed opens them at your word, and then looks around the circle and identifies the friend who is missing.
30. It's Me	Seat the children in a circle formation, and place a chair in the center. Choose one child to sit on a chair in the circle, closing his or her eyes. After this, ask another child to walk up softly behind the chair and tap the child on the shoulder. The seated child asks, "Who is tapping?" The other child replies, "It's me." By listening to the response, the seated child identifies the other child.

31. Feeling and Naming

Ask a child to stand with his or her back to you, placing his or her hands behind him or her. Then place an object in the child's hands for identification by feeling it. Nature materials can be used, such as leaves, shells, fruit, etc. A ball, doll, block, Lego piece, puzzle piece, crayon, and so forth may also be used.

32. Doggy, Doggy, Where's Your Bone?

Sit the children in a circle formation. Then place a chair in the center of the circle. Place a block under the chair. Select one child, the dog, to sit on the chair and close his or her eyes. Then point to another child. This child must try to get the dog's bone from under the chair without making a noise. After the child returns to his or her place in the circle, all the children place their hands behind them. Then, in unison, the children say, "Doggy, Doggy, where's your bone?" During the game, each dog has three guesses as to who has the bone.